A History of the Russian-American Company

ARCTIC OCEAN

PACIFIC OCEAN

BERING SEA

SEA OF OKHOTSK

SIBERIA

ALASKA

KAMCHATKA

ALEUTIAN ISLANDS

KURILE IS.

HOKKAIDO

Mackenzie R.

Vancouver I.

Sitka
Alexander Arch.

Prince William Sd.

Afognak I.
Kodiak I.

Shumagin I.

Bristol Bay

Yukon R.

Unimak I.
Unalaska I.
Fox I.

Umnak I.
Andreianov I.
Atka I.

Near I.
Rat I.
Attu I.
Agattu I.

C. Liburne
Kotzebue Sd.
Prince of Wales
Norton Sd.
Bering Strait
Chukchi Pen.

St. Lawrence I.

St. Matthew I.

Karaginski I.

Bering I.
Commander I.

Nizhne-Kolymsk

Kolyma R.

Indigirka R.

Verkhoiansk

Lena R.

Iakutsk

Maia R.

Aian

Okhotsk

Nikolaevsk

Amur R.

Tatar Strait

Urup I.

Siberia and Russian America

A History of the Russian-American Company

By P. A. Tikhmenev

Translated and edited
by
Richard A. Pierce
and
Alton S. Donnelly

University of Washington Press   *Seattle and London*

Library of Congress Cataloging in Publication Data

Tikhmenev, Petr Aleksandrovich, d. 1888.
    A history of the Russian-American Company.

    Translation of Istoricheskoe obozrenie obrazovaniia
Rossiĭsko-Amerikanskoĭ kompanii.
    Includes bibliographical references and index.
    1. Rossiisko-Amerikanskaia kompaniia--History.
2. Fur trade--Alaska--History. 3. Russia--Colonies--
North America. 4. Alaska--History--To 1867.
I. Pierce, Richard A. II. Donnelly, Alton S.
III. Rossiisko-amerikanskaia kompaniia. IV. Title.
F907.T5613 1977   979.8'02   77-73318
ISBN 0-295-95564-3

Preface

The Russian phase of North American history lasted nearly 130 years, from the 1740s to 1867. During that time the Russians explored the coasts and islands and some of the interior of the northwestern part of the continent, established settlements, acquainted the indigenous population with the benefits and detriments of civilization, propagated Orthodox Christianity, developed communications, and began exploitation of the region's natural resources. Chief among these were furs, but some attention was given to fish, minerals, timber, and agriculture. Russia played an important part in early Pacific trade and diplomacy, and her ambitions at various times extended as far as California, Hawaii, the Philippines, and China. Modern Alaska retains hundreds of Russian place names, has boundaries that were worked out during the Russian period, and has living reminders of the earlier time in the spiritual force still exerted by the Orthodox Church in many communities and in survival of the Russian language.

Petr Aleksandrovich Tikhmenev's *Istoricheskoe obozrenie obrazo-vaniia Rossiisko-Amerikanskoi kompanii i deistvii eia do nastoiashchago vremeni* [A historical survey of the formation and activities of the Russian-American Company until the present time], published in St. Petersburg in two volumes in 1861-63, is an indispensable source concerning this long and colorful period. Compiled near the end of the company's existence, largely from primary materials, many subsequently lost in the destruction of the company archives in the 1870s, this massive work is unique.

Little is known about Tikhmenev himself. He was born in the late 1820s; in 1837 he entered the naval academy as a cadet. In 1852-54 he served as a lieutenant on the frigate *Pallada*, on its voyage from Kronshtadt around the Cape of Good Hope to the Far East. I. A. Goncharov, who recounts the voyage in his sea classic, *Fregat*

"*Pallada*", refers to Tikhmenev as "our diminutive, kindly, obliging manager of the officers' table." Tikhmenev returned to Europe overland, across Siberia, and in 1857 left regular naval service to enter the St. Petersburg headquarters of the Russian-American Company. There he was given the formidable task of writing a history of the company. The charter would run out in 1863, and influential foes of the company, headed by the Grand Duke Constantine, were urging a drastic curtailment of its privileges and monopoly status. The book was evidently intended, though this is nowhere clearly stated, to help influence official opinion in the company's favor.

Tikhmenev sets forth his immediate aims in his introduction. He is aware of the difficulty of his task, the complexity of his subject, the diversity of the materials he had to work with, and the lack of any information on certain matters. He follows a generally chronological scheme, but where necessary he deals at length with individual subjects. He is apologetic concerning his abilities as a writer and historian.

The book does indeed have shortcomings. Tikhmenev's style is pedestrian; he leaves many questions unanswered; he does not provide enough personal details about company managers and directors, and tells little about the daily life of the promyshlenniks, creoles, and natives. He neglects the origins of the Imperial ukaz of 1821 which excluded foreign vessels from trade in Russian America and eastern Siberia, and the subsequent conventions of 1824 and 1825 with the U.S. and England which set boundaries that have lasted to the present day. He underplays—or perhaps was not yet aware of—the decline of company fortunes which set in in the 1850s.

Nor does Tikhmenev pursue effectively what ought to have been his main purpose, to create pro-company sentiment. Except in his introduction he never states what he intends to do, and he does not sum up at the ends of chapters or at the end of the book. His final chapter is a catch-all of geographical and ethnographical information which he had not been able to work in elsewhere. He makes no active defense against the critics of the company. Instead, in a relatively dispassionate account, he indicates what the company achieved, but does not hide its failures.

In defense of the book, it can be said that additional details on personalities would have made it excessively long and would not have been in accord with its presumed aim. And, had it been either a more polished literary work or a more effective propaganda piece, it would have been less useful today as a historical source. In any case, Tikhmenev's minimal aim, "to provide useful material for the future historian of the Russian possessions on the Eastern Ocean," is achieved, while in his encyclopedic account there is abundant variety, color and drama, and indication of the important role played by Russia on both shores of the North Pacific for more than a century after Bering's second expedition.

Tikhmenev's book was received with interest and had favorable reviews; the exploits of fellow-countrymen in the remote and exotic North American colonies were looked upon with pride by many in the Russian educated class. Each volume received the Demidov Prize, a prestigious literary award of the time. Soon after completion of the work, in 1864, Tikhmenev left the company and a few months later retired from the navy as a captain of first rank. In 1878 and 1881 he was elected justice of the peace in Kostroma gubernia. He died on 7 September 1888.

Tikhmenev's work has been translated into English several times. Ivan Petroff, a Russian immigrant to the United States in the early 1860s, and one of the first American authorities on Alaska, translated a large part of it for Hubert Howe Bancroft during preparation of the latter's *History of Alaska* (San Francisco, 1885). Petroff's version, filed with others of his translations in the Bancroft Library of the University of California under the collective heading "Russian America," is still consulted, but is inaccurate. Another translation was made in Japan by Nichiro Kyokai and published in Tokyo in 1918; it is very rare; no copy could be found. In the 1930s, two Russian emigres, Dimitri Krenov and Michael Dobrynin, on parallel projects, produced *two* separate translations for the Works Progress Administration. Their versions, available in typescript, handwriting, and microfilm in several libraries, are generally reliable, but the English is faulty. In the 1960s, Norman Terrell translated most of Volume 1 for the University of Washington Press. The present translation spans the entire work; it is essentially new, but has benefitted from consultation with earlier versions.

The effort here has been to balance fidelity to the original text with readability, and consistency with common sense. A modified version of the Library of Congress system of transliteration is used. Russian forms of most names and of many terms have been retained in order to indicate usage during the period concerned. Square brackets [ ] in the text enclose matter inserted for explanation. Terms with special connotations are used in the original form, usually first in italics, with explanation in brackets, and thereafter as terms in ordinary use. Thus, the words *promyshlennik, baidarshchik, odinochka,* and *zimov'ia* are used rather than any attempt at translation, but chief manager or governor are used instead of *glavnyi pravitel'*, and main office, head office, or board of directors, are used instead of *glavnoe upravlenie*. Names of birds, animals, and plants were troublesome because of the absence of scientific names, and thus it was necessary to exchange one popular name for another. Thus, *shiksha* and *moroshka* become crowberry and cloudberry, but certain other plants are less certain. *Morskoi bobr*, literally "sea beaver," becomes sea otter, as distinct from "land beaver" and "land otter." Most fish have ready equivalents, but a few, such as *nerka, nel'ma,* and *motuk*, have no English names. *Olen'* is translated sometimes as "caribou" and sometimes as "deer." However, imperfect though they are, Tikhmenev's descriptions can help to establish earlier distribution of plant and animal species.

For consistency, and to indicate usage in Tikhmenev's time, Russian forms of place names are generally used instead of the forms on modern maps, thus Pribylov, Kad'iak, Sitkha, and Mikhailovskii redoubt instead of Pribilof, Kodiak, Sitka, or Fort St. Michael. Exceptions have been made in certain cases, such as New Archangel for Novoarkhangel'sk, Marmot Island instead of Evrashech'ia Island, Near Islands instead of Blizhnie Islands, Paul's Harbor instead of Pavlovsk. Aliaska refers only to the Alaska Peninsula, since "Alaska" in the modern sense was not coined, to supplant "Russian America," until 1867. Ship names usually follow the Russian forms, thus *Otkrytie* instead of *Discovery, Tri Sviatitelia* instead of *Three Saints*, but the more familiar *Juno* instead of *Tunona*, and *Phoenix* instead of *Feniks*. In most cases the Russian terms *zaliv, bukhta,* and *guba* have been translated simply as "bay" rather than trying to match the Russian terms with "gulf," "inlet," "sound," "bay," or "cove."

Monetary values are as indicated in the original, either in silver or paper rubles. The glossary indicates equivalents of terms of value, measurement, and weight. Latitudes and longitudes are as given by Tikhmenev; many are of course different today because of more precise measurements. Dates are kept in the old style Julian calendar except in a few cases where the Gregorian system is also used, as in the 1824 and 1825 conventions with the United States and Great Britain. Thus eighteenth-century dates are twelve days behind the countries using the Gregorian calendar, and nineteenth-century dates are thirteen days behind.

Personal names are as given by Tikhmenev, except for those of foreign origin—thus Wrangell and Etholen instead of the russified Vrangel' and Etolin. Variants are shown in the index.

The lengthy appendices to the Russian edition include correspon-

dence between Shelikhov, Baranov, Rezanov, and other company fig-
ures, the three company charters, the ukaz of 1821 and regulations
excluding foreign shipping from company waters, the regulations of the
Russo-Finnish Whaling Company, and many other valuable documents.
These documents, part of Tikhmenev's source material, will be pub-
lished separately under the title *Documents on Russian America*,
P. A. Tikhmenev, compiler, by the Limestone Press of Kingston,
Ontario.

Other documents that Tikhmenev used may be found in the Russian-
American Company *Correspondence* (dispatches from the main office
to the governors at Sitka) and *Journals of Correspondence* (copies of
dispatches sent by the governors at Sitka to the main office) in the
U. S. National Archives. It has not been possible to comb this vast,
unindexed archive to identify all of these. Other documents may be
found in several published collections of documents. Several may be
found in *K istorii Rossiisko-Amerikanskoi Kompanii (Sbornik
dokumental'nykh materialov)* [On the history of the Russian-American
Company. A collection of documentary materials] (Krasnoiarsk, 1957),
published in translation as *Documents on the History of the Russian-
American Company* (Kingston, Ontario: The Limestone Press, 1975);
and in A. I. Andreev, editor, *Russkie otkrytiia v Tikhom Okeane i
Severnoi Amerike v XVIII veke* [Russian discoveries in the Pacific
Ocean and North America in the 18th century] (Moscow, 1948).
An earlier, shorter edition was translated by Carl Ginsburg as *Russian
discoveries in the Pacific and in North America in the Eighteenth and
Nineteenth Centuries* (Ann Arbor, 1952). A few documents on the
Russian-American Company also appear in the multivolumed series
*Vneshniaia politika Rossii XIX i nachala XX veka. Dokumenty
Rossiiskogo Ministerstva Inostrannykh Del* [Foreign policy of Russia
of the 19th and beginning of the 20th century. Documents of the
Russian Ministry of Foreign Affairs]. Copies of other documents that
Tikhmenev used, along with supplementary material, may yet turn up
in Soviet archives.

Tikhmenev's notes have been supplemented by citations in square
brackets of some sources that he used but does not identify and also by
references to some relevant works that have appeared since his history
was published. A few of his shorter notes have been incorporated in
the text.

The original work has only four illustrations: portraits of Shelikhov,
Baranov, and Rezanov, and a late view of Novo-Arkhangel'sk. Views of
various company establishments have been added.

The maps in the original work are so detailed that it would not have been practical to redo them in transliteration. Instead, several smaller maps have been included.

Richard A. Pierce
Queen's University
Kingston, Canada

Alton S. Donnelly
State University of New York
Binghamton, New York

Contents

Illustrations

A History of the Russian-American Company

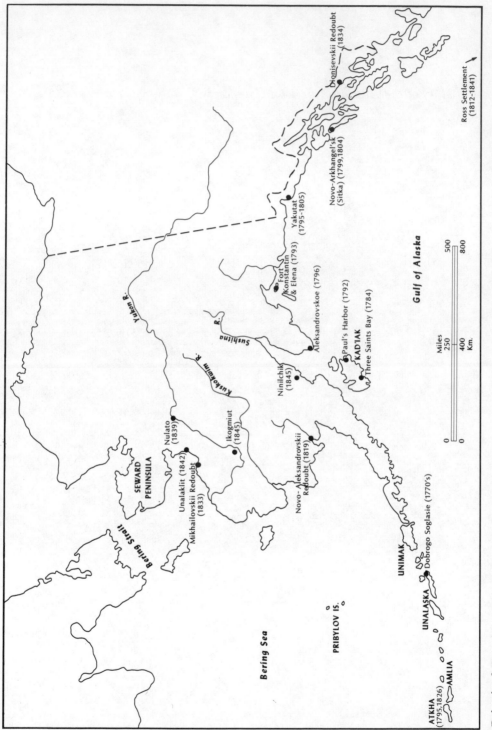

Principal Russian establishments in Alaska

Droiisevskii Redoubt (1834)

Ross Settlement (1812–1841)

Novo-Arkhangel'sk (Sitka) (1799,1804)

Yakutat (1795–1805)

Fort Konstantin & Elena (1793)

Aleksandrovskoe (1796)

Paul's Harbor (1792)

KAD'IAK

Three Saints Bay (1784)

Ninilchik (1845)

Gulf of Alaska

Sushitna R.

Yukon R.

Kuskokwim R.

Nulato (1839)

Ikogmiut (1845)

Unalakiit (1842)

Mikhailovskii Redoubt (1833)

Novo–Aleksandrovskii Redoubt (1819)

SEWARD PENINSULA

Bering Strait

Bering Sea

PRIBYLOV IS.

UNIMAK

Dobrogo Soglasie (1770's)

UNALASKA

ATKHA (1795,1826)

AMLIA

Miles
250   500

Km.
400   800

Author's Introduction
(1861)

In publishing this historical survey of the organization of the Russian-American Company and its activity to the present time, compiled from official sources, I must first make certain explanations. First of all, it may be asked why these materials are termed "official," and second, what purpose I had in combining them in a single whole.

The materials consist mainly of historical documents that are preserved in the archive of the main office of the company; the main office's correspondence with departments and individuals governing and administering the region controlled by the company; the decisions of the company's shareholders and the council of several shareholders established at the main office to consider and decide on matters of special importance; the orders issued by the main office and the colonial administration; reports to the latter from local administrators; and, finally, the accounts of the latter.

In compiling this survey from such documents my aim was to present briefly, as already indicated in the title, the organization and activity of the company from its foundation to the present time, and to show why private entrepreneurs combined their capital for joint action, or, in other words, established a company that, while fulfilling commercial expectations, could also promote government aims and satisfy the needs of the region. The vastness of the field in which the company operated, combining in itself so many multilateral obligations, made the task of describing everything pertaining to it far from easy, at least for me. Finally, the unorganized nature of the data itself, and even the complete lack of certain essential details, deprive my work of the completeness to be expected from a combination of the historical and statistical data regarding Russian possessions on the shores of the

Eastern Ocean. In any event, until a more capable and experienced person than I am undertakes this task, and until the possibility of explaining certain circumstances of the life of the colonies enables the compilation of a history satisfactory in all respects, I venture to present my work as it is. Even if it only partially explains certain questions or circumstances that have remained little known until now, I shall consider my aim to some extent attained. Even if this survey is regarded as no more than useful material for the future historian of the Russian possessions on the Eastern Ocean, I shall feel that my work was not in vain.

Needless to say, any indication of omission or error in my description of any event will be gratefully received.

The order I followed in presenting the historical facts seemed to me the only way to compile a description of the company's activity which would be as brief and clear as possible.

A general picture of the company's activity had also, in my opinion, to contain separate sketches of its most important activities in various instances. Thus, life in the colonies, the supply of the region with necessities, the expeditions fitted out by the company for this purpose and for hydrographic, ethnographic, and economic study, and the spread of religious and moral education among the natives are each presented separately during a certain period. Although with this order of presentation it is necessary sometimes to return to the time considered under other circumstances, or to mention in different places one and the same event or company order, such repetition is unavoidable, and provides greater clarity.

But the most appropriate and convenient way to delimit such periods is by the main events in the company's existence, and the periodic renewal of its privileges.

Two distinct periods stand out in the development of our colonies. First, the preparation of the previously wild and unknown region for acceptance of principles of social organization, and second, the introduction and gradual spread of enlightenment in accordance with the requirements of the natives. In the first period there was a special need for men of action endowed with strong will, vision, intelligence, and readiness for self-denial. A double struggle—on the one hand with the unbridled passions of primitive savages, foreign to any order and sense of love for man, and on the other with all kinds of privations because of the company's very meager means in this country, very poorly endowed by nature—presented many obstacles to its aims and expectations. The company had such men in the person of Shelikhov, a man of unusual mind, who was ahead of his time in his view of the significance and importance of the field he selected; of Baranov, who was endowed with great energy, indefatigable activity, and abundant wisdom in the most difficult circumstances; and finally of Rezanov, educated, benign, but nevertheless willing to sacrifice himself wherever duty required. Circumstances themselves, and necessity, caused this period to be distinguished by cruelty, arbitrariness, and in general, disorder of every kind. Thus it was wherever the European entered the environment of savages, whom he had simultaneously to subjugate and introduce to a new and better order which, if not always for their own welfare, at least was for the benefit of their descendants.

In the second period of the development of the colonies there is already a noticeable predominance of the spirit of peace and order which was instilled in the colonial government by administrators from naval ranks. This became especially apparent after 1821, when the combination in one individual of governmental and company duties made it possible to carry out government orders more exactly and to protect the natives from arbitrary rule more effectively. The zealous cooperation of the missionaries or, better put, the labors of the Orthodox bearers of glad tidings in this region—among whom stands out sharply the enlightened and tireless Innokentii, the prelate of the colonial church, who began his service there as a priest—assisted in the spread of the Gospel and the bases of spiritual and moral enlightenment even among the natives, whose hearts long remained foreign to reception of the True Word and Christian love toward fellow men. The heroic example of Shelikhov's wife, who decided to share her husband's dangers and labors in the wild and remote country, was followed by the Baroness Elisabeth Vasil'evna Wrangell, the first educated woman after Shelikhova who decided to accompany her husband when he was appointed chief manager of the colonies. The resoluteness of the Baroness Wrangell is much more important in its social significance, for her example was followed in the families of other persons entering the service of the company. Thereafter, the principles of the family order began gradually to take root among people cast by fortune so far away, and social life acquired more moral direction. Establishment in Novo-Arkhangel'sk by the former chief manager A. K. Etholen of a club for the officers and other employees also aided greatly in the development of social life. In addition, uniting the natives into common villages, which were built at the company's expense; the making of new rules for governing the tribes under the company jurisdiction; the establishment of the class of colonial citizens from company employees with large families who wish to settle in the colonies, and outfitting them with all household necessities at company expense; the founding of a pension capital, and in general taking care of persons incapable of further colonial service on account of age or illness; the establishment of a port with necessary shops for building and repair of sail and steam boats; and finally the spread of education in the colonies, recently on a more positive principle, also belong to the second period of the development of the colonies. To all of this ought also to be added the carrying out of many tasks for the government by the company with its own colonial resources.

The first part of this survey [Chapters 1-11] covers events in the colonies until 1841. The second part [Chapters 12-20] will describe the colonies during the current twenty-year period.

In now presenting my work to the reading public, I again commend it to the attention of persons particularly acquainted with the subject, in order that its shortcomings may be pointed out and thereby avoided in the second part.

PART ONE

1. *The Organization of Fur-Trading Companies and the Operations of Shelikhov's Company until His Death in 1795*

Early trading companies, to 1781. The second Northern Seas expedition, outfitted in 1733 by command of Empress Anna, was placed under the command of Captain Bering, who had also led the first expedition.[1] Although plagued by misfortune, the expedition showed Russian seafarers the way to the coasts and adjacent islands of North America, lands until then almost unknown. While the information it acquired was largely superficial, it at least gave Russians some knowledge of lands previously thought of as legendary. This expedition discovered the North American coast at approximately 58° 50' north latitude,[2] the Aleutian Islands, extending westward from there, and most of the Kurile Islands. Some of the latter were vaguely known even at the end of the sixteenth century; but for our first accurate information on all these places we are indebted to their conquerors, the Russian promyshlenniks [fur traders], daring fortune hunters in a country purported to be an inexhaustible source of valuable furs. Even Bering's expedition was sent forth because of the riches which had been brought back from the North Pacific islands.[3]

Almost nothing is known of fur-gathering voyages into these regions before 1743. From that time, however, for almost sixty years, many merchants and other persons, singly or in companies, sent out parties on one or more vessels to the Aleutian and Kurile islands, and we have reliable documentary evidence of several of these expeditions. Over forty such merchants and companies are known. We will mention here for the most part only those expeditions which made either new discoveries, or more detailed investigations of regions already known.

Emel'ian Basov, a sergeant of the Nizhne-Kamchatsk command, may be considered the first to engage in this trade. In 1743, 1745, 1747, and 1749 he sailed his own vessel to the Bering and Copper [Mednyi] Islands.[4]

In 1745, Nevodchikov, who had been a sailor under Captain Bering, went to sea as commander of a vessel belonging to the Chuprov company, and visited Attu[5] and Agatu, later called the Near [Blizhnie] Islands. At the same time the small islands lying nearby became known by the native name of Semiia or Semichi.

In 1749, a vessel belonging to the merchant Trapeznikov visited Atkha and several adjacent islands of the Andreianov group. However, the discovery of these islands has been given a later date, probably owing to the inadequacy of Trapeznikov's data.

In 1759, the promyshlennik Glotov, on a vessel belonging to the merchant Nikiforov, reached Umnak Island; and subsequently all of the Fox Islands—probably so called because of the foxes found there—extending as far as the Aliaska Peninsula, were discovered. Some authorities ascribe the discovery of these islands to Bashmakov, commander of a vessel belonging to the merchant Serebrennikov, comparing the position of the Aleutian chain with data obtained by this promyshlennik; but others consider it doubtful that Bashmakov was ever on Umnak Island or the other Fox Islands. They doubt this because no foxes were exported from these islands before 1762, that is, before Glotov, after spending more than two years on Umnak, returned from there with a large number of fox furs. Furthermore, the Aleuts spoke of Glotov as their first visitor, remembered because he baptized many of the natives. Glotov was also the first to furnish the government with a good map of these regions. This map, quite detailed for its time, depicted the eight large islands lying east of Unalashka. They were described by the Cossack Ponomarev. In 1763 Glotov also visited Kad'-iak Island.

In 1760, the merchant Andriian Tolstykh arrived at Adakh Island and over the next three years made a detailed census of the island's inhabitants, as well as those of five neighboring islands (Atkha, Amlia, Sitkhin, etc.), to all of whom he gave Russian citizenship. From his Christian name these islands are called the Andreianovs.[6]

In 1761, a vessel belonging to the merchant Bechevin visited the Aliaska Peninsula and, according to the Aleuts, wintered in Protasov Bay, in Issanakh Strait.

In 1762, a ship belonging to the mercantile company of Posnikov, Krasil'nikov and the Kul'kovs, commanded by the merchant Druzhinin, reached Unalashka Island. Unfortunately, the natives destroyed this vessel with its entire crew, as well as three other ships of the same company that visited there somewhat later. Of the members of these expeditions, only those who were absent at the time of the attack were saved. The first of these vessels is credited with discovering Koshigin [Kashega] Bay on Unalashka Island; but, according to the natives, Druzhinin's visit was preceded by that of another ship, which stood off the east side of Akutan Island and put out to sea unharmed.

Meanwhile, information concerning the discoveries made by Glotov, Ponomarev, and other traders prompted the governor of Siberia, Chicherin, to petition in 1763 for a more exact study of the newly discovered lands. In his memorandum to Empress Catherine II, Chicherin congratulated Her Majesty on the acquisiton of heretofore unknown places and the establishment of a new trade, all of which had been accomplished by the simplest and most unlearned men. Then the governor mentioned the necessity of assigning to trading vessels naval officers, who, neither hindering trade nor taking command of the vessels, should keep detailed journals and descriptions of the voyages.

The empress approved Chicherin's proposal, and ordered enough officers and mates sent to fulfill this purpose. Captains Krenitsyn and Levashov were chosen by the Admiralty College to carry out the sovereign's will. However, it was left to the governor's discretion whether to send government ships independently of private vessels. On this basis, in 1766 Krenitsyn and Levashov set out from Okhotsk in government galiots for a voyage to the Aleutian Islands. However, Krenitsyn's vessel was wrecked at Bol'sheretsk, delaying the expedition until 1768. In that year Krenitsyn and Levashov again set sail, and the former wintered at Unimak Island and the latter at Unalashka. This expedition, however, does not appear to have been especially effective. Although Levashov's journal contains four articles on Unalashka, the description of this island is quite superficial[7] and adds nothing to what was already known from other mariners. Furthermore, this expedition's clashes with the natives aroused lasting antagonism and of course led to new difficulties which later visitors to the island had to overcome.

Meanwhile, the government sought in every way to encourage the emerging trade. The mariners who had discovered the new lands were rewarded with medals and encouraged by various immunities. In the Imperial Decree to Siberian Governor Chicherin in September 1764, and in the Senatorial Decree to the Bol'sheretsk Chancellory in April of the same year, government officials were strictly ordered not to interfere with traders putting out to sea, to help them in any way possible with government funds and to defer repayment until their vessels returned.

Shelikhov's activities, to 1781. The early 1780s marked a new era in the history of the Russian fur trade in the islands of the Eastern

[Pacific] Ocean. For some years prior to this Grigorii Ivanovich Shelikhov, an honored citizen of Ryl'sk, had made a name for himself as an active participant in this trade. Shelikhov arrived in Siberia with Ivan Larionovich Golikov, a merchant of Kursk, and served for some time as his business manager. Then Shelikhov, in company with Golikov and other Siberian merchants, sent out several fur trading expeditions to the Kurile and Aleutian Islands. From the results of these expeditions, Shelikhov noticed that the fur trade was declining each year. Several factors, including the visible decrease in furs, the hostility of the natives toward the uninvited newcomers, and the violent conduct of the traders themselves, urgently required a basic reform in the conduct of affairs in these regions and the institution of measures for systematically developing the industry. Furthermore, the inadequacy of information concerning the Aleutian Islands and the uncertainty of Russia's rights to their possession caused Shelikhov to consider establishing closer ties between the new country and Russia proper. With this aim he himself decided to set out for the Aleutian Islands and the coasts of North America.

A company is organized for fur trading and the discovery of unknown lands. In order to carry out his plans Shelikhov persuaded his associate Golikov and another Golikov, Captain Mikhail Sergeevich, to set up a special company for ten years. The company was capitalized at 70,000 rubles, divided into 120 *investment* shares, in addition to *donative* shares and shares given *on landing.*[8]

This capital was to be used to build two or three ships, to be placed under Shelikhov's personal command and to be sent (in the words of the incorporation agreement) "to the land of Aliaksa [sic], which is called America, to islands known and unknown, in order to trade in furs, to make explorations and to arrange voluntary trade with the natives."

The three ships set out for the Aleutian Islands. Shelikhov equipped three galiots, called the *Tri Sviatitelia* [Three Saints], the *Arkhistratig Mikhail* [Archangel Michael], and the *Simeon Bogopriimets Anna Prorochitsa* [Saint Simeon and Saint Anna the Prophetess], and on 16 August 1783 he set sail from Okhotsk. He and his wife sailed on the *Tri Sviatitelia*:[9] The expedition encountered bad weather and while the ships were separated by a storm the *Arkhistratig Mikhail* disappeared. Shelikhov was forced to spend the winter on Bering Island.

The next year Shelikhov visited the Unalashka Island and there made such repairs to the ships as were possible. Then, along with two interpreters and ten natives who had volunteered to serve with him, he set

Печ. Дарленгъ.   Рис. Смирновъ.

Grigorii Ivanovich Shelikhov

out for Kad'iak Island, leaving orders to the commander of the *Ark-histratig Mikhail* to follow him. On 3 August 1784, the ships arrived at the island and entered a harbor which they named *Three Saints Harbor*, after the ship.

Shelikhov settles on Kad'iak Island. A party was sent in baidarkas[10] to find out if the island was inhabited. The men returned with one of the natives, whom Shelikhov tried to entertain as well as possible and the next day permitted to return home. The reception given by the Russians must have pleased the savage, because on the following day he reappeared and remained with Shelikhov until the expedition departed on the return voyage. Not only did he constantly accompany Shelikhov on all his trips around the island, but he cautioned him against hostile attempts by his fellow islanders.

The natives' unfriendly intentions were soon revealed: men sent in baidarkas to survey the island and its animal breeding grounds, with orders to go as far as possible, observed a large number of Koniagas (as the natives of Kad'iak called themselves), as many as four thousand,[11] who had gathered on a rocky islet some distance from the shore and inaccessible from the sea. Suspicious of such a gathering, Shelikhov sent a deputation to them with a proposal to begin trade and live in peace; but the natives answered with menacing demands that the Rusrians leave the island immediately and never again dare to approach it. Then Shelikhov himself, along with his hunters, went to their gathering and again attempted to persuade the Koniagas to enter into friendly relations with him, assuring them that he had not come to quarrel with them but to help them. His words were of no avail; the Koniagas shot several arrows, and the party was forced to return to the ships and guard against a surprise attack. In fact, several days later, in the middle of the night, the savages approached the harbor unnoticed and threw themselves on the Russians. The struggle continued until dawn with equal fierceness on both sides. Self-preservation forced the traders to fight with reckless daring, and finally the enemy, though greatly superior in numbers, took flight. This first victory, however, did not lessen the danger. One of the natives who had gone over to the Russian side revealed that the Kad'iak islanders were expecting considerable reinforcements from neighboring tribes and were firmly resolved to renew the attack on the newcomers and to destroy them to the last man. Delay could only lead to disaster, so Shelikhov proposed to seize at all costs their main haunt on the islet. With a selected party he besieged the Koniagas in their refuge, which they considered inaccessible, and with a few good shots at their huts from his five two-pound cannons he reduced them to such terror that they abandoned all their possessions and fled in all directions, leaving the islet and numerous prisoners in Shelikhov's hands. On the victors' side several men were seriously wounded.

In accordance with their wishes, Shelikhov settled the prisoners fifty versts from the harbor and provided them with everything they needed for fur gathering; but to ensure their loyalty he took twenty of their children as hostages. Subsequently, although attacks by the natives continued for some time, they took place far from Shelikhov's main base and only against small parties of traders sent out to survey the island; but since the Russians now had the advantage of a higher morale, all these attacks were repulsed with considerable loss to the savages. Shelikhov's determination to crush with one blow the main force of the natives and to drive them from their stronghold was important since it shook the islanders' self-confidence, maintained by their successful clashes with other trading companies, whom they had always forced to leave their shores. They clearly understood that this time they would not succeed, as before, in ridding themselves of the troublesome newcomers. Most of all, the impression produced by Shelikhov's fearlessness forced the natives to make peace with a man in whom they acknowledged something supernatural and against whom, therefore, they did not feel themselves able to struggle.

The beginning of Christianity and education among the natives. Now that Shelikhov had established himself on the inhospitable island, he set his entire force to erecting fortifications and dwellings, which were finished only with some difficulty. Meanwhile, his gifts and friendly dealings began gradually to win over the Kad'iak islanders and his repeated assurances that he had come not to wage war but to live in friendship, and that the great Russian empress wished to protect them and ease their existence pacified them completely. Moreover, everything about the Russians' domestic life excited the natives' curiosity, and the knowledge and skill with which their new neighbors erected buildings and in general organized whatever they needed made the savages eager to imitate them, even to take part in their labors. Thus, circumstances drew ever closer together two peoples that so recently had been quite alien to each other. Shelikhov's constant readiness to satisfy, if possible, the islanders' needs and his continuing attention to everything that concerned them soon won them over to such a degree that they even began bringing their children in as hostages.

Although Shelikhov had no need whatsoever for most of them, in order not to give offense he always accepted and provided for them. Convinced that the light of Christianity would quickly instill good principles in them, Shelikhov attempted, little by little, to explain to children and adults alike God's law in simple and intelligible terms, encouraging them to become Christians. His efforts were successful— by the time he departed from Kad'iak Island forty natives had asked to receive Holy Baptism. After the sacrament was performed, according to the rite permitted to any Christian in the absence of a priest, it became obvious that these newly enlightened ones were beginning to convince the rest of the islanders. Similarly Shelikhov gave them their first ideas of civilization and superior authority, and under his guidance they began to feel the need to accept Russian sovereignty and laws. However, for fear of antagonizing them, he never mentioned the payment of iasak [fur tribute], leaving this question to the government.

Shelikhov's further activities on Kad'iak Island and the attempt by the Kenais to expel the Russians. As soon as possible, Shelikhov detached a party of 52 men who set out eastward in four baidaras, accompanied by 11 Fox islanders and 110 Koniagas. They were to explore as far as Kenai Bay [Cook Inlet] and to meet the tribes inhabiting the islands and coasts of these regions, gathering appropriate data. Throughout the voyage, which followed the north shore of Kad'iak Island through the strait [now Shelikof Strait] separating the island from the mainland, the party encountered no opposition from the Koniagas, the Kenais, or the Chugach, and even accepted about twenty hostages from these tribes. But trade with the natives was insignificant, owing both to the limited time available and to the novelty of commerce to the inhabitants of those regions. After returning to Kad'iak Island the detachment wintered at the settlement of Karluk, and from here they traveled along the north and west sides of the island and along the coast of Aliaska as far as Kamyshak Bay, obtaining hostages from all the surrounding tribes as a guarantee of trust and alliance. Trade was carried on without interference.

Other parties of the promyshlenniks remaining in the harbor were sent out to explore the south and west sides of Kad'iak Island, the adjoining islands, and Kenai Bay. Some of the goods dispatched with these parties for trade with the natives were entrusted to the toion [chief] of Shuiakh Island, who was a hostage of the Russians, but this proved an unfortunate choice. The toion turned traitor, killing the men who were sent with him, and incited the Kenais to rebel against the Russians. A thousand Kenais set out from their shores to attack Shelikhov's stronghold. When Shelikhov heard of this at the beginning of 1786, he immediately sent two parties to repulse them, one consisting of Russian promyshlenniks and the other of Koniagas and Fox Island Aleuts. At the same time promyshlenniks were sent to Afognak Island to occupy a suitable harbor where a small fort could be built. Soon word was received that the detachments had successfully dispersed the Kenais, destroying their conspiracy, and that forts had been established on Afognak Island and on Kenai Bay. Then Shelikhov sent a party of promyshlenniks and natives to Cape St. Elias, to build a small fort there, and to complete the explorations which had been begun the previous year. All of the parties were enjoined to conciliate, if possible, the tribes with whom relations had not yet been established, and to place crosses and other signs along the coasts.

In 1786 both the harbor and the outposts saw the natives coming over from the mainland every day and in much greater numbers than before. Shelikhov ordered the Russians to befriend the visitors in every way and to inspire their confidence.

After preparing his ship, the *Tri Sviatitelia,* for the return voyage, Shelikhov entrusted the command of all the establishments on Kad'iak Island to Samoilov, the foreman in charge of the hunters, and on 22 May 1786 he put to sea, accompanied by the toions and elders of the neighboring tribes. As they set out they sighted the *Arkhistratig Mikhail* heading for the island. According to her commander, Second Navigator Olesov, after being separated from the other vessels, they had wintered on the first Kurile Island [Shumshu] and the next year they had arrived at Unalashka. The following spring, while leaving the harbor at Unalashka, they had hit a rock through the captain's error, and again had to spend the winter in port. Finally, after almost three years, they had reached Kad'iak. Replacing Olesov, Shelikhov ordered the *Arkhistratig Mikhail* to proceed to the harbor at Afognak Island, and from there both vessels were to sail according to the following plan: one vessel was to explore the region from 40° to 75° north latitude, reckoned east of the Okhotsk meridian, the other was to sail north to the point where the two continents came together, discovering new lands and islands and supplementing discoveries already made.

Shelikhov's return voyage was uneventful. On 8 August his galiot arrived at Bol'sheretsk. Many men had been sick during the voyage, and the islanders accompanying Shelikhov had acted as sailors, helping considerably. While Shelikhov was ashore, a gale tore the vessel from its anchors and carried it out to sea, forcing him to travel to Okhotsk by land. He reached there in January 1787 and immediately set out for Irkutsk.

The travails of the long journey were far from ended for Shelikhov and his wife. Everything seems to have conspired to try the patience of the travelers on their grueling passage from Okhotsk. The severity of the winter, and particularly the heavy blizzards which were constantly encountered in open places, not only delayed their journey but made it almost unendurable. Several times they were forced to lie in snow drifts for two, three, or even five days, eating only sugar and quenching their thirst with snow because it was impossible to build a fire; the weariness of the horses, dogs, and reindeer compelled them to travel on foot, until they were almost exhausted. Finally, on 6 April, they arrived at Irkutsk, and thus Shelikhov terminated his journey to America, which was destined to have far-reaching consequences. All of Shelikhov's deeds in a distant land known only by vague and conflicting rumors speak for themselves. Everyone must agree that not gain alone but also self-sacrifice for the common good could have inspired the daring traveler to make such a journey and summon strength to endure all the difficulties, dangers, and privations which he experienced in his steadfast desire to attain the goal he had set himself.

Shelikhov reports on his voyage to Iakobii, governor-general of Siberia, and requests imperial patronage for his undertaking. Upon his return, Shelikhov gave Governor-General Iakobii a detailed description of his voyage, a map of the lands he had visited, and plans of the forts he had built. At the same time he asked the governor-general for instructions regarding his conduct toward the peoples he had brought under Russian dominion and assistance in obtaining Her Majesty's acceptance of his efforts for the benefit of the state. It is fitting to present here the actual words with which his report closed:

> Without our Monarch's approval my labor will be small and insignificant, for I have undertaken this matter solely to see for myself the lands and islands in that sea, to observe their advantages, and to establish in suitable places secure outposts, that other powers might be confounded and that they might serve our Majesty's glory for Her benefit and the benefit of my fellow countrymen. I believe and hope that in future my efforts will provide a source of revenue not only to myself, but also to the state.

At the same time, in view of the cessation of trade at Kiakhta, Shelikhov asked the governor-general's permission to send several ships "under some suitable flag" to Chinese ports in order to trade merchandise for furs or for money.

Empress Catherine II's interest in the company. Meanwhile the merchant Golikov was permitted to deliver in person to Her Majesty, as she passed through Kursk, a map of Shelikhov's voyage. The empress inquired in detail about the company's operations and ordered that Shelikhov be brought to Saint Petersburg so that he and Golikov might appear before her.

The imperial command to send two expeditions to the Eastern Ocean. At the same time Her Majesty, wishing to insure safer means of navigation for her subjects who were engaged in trade in the Pacific Ocean, and to obtain new information about the newly discovered lands, ordered a squadron of four warships, under Captain Mulovskii, to be outfitted in the Baltic Sea. Upon reaching the Eastern Ocean, part of the expedition, under Mulovskii, was to sail for America, the other for the Kurile Islands.[12] An expedition from Okhotsk under Captain Billings had already been ordered to those waters. In addition to other duties, Captain Billings was directed to observe and describe the islands lying between Kamchatka and America.[13] The outbreak of war with Sweden forced cancellation of Mulovskii's expedition, but the ships under Billings sailed for the Aleutian Islands in 1790 and visited Unalashka, Kad'iak, and several other islands. The hydrography of those waters was greatly enriched by data obtained by Captain Sarychev, who was assigned to the expedition.

The empress then ordered Governor-General Iakobii to recommend the best means of consolidating Russian rule on the islands of the Pacific and the coasts of America, of governing the native peoples, and of improving their way of life.

Iakobii's opinion regarding the best means to consolidate Russian rule on the Eastern Ocean and his petition for government assistance of Shelikhov's enterprises. Governor-General Iakobii submitted three proposals:[14]

1. The dispatch of a flotilla from the Baltic Sea and the construction of a port at the mouth of the Uda River would eliminate most of the foreign pretensions to Russia's dominions, and also increase her prestige, particularly since the Uda port would eliminate many of the difficulties associated with the route to Okhotsk, and was better situated for the defense of these areas. Needless to say, it would take a long time to build such a port, even though at the empress' command preliminary measures had already been taken. A start had also been made in determining the rules under which foreigners might trade in Russia's Pacific ports. With a view to averting the claims of other powers to the new lands of America that were Russia's by right of discovery and

exploration, thirty copper crests of the Russian Empire and the same number of plates bearing a cross and the words "Russian Territory" [*Zemlia rossiiskago vladeniia*] had been sent for placing in America and on the nearby islands. Most of these markers had been entrusted to one of the agents of Shelikhov and Golikov charged with the exploration and description of these areas. Instructions had been given on the use and placement of the markers.

2. If the iasak were changed into a voluntary assessment, the natives could be brought to understand more quickly Her Majesty's great concern for their welfare.[15] In this way abuse of the natives could be avoided, for one could truthfully say that those charged with collecting the iasak had often misused their powers, and the savages, exasperated by the arrogance and violence of the tribute gatherers, had shunned any allegiance and had attempted to take vengeance on the Russians in any way they could.

By rousing the hostility of the natives toward all visitors, the promyshlenniks had deprived themselves of the successes they might have obtained by treating them gently and fairly, and they had often paid with their lives and fortunes for the wrongs of others. Since, on the other hand, excessive indulgence toward the natives might give rise to other evils, it was recommended that a reliable man impress upon them the advantages enjoyed by Her Majesty's subjects. It might be pointed out that her charity extended even to distant peoples, as proved by her wish to eliminate the previous taxes and replace them with a payment determined at each native's discretion.

Furthermore, the fur trade itself might gain from changing the iasak to a voluntary assessment. Many indications pointed to a considerable decrease every year in the number of fur-bearing animals, which was not surprising, considering the millions of pelts taken and the constant increase in the number of promyshlenniks. From this gradual decrease in the fur trade it might be inferred that in a few years, unless steps were taken to stop the indiscriminate destruction of fur-bearing animals, the trade might cease, or at least not merit the cost of taking the pelts.

3. Having set forth means by which Her Majesty's will might be fulfilled toward improving her subjects' way of life and enlightening them as much as possible, both for the benefit of the nation and for their own welfare, it was impossible not to overlook Shelikhov's activities in his visit to the islands lying near the American continent. Without going into the details of his trip, which had already been brought to Her Majesty's attention, Iakobii mentioned that everything Shelikhov

did was done much more from zeal for the good of the country than for his own personal advantage. The way he had made savage and hostile peoples see the advantage of dealing peacefully with visitors to their shores was truly amazing. After they had shown clear hostility toward Shelikhov and his men, he not only pacified them to the point where they entrusted themselves to his leadership and defended his interests against other natives, but he persuaded them to give him their children as voluntary hostages. When Shelikhov taught these children reading, writing, and Christian doctrine, their fathers were favorably impressed, proving Shelikhov's great patience in carrying out a plan of action. His tales of the progress, order, peace, and safety prevailing in Russia so fired the curiosity of the natives that forty of them asked to see that country. Some of these were even now in Irkutsk. Finally, there could be no doubt that Shelikhov had actually done all these things in the lands he visited, for the establishments he had founded were themselves a proof of his energies. Equally certain was the fact that some of the natives had accepted the Orthodox faith. Even if one admitted that the natives were not convinced that they needed to be christened or did not comprehend the purpose of this rite, still it was obvious that their consenting to become Christians had laid the groundwork for their future enlightenment and progress.

In view of his account, Iakobii felt that it was necessary to support the first steps Shelikhov had taken and to prevent ignorance and greed from destroying all he had created. Therefore, he considered himself obligated humbly to indicate to Her Majesty the justice of rewarding Shelikhov's company with the exclusive fur trading rights in those places discovered by its own vessels, that is, from 49° to 60° north latitude and from longitude 53° to 63° west. [16]

Iakobii then supplemented his proposal for the new regions with further proofs of the need to bestow an exclusive charter on Shelikhov and his company. We quote his words:

I should hardly dare present my opinion for Your Majesty's consideration, were I not convinced of the following:

1. The necessity of exclusive fur trading rights for Shelikhov and his company in the above-mentioned places derives from the fact that, if Shelikhov was able to attract to himself the inhabitants of Kad'iak, Afognak, etc., which is proven by the fact that he managed, according to his companions, with one Russian for each thousand natives, then his loyal zeal, encouraged by Your Majesty's favor, would make him redouble his efforts to instruct these peoples, who, because of their confidence in him, would certainly follow the path he showed them.

2. In any event, it is not this alone that has induced me to petition Your Majesty for a franchise for Shelikhov and his company. The advantages which in my opinion must accrue from granting a franchise have compelled me to approach Your Majesty, particularly when one considers those lands which trading companies of various European powers have already occupied in various parts of the world. My petition is inspired largely by the fact that the field in which Shelikhov and his company propose to operate is removed from Russia proper, where because of the numerous traders the very notion of monopoly would be inappropriate, hampering Russian subjects in acquiring that which each can gain by his labors under free trade. Furthermore, the fur trade in the Eastern Ocean regions demands much greater capital, and there are very few promyshlenniks there compared to Russia proper. And, of course, no one else has ever been able to gather furs where Shelikhov has even established the basis of imperial control, for although in 1761 to 1767 and in 1780 several vessels ventured there, the promyshlenniks from these vessels could not even establish themselves on a cape of Kad'iak Island called Aekhtalik,[17] but were driven from there with sizable losses by the natives, and not permitted to hunt, although the Russians were numerous enough to repulse any attack. And now, if other promyshlenniks are to capitalize on the natives' peaceful willingness to respect the suggestions of a man whom they acknowledge their friend, it will be impossible to ensure that Shelikhov's successful beginnings will not be disrupted and destroyed. Most probably, in fact, the native peoples will resist the promyshlenniks by war to the death, because they could hardly expect identical treatment at the hands of most visitors. Therefore, it would seem better to entrust relations with the natives to the one man already known by his works, than to many guided mainly by greed.[18]

The views of the College of Commerce. When the empress received Iakobii's report and Shelikhov and Golikov's request to continue exploring and trading in the islands and along the shores of America and to establish posts there, she ordered the College of Commerce, under the presidency of Count Chernyshev, to study factors relating to the conduct and expansion of trade on the Eastern Ocean.

In March 1788 the College of Commerce delivered the following opinion.[19] To avoid repetition, I give only the conclusion:

The important successes resulting from the indefatigable industry of Shelikhov's company deserve not only approval to continue what has begun, but also possible future aid, particularly in view of the expenses amounting already to 250,000 rubles, and likely to exceed 200,000 more in the near future. The continuation of Shelikhov's enterprise on an appropriate scale is particularly important at present, owing to the cessation of the China trade, which not only will damage Siberia but is hurting all Russian commerce. For those goods intended by Russian merchants for export to China are lying unproductive, to the irreparable loss of the owners, who will be unable to realize their investment. The goods Russia has imported from China, both for her own use and for export to Poland, such as nankeen and tea, particularly the latter, she is now having to acquire through other European powers, which has caused, among other things, the weakening here of the ruble in the rate of exchange. Finally, the great expense of outfitting vessels and equipping them with everything needed for establishing settlements on the shores of the Eastern Ocean and, in general, all of the company's activities may serve as valid reasons for asking from the treasury help which the company would find it difficult to do without.

On this basis, the college presumes to recommend to Her Majesty, in accordance with Shelikhov and Golikov's request, that their undertaking, which promises such great future benefit, be supported by a noninterest-bearing loan of 200,000 rubles, to be repaid in installments over twenty years and guaranteed by the pledging of suitable security. Such a boon will give the company the means to continue what it so successfully has begun, will encourage the turnover of capital, and, in addition to spreading Your Majesty's power and developing trade and industry, will enable the treasury itself to derive a profit, by collecting 10 percent duties for imported and exported goods.

Imperial patronage for Shelikhov and Golikov's company will be beneficial in that it will offer a firm defense against the destruction or impairment of what this company has created. The charter of the regions where posts have been set up to the company's exclusive use is particularly significant in view of the causes of depopulation of the Fox Islands, the blame for which rests, of course, with the promyshlenniks. Most of the inhabitants of these islands, owing to ceaseless squabbles with visitors to their shores, moved to more distant lands or to the mainland, while some perished in wars. These circumstances compel Shelikhov and his company to fear such interference in the fur trade, for if other promyshlenniks have the same rights in the lands Shelikhov found, then the same consequences will naturally follow as in the Fox Islands.[20]

In general the College of Commerce agrees totally with the views of Governor-General Iakobii in respect to furnishing the company with its needs from the treasury, but would, however, interpose the following: the appointment of the commander of a fort, or, more properly, a settlement, should be removed from the prerogative of the governor-general of Siberia and reserved to the recommendation of those sharing in the enterprise. They, having to retain employees in the outposts at their own expense, will certainly, in their own interests, choose for these offices men who may be relied upon to provide the greatest satisfaction in the performance of their duties.

The empress rewards Shelikhov and Golikov. On receiving this report, Her Majesty consented to bestow rewards on Shelikhov and Golikov. The Imperial Ukaz of 28 September 1788 says:

To reward the zeal of the merchants Shelikhov and Golikov, who have discovered new lands and peoples for the benefit of the state, We bestow on each of them a sword and a gold medal to wear about the neck, with Our portrait on one side and the reasons for its award on the other, and We command that the Ruling Senate give them citations setting forth all their high-minded exploits and activities for the benefit of society.

With regard to iasak and aid from the treasury the decree adds:

Her Majesty desires to know by what decree iasak was imposed on the Aleutian Islands, and should there be none, merchants are forbidden to make exactions not set by legal authority.

All promyshlenniks are strictly enjoined to avoid any disputes with the Chinese over possession of the Kurile Islands and likewise not to touch islands under the dominion of other powers.

At present it will be impossible to provide the company with money or with a military detachment, because of the need for troops in Siberia, where there are hardly enough for present demands.[21]

The further activities of Shelikhov's company in the Aleutian Islands and on the American mainland. After returning to Irkutsk, Shelikhov equipped two ships for long-range exploration: one for the Kurile Islands, and the other for the Aleutian Islands and the coast of America.[22] As soon as circumstances permitted, he proposed to move south along the American coast and establish settlements there. In the summer of 1787 he sent a ship from Okhotsk to the islands with necessary supplies and equipment for the company's posts.

In the spring of 1788 the *Tri Sviatitelia*, under the command of navigators Izmailov and Bocharov, set sail from Kad'iak Island. They had been ordered by Delarov, a Greek who had been sent to Kad'iak as head of the company's establishment, to explore the American coasts and to establish the empress' rule over all the newly described places. To this end they were given special markers, which were to be placed in specific locations. In May the galiot arrived at Chugach Bay [Prince William Sound], where the company's agents did a little trading with the Chugach, paying them eight or nine strings of blue beads and three or four corals for a sea otter and five corals each for otter tails. Next Izmailov and Bocharov visited Nuchek Bay [Port Etches], where they anchored in one of its arms on the northwestern side, which they proposed to name Saints Konstantin and Elena Bay. Meanwhile, one of the leading natives of Suklia [Montague] Island, who visited the ship, was entrusted with a copper crest, since it was quite impossible to place it in a suitable spot, as Iakobii had instructed. This was because the islanders manifested a singular proclivity to steal and at every opportunity they would pilfer what they could from the ship, particularly metal objects. From Nuchek Bay the ship proceeded to what the natives called Yakutat Bay (known to the Russians as Bering Bay), and there dropped anchor. The toion of this region was also entrusted with a crest and in addition he requested, and enthusiastically received, a portrait of Grand Duke Paul Petrovich, heir to the throne. After visiting several other places along the American coast, including L'tua Bay, the ship had to return in July to Kad'iak Island, owing to the large number of sick on board.[23] In 1789 Izmailov described the southwestern side of Kenai Bay and Kamyshak Bay.[24]

Delarov remained manager until July 1791 when he was replaced by Baranov, a merchant. Under Delarov the inhabitants of Kad'iak Island enjoyed the same relations with the Russians as they had under Shelikhov. The promyshlenniks gathered furs, explored the nearby islands, and sought suitable locations for company outposts. Delarov also sent a detachment to the mainland at the entrance of Kenai Bay, where fort Aleksandrovsk was subsequently founded. But the inhabitants of Aliaska Peninsula still refused adamantly to allow settlements on their land.

The discovery of Paul and George Islands. The diminishing number of otters on Unalashka and the constant northward migration of fur seals and their return from the north with young led the promyshlenniks to postulate the existence of still unknown seal rookeries somewhere north of the Aleutian Islands. And, in fact, in June 1786 the *Sv. Georgii* [St. George], a vessel belonging to the merchant Lebedev Lastochkin, discovered in that direction an island, which was named St. George Island after the ship. All the promyshlenniks on the ship were left for the winter on the island. But the vessel itself could not find a suitable harbor there and wintered in the Andreianov Islands, in order to conceal the discovery from the other promyshlenniks on Unalashka. The next year Lebedev's promyshlenniks sighted another island, not far to the north of St. George, which was named St. Paul Island, in honor of the holy apostles Peter and Paul whose feast day it was. When the island was explored, signs were found that some earlier explorer had already visited it. The Russians gave a number of names to these islands. At first they were called the "New Islands"; then the "Lebedev Islands." Shelikhov named them the "Zubov Islands" in honor of his "benefactor and patron" as he states in his notes. The promyshlenniks knew them as the "Northern" or "Seal Islands" and in the settlements they were called merely the "little islands."

Also in 1786 another of Lebedev's vessels, the *Sv. Pavel* [St. Paul], arrived at Kad'iak Island. When the promyshlenniks on this ship heard from Shelikhov's men of the abundance of sea otters in Kenai Bay, they sailed there, and thirty-eight men, under the leadership of the foreman Kolomin, settled on a small cove at the mouth of the Kasila or Kasilovka River, which later became known as Nikolaevsk Harbor. In 1791 they were joined by the promyshlenniks of the *Sv. Georgii*. The foreman Konovalov relieved Kolomin of command and built a fort and several store buildings. In this way Lebedev's traders occupied the half-completed settlements which had belonged to Shelikhov's company since 1785. They took advantage of the absence of Shelikhov's men to punish the Aliaskans who had taken part in looting the Katmai outpost and after that they finally consolidated themselves in all of Shelikhov's establishments on Kenai Bay.

The export of furs. Besides Lebedev's company[25] detachments from other merchants and trading associations were located on various islands of the Aleutian chain, but they remained only for the trading season and did not establish settlements. From 1747 through 1791 furs worth 6,310,756 paper rubles were exported by all companies from the Aleutian Islands, and almost seventy vessels, some of which made several voyages, were outfitted for this trade.

Ships of other powers explore the Pacific islands and American coasts. Foreign governments also undertook to explore the American coast and the nearby islands. Between 1769 and 1780 Spain sent out three expeditions, under the command of Captains Vila, Perez, Bodega, and Artela. The second and third of these reached 50° north latitude. In 1775 the Spanish Captain Quadra reached the entrance to Sitkha Bay. In 1778 Cook, the famous English captain, touched many points on the shores of northwestern America and surveyed Bristol, Chugach, and Kenai bays, and the east shores of Kad'iak Island, as well as several other islands. After him the private English captains Dixon, Portlock, and Mears visited the American coasts. Portlock discovered in Kenai Bay north of Cape Bede [now Point Adam] the so-called Graham's Harbor, known in the colonies as English Bay [*Angliiskaia bukhta*]. In 1786 a French expedition, under La Perouse, visited North America and entered L'tua Bay, which La Perouse named "le port des Francais." Finally, about the same time, the Spanish navigators Fidalgo and Malespina were also in these waters.

Shelikhov forms more trading companies. Recognizing the need to expand his operations in the Aleutian Islands, Shelikhov founded in 1790 two more companies: the Northeastern Company and the Baptist Company (the latter named after the vessel employed in the fur trade). In 1791 he founded still another, the Unalashka Company, which was intended to operate from that island.

Baranov is appointed manager of Kad'iak Island. In the meantime, convinced that all he had created on the islands would fall into ruin without an experienced leader, Shelikhov sought a man capable of governing the settlements, and with enough industry and enterprise to guarantee the realization of the founder's goals. Shelikhov considered Baranov, a merchant of Kargopol, to be such a man, and his choice

Печ. Дарленгъ.   Рис. Смирновъ.

Aleksandr Andreevich Baranov

proved correct. Several times Shelikhov had offered Baranov the managership of his establishments on Kad'iak Island, but Baranov's prosperous and independent business affairs prompted him to decline these
offers. However, all of Baranov's undertakings soon took a turn for the
worse; in particular, the complete breakdown of his trade with the
Chukchi, who looted and destroyed his stores at Anadyrsk, compelled
him to enter Shelikhov's service. He was rewarded with ten donative
shares.

The agreement determining Baranov's relations with the company
was concluded on 18 August 1790. Besides provisions for mild treatment of the natives and a detailed exposition of the company's goals,
it included the following provisions:

1. An expedition was to be sent north of the Aliaksa Peninsula to
discover new islands. It was to spend the winter "in the first bay from
Aliaksa Peninsula and there to find a suitable harbor." Then, the expedition was instructed to obtain detailed data on the shortest distance
between this harbor and Kenai Bay, through the isthmus, and to
describe this route carefully in case it proved necessary to transport
goods and supplies in the event of an attack on the company by hostile
tribes.

2. In accordance with secret orders from the empress, measures
were taken against possible attack on the company's outposts by privateers commissioned by the Swedish government and commanded by
English captains. All possible steps were to be taken to avert the
impending danger to the hunters and to the company's property. But
if, despite all precautions, such privateers were to enter Russian harbors
or land raiding parties, means should be sought to repulse or even capture the enemy. The contract goes on:

> A detachment of Americans [natives] accompanied by Russians who are swar-
> thy or painted like natives, should go out to the vessel in two- or three-man
> baidarkas, showing signs of wonder and devotion. The enemy should be lured
> ashore by showing them, or even giving them, sea otters. Thus having lured
> ashore as many as possible, the Americans [natives] should meet them with
> joyous dances and happy looks, attempting to lead the vessels into dangerous
> places. The Russians should remain hidden, preparing a fitting reception for
> their guests. When these are enticed into defiles or other suitable places, then on
> both land and on water strong parties should at the first signal fall immediately
> on the vessel and on the landing party and throw them into panic, attempting
> to take their leader. . . ."

The following passage deals with damaging the enemy ship:

> Meanwhile, several brave Russians or Americans might hide in the baidarkas,

appearing with their tools when the enemy were not watching and drilling holes in the bottom of the vessel or somehow setting it on fire. . . .

3. A detachment should be sent in a ship to Cape St. Elias and thence toward Nootka Island to learn the exact point where the Spanish borders begin and to discover if there are settlements of any other power between our possessions and those of Spain. If so, they should try to describe suitable places and harbors and to form friendly relations with the tribes dwelling thereabouts. They shall also be permitted to be friendly with the settlements of other powers, particularly with those of Spain, and to carry on trade, if it appears advantageous. But in no case are they to divulge needlessly either the number of Russians engaged in trade or the extent of our possessions.

4. Relations were to be established with the English merchant McIntosh, "who has trading establishments in the East Indies, near China. A trade should be arranged, whereby he is provided with our colonial products in exchange for goods they might need. . . ."

Baranov's voyage to the colonies. The day after concluding the agreement, Baranov set sail in the *Tri Sviatitelia*, under the command of navigator Bocharov. The voyage began badly. As soon as they left Okhotsk, sickness began to break out, owing to lack of water, which had been stored in leaky barrels. The ship had to land at Unalashka Island. Immediately thereafter, a violent storm destroyed the ship and all their possessions. Yet an eight-month sojourn on the barren island amid constant privation did not break Baranov's spirit. He attempted by all means to bolster his comrades' flagging spirits with the hope of early rescue, although his first plans were immediately thwarted. The promyshlennik whom he had sent for help to Kad'iak Island was attacked by the Aliaksintsy [natives of the Aliaska Peninsula]; he and the handful of Aleuts accompanying him barely escaped with their lives by fleeing to Unga Island, where they remained, waiting for Baranov. With the arrival of spring, Baranov set about building three large baidaras. Two of these, under Bocharov's command, were sent to explore the north shore of Aliaska Peninsula; Baranov himself sailed in the third baidara directly to Kad'iak Island, where he arrived on 27 July 1791.

Bocharov explores Aliaska Peninsula. Bocharov began his explorations at Issanakh [Bechevin] Bay, which separates Unimak Island from the mainland, continuing along the north coast of Aliaska Peninsula as far as the Kviichak River. He wished to continue farther, but his baidaras were damaged and his crews were small. The approach of autumn, with its stormy and rainy weather, and lack of food forced him to return to Kad'iak. He did not, however, retrace his steps, but set out across the unexplored isthmus. Thus he discovered the shortest and most convenient route from the north to the south coast of the peninsula. He reached the south shore at a bay lying less than seven [actually about thirty-five] miles from Kad'iak Island.

From all indications, the natives valued gifts of crests highly. Thus, in Bocharov's journey around Aliaska Peninsula he gave a crest to the toion of one of the most populous tribes. In the spring of 1792 the toion appeared in the company's settlement with hostages. He promised Baranov that all his people would live in peace with the Russians and asked for protection from tribes living outside the Russian realm. To give greater assurance that his words were in good faith, he wished to take up residence with many of his relatives not far from the company's post.

Delarov returns from Kad'iak Island and reports on the company's activities. In July 1792, Delarov returned to Irkutsk from Kad'iak Island, bringing with him the furs obtained while he had been manager there.

Delarov reported as follows on the activities of the company:

1. Forts had been built on all major islands of Aleutian chain and at several places along the Aliaska coast.[26] Here many natives of various tribes lived together with the promyshlenniks. Near each settlement suitable places for fur trapping had been surveyed, and rules were established regulating the conduct of trade and the annual storing of provisions. Possible future outposts for agriculture and cattle-raising had been noted. Several places had been fixed as harbors and others for erecting various buildings, owing to their proximity to forests. Finally, places had been found along the American coast on great rivers, where a mutually advantageous trade might be carried on with the natives of the interior.

2. As directed by the government, plates and crests had been placed along the American coast far beyond Cape St. Elias.

3. As to foreign navigation in Russian waters, Delarov reported that during his stay on Kad'iak Island several Spanish ships had arrived at the company's outposts every year. In 1791 three of them entered Chugach Bay and Baranov tried to discover their intentions through a Serbian interpreter on one of the vessels who appeared to be friendly toward the Russians. According to the interpreter, these vessels had been sent out by the Mexican viceroy for the sole purpose of surveying St. Lawrence (Nootka) Sound. He also said that up to now the Spaniards had established no colonies along the American coast,[27] but they considered it vital to do so north of San Francisco, in order to prevent the English from occupying the region between the Spanish

and Russian possessions. He added that the Spanish were in complete sympathy with further Russian expansion to the east and southeast, since this would leave the English no hope of occupying this area. As to the Spanish interest in the fur trade, Delarov said that they expressed no desire to barter beavers, otters, and martens, because they considered the trade, particularly in beavers, unprofitable since they had no markets for the furs. This was confirmed by the fact that they sold the best beaver furs to the Russians for ten to twelve rubles, or for three or four German cotton shawls.

Furthermore, the English trade around Namchatka and, in particular, along the coast of America, deprived the Russians of large profits. There were cases where ships of the East India Company had obtained as many as eight hundred otters in a very short time.

Several times Shelikhov had petitioned the government for protection of fur-trading companies from foreign incursions, but, as will be seen below, his efforts and those of his successors in the management of the company long proved fruitless.

Company operations from 1791 to 1795 and the beginning of shipbuilding in the colonies. Shortly after becoming manager of the company, Baranov, finding Three Saints Harbor unsuitable, decided to transfer all the establishments to Chiniak Bay, where he chose a suitable harbor and erected a fort, naming the settlement Pavlovsk or Paul's Harbor in honor of Prince Paul, heir to the Russian throne.

Early in the spring of 1793, Baranov and thirty Russians in two large baidaras set out for Kenai Bay to investigate at first hand the fur hunting there. The number of sea otters taken in the bay had been decreasing every year. Up to this time from one thousand to two thousand pelts had been taken, but in 1793 it proved difficult to obtain even four hundred. For this reason Baranov and his party set out for Chugach Bay. Baranov wished to survey the coastline and the interior in order to establish additional outposts, and through kind treatment befriend the local tribes and thus forestall foreign efforts to seize this portion of the coast. He navigated and surveyed all of Chugach Bay and obtained hostages from three large native settlements with no bloodshed—"by humanitarian means," he wrote to Shelikhov, "and the rest of them promised to visit the place where I decided to establish a winter outpost." In the interior of the Aliaska Peninsula hostages were taken from four other villages. In Nuchek Bay Baranov encountered Izmailov, who had been sent out in the *Sv. Simeon* to make new discoveries. However, he had found nothing except doubtful signs of a possible island.

Baranov sent part of his men to survey Suklia Island and landed on

1 Dwelling Church
2 Astronomical Tent
3 {illegible} build on shore

The North extremity of the Island Tanaga bearing South distant 15 Miles.

Island of Atcha 22 June 1791 bearing S.E.

Published Feb. 22.t 1802. by Cadell & Davies Strand.

Three Saints Bay, about 1790

the mainland with the rest. A large band of Kolosh,[28] who were looking for Chugach in order to avenge some recent injury, noticed the Russians and decided to attack them and seize their possessions. Under the
cover of darkness they surrounded Baranov's camp unnoticed. Suddenly wakened, Baranov's men could not come to their senses. The
enemy took advantage of this confusion to strike out at everyone they
met. Furthermore, the panic of the Aleuts who were with the Russians
intensified the confusion. Milling around in disorder, they blocked the
use of the party's cannon. Finally, the arrival of dawn and timely assistance from Izmailov forced the enemy to retreat. They left twelve dead,
but carried their wounded away with them. On the Russian side, two
traders and nine Aleuts were killed and more than fifteen men were
wounded. "God shielded me" wrote Baranov, "for although a spear
pierced my shirt and arrows fell all around me, I was unhurt. Jumping
up from my sleep, with no time to dress, I rushed about encouraging
the men and directing the cannon fire to the points of greatest danger."[29]

According to Shelikhov's wishes, Baranov set about building the first
ship in the colonies. In the autumn of 1791, Shelikhov had sent the
Severnyi Orel to Kad'iak Island loaded with shipbuilding material and
under the command of Second Lieutenant Shields, a shipbuilder.
"Herewith," wrote Shelikhov, "we send you iron, rigging, and sails
for one ship, which you will build with Shields' help. Using him to advantage, you should also begin two or three other ships of various sizes,
bringing them to the point where you can finish them yourselves, without a shipbuilder's aid. Everything you need for this will be sent later.
Teach the natives to be sail-makers, riggers, and blacksmiths."

For his shipyard Baranov chose one of the harbors of Chugach Bay,
and there he built the necessary works and dwellings, calling the place
Resurrection Harbor [*Voskresenskaia Gavan*, now Seward]. The wood
for the vessel's hull was obtained from nearby Greek Island. The work
proceeded rapidly under Baranov's personal direction and in 1794 the
ship was completed and christened the *Phoenix* [Feniks]. A three-
master with two decks, she was 73 feet long, 23 feet wide, and 13½ feet
deep, and of 180 tons capacity. In place of pitch and tar Baranov
caulked her with a durable compound of his own invention consisting
of fir pitch, sulfur, ocher, and whale oil.

After launching the *Phoenix,* Baranov started the hulls for two more
fir sailing vessels, each forty feet long. By the summer of 1795 these
ships had been finished and christened the *Del'fin* [Dolphin] and the
Ol'ga [Olga].

Soon Baranov sent the *Phoenix* to Kad'iak Island. From there, on

Voskresenskaia Gavan' (now Seward), in 1794

Shelikhov's instructions, she sailed for Okhotsk with a three-year catch of furs. During 1793 and 1794 Shields sailed the *Severnyi Orel* in search of land which had been observed by several navigators. He traveled the American coast as far as Yakutat Bay escorting a fur trading party and trading with the natives, trying to make friends with them.

The hunting party, consisting of 170 baidarkas, took almost 2,000 otter pelts in Yakutat Bay alone. Purtov, leader of the party, became friendly with many of the natives, receiving fifteen hostages from tribes living around Cape St. Elias, in Yakutat Bay, and farther toward L'tua Bay. Upon arrival at Kad'iak they were baptized.

Aggressive acts by Lebedev-Lastochkin's men. In 1793 Baranov became greatly harassed in Kenai Bay by the men of Lebedev-Lastochkin's company. That company's promyshlenniks began telling him that Kenai Bay belonged entirely to them, in spite of the agreement defining the territory of both companies, previously concluded with Lebedev, and notwithstanding the rights of first occupation enjoyed, of course, by Shelikhov's company. Then they stirred up in every way not only the Kenais, but also Baranov's men, particularly the foreigners serving on the vessel under Shields.

The inhuman behavior of one of Lebedev's foremen forced Baranov to send him to Okhotsk and to inform the governor of Okhotsk of what had happened. But this did not stop the disorders, and finally the violence of Lebedev's traders reached the point where they began to pillage and destroy many of Shelikhov's outposts in Kenai and Chugach Bays.

The natives observed all this, and consequently their faith in the Russians inspired by the just behavior of Shelikhov and his successor Baranov was considerably weakened.

Vancouver's expedition to North America. In 1794 two English vessels, the *Discovery* and the *Chatham*, sailed the American coast under Captain Vancouver. They accurately described Kenai, Yakutat, and Chugach Bays, but the expedition is best known for its description and exploration of the many straits and passages lying between Icy Strait and the Strait of Juan de Fuca. "Circumstances prevented me from seeing them," wrote Baranov to Shelikhov, "although they invited me and waited several days around Kenai Bay. My subordinates, however, showed them all hospitality."[30] Presumably Baranov avoided meeting the English captain, since it was thought that his expedition was intended to discover how far the Russians wished to extend their territory along the American coast.

The empress orders a religious mission and several exiled families to be sent to the colonies. Shelikhov and Golikov, seeing the absolute need of instructing the natives in Christianity, asked that a clerical mission be assigned to the Aleutian Islands, that several natives be permitted to study for the priesthood in the seminary at Irkutsk, and that permission be given to build a temporary church in the colonies. They agreed to bear the expense of providing a church vestry, of maintaining the clergymen, and of instructing the natives in the seminary.

Catherine II, in the Imperial Decree of 30 June 1793, approved this request, entrusting the matter to Synodist Gavriil, Metropolitan of St. Petersburg.

Archimandrite Ioasaf was named head of the mission, which included seven priests (the hieromonks Iuvenalii [Juvenal], Makarii, and Afanasii; the archdeacons Stefan and Nektarii; and the monks German and Ioasaf) and two novices.

At the same time Shelikhov asked Pil', governor-general of Irkutsk, to petition the empress to assign as settlers in the colonies several exiles who knew blacksmithing, locksmithing, and casting, as well as ten families of peasants.

In the Imperial Decree of 31 December 1793, the Empress granted this request.[31]

On 13 August 1794 the religious mission and the settlers sailed for Kad'iak Island in two company ships, the *Tri Ierarkha* [Three Hierarchs] and the *Sv. Ekaterina* [St. Catherine]. The first ship carried 126 passengers, including ten clergymen, two prikashchiks, and sixty-two promyshlenniks, along with fowl, cattle, seed grain, agricultural tools, and provisions, so that in addition to the crew and 120 barrels of fresh water she was laden with 13,000 puds.

The other ship carried its crew, two more prikashchiks, five Aleuts, fifty-nine promyshlenniks, and the remaining cargo.

Both ships had recently been built in Okhotsk. The *Tri Ierarkha* had two decks and was sixty-three feet long and the *Sv. Ekaterina* had one deck and was fifty-one feet long. "I commend to you your guests," Shelikhov wrote Baranov,

> Archimandrite Iosaf and his brothers, chosen by Her Majesty to preach God's word in America. I am certain that you, no less than I, will feel gratified that the country where I labored before and where you are now laboring for the glory of Russia will find in these men a sturdy bulwark to its future welfare. God grant that this good may be fulfilled while we are still in a position to do the bidding of our wise Sovereign."[32]

A colony is established on Urup Island. Shelikhov left four exile families at Okhotsk, intending to settle them on Urup Island. The

establishment of this colony was motivated by the fact that Shelikhov's agents, sent to the Kurile Islands in 1777 by the Lebedev-
Lastochkin company, had encountered some Japanese, gone with them
to the port of Atkis on the island of Matsmai, and had returned with
hopes of establishing trade relations with Japan. When the settlers set
out, Shelikhov wrote to Baranov:

> Besides establishing agriculture on Urup Island I wish to maintain a trading
> company there. As you know, Urup lies close to Japan, where a mission under
> Lieutenant Laksman was sent in 1792. Therefore, the foreman on this island is
> to be ordered to treat with kindness and friendship and without the least sus-
> picion any Japanese who appear. From the Kurile Islanders he should attempt to
> learn of Japan, particularly of their resources, the occupation of their inhabi-
> tants, etc. Measures should also be taken to befriend the Kurile Islanders, and to
> try to obtain food and supplies from them and through them to establish trade
> with the Japanese. Induce the Kurile Islanders to settle on Urup Island and take
> up agriculture, particularly since it is known that the inhabitants of Number 18
> (Urup) and Number 19 (Iturup) are hostile to one another.

In 1794 the colonists and about twenty hunters under the leadership
of foreman Zvezdochetov were sent to Urup Island.

*The company ship "Ioann Predtecha" is wrecked and Shelikhov
founds the North American Company.* In 1790 Shelikhov had established the Baptist [*Predtechenskaia*] Company. Sent out in the autumn
in the ship *Ioann Predtecha* [John the Baptist] under the command of
navigator Shirokov, this company had set up trading posts on the Fox
and Pribylov Islands.

While engaged in exploration the *Ioann Predtecha* was wrecked on
St. Paul Island in the autum of 1791. On a matter of extreme importance Baranov ordered Captain Izmailov to sail the *Sv. Simeon* to Okhotsk in 1793. But storms prevented Izmailov from reaching Okhotsk
in that year and he was forced to winter on Unalashka Island. There he
heard of the bad luck of the *Ioann Predtecha* and hurried to help her
crew. About sixty thousand sea otter skins were transshipped from the
wrecked vessel. With a letter from the foreman and the *Predtecha's*
supercargo, Izmailov set sail for Okhotsk, where he arrived in 1794.
"Shirokov has lost the *Predtecha*," Shelikhov wrote Baranov, "but for
that we dare not reproach him, for such men are needed."[33]

Shelikhov knew that the lack of trees in the islands would prevent
the building of another ship. With this in mind, and wishing to occupy
the mainland coast as far north as possible, he decided to form the
north as possible, he decided to form the North American Company.
This company was intended to establish permanent settlements and

was to be provided with vessels for transporting various cargoes. The company was to have a complement of about 120 men, but it was decided to send about seventy out immediately, in July 1794. The next year over thirty additional men were sent to join them.

Shelikhov considered that this new company would provide greater means for averting foreign claims to trade with the natives, for protecting and expanding the fur trade from Unalashka Island to the shores of the Arctic Sea, and for establishing trade with the natives of the American continent opposite the Chukotsk Peninsula. Furthermore, Shelikhov wished to find out what discoveries could be made along the American coast to the north and northeast, particularly whether there might be a passage to Baffin Bay, even over dry land.[34] Subsequently, the North American Company was to combine with other companies to form the United American Company, and ultimately, the Russian-American Company.[35]

The establishment of a head office in Irkutsk. In 1794, after seeing his ship off to America, Shelikhov returned from Okhotsk to Irkutsk. Now that all his companies had been placed on a more permanent footing, he felt it necessary to establish a head office and provide it with a set of rules, so that its business might be carried on efficiently in his absence. The office began operations in 1795.

Trade is resumed at Kiakhta. In 1794 trade with the Chinese was reopened at Kiakhta. On 25 November, the governor-general of Irkutsk reported to the empress: "Shelikhov has contributed a great deal to the development of the Kiakhta trade and has supported a profitable rate of exchange for our goods, despite many Chinese efforts to the contrary."

Shelikhov's death and the plans he left unfulfilled. Shelikhov was unable to continue his efforts for his country's good. He died on 20 July 1795, in Irkutsk, and was buried in the convent there.

Besides the many things this remarkable man accomplished during his lifetime, he presented to the government numerous proposals which were left unrealized either because of the vast resources necessary for their execution or because of various obstacles blocking them. For example, in his report of 18 November 1794 he petitioned the governor-general of Irkutsk for permission to equip a private expedition to find a better route from Irkutsk to Okhotsk in the direction of the Amur and Uda Rivers, and to build a harbor with wharfs and dockyards for company ships near the mouth of the Amur.[36] Since this expedition's route would have to pass through Chinese territory, the governor-general was compelled to decline this proposal for fear of clashes with the Chinese.[37] Shelikhov also sought permission to

Печ. Дарленгъ.   Рис. Смирновъ.

Nikolai Petrovich Rezanov

build dockyards for his ships at the Ul'ia River (entering the sea thirty-five versts from Okhotsk) or at the Urak River (fifteen versts from Okhotsk). He requested licenses to trade with Japan, China, India, the Philippine Islands, etc., and petitioned, in the interests of improving foreign trade, for the appointment of "competent and responsible individuals" as consular officers in certain places. In time, all of these proposals were presented to the empress. The most important of them, to trade with the Chinese in the southern port of Canton, was thwarted by disturbances in Europe. "Our intentions in Canton," Shelikhov wrote to Baranov, "have been cut short, for the French are forcing the whole world to fight them. We will not abandon this project however, for it is also necessary for Okhotsk."

Shelikhov's deeds and plans, daring for their time, but soundly conceived, as circumstances have proven, testify to the wisdom and intelligence of this man and give him a respected place in history.

After Shelikhov's death, his widow directed the company from 1795 to 1797, aided by her husband's associates. She attempted to expand the company's activities and to strengthen its finances, particularly since the property of her partner, Ivan Golikov, was at that time sequestered by a government lien and could not be used for the company's needs. (The other Golikov, Mikhail, had died a few years before Shelikhov.)

N. P. Rezanov, her son-in-law, was of great help to Madam Shelikhov in directing the colonies after her husband's death. His broad education, good connections to St. Petersburg, quick and persuasive intellect, tireless energy, and devotion to Shelikhov's undertakings entitled him to be called one of the principal figures in the settlement of the Pacific coasts. Although separated by an enormous gulf, Rezanov and Baranov were nevertheless united by a common purpose—to use all means possible to fulfill Shelikhov's dreams in this new, almost unknown land. Rezanov enjoyed Shelikhov's full confidence and he, more than anyone else, was familiar with Shelikhov's plans and ideas. Fully recognizing that with Shelikhov's death the smallest error could damage the undertaking or even destroy what had already been built, Rezanov assumed all the main duties, to the point of sacrificing himself, as we shall see, to accomplish Shelikhov's aims. Obviously, his business success owed much to the merger in 1797 of all the fur-trading companies into one company under government franchise. Rezanov's personal appearance on several occasions before the Emperors Paul and Alexander saved the company from many slanderers and detractors and exercised profound influence on the welfare of the regions under its care.

2. The Merger of Shelikhov's Companies and Others to Form the Russian-American Company

Baranov proposes to establish a settlement on the mainland in accordance with Shelikhov's wishes. Shelikhov had constantly thought of establishing a settlement beyond Cape St. Elias and of building ships there. "I have proposed to the government," he wrote to Baranov [1794], "to carry on agriculture and shipbuilding beyond Cape St. Elias. While I was still on Kad'iak, I knew that the mainland coast, beginning at the limits of the Unalashka tribes, i.e., above Unga Island, and continuing to the limits of the Kenais, had a better climate than Kad'iak, ample arable soil, forests, and so forth."[1]

Baranov replied that he had no hope whatsoever of pursuing agriculture west of Yakutat Bay, particularly along the sea coast, since these regions lay around latitude 59° or 60°. Kenai Bay and Chugach Bay were both surrounded by high mountain ranges, and the soil was unsuitable for growing grain. "In any case," Baranov wrote, "I am entrusting a more detailed investigation to the good archimandrite, who intends to leave immediately [1795] on the small *Sv. Ol'ga* for Kenai Bay and thence as far as Yakutat Bay."

In the meantime Baranov sent the *Tri Sviatitelia* to Yakutat Bay. With her sailed part of the religious mission, some settlers, and around thirty traders. The cargo consisted of various provisions and materials. Another vessel, the *Del'fin*, under Shields, was sent to survey and describe the shores and harbors between L'tua Bay and the Queen Charlotte Islands. Baranov himself also decided to go to Yakutat in order to select a site for a settlement, designating Chil'kat Bay as a rendezvous for the ships.

In submitting his program for 1795, Baranov again complained bitterly of foreigners who were freely trading for furs in Russian territory and carrying them off for sale in Canton and Macao. The thought that foreigners might occupy the region between Kenai Bay and Nootka Sound, or at least found a settlement there, constantly troubled him and he determined to establish a settlement below L'tua Bay at the first opportunity.

Toward this end, Polomoshnoi, a company prikashchik [agent] was sent to Yakutat Bay to find a suitable location for buildings and to experiment with planting various grains and garden vegetables. Even before Baranov's arrival, he was to begin constructing the essential buildings. To protect the settlement from attack by the natives, Chertovitsyn, an ensign in the company's service, was instructed to assume military command of the traders and settlers, keeping firearms in order and maintaining constant watch both night and day.

In the middle of June 1795 Baranov set sail in the *Sv. Ol'ga*. The voyage began badly. On the second day at sea the ship sprang a large leak and almost sank. A favorable wind blowing toward Evrashech'ia [Marmot] Island saved the cutter from sinking. Repairing the damage as best he could, Baranov set out for Kenai Bay. There he learned that natives from Copper River had killed thirteen of Lebedev-Lastochkin's men, torturing to death the foreman, Samoilov. He spent several days in Kenai Bay on various business matters, including experimenting with coal from English Bay. From there he proceeded to Chugach Bay and then to Nuchek Bay [Port Etches]. Here, at the archimandrite's wish, he settled various disputes between Lebedev's traders and also investigated the murder of Samoilov and his men. It appeared that they had not been killed by Copper River natives, but by Kol'chane, and even then the attack had been provoked. This view was supported by the fact that both groups of natives came to Baranov, bringing furs for barter, and generally showed themselves well disposed toward the Russians.[2]

While he was at Nuchek Bay, Baranov learned that many of the natives who traded with his men at Yakutat Bay had left there, fearing an attack by the Kolosh, a warlike tribe who always had an abundance of guns, powder, and bullets, provided them by the English. In this case one must recall the influence which Baranov exerted on everyone around him. The natives not only listened submissively to his reproaches, but even bore punishments. Sometimes, of course, they would deviate from his orders, but never in his presence, whereas they did not even wish to know many other Russians who were considered important men in Shelikhov's company. "For his flight from Yakutat," wrote Baranov, "I had the Kenai toion lightly punished by cutting off half his beard and mustaches as a warning against future irregularities:

for he had shown the first bad example by arbitrarily leaving with ten baidarkas of Kenais, thus depriving the company of trade." Even the leaders of other companies visiting the Aleutian Islands would ask Baranov to settle disputes between them, abiding unconditionally by his decision.

Baranov arrived at Yakutat in August and persuaded many hitherto hostile tribes to become friendly with the Russians. He planted the flag and crest of the Russian empire on their shores amist gun salutes, beating of drums and shouts of "Hurrah!" while everyone with Baranov was drawn up in formation and performed military maneuvers.

Having left thirty men in Yakutat due to lack of space and provisions in his ship, Baranov immediately set out for Chil'kat Bay but there he did not find any of his ships. One of the inlets which presented an adequate harbor was named Olga Bay, and the island located in it was named St. Catherine Island. On heights and prominent places on the shore[3] Baranov set crosses with the inscription "Russian territory." The inhabitants of this inlet did not take well to the Russians, and although they came to trade furs, they were unfriendly and even tried to lure the ship into a narrow strait where it would have been in great danger.

Baranov then sailed again for Kenai Bay. The voyage was accompanied by continuous bad weather and strong winds, and lack of food and water exhausted the crew. On reading of the bad condition of the *Sv. Ol'ga* (in Baranov's words, "the main framework is not held together with bolts, but with barbed nails") one can only wonder at the self-sacrifice and courage with which the men of that time put to sea in their poorly constructed and inadequately supplied ships. Toward the end of autumn Baranov reached Kad'iak. Pribylov and Shields had also returned with their ships sometime before.

Novorossiisk settlement is founded on Yakutat Bay. In the summer of 1796 Baranov once again set out for Yakutat Bay. Despite Polomoshnoi's report of the obstacles to establishing a settlement there, Baranov decided to found one. Bad weather, however, delayed work until the middle of August. After hasty construction of baraboras,[4] promyshlenniks and settlers moved into the new village. The ship was taken to a nearby harbor designed for the settlement's use. Then essential structures were laid out. During his two-month stay at Yakutat, Baranov and his sixty men completed barracks and stores. Before returning to Kad'iak, Baranov instructed Polomoshnoi to continue building according to the plans and gave him orders as to laying up provisions, cultivating gardens, etc. Altogether, about eighty people, including traders and settlers with their wives and children, were left to winter at Yakutat. Baranov named the settlement Novorossiisk [New Russia].

During his stay at Yakutat, Baranov was visited by the main toion for that region, accompanied by numerous natives. They arrived with high ceremony, that is, singing and dancing in full array. This solemn visit was occasioned by their wish to establish friendly relations. At Baranov's order, the chief gave his children and relatives as hostages to show his sincerity. Because of their toion's advanced age, the natives asked that his nephew be chosen in his place. As a sign of his irrevocable elevation to this office, the natives asked that he be given a paper signed by Baranov. The Ugalakhmiuts, who lived further inland from Yakutat Bay, also presented hostages, for which they received a written assurance that the Russians would not injure or persecute them in any way.

Unfortunately, constant disagreement between the head of the settlement and its members and ignorance of how to treat the natives caused the Russians in Yakutat much harm. Moreoever, diseases, which broke out because of unsatisfactory quarters, the severity of the climate, and lack of fresh supplies undermined the success of the undertaking. During the winter thirty persons died. This weakening of the company's forces endangered the new settlement's survival, especially in view of the natives' hatred for the foreman. Although Polomoshnoi's removal quelled the general dissatisfaction for awhile, it could not erase the bad impression produced on the natives by the Russians' presence among them. Later this hostility was to make itself felt.

First explorations of Sitkha Island and Bay, and Baranov's proposal to found a settlement there. In the summer of 1796 Baranov ordered Shields to proceed with a survey of Chil'kat Bay, concentrating on its east side, where there were two native settlements. One of these was located on Sitkha [now Baranof] Island, which had a good harbor where foreign vessels often came to trade. "If you should happen to see the main Chil'kat toion," Baranov wrote to Shields, "befriend him and give him a baize cloak with ermines and a velveteen cap, and also from six to ten sazhen of blue beads. Ask him if any of his relatives would not like to live with us on Kad'iak, and if so, then take them, but no more than two. In this respect be as careful as possible of their cunning, for in those parts they have a passion for deceit."

With these orders the *Severnyi Orel* set out for Sitkha Island. There they found an English ship [the brig *Arthur*, from Bengal] under the command of Captain Barber. During their stay at the island, the English had traded with the natives, sent an armed launch to explore the straits and passages and attempted to rescue a sailor whom the Kolosh had taken from the ship. The main toion on Sitkha Island was angry at the violence of the English. They, had, for example, taken several natives, thrown them in irons and held them until they were given a required number of sea otters.

Beginning in 1796, hunting parties were sent regularly to the passages around Sitkha Island and a particularly large otter catch was taken from those regions in 1798. A party of five hundred baidarkas trapped and bartered in a short time more than twelve hundred otter skins, as well as other kinds of furs. The favorable position of Sitkha Island resolved Baranov to found a settlement there at the earliest opportunity. But this intention was not to be realized for several more years, and even then, as we shall see, only at great cost.

The wreck of the "Tri Sviatitelia." In 1796 the *Tri Sviatitelia* was also sent to Yakutat Bay, under the command of the foreman Medvednikov, skipper Pribylov having died in April of the same year. In the vicinity of Afognak and Marmot Islands she was overtaken by a violent storm and driven ashore in Kamyshak Bay, with the loss of two men and two women and much of the cargo, which consisted of furs and other goods. The ship was badly damaged and in the spring of 1797 Baranov sent a ship carpenter to repair her, but this proved impossible.

The building of forts at company settlements and the relinquishment of the posts by Lebedev's company. In 1795 the fort in Kenai Bay at the mouth of the Kaknu [Kenai] River was completed. All the buildings were transferred to the elevated right bank to avoid winter floods and heavy seas. Redoubts were also finished at Chugach Bay and Resurrection Harbor. In 1798 Baranov went to Nuchek Bay to choose a new and better site for a fort.

These forts offered necessary protection and defense against attack by the natives, who were frequently angered by the excesses of some of Baranov's subordinates and, particularly, of other companies' promyshlenniks, who were constantly feuding among themselves. This hostility also seriously affected the interrelations of the islanders, since the promyshlenniks, in an effort to defend their own interests, frequently set friendly tribes against each other.

Lebedev-Lastochkin's men removed their foreman, Konovalov, and presented him to Baranov in chains, that he might be sent off to Okhotsk [but the authorities there sent him back]. At Archimandrite Ioasaf's request, Baranov tried to reconcile the men with Konovalov, but from the time when Konovalov again became Lebedev's foreman at one of his main artels, the so-called fort Konstantin at Nuchek Bay, the quarrels and other troubles were renewed. The promyshlenniks complained unceasingly of each other to Baranov, or even fought openly, completely neglecting the fur trade. Meanwhile, the Kenais and Chugach took advantage of the dissension among the hunters to avenge wrongs, killing several Russians at various outposts and Lebedev's stores. The impotence of Lebedev's company and the hatred of the natives forced Konovalov and all his men to depart for Okhotsk. Kuskov, a merchant of Tot'ma who was Baranov's assistant on the island, took charge of the Nuchek Bay outpost and Lebedev's ship, the *Sv. Georgii*, set sail in early July 1797. Khlebnikov speaks of the incident in his biography of Baranov:[5]

> Baranov was quite pleased to gain influence over this area. The Chugach are of the same origin as the people of Kad'iak, but because they are surrounded by peoples who are their historical enemies, they were subject to attack by the Kolosh from the sea and by the inhabitants of the Copper River area from land. They were therefore warlike, extremely wary, and energetic. When the first Russian ships visited their shores, they were completely unapproachable; in 1783 they fell upon one of the Panov company's ships and drove it off; and in 1791 they resisted landing parties from Captain Billings' expedition.

Zaikov, captain of another of Lebedev's ships, the *Ioann Bogoslov* [St. John the Divine], remained for some time in Kenai Bay with sixty hunters. Dissension among the Russians and persecution of the natives reached such an extreme that the infuriated Kenais destroyed the two outposts at Iliamna and Tuiunak, killing twenty Russians and almost one hundred subject natives. When Baranov learned of the extreme danger threatening the remnants of Lebedev's company, he sent Malakhov to their aid with a well-armed party, who fortunately arrived in time. They found the fort under siege by the Kenais, who were preparing to set fire to it. In May 1798 Lebedev's traders left Kenai Bay, but they could not reach Okhotsk that year. They put in at Nizhne-Kamchatsk, where they found the *Sv. Georgii*, which had sailed from Nuchek Bay but was so dilapidated that she could go no farther. Thus, of Lebedev-Lastochkin's three ships only one returned, and of the two hundred men who set out on them fewer than eighty were left.

Baranov was pleased, of course, to be rid of his restless neighbors and competitors. Although other companies' outposts were still scattered here and there, they were not strong nor influential enough to disrupt his plans for placing the region on a sound administrative basis. It was obviously necessary to centralize the control of Russian settlements in the Eastern Ocean, and Baranov was justified in attempting to bring other jurisdictions under his control.

Missionary activities. From Baranov's letters to friends and business associates it is obvious that the presence of a religious mission in the colonies afforded him real satisfaction and that he cooperated fully with its efforts to spread God's word. "My heart rejoices," he wrote to Shelikhov, "in the introduction and propagation of the Holy Gospel here. My zeal has compelled me to give to the Church and the missionaries 1,500 rubles on my own account, as well as 500 rubles collected from various employees."

The mission succeeded in baptizing and marrying many natives: over twelve thousand persons of both sexes, according to Archimandrite Iosaf's report to the Holy Synod. In 1796 a church was built on Kad'iak. "In the new church there are holy services and ringing of bells," Baranov wrote with rapture to Kondakov, a promyshlennik.

Hieromonakh Juvenal set out around Aliaska Peninsula to preach the Gospel to the natives and to perform the Holy Sacraments among them, but his zeal proved to be his undoing. In 1795 he was killed by natives at Lake Iliamna. Generally speaking, the missionaries' efforts to spread immediately and everywhere among the native population Christian teachings, which were alien to many of that population's concepts were, to say the least, premature, particularly in view of the fact that confirming the natives in Christianity could only have taken place slowly. In their fervor, however, the colonial clergy compelled the newly converted natives to observe strictly those church ordinances which in time might well have overcome their indigenous customs and ancient prejudices.[6] This haste only thwarted their good intentions. Furthermore, the missionaries' ignorance of native dialects rendered their teachings useless to most of the natives and further hindered the attainment of their goals. Thus, the propagation of Christianity in the colonies, initially successful, soon came to a halt. Not only did the number of converts cease to grow, it even began to diminish, and the efforts of the clergy to reattract the natives were futile. When Archimandrite Ioasaf was recalled to Irkutsk by imperial ukaz [19 July 1796] to be consecrated a bishop, disorders broke out among the missionaries remaining in the colonies and their relations with the secular authorities began to deteriorate. This dissension did not cease from the time of the archimandrite's departure from the colonies in the summer of 1798 until Rezanov's arrival [in 1805] and during this entire time no church services were performed.

In the winter of 1795-1796, Barnov personally conducted a census of the inhabitants of Kad'iak Island, who numbered more than 6,200 persons: 3,221 men and 2,985 women. The numbers of natives in other places remained unknown.

Shelikhov's company merges with a company of Irkutsk merchants to form the United American Company. The merchants of Irkutsk constantly reproached Shelikhov for enriching himself at their expense by denying to them the means of trading with the natives of the islands and the American mainland. Their pretensions reached the point where they circulated scandalous letters in all of Shelikhov's overseas establishments and even sent men to incite Shelikhov's employees to petition the government and submit reports concerning the company's evil activities. Although these reports were so absurd that they were almost always ignored, they still produced an unfavorable impression. After Shelikhov's death all manner of malevolence was directed against his widow. The merchants of Irkutsk constantly brought lawsuits against her and seized every opportunity to slander her to people upon whose good will the company's welfare rested. They were particularly energetic in employing dishonorable means to undermine her credit. The chief participant in all the hostility against Madam Shelikhov was the merchant Myl'nikov, and finally her partner, Golikov, who had just concluded successfully his difficulty with the treasury, also turned against her. If the governor of Irkutsk, Acting Privy Counsellor Nagel', had not defended her, Madam Shelikhov could not have withstood her opponents' hostility.

Early in 1797 Myl'nikov decided to form a special maritime trading company consisting of ten or twelve partners. He proposed to capitalize the company at 129,000 rubles. Myl'nikov and his partners raised this sum by putting up their tanneries and various goods from their stores in Irkutsk and selling promissory notes with various maturities. Having undertaken to build a ship destined to sail for the very regions which Shelikhov's company already occupied, Myl'nikov decided that 120,000 rubles of capital was quite inadequate and that unless considerable sums were added to it, the company would surely go bankrupt within five months. Furthermore, the company's position was unenviable in that it had carelessly pledged goods to outside merchants who had lent it large sums of money. The debts were now due, but previous expenses had left the company with very little money to repay its creditors. In this difficult position the Irkutsk merchants decided to approach Golikov and persuade him to join them. Golikov accepted their offer, but insisted that Madam Shelikhov not be permitted to take part in the company. His wishes, however, could not be followed. Myl'nikov and the other partners knew very well that they could not get along without Madam Shelikhov's cooperation, and for this reason invited her to join them. Madam Shelikhov, wishing to eliminate their rivalry and hoping that the merger of the two companies would quickly

end her quarrel with Golikov, decided to join Myl'nikov and his partners. She hoped that the imperial patronage would extend from Shelikhov's company to the united company, which would, through the participation of many more people, have greater means to carry out her
husband's projects in the Aleutian Islands and on the coasts of America. Thus the merger took place on 20 July 1797.[7]

In concluding the merger Madam Shelikhov ceded to the new company for 600,000 rubles all the assets of her company, which had been
appraised at 688,460 paper rubles. Of these 600,000 rubles she agreed
to subscribe 200,000 into the capital of the new company, letting the
company pay the remaining 400,000 without interest in installments
over a two-and-one-half-year period, on condition that after this time
her capital would earn 5 percent if it were necessary to retain it in the
company. In such case, Madam Shelikhov agreed not to demand repayment of more than 100,000 rubles per year, so the company's
operations would not be disrupted by excessive payments.

Moreover, the united company took on itself a debt of 96,370
rubles which Madam Shelikhov had incurred for various commercial
operations.

Madam Shelikhov also sold to the new company for 70,000 rubles
the ship *Dobroe Predpriiatie Sv. Aleksandry* [Good Enterprise of St.
Aleksandr] , which was her own personal property.

The Irkutsk merchants agreed to subscribe 400,000 rubles to the
capital of the company by 1 January 1798, and on top of this Golikov had to pay in 200,000 rubles. These amounts, together with
Madam Shelikhov's subscription, capitalized the company at a total
of 800,000 rubles. Subsequently the capital was reduced to 723,000
rubles, divided into 723 shares with a par value of 1,000 paper rubles.

Through this merger then, the Irkutsk merchants acquired the
following:

Nine ships and the rest of the assets of Shelikhov's company, consisting of various ship's equipment and goods located in America and
in Siberia, valued at 600,000 rubles (the amount conceded by Madam
Shelikhov). This sum together with the capital of the other partners
provided the new company with over 1,100,000 rubles. The new
company also acquired other assets not included in this accounting:
various buildings in Aliaska and the Aleutian Islands, agricultural
provisions, shipbuilding stores and supplies, etc.

Meanwhile Kiselev, another merchant of Irkutsk active in the American fur trade, refused to participate in the company, and made every
effort to injure it. He presented the directors with various claims
against the company, accusing it of taking away his means of trade.

He secretly bought up from the promyshlenniks the furs they had acquired through their shares and obtaining their powers of attorney in dealing with the company, brought lawsuits against it. Moreover, he employed agents to convince one of the missionaries, the hieromonk Makarii, to go secretly to St. Petersburg and inform against the company directors' allegedly harsh treatment of the natives and to take with him several Aleuts to attest to the truth of his report. To this end, Kiselev ordered his own vessel to take the hieromonk and his natives from Unalashka Island. Despite all these efforts, Makarii was unable to incriminate the company and was sent back to Irkutsk to do penance before Archimandrite Ioasaf for going off to St. Petersburg without the latter's knowledge. Subsequently, Kiselev saw that his schemes had backfired and sent to the company requests for a merger or even for permission to carry on trade, but all his pleas were rejected.

After the merger agreement was completed, Madam Shelikhov went to St. Petersburg both to petition the government to ratify the merger and to settle several outstanding disagreements with her partners. These matters were all settled by imperial decree in Madam Shelikhov's favor. The emperor also gave his approval to a recommendation of the College of Commerce that other Russian subjects of all classes be allowed to participate in the new company. At the same time Madam Shelikhov was elevated to the nobility. On 3 August 1798 the merger was confirmed. The firm was known as the United American Company.[8]

The management of the United American Company. Article 8 of the Act of Incorporation provided for the appointment of two to four directors. The partners elected to these posts Merchant of the First Guild Dmitrii Myl'nikov of Irkutsk and Merchant of the Third Guild Ivan Shelikhov of Ryl'sk.

The Act of Incorporation stipulated that small traders might join the company under the following conditions: their assets were to be paid into the general capital of the company and new shares were to be issued with the same rights as the original shares. According to these general rules, Lebedev's company was also to be integrated into the united company.

Early in 1799 the company sent director Dmitrii Myl'nikov to Kiakhta to trade with the Chinese and to take over the management of the company's activities in that city. He replaced Shmatov, a merchant of Kursk who until that year had been the company's agent. Iakov Myl'nikov, Dmitrii's brother, was named director in his place.

The manager of the former Northeastern American Company,

Baranov, was assigned twenty donative shares from the general profits for his past services, with the right to use these shares to reward any assistants which he might employ and to consider himself, if he wished, a full partner in the United American Company. Moreover, it was decided to issue to him gratis twenty ordinary shares worth 2,500 paper rubles each.[9] Two-thirds of the profits on these twenty shares were to be retained by the company until the total sum of 50,000 rubles had been repaid, and one-third of the profits were to be given to Baranov. Baranov, however, refused this loan and paid the full 50,000 rubles for his shares.

In addition to the head office at Irkutsk it was decided to establish three other offices: on the Urak River, at Kad'iak and on Unalashka Island, and if necessary another in the Kurile Islands.

One of the partners, the Irkutsk merchant Larionov, was named head of the company's Unalashka district. In case Baranov should leave the colonies, Larionov was to take his place. In the meantime Larionov was placed in charge of the islands from Atkha to the Aliaska Peninsula and north to Bering Strait.

The Atkha Company. In 1799 the United American Company sent the townsman Ladygin to Atkha Island. Up to that time the vessel *Dobroe Predpriiatie Sv. Aleksandry* had been at Atkha. It had been sent there in 1795 from Okhotsk, returning in 1798 with a cargo of furs, under the command of Ladygin. After his departure a trading party of forty-one men, referred to as the Atkha Company, had remained to Atkha and the neighboring islands. The territory of this company comprised the Andreianov and Near Islands and, in general, all of the Aleutians lying toward Kamchatka, including Komandorskie and Mednyi islands, as well as all the Kurile Islands, including the detachment on Urup, under the command of Zvezdochetov. It was proposed to man the company with one hundred promyshlenniks, thirty or forty of whom Ladygin was to send to trade in the Priblov Islands.

The supplying of the Atkha Company, the hiring of its personnel, and the export of its fur catch from the islands were all the direct responsibility of the Okhotsk office, independer.t of the management of the other settlements, that is, of Baranov or Larionov.

Shortcomings of company shipping. Larionov left Okhotsk in the autumn of 1797 on the company ship *Sv. apostoly Petr i Pavel i chudotvorets Nikolai* (Apostles Peter and Paul and Nicholas, the miracle worker). The vessel was wrecked on the coast of Kamchatka. According to Larionov's report the wreck was caused by the complete ignorance of the captain, sub-navigator Kozlov, of reckoning and of the position of the coasts. The dearth of fresh water aboard the ship was extreme. Nine men died of exhaustion or of excessive consumption of water upon their arrival ashore. In the summer of 1798 Larionov sailed from Kamchatka for Unalashka on another company ship, the *Sv. Simeon.*

Unfortunately for all companies engaged in the fur trade, the lack of good captains and the general weakness of theoretical knowledge of navigation on the part of their vessel commanders frequently led to the loss of ships, crews, and cargo.

It is fitting to record here, as a striking example of the complete ignorance of those early captains, the tale of the voyage of Kiselev's ship, the *Sv. Zosima i Savatii* [Sts. Zosima and Savatii] under the command of the "experienced voyager" [*starovoiazhnyi*] boatswain Sapozhnikov. This story is taken from a letter from Kozhin, a merchant of Iakutsk who was a passenger on this voyage, to one of the employees of Zhigarev, a partner in Kiselev's company. Through the captain's ignorance, the ship strayed about eighteen hundred versts south of its course, until finally a happy change of wind blew her to Afognak Island, where she arrived in very bad straits. This voyage is so interesting that we will reprint Kozhin's account.

> You know of our departure from Okhotsk. We got out of the bay successfully and passed through the first Kurile strait into the open sea, setting our course for Unalashka. After we had left the Kurile Islands, we saw no land and finally reached a point where it was impossible to wear clothing, the air was so heavy with heat, even at night on the deck. The gear and tackle were burning hot, all around the ship we saw many worms and the water was almost boiling. The vessel leaked so badly that the pumps had to be manned constantly. Water was pumped out around the clock and the sailors dropped from exhaustion. But God did not wish to see his creatures perish, so the water was successfully kept out. The heat was everywhere; there was no escaping it either in the cabin or in the hold—it was impossible to live. Soon the men began asking why it had become so hot. To this our captain answered that the water was always that hot in the winter, and moreover that the continuing southerly winds had driven all the warm water together. Then the men asked, "Where are we going?" The captain replied, "I still have to continue southwards, because I have not reached the line where I will change course." At this the crew began to have misgivings and to talk of choosing another captain. Finally, despairing of their lives, since there was only one more barrel of water, they chose another captain and gave themselves up to the power of the Omniscient God, singing acathisti to the Holy Virgin and to St. Nicholas, the Miracle Worker, and to Sts. Zosima and Savatii, the miracle workers of Solvetskii Island. After the services were ended, they carried images of the Holy Virgin and the Saints onto the deck and, in place of confession, kissed them and prayed to them with weeping. They prayed that God might send them any wind and thither would they go, because now they knew not whether they were going north or south and they yet had found no

land. Then in a short time a south wind came, the sails were filled and we kept the same course for eighteen hundred versts, quenching our thirst with rainwater. Thus, by accident, we came to land, which chanced to be the island of Shuiakh.[10]

Instructions to Baranov. The United American Company gave Baranov detailed instructions concerning the conduct of trade and the barter of furs from the natives. He was ordered to pay them according to voluntary negotiations and to make all possible concessions, so that they might be won over by his kind and friendly behavior.

The company also informed Baranov that thereafter its accounts with the promyshlenniks were to be settled not in furs, but in cash according to a special table of prices, which was to be established immediately on the basis of a mutually agreeable and advantageous assessment of the value of furs. In case any promyshlenniks should be dissatisfied with this arrangement, Baranov could let them return to Okhotsk, replacing them with Aleuts, who were to be paid for their services with goods that they might choose from the company stores, to the value of 50 or 60 paper rubles per year.

At the same time the company concluded an employment contract with Banner, a gubernia secretary. He was to set out in a company ship for the Chukotka Peninsula and try to carry on barter trade there and on the opposite coast of America. This proposal, however, came to nothing and the expedition was cancelled, even though Banner had already set out.

The company shares increase in value. In 1798 the company ships *Phoenix* and *Predpriiatie Sv. Aleksandry* arrived from the colonies with large cargoes of furs. Part of the company's furs, about sixty-six thousand fur-seal pelts, were obtained by one of Lebedev's ships which returned in the same year. In all, the United American Company obtained furs worth more than a million rubles. By the next official accounting each share of the company's stock had appreciated to thirty-five hundred paper rubles, and this was the price that new shareholders had to pay. In appraising this increase in value we must also consider profits from goods sent overland by Madam Shelikhov to Kamchatka, Okhotsk, Gizhiga, Iakutsk, Kiakhta, and Moscow.

Archimandrite Ioasaf arrived from the colonies on the *Phoenix* and immediately set out for Irkutsk.

The Russian-American Company obtains imperial patronage and is granted rules and privileges. In 1799 Emperor Paul granted the company rules and privileges.[11] This event was significant not only in consolidating the company's position, but also because it enabled the company to introduce proper government to the country under its control.

The Imperial Decree to the Governing Senate of 8 July 1799 states:

> The benefits and advantages resulting to Our Empire from the trade being carried on by our loyal subjects in the Northeastern Sea and along the coasts of America have attracted Our attention and high regard. For this reason we place under our immediate protection the company which has been formed to carry out this trade and we order that it be called "the Russian-American Company under Our Highest Protection," and authorize that our military commanders utilize all possible land and naval forces to support the company's requirements. For the guidance of the company and for its relief and encouragement we have provided it with rules and privileges which shall continue in force for a period of twenty years. We order that both of these Imperial Decrees, as well as the Act of Incorporation composed in Irkutsk, which in every respect are worthy of our approval and are in no way annulled by our rules, be carried to Our Senate, and that there an appropriate document be prepared in accordance with the above-mentioned privileges and that it be presented for our signature, and that, in general, all necessary arrangements be carried out.

Here is a short extract of the most important rules imposed on the company:

1. To the existing 723 shares were to be added another thousand. These shares[12] might be acquired by any Russian subject, regardless of his rank or class, and also by any foreigner who had accepted Russian citizenship and resided in the Russian empire.

2. The capitalized value of the shares was to remain constant, but each shareholder might dispose of his shares as he saw fit. The profits were to be divided by general agreement of the shareholders, but at least a tenth of them were to be left in the company to strengthen its position.

3. The managing body of the company in Irkutsk was to be known as the "Main Administration of the Russian-American Company under Highest Protection of His Imperial Majesty." This body was obliged to report directly to the Emperor on everything concerning the company's affairs, including both its decisions and its progress. Four directors were to be chosen.

The privileges conferred on the company included the following:

1. To make use of all hunting grounds and establishments now existing on the northwestern coast of America from 55° north latitude to Bering Strait and beyond, and also on the Aleutian, Kurile, and other islands situated in the Northeastern Ocean, and everything which had been or might be discovered in those localities, on the surface and in the interior of the earth, without competition from others.

2. To make discoveries north of 55° latitude, and to the south,

and to occupy newly discovered lands in the name of Russia, according to previously prescribed rules,[13] if they had not been previously occupied by or been dependent on any other nation.

3. To establish settlements and to fortify them wherever the company, at its best judgment, might find them needful.

4. To extend navigation to all adjoining nations and to trade with all nearby Powers, upon obtaining their free consent and on the confirmation of the Sovereign. For its use and advantage the company might hire free men of any class for navigation, hunting and all other business.

Formation of the board of directors. A special imperial decree followed. "One of the four directors of the company is to be trustee of the interests of the Shelikhov family." On the basis of this decree, Madam Shelikhov asked that her son-in-law, Mikhail Matveevich Buldakov, a merchant of Velikii Ustiug, be named to this post, and this was done.

Baranov, head of the company in America and the islands, was rewarded with a gold medal to be worn around the neck.

The convening of the board of directors was celebrated with particular pomp for several days. In addition to the previous directors and the newly appointed Buldakov, the merchant Startsov was also elected to the board. All the directors took an oath of office. Buldakov was named chairman of the board.

At the first board meeting (16 September 1799) a motion was proposed by Madam Shelikhov and carried whereby the company was to donate sixty thousand paper rubles at the rate of three thousand rubles per year to build barracks in Irkutsk, as a sign of devotion to the emperor. In addition, five hundred rubles were to be given to the military hospital and seven hundred rubles to civilian hospitals for the poor.

To protect and advance the company's interests in St. Petersburg, Rezanov accepted the post of company representative there. The appointment was confirmed by the emperor at the request of the board of directors.

The transfer of the main office to St. Petersburg and the split of the company's stock. In the Imperial Decree to the Governing Senate of 19 October 1800 the Emperor Paul ordered:

1. That the main office be transferred from Irkutsk to St. Petersburg. The board of directors was permitted to establish at Irkutsk a secondary office for carrying on trade, dispatching goods to America, enlisting crews for ships, etc. This decree was immediately put into

effect, and the board ordered all other establishments and outposts to obey the instructions of the Irkutsk office, as being second in authority only to itself.

2. That the College of Commerce consider to what value the shares of the Russian-American Company might be split, in view of the greatly increased value of the company's shares, which made it difficult for new shareholders to be brought in. The determination of the new value was to be submitted to the sovereign's confirmation.[14]

The College of Commerce, after considering the assets of the company and the suggestions of the board of directors, found it proper to split the old shares (which had risen to 3,727 rubles 27 3/4 kopeks) into new shares worth 500 rubles each. In place of the former 1,723 shares, there were now to be a total of 7,350 shares, which the company was permitted to utilize for the purposes set forth in its Imperial Charter before the expiration of the term of its privileges.

The Emperor confirmed the proposal of the College of Commerce on 17 August 1801.[15]

Members of the imperial family become shareholders. On 25 March 1802 the emperor sent to the directors the following rescript:

> To the Directors of the Russian-American Company: Gentlemen! Wishing to signify how beneficial I find the commercial enterprise which you direct and how pleasing to me it is to view its growth, I have seen fit to purchase twenty shares for 10,000 rubles for the benefit of the poor, which the company is to issue in the name of the head of the Cabinet. It will please me if my example strengthens the general confidence in this enterprise and more closely acquaints private persons with this new branch of Russian industry, which unites so intimately private profit and the good of the State. I remain your benevolent Alexander.

The Dowager Empress Maria Feodorovna bought four 500-ruble shares, assigning both the shares and their dividends to the benefit of the School of Commerce.

The emperor also subscribed two thousand rubles in the name of Empress Elizabeth for four shares which would be used for the benefit of the poor.

Tsarevich Constantine wished to acquire two shares.

In the same year, the general meeting of stockholders, as a sign of the company's gratitude to its imperial protector, voted to set aside .5 percent of each dividend for the benefit of the poor.

Also in 1802 the emperor sent to the directors the following rescript on the occasion of their having provided vessels for the transport of women settlers from Irkutsk to Kamchatka:

To the Directors of the Russian-American Company: Gentlemen! The Commandant of Nizhne-Kamchatsk, Major General Koshelev, has reported to me that the Russian-American Company has provided the women settlers en route from Irkutsk for Kamchatka with a large river boat at company expense and thus has permitted them to depart with the rapidity so necessary to the establishment of the Landmilitsiia in Kamchatka. Such zealous and praiseworthy conduct by the Directors of the Russian-American Company I find worthy of my favor and gratitude, with which I remain your benevolent Alexander.

Orders of the board of directors regarding the colonies and to the company's Siberian offices. The board of directors, in accordance with the decision of the general meeting of stockholders, appointed Baranov chief manager of all the colonies in America and on the islands and gave him the following orders:

1. All company artels and detachments on the islands (excepting those of the Atkha Company) were to be united under the direction of the chief manager of the colonies and subject to his orders. In order to manage the affairs of all of these outposts and detachments, an American head office was to be established, which in turn was to distribute the men in America and on the islands and to organize the hunting and trade.

2. The promyshlenniks were to be paid for furs credited to their accounts according to the following table of rates [in paper rubles], established with their general agreement:[16]

Furs	Price per pelt	
	r.	k.
Sea otters of the 1st, 2nd, & 3rd grades	50	—
Young sea otters	20	—
Sea otter pups and tails of all grades, except young beaver tails	3	—
Fur seals	1	
Foxes: Kad'iak silver	10	—
" " " (not well furred)	5	—
" Unalashka silver	15	—
" " " (not well furred)	7	50
" " " (summer-furred)	2	—
" Kad'iak cross	3	—
" Unalashka and mainland cross	5	—
" " " " " (not well furred)	1 r. 75 k. to 2	50
" red	2 r. to 3	50
Arctic foxes: St. George Island and mainland	5	—
" " Commander Islands	2	50
" " island and mainland white	1	—
Otters	3 r. to 8	—
River beavers	3 r. to 6	
Wolves	2 r. to 5	—
Minks	—	50

Furs	Price per pelt	
	r.	k.
Martens and American sables	50 k. to 1	—
Wolverines	2 r. to 5	—
Walrus tusks (from 6 to 9 tusks per pud)	per Pud: 12	—
" " (more [?] than 6 tusks per pud)	per Pud: 10	—

3. Some Russian employees located at Okhotsk and other company establishments and at sea were to be replaced by natives, no more than 100 or 120 men per detachment, paying them with goods from the company stores at their value in Okhotsk, with additional charges for transportation to the colonies.[17]

4. Special attention was to be paid to ethnographic, statistical, and hydrographic investigations on the American mainland, and accurate and detailed maps were to be prepared for all the areas surveyed.

5. Special attention was to be paid to agriculture, animal husbandry, various metallic ores and salts, etc., and to reporting observations in these fields.

6. Special attention was to be paid to the school which had been established and to furnishing information on the results of education and on the willingness of the natives to learn. A catalog of books available in the Kad'iak library was to be compiled so that the head office might supplement this collection with standard and newly published works in Russian and in foreign languages.

7. Data were to be sent on what manual arts and crafts were currently being practiced in the colonies and also on what kinds of tools and craftsmen were needed, so that the company might immediately send them out.

8. Bearing in mind the abundance of whales in colonial waters, a report was to be submitted on the number of whales washed up on Kad'iak and the Unalashka each year, their size and the approximate amount of oil, bone, etc. which might be extracted from them, including observations on the best means to catch whales.

9. In view of the remoteness of the colonies, Baranov was permitted, in accordance with his own request, to make changes in the orders of the head office and the Irkutsk office, if he considered that certain provisions were unsuited to local conditions. This right, however, was accorded only to Baranov, and then only if such changes did not destroy the essence of the orders.

In 1802, A. E. Polevoi, a merchant of Kursk, was named head of the Okhotsk office. He was also entrusted with the management of the company establishments in Iakutsk, Kamchatka, Gizhiga, America[?], on the islands etc., so that he became in effect chief manager of all the company's posts in Siberia except Irkutsk, where Director Startsov had taken over after the death of Myl'nikov. Polevoi was also made responsible for supplying the colonies with their needs.

Company losses in 1799. In spite of the many favors which the emperor showed to the company in 1799, this year proved to be a very unfortunate one, owing to the loss of several ships with their passengers intended for service in the colonies. The greatest of these disasters was the wreck of the *Phoenix*, lost somewhere between Okhotsk and the colonies. This ship carried eighty-eight men, including the Most Reverend Ioasaf, who was on his way to his duties after being consecrated bishop. The cargo, both company and private, lost with the ship was valued at more than five hundred thousand paper rubles.

For a long time it was hoped that the *Phoenix* had found shelter somewhere from the storms which were then raging, but the subsequent casting ashore at Sitkha, Kad'iak, and Otter Bay of many items belonging to the ship finally forced acceptance of the sad truth.

It was suspected that the loss of the ship was caused by the terrible fever then raging in Okhotsk and Kamchatka. If the crew succumbed to this infection, owing to the poor and crowded conditions on board, they may have been unable to bring the ship to its destination.

During the same year the company vessel *Severnyi Orel*, under command of navigator Talin, was wrecked on Suklia Island while returning from Yakutat to Kad'iak, with 22,000 furs and many other goods. In addition the vessel *Sv. Simeon i Anna* was wrecked on St. Paul Island, although without loss to personnel or cargo.

Ships are built for the company fleet and naval officers are detached to command them. In 1799 the ship *Sv. Dmitrii* was built for the company in Okhotsk; in 1801 the *Sv. Petr i Pavel* and the *Sv. Kniaz Aleksandr Nevskii*; in 1802 the *Zakhariia i Elisaveta*; and 1804 the *Sv. Mariia Magdalina* and the cutter *Konstantin*. The directors petitioned the Empress Dowager Maria Feodorovna for permission to name one of the newly built ships after her. On 17 December Her Majesty replied to the chairman of the board with the following rescript: "Mr. Buldakov! The reported action of the board of directors of the Russian-American Company touches me deeply and truly evidences its zeal toward me, for which I desire to express to the Board my gratitude and favor and to assure it that I sincerely wish it the greatest success in its undertakings. I remain your benevolent Maria."

The board of directors was compelled to discontinue shipbuilding in Okhotsk and ordered Baranov to build ships in the colonies, if there should be need for them there, or to purchase them from Englishmen and Americans who came to those regions, bearing in mind the cost of building them in Okhotsk, from 15,000 to 25,000 paper rubles each.

From the time the company passed under imperial patronage, naval officers were detached to its service. In an imperial decree two experi-enced navigators, Petrov and Bulygin, were assigned to the command of company ships in 1801 and the two sub-navigators [first mates] were detached from government service at Okhotsk. In 1802 two naval officers were taken into the company's service, Lieutenant Khvostov and Midshipman Davydov, and in 1804 Lieutenants Mashin and Sukin, Midshipman Karpinskii, and one first mate.

The company's Kiakhta trade in 1798 and 1799 and the prohibi-tion on the import of fur seals. Since the renewal of the Kiakhta trade with the Chinese, the exchange of the company's furs for tea had gone as usual, and since most of the furs were in the company's hands, the prices were well maintained in 1798 and 1799, particularly in the case of fur seals, which brought almost five paper rubles per pelt. Sea otters brought no more than 100 rubles. Young otters and female otters were priced according to their quality. Otter tails fetched from 7 to 9 rubles, otters around 18 rubles. River beavers dressed in the old manner brought 10 rubles, and when dressed in the European manner brought considerably more. Silver foxes were priced at 20 rubles, cross foxes at 10 rubles, and red foxes at 4 or 5 rubles. Lynx brought 13 rubles.

On the company's petition that imported fur seals, under the name of gray beavers, were undermining the company's sale of the furs obtained in the Pacific islands and America, the following Imperial Rescript was issued in August 1802 addressed to the Minister of Com-merce:

Count Nikolai Petrovich! Deferring to the request of the Russian-American Company, in which it is explained that the customs house here, on the orders of the College of Commerce, permits the importing of gray beavers from a certain Kap [cape?] Island, which the Russian merchants consider to be fur seals, I command that the importation of these furs from foreign lands be prohibited, since the company's business in America is being hampered, and those furs which have been ordered or are now in the customs house be sent back under surveillance during the present navigation season, but without confiscating them or subjecting them to public sale; with the arrival of the new year, however, I order that any such goods imported be dealt with ac-cording to the Decree of 1793 in regard to prohibited goods. I remain your benevolent Alexander.

3. The Extension of Russian Colonies along the Northwest Coast of America, the Imperial Appointment of a Delegation to Japan, and the Company's Round-the-World Expedition of 1803

The occupation of Sitkha Island. In 1799 Baranov decided to carry out his plan of establishing a settlement on Sitkha [Baranof] Island. A year-round ice-free harbor and other conveniences made it better for Russian settlement than Yakutat. With this aim, the ship *Sv. Ekaterina*, under the command of Podgazh, a foreigner, was ordered to sail to the port of Bucarelli and then to meet Baranov and a trading party at Sitkha. Among other things, she was supposed to obtain there building materials for a fort and essential buildings.

When he arrived at Sitkha, Baranov did not find the fur hunting party, which had suffered a great disaster on the return trip. One hundred fifteen natives in the party had died in a few hours from eating mussels found on the shore. In their terror the survivors took flight, and could hardly be held as a party. In spite of this, however, the catch of sea otters was abundant. Almost fifteen hundred pelts were taken in the neighborhood of Sitkha, as well as three hundred obtained at Yakutat in the same year.

In the winter of 1799-1800 Baranov built a fort and several essential buildings for himself and for his workers. His self-denial for the common good was remarkable. Until late autumn he endured living in a tent torn by the winds, and then for several months he suffered from the smoke in a miserable shack. Subsequently the fort was improved and yurts were built for the hunters and workmen. Only twenty men took part in the work.

Company losses from trade with the natives by foreigners. In the spring of 1800 several American and English vessels arrived at the new Russian settlement. In plain view of the Russians, the English bartered over 2,000 sea otters from the natives. They paid the Kolosh for the furs with more and better goods than the Russians had to offer, completely disrupting the company's trade yet complaining all the while that the Americans were cutting them out of the fur trade. The Americans for their part attempted to obtain furs from the natives in exchange for guns, powder, and ammunition. Baranov, seeing this, urged the Americans not to give the natives arms, but they replied that having come more than fifteen thousand miles in search of profit, they had to market whatever paid best.

Relations with the natives at the new settlement. While the Russians were building, the Kolosh did all they could to harm them. Only Baranov's firmness and his fearlessness saved the new settlemen. When the Kolosh injured a female interpreter sent to ask her people to a celebration on the occasion of the dedication of the fort,[1] Baranov appeared in the Kolosh settlement amid three hundred armed natives with only twenty-two men, demanding satisfaction. After that, the Kolosh evidently abandoned all attempts to drive the Russians from Sitkha Island. However, trade with them was not very satisfactory. The Kolosh constantly pointed out that the English and Americans gave them more goods and that they would wait for the arrival of their ships to barter their furs.

The disorders which Baranov found on Kad'iak after his return there, and his intention to resign the chief managership. Upon his return to Kad'iak from Sitkha, Baranov found much disorder. Most of the company's employees, and particularly the clergy, wished to ignore the orders of Kushov, who had acted as Baranov's deputy in his absence. Moreover, the disaster which overtook the hunting party in 1799 worked so strongly on the natives' imagination that they had no wish whatever to go out hunting for sea otter again, being confirmed in their resistance by the monks, who attempted to undermine secular authority. Despite Baranov's strength of character, which was especially evident in the face of obstacles, these troubles strongly affected him. In many of his letters to Larionov, he attempted to persuade him to accept the post of chief manager of the colonies. Larionov could not bring himself to assume this responsibility, understanding the significance of Baranov's position in the founding of the colonies. Closely acquainted with the affairs of the company, he knew well that many difficulties would be encountered in building Russian settlements on the Eastern Ocean and, convinced of his own inadequacy, was unwilling to undertake this job. For these reasons Larionov did all he could to refuse Baranov's offer.

It seems that fate itself preserved Baranov for a land which would owe everything to his energy and enterprise.

Shortage of goods and supplies. Meanwhile the colonies were suffering one ordeal after another. The loss of the *Phoenix*, which had been sent to the colonies with a large cargo, produced a shortage of essential items, and this continued throughout 1801. The *Sv. Arkhistrati Mikhail* [Archangel Mikhail], under the command of navigator Mukhoplev, which sailed from Okhotsk for Unalashka and Kad'iak in 1800 with a cargo of materials and supplies and twenty-seven workmen, barely escaped destruction from contrary winds and violent storms, and one-third of the cargo had to be jettisoned in order to save the ship. The captain and his mate Beliaev failed through negligence to set the correct course, deviated toward Bol'sheretsk and ran aground near there. Navigator Mukhoplev perished and his crew wintered on various small islands. During the winter the workmen were so deprived that after a two-month voyage they arrived at Unalashka under Beliaev's command with almost no clothing. Here they were driven ashore by a violent wind. The ship was wrecked, and although part of the cargo was saved, it was soaked through and almost completely unusable.

Meanwhile, the inhabitants of Unalashka had been awaiting supplies from Okhotsk with great impatience. Finally, a ship appeared at the entrance to Unalashka Bay, but the joy was short lived. She was the *Predpriiatie Sv. Aleksandry*, sent to the Chukotka Peninsula with Banner. After two winters on the voyage from Okhotsk, first in the Kurile Islands and then on Atkha Island, she had barely reached Unalashka. By that time her crew had consumed most of the supplies on board. Banner's command was unsatisfactory in all respects, and the directors, hearing of the unsuccessful beginning of the expedition, canceled it until a more favorable time and transferred Banner to service in the colonies. Baranov put him in command at Kad'iak on the frequent occasions when he and Kuskov were absent from the island. Larionov, having some essential company business on St. George Island, decided to go there himself and enroute to try his luck at discovering some islands which were rumored to exist. Beliaev and his crew, assigned to the *Predpriiatie Sv. Aleksandry*, displayed brilliantly indeed their knowledge of the sea. Far from making new discoveries, they were quite unable even to find St. George Island. "We sailed toward Umnak Island," wrote Larionov, "and found ourselves at Unimak. After sailing for twenty days, having provisions for only one more day, we again sighted Unalashka. A second effort to reach the Pribylov Islands also failed, the ship barely escaping destruction from a strong contrary wind."

Fortunately for Baranov and his companions an American ship [the *Enterprise*, Scott] arrived from New York [on 24 June 1800], and the

Russians were able to barter for more than 12,000 paper rubles worth of goods and supplies, which saved them from imminent starvation.

Baranov's visit to Kenai and Chugach bays and the ordeals of the company ships "Sv. Ekaterina" and "Predprüatie Sv. Akeksandry." In the spring of 1801 Baranov sent the *Sv. Ekaterina* to Yakutat and Sitkha with provisions and went himself to Kenai Bay, where there had been clashes with the natives. Having calmed the traders and pacified the Kenais as far as possible, he gathered the fur catch and set out for Chugach Bay. In Nuchek Bay he met Kuskov, returning with a party of traders and a quantity of furs abundant beyond expectation. Baranov followed the party to Kad'iak, where he and his ship successfully arrived in September.

The *Sv. Ekaterina* arrived from Sitkha late in the autumn, having suffered greatly on the voyage because of bad weather and shortage of provisions, so that finally the crew were reduced to eating seal skins. During the ship's stay at Sitkha good progress was made in erecting the various buildings, thanks to the help of the men on the ship. The fort and the barracks were almost completed; several storehouses were still lacking and they proposed to build them the following year.

The same year the *Predprüatie Sv. Aleksandry* sailed for Okhotsk with a cargo of furs, but could not make port before the onset of freezing weather. They wintered in Kamchatka. The following year, 1802, the vessel was completely destroyed at the mouth of the Urak, but the crew and cargo were saved.

Continued shortages in the colonies and some of Baranov's measures on Kad'iak. The goods and supplies which had been bartered from the American ship were soon exhausted, and the colonies again began to feel acute shortages of everything. The causes for this were the extremely limited cargo sent by the Okhotsk office on the ship *Zakhariia i Elisaveta* and the delayed arrival at Kad'iak of two company ships sent out in 1801 with various supplies. One of these, the *Aleksandr Nevskii*, wintered on Atkha and reached Unalashka only in midsummer. There it had to leave most of its cargo, bringing back almost nothing for Kad'iak. The other, the *Petr i Pavel* was ordered first to discharge a government cargo at Kamchatka and then, owing to the lateness of the season, was forced to winter there. Admiral Mordvinov informed Buldakov that the emperor had received a report that the company's agent, having free space on this vessel for 2,200 puds, had accepted without charge a government cargo for Petropavlovsk, for which the emperor had expressed his gratitude to Buldakov, as chairman of the board.

Having sent what men and supplies he could to Yakutat and Sitkha, Baranov decided to devote the year 1802 to various projects on Kad'-iak, including the planting of vegetable gardens. Also, in view of rumors of war with England, he planned to prepare places several miles from the harbor where furs could be safe from the enemy, and to build batteries. Mainly, of course, this was done for appearances, since his small caliber guns could be of little use. Later he went to Afognak Island to inspect the artels [posts] there.

Natives sack the settlement on Sitkha Island. During Baranov's absence from Kad'iak, news was received of a terrible disaster which had overtaken the Sitkha settlement. The English Captain Barber, upon arrival in Kad'iak with his ship, related that the Kolosh had attacked the Russian fort when he was nearby. Although he had hastened there, he found only smoking ruins and dead and horribly mutilated promyshlenniks. According to survivors, who had fled to Barber to avoid capture, an enormous horde of armed natives, profiting by the absence of half the Russians, who were working outside the fort, surrounded the barracks and began shooting through the windows. For a long time the Russians managed to repulse the enemy, but when the natives set fire to the buildings, the defenders had to flee, whereupon the Kolosh cut down and slew them one at a time. There were some fifteen men in the barracks. The other promyshlenniks and Aleuts hastened to their aid, but could do nothing to save them and were almost all killed themselves. In all, twenty Russians perished at Sitkha, including their leader, foreman Medvednikov, along with 130 Aleuts. Three thousand otter and other pelts were stolen and the vessel built for the company was burned. The English rescued from the hands of the Kolosh three Russians and five Aleut men, eighteen women, and six children.

According to the Englishmen, when they took aboard their vessel Russian promyshlenniks who had fled from the ruined village, the Kolosh chief who came aboard presumed to demand their surrender, but the English put him in chains and, after the Kolosh refused to release immediately their other prisoners, opened fire on their boats and sank many of them. The Kolosh then brought all of their prisoners and the English released the chief. Captain Barber did not want to hand over the rescued Russians until Baranov had compensated him both for the special and unnecessary voyage to Kad'iak and for their provisioning on board, claiming also that his actions had cost him the friendship of the Kolosh. He demanded a total of 50,000 paper rubles. After long bargaining both sides finally agreed on 10,000 rubles, to be paid in furs, particularly foxes, river beavers, and beaver tails. In addition, the

Russians bartered from the English 27,000 rubles worth of various items, including several cannon, around fifty rifles, and a large quantity of ammunition.

It was later said that when Barber learned in the Sandwich Islands of the break between Russia and England, he was furious that he had not taken advantage of the Kolosh attack on the Russian settlement at Sitkha and wished to return immediately to Kad'iak for hostile purposes. But just then news arrived of the peace between the two powers and his wish to destroy the Russian colony came to nothing.

Investigations have revealed that the English played a very great part in encouraging the natives to destroy the fort at Sitkha, both by their advice and by providing the natives with guns and powder. This is the more likely since Barber and his countrymen, according to the promyshlenniks, kept aloof during the native attack and took action only when everything had been burned and destroyed, despite their stories that they did everything possible to save the Russian settlement. However, according to other accounts it was not only the English who took part. A few fugitive American sailors were in league with the Kolosh and ruthlessly looted and destroyed everything they could.

The Yakutat natives' hostility toward Kuskov's hunting party. While the Kolosh were destroying the Sitkha settlement, Kuskov arrived at Yakutat Bay with a party of hunters. When their baidaras overturned, the party stopped at one of the native settlements so that the men could dry out their furs. Encouraged by their tribesmens' successful attack on Sitkha, which they had kept a secret among themselves, these Kolosh also reversed their behavior toward the Russians. The toions came to Kuskov's tent and complained that the Russians not only were depriving them of their fur-bearing animals, but were also stealing things which had been placed in the graves of their dead. Then they announced that they were breaking off friendship with the Russians. Kuskov attempted to show them the absurdity of their accusations, but they would not even listen to him and began picking quarrels on the most insignificant pretexts. Finally they attacked the Russians, who courageously sustained their first onslaught. Drawing themselves into ranks and placing their cannon on their flanks, they stubbornly defended each step of ground, but finally had to yield to the superior numbers of the enemy and to retire to their baidaras. This time the Kolosh were driven off with large losses and were forced to sue for peace, although the Russian losses were quite small. Since the party had very little powder and very few provisions left, Kuskov consented to their request, first demanding that they fulfill their previous obligations. The Kolosh returned only half the things they had taken in the first attack, but they did give over hostages. Kuskov decided to proceed to the settlement at Yakutat, both to renew his supplies and to give aid in case the natives also attacked the settlement. Upon his arrival he found many natives, even from unusual places. The Kolosh maintained that they had only come to trade in friendship, but the Russians continued to take all possible precautions against treachery. Kuskov learned from them that they intended to go to war against the tribes living near Sitkha Island. Foreseeing undesirable consequences, he decided to detach six baidara-loads of men to the leader at Sitkha, so that they might advise him of the Kolosh plans and reinforce his garrison. The news of the destruction of the Sitkha settlement, which was received soon thereafter, so affected all the promyshlenniks, particularly those living at Yakutat, that they threatened to leave there of their own volition if they were not immediately transported away. Since they were already getting ready to leave, Kuskov agreed to do as they wished, but he delayed the departure in the hope that their fears would diminish. Finally he persuaded them to await his return from Sitkha, where, he assured them, he had to go in order to find out if any of the Russians or Aleuts who were in the fort were still alive. All of the Kolosh in Yakutat unanimously confirmed that the plot to destroy the Sitkha settlement had been planned for a long time, that Medvednikov had frequently been warned of the natives' plans and that many foreign sea captains had incited them to drive the Russians from their lands.[3]

It must be admitted, however, that by their own indiscretions the Russians had more than once exposed themselves to almost certain destruction. Often the natives were roused by actions contrary to Baranov's orders by those who thought their status gave them the right to reject his orders. For example, almost coinciding with the destruction of the Russian settlement, and when the natives in general felt that the Russians were powerless to repulse and punish them, Talin, a navigator in the company's service, encouraged by the clergy, decided to summon natives from many places to Kad'iak in order to pledge allegiance to Emperor Alexander I, who had just acceded to the throne. This was done solely to annoy Baranov, on the pretext of orders issued to Talin by the commandant at Okhotsk, who had no relation to the company. Besides the fact that it was impossible to feed such an enormous number of natives gathered in one place and that the natives' very presence together could precipitate an attack on the Russians, the arrangements to bring them there were made without Baranov's knowledge. He barely managed to avert this gathering, later fulfilling the commandant's wishes in a gradual fashion.

In 1803 Baranov again sent Kuskov to Yakutat to inspect the settlement, ordering him in case of attack by the Kolosh to take the field with all of his men, but with great caution.

Baranov prepares to reoccupy Sitkha. The lack of means to retake Sitkha seems to have troubled Baranov greatly. Several times he decided to assemble all the men at his disposal and proceed to Sitkha either to punish the guilty natives or to mount an armed attack. But discretion prevailed and that year he limited himself to ordering Kuskov to build two new ships during his stay in Yakutat, to strengthen his forces so that by the spring of 1804 he would match the Kolosh.

American captains propose permanent trade relations. In that year Baranov bartered 37,000 paper rubles worth of goods and supplies, including two cannon, from American ships visiting Kad'iak. These vessels also brought several Aleuts and one Russian rescued from Kolosh captivity. The Americans proposed to establish continuing trade with the colonies, and Baranov gave them a list of things he needed. One of the American captains, O'Cain [with the ship *O'Cain*], who was on his second trip to the colonies, informed Baranov that during the voyage he had observed an uncharted island. Baranov decided to give him fifteen baidarkas with thirty-four natives, under the command of a Russian, to make a careful exploration of this island and to gather furs. Although this island turned out to be nothing more than the coast of California, and probably served O'Cain as a mere pretext to obtain a hunting party from Baranov, the venture nevertheless provided the company with more than six hundred sea otter pelts.

The export of furs from the colonies. At the beginning of the year Baranov sent the *Zakhariia i Elisaveta*, under Khvostov's command, back to Okhotsk with a rich cargo of furs, then worth more than one million rubles. In that year three ships arrived from the colonies with furs worth almost 2.5 million paper rubles. These included more than 15,000 sea otter pelts and almost 280,000 fur seal pelts.

Although such a large number of fur seals had been exported, the colonial warehouses still held almost 500,000 more fur seal pelts, either previously accumulated or bought up from other traders to destroy competition in the market. Because of poor dressing most of them must have had a very low value. Moreover, the inordinate destruction of fur seals in previous years by the numerous hunters visiting the Pribylov Islands had so diminished these animals, that their extinction was feared. When the directors heard of this, they immediately ordered a temporary halt in the fur seal catch.

The wreck of the "Sv. Dmitrii" and the state of the company fleet in 1804. In 1803 the company lost another newly built ship. The *Sv.*

Dmitrii was completely destroyed near Umnak Island. Everyone on board was saved, but most of the cargo was lost. Frequent wrecks had substantially reduced the company's fleet, which in 1804 included only the *Sv. Aleksandr Nevskii*, a 115-ton two-master; the *Zakhariia i Elisaveta*, a 150-ton two-master; and the dilapidated *Sv. Ol'ga*, a small vessel with only one mast and one deck. Full credit for their energy and experience must be given to Lieutenant Khvostov and Midshipman Davydov, who taught shipfitting and the use of cannon in the colonies, and made voyages between the colonies and Okhotsk with unheard-of speed. Most of the captains whom the company had to employ, in the absence of better, could not make this passage in a single year. Thus, not to speak of the unnecessary expense connected with these delays, many orders from the board of directors, colonial administrators, and the Okhotsk office could not be executed promptly and the colonies frequently suffered shortages of essential supplies.

These continual failures to supply the colonies with goods and necessities by sea from Okhotsk and the extraordinary difficulties of transporting them to this port through Siberia frequently prevented the company from satisfying the ever growing demands of such a remote area. The absence of satisfactory communications across the enormous wastes of Siberia, particularly in the last thousand versts to Okhotsk, imposed continual obstacles to transporting any unwieldy objects. After the Lena River turned due north, all freight had to be transported overland, on Yakut pack horses.

In the overland part of the journey, guns to defend the colonial settlements and anchors for the company's ships (the latter sawed into several pieces) were placed on sledges and dragged between two horses. Besides these inconveniences, the rewelded anchors were not safe for the ships to use and, furthermore, the cannons and the anchors rarely reached their intended destinations. In the impassable parts of the tundra and marshes, the heavy packs exhausted the horses and were frequently discarded and lost. Other items were also damaged in transit and sometimes, when they were sorted out in Okhotsk, proved to be nothing more than heaps of soaked and useless rubbish. These conditions, as well as the expense of freight from Yakutsk to Okhotsk—which was as high as 9 paper rubles a pud—caused losses which seriously influenced the company's future plans.

A round-the-world expedition is proposed to ease the problem of supply. This state of affairs, of course, urgently required the directors to find other, more suitable means of supplying the colonies. Shelikhov's idea of outfitting large vessels in the Baltic and sending them on round-the-world voyages to the colonies was taken up by Rezanov. It was all the more attractive since a suitable market could be found for the colonies' furs on the return voyage in the southern ports of China. The enormous profits which many Englishmen and Americans had obtained from similar operations guaranteed to some extent the feasibility and profitability of this plan. Count N. P. Rumiantsov, whom Alexander I had made minister of commerce on his accession to the throne, was in full agreement with Rezanov's plan and undertook to petition the emperor to authorize it.

The emperor was pleased to grant the company permission to equip a round-the-world expedition.

At first the directors considered buying a fully outfitted ship in Hamburg and sending it to the colonies,[4] but subsequently, on the advice of Admiral N. S. Mordvinov, a shareholder, they decided to send two ships, so that the maximum amount of supplies could be taken to America and the ships could help each other in case of difficulties during the voyage.

They entrusted command of these vessels to two of the finest naval officers available, Captain-Lieutenants Iu. F. Lisianskii and I. F. Krusenstern. Lisianskii had asked for the command when it was proposed to send only one ship to the colonies. Krusenstern was known to the company not only as an experienced seaman who had made several voyages to distant seas with the English navy, but also as a well-educated man familiar with the state of trade in China. From personal observations he had written a description of political conditions throughout the Chinese Empire and in the East Indies, and put forward plans for successfully expanding Russian trade in foreign ports and for improving the knowledge of Russian naval officers by means of frequent round-the-world voyages. He attracted the attention of Count Rumiantsov, who persuaded the directors to entrust him with command of the round-the-world expedition.

Having calculated that equipping a two-ship expedition might demand greater means than the company had at its disposal, the board of directors, with the approval of a general meeting of stockholders, proposed to obtain more exact details on the expedition and then to petition the emperor (1) to finance the needs of the expedition with a 250,000-ruble (paper) loan at legal interest from the state bank, (2) to man the ships with naval officers and sailors and navy doctors, in addition to Krusenstern and Lisianskii, and to provide the expedition with two students from the Academy of Sciences and Mining to carry out research in the colonies, and (3) to let the company purchase needed equipment and supplies from government warehouses at commonly established prices. The emperor approved the company's request at once. In response to the directors' petition, Baranov, chief manager of the colonies, was made Collegiate Counsellor in honor of his exceptional services.[5]

To initiate its project the directors immediately ordered Lisianskii and Razumov, a shipbuilder, to go to Hamburg to buy ships. If suitable vessels could not be found there, they were ordered to proceed to England to purchase them.

Soon Lisianskii had acquired two ships in London: the *Leander*, renamed the *Nadezhda*, 430 tons and 16 cannon for 82,024 paper rubles; and the *Thames*, renamed the *Neva*, 373 tons and 14 cannon for 89,914 paper rubles. Both ships reached Kronshtadt early in the summer of 1803 and preparations immediately began for the round-the-world voyage. Krusenstern assumed command of the *Nadezhda* and of the expedition. Lisianskii was made captain of the *Neva*. The captains chose officers and crews, which were assigned to the ships by the Admiralty College.

To the *Nadezhda* were assigned Lieutenants Ratmanov, Romberg, Golovachev, and Levenshtern, Midshipman Bellingshausen, Navigator Kamenshchikov, Second Navigator Spolokhov, Surgeon Espenberg, Surgeon's Assistant Sydham, Horner, an astronomer, Tilesius and Langsdorf, naturalists, two cadets, O. and M. Kotzebue, of the Infantry Corps, Artillery Sergeant Raevskii and forty-eight men of lower ranks. To the *Neva* were assigned Lieutenants Arbuzov and Povalishin, Midshipmen Kovediaev and Berkh, Surgeon Laband, Navigator Kalinin, and forty-five men of lower ranks.

The emperor orders the organization of Russian settlements in the Pacific region and the dispatch of an embassy to Japan with the expedition. In the meantime, while the ships were being readied to sail, several basic changes were made in the original plan of the expedition, particularly the emperor's order that the ships carry an embassy to Japan.

These changes were prompted by several reasons. The Russian settlements in the Pacific regions were in a hopeless position because of the lack of means to maintain them even with bare necessities, and could hardly be protected from the attacks of natives or the claims of foreigners. Rezanov understood that all the difficulties of building a new country and expanding the company's operations could not be overcome by the will of any one man, even one such as Baranov. Therefore, he persuaded Count Rumiantsov to send to the colonies a man vested with full authority by the government. His duties would consist of examination of the needs of the colonies and, so far as possible, of the use of his powers to provide for these needs. No one, of course, was more qualified than Rezanov to satisfy the various requirements of this post. When Count Rumiantsov asked him to accept this commission from the government, Rezanov agreed to sacrifice his comfort and repose for the sake of an idea close to his heart: the flourishing of a country whose troubles he had inherited, mainly, from the illustrious founder of Russian settlement on the Pacific shores. Furthermore, sending a government appointee to those regions gave a more positive basis for establishing trade relations with Japan—another of Shelikhov's plans, which he had been unable to carry out in his lifetime.

Lieutenant Laksman had visited Japan by orders of Empress Catherine II in 1792, under the pretext of repatriating some ship-wrecked Japanese.[6] This visit gave reason to expect success from a second attempt by the Russians to establish relations with the Japanese, particularly as a recent Japanese shipwreck provided the means to realize these aims. It appeared that on Laksman's voyage he had been well received by the Japanese officials, although they had refused to accept a letter sent to them by the governor general of Irkutsk, on the grounds that such a letter could only be delivered at Nagasaki. At the conclusion of his discussions Laksman had received a paper with the seal of the Japanese emperor permitting one Russian ship to visit Nagasaki in order to carry on conversations with the Japanese government.[7]

On this basis Rezanov was made minister plenipotentiary to the Japanese court. The emperor ordered that several officers and officials (Major Frideritsii, of the Suite of His Imperial Majesty, Lieutenant of the Guard Tolstoi, Court Counsellor Foss, Doctor Brinkin, M.D., Hieromonk Gedeon, and Kurliandtsov, an artist) be appointed to his suite and that he be provided with appropriate gifts for the Japanese emperor and for the various officials with whom the mission would have to deal. So he could better fulfill his assignments, Rezanov received detailed instructions on all relevant matters and three hundred gold and silver medals to give out to those who had distinguished themselves in colonial service. The company gave Rezanov full command of commercial transactions during the voyage and of all company affairs in the colonies. Consequently, a supplement was added to the instructions given by the board of directors to the expedition commander. In essence, this stated that the powers conferred on Rezanov by the government left to Krusenstern only the command of the ships and their crews during the actual voyage.[8] This supplement completely changed the nature of the original instructions and made Krusenstern immediately subordinate to Rezanov. Furthermore, the directors gave

Rezanov all the information which, in their opinion, would let him improve conditions among the company's employees in the colonies and among the natives under its charge.

The instructions ordered the expedition to proceed around the Cape of Good Hope and, after conveying the mission to Japan and the cargo of goods and supplies to the colonies, to load furs at Kad'iak and Okhotsk and call at Canton on the return voyage, to discover whether furs might be favorably traded for Chinese goods. Moreover, if conditions permitted, the vessels were to survey the islands lying in the North Pacific Ocean and along the American coast as far as 55° north and farther with greater accuracy and detail than previously possible.

The ships' cargo consisted of anchors, guns, iron, lead, copper vessels, rope, sailcloth, victuals, vodka, and other provisions and supplies worth over six hundred thousand paper rubles. Rezanov delegated control of the cargo, payment of the crews and other expenses during the voyage, as well as the conduct of trade, to specially selected commissioners.[9]

In view of the fact that the mission to Japan and the large number of gifts for the Japanese occupied more than half of the space on the ships, the emperor ordered that the treasury bear the cost of one of the vessels, namely the *Nadezhda*, which was occupied by Rezanov and his suite, as well as all the expense of equipping this ship, and all expenditures and wages during the voyage.

The voyage of the expedition and the arrival of the "Nadezhda" at Kamchatka and the "Neva" in the colonies. When the ships were ready for the voyage, they were visited by the emperor. Then, after taking on additional cargo in the roadstead, they set sail on 26 July 1803.

Completing their provisioning at Helsingfors and Falmouth, the expedition proceeded to Tenerife Island. Remaining there a short time, they set out for St. Catherine Island (Brazil).[10] Here, the *Neva's* masts proved to be so badly damaged that they had to be replaced, delaying the expedition much longer than had been planned. As a consequence, Krusenstern ordered the ships to proceed directly to Kamchatka, and from there to Japan. From St. Catherine Island Rezanov wrote to the board of directors that after he finished his mission in Japan and returned to Petropavlovsk he would send Krusenstern alone to Canton with the cargo, since the insubordination and conflicting orders of the captains made it impossible for him to continue as head of the expedition. Unfortunately the captains' refusal to agree with any of Rezanov's proposals led to many clashes which destroyed general accord and harmony. It is impossible to say definitely to what extent these disagreements affected the expedition's success.[11] In any case, however, it is obvious from Rezanov's reports that genuine agreement between himself and the captains might have led to fuller attainment of its goals.

The ships parted at the Sandwich Islands. The *Nadezhda* sailed for Kamchatka, where she arrived in mid-July 1804. The *Neva* was sent straight to the colonies and reached Kad'iak early in the same month.

The reconquest of Sitkha Island and founding of the New Archangel fort. Meanwhile Baranov was en route to Sitkha Island, firmly resolved to fight the Kolosh and restore what had been lost, and Lisianskii hurriedly set sail from Kad'iak to join Baranov and his men.

Baranov's fleet consisted of the *Aleksander Nevskii* and the *Ekaterina* and two ships which Kuskov had recently built in Yakutat, the *Ermak* and the *Rostislav*. The *Ermak* was fifty-one feet long and had over one hundred tons capacity; the *Rostislav* was forty-one feet long with almost eight-five tons capacity. The iron for these vessels was taken from the wrecked cutter *Sv. Ol'ga* and for rigging the rotten ropes from the *Sv. Ol'ga* were utilized, with tree roots and whale bone mixed in with the hemp for greater durability.

On his way to Sitkha, Baranov called at Yakutat, where he negotiated with the most important inhabitants of Icy Strait, those at the native settlements of Chilkat and Khutsnov. The fact that the Russians had taken the main toion's son as a hostage contributed to the success of these negotiations. By the terms of the agreements, the natives were forgiven their hostile actions of 1802, as well as their attack on Kuskov's party. To celebrate the conclusion of peace the *Sv. Ol'ga* was burned by salvos from guns and cannon hidden nearby.

Leaving about twenty-five men in Yakutat, including settlers, Baranov ordered the *Ekaterina* and *Aleksandr Nevskii* to proceed to Cross Sound and there await his return with all possible caution. He took the other ships to the straits and passages farther south, where he intended to discover the plans of the Kolosh, who were expecting Russian vengeance for the destruction of the settlement. Upon arriving at Sitkha, Baranov was very pleased to find the *Neva*, which had already been waiting for him more than a month.

Lisianskii and Baranov first offered peace to the Kolosh, but on condition that they immediately quit their fort and surrender the entire area to the Russians unconditionally. Meeting with an abrupt refusal, Baranov decided to attack. Three sailors from the crew of the *Neva* were killed, and the wounded included Baranov, Lieutenant Arbuzov, Midshipman Povalishin, a surgeon's assistant, eight promyshlenniks, and several Aleuts. The battle was halted by darkness. On the second day the ships drew near the fort and opened fire on it. The bombardment lasted until evening, but the Kolosh would not accept the Russian terms. The natives would concede to the Russians only one hostage, so on the third day the attack was renewed with full force. Later, it was discovered that their expectation of strong reinforcements from neighboring tribes had induced the Kolosh to defend the fortress so stubbornly. On the seventh day, however, they surrendered. They retired to a place on Kondakov (Chatham) Strait about 150 miles from Sitkha, and there and at other nearby places they built several fortifications.

Baranov built a new fort, New Archangel [Novo-Arkhangel'sk, now called Sitka], on a height in the middle of the abandoned Kolosh settlement. He had considered occupying this hill in 1799, but wishing to show the Sitkhans that he had no intention of oppressing them, he had chosen the site which they had razed two years previously. Lisianskii had his men assist as much as possible in building the fort and essential buildings, but they left to spend the winter in Kad'iak. In the spring of 1805, when the natives were gathering around Sitkha Island for fishing, he returned to New Archangel. Here he remained until autumn. Loading the cargo of furs, Lisianskii set sail for Canton, where he was to be met by Krusenstern after the latter had completed his assignment with Rezanov.

The failure of the mission to Japan. At the end of August, the *Nadezhda* had left Kamchatka for Japan, and after six weeks at sea reached Nagasaki. Rezanov had to promise that the mission, during its residence ashore, would have limited freedom and would particularly observe and respect Japanese laws and customs. These concessions, however, were of no avail. The total failure of Rezanov's mission was caused by the preponderance in the Japanese state council of a hostile party, who opposed relations with any foreigners, even with the Dutch, who suffered severe restraint and even occasional humiliations for the pitiful privilege of sending one trading ship per year to Japan. Rezanov was not even permitted to transmit the official letter of the Russian government or to hand over his gifts. According to the interpreters and other Japanese officials taking part in the negotiations, subsequently confirmirmed on Khvostov's visit to Japan, the refusal to enter into relations with Russia produced a very unfavorable impression on the people. Many of the Japanese urged Rezanov to take measures to show his government's dissatisfaction at the Japanese refusal to establish relations. They assured him that in that case the opposing members of the Japanese council would have to give way and concessions by the Japanese government could therefore be expected. This outcome was even more probable because several government officials who enjoyed great authority in Japan had clearly expressed their approval of relations with foreign countries. Be that as it may, the aims of the mission

Novo-Arkhangel'sk (Sitka), in 1805

were not realized and Rezanov returned to Kamchatka at the beginning
of June 1805, disappointed, but firmly resolved at some time to force
Japan to conclude a trade treaty with Russia.[12]

The company settlement on Urup Island. On the return trip from
Japan, Rezanov ordered Krusenstern to approach the island of Urup to
discover the condition of the company settlement, numbering thirty-
five men and three women, left there in 1795. The lack of any news
from them for such a long period of time disturbed the company management. Krusenstern said it was impossible to carry out this order
because the water was too shallow for his ship to approach the island,
and for many other reasons lying, as he expressed it, in the realm of
his personal responsibility. The commander's reply probably had some
basis in fact, particularly the lack of knowledge then concerning the
geography of the Kurile Islands, but nevertheless it could hardly fail to
vex Rezanov. The state of the settlement, left without help for so many
years under unfavorable conditions, must have concerned any man who
thought himself under the slightest obligation to help his fellow countrymen. Furthermore, Rezanov knew that under the prevailing condition of the company fleet, a similar opportunity to visit the island
would hardly arise soon.

According to information received later, the leader of the settlement, foreman Zvezdochetov, died in April of the same year and the
settlers, having no means to exist, left Urup some time afterward,
thus long depriving the company of profits from the Kurile fur trade.
Rezanov's visit and his reinforcements in men and supplies might have
forestalled this, but unfortunately the visit did not take place.

The unfortunate selection of Zvezdochetov as leader of the settlement also helped to deprive the company of the advantage which might
have been expected from the Urup settlement's proximity to islands
belonging to Japan. Zvezdochetov's bungling behavior with the natives
forced them to break off all relations with the Russians and to resettle
on Iturup, whereas continuing contact could have enabled the settlement to maintain an indirect communication with the Japanese. Furthermore, Zvezdochetov's high-handed and barbarous treatment of his
subordinates caused constant disorders almost from the first days of
the settlement. Finally, the promyshlenniks removed Zvezdochetov
from his office and deported him to a nearby island, from which the
natives were to carry him back to Kamchatka with a report on his
behavior. Zvezdochetov, however, was able to deceive the Kurile
Islanders and, winning them over by means of gifts, used their help to
regain authority. He threw the suspected instigators of the revolt into
chains and sent them to Kamchatka. After that his cruelty became

extreme. He so terrified his coworkers that none dared oppose his orders. To prevent any further plotting, Zvezdochetov divided the work parties of hunters into very small units, continually rotating the members. As if this were not enough, he ordered fourteen men to return to Russia by way of Kamchatka to ask for reinforcements for the settlement. To build the baidaras necessary for the journey, he removed these men to the opposite side of the island, supplying them with the scantiest provisions. Thus these wretched men spent the winter of 1797-1798 in a barren and uninhabited place, deprived of almost all necessities. When they returned to the settlement in the spring, they were met on the shore by Zvezdochetov and several of his men, all armed to the teeth. The leader of the settlement promised to shoot them all if they attempted to land. He permitted two or three men to come ashore to get their possessions, but on condition that they should all set out on the next day. They had to obey. After a rugged pilgrimage through the Kurile Islands, they reached Shumshu Island, where they joined Banner, who was there with his detachment. The remaining sixteen hunters (five had died during their stay on Urup) arrived at Kamchatka only after Zvezdochetov's death and after having buried the guns and ammunition of the settlement on the island.

The further voyage of the round-the-world expedition and its return to Kronshtadt. After returning to Kamchatka, Rezanov ordered Krusenstern to survey Sakhalin Island and then to return to Petropavlovsk to take on a cargo of furs. Then he was to proceed immediately to Canton to barter the furs for Chinese products. The *Neva* was supposed to join Krusenstern in Canton. In order to avoid further disagreements with the captain of the *Nadezhda*, Rezanov decided to go to the colonies on the company ship *Mariia Magdalina*, which had just arrived from Okhotsk.

The *Nadezhda* reached Kamchatka in August and in only two months was in Canton. The *Neva* reached China two weeks after the *Nadezhda*. Her voyage had been delayed by fresh winds and a severe storm, during which Lisianskii, in order to lighten the ship, had had to throw overboard almost thirty thousand paper rubles worth of furs. In addition, he took time to survey several islands in the Pacific Ocean, in order to complete and correct hydrographic data on that region.

The Chinese authorities imposed obstacles to the barter of furs, but these were removed by the efforts of Drummond, the president of the English factory. The prices offered were quite low, but since they still exceeded the prices then prevailing in the home market, the company's chief commissioner Shemelin accepted them with only minor changes. Sea otters fetched from 17 to 20 piasters (10 otter tails were considered as equal to one otter); river beavers, 2½ piasters; otters, 4;

100 red foxes, 120; 100 cross foxes, 60; 100 silver foxes, 200; white arctic foxes, 1 piaster each; blue arctic foxes, 1½ piasters each; and 100 fur seals, 75 piasters. It seemed more profitable to Shemelin, however, to retain sea otters of the highest quality, sea otter pups, blue foxes, and the best grade of other foxes for sale in Petersburg. The whole fur cargo, with these exceptions, was sold for 191,623 piasters. It was decided to take half this sum in teas, amounting to some 2,105 chests. The other half was taken in nankeen, silk, porcelain, and other Chinese goods.

The trading was finished, the ships were readied for sea, and on 29 January 1806 Krusenstern and Lisianskii left Canton. The unsuccessful mission of Count Golovkin, president of the College of Commerce, to China[13] caused the Peking government to send an order to detain the Russian ships, but fortunately it did not arrive until several days after their departure. The *Neva* reached Kronshtadt on 26 July and the *Nadezhda* on 7 August 1806.

The emperor rewarded all of the participants in the expedition. Rezanov was given a gold snuffbox with the emperor's monogram, and his son was made a page. The captains of the ships were promoted and received Orders of St. Vladimir (fourth class), three thousand rubles each, and pensions corresponding to their salary. The officers were promoted and received pensions and one thousand rubles each. The lower ranks received pensions of from fifty to seventy rubles and were permitted to retire. The company directors were also rewarded. Buldakov was given the Order of St. Vladimir (fourth class), and Delarov and Shelikhov received gold medals studded with diamonds.

The ships' cargoes were admitted duty-free, by imperial decree, and were all sold, although at only a small profit.

The results of the expedition in respect to trade, and the state of the company's affairs. The sale of the company's goods in Canton and the subsequent delivery of numerous furs to St. Petersburg greatly bolstered the company's affairs, which were in great difficulties due to the frequent wrecks of ships bearing cargoes to the colonies, and the unprofitable course of the Kiakhta trade from 1802 to 1803. The Chinese continually lowered their buying prices for furs, since they could obtain them more cheaply from the English in Canton. Fur seals, in particular, had almost no market, and other furs could not be traded profitably in Kiakhta. Sea otters, for instance, excluding duties and carriage, only brought about fifty-five rubles. Only river beavers and land otters partly sustained the trade.

To these factors were also joined additional unsatisfactory circumstances. In Moscow in 1804 something of the nature of a financial crisis occurred. Many bankruptcies were declared in a short time, so that the company experienced great difficulties selling furs on the local market. The circulation of money was sluggish, and the resulting stagnation of trade made many bankers reluctant to accept bills of exchange drawn by the most reliable people. Funds transferred from Irkutsk to the Makar'ev fair were discounted at least 17 percent. In consequence, most of the furs brought on the *Zakhariia i Elisaveta* remained unsold and, generally speaking, all of the furs in the company's warehouses in Russia could not possibly have been sold in less than three years.

The establishment of a temporary committee at the Main Office to consider special matters. Deciding important questions relating to the Russian colonies in America, and the execution of reforms entrusted to Rezanov and incumbent partly on the directors frequently exceeded the authority granted to the board at the organization of the company. Furthermore, such matters could not always be presented for disposition by a general stockholders' meeting, because of their close relation to Russia's political relations with other powers. For this reason, the directors determined in 1804 to petition the sovereign for permission to establish a temporary committee of three stockholders. These would sit at the head office and would be empowered, with the board of directors, to determine, with the full authority vested in a general meeting, questions which required secrecy because of political or administrative considerations.

The emperor, through the minister of commerce, ordered the board of directors to be informed that "in consideration of the necessity of conferring on urgent matters in respect to America, His Majesty permits the establishment for this object of a committee, appointing thereto the three nominees: Admiral Mordvinov, Count Stroganov, and Privy Counsellor Veidemeier."

4. The Colonies after Formation of the Russian-American Company, and Chamberlain Rezanov's Inspection and Reorganization

The state of the colonies in 1803. In considering Baranov's career, it is amazing what he managed to accomplish in the company's settlements in a little more than ten years, and with a constant shortage of men and materials. The following description of the colonies in 1803 is based upon Baranov's reports and will give a clearer idea of his value to the region entrusted to him.

Forts and other establishments. By 1803 the company had the fllowing forts in the colonies: two on Kad'iak Island, one established by Shelikhov at Three Saints Harbor, and the other at Pavlovsk Harbor [now the town of Kodiak]; one on Afognak Island; fort Aleksandr [Aleksandrovsk or English Bay] on Cape Kenai; forts Georgievskoe, Pavlovskoe, and Nikolaevskoe on Kenai Bay; two on Chugach Bay [Prince William Sound] — one on Nuchek Bay [Port Etches] at Konstantin and Elena Harbor, and the other at Delarov Harbor (Zaikov Bay) [on Montague Island] where the English wintered in 1785. When a Russian detachment arrived there from Kad'iak, they found the fort burned, but it is not known whether this was done by the English upon leaving the harbor or afterwards by the natives. Finally there were fort Simeon at Cape St. Elias, two forts on Yakutat Bay, and New Archangel on Sitkha [Baranof] Island.

Most of these forts were armed with brass three-pounders, there being very few cast iron cannon. There were about fifteen hundred small arms, such as muskets, rifles, and carbines. Generally speaking, if properly guarded, all of these forts could be strongly defended against hostile natives, even the Kolosh, who were just as well armed as the Russians. Only negligence, as often proven, could endanger the forts, particularly since the garrisons were always adequate, even though the colonial population was small. Usually hunting crews were located at the forts and, in many places there were also temporary parties which hunted and traded with the natives. Offices at the settlements on Unalashka and Kad'iak which were in charge of their respective districts, were under the immediate supervision of the chief manager of the colonies.

In 1805 the company had a total of 470 employees in the colonies. Of this number sixty-nine were hunters on Unalashka and the Pribylov Islands.

Native tribal divisions. The following native tribes were subject to the colonial administration:[1] the Kad'iak islanders and the adjacent coastal natives of Aliaksa [Alaska Peninsula] constituted one tribe. In the interior of Aliaksa there was another tribe, divided into the following settlements: Kanigomiuts, Kats, and Nunalits, and, along the northern coast of the peninsula, Ugashentsi, Aliagomiuts, and Kuikhpagomiuts. Aliaksa also had other native tribes, distinguished from each other and from the above-named groups by both language and customs. Then came the Kenais, of whom the Akoi, who lived near the sea, were much like the tribes in the interior of Aliaksa. The independent tribes included the Chugach, the Mednovtsy [Copper River natives], and the Ugalakhmiuts, who lived between the Copper River and Yakutat. The coastal inhabitants of these regions differed in language from the Chugach, Mednovtsy, and Yakutats. The Yakutat, Kanout, Khutsnov, Chil'kat, Sitkhin, Akutaku, Stakhin, Kekakuiu, Kigan, and Kaigan tribes and natives of neighboring areas were known collectively as the Kolivzh or Kolosh [Tlingits]. The Kolosh tribes living in different localities had different dialects, some with little resemblance to the common language of this people, but in any case all the Kolosh called themselves *klinkit*, that is, *people*. Different groups were frequently hostile to one another. The inhabitants of the Queen Charlotte Islands and neighboring regions had a completely different language than the Kolosh and were known by the latter as "*Tekina*."

Education of the natives and some of their ceremonies and games. The instruction of the natives in the principles of the Christian religion, as we have mentioned, was unsuccessful, particularly in more recent times. The native religion, according to Baranov, contained no remarkable rites. Among all tribes, shamanism played a major role in various circumstances. The outstanding feature of native games (masquerades) was the impersonation of evil spirits. The master of ceremonies was usually called *koziak* (scholar), a hereditary title. During the games the koziaks did not admit women or children, hoping perhaps to lend secrecy to the games and thereby increase their importance in the eyes

of their more naive comrades. Only a koziak could explain the significance of the games, but they were very reluctant to do so; the other
natives professed complete ignorance of their meaning.

   The condition of the school for natives and creoles (offspring of Russian men and native women) was far from satisfactory. There were
less than thirty pupils. The main problem was the lack of qualified
teachers. Until 1803 the school teacher was a graduate of the commercial class of a foundling home [*vospitatel'nyi dom*], but he died and for
some time it was impossible to replace him. For this reason, from 1804
the students of the Kad'iak school taught each other reading and writing. Eight of the former students obtained quite satisfactory knowledge
of arithmetic and a little navigation, and four had some handicraft
training. The monks also took four young boys to raise, but used them
only as church attendants. This hardly furthered their education, particularly because for a long time no services were held.

   The state of public health. The Russians employed in the colonies
needed great strength to live the life of fur hunters. They spent much
time outside in harsh weather facing privations caused by the remoteness of the country. In spite of these conditions, the state of public
health was satisfactory. The natives, of course, were accustomed to this
life, but the new ways which they learned from the Russians were
mainly harmful. The most common disorders were colic, festering sores,
cancer, and scurvy, the latter being particularly prevalent among Russians who had recently arrived or were newly transferred. Syphilis was
widespread among natives of both sexes, chiefly among the native
women in Kenai Bay, undoubtedly owing to the Europeans who had
visited these regions. It is remarkable this disease was then quite rare
among the Kolosh. Eye diseases were common every spring. There were
very few epidemics. Smallpox sometimes appeared among the natives
living south of Sitkha, who considered it a punishment sent down by
an evil spirit in the form of an unusually large raven who dwelled on
the distant mountain peaks. They feared this greatly, but they did not
worship or make sacrifices to it.

   The lack of doctors in the colonies at that time contributed to the
development of diseases and their unfavorable outcome.[2] In addition,
the usual diet for patients, consisting sometimes of nothing but dried
fish, greatly hindered a cure.

   Agriculture and gardening. Agricultural experiments conducted
under Baranov's supervision at Kad'iak, Kenai Bay, Yakutat, and near
Sitkha showed that rye and wheat would not grow. Barley, although
of very poor quality, would grow in several places.[3] Radishes, turnips,
potatoes, cabbages, and other garden vegetables could be raised if

good seed were used. There was very little fertile soil, and this only in patches, with no black soil anywhere, but only gravely, rocky, and sandy ground. Since all of these places were almost completely surrounded by high mountains, the cold which drifted down from the summits and the rain and fog greatly inhibited the growth of vegetation, except for conifers. Although tobacco could be grown, it would not yield good seed. On the coast of the mainland, near Sitkha, a small-leafed plant about the height of tobacco and somewhat like laurel grew, which the natives mixed with lime calcined from shells and used for smoking and for chewing. This mixture was not strong, but when burned, it gave out a pleasant odor. The natives did a good trade in it.

Livestock breeding. Cattle were raised successfully on Kad'iak. Over thirteen wild goats [*iaman'*][4] were kept on Kad'iak for more than five years, but they would not breed. There were quite a few swine, and various fowl. No horses were raised because they were useless without roads.

The local food supply. Fish in all forms was the main item of diet, particularly for the natives. The fish were caught in nets or traps placed in rivers, and cured by drying in the air; on Kad'iak alone over one-half million fish were preserved this way. Dried fish (*iukola*) was widely used not only among the Russians, but also among the natives in the company's service, but they did not always have time to store enough of it. Hunting parties and other expeditions made extensive use of this food. The fish caught on Kad'iak were chiefly of the salmon family [*losos'*], under various names: humpback [*gorbusha*], blueback [*krasnaia*], dog salmon [*khaigo*], silver salmon [*kizhuch*], and king salmon [*chovycha*]. The last were fatter and tastier than the others. Occasionally the natives also caught true salmon [*semga*] but these did not taste like the Russian variety and were quite unsuitable for pickling. Cod [*treska*] and halibut [*paltus*] were quite common in the summer; herring [*sel'd*] and navaga (called *vakhnia* by the natives) were each caught in their own season. Geese and swans flew to Kad'iak seasonally. Gulls [*chaika*], cormorants [*uril*], and various ducks abounded. Snipe [*kulik*] and woodcock [*val'dshnep* and *dupel'shnep*] were sometimes found in marshy places.

Fish of the salmon family were also plentiful in Kenai Bay. They were preserved by smoking, since the Kenais and almost all the neighboring tribes used no salt. At the mouth of the Sushitna River, which flows into the northeastern part of Kenai Bay, many fish called *talkha* were caught. Fat was obtained from these. Many herring were caught near the Russian settlement on Sitkha Island and in the springtime, natives from surrounding areas gathered there for fishing.

The diet also included seal meat, bird eggs, various berries, and many kinds of plants, such as wild onion, lily [*sarana*], and snakeweed [*makarsha*].

Whaling was an essential industry for both Russians and Aleuts, particularly since the Aleuts required whale blubber with every kind of food, and used it several times a year for greasing their baidaras. The Kad'iak islanders also engaged in whale hunting, but none of the other natives took any interest in this occupation. Nowhere on the mainland coast was whale meat or blubber used as food, but whale blubber was the main food item in the Russian stores at Sitkha. In all, there were only about twenty whale hunters on Kad'iak, Afognak, and the neighboring islands. Although Russians and natives were sent from Kad'iak to Kenai and Chugach Bays to teach whaling, no one took up this occupation in those places, although whales were plentiful. Around Kad'iak only small whales without whalebone were caught. Each of them yielded no more than three barrels of blubber and sometimes yielded only one. The Kad'iak islanders feared the large whales, which rarely approached the island, although dead ones were frequently washed up on shore. The whaler's weapon was a long, barbed, javelin-like harpoon. An air-filled bladder was attached to the middle of the shaft so that the harpoon would float on the water. After a while the wounded whale would be washed ashore, where the ownership of the catch was determined by distinctive markings on the harpoons.

Fur hunting. The islanders shot sea otters with darts, but the mainland natives used the bow and arrow. Usually, a party of twenty or more baidarkas would set out to sea in calm weather and, sighting an otter, would surround it and throw darts at it. When wounded, the otter could not remain long under water and, once he emerged, he was usually caught, unless the sea swells or strong winds carried him from the hunters' sight. Seals were hunted by the natives with nets and small hand harpoons and by the Russians with firearms. The natives killed bears with spears. Otters, wolverines, and lynxes were either shot or baited with dogs. Sables were caught in snares. Beaver lodges, usually located on rivers or lakes, were hunted out by dogs, then the escape holes were stopped up and the animals were killed through a hole in the roof. The natives snared caribou [*olen'*] or, when they swam in herds across rivers and lakes, speared them from boats. The Russians hunted foxes and otters with traps[5] and sometimes with firearms, as they did with bears and caribou. It is interesting to note that besides the ordinary kinds of foxes (red, cross, and silver), all-white foxes were also found, although very rarely. In 1802 one of these white foxes was caught on the Aliaska Peninsula and another in Kenai Bay. According to native superstition, white foxes always foretold some misfortune, which was proven to some extent by the destruction of Sitkha. The Russians did not hunt beavers, but bartered them from the Kenais. It should be observed that the hunting of beavers and caribou posed incomparably greater difficulties than that of any other animal. To hunt these animals the natives had to leave their houses along the rivers and lakes in the autumn and wander for two months over 150 or 200 miles of tundra, each hunter crossing rivers, swamps, and high mountains with his family. Often they went for several days without food, and early snowfalls would block their way, causing many to perish. Sometimes before they returned home, they had eaten their entire catch, even including the skins. Finally, encounters with hostile tribes led to fighting, in which the natives ruthlessly slaughtered each other.[6]

Timber. Trees suitable for shipbuilding, called American larch [*listvennitsa*] by the Russians, were found in the colonies in many places, such as Chugach Bay, Yakutat Bay, Sitkha Island, and the Kolosh (Vancouver) Straits. The Russians preferred to obtain wood from the straits rather than from the other places, since they could then barter with distant native tribes and hunt furs.

Mining and other colonial industries. Every effort was made to smelt iron from ores found on the Aliaska Peninsula, but this proved extremely difficult, since Baranov had no skilled man who could smelt the metal on hand-operated hearths and then forge it into the desired objects. The clay used in smelting was of poor quality, being very loamy and guttering at high temperature. The first attempts at smelting and forging iron were carried out by Baranov, who had brought the clay for this purpose from Issanakh [Bechevin] Bay on a baidara expedition from Unalashka in 1791. It proved superior to that obtained elsewhere. Subsequently, however, there were no opportunities to obtain it there. Special pains were taken to locate copper ore, but they failed because of the company's inadequate resources. The inhabitants of Copper River, in whose neighborhood copper ores were supposed to exist, agreed to show a Russian from the trading post in Chugach Bay places rich in copper, but they took him only about three hundred versts up the river, far from the mountain summits, on the pretext that they were enemies of the mountain tribes who, according to them, lived by war and even slept with their weapons. "The Copper River people," wrote Baranov, "gave ten men as hostages, but pay little attention to that, for they have a brutal character and deceive the Russians constantly."

In the first years, mica was obtained in Kenai Bay in small quantities for colonial use, but later the natives quit supplying it or even showing the places where it was found, deceiving the Russians just as the Copper River Indians did.

Every year from three to six thousand bricks were made on Kad'iak Island, and their production might have been increased to fifteen thousand, if there had been more lime, which had to be burned from shells, and clay suitable for brickmaking. The lack of men familiar with building arches and with other stone work was also acutely felt. "It would do no harm," wrote Baranov, "to send a couple of men skilled in erecting buildings. We were going to build a stone powder magazine, but the lack of experienced people prevented us last year (1802), and now there are still fewer."

Goods brought on the "Nadezhda" and the "Neva" are sold in Kamchatka. When he reached Kamchatka, Rezanov immediately set about selling some of the goods brought there by the *Nadezhda*. This action helped that region, since trade there was in the hands of a few monopolists, who, taking advantage of the infrequent supply of goods to Kamchatka, raised their prices at will, disregarding the poverty and the desperate need of most of the inhabitants. To give a better idea of the revolution which the company's trade produced, we will present here a comparison between the prices established for goods brought on the *Nadezhda* and the prices prevailing for similar objects before Rezanov's arrival in Petropavlovsk.

Prices before Rezanov's arrival			*Prices established by Rezanov*		
	r.	k.		r.	k.
Fruit vodka mixed with water — [shtof]	20	—	Spirits — shtof	6	
			French vodka or double cognac — shtof	8	
Sugar — pud	140		Refined sugar — pud	48	
Tobacco — pound	2	50	do. [ditto]	—	75
Soap	2	50	do.	—	50
Coarse cotton cloth — piece	14	—	do.	7	—
Printed calico — arshin	4	—	do — better quality English	2	60
			do. — wider	2	25
East Indian handkerchiefs — each	3	50	do.	2	25
			and	2	75
Sackcloth — arshin	—	65	do.	—	30
Printed linen	1	50	do.	1	15
Baize	2	50	do.	1	80
Ververet	4	—	do. — smooth	2	25
			do. — ribbed	2	50

Prices before Rezanov's arrival				Prices established by Rezanov		
	r.	k.			r.	k.
Demi-cotton	3	50	do.		1	30
				and	1	10
Tow — pound	2	50	do.		1	—
Tea cups — dozen	40	—	do.		30	—

In all cases, according to Rezanov, the goods the company offered were of far better quality than the goods of the other merchants. In order to avoid inordinate price rises in the future, as well as to expand trade in Kamchatka, Rezanov arranged to establish in Petropavlovsk a permanent depot for the company's goods and, at the first opportunity, trading posts. To carry out this plan, the Okhotsk office was ordered to send twenty workers and several horses, which were greatly needed in Kamchatka. Thirteen hundred puds of salt, which Rezanov had brought from Japan, were made available to the inhabitants of Kamchatka, who were suffering from lack of salt. The hostile attitude of Koshelev, the governor of Kamchatka, hampered the company's activities in many instances and often halted trade completely. For example, Khlebnikov, the company *prikashchik* [agent or factor], was held for three months in the guardhouse on Koshelev's orders, because he would not change the established prices of the company's goods without informing the manager of the Okhotsk office. Under other administrations, however, trade in Kamchatka was conducted with much greater success.

Rezanov goes to the colonies on a tour of inspection. Setting out from Kamchatka on the *Mariia Magdalina*, Rezanov proceeded along the north side of the Aleutian Islands to begin his inspection of the company settlements with Unalashka Island. Contrary winds prevented the ship from entering Kapitanskaia [Dutch] Harbor and it was necessary to go on to the Pribylov Islands. Describing his inspection of these islands, Rezanov wrote:

> The number of fur seals on this island is unbelievable. The shores are covered with them. It is very easy to kill them, and lacking meat, we killed about eighty in a half hour. Even at that I was told that there are only a tenth as many as there used to be. Up to the present more than a million seal skins have been taken on the islands. I ordered that the killing be stopped, lest they be exterminated, and set the men to obtaining walrus tusks, since near St. Paul Island there is an island covered with walruses.[7]

On his arrival at Unalashka Island, Rezanov found the storehouses full of useless goods that did not serve the needs of the population. The responsibility for this negligence lay, of course, on the Okhotsk office, which not only sent poor-quality goods to the colonies, but also set high prices on the goods. Rezanov wrote directly to the directors of the company, telling them that Director Delarov, who had been sent by the board in 1804 to reform the company's Siberian offices, had been completely deceived by their managers.

Rezanov found the settlement on Unalashka in good order. The exceptional amity which he observed between the inhabitants prompted him to call the settlement Soglasiia [Harmony]. He wrote, among other things: "Iurts take the place of houses on Unalashka. Each of them contains several rooms with quite large windows. Outbuildings stand apart. As a whole, the accommodation in the iurts is quite comfortable. Besides the iurts, I found storehouses, company barracks, a smithy, a locksmith's shop, an arrangement for melting down blubber, storehouses for fish, and several gardens."

Gathering together the toions of the neighboring native tribes and several of the natives, Rezanov asked if they had any complaints. He received the unanimous reply that they were satisfied with everything, that they were receiving due recompense for company work, and that they wished only that Larionov, the manager of the island, would continue to treat them as he had in the past. As a reward for his intelligent conduct with the natives, Rezanov conferred a medal on Larionov. On the other hand, he assured several of the promyshlenniks who had taken the law into their own hands that they would be sent back to Okhotsk as criminals, and one of them, the manager of the Atkha post, who had treated the natives illegally, was thrown into irons and informed that he would be turned over to the courts.[8]

Rezanov left Unalashka on 25 July 1805 and reached Kad'iak on 31 July. There he spent three weeks investigating the condition of the natives and their relations with the Russians. On inspecting the Kad'iak storehouses, he found for the most part the same poor-quality goods as in Unalashka. At the end of August Rezanov reached New Archangel.

Rezanov's arrival at New Archangel and some of his observations on the settlement and on Baranov. Describing his arrival, Rezanov observed:

> I found that Baranov has installed himself permanently here . . . and has built numerous log buildings with stone foundations. . . . We are quite crowded, but the winner of this land lives in worse conditions than any of us, in a sort of plank iurt, so damp that the mildew has to be wiped off every day and with the continuous rains it leaks like a sieve. An amazing man! He thinks only of the comfort of others, but is so careless of his own that once I found his bed standing in water and asked him: "Perhaps the wind tore off a board somewhere?"

"No," he replied calmly, "it seems to have flowed in under the floor," and went about his business. I tell you, Dear Sirs, that Baranov is a quite unique and happy creation of nature. His name is heard all along the west coast as far as California. The Bostonians respect and honor him, and the natives, even from the most distant places, fear him and offer him their friendship. [...] The true patriot will value him highly, in spite of his human failings and weaknesses, which are the fault either of his upbringing or habit of long standing. [...] Cast by fate into a mass of violent spirits, he had to feign their way of life to some degree in order to win their love and obedience. Having had to force himself to adopt ways that were alien to his mind and heart he has accustomed himself to disregard in others weaknesses which are morally insupportable.[9]

Here it would be appropriate to present several opinions of other contemporaries on Baranov's personality and qualities, since the details on a man on whom the fate of so many lives depended can but refute the unjust criticism of him by some of our Russian travelers and writers, who, if they did not completely reject, at least attempted greatly to diminish his services to Russian America. Krusenstern in particular drew false conclusions which were based on nothing but rumor. In describing his voyage he speaks thus:

I have not been on Kad'iak, Unalashka, or Sitkha, but judging by all I saw on the ship *Mariia* and by what I heard of the company's establishments in the American colonies from quite reliable men who had been there, nothing more distressing can be conceived than a residence in their possessions. Anyone would run away from even the most beautiful and bountiful land, if he knew that he should be exposed in it to the boundless will of a single person, often of a most immoral and cruel character.[10]

Lisianskii, Krusenstern's companion on the voyage, knew Baranov personally and wrote of him in *Voyage to the Colonies of the Ship Neva*: "Baranov's talents merit our respect. In my opinion the Russian-American Company could not have a better representative in America, for, besides his abilities, he has made it his custom to undertake any labor and does not spare his own fortune for the general good."[11]

Later in this same book, Lisianskii, pointing out certain inadequacies in the government of the Kad'iak islanders, observes: "Full credit must be given to the present governor, Baranov, and to his helpers, who have abandoned the former practices and deal with the Kadiak Islanders leniently."

Davydov, in his *Two Voyages to America*, says the following: "I could not but look with respect on a man who has devoted his life to the improvement of trade in its various forms. He had already lived in America for twelve years, in the company of wild and primitive people, surrounded by constant danger. He had been struggling with the deep-rooted depravity of the Russians living here, working constantly, in need of many things. . . ." And further: "His firmness of spirit and constant presence of mind are the reason why the savages respect him without loving him, and the fame of the name of Baranov resounds among all the savage peoples who live on the northwest coast of America."[12]

Such statements are completely opposed to the words of Krusenstern and should prove where the truth lies.

"Davydov has given a true and impartial character sketch of Baranov," says the famous Russian navigator, Liitke, in the account of his voyage on the sloop *Seniavin*.[13]

As soon as he arrived in New Archangel, Rezanov set about reforming the company's management system, introducing changes which he felt were more suitable to the needs of the time and of the country. "The company cannot sustain itself solely through fur trading," he wrote to the directors.

> It is absolutely essential to organize local administrative districts, and we must also seek profit in expanded trade by the many paths which are open to us here, particularly in view of the continually diminishing number of fur-bearing animals. If Baranov had not retaken Sitkha, the company would have been ruined in the same year, because, including even the furs taken on Sitkha Island through 1 May 1805, the average share value taken for two years equals only 280 rubles, as opposed to the former 1,000 rubles. Thus, when the promyshlenniks obtained their half-share of 140 rubles, they were toiling for nothing, since their food and drink costs them more than this. I have computed that the expenditure of each promyshlennik at present prices must be at least 317 rubles per year.

The directors understood very well that if the promyshlenniks were so limited in their income and spent so much on their living they could hardly observe any work regulations, but would concentrate on obtaining as much profit as possible. It was obvious that this could lead only to the complete extinction of fur-bearing animals. For this reason they immediately accepted all of Rezanov's proposals.

Rezanov found it desirable to discontinue the employees' sharing company revenue, replacing this with daily wages at a yearly rate of at least two hundred rubles. He thought this amount would be adequate, because when the management of the company stores was put in good order, the prices on all goods would inevitably go down. In case shoddy goods were sent to the colonies, the hunters had the right to obtain them at a price appraisal made by a committee of their own choosing; the resulting loss should then be borne by the office responsible for sending the goods out. Furthermore, fixed wages would lead to the circulation of money in the colonies, which, as Baranov had already pointed out to the directors, would prevent employees from incurring bad debts against goods taken for their own use from the company stores and would thus save both them and the company from inevitable losses.

Rezanov also ordered a census of all friendly natives and arranged that the directors should be informed each year of their numbers. When this information was compiled, it was revealed that 1,652 male and 1,566 female Kad'iak islanders[14] lived under the control of the colonial administration and that 997 men and 1,019 women lived within the realm of the Unalashka office. This made a total of 5,234 people, of whom 1,509 were children.

Rezanov reopened the boys' school, with no limitation on the number of pupils. Until standard organizational lists could be promulgated for the colonies, it was proposed to accept into the school at company expense all male children regardless of their family origin. Rezanov also ordered that ten of these pupils be sent to Irkutsk with each transport and from there, after smallpox vaccinations had been administered, to Moscow or St. Petersburg, where they were to be taught science, engineering, and trades. After five years these boys were to return to America and others would be sent in their place.

Having secretly reproved the monks for their disobedience to the chief manager's orders, Rezanov put Father Nektarii in charge of the school and entrusted twenty boys to Father German to be taught practical agriculture; in the winter, however, the boys were to be returned to the school to study reading and writing. Rezanov also ordered that five selected pupils of the school be placed under the supervision of the bookkeeper at Kad'iak, who would teach them bookkeeping and clerical work, in order to prepare them for office work in the colonial administration.

All of the colonial employees without exception were so pleased with Rezanov's plans in this regard that they wrote him a letter expressing their wish to donate part of their salaries to maintaining the school. After preliminary examinations were given to students of the old school and to applicants for new admission, the school was opened on Kad'iak with an initial attendance of ninety-one students.

Furthermore, Rezanov proposed to establish a girls' school which was to admit initially up to one hundred pupils and be called the Home of Mary's Beneficence [*Dom blagotvoreniia Marii*]. This was also opened in the autumn of 1805, and sixteen creole girls were enrolled under the supervision of Banner's wife. Four of these pupils were sent

to Okhotsk on the *Mariia Magdalina* and from there went to St. Petersburg to study home economics and handicrafts.

On Baranov's orders four creole boys had been sent to Russia on the
ships of the first round-the-world expedition. The emperor commanded
that they be sent to study navigation in the school at Kronshtadt.

After organizing educational institutions in the colonies, Rezanov
proposed to found a hospital for the use of the company's Russian
employees and those natives who might apply to the Russians for medical aid.

In addition to the organizational lists compiled by Rezanov, showing
the number of Russian and native colonial employees needed for company operations[15] and the applicable salary for each position, it was
determined to spend a certain time on port works and to create a court
called the Tribunal of Promyshlenniks and Americans [*Rasprava
promyshlenykh i amerikantsov*]. Rezanov's chief aim in establishing
this court was gradually to accustom the citizens of the colonies to try
their own civil cases and to avert the abuses which up to then had taken
place mostly in places far removed from the residence of the colonial
administrator—places where strength almost always overcame justice.
This court was to try all disputes between promyshlenniks, complaints
of injury, oppression, assault and fraud, creditors' claims, and, finally,
disputes between natives and Russians. It was proposed to name two
Russians and two natives as members of the court, under the presidency
of one of the company's high-ranking officers. The natives could participate only in cases which concerned them. All cases were to be
decided by a majority vote.

One of Rezanov's next orders charged the colonial clergy with learning the native language. In order to promote this, Rezanov took it upon
himself to collect native words for a dictionary, which he subsequently
presented to the board of directors with a request to print it and sell
it to people setting out for America, using the proceeds for the benefit
of colonial schools.[16]

To guide Baranov, Rezanov gave him several written orders. The
main ones are presented here:

1. In view of the small population of the colonies, which hindered
not only the expansion of Russian settlement on the American [main-
land] coast, but also the continuance of the company's present establishments, the board of directors were to be advised of the need to
increase the complement of employees working for wages rather than
for shares, a practice already observed with the promyshlenniks.

2. Special attention should be paid to the instruction of colonial

artisans, rewarding the best of them with such sums as were left unexpended because of the incomplete complement of employees, until a special fund could be established for that purpose. These rewards should be so distributed that they would not tend to increase the pay of only a few artisans.

3. Considering the weak and unhealthy condition of workers being sent from Russia, the board of directors was asked to pay strict attention to health in selecting men for service in the colonies.

4. The enlistment of a permanent garrison of subject natives and company pupils for colonial defense should be undertaken. The board directors were also asked to send artillery.

5. In view of the critical lack of ships in the colonies and the impossibility of building them because of the few men available, ships were to be bought from the Americans under satisfactory conditions even if the price was somewhat high. For this purpose a letter of credit was left in the colonies. It would be honored, by notification of the directors, in Amsterdam by Hoppe and Co., and in London by both Bering and Co. and Garman and Co.

6. Rezanov considered it essential to have a port captain, who would supervise all work in port and would be responsible for relations with the company's maritime employees and for furnishing ships with supplies. He would be directly under the chief manager of the colonies and might be of great help to him in the colonial administration.

7. Rezanov promised to pay particular attention to affairs in the company offices when he returned through Siberia. He would make regulations to determine the prices of all goods on the basis of their cost, with fixed percentages added for transportation, insurance, and profit. He was fully convinced that such orderly procedures would substantially lower the price of goods in America, particularly since responsibility for their quality lay entirely on the offices.

8. Rezanov promised that all information on the needs of the colonies would certainly be considered, particularly in view of the fact that heretofore the directors had been unable to calculate all of that country's needs, permitting abuses to take root in the company's Siberian offices.

9. Since Okhotsk could not provide the colonies with sufficient bread, the opening of trade with California would be considered. As other sources of supply, Rezanov proposed the Philippine Islands and, particularly, the shores of New Albion, where no efforts should be spared to raise wheat. Finally, in case of need, the colonies would have to turn to Boston, where grain could still be obtained cheaper than from Okhotsk, as well as to Canton and even Japan.

10. A head office, in New Archangel, should be established and secondary offices in other locations. The school should educate clerks and bookkeepers, as well as copyists. For the present, however, these positions would be occupied by qualified personnel sent from Russia.

11. Attention should be paid to the morals of colonial employees, it being especially important to restrain the men from drunkenness.

12. Almshouses should be established in the colonies for aged employees, both Russians and natives. They would be supported by a special fund, derived from annual sums withheld from the wages of colonial employees for whom the company provided native servants.

13. The directors would send the necessary materials for building a sawmill in the colonies.

Later, during his stay in Okhotsk, Rezanov sent ten exiles to the colonies, paying them an annual salary of one hundred rubles, with their rations and clothing provided out of the treasury. In a memorandum to Minister of Commerce Count Rumiantsov, Rezanov pointed out the value of settling from 150 to 200 exiles in America. He also asked that the directors petition the emperor for permission to settle freely in the colonies anyone who might wish to go there.

Shipbuilding is resumed and a ship and cargo are purchased. While at New Archangel, Rezanov saw to the immediate construction of two shipbuilding slips, on which were begun two ships of his own design—a tender and a brig. In 1805 several American ships came to Sitkha, including the *Juno* [*Iunona*], under the command of its Bostonian owner, D'Wolf.

Rezanov adroitly let the Americans know that the Russian emperor would soon prohibit trade with the natives. Rezanov suggested that the Americans should instead trade directly with the Russians, and as a first experiment bartered 20,000 rubles worth of goods from them. The rapid growth of the Russian settlement on Sitkha Island, the activity everywhere, and the thought of the possible profits impressed the Americans. In accordance with Rezanov's proposal, D'Wolf decided to sell to the company the *Juno* and all of its cargo for 54,637½ Spanish piasters, which at that time equaled 109,821 paper rubles 37½ kopeks. This ship had 206 tons capacity and was sheathed with copper. Her acquisition greatly aided the colonies, particularly in view of the deprivations which the employees there were suffering because of the wreck of the *Zakhariia i Elisaveta*, lost under Midshipman Karpinskii on her return voyage from Kad'iak to New Archangel, and the delayed arrival of another company ship from Okhotsk. The need for essential supplies in the colonies had reached the point where two hundred men were being rationed only a pound of bread per week, and even that could not continue beyond 1 October. Fish were no longer being caught. The only food in New Archangel consisted of iukola, sea lions, and occasional seals. Through necessity they scorned nothing: they ate eagles, crows, cuttlefish, and, in general, anything they could find. Only those afflicted with scurvy, which was endemic in the settlement, were given millet with molasses and beer brewed from fir cones. "If you visited here," Rezanov wrote to the board of directors, "you might think at first that we are living in the Elysian Fields, but you would be absolutely wrong: it is Sitkha we live in and we are waiting to be moved out."

Rezanov's trip to California.[17] This hopeless state of affairs, certain to last at least several more months, convinced Rezanov that he must go to California to obtain grain and perhaps furs, if not with the viceroy's permission, then privately, through the missionaries. The shortage of necessities in the Spanish settlements and the prohibition against trade with foreigners frequently forced the settlers there to obtain supplies secretly from mariners, and apparently the missionaries were the chief participants in this contraband trade.

At the end of February 1807 Rezanov put to sea in the *Juno*, under Lieutenant Khvostov. The crew, weakened by starvation, soon began to contract scurvy, so that hardly half of them could turn out to man the ship. Their condition forced Rezanov to consider putting in at some port. He decided to attempt to obtain fresh provisions at the nearby Columbia River but violent winds and a strong current prevented the ship from anchoring.

After a month of sailing, the *Juno* reached San Francisco Bay. Knowing the Spaniards to be suspicious, Rezanov decided to enter the port without asking permission, as if it had already been obtained. When they drew even with the fort they were hailed and ordered to drop anchor. They pretended to comply by immediately answering "Si Señor," then continued under a favorable wind straight for the harbor, where they dropped anchor within cannon shot of the fort. A boat soon arrived carrying a missionary and the son of the commandant, Don Luis de Arguello, who was commanding the fort in the absence of his father. Rezanov told him that he was on his way to Monterey, but a violent wind and need of repairs had forced him to enter the first port he encountered. He added that the Spanish government had surely informed them of his arrival. The son of the commandant replied courteously that he had actually received such a communication; he invited Rezanov and his officers to call on him and immediately sent to the ship fresh supplies, which greatly restored the crew.

When asked the whereabouts of the *Neva* and the *Nadezhda*, which the Spaniards had heard were going to arrive, Rezanov said he had sent them back to Russia. He also said that the Russian emperor had named him commander-in-chief of the American realms [*Slavnyi nachal'nik amerikanskikh oblastei*] (a title which he assumed on the spur of the moment) and that he wished to discuss with the governor the mutual benefit of their neighboring domains. To refute rumors spread by the Americans of the poverty of the Russian colonies, Rezanov sent expensive gifts to all the important people in the fort, winning their favor; the first result of this was a promise to provide the ship with necessary provisions.

Noticing from the missionaries' conversation that the Spaniards did not forswear trade and that the cargo of provisions necessary for the colonies could be purchased on the spot, Rezanov wrote to the governor of California asking permission to go to Monterey for a personal interview. Don Arillaga, the governor, answered that he could not permit Rezanov to do this (doubtless out of fear of incurring the government's indignation for allowing foreigners into the interior of the country), but he himself would hasten to San Francisco, to meet the commander-in-chief of the Russian colonies, adding that he had received orders to fulfill all the wishes of the honored guest.

The healthy California climate and the abundant fresh food restored the health of the ship's crew. Soon there was not one sick man remaining. Several sailors, in fact, felt well enough to attempt to desert, two of them succeeding.

While awaiting the governor, Rezanov and his officers spent every day in Don Arguello's hospitable house. The favor one of the commandant's beautiful daughters showed toward Rezanov was the chief reason for the friendly relations between the Russians and Spaniards so essential for the success of Rezanov's visit. This representative of the fair sex played an important role in saving Sitkha, if not from death by starvation, then at least from diseases associated with malnutrition. Doña Concepcion was known as the most beautiful woman in California, and it was to her ambition, and perhaps Rezanov's special charm, that abundance replaced absolute need in the colonies. Moreover, the favorable repute of the Russians, which spread all the way to Monterey, won the governor's favor.

After the governor's arrival in San Francisco, cordiality soon replaced ceremonial constraint between the representatives of Russia and Spain. Rezanov immediately got down to business, but despite the fact that he had most favorably impressed the governor, Don Arillaga could not at first bring himself to grant his request, but suggested that he might more conveniently fulfill his wishes through the commandant and the missionaries, who were already completely on Rezanov's side. Among other things, the governor pointed out the present position of both of their governments and the necessity of quickly ridding himself of his uninvited guests, so that he should not incur the dissatisfaction of the Spanish court.

At their next meeting, Arillaga promised to give them grain, but appeared to waver in keeping his promise. Soon, however, news came of the break between Russia and France, a power friendly with Spain, and this put him into the utmost confusion. He considered it necessary to call part of the garrison from Monterey and station them near San Francisco. This action could not be concealed from Rezanov, however, despite the secrecy with which it was carried out. Furthermore, the expected arrival in California of a Spanish cruiser and the clearly expressed intention of some of the foreigners in the *Juno's* crew to betray the Russians at the first opportunity, put them in a critical position, although their friendly relations with the Californian authorities appeared to be unchanged.

Rezanov carefully weighed what course he should take and decided to attain his goals by other means. Every day he managed to see Doña Concepcion and observed her unusual independence of thought and her boundless ambition. He decided to profit by her influence on the other members of the commandant's family and on the close relations this family enjoyed with the governor. Attempting to instill in this young lady thoughts of the charming life in the Russian capital, the splendor of the Emperor's court, etc., he soon inspired in her a desire to become the wife of the Russian chamberlain. The first hint from Rezanov that she held the key to his success was quite enough to assure that she would act in accordance with his wishes.

Although Doña Concepcion's wish to marry a Russian astonished her parents because of Spanish zealotry against mixed marriages, Rezanov managed to become engaged. The final resolution of this matter rested on the Pope's permission. Now that Rezanov had become a future close relative of the commandant, he could work more adeptly to attain his goal. The Arguello family now kept no secrets from him, even those quite apart from family relations. The very port and all those who were stationed there found themselves increasingly at his disposal. The governor, urged from all sides to grant Rezanov's request to provide the colonies with grain, felt obliged to give him the required provisions, and even ordered his own men to help Rezanov load the ship.

Doña Concepcion's brothers had previously readied most of the grain, and the missionaries vied with each other to obtain the rest. The loading proceeded rapidly, and Rezanov, seeming to pay no heed to the ever current rumors of war, gave the Spaniards an unbroken series of parties and dinners, attempting thus to stifle the very thought of possibly imminent hostilities between the two powers.

The ship held only 4,600 puds of cargo, consisting of wheat, flour, barley, peas, beans, lard, salt, and a small quantity (26½ puds) of dried meat.

On 8 May 1806 Rezanov left California and in early June reached New Archangel without incident. In his absence scurvy raged on Sitkha Island and on Kad'iak. Seventeen Russians had died and sixty others had lain almost immobile. The natives had also suffered from this disease and many had died. Fortunately, the herring appeared around the end of March and health began to improve because of the fresh food, so that Rezanov found only six persons dangerously ill and five walking on crutches.

Kolosh hostility and the destruction of the Yakutat settlement.[18] In the meantime, the Kolosh, taking advantage of the weakened New Archangel garrison, attempted more than once to attack the new settlement. Although their self-confidence had been greatly shaken by their expulsion from Sitkha during the *Neva's* stay, the Kolosh persisted in sending armed parties to scout the fort, to discover whether they could attack decisively from any direction. Experience had taught the Russians to be very cautious. The inhabitants of New Archangel were ready at any time of day or night to appear at their designated posts; their guns were always loaded and no one parted with his weapon, even while he was asleep. Moreover, Baranov fenced the fort with a high log palisade to prevent a sudden break in. The other tribes of the Kolosh nation sympathized with the Sitkha tribe. According to rumor, the Khutsnov Kolosh, on Admiralty Island, had seventeen hundred well-armed men and intended to attack a fur hunting party. For some time the Kenais had been making peculiar claims. In general, unusual activity was observed everywhere. In particular, the Russians were kept in constant anxiety by a migration of Kolosh, numbering more than a thousand, toward New Archangel in the spring of 1806, for the usual herring fishing of that season. Finally, the destruction of the Yakutat settlement by the Ugalakhmiuts in the autumn of 1805 and, soon thereafter, the massacre of a fur hunting party of three hundred crowned the distresses experienced by the colonies at that time.

There were forty persons in the Yakutat settlement. Of these only eight men, two women, and three boys escaped death, and they only because they were working in the forest when Kolosh attacked. Subsequently, they too were captured. The fort was armed with five small-caliber cannon and 180 pounds of powder. Some time later it was discovered that the native employees [*kaiurs*] of the settlement had also taken part in the destruction of the fort. The old friend of the Russian colonies, the Englishman Barber, who had made a good profit returning to Kad'iak Russians saved when Sitkha was destroyed in 1802, found out about the fate of Yakutat and immediately arrived at Kad'iak. His obvious aim was to attack the Russian settlement at the earliest opportunity. Noticing, however, that there was a company ship in the harbor, he quickly left, offering as a pretext for his visit the need to see Baranov, although he must have known that the latter was at New Archangel. Rezanov's arrival from California with supplies and the reinforcement of the garrison with the crew of the *Juno* completely reanimated New Archangel.

Rezanov and Baranov agreed that the cargo should be sold in the colonies at the following prices: wheat, three paper rubles per pud; beans and peas, four rubles; butter, eight rubles; and beef suet, six rubles. "Such low prices were set," wrote Rezanov, "in order to show the people the benefit of trade and to dispose them favorably toward voyages for that purpose." Providing the colonies with provisions from California seemed so advantageous and convenient to Rezanov that he hoped in future to supply grain in this way to Okhotsk and Kamchatka at prices more than one and a half times less than those which had prevailed over the last three years (1804-1806) in those ports, when a quarter [*chetvert'*] of grain, weighing 7 puds, 10 pounds cost from thirty-four to thirty-five rubles, and groats from fifty-four rubles to sixty rubles sixty-eight kopeks. For this reason, Rezanov's favorite dream was of Russian occupation of the regions which, according to the convention of 1790, were under the condominium of England and Spain. In his opinion, this matter could be settled through the Russian government, particularly since neither England or Spain had colonies there. First he proposed to establish a settlement in the Strait of Juan de Fuca at Discovery Bay, where, according to Capt. Vancouver, the land was extremely fruitful. He thought two hundred men to be sufficient to occupy Discovery Bay, Gray's Harbor, and the Columbia River. Having settled there and befriended the natives, it would be an easy matter, in his opinion, to move gradually toward California and thus to become the Spaniards' close neighbor. The advantageous location of the port of San Francisco must inevitably attract to it traders from all over the world. In his notes on California Rezanov wrote that, "if the far-reaching plans of Peter the Great, who with insignificant resources dispatched the Bering expedition, had been properly executed, California would never have been a Spanish possession, for only in 1760 did the Spaniards turn their attention to that country and they strengthened their hold on this incomparable territory solely through the work of missionaries."

Considering the family ties and friendship which he developed in California, Rezanov's enterprise might have aided the realization of his aims there, but fate determined otherwise.

Rezanov orders an expedition to Japan. One of Rezanov's last acts in the colonies was to order a secret expedition to Japan by the company vessels *Juno* and *Avos'*, under the command of Lieutenant Khvostov and Midshipman Davydov. Ascribing the refusal of the Japanese government to conclude a trade treaty with Russia solely to the opposition of one influential minister who, as mentioned above, stood for the absolute isolation of Japan, Rezanov decided that it would be necessary to use force. While he was still on Unalashka, he had written to the Emperor:

> By strengthening our American establishments and building ships, we may oblige the Japanese government to open the trade which their people most earnestly desire. I do not believe that Your Majesty will consider it criminal when, aided by such worthy assistants as Khvostov and Davydov, I build ships and set out next year for Japan to destroy their settlement on Matmai [Hokkaido], to push them from Sakhalin and to ravage their coasts. By cutting off their supply of fish and depriving 200,000 people of their food we will force them to open trade with us. I hear that they have even dared to establish a trading post on Urup. If it be Your Will, Most Gracious Sovereign, punish me as a criminal for taking action without awaiting your command; but my conscience will reproach me even more if I let time pass in vain and do not make this sacrifice to your glory, particularly when I see that I may help effectuate the fulfillment of Your Imperial Majesty's high intentions.

In Rezanov's opinion, the immediate results of the expedition would be the following:

1. A Russian colony on Sakhalin Island, protected by armed forces with artillery, could pay for its upkeep in furs obtained, and even return a profit, while gradually giving the Russians a closer acquaintance with the Japanese and forcing the Japanese to seek trade ties with the Russians by holding their settlement on Matsmai under constant threat.

2. The fact that mountainous topography of Japan and fast-flowing rivers which frequently overflowed their banks forced the Japanese to conduct most of their trade by sea might greatly assist the Russians in attaining their goals. The thousands of cargo-laden boats, unsuitable for venturing more than three or four miles from the coast, which scampered for shore at the slightest fresh wind, could easily be cut off and captured by company cruisers. Such raids, particularly if repeated

several times, would cause popular unrest in Japan which would compel the government to agree to a mutually profitable peaceful agreement between the two countries.

Rezanov received no answer to his report.

At first Rezanov decided to lead the expedition personally, and departed from New Archangel with both ships on July 27. On the way, however, he suddenly changed his mind and ordered Khvostov to proceed to Okhotsk and the tender *Avos* to Aniva Bay, in southern part of Sakhalin, there to await the arrival of the *Juno*. Khvostov received instructions from Rezanov which also contained information on the Urup settlement and a description of that island. Essentially, Khvostov was ordered to enter Aniva Bay and, if there were any Japanese ships there, to destroy them, taking with him the fit and healthy Japanese crewmen, leaving the unfit ones to make their way to the northern part of Matsmai Island with orders never again to visit Sakhalin, a Russian possession, except for trade, for which the Russians would always be ready. An effort should be made to include artisans and craftsmen among the prisoners.

The orders went on to discuss the destruction of commercial stores on Sakhalin, after removing from them all possible goods; the kind treatment of the natives of Sakahlin, promising them a calm and peaceful life under the Russian emperor's rule; and, finally, the removal from Sakhalin to America of all idols from heathen temples and, if possible, at least one bonze (priest), "in order," wrote Rezanov, "that the Japanese, in the free conduct of their faith, might be more satisfied with relocation and might eventually settle down, thus attracting their fellow-countrymen." In conclusion Khvostov was ordered to bind the crew of the ships by a signed promise to keep the purpose of the expedition absolutely secret.

After arriving in Okhotsk, Rezanov requested that Khvostov return the orders, to which he made the following supplement:

The recent break in the foremast, contrary winds hindering your navigation and the lateness of the autumn season oblige you now to hasten to America. The designated time for your meeting with the tender in Aniva Bay has passed. Since the fishing season has ended there, the hoped-for successes can no longer be realized, so, everything considered, I find it better for you to abandon the previous orders and proceed to America, so that your men can reinforce the port of New Archangel. The tender *Avos* should return, whether ordered to or not. But if the winds will allow you to go to Aniva Bay without loss of time, attempt to win the natives' favor with gifts and medals and observe the condition of the Japanese settlement there. You will have enough honor in doing this, but first and foremost your efforts should be directed toward returning to

America, which will yield real benefit. Therefore, provide the tender with the same admonition, if you should encounter it. I, for my part, am extremely sorry that this port is unsuitable for changing the mast and that the course of events has obliged me to change the plan.

When Khvostov received the new orders, he hurried to Rezanov to receive an oral explanation, but to his surprise he discovered that Rezanov had already left Okhotsk. "The ambiguity of this supplement," wrote Vice-Admiral Shishkov in his foreword to the account of Khvostov and Davydov's expedition, "placed Khvostov in no little difficulty. However, considering that Rezanov by himself could not have canceled an expedition of which he had already informed the Emperor, and that nothing in the supplement would indicate that the change was in the nature of an order received from the sovereign, and since Rezanov apparently had not canceled the expedition entirely, but merely postponed it, Khvostov decided to go to Sakhalin."

Shishkov's words lead to the inevitable conclusion that Rezanov issued the new orders in order to avoid responsibility for dispatching the expedition, while wishing nevertheless that it might take place. It is apparent from his subsequent correspondence with Baranov that, despite the urgency with which he made preparations for the expedition, he later thought it might be premature and it would be better to await the government's decision on it. Still, he did not wish to say this explicitly in his last orders, perhaps out of gratitude to his co-workers, who had worked hard to equip the ships rapidly. He knew Baranov's opinion that detaching men for this undertaking considerably weakened the colonies at a dangerous time, and he could not believe that, once the ships had arrived in America, the chief manager would at his own discretion release Khvostov and Davydov the next year to undertake a voyage to the shores of Japan. Be that as it may, Khvostov, regardless of the supplement to the instructions, decided to undertake the expedition, which ended without accomplishing any of its main aims and had as a further result the capture [in 1811] of Golovnin, the captain of the naval sloop *Kamchatka*. The enmity aroused in the Japanese by this incursion on their shores made good relations between Russia and Japan even more remote, while without outside help the colonies were not strong enough, even in case of need, to renew the expedition even once in order to compel Japan to accept the Russian proposals, as had been suggested by Rezanov. Rezanov's realization of the truth of this, although it came late and untimely, was probably one of the main reasons for his cancelation of the expedition.

Khvostov's and Davydov's operations against the Japanese. When he arrived at Aniva Bay, Khvostov took away from the Japanese around 1,200 puds of groats and loaded them aboard his ship. In addition, he took dishes, clothes, and other articles from some of the houses and burned the settlement. Suffering some damage from strong winds, the *Juno* with four captured Japanese arrived in Kamchatka late in autumn, to find that the tender had also reached there several days before.

The following year, 1807, both ships set out again for Aniva Bay in early spring. They entered the harbor at Iturup, seized four Japanese who were in the settlement, and took them on board, after destroying the settlement. Several days later they arrived at another inlet on the same island and sent a party ashore in three gigs to attack the settlement. The inhabitants opened fire from behind their buildings and forced the Russians to withdraw. Then they fired on the tender with their cannon and several shells hit the hull of the ship, but without causing any serious damage. The next day the Japanese began moving out of their houses and set fire to all of the buildings. Khvostov again landed a party and three cannon in five gigs and occupied the village, removing several things from it. The information obtained from the captured Japanese indicated that there were more than one hundred inhabitants in that settlement and about fifty more nearby. When he set sail, Khvostov released one of the Japanese on shore with a letter which explained why the Russians were acting in a hostile manner against Japanese possessions.

The ships visit Urup. When he visited Urup Island, Khvostov found no Russians, but only their living quarters and a few graves. On one of the latter was an inscription that Zvezdochetov had died in April 1805. In the meantime, the last seven members of Zvezdochetov's party had reached Kamchatka from Shimushu, bringing with them a large quantity of furs.

Returning to Aniva Bay, Khvostov and Davydov burned three sheds full of fish. Near the bay they noticed three unmanned Japanese vessels, took the salt, fish, and 190 sacks of millet which were on board, and burned the ships. They did the same with two other ships which stood off a nearby Japanese settlement. Finally, on the return voyage Khvostov released all of the captured Japanese except two, whom he kept on the ship for some unknown reason.

When they arrived in Okhotsk, Khvostov and Davydov, as well as their ships and cargo, were arrested by order of the port commander, Captain of Second Rank Bukharin, on the grounds that the captains of the ships had undertaken the expedition without authority.[19]

From Davydov's letters one may conclude that the main reason for the arrests was his unfriendly relations with Bukharin, who claimed remuneration from the company.

From the company archives it is seen that on the decision of a general meeting of stockholders, the board of directors informed the authorities of Bukharin's actions and as a result the Japanese goods which he had seized in arresting the ships were taken from him. Part of the booty was delivered to St. Petersburg and two Portuguese cannon and a Japanese falconet were placed by Imperial command in the arsenal; the other falconet taken by Khvostov was presented by the company to His Imperial Highness Grand Prince Nikolai Pavlovich.

Fortunately, Khvostov and Davydov escaped Bukharin's persecution and reached Iakutsk, whence, on the petition of the board of directors they were sent to St. Petersburg.[20]

Rezanov's inspection of the company offices in Siberia and his opinion of the company's trade. When Rezanov inspected the affairs of the company offices on his way through Siberia, he found great disorders in accounting, arising for the most part from the unscrupulousness of the manager and employees of the offices. In Okhotsk, for example, all of the company buildings, despite their quite ramshackle condition, were kept on the books at their original cost, with additions for all remodeling expenses: reappraisals were never made. In this way the capital value grew only on paper and produced a muddle in the company's accounts. Postal expenses alone in some Siberian offices reached twenty-five rubles daily, because employees were sending their personal letters and parcels at company expense, and also those of outsiders.

After he had eliminated all shortcomings that he could and investigated conditions on the spot, Rezanov established rules, based on those set forth above in the instructions to Baranov, relative to the transport of goods to the colonies, and toward determining their price. Furthermore, he considered it essential that the company establish an insurance fund (or capital reserve). He ordered the Okhotsk office, on each shipment of goods to America, to set aside 12 percent of the total value in order to capitalize this program. He ordered the Irkutsk office, at each shipment of furs from the warehouse, to lay aside the same percentage of cash, based on the colonial schedule of fur values. The rules on expenditure from this fund he left to the determination of the directors.

In Rezanov's opinion the company operations at Okhotsk, Gizhiga, and Anadyrsk were quite unprofitable. The Kamchatka trade, on the other hand, consistently showed returns of up to 20 percent. Kiakhta did not return good profits; Rezanov felt that carrying cloth to Kiakhta to trade with the Chinese was completely unjustified and that only furs should be marketed there. In his proposals concerning increased fur trading in Kiakhta, Rezanov wrote:

> They should be imported through Okhotsk and thence by water to Chita via the Amur, Shilka, and Ingoda rivers. An audacious plan, they tell me, but I say that it is possible and it will be a shame for Russia if it is not put into effect. However sweet the trading profits from the Amur River may be, the government will never be able to touch them without its American realms. But by strengthening the colonies there and on Sakhalin, dockyards may be built in America, and the ships built there from time to time will pay for themselves by trading with California. In the meanwhile, trade with the Japanese would offer means to fortify the Kurile and Sakahlin colonies, and when this plan bore fruit, it would be possible to demand of the Chinese immediate rights to free use of the Amur and, in case they refused, to send several warships up the Amur and force the court of Peking to accept our terms.

Rezanov's death. When he left Okhotsk on 24 September 1806, Rezanov, driven by his inexhaustible energy, traveled very fast; this had disastrous effects on his health, weakened for more than three years by hard work, disappointment, and care. He was forced to cross rivers already covered with the first autumn ice and to spend several nights in the snow. Forty miles east of the Aldan River he was seized by a severe fever and was carried unconscious to a Iakut yurt. He rested for twenty days and set out again; in Iakutsk he once more took to bed, but continued his trip while still ill. When he reached Krasnoiarsk, he again fell ill and on 1 March 1807 he died.

With the death of Rezanov, the company lost one of its most valuable workers in the field of colonial development. Had he lived to reach Petersburg, Rezanov would probably have personally presented the measures which he thought essential, calling on his first-hand acquaintance with the needs of the colonies and with the relations which existed with neighboring powers. The value of his personal participation in the colonial administration was unquestionable. There must have been many projects which he intended to present to the government and to the board of directors upon his return to the capital. If Rezanov's life had not been cut short so soon, certain of his plans would certainly have been carried out much earlier than was actually the case and certain others would not have been completely ignored. Few men would have undertaken what he accomplished with such self-sacrifice. His works for the common good were valued too little in his own time and were even frequently misinterpreted. Some people even considered him to be nothing more than a dreamer, capable only of creating plans on paper. However, neither setbacks, nor annoyances, nor obstacles prevented him from pursuing his goal. Ultimately he proved that despite extraordinary kindness and gentleness of character, a man such as he could accomplish much.

5. Maintenance and Supply of the Colonies and Trading Expeditions Sent Out by the Colonial Administration, 1806–21

The second round-the-world expedition of the "Neva." In August 1806 a general meeting of the stockholders instructed the board of directors to send the *Neva* back to the colonies that same autumn. This action was prompted by Baranov's dispatches on the need for a large cruiser in colonial waters to protect the company's settlements from hostile actions by the natives or the various foreigners who came for trade and furnishing the colonies with needed goods and supplies.

The directors placed Lieutenant Hagemeister in command of the *Neva*. Others on the vessel included Lieutenants Berkh and Kozliainov, ship's doctor Mardgorst, navigator fourteenth class Vasil'ev, assistant navigator Klochkov, commissioner Zakharov (supercargo), thirty-one seamen, and two Kad'iak Aleuts. The officers and crew agreed to spend four years in the company's service. The cargo consisted of articles needed in the colonies, such as anchors, guns, shells, powder, canvas, resin, food, tobacco, etc.

At the same time the emperor ordered that a naval ship accompany the *Neva* in order to protect it in case of enemy attack. But because of various circumstances the sloop *Diana*, chosen for this purpose, was unable to join the expedition until 1807. Therefore the *Neva* was forced to sail alone. She left Kronshtadt October 1806 and reached New Archangel on 12 September 1807. After leaving part of her cargo she proceeded to Kad'iak for the winter.

When Lieutenants Berkh and Kozliainov learned that a proposed expedition to Canton could not take place, they declined the high positions offered them by Baranov and asked to be sent back through Siberia. Lieutenant Hagemeister assumed their duties himself, retaining as his assistants only the two navigators, Vasil'ev and Klochkov.

In April 1808, during the usual spring gathering of natives from various places around Sitkha for fishing, Baranov sent the *Neva* to New Archangel. The presence of a well-armed vessel was necessary as it had been known for some time that the natives at Chugach Bay, encouraged by the small number of Russians there, and by rumors of a second destruction of the settlement on Sitkha Island, were preparing to attack Fort Konstantin.

In the spring of 1807 [*sic.* Actually November 1808-Ed.], Baranov dispatched the *Neva* to visit some of the colonial districts, instructing the commander at the same time to seek the island of Rico-de-Oro and Rico-de-Plata, situated between Japan and the Sandwich Islands, reported by seventeenth-century navigators. He was also to visit the island of Oahu of the latter group.[1]

The search for the unknown islands proved unsuccessful. From Hagemeister's observations on the Sandwich Islands,[2] it appeared that there was no possibility of opening trade there, since the principal chief, the so-called king, Kamehameha [in original Tomeomeo] kept all trade in his own hands, and would allow neither his subjects nor the foreigners living in his possessions to engage in it. Though his stores were overstocked with European goods, he would sell nothing at a reasonable price, although much of his wealth was said to be spoiling from long storage. Among other things, Hagemeister wrote that any of the Sandwich Islands could provide everything necessary for the Russian colonies and ports on the Eastern Ocean. Sugar cane, for manufacture of rum and sugar, rice, and finally the native bread plant, called taro, which is equal to any cereal, all grew there abundantly.

The king, having learned from the Americans that the Russians wished to settle in his possessions, at first seemed a little afraid of such neighbors, but finally became reconciled to the idea and spoke of it favorably. Rumors that a vessel would be sent from New Archangel to establish the settlement spread so widely that an English frigate came to the Sandwich Islands to ascertain the truth of the matter.[3]

On his visit to Oahu, Hagemeister succeeded in obtaining baked and ground taro for his crew. But for the colonies he could get nothing, although the king promised to send immediately but never delivered 1,000 barrels of taro. Nevertheless, Hagemeister did succeed in bartering 1,805 fur seals for some 1,200 puds of fairly good salt, and obtained a considerable amount of sandalwood. He also obtained a number of good pearls in exchange for walrus tusks. Subsequently, these pearls were sold at Canton at 9 piasters per zolotnik [1/96 of the Russian pound].

The *Neva* then went to Kamchatka, and at the beginning of the autumn [of 1809] returned to New Archangel. Hagemeister intended to return to Petropavlovsk the same month and thence to St. Petersburg; but when he got to Kad'iak to load a cargo of furs, he had to winter there and went to Kamchatka only in the spring of 1810 with furs worth 778,526 paper rubles.

The company was very dissatisfied with Hagemeister for taking his vessel to Kamchatka since there was no immediate prospect of getting the cargo to Okhotsk or Irkutsk because of lack of a commander for the vessels, and capital invested [in the furs] had to lie idle.

All of these furs were shipped on government vessels, with permission of the governor of Irkutsk, during 1810 and 1811 with payment in furs, namely one red fox per pud, totalling 10,000 paper rubles.

Transactions with foreign administrators. Because of lack of everything in the colonies, especially provisions, the inconvenience of obtaining them through Siberia and the impossibility of sending round-the-world expeditions from Russia annually, Baranov sought to encourage foreigners to supply the colonies with necessities, and tried to use local resources to supply the settlement in an effort to lighten the men's privations.

Thus, even before the departure of the *Neva*, Baranov made a contract [in May 1806] regarding hunting in partnership with Winship, an American, who came to Kad'iak on his own vessel [the *O'Cain*]. By this agreement, Winship was bound to escort a party of fifty baidarkas fitted out for hunting, each of them containing two Aleuts, under command of Slobodchikov and two assistants, to the shores of New Albion, to the Bay of Trinidad and farther on to [Spanish] California, not touching, however, on the Spanish possessions without special permission. In case Winship desired to go to California, he was to leave the party at New Albion under armed protection. The furs secured by the Aleuts, and those traded from the natives of the vicinity were to be divided equally, and of Winship's share, a percentage was to be paid to the company (5 paper rubles for a grown sea otter and of 1 ruble for pups) to indemnify it for furnishing him with men and equipment for the fur hunt, which was to be conducted only in the presence of the company's agent. If Winship obtained any provisions in California, he was to deliver them to Kad'iak, receiving 10 percent of their value for freight. For any goods from his cargo needed in the colony, he was to be paid in furs at the same rate as they were sold to his countrymen, i.e., 80 rubles for a grown sea otter, 40 for a cub, 6 for a beaver, and 5 for a fox.

Winship and his party went to California and in spite of the hostility existing between Russia and Spain, then an ally of Russia's enemy,

France, traded with the commanders of the California forts and the missionaries without any difficulties.

At the end of the agreed term for hunting in partnership, Slobodchikov succeeded in buying on the coast of California, on very good terms, a small American vessel [renamed the *Nikolai*] with all its armament and equipment for one hundred sea otters and fifty yearlings. Having loaded his vessel with the company's share of the furs, valued at 100,000 rubles, Slobodchikov persuaded the former skipper of this vessel to accompany him to New Albion whence he hoped to reach Kad'iak without any further assistance. However, for various reasons he had to change his plans and go to the Sandwich Islands first. King Kamehameha received the Russians very kindly and sent to Baranov, of whom he had heard much from the American captains, a colorful feather helmet and cloak, as a sign of his special respect. Slobodchikov managed to get some provisions from the company in exchange for some of his furs, but for the reasons mentioned above, he could do no business there. Meanwhile, the skipper refused to go back with him. This placed him in a very difficult situation, for the crew consisted of one foreign sailor, who was a runaway from a merchant ship, and several Aleuts, who had no idea whatsoever about navigation. However, in spite of this crew Slobodchikov sailed to the colonies, relying on divine help and his own common sense. Fortunately, he reached Paul's Harbor safely, with the loss of only two men and a baidarka [and Sitkha on 22 August 1807].

In the same year [1806], Baranov made a contract with his old friend O'Cain—who had come to the colonies in his own vessel [the *Eclipse*]—to exchange colonial furs in Japan for needed goods, under supervision of the company's own commissioner. Baranov's expectations of profit from this transaction were based on representations by O'Cain, who had considerable knowledge of the trade of that country, and who asserted that it was possible to open trade with Japan. Having loaded a cargo of furs valued at more than 300,000 paper rubles, O'Cain first went to the Sandwich Islands where he had thought of taking aboard his ship for transport to Nagasaki several recently shipwrecked Japanese, hoping to attain his goal more easily with their help. Finding upon arrival at the island of Oahu that the Japanese had already departed for their country on another vessel, O'Cain resolved to go straight to Canton. After learning in Canton that Russia and China were on unfriendly terms, and that the ships *Neva* and *Nadezhda* had barely missed being seized there, O'Cain decided to remove Baranov's commissioners from participation in the trade and send them to

Macao under the pretext that their presence might be disadvantageous. An assistant of the Swedish Consul, Ljungstedt, who had lived some time in Russia, assured the commissioners that they would be in no danger; but the crafty American refused to change his plans, and excluded the commissioners from all participation in selling the furs. When the trading was finished, O'Cain had obtained the lowest prices on all furs, namely 27 paper rubles for sea otters, and only 80 kopeks per skin for fur seals. He asserted that he had received no more than 245,000 rubles worth of Chinese goods in the exchange. Moreoever, he did not sail to New Archangel from Canton, but to Kamchatka where, contrary to the agreement, he turned over most of the things he had brought to the local company commissioner instead of to Baranov's agent who had been sent along with him.

Thus, the transaction had resulted in a loss. On the other hand, certain benefits had accrued since the goods received in Kamchatka had been critically needed at a time when shipping was unavailable. We must also remember that many of the fur seal skins exchanged had little selling value because they were poorly dressed or had been lying too long in the storehouses. As a result the capital invested in them had to remain idle and thus was only a liability for the company. Having concluded his business, O'Cain left Kamchatka in August 1807, but near Kad'iak his vessel was wrecked on a reef. Fortunately, the crew was saved, but the cargo of sugar and rice was lost. The remaining cargo was saved by Aleuts sent from Kad'iak, under the supervision of navigator Petrov, the commander of the company's ship *Aleksandr Nevskii.*

In 1807, the American ship *Derby* came to Kad'iak from Canton under the command of Captain Swift. He proposed to exchange his cargo of Chinese goods for furs on condition that he should be furnished with thirty baidarkas for hunting in partnership, as Winship had done. Baranov did not want to make any more such agreements for fear of incurring the company's dissatisfaction by possible failures. However, induced by the obvious advantages of the proposed deal, and by the fact that the supplies remaining from the ship *Neva's* cargo were nearly exhausted, he decided to give Swift twenty-five baidarkas with fifty natives under command of two promyshlenniks.

Subsequently, Baranov made similar deals with other American skippers who brought goods to the colonies. He also employed American vessels for other purposes, for instance, to punish the natives who destroyed the Russian settlement at Yakutat, and to obtain the release of the Russians and Aleuts captured on that occasion. In accordance with Baranov's wish, Captain Kimball [brig *Peacock*], cruised along the Yakutat coast [1806] and managed to capture several natives as hostages and to liberate two Kad'iak men. For this he received, according to agreement, twelve baidarkas, with the natives needed for them, under command of one Russian promyshlennik. These joint hunting arrangements were generally made only with those foreign skippers who had gained Baranov's special confidence by some service rendered or by long honest business relations, who could be trusted to look after the company's interests. Such deals were arranged with foreigners quite often up to 1814. The expeditions for hunting in partnership on the California coast, under contracts concluded in 1811, 1812, and 1813 with skippers Whittemore [brig *Charon*], Blanchard [*Katherine*], and Meek [*Amethyst*], yielded the company more than 270,000 paper rubles worth of furs.

Meanwhile, against all expectations, payment in fur seals for goods purchased from American skippers proved disadvantageous to the company. Skipper Bennett, who had received fur seals for his cargo of supplies brought to the colonies, took the skins to Okhotsk for sale, and in order to prevent them from falling into rival hands and creating dangerous competition in the market the company's office there had to buy them for much more than Bennett had paid Baranov. When the directors heard of the company's loss from this transaction, Baranov was ordered to limit such deals with foreigners, and to store up fur seals, which had a good market at Kiakhta, as a commodity necessary for trade with China. Skipper Pigot later obtained the same kind of furs at New Archangel as payment, at 2 rubles 50 kopeks apiece, and brought them to Kamchatka. Pigot had already succeeded in selling them to the Kamchatka commissioner, with payment to be made by the directors at the rate of 15 paper rubles per skin, amounting to 61,000 rubles, and the fur seals had already been transported on a company vessel to Okhotsk. However, the main office refused to pay and after intercession with higher authorities charged him 35,000 paper rubles for transporting the furs, on the grounds that the colonial rules regarding the resale of furs were well known to the buyer, and he was ordered to take the furs beyond the boundaries of Russia.[4]

The American Fur Company project. The order to limit transactions with foreigners naturally caused Baranov to ask whether the directors, after preventing him from provisioning the colonies in this manner, would be able to satisfy the colonies' wants by shipping supplies through Siberia or around the world. Nevertheless he strove to obey his instructions as far as possible. In 1816, fifteen foreign vessels came to the colony, but Baranov purchased only a small quantity of provisions and refused to enter into any business transactions with the other captains, especially because they would not accept in payment notes on the board of directors, but demanded payment in Spanish dollars, counting each only at somewhat above 2 paper rubles, whereas the dollar was worth 5 rubles 50 kopeks on the St. Petersburg exchange.

The directors understood very well the great cost of sending provisions to the colony around the world or by way of Okhotsk, and the advantages of buying them from the Americans under former arrangements, but, taking into consideration the abuses involved in such transactions, they resolved to prevent as far as possible foreign skippers from trading with the colony.

Fearing, however, that suddenly cutting off the colonies' supplies in that way might cause too great a scarcity of provisions and goods, especially if an accident befell the vessel sent annually from Okhotsk, the directors decided to provision the colony through the newly organized American Fur Company. Besides allaying all anxiety regarding provisions, the new company offered the advantage of forestalling the disasters likely to follow the relations of the independent natives (the Kolosh) with foreign skippers who often incited them against the Russians.

Long convinced of the need for this measure, the directors had petitioned the government several times to cooperate with the company in this case. In 1809 they again asked the emperor's consent to take more effective steps than the useless repetition of the same old request in regard to those skippers who despite the prohibition continued to sell the Kolosh firearms, powder, and ammunition.

In response to this request, the emperor instructed Count Pahlen, the Russian Ambassador to the United States, to request that American citizens be prohibited from trade with the natives injurious to the colonies, and to exert similar pressure on the American ambassador Adams at St. Petersburg.

Count Pahlen informed the Imperial Chancellor that in spite of repeated representations on this subject, the American government had neither power nor desire to take any steps to prohibit its citizens from trading with the natives on the coast of northwestern America and particularly the trade in arms, which was not prohibited by law and was subject only to general regulations. These restrictions referred to American vessels shipping contraband of war to one of two contending powers when the American government was neutral. Under these circumstances, Count Pahlen thought it incompatible with Russia's dignity to reopen negotiations with the United States on this subject, especially since many of the most important persons in America, who had great influence in the Eastern States, and who were very ill-disposed toward the administration, participated in the profits of this trade, and the administration feared irritating them by acting against their interests. Finally, the very principles on which the trade on the American coasts was conducted were conducive to developing abuses, for the skippers and supercargoes of the vessels received no salaries from the owners, but shared in the general profits, and consequently were anxious to increase their share by selling everything they could find a market for, whether in accordance with law or not. Also, the American government had shortly before given the privilege of settle ment on the Columbia River to a company composed mainly of American citizens for trading and hunting for furs. In our ambassador's opinion, arrangements with that company, based upon mutual advantage, would provide the only means under existing circumstances of fulfilling the wishes of the Russian-American Company.[5]

After some time, The American Fur Company, through its founder and principal business manager, the Boston citizen Astor, proposed to cooperate with the Russian-American Company with all means at its disposal in preventing the trade in contraband of war in their respective colonies, without any government participation, and at the same time supply the colony with provisions, agreeing to combine forces in case of need in localities occupied by settlements of both companies.[6]

Astor's main object in establishing the company, and his subsequent proposal to the Russians, was to weaken the influence of the English, who were extending their trading operations in America to the detriment of American citizens. The English Hudson's Bay, Northwest, and Mackinac companies threatened to seize the whole interior trade of the American continent. The first of these was established under a charter granted by King Charles II in 1670 to Prince Rupert and other English citizens, who had sent an expedition to the North America, in an area adjoining Hudson's Bay, known as "Rupert's Land." Soon the Hudson's Bay Company became a strong competitor of the French trappers, who a few decades before had selected Canada as their main field of activity, and who had attained some degree of monopoly in the fur trade with the surrounding natives. Despite the competition of these trappers, especially during the first thirty years of its existence, the Hudson's Bay Company grew steadily. When France ceded Canada to England in 1763, many of the English trappers hastened to replace the French in trapping and trade with the natives. Hostilities between the different groups considerably reduced the profits from the fur industry, and the main participants resolved in 1783 to form another English company which, having removed all reason for competition, could in case of need compete with the powerful Hudson's Bay Company. Thus began the Northwest Company, with its main office at Montreal. Its goal was a gradual expansion of its establishments and trade to the northwest of the Canadian lakes, into New Caledonia. Soon after this, a third company was formed on the strait uniting Lakes Huron and Michigan, which was called Michilimackinac or Mackinac. The company known by this name directed its activity to the southwest, reaching gradually along the Fox, Mississippi, and other rivers into the United States, where it exerted a strong influence on the native trade.[7]

Aiming mainly to stop this forced intrusion, and in general to limit the extension of the English trade, Astor, on obtaining the privilege of founding a factory on the Columbia River, which had been surveyed by a commission of the American government in 1804, succeeded [in 1810][8] in buying the shares of the Mackinac Company, and thus annexed it to his own. In his opinion, the establishment of an American trading post at the mouth of the Columbia, and other trading posts up that river, which would communicate with similar posts on the Missouri, and with Russian settlements south of the same river, could not only prevent the English seizing the coast, but also destroy their profits from the trading and trapping operations of the Northwest Company. In addition, the latter, restricted by the East India Company's monopoly on Pacific Ocean navigation, could communicate with its posts on the east side of the Rocky Mountains and supply them with provisions and trade goods only by the inconvenient and dangerous overland route, over 6,000 Italian miles long, whereas the Americans could use sea transport, a cheaper and better way that would inevitably affect the prices of the goods. These considerations convinced Astor of the advantages of competition and the assurance of success for his enterprise.

Under these circumstances, it seemed possible that the combined efforts of the Russian and American companies would be sufficient to drive from the colonial coasts all the other American traders who were damaging both by their contraband trade with the natives. At the same time supplying the Russian colonies with provisions on the Astor ships would guarantee their material well being, while enabling them to obtain necessity articles at a more reasonable price than before.

As a reward for providing these benefits to the Russians, the American Fur Company petitioned to be permitted to import into Russia annually 2,000 black bear skins as well as raccoon and skunk furs, duty free.[9]

On 4 October 1811, the minister of commerce informed the directors of the company, that after a report to the emperor about Astor's proposal, His Majesty permitted the company to undertake negotiations on all subjects related to its advantages with the Astor representative, the councilor of the Danish King and member of the administration of the Danish West Indies, Mr. Benson [Bentzon], if the company itself so desired, on condition, however, that all the agreements be first presented to the minister of commerce for consideration.[10]

With this imperial sanction, the directors replied that permission to the American Fur Company to import to Russia the above-mentioned furs, even on condition that they export from Russia goods equal in value to the furs imported, would nevertheless undermine the Russian fur trade, and in their opinion, such a request should not be granted.

A temporary committee on colonial affairs, along with the board of directors, acting on authority of the stockholders, considered the various questions relating to an agreement with the American Fur Company and ordered that a contract be made between the two companies in accordance with the suggestions of Benson and Astor. The contract term was five years, and the provisions were essentially as follows:

1. Neither company would carry on fur hunting or trade with the natives in areas where the other company had settlements.

2. Neither company would sell firearms or ammunition to natives living in its areas.

3. The American Fur Company agreed to supply the Russian colonies at prices established between the chief manager of the Russian colonies and the agents of the American Fur Company.

4. Each company would show the other prompt aid and cooperation in preventing the operation of outside traders in the territory of both companies.

5. In case the chief manager should find it inconvenient to send his own vessels, the American Fur Company would undertake to transport the Russian-American Company's furs on its own ships to any designated port and to barter them, with the Russian-American Company's commissioners participating.[11]

While the contract was being negotiated, Baranov, as Dashkov, the Russian consul in the United States, recommended, began dealing with Astor and bartered 54,000 paper rubles worth of goods from the American agent Ebbets, who had come to the colonies on a ship [the *Enterprise*] of the American Fur Company. Although the American goods cost 50 percent more than similar goods obtained locally, Baranov decided to accept Ebbets' cargo. Ebbets agreed to transport to Canton 146,000 paper rubles worth of colonial furs, receiving in payment all of the American expenses and 36,000 rubles in freight charges.[12]

Ebbets sold the furs in Canton quite profitably, receiving more than 150,000 paper rubles worth of Chinese goods.

The goods were resold in the colonies to the company's employees at the following prices:

Sugar candy	per pud	16 r.,	50 k.
Rice	do.	5 r.,	50 k.
Nankeen [*kitaika*] , per piece		3 to 8 r.,	80 k.
Jean [*demi-coton*] , per piece		5 r.	
Bengal, per piece		22 r.	
Velvet, per piece		89 r.,	60 k.
Taffeta, per piece		29 r.	
Foulard, (*fanza*) per piece		22 r.	
Canvas [*kanfa*]		65 r.	
Kangan, per piece		42 r.	
Thread, per pound		3 r.	
Tea service		12 r.	
Dinner service		80 r.	
Best green tea, per pound		2. r.,	25 k.
Ordinary green tea		1 r.,	7 k.
Aromatic black tea		2 r.	
Ordinary black tea		1 r.,	30 k.[13]

After his own voyage Ebbets sent his ship *Beaver* to New Archangel, under Captain Soule, carrying various goods and supplies. But the war between America and England had made the prices higher than those previously agreed upon, and Baranov did not accept the entire cargo, but only part of it valued at 124,000 paper rubles. Payment was made in fur seals, which Soule had to fetch from the Pribylov Islands because of the lack of company ships.

By 1812 the state of the American Fur Company's fortifications and settlements at the mouth of the Columbia River was so good that merchandise could be stored there secure from native attack. A major event in that region was the American discovery of a convenient route from the Columbia River through the Rocky Mountains and along the La Platte [Platte] River to the American posts on the Missouri and the Mississippi.

In the meantime the Northwest Company, in order to block the Americans, quickly established several trading posts along the west side of the Rocky Mountains somewhat north of the Columbia River and that area which lay between the Russian and American possessions and is now known as British Columbia. The clashes between the two companies had favored the Americans, but in 1812, during the war between England and America, the English government, understanding the great importance of the post at the mouth of the Columbia, sent several war ships there and destroyed Astoria. Astor's agent Hunt, and many of the company's employees went to New Archangel and remained there idle for almost two years. The Northwest Company immediately established a fort on the Columbia River, calling it Vancouver.

Despite the fact that the peace treaty of 1814 between America and England affirmed the American boundaries that had been established by a previous treaty, mainly the 49th parallel, the American post on the Columbia River was not reoccupied for some reason, and the Northwest Company, taking advantage of this, expanded its activities from the Rocky Mountains to the Pacific Ocean. It is obvious from Baranov's reports that he greatly feared English competition in the fur trade. The Northwest Company's agent frequently proposed to the colonial government joint activities along the northwest coast of America, but these proposals were not favorable to the Russian-American Company and were always rejected.

Subsequently, the Americans attempted several times to recoup their losses, and in 1820 Astor's company, in conjunction with another American company formed to take furs and fish in American rivers, nearly succeeded in doing so. The Americans founded several posts along the Columbia and its tributaries, but strong interference from the Northwest Company and a lack of capital forced the Americans to sell their establishments to the English, who were able to fulfill Astor's plan.

Even before the destruction of Astoria, the loss of several ships in a short time prevented Astor from fulfilling his contract to supply the Russian-American Company with goods and supplies. One of these ships was wrecked in the Sandwich Islands, through the neglect of the captain; the crew of another was massacred by natives in Nootka Sound, and in desperation one of the surviving sailors blew up the ship along with himself and all of the Indians who had taken part in the attack.

Thus the agreement between the Russian-American Company and the American Fur Company lapsed. This was, of course, no great loss for the colonies, since, except for the first cargo which Ebbets brought, many of the American goods were overpriced. The Americans continued to supply the natives with guns and powder secretly, in violation of their agreement. The commander [V. M. Golovnin] of the naval sloop *Diana* happened to see an order to Ebbets to trade with the natives on the voyage to the Russian colonies, whereas Baranov had been told that the vessel would proceed directly to the Russian colonies from America.[14] This show of bad faith indicated that the other terms of the agreement would not have been carried out and the arrangement would have brought no good to the Russians.

The third round-the-world expedition under Lieutenant Lazarev.
The company planned to send a shipload of necessities to the colonies
in 1813. The directors bought a 335-ton ship from an American in
Kronshtadt and renamed it the *Suvorov.*

The command of this ship was entrusted at first to Lieutenant-
Captain Makarov, but circumstances forced the directors to release him,
and she was placed under the command of Lieutenant M. P. Lazarev.
Under Lazarev were placed Lieutenants Unkovskii and Shveikovskii,
navigators Rossiiskii and Desilve, Assistant Navigator 14-class Samson-
ov, Doctor Schäffer, Supercargo Molvo, twenty-three naval seamen,
nine hired seamen, and seven hunters, who were passengers to the
colonies.

The *Suvorov* left Kronshtadt 8 October 1813. Upon reaching Karl-
skrona, she joined an English convoy, which she accompanied to
England and then to Brazil. Then she visited New Holland [Australia]
and, enroute from there to the colonies, discovered several uninhabited
islands at 13° 13' 15" south latitude and longitude 163° 31' 4" west,
which were called the Suvorov Islands. On 14 November 1814, the
Suvorov reached New Archangel, having completed the voyage from
England to the colonies in eight and one-half months.

In the spring of 1815 Baranov ordered Lazarev to proceed to the
Pribylov Islands for a cargo of fur-seal furs. He was then to go to the
Sandwich Islands for sandalwood and from there to Macao, where
sandalwood, which had great value on the Chinese market, and many
of the furs were to be traded for needed colonial supplies. But the
price of fur seals was rising in Kiakhta, and Baranov changed his orders,
sending Lazarev and his ship to Okhotsk, so the furs could be taken
directly to Kiakhta through Siberia. Presumably,[15] this decision was
the main cause of the disagreements which arose between Baranov and
Lazarev. Another important reason for these disagreements was the
conduct of Hunt, Astor's agent, who, Baranov felt, was violating
colonial orders, which he demanded that the former agent of the
American Fur Company must strictly obey. Baranov was already
irritated with Lazarev for evading his assigned duty, and when Lazarev
attempted to justify certain of Hunt's actions, Baranov threatened
to replace him as commander of the *Suvorov.* Finally, probably aiming
to force Lazarev to obey unconditionally the colonial administration's
orders, Baranov ordered him to anchor his ship under the guns of the
fort. Instead of obeying, Lazarev decided to leave New Archangel
altogether, and despite several cannon shots, which Baranov hoped
would force him to return, Lazarev went on his way with the *Suvorov.*

Stopping briefly in San Francisco to refresh the crew, Lazarev set

out for Quito and Lima, where he purchased for the company cin-
chona, ritania, Peruvian balsam, sarsaparilla, cotton, and wool. He
continued his voyage around Cape Horn and arrived in Kronshtadt on
15 July 1816.[16] In addition to these goods, the *Suvorov* carried a
large quantity of furs, so that the value of the whole cargo reached a
million rubles.

Baranov sends an expedition to the Sandwich Islands. After the
visits of Hagemeister and Slobodchikov to the Sandwich Islands, King
Kamehameha, through the Americans, proposed to Baranov that his
kingdom and the colonies establish trade relations. He even wished to
come to New Archangel to settle the terms of the agreement. Baranov
wanted to maintain friendly relations with the islands, where the fruitful soil offered a rich source of supply, and ordered Captain Bennett
to visit the islands in 1814 with the company ship *Bering* to purchase
provisions. A violent wind drove the ship ashore on Kauai Island,
where the cargo was looted by the natives. When the king of the island,
Kaumualii, was asked to return the goods, he flatly refused, alleging
that things washed onto his shore became his property. The king permitted the crew of the vessel only very meager provisions. In the end
they were rescued by Captain Smith, an American.[17] In 1815, Baranov
sent Doctor Schäffer, who had remained in New Archangel after
disagreements with the commander and officers of the Suvorov, to
King Kamehameha, who lived on Oahu and was considered the chief
ruler in the islands.[18] Schäffer was to seek Kamehameha's cooperation
in gaining the return of the cargo and vessel or in obtaining compensation in sandalwood, which commanded high prices on the Chinese
market. Finally, if circumstances permitted, Schäffer was to attempt
to establish trade relations with the king. At first Kamehameha received
Schäffer very favorably, but he was influenced by rumors spread by
Hunt, the American expelled from New Archangel, saying that Schäffer
had been sent by the Russians to find out how best to conquer the
islands. This forced the doctor to flee to Kauai Island, ruled by King
Kaumualii. Schäffer cured Kaumualii of dropsy and his wife of an ague,
winning the king's favor and boundless trust. He agreed to fulfill all
of Baranov's demands and concluded the following agreement with
Schäffer: (1) the *Bering* and its cargo were to be returned to the Russians, except for certain goods needed by the king, for which he agreed
to pay in sandalwood; (2) the king agreed to provide the colonies with
a full shipload of dried taro each year; (3) all the sandalwood on the
islands was placed at Schäffer's disposal, and trade in this commodity
was to be carried out only with the company; (4) the Russians received
the right to establish trading posts in any part of Kaumualli's realm.

For his part, the doctor promised to obtain for Kaumualii five hundred men and several armed ships, in order to capture Kamehameha's islands. The king promised to pay for this assistance in sandalwood. Moreover, Schäffer took command of Kaumualii's troops, on condition that the company was to be ceded half of Oahu Island. Finally, by common agreement, King Kaumualii and all his subjects were placed under the patronage of the Russian emperor.

Before news of Schäffer's activities reached him, Baranov sent two ships to strengthen his demands for the return of the company ship and its cargo. He also asked the doctor to attempt, if possible, to obtain King Kamehameha's permission to establish trading posts on Oahu Island, where an American establishment had existed for several years, under the American Winship brothers, who enjoyed the king's special favor.

Meanwhile, Schäffer, in order to carry out his promises to Kaumualii, bought an American schooner [Lydia] for 21,000 paper rubles and ship [Avon] for 200,000 rubles. He paid for these in company furs, which he bartered at a very low price.

When he heard of the doctor's arrangements, Baranov quickly wrote that he could not approve the agreement with Kaumualii without the permission of the board of directors, particularly since the Sandwich Islands were rumored to be under the protection of England. Furthermore he refused to acknowledge the purchase of the ships, asserting that Schäffer had deviated from his instructions. Baranov even urged the doctor to send immediately to New Archangel the brig Il'men, which had arrived in the Sandwich Islands from the shores of New Albion with a general cargo worth 65,000 paper rubles, in addition to a number of furs.

Ignoring the voice of reason and driven solely by the ambition to earn glory as the founder of new colonies for the company, Schäffer had already begun building a fort and trading post, using timber which he had taken from one of the ships that arrived from New Archangel, and planting orchards and gardens with which he hoped to provision the colonies.

When the emperor received King Kaumualii's request for protection, His Majesty responded that he did not consider it advantageous to fulfill the request and ordered the company to refuse, in as friendly a manner as possible, the request of the king, to return to him the document which Kaumualii had signed, and to confine future relations with the islands to those of friendly trade. As to the lands Kaumualii had ceded to the company, the emperor permitted them to be retained and used, if this should prove convenient.

The board of directors ordered Baranov to entrust the emperor's orders to someone more suitable for that purpose than Schäffer and, for his rash actions, to immediately recall Schäffer from the Sandwich Islands to the colonies.

Later, the order to return the protection agreement to the king was rescinded. The emperor, on the recommendation of the board of directors and the company council bestowed on Kaumualii a golden order of St. Anna with the inscription, "To Kaumualii, Lord of the Sandwich Islands in recognition of his friendship for the Russians." He was also given a highly decorated cutlass and a scarlet cloak with golden tassels and galloon.

In the meantime, the Americans who were trading in the Sandwich Islands were using every device to agitate the natives against the Russians. In 1816 Kaumualii permitted them to establish trading posts. They purchased land, plantations, and sandalwood for whatever prices the king demanded. Furthermore, they bought up a whole year's supply of dried taro, salt, coconuts, and so forth, which Kaumualii had agreed to give to the Russians for the 12,000 paper rubles worth of goods which he had taken from them. The Americans constantly urged the king to take down the Russian flag, which he had raised as a sign of Russian protection. Finally, they paid generously the king's chief agent, a fugitive Englishman who had gained great influence over the king, to expel the Russians. Under his leadership, the Americans destroyed the trading post which Schäffer had established on Oahu Island, forcing the inhabitants to flee. They tried to do the same thing on Kauai Island, where Schäffer had also started several establishments, but initially they failed. Then they resorted to spreading rumors that five American ships would soon arrive at the island and, if the king did not take down the Russian flag, their crews would kill all the Sandwich islanders. These Americans were joined by their countrymen in the service of the Russian-American Company, who abandoned the Russians. These included Vozdvit [Wadsworth?], commander of the brig *Il'men*, who left his ship without ceremony. Finally, the natives seized the Russians' possessions and drove them to their ships under threats that if they did not leave the island immediately, they would regret their stubborness. They tried to drown the doctor by setting him adrift in a rowboat with holes in the bottom, but by some miracle he saved himself. When the Russians tried to come ashore again for their lost possessions, the natives opened fire on them from the shore and forced them to return to their ship. It is not difficult to imagine the dreadful position that Schäffer and his men found themselves in. They were forced to sail without provisions, essential clothing, or any means

of defense. The company ship *Kad'iak* was in particularly bad condition. The ship's hull had sprung a serious leak and the hold was full o
water, subjecting the crew of sixty to the danger of drowning. Schäffer
sent a message to the king reminding him of their agreement, but he replied that he was in no position to help. Fortunately, the American
commander of the *Kad'iak*, Young, did not abandon the Russians.
Schäffer transferred him to the brig *Il'men* and sent him to Baranov
with news of the disaster. Schäffer himself decided to take the *Kad'iak*
to the port of Honolulu, the only safe refuge remaining open to him.
Calm weather helped the ship to reach port, but she was not admitted
until all weapons had been handed over. King Kamehameha's minister,
Young (also a fugitive sailor), urged the Russians to betray Schäffer,
but they refused to do so. The Americans roused such hatred toward
the doctor among the natives that he would certainly have lost his life
if an old friend, Captain Lewis, had not offered to take him to Canton,
from which he could reach Petersburg safely. Leaving the Russians on
Oahu Island under the command of Tarakanov, a hunter, Schäffer set
out in July 1817.

Thus vanished all of Schäffer's plans for a permanent Russian settlement in the Sandwich Islands. This experiment cost the company
around 230,000 paper rubles.

Several times afterward ships were sent from the colonies to the
Sandwich Islands to collect Kaumualii's debt, but they returned without success. In 1819 a company commissioner, Schmidt, saw Kaumualii
on Oahu Island. Kaumualii expressed readiness to pay for the things he
had taken from Schäffer, but he never did. The *Kad'iak*, which had
been left in the islands, was sold by the company to a foreigner for a
small amount.

In 1818 Tarakanov and his men reached an agreement with an
American named Jones to take them aboard his ship to hunt furs along
the California coast, and after that they reached New Archangel.

In 1818 Schäffer presented to the minister of internal affairs a
memorandum, explaining in detail all the advantages of trading with
the Sandwich Islands and of seizing one of them to establish a Russian
trading post. He submitted the number of ships and men necessary to
achieve this undertaking. The minister asked the company's opinion
of Schäffer's project. The company counsel and the directors set forth
all the circumstances associated with the previous attempt to establish
a settlement in the Sandwich Islands. They answered that they acknowledged the truth of Schäffer's arguments on the advantages to the
colonies, Kamchatka and Okhotsk of obtaining supplies in the Sandwich Islands, particularly if one of the islands were in Russian hands.

But, before entering into the undertaking with adequate means for its accomplishment, the company would await the government's orders.

When His Majesty was informed of the proposal and the opinion of the council and the directors, he replied,

> that, when he had ordered the company, under the most favorable circumstances, that is with the good will of Kaumualii toward the Russians and his free request for Russian protection, to decline this proposal and to confine themselves to friendly and commercial relations with the Sandwich Islands, His Majesty had based his wish on a firm conviction of the unwisdom of closer relations with this ruler, which has been justified by subsequent events. Consequently, at the present time His Majesty finds the thought of Russian settlements on one of the Sandwich Islands even less sensible. However, His Majesty approves the company's intention of re-establishing friendly ties with the rulers of the islands and wishes them success, hoping that with prudent and careful choice of company agents, it will enjoy the same advantages as it would have had from occupying the islands. All commanders of naval ships proceeding around the world would be ordered to spread the word that the company enjoys His Majesty's protection. As to gifts to the ruler Kaumualii made in the name of His Majesty, the company may use them at its discretion.

On the basis of this imperial order, the company's relations with the Sandwich Islands were thereafter confined to obtaining occasional provisions there, particularly salt.

Baranov sends an expedition to the Philippine Islands. In 1816 the American ship *Isabella* returned from Manila. Baranov had sent her there with one of his agents to find out whether the colonies could purchase supplies and trade in the Philippine Islands profitably. The expedition was completely unsuccessful. Baranov's envoys brought back to the colonies only large amounts of rum, and very little else. This expedition had been undertaken chiefly because of a plan presented to the emperor by Dobell, an American, who spoke of the profits the colonies could obtain from trade with the Philippine Islands. Dobell was appointed Russian consul in Manila, but the Spanish government would not acknowledge him. In 1817 he reached Kamchatka, where he concentrated on other matters, particularly trading the goods he had brought with him. Moreover, he made an offer to Rikord, commandant of Kamchatka, to import various provisions from overseas.

The company undertakes to supply provisions to Okhotsk and Kamchatka. In the same year the English vessel *Seven Brothers* arrived in Okhotsk with a cargo of manufactured articles and provisions, particularly alcoholic beverages, which the skipper proceeded to trade.

When the local company office informed the directors of this, they presented their thoughts on the matter to the minister of internal affairs, excerpts of which follow.

1. If foreign ships could import various food supplies to Okhotsk at prices not exceeding those paid for the same items obtained by way of Siberia (which was almost impossible, because of the small profits in these goods and the large space they occupied in a ship), this trade might be advantageous to the country. But if foreigners brought luxury items, such as alcoholic beverages, it would inevitably harm Russian trade, particularly since shipment of foreign goods into the interior of Siberia from Okhotsk or Kamchatka would be completely impossible in view of their high price.

2. Most of the furs obtained in the Kamchatka-Okhotsk area would inevitably pass to foreign merchants, which already was confirmed to some extent in this case, since the number of furs obtained had considerably decreased with the arrival of the *Seven Brothers*.

3. Thus the government would lose large sums from customs duties collected from the export of furs to China, Persia, and Turkey. These duties would amount to more than a million rubles, whereas, if foreigners imported goods to Okhotsk and exported furs from there, it would be impossible to obtain more than 50,000 to 100,000 rubles. Finally, when foreigners sold their furs in Canton, they would receive profits which might have been enjoyed by Russian merchants.

Then the Englishman Pigot arrived in Petropavlovsk with an offer to conduct fishing and whaling along the shores of Kamchatka for a period of ten years. Rikord zealously supported this project, as well as trade with Dobell. The board of directors considered that the foreigners could catch fish only in the islands of the Aleutian chain or in the waters of Bering Strait and the Arctic Ocean (from which whales occasionally chased small fish) and consequently hoped in time to establish a permanent settlement in one of the company's possessions. Finally, under the pretext of catching whales, the oil of which provided the crown with an income of only 50 kopeks per pud, they would surely attempt to carry on fur trading with the natives, and perhaps even fur trapping. This being so, the board of directors found it necesary to inform the minister of internal affairs that permitting Pigot's project would not only violate the company's imperial privileges, which granted it the exclusive use of all the area extending northward from latitude 55° north and south to Japan, but would harm the inhabitants of Kamchatka to the benefit of the foreigners, since fishing was absolutely necessary to the economy of Kamchatka.

When M. M. Speranskii, governor general of Siberia, learned of Pigot and Dobell's proposals and of the company's view, he informed the directors that he had taken note of the circumstances and shared their opinion of foreign trade in Kamchatka and that he would use all means at his disposal to see that the company's rights and advantages were not violated.[19] As to Dobell's proposal to furnish supplies for the soldiers and citizens of Kamchatka and Okhotsk, Speranskii asked the board of directors if they did not consider it possible for the company to provision these places with their own vessels. The minister of finance repeated this proposal at the same time, and the board of directors, in order to obviate the harmful effect on the company of foreign trade in the Pacific ports, decided to carry out the government's wishes.

On this basis most of the rye carried by the round-the-world expedition of 1821 was designated for these ports. But when the ministry of finance asked if this practice could be continued, the board of directors showed the unfeasibility of bringing provisions on company ships, and thus the company was freed from this obligation (see Chapter 10).

As to the other proposals of the foreigners, the minister of finance informed the directors that he had presented them to the emperor and obtained the following reply:

1. The government will not ratify the contract concluded with the Englishman Pigot. However, since whaling could be useful as a means of augmenting the food supply of the inhabitants of Kamchatka and Okhotsk in case of a bad catch of fish and as an additional profitable enterprise for the Russian-American Company, His Majesty wishes that the company turn their attention to this matter and use in this industry one ship, equipping it with all necessary equipment and experienced men.

2. The government of the Irkutsk Gubernia will forbid any foreigner, unless he be a Russian subject, from enrolling in the merchants' guilds or settling in Kamchatka or Okhotsk. In addition it will prohibit all foreign merchant ships from trading in these places or putting into the ports of East Siberia, except in case of accident, in which case care will be taken that they do not unload anything or sell to anyone, under threat of confiscation of the entire ship. The same government will inform the Englishman Pigot in Okhotsk and Commissioner Dobell in Kamchatka that the government no longer permits them to stay in those places, and even less to erect homes or other immovable possessions. The local government is to assist them in selling their possessions and in leaving. Dobell, however, will be instructed that the ship which he has proposed to sail from the Philippine Islands to Kamchatka will be permitted on this occasion, and the goods and food supplies brought on it may be sold. But in the future, he will be prohibited from making such voyages and will be confined to supplying Russian ships, which will be sent to Manila for food stuffs and supplies either by the government or by the Russian-American Company.

3. Dobell will be refused permission to bring two ships to Kronshtadt with tea and other Chinese goods, since this does not coincide with the views of the government. It will be explained that he is now asked merely to furnish

information on what prices may be obtained in Manila for Chinese goods and what products of Eastern Siberia may be profitably sold there, to the end of using this information in the general trading considerations of the Russian-American Company.

The fourth round-the-world expedition under Captain-Lieutenant Hagemeister. The fourth round-the-world expedition was proposed by the directors in 1815, under the former commander of the *Neva*, Captain-Lieutenant Hagemeister. For this purpose a 525-ton ship, the *Kutuzov*, was purchased in Havre for £6,000. On 15 July 1816, she was ready to sail, but on that same day the *Suvorov* arrived in the Kronshtadt roadstead from the colonies, and the sailing of the *Kutuzov* was delayed. Inspection of the *Suvorov* revealed that with minor repairs and some replacement of some of her copper sheathing, she could set out again on a long voyage, and the directors decided to send her to the colonies with the *Kutuzov* under the general command of Hagemeister.

The command of the *Suvorov* was entrusted to Lieutenant Ponafidin. The crew consisted of Lieutenants Ianovskii and Novosiltsov, Doctor-Surgeon Berve, Assistant Navigators Zarembo and Domashnev, Commissioner Krasil'nikov, supercargo, thirty naval ranks, and four promyshlenniks as passengers to the colonies.

The crew of the *Kutuzov* consisted of Lieutenants Selivanov and Kropotov, Navigators Klochkov and Kislakovskii, Staff Doctor Kerner, Commissioner Khlebnikov and Tumanov, a commercial student, supercargo, forty-five naval ranks, seven promyshlenniks as passengers to the colonies, and Blek, a Siamese who had been brought to New Archangel by the Englishman Barber and there had accepted the Christian faith.

The cargoes of the two ships consisted of more than a million paper rubles worth of supplies and foodstuffs for the colonies.

The ships proceeded together as far as the Port of Callao. From there the *Suvorov* went straight to New Archangel, arriving 22 July 1817. The *Kutuzov*, however, called at several ports on the way and did not reach New Archangel until 22 November.

On 14 January 1818, the *Suvorov* began the return voyage to Kronshtadt. It arrived on 18 October, bringing news of Hagemeister's replacement of Baranov as chief manager of the colonies (see Chapter 7). In Rio de Janeiro Ponafidin had obtained for the company 260 puds of granulated sugar. In addition he brought from the colonies a large number of furs. The total cargo of the *Suvorov* was worth more than 900,000 paper rubles.

In the meantime the *Kutuzov* had sailed to Ross settlement and to San Francisco for foodstuffs and brought a large quantity back to New Archangel.

The *Kutuzov* stayed in the colonies until 26 November 1818, when she set out on the return voyage. In Batavia Hagemeister traded 200,000 rubles worth of colonial furs for various goods. The *Kutuzov* reached Kronshtadt on 7 September 1819.

The *Kutuzov* brought more than one million paper rubles worth of furs.

The fifth round-the-world expedition under Lieutenant Ponafidin. For the fifth expedition to the colonies the company bought in England a ship of over 600 tons, which was named the *Borodino*. The command of this vessel was entrusted to the former commander of the *Suvorov*, Lieutenant Ponafidin. The crew consisted of Lieutenants Chistiakov (II), Ponafidin (II), and Nikol'skii, Doctor Planten, Navigators Zarembo, Prokof'ev, Kal'khin and Raunen, Commissioner Krasil'nikov, supercargo, and two assistants, seventy-nine naval ranks, and thirty-three promyshlenniks as passengers to the colonies.

Although the goods brought on the *Kutuzov* from Batavia were sold at a profit, uncertainty of trading conditions in some foreign markets prompted the directors to instruct the commanders of vessels proceeding to the colonies around the world to visit various ports during their voyages and to experiment in trading small quantities of goods, provided for that purpose. Ponafidin was able to do this in Rio de Janeiro and in Manila, but the trade was not profitable in either port. In Rio de Janeiro glass and candles were sold at good prices, but in Manila these goods brought very little.

The ship returned to Kronshtadt 15 September 1821, after much sickness on the voyage; forty men died. The emperor ordered a commission to investigate the causes and circumstances of the illnesses and deaths. It reported that the commander and the doctor had in no way neglected the crew's health, and that the illness probably resulted from local causes.

The *Borodino* brought about 800,000 paper rubles worth of furs from the colonies.

The sixth round-the-world expedition under Lieutenant Dokhturov. The *Kutuzov* was equipped for the sixth round-the-world expedition to the colonies and set sail from Kronshtadt on 7 September 1820 under the command of Lieutenant Dokhturov. Her crew consisted of Lieutenants Novosiltsov, Naumov and Romanov, Navigator Ingstrem and two assistants, Doctor-Surgeon Berve, Commissioner Chernyshov and his assistants, forty-two naval ranks, and three creoles, twenty-eight promyshlenniks, and two foreigners as passengers to America.

During the voyage the ship visited Rio de Janeiro, whence she took dispatches and four Spanish officers to Callao, at the Spanish minister's request. As the ship neared Callao, insurgents who were only two miles from the port demanded that the Russians conduct no trade with the Spaniards, and Dokhturov, fearing a clash, refused to trade his goods, despite the fact that the viceroy offered high prices for some of them. In the middle of June the ship reached Ross settlement, where she discharged some of her cargo. She then set out for the ports of Monterey and Santa Cruz, where she obtained, with the governor's aid, a large quantity of wheat. The *Kutuzov* reached New Archangel on 24 October 1821. There she discharged her cargo and took on furs valued by the directors at 1,109,368 paper rubles 50 kopeks. The ship arrived at Kronshtadt on 21 October 1822.

Company cargoes were sometimes carried to the colonies on war ships, as for example from Kamchatka on the sloop *Diana* at a cost of 4 paper rubles per pud, and from Kronshtadt on the sloop *Kamchatka* at 10 rubles per pud.

6. *Trade with California and the Establishment of Ross Settlement*

Trade with California.[1] Making every effort to obtain for the colonies an assured food supply and having in mind that California, with its fertile soil and proximity to the company settlements, presented the best solution to that end in comparison with other sources of supply, the board of directors repeatedly asked the government to petition the Spanish court for permission to trade with California and constantly reminded Baranov to maintain trade relations with that country.

When in 1808 the company first asked permission to trade with California, the state chancellor replied that the government was now approaching Spain on this subject, but that no answer had yet been received.[2] In 1809 the directors again asked the government to renew its efforts in Madrid. They explained that the inhabitants of California, forbidden trade relations with foreigners, were forced to sell their native products secretly to the American captains who ran contraband on the California coast. The emperor instructed Count Rumiantsov to inform the company that it should push its own way into this trade. Then the directors ordered Baranov to send a vessel to San Francisco with a cargo of the goods most commonly used by the Californians, with a proclamation from the government on the Russian-American Company's wish to provide this country with necessary goods in exchange for California products. In 1812 Baranov sent his agent on the ship [*Mercury*] of an American captain, Ayres, instructing him to use his best efforts to inform the Mexican viceroy of the company's proposal through the medium of the missionaries.[3] Pending the viceroy's answer, the California governor replied that although all the inhabitants of San Francisco and the surrounding country would be pleased to have trade relations with the Russian colonies, they dared not violate the established restriction without the agreement of their government. Therefore, they asked the company, through the Russian minister of foreign affairs, to petition the Spanish Court for permission to import goods from New Archangel into California. The Spanish consul in St. Petersburg, Céa de Bermúdez, also wrote to Madrid, citing all the advantages that would follow from an exchange of goods and provisions. The directors brought the California administration's appeal to Count Rumiantsov's attention, repeating its request for aid in establishing those trade relations which were necessary to the welfare of the colonies.

Moves to establish a settlement in California. Meanwhile, the directors had borne in mind the impossibility of carrying on agriculture in any of the places in the company's control because of climate, particularly the heavy rains which prevented grain from ripening. Therefore, it was proposed to establish a company settlement in a more favorable climate, on the coast of New Albion adjacent to the Russian colonies. This seemed the more possible since these shores were neither occupied by any foreign power nor claimed by any other country by right of first occupation.

The English navigator Drake had named this coast New Albion. Although Spain pretended to the possession of the Northwest Coast of America as far as the Strait of Juan de Fuca, her rights to these lands were based only on the fact that two Spanish ships had penetrated these waters in 1788 and had established one settlement in Nootka Sound. Thus these rights were very dubious. The impermanence of the Spanish possessions in these regions was emphasized by the fact that, when the Spaniards captured an English merchant ship in Nootka Sound, the English government compelled them to make full reparations to ship owners. Subsequently, under the treaty of 1790 between Spain and England, the settlement itself was destroyed and all the ports north of San Francisco were thrown open to subjects of both powers.

Later, when the Americans established forts and trading posts along the Columbia River with no objection from the Spanish government, Spain's claims to the coast of northwestern America above California were conclusively destroyed.

With these facts in mind, the board of directors asked the emperor in 1809 for permission to establish a settlement on the shores of New Albion and for the government's protection in case of opposition by the Americans. The board also presented its views on direct government action in establishing this settlement, in view of the small number of men in the colonies.

The emperor gave permission for the company to establish the settlement itself, under imperial patronage.

The expedition of the "Kad'iak" and "Nikolai." The directors ordered that an advance party investigate this coast and choose a suitable place for a settlement. In the autumn of 1808, Baranov therefore dispatched two ships under his assistant Kuskov, who was also to supervise the fur-hunting party which proceeded under the protection of these ships. The schooner *Nikolai*, with a party of hunters under the command of Tarakanov, was ordered to use all possible means to open trade with the natives at the mouth of the Columbia River, and then to proceed to Gray's Harbor, where it would join Kuskov with the *Kad'iak*. But near Gray's Harbor the schooner was wrecked and the natives attacked the crew. One sailor was killed, several others were wounded, and four women were taken prisoners, including the wife of Navigator Bulygin, commander of the schooner. The rest of the men escaped into the forest, where they wandered for a long time with almost no means of survival. They spent the winter in a hut built of tree branches. In the spring they built a boat, in which they intended to make their way somehow to the colonies. But the survivors were so weakened by illness and deprivation that the natives took them without resistance and held them in various settlements around the Strait of Juan de Fuca. Early in 1809 Bulygin, his wife, two other Russians, two Kad'iak islanders, and two other islanders died, and several months later the rest were freed into the hands of Captain Brown [brig *Lydia*], an American, who took them to New Archangel. In the meantime the *Kad'iak* had successfully returned from her voyage with 2,350 sea otters. In the neighborhood of Rumiantsov (Little Bodega) Bay, Kuskov had noticed a suitable place for settlement and had considered establishing himself there, but a shortage of building materials and the wish of many of the Russians and Aleuts to run away forced him to wait until a better time.[4]

In 1810 Kuskov again set out for New Albion, this time in the *Juno*, in order to make a more detailed survey of the region. The results, however, were even less successful. All of his plans were upset when a large number of well-armed natives attacked his trading party near the Queen Charlotte Islands. He lost eight hunters and had to return to New Archangel.

The Ross settlement. In 1811 Kuskov finally succeeded in founding a settlement to the south. During the winter he met some of the native leaders and gave them medals and gifts, for which they agreed to surrender voluntarily the area that he needed for the settlement. Later in the year he returned to New Archangel for further conferences with Baranov. In March 1812 he returned to the site of his settlement with everything he needed to get started. The place that he and Baranov had agreed upon was located on a small inlet, about fifteen Italian miles from Rumiantsov Bay, at 38° north latitude and longitude 123° west. On 30 August, the emperor's namesday, the fort and all of its outbuildings were ready and were solemnly named Ross.

The fort, armed with ten cannon, was situated on a small hill 110 feet above sea level. The hill inclined toward the sea and ended in a 70-foot cliff. On the slope the Aleuts built their houses, imitating the Russians in their usually careful construction, so that there were very few simple mud huts. Red pine (*chaga*, a wood similar to larch [redwood]) was used for all the structures. So that the Aleuts might have what, in their opinion, were the best possible living quarters, Kuskov permitted them to place their houses wherever they wished, disregarding a regular street layout and allowing structural eccentricities. It was proposed to build cattle sheds to the west of the settlement, but no pains were to be taken to breed cattle, since they could be left on green pasture throughout the year round, which greatly reduced their cost of maintenance. Their other needs could be met with little trouble.

The settlement did not have a good roadstead, so ships could stand safely only when the wind was from the northwest. There were many submerged rocks near the shore. The Slavianka [Russian] River, called Shabakai by the natives, ran to the sea halfway between the fort and Little Bodega Bay. The river originated in a large lake. Its mouth was obstructed by a bar, and when the wind blew strongly from the southwest, usually accompanied by rain, so much sand piled up that the river and the sea had difficulty forcing a narrow passage. Some distance from the sea the river had many rapids. and had cut a passage through an enormous rock.

The landing was located in a small bay south of the fort. At the landing were built a dockyard (where in 1818 and 1819 Kuskov built the brigantine *Rumiantsov* and the brig *Buldakov*) and a large shed for storing baidaras and building ships in bad weather. The smithy was a short distance away. The hollow between the landing and the fort was bordered with garden plots, most of which belonged to the settlement. They produced enough vegetables to supply the settlers. There were two potato crops each year. Yields were at least 11 times the number of seed potatoes planted, and there were even cases where the multiple was 250. Consequently, this one product would have guaranteed the entire settlement's food supply had it not been for the numerous moles [gophers?], which ate many of the potatoes and greatly reduced the company stores. The diet also included the meat of fur seals and sea birds, both salted and dried. These were obtained from the rocky Farallon Islands, which lie west of the entrance to San Francisco Bay. Kuskov ordered that a party of Russians and Aleuts be stationed on the largest of these islands. A fish somewhat like sturgeon was sometimes caught in the Slavianka River. Bison [!], wild goats, sheep, and seals were also hunted near the settlement.

In order to expand animal husbandry Kuskov acquired horses and cattle from neighboring tribes, and imported on the *Il'men* several animals, including domestic sheep, from [Spanish] California.

In the early days of the Ross settlement the fur trade went badly, because building operations left very few men for hunting, and then only near the settlement. Despite Kuskov's efforts, the Spaniards would not permit otter hunting in San Francisco Bay. Elsewhere, around Drake's Bay, Big Bodega Bay, and north to Cape Mendocino there were very few fur-bearing animals. Later a hunting party under Tarakanov ranged along the entire California coast, and a ship built at the settlement carried necessary supplies to the party and took furs from them. Another party worked on the Farallon Islands catching fur seals.

By 1817 sea otters had become extinct from Trinidad Bay to San Antonio Bay, not far from the entrance to San Francisco Bay. The fur seals on the Farallon Islands had also been destroyed by then. There was no alternative but to transport the parties to islands quite far from the California coast.

No great successes had been expected from agriculture in Ross, a view which was later justified. The Aleuts, creoles, and Indians were not suited to this occupation. The Russian promyshlenniks sent to the settlement from New Archangel tried to avoid farming. This was one of the main obstacles to the spread of agriculture. Moreover, the moist sea air and the frequent fogs retarded the growth of grain. For example, the fogs of July and August 1817 so affected the harvest that it was not even possible to get seed for future sowing. The first experiments fell far short of even the most modest expectations. In the first five years the results of the harvest were as follows:

In 1813	1 pud 25 pounds sown	4 puds 5 pounds harvested
In 1814	5 puds sown	22 puds 2 pounds harvested
In 1815	5 puds sown	8 puds harvested
In 1816	14 puds 14 pounds sown	48 puds 23 pounds harvested
In 1817		nothing harvested

These failures showed that the main aim in founding the settlement, to create a grainery for the other Russian colonies, could hardly be achieved, and this led to criticism of Baranov and Kuskov, who were chiefly responsible for choosing the unsatisfactory location. But a question arises: could they have imagined that the area occupied by the settlement would remain long within its original bounds and that with time the company's possessions in that region would not expand? From this point of view, did not Baranov's selection of a site on a shore thought to be inaccessible to enemy attack and located less than eighteen miles from Rumiantsov Bay promise future expansion of Russia and Russian influence to the very boundaries of [Spanish] California and offer a potential source of prosperity for all of the company's possessions? Local conditions and other changes in the general make-up of the country surrounding Ross settlement had the very opposite effect and made this settlement a burden from which the company had to try to save itself, lest even worse should follow.

When the directors received Baranov's report on the establishment of the settlement, they did not share his view on the advantages enjoyed by the location of the new company possession, but found that Ross was too close to the port of San Francisco, had neither a harbor nor a good roadstead, was far from Slavianka River and, finally, that the fort did not command the surrounding territory and that, in case defense became necessary, a proper fort could not be built on that site.

For some time after the founding of Ross, Kuskov saw no Spaniards. Only in mid-October did an officer and seven soldiers from San Francisco appear at the fort. They asked permission to enter and looked around very attentively. Then they asked why the Russians had settled in this place. In reply Kuskov showed the officer the statement of the directors that the settlement had been established with a view to securing a food supply for the colonies. He also explained the advantages of trade relations between California and the Russian colonies. For his part, the officer in turn promised to try to obtain the governor's permission for such trade, observing that everyone in California would be quite happy to obtain certain goods which they desperately needed. Early in 1813 the officer reappeared at the settlement with the commandant's brother and announced verbally that Governor Don Arillaga would permit trade, but on condition that until official permission was obtained the company's vessels would not enter the port and goods would be brought ashore in rowboats. As a gift to the settlement the Spaniards brought along about twenty cattle and three horses. Kuskov immediately sent the agent Slobodchikov to San Francisco with goods. Slobodchikov settled prices for the goods with the commandant and sold them for 1,400 piasters, receiving grain in exchange. After that trade with California continued uninterrupted throughout all of 1813. Goods brought to New Archangel on the brig *Il'men* brought particularly high prices. Elliot, an American who sailed on the *Il'men* as company commissioner, visited the Spanish presidios of Santa Barbara and San Pedro and other places along the California coast, where he was able to make several useful business acquaintances. He took on a full cargo of various foodstuffs, discharged them at Ross and returned again to the California coast.

At the same time Kuskov sent to California for food supplies an American ship [the brig *Pedler*, Northrop], which had arrived from New Archangel with annual provisions for the settlement. Not far from the Presidio of Santa Barbara, this ship, being American, was captured by two Spanish war ships cruising in those waters and taken to the port of San Pedro. Ascertaining that the cargo and most of the crew belonged to the company, the governor of California ordered the ship immediately released, and she returned safely to Ross.

Soon Kuskov received a letter from the governor, asking on behalf of the viceroy for detailed information as to why the Russians had settled at Bodega Bay and who had given the orders to found the settlement. Kuskov asked Baranov how he should answer this letter and, in the meantime, told the Spaniards that it would be impossible to reply exactly to the governor's request without a Spanish translator.

Despite these exchanges, the commandant of San Francisco and the head of the religious mission, also an important man, continued to be friendly with Kuskov and several times agreed to visit Ross, but this resolve was prevented by the death of Governor Arillaga, which produced many changes in the relations of the California authorities with the Russians.

Don Arillaga's death was undoubtedly a great loss for the Russian colonies. From his first acquaintance with Rezanov he continued to be friendly with the Russians and to carry out as far as possible everything they wished, despite the suspicions of the Spanish government and the limitations of his own authority. In time his influence might even have led to more permanent occupation of Ross and to the expansion of the area of Russian settlement in this area.

José de Arguello, who temporarily assumed the post of governor, formally demanded on the Viceroy's orders that Kuskov destroy the Ross settlement, expressing surprise that the company had directed its proclamation to the inhabitants of California, and not to the viceroy, who was over them. Kuskov replied that the colonial government had no authority to carry out the wishes of the California authorities until it received word from St. Petersburg.

The growing unease of the Spaniards at the existence of a Russian colony in their neighborhood was no doubt partially founded on rumors which American and English sea captains attempted to spread in California. Some of them even asserted that they knew for a fact that the Russians intended to seize San Francisco and that Kuskov had already secretly approached the fort several times in order to discover a suitable point of attack. Because of such stories one of the American ships which Baranov had sent to San Francisco for trade was seized. Her cargo was taken, and certain of Baranov's papers in possession of the captain also remained in the hands of the California government. Several men who had fled from Ross settlement were retained by the Spaniards and later used as interpreters in negotiations with the Russians.

After the demand to destroy Ross settlement, Kuskov received another official communication forbidding all foreigners to trade with California and ordering all ships proceeding from the Russian colonies to stay clear of Spanish ports. With the arrival of the new governor, Lieutenant Pablo Vicente de Sola, in 1815, company affairs in California took a turn for the worse. Not only were trading and fur trapping stopped entirely, but the governor ordered the arrest of many of the colonial commissioners and promyshlenniks who had not left in time, including the American, Elliot. The California government treated them poorly, working them alongside the natives. According to Kuskov's reports, one of the baptized Kad'iak Aleuts was tortured to death by the head of the religious mission in San Francisco for refusing to accept Catholicism. Several of the prisoners managed to escape in a baidara, taking advantage of the negligence of the Spaniards, who sent them beaver hunting. They reached Ross settlement successfully after spending four days at sea without food or fresh water. Since trade and trapping had been carried on with the previous governor's knowledge, and all colonial commissioners and parties had been recalled after the new governor's prohibition on relations with California, Kuskov repeatedly demanded that the commandant of San Francisco free the captured men. This was promised, but soon the governor ordered all relations with the Russians to cease and the matter of the men's release remained unsettled.

In 1816, when Baranov received word of the Spaniards' violence, he sent Lieutenant Podushkin to Monterey in a company ship [*Otkry-tie*] instructing him to explain to the governor the legality of Russia's occupation of Ross and to demand the immediate release of company employees. Podushkin was also to attempt to win the governor's permission to gather furs in San Francisco Bay, whereby the company would pay the Spaniards for their share of the furs taken, at the rate of fifteen to twenty piasters for a full-grown sea otter and three piasters for a pup. The governor received Podushkin amicably and, in accordance with Baranov's wishes, ordered fifteen Russians and Aleuts freed, promising to do the same with other prisoners who had been sent further down the California coast. The governor fully agreed on the advantages of trade with the colonies and assured Podushkin that he would use his best efforts to obtain permission to trade and hunt with the Russians. But, as to the Ross settlement, he could not be swayed and wrote to Baranov again demanding its destruction. Some reason for this insistence may be found in the actions of Lieutenant-Captain Kotzebue, captain of the brig *Rurik*, who was sent at State Chancellor Count Rumiantsov's expense to explore the northern part of the Pacific Ocean. Without any authority he interfered in colonial relations with California and forced Kuskov to confirm a decree, which he had already signed, designating the Strait of Juan de Fuca as the northern border of the Spanish dominions. He also demanded that Kuskov explain why the company had dared to establish a settlement on a foreign coast without the government's permission, and finally he refused to accept some of the prisoners who were being returned by the governor, taking aboard his brig only three fugitives from the settlement.

In the meantime, the directors were trying in every way to strengthen the company's hold on the Ross settlement. In 1817 the Spanish ambassador presented a note to Minister of Foreign Affairs Count Nesselrode, in which the Russians were reproached for their aggressive occupation of foreign territory for commercial reasons and demanding in the king's name that the settlement be destroyed. The directors answered strongly in defense of their rights,[5] and for some time the demands that the Russians leave California ceased.

The directors did not abandon hope of renewing trade relations with Spanish California. One of the orders issued to Lieutenant-Captain Hagemeister, commander of the company's fourth round-the-world expedition, was to visit San Francisco and negotiate with the governor regarding trade. He was also to observe the condition of the Ross settlement and the relations between the Russians and the natives.

While at the settlement, Hagemeister considered it necessary to extend somewhat the territory occupied by Kuskov. He met with the main toions of the area surrounding Rumiantsov Bay, Chu-chu-oana and Vale-lii-l'e, and many other prominent natives, and asked them if they would agree to Russian occupation of the coast as far as the isthmus on which several local native settlements were located. The chiefs and other natives unanimously answered that they were quite satisfied with the Russians establishing a settlement in their midst and were prepared to give them the necessary land. Furthermore, they declared that they expected an attack by the natives under Spanish control and that all the independent tribes hoped to find protection from the enemy in the Russian fort. Hagemeister promised to help them and gave them several gifts in reward for their friendliness.

The desire of the natives to benefit by the Russian presence strongly justified the occupation of the shores near Rumiantsov Bay, especially since the Spaniards, who had been close to these places for a very long time, had shown no wish to enter into relations with the inhabitants. Rumors of the oppression by the Californians of their native subjects, particularly when compared to Kuskov's behavior toward his neighbors, compelled the inhabitants of Rumiantsov Bay to fear falling under the authority of the Spanish presidios and Catholic monks, who had turned everything to their own advantage. The bonds between the Russians and the natives were soon strengthened by family ties between the latter and many of the newly arrived Aleuts, so that many of the natives did not confine themselves to ordinary visits with their new relatives, but came voluntarily to help them in their work, and Kuskov tried constantly to reward them with various gifts.

With the aim of reconciling Kuskov with the Spaniards, Hagemeister brought him to San Francisco.[6] The pretext for this visit was the collection of money which the Californians owed for goods they had previously purchased and the need to determine exactly the number of Aleuts and other company employees remaining in the hands of the Spaniards. Despite the obvious wish of the commandant and the head of the religious mission to let the Russians conduct mutually profitable fur trapping, this matter remained unsettled. As for trade and the visits of company ships to California ports, the governor finally expressed his consent in a letter to the directors. Such readiness on his part to comply with the Russian aims was undoubtedly prompted by the shortages experienced by his subjects, particularly the soldiers, who for seven years had received nothing but food. Taking advantage of this, Hagemeister obtained for the colonies and for the *Kutuzov's* crew large quantities of food. When, however, the governor proposed to accept the ship's entire cargo with remittance of payment in Guadalajara, Hagemeister felt obliged to decline the offer until an answer had been received on the question of common trapping, in view of the poor financial condition of the Spanish colonies, particularly in those troubled times.[7] There was almost no money in circulation, aside from a small quantity of coin which had been issued by the insurgents and was supported by the Spanish government until better times. It should be observed that the only crown property in California was a herd of livestock which had been recently imported. Although the missions, who used the labor of natives gathered under the pretext of converting them to Christianity, had enough grain, most of this went to support these natives or the soldiers stationed in the presidios. Payment for the soldiers' food was also made in bills of exchange drawn on Guadalajara. Thus little of the food produced could be sold to passing ships. However, foreign flags, aside from the Russian flag, rarely appeared off the California coast, particularly in more recent times, and the demands of the missions were confined to purchasing iron and simple tools worth only 2,500 piasters annually, so that one ship sent from the colonies each year could adequately sustain the California trade.

Finally, the occupation of California by insurgents at the end of 1818 and the declaration of independence in the Spanish possessions in America gave matters a completely different turn, which later affected the Ross settlement.

Under more diligent efforts to cultivate the newly increased field area at Ross, agriculture improved, but not to an extent that could be called satisfactory. Grain grown near the shore was covered with rust, caused by salt spray. Straw grew as thick as cane. In the last four years of Kuskov's administration, 1818-1821, wheat yielded between three and four times, and only in 1821 was the harvest six times greater than the sowing; i.e., 37 puds 25 pounds were sown and 235 puds 33 pounds were gathered; however, a sowing of 11 puds 20 pounds of barley yielded only 26 puds 10 pounds.

Thus, in its first ten years the Ross settlement provided the company with nothing but heavy expenses for its maintenance and relief for ships sent from New Archangel to Spanish California. These ships, taking advantage of the settlement's proximity to Spanish possessions, could carry out their trade more conveniently and bring back from Ross the food supplies necessary for the colonies. The following quantities of foodstuffs were obtained from Ross settlement through 1822:

wheat, 8,127 fanegas	flour, 1,135 arrobas
peas and beans, 1,458 fanegas	lard, 3,200 arrobas
barley, 1,192 fanegas	dried meat, 1,354 arrobas

One pud of wheat bartered in California brought the company from 3 to 4 paper rubles 50 kopeks, one pud of barley from 3 rubles 60 kopeks to 4 rubles, and one pud of wheat flour around 9 rubles.

Generally speaking, the failure to establish trade with Spanish California, which was particularly essential to the colonies then, was closely related to the very existence of Ross. If the company had considered it possible at any time to open this trade, it would probably not have bothered to retain the controversial settlement, particularly when the hope of realizing satisfactory profits from it was gradually fading.

This view is fully supported by the contents of a memorandum from the directors to Count Nesselrode, minister of foreign affairs, in January of 1820, concerning new negotiations in connection with Hagemeister's discussions with the California governor on the subject of trade and the existence of Ross. The directors wrote as follows:

> Although the considerable amount of capital used to establish this settlement (Ross) has not given the company the expected return, owing to the short period and the fact that the company still lacks men to settle there permanently with their families, work their own land and pass the fruits of their labors on to the company, the Spanish government of New California nevertheless continually demands the destruction of this settlement and the removal of Russian subjects, considering the land that they occupy, and even the entire coast of New Albion, a possession of the Spanish crown by reason of Columbus' discovery of America, and perhaps to this day they would resort to the use of force, if they were in a position to do so.

> Under these circumstances, the Russian-American Company would willingly destroy this settlement, which rouses the Spaniards to envy and fear, and would never again consider seeking another place on the Albion coast, if the loss of this settlement could be exchanged for regular trade with New California, to which foreigners are not admitted both by colonial law and by the fear of revealing the remarkable insecurity and weakness of the government.[8]

There was no reply to this report, probably because of the particular circumstances in California at that time, and the question of whether there was to be or not to be a Russian settlement on the Pacific coast remained undecided.

7. Measures of the Board of Directors and the State of the Colonies to the Expiration of the Company's First Charter

Several times in describing his round-the-world voyage, Krusenstern accused the colonial administration of improper conduct with respect to the natives under its control. When the board of directors read this, they ordered Baranov to respond to each point of these accusations, as far as possible, with a detailed explanation and also instructed him to carry out the following:

1. In no case are Aleuts and other islanders of either sex to be used in any work against their will and without previous agreement on the payment for their efforts on behalf of the company. Nor are levies [*obrok*] to be imposed on them, i.e. shares to be taken for berrypicking or anything else, since the company has never authorized this. Those natives who agree to work for the company should be paid promptly, so that not only will they have no complaints but also so that no outsider may slander the company for any reason. Your opinion that islanders and their families should be settled near the main colonial establishments is considered by the board of directors from all indications to be sound, feasible, and useful.

2. The 167 Aleuts moved in 1807 from the Aleutian Islands to Sitkha are to be settled there permanently, if a need for them is foreseen, and joined by their families at the first opportunity, particularly by their wives and children, and long separations from their families are not to be permitted under any pretext.

3. If it is correct that traces of the former malpractices can still be found in places under the jurisdiction of the colonial administration, the board of directors charge Mr. Baranov with the sacred duty of using all means at his command to suppress and eradicate them completely. In accordance with previous directives and the instructions given herein, he is to reestablish good order in all places, so that it will not be shameful for us to stand in the presence of the emperor.

The board of directors also ordered Baranov to observe the following rules with respect to the creoles and Aleuts:

1. An effort should be made to improve the condition of all creoles and Aleuts who have families and work for the company, particularly in the following ways: providing the necessary homes, gardens and orchards, and all other things required for household and economic tasks, so that in time they might see the success of their efforts and enjoy their own possessions. In short, all possible measures should be employed, even at some sacrifice to the company, to elevate these people to that degree of civilization which will make them useful not only to themselves, but to the state.

2. When the creoles reach legal age, they should be encouraged to start families, obtaining wives from among the natives if there are no creole girls, and then be introduced into various company occupations and provided with farms.

3. Creoles who appear incapable of filling offices in the colonial administration should be taken to the Ross settlement, where agriculture and animal husbandry can provide them and their families with a secure living. Their surplus produce and other home manufactures should be purchased by the company in order to encourage them.

In 1815, on Baranov's suggestion, the board of directors decided to increase the payments to those engaged in the fur trade for their diligent labor and zeal. Furs obtained from them were to be bought at higher prices than those set out in the schedule established in 1804, namely, instead of 20 rubles for a sea otter, the hunter was to be credited with 30 to 50 rubles per pelt, depending on the size, and for a fur seal, double the prices in the schedule (with the exception of those obtained in the Farallon Islands).

Furthermore, in order to facilitate settling accounts with the hunters, the board of directors sent the colonies parchment tokens [marki] with the government's permission. They were to take the place of money and were distinguished in color and shape according to their value—1, 5, 10, or 25 paper rubles, and 10, 25, or 50 kopeks. Baranov was ordered to pay the salary of each employee in the colonies with these tokens. Goods and supplies in the company stores were to be sold in exchange for the tokens, with certain restrictions on alcoholic beverages (the sale of which was rationed) and luxury articles (which would deprive the purchaser of necessities if their value exceeded his means). On payday, when the tokens were distributed, company stores were to return the tokens they had received during that period. Forgers of the tokens, should any such appear, were to be treated as criminals.[1]

Meanwhile, on 15 December 1811, the emperor ordered that the Russian-American Company be placed under the control of the Ministry of Internal Affairs. The imperial rescript on this subject addressed to the minister of internal affairs said:

The position of the company, which has been placed under special imperial patronage, makes it even more necessary that the Ministry of Internal Affairs be the company's trustee in all of its dealings and its representative before me for all its needs. In consequence of this, I instruct you to devote particular attention to this important organization, which to fulfill the aim of its operations, must make large profits, not merely for the company directors, but also for all the stockholders and for the nation as a whole. For this reason do not fail to demand immediately of the board of directors of the company the most detailed data on all its activities, no matter what their nature, on its operations, its proposed undertakings, and its successes. The board of directors must lay such data before me through the Ministry of Internal Affairs, so that all its activities will be known in detail at all times.

In compliance with the imperial will, the board of directors immediately presented the minister with a report on all the company's divisions and their activities, indicating those administrative and commercial measures which it regarded as useful for the welfare of the region under its control and requesting at the same time the necessary government assistance to achieve this aim.

All the directors' proposals were subsequently carried out with the emperor's approval, and they will be discussed below.

A council is established at the head office to confer with the board of directors on matters of particular importance, and two more directors are chosen. In 1812 a general meeting of stockholders was called to consider expanding the company's sphere of activity and also those matters of particular importance which were beyond the authority of the directors. This meeting authorized the directors to petition the government again to establish at the head office a council similar to the former temporary committee for solving such matters. This council, consisting of three stockholders each having a vote, together with the board of directors, would decide questions without interference from the stockholders, which demanded particular attention for political and trade reasons. On the advice of the Committee of Ministers the emperor authorized the establishment of the council on 16 December 1814.

By majority vote the following stockholders were elected members of the council: Ivan Andreevich Vedemeier, Petr Stepanovich Molchanov, and Iakov Aleksandrovich Druzhinin.

In this same election two more directors, Andrei Ivanovich Severin and Sidor Andreevich Shelikhov, were added to the board, which then consisted of Mikhail Matveevich Buldakov and Benedikt Benediktovich Kramer.

Directors Delarov and Ivan Andreevich Shelikhov, at their own request, had been relieved of their duties in 1807.

Divine worship is introduced to New Archangel. In 1808, at Rez-anov's suggestion and with the approval of the board of directors, Baranov transferred the colonial administration from Kad'iak to New Archangel. From that time until 1816 the inhabitants of New Archangel, both Russians and baptized natives, had never had the satisfaction of seeing the liturgy performed by clergymen. Several years before, one of the company's trainees, Father Lavrov, had been assigned to New Archangel, but had remained in Kamchatka instead. The surviving members of the former clerical missions, German, Ioasaf, and Afanasii, decrepit old men, lived in and around Kad'iak and could not bring themselves to undertake a long sea voyage. In the absence of a priest in New Archangel all those holy sacraments that did not demand the participation of a clergyman, such as christenings, burials, and so forth, were performed by Beliaev, a company employee. On the request of all the inhabitants of the colonies, Baranov urgently requested the board of directors to ask the Holy Synod to consecrate Beliaev a priest as a reward for his untiring efforts and zeal in fulfilling these religious duties and also for his exceptional ecclesiastical knowledge; but the Synod did not see fit to fulfill this request. Finally, in 1816 Father Sokolov was sent to serve in the colonies and reached New Archangel safely. With Father Sokolov the board of directors sent a beautifully decorated icon of the Archangel Michael, patron saint of the colonies. Soon after Father Sokolov's arrival, the chapel was converted into a temporary church. The iconostas was made from icons cast ashore from the wreck of the *Neva*, and, as Baranov wrote, "the icon of Saint Michael shone among them." The church's vessels were made from Spanish silver by local craftsmen, and the altar cloth and priestly vestments were sewn from Chinese materials. "Glory to the Almighty," wrote Baranov in the same letter, "there is another church in America, and I have built it."

The colonial fleet and the loss of several ships. Recognizing the great importance of reliable transportation in moving goods to, and furs from, the colonies and also recognizing the inadequacy of colonial fortifications to withstand attack by foreigners or independent native tribes, Baranov seized every opportunity to increase the number of ships in the colonial fleet. In 1807, while he was still on Kad'iak, he had paid 42,000 Spanish piasters for a fully loaded English ship, the *Myrtle*, which he had renamed the *Kad'iak*. Among the items which he acquired in the bargain were twelve cannon, quite essential to the colonies at that time. They included four twelve-pounders, four four-pounders, and four one-pound falconets.

At the same time a two-master, called the *Sitkha*, was built in New Archangel by Lincoln, an American in the company's service. In May 1807 it was sent to Kad'iak. Baranov contracted with Barber, former commander of the *Myrtle*, to take the *Sitkha* under his command to Okhotsk with a cargo of furs. The *Sitkha* also carried back to Russia Hieromonakh Gedeon, who had given over leadership of the church mission in America to Father German, and Banner, who had been sent to review the affairs of the Unalashka office and to inspect the cutter *Konstantin*, which had been wrecked near Captain's Harbor. Strong contrary winds forced the *Sitkha* to land in Kamchatka in late autumn. The company commissioner unloaded the furs and sent Barber and the ship to Nizhne-Kamchatsk to sell about 100,000 rubles worth of goods imported from Canton and Okhotsk. At the mouth of the Kamchatka River the vessel hit a shoal, rolled over on its side and, just as the crew had succeeded in abandoning ship, was blown to sea by a strong wind. Very little of the cargo was saved. At almost the same time the government vessel *Ioann Bogoslov* was torn from its anchor by a storm and sank with several sailors and all the cargo on board. Many of the merchants in Kamchatka lost their entire fortunes in this disaster, and the company lost more than 6,000 paper rubles worth of goods which had been sent from Okhotsk on the vessel.

In the spring of the next year, 1808, the *Mariia Magdalina*, which was being sent from Okhotsk under the command of an Assistant Navigator [Petrov], ran aground near the entrance to the Okhota River due to an error in navigation and almost broke up. Instead of repairing the *Mariia Magdalina*, the director of the Okhotsk office built a new ship, the *Finliandiia*. Because of insufficient manpower, but even more because of the ill will of the Okhotsk office, the work proceeded very slowly, and the ship was not ready until the end of 1809.

In 1808 the company tender *Avos'* under the command of Lieutenant Sukin was also lost near Unalashka Island. Sukin was seeking an island which Sarychev and rumors from the islanders placed somewhere between Umnak and the Islands of the Four Volcanos. The *Avos'* was carrying cargo and dispatches. The crew was saved, but the articles carried on the tender must have been stolen by the islanders, since a party sent from New Archangel to fetch back the cargo found nothing. Someone had even dragged the ropes and anchors from the water and stolen them.

At that time the company was suffering from a serious shortage of good navigators. Because of the war, the Navy had to discontinue detaching fleet officers and navigators for company service; and, despite the efforts of the board of directors to find good ship captains in Finland, newly annexed to Russia, none of the Finnish captains were willing to travel so far. Furthermore, the Okhotsk authorities sometimes treated the company quite unfairly, removing assistant navigators and apprentices, as Baranov complained, from company service without the knowledge of the board of directors or the colonial administration. Since some of those removed were in the company's debt because of salary advances, such arbitrary actions cost the company considerable sums of money.

In 1809 Lincoln launched two more ships from the dockyard at New Archangel. One, a 306-ton brigantine, was called the *Otkrytie* [*Discovery*], and the other was a 120-ton schooner, the *Chirikov*.

In 1811 Baranov sent the *Juno* to Kamchatka under command of Navigator Martynov with a cargo of more than 200,000 paper rubles worth of Chinese goods bartered in Canton by Captain Ebbets, Astor's agent. About twenty-five miles from Petropavlovsk, at the mouth of the Viliui River, the *Juno* was driven ashore by a terrible storm and was completely destroyed. Strong contrary winds had held the ship at sea more than three months and then for nineteen days in sight of the port, and the men were extremely exhausted because of the lack of fresh food and water. The ship's captain died on the morning of the wreck and by evening his ship was gone. Of the crew only three were saved; twenty-three were sacrificed to the waves. Very little of the cargo was salvaged. Shortly afterward the government ship *Feodosiia*, bound from Okhotsk to Kamchatka and carrying the company commissioner Iudin and a large quantity of company goods and money was lost on [Shimushu] the first Kurile island.

The *Neva*, returning to the colonies from a fur-selling voyage to Okhotsk under the command of Lieutenant Podushkin, was also lost on the shores of Sitkha Island on 9 January 1813, along with more than half of its sixty-two passengers and crew. The *Neva* had set sail at the end of August 1812. Stormy weather prevented the vessel from entering any port, and the scarcity of fresh water was acutely felt. Scurvy ravaged the ship, constantly taking new victims. Finally, on the day of the wreck, intensified winds and currents drove the ship ashore in view of Mount Edgecumbe, where it broke up. Thirty-seven of those aboard were drowned, including Collegiate Counsellor Bornovolokov, who was coming to the colonies to replace Baranov; Navigator Kalinin; the wife of Navigator Nerodov and her small son; an apprentice navigator; the supercargo; and three other women. In addition to the value of the ship and all its equipment, the company's loss in the accident amounted to more than 250,000 paper rubles.

Disaster followed disaster. In July of the same year the company ship *Aleksandr Nevskii* [navigator Petrov] was wrecked and completely lost in the Kurile Islands. It was proceeding from the colonies to Okhotsk with a cargo of furs and Chinese and American goods. Fortunately, all the men on board were saved and reached Bol'sheretsk in baidaras. The total material loss was around 500,000 paper rubles, including the ship itself, which was worth 30,000 rubles. Only 320,000 rubles worth of furs was saved.

To all of these misfortunes must be added the loss of the ship *Nadezhda*, although in this case the company did not suffer heavy damages because the ship had been let to an American to carry various goods from the colonies under bond almost equal in value to the value of the ship and her cargo. The ship was sent out under these terms in 1808 because of the war, which did not permit it to be sailed around the world under the company flag.[2] In the winter of 1808 the ship was icebound off the coast of Denmark and the cargo was looted by Danish privateers.

In 1813 and 1814 Baranov bought from some Americans in exchange for sea otters three fully-equipped copper-sheathed ships, two three-masters, the *Truvor* and the [*Atahualpa*, renamed] *Bering*, and one two-master [the *Lydia* or *Lady*] renamed the *Il'men*. The *Truvor* soon proved unseaworthy and the company lost money on its purchase, even though the price had been very low (10,000 paper rubles). The *Bering*, after one voyage to Okhotsk with a cargo of furs, ran aground in the Sandwich Islands and was permitted to remain in disrepair for a long time, after which it proved unseaworthy.

In 1816 the company lost another ship, although the loss sustained in this case was quite small. In 1808 the *Mariia Magdalina* had been damaged near Okhotsk and repaired. It was again put in service and on a voyage from New Archangel to Okhotsk it was unable to enter the mouth of the Okhota River because of strong contrary winds and was forced to tack for several days within sight of the port. Finally Navigator Nerodov, captain of the *Mariia Magdalina*, dropped anchor 2½ versts from the shore. The violent wind drove the ship out to sea and the captain, in order to save the crew and the cargo, decided on a desperate course of action—he cut the cables and ran the ship aground. The crew was saved, but the ship was lost. Most of the furs were soaked, but drying restored them. The other goods, such as wheat, beans, peas, sugar, and other food stuffs, were ruined. The total loss did not exceed 15,000 Spanish piasters, or about 80,000 paper rubles at the current rate of exchange.

From 1817 through 1819 two schooners were built in the New Archangel dockyards, the *Platov* and the *Baranov*. The 199-ton American vessel *Brutus*, renamed the *Golovnin*, after the Russian navigator V. M. Golovnin, was obtained in exchange for 5,000 fur-seal pelts worth around 40,000 paper rubles. The brigantine *Rumiantsov* and the brig *Buldakov* were built at the Ross settlement. In addition to these, the colonial fleet was quite unexpectedly enriched by the acquisition in 1819 of a small ship called the *Fortuna*. She was acquired as follows. From the New Archangel fort a ship apparently in distress was sighted at sea and a pilot and launch were sent to tow it into port. Surprisingly, it had seven Sandwich islanders aboard but no Europeans. The Sandwich islanders unanimously declared that the leader of the Spanish insurgents had impressed them as sailors from their home islands and had placed them aboard his two frigates. He had bombarded Monterey and San Francisco and at Monterey had taken this schooner as his lawful prize and placed the Sandwich Islanders and three Europeans aboard it, the Spanish crew having escaped. During an uprising on the frigates, the commander and other officers were killed. The Europeans aboard the schooner took what cargo they could and transferred it to a frigate, ordering the Sandwich islanders to follow them. Under the command of one of the islanders who barely knew how to use the compass, the schooner fell behind. After an eighty-two-day voyage they found themselves, not at the Sandwich Islands as their new skipper had intended, but at New Archangel, having only a two-day supply of provisions and several casks of fresh water left. Upon inspection the schooner was found to be leaking badly, and in need of retimbering. When a thorough search failed to disclose the real owner, it was put into service in colonial waters. The Sandwich islanders were returned to their homeland.

In 1821 the colonial fleet consisted of the following ships:

Otkrytie	brigantine	306 tons
Finliandia	brig	250 tons
Il'men	brig	200 tons
Buldakov	brig	200 tons
Rumiantsov	brigantine [*goelet*]	120 tons
Chirikov	schooner	120 tons
Fortuna	schooner	60 tons
Konstantin	sloop	60 tons
Baranov	sloop	30 tons
Platov	sloop	30 tons

During the company's first period of incorporation, i.e. from 1799 to 1821, the following ships were obtained: five foreign ships for round-the-world expeditions, eight for sailing in colonial waters, and fifteen built in colonial dockyards or in Okhotsk. Of these, sixteen were lost, five were retired because of age, and three were sold.

The state of the colonial fur trade and several experiments made by Baranov to develop colonial industry. Despite the great success of fur exports from the colonies during the first twenty years of the company's existence, it must be observed that the catch of furs, particularly those of sea otters and fur seals, declined, even if compared with Baranov's first years as governor. The first sea otters were trapped in Kenai Bay by Delarov; in the first year he took around 3,000 furs, and in the second around 2,000, but in the third year, when Baranov became governor, only 800 were taken. The following year 600 sea otter pelts were taken. Thus, the number of pelts declined from year to year, until in 1812 only 100 sea otters were taken, and in subsequent years even fewer. When Baranov first visited Chugach Bay, it abounded in sea otters. Around 1812 the catch there had also decreased to fifty furs, and in subsequent years even fewer were taken. Farther beyond Chugach Bay in the direction of New Archangel, around Cape St. Elias, Yakutat, Icy Bay, and Iakobi Island, sea otters were found everywhere, but five years after hunting had begun they were almost extinct, and were a great rarity in those parts by the second decade of the nineteenth century. Sea otters abounded throughout the entire Vancouver Straits [Alexander Archipelago] area, around Bobrovaia [Bucareli or Iphigenia] Bay and the Queen Charlotte Islands, near the shore of the mainland, and among the islands as far as Nootka Sound. Each year the Americans bartered about 8,000 pelts from the natives, but the Russians obtained them in far fewer numbers and with greater difficulty than the foreigners, because the Kolosh used their ample firearms and ammunition to prevent their neighbors from fur hunting. The Kolosh only bartered with the Russians very unwillingly, since they received better terms from the Americans.

In 1816, during the unpleasantness between Baranov and Hunt, an American who had been in New Archangel for about two years (see Chapter 5), the board of directors again requested the Ministry of Internal Affairs to petition the emperor for permission to forbid foreigners to trade with the natives, since this undermined the company's very foundation and caused a considerable loss. Until 1821 this matter remained unchanged. But when the company's charter was being renewed, the matter was again brought up by the board of directors in accordance with the opinion of Captain Golovnin, who had just visited the colonies. Golovnin thought it essential to protect the colonies against the actions of the American sea captains, which harmed the company's trade and the relations between the Russians and the independent natives. An imperial decree was published setting forth regulations outlining the limits of navigation for foreign ships, the conduct of maritime trade along the shores of eastern Siberia, northwestern America and the Kurile and Aleutian Islands, and the defense of the colonies by armed cruisers.

A survey of sea otter hunting both in the above-mentioned places and in other parts of the colonies revealed that otters quickly became extinct in those areas where they were hunted, that they sought refuge in places where they would not be destroyed by hunters, and that in hunting these animals much care and the principles of good economic management must be observed, or they would become completely extinct. The truth of this view was sustained by the excessive and wanton destruction of fur-bearing animals by the first fur hunters. When the Pribylov Islands were first discovered, Lukanin and Zaikov obtained many otter pelts there, particularly Lukanin, who took more than five thousand skins. Subsequently, the yearly catch decreased to two hundred skins and then completely ceased. The same thing occurred in the Commander Islands, on Copper Island, and on Unalashka, where the catch was abundant at first and then gradually declined.

From 1814 to 1822 sea otters were also caught off the shores of Kamchatka, particularly around Cape Kamchatka, but with quite negligible success, only forty-nine sea otters being taken throughout the entire period.

Fur seal hunting was accompanied by disregard for preserving these animals, especially during the period from the opening of the rookeries until the end of the company's first charter. The suspension of hunting in 1804, when the board of directors forbade it, produced a substantial increase in the numbers of fur seals, but they were still not as abundant as before. In 1808 the prohibition was removed, but the yearly catch was to be limited to 40,000 pelts, with an order to pay special attention to their selection, since most fur seals taken when the supply was virtually exhausted had fetched a poor price or were even destroyed without any profit to the company. The necessity of providing the colonies with supplies and of obtaining foreign ships frequently forced Baranov to demand the largest possible number of pelts. Because of the scanty colonial fleet he sometimes sent to the islands the same foreign captains who had brought needed supplies to the colonies. Under these circumstances the hunters naturally paid no heed to conservation, and fur hunting was based more on carrying out the wishes of the colonial governor exactly and rapidly. Perhaps Baranov had the same opinion as those who had taken part in the earliest expeditions, who maintained, according to Veniaminov,[3] that a closed season on the fur seals, or interruption of hunting for several years, was useless as far as the animals' propagation was concerned and would even lead to the destruction of the industry. To support their allegations they referred to several examples of diminution in the number of fur seals after hunting had been halted temporarily, but subsequent experiments completely refuted this theory.

The yield of other fur-bearing animals varied normally, increasing or decreasing on various local conditions.

In 1808 the responsibility for sorting furs for export from the colonies to Kiakhta and Moscow was entrusted to the Irkutsk office.

In the period from 1797 through 1821 fur exports from the colonies were as follows:

Sea otters, male, female, and young	72,894
River beavers	34,546
Beaver tails	59,530
Otters	14,969
Fur seals	1,232,374
Black and silver foxes	13,702
Blue foxes	21,890
Red foxes	30,950
Sables	17,298
Wolverines	1,151
Lynx	1,389
Minks	4,802
Blue polar foxes	36,362
White polar foxes	4,234
Wolves	121
Bears	1,602
Sea lions	27
Walrus tusks	1,616 puds 20 pounds
Whale bone	1,173 puds
Castoreum	21½ pounds

The total value of these exports at the prices existing at the various times was 16,376,695 paper rubles 95 kopeks.

Of this amount 3,647,002 paper rubles was exchanged with the Americans in Canton for goods and supplies.

Most of the remaining furs were traded to the Chinese in Kiakhta, and some, usually the best quality foxes, were sold to foreign merchants for the Constantinople trade.

The treasury earned around 2,000,000 paper rubles in duties for the export of furs to China and the import of Chinese goods in exchange.

Besides his other occupations in the colonies, Baranov experimented with using furs for the manufacture of various products. He attempted to manufacture fur seal pelts into gloves, stockings, caps, and hats, but the fur proved too short for yarn and not durable enough for knitting. Thus the attempt to use it in manufactures was abandoned as unsuccessful.

In addition Baranov sent to the board of directors several arshins of cloth woven in the colonies from California wool, but the difficulty of obtaining wool from California and the diversion of men to other tasks halted further experiments in this direction.

Relations between the Kolosh and the Russians. After the destruction of the settlement at Yakutat, Baranov demanded hostages from the Kolosh and unsuccessfully attempted to renew peaceful relations with them. The inhabitants of New Archangel were held in a constant state of terror by the treachery of the Kolosh. Their hostility toward the Russians was made evident in 1809 and particulary in 1813, when they incited neighboring tribes to attack the fortress and secretly prepared a large quantity of arms, ammunition, and various incendiary substances. Fortunately, the plot was discovered in time and the careful defensive measures taken by the colonial government forced them to abandon further attempts. From the time they had been driven out of the Russian fortress they had seized on Sitkha, the Kolosh, although they were careful to offer no pretext for open hostility, used every opportunity to harm the Russians, stealing and murdering, particularly when company employees were traveling through the straits. In such cases the culprits were always clever enough to cover their tracks and were almost never exposed, despite careful investigation. The matter would invariably end in mere negotiations with the chief and fruitless assurances that the unfriendly actions would cease in the future.

During Hagemeister's stay in the colonies in 1818, the Kolosh' unceasing thievery and attacks, despite the presence in New Archangel of a well-armed ship, forced the Russians either to begin to use force against them or to attempt once more to appease them with more conciliatory measures. When hostages were demanded, the Kolosh replied that they could never agree to this until they had received hostages from the Russians. The colonial administration decided to make this concession and gave them two creole boys in exchange for their chief's blood relatives. Several days later the exchange of hostages was carried out amid great ceremony and solemnity. For some time this resulted in a cessation of hostilities and an increase in the number of furs obtained from the Kolosh. Soon the Kolosh brought back the Russian hostages and asked that their own be returned, which was done. It seems that this new proof of the colonial government's desire to maintain peaceful relations with the Kolosh had favorably influenced them, because hostile activities were not renewed for a long time, at least toward the Russians themselves.

Some of the hunters plot against Baranov. One of the most remarkable events in the colonies during Baranov's administration was a plot in 1809 among several company employees against the chief manager and anyone else who refused to join them. Two hunters stationed at Sitkha, Naplavkov and Popov, and a number of conspirators decided to kill Baranov and his retinue, take one of the company ships, all the artillery and ammunition, provisions, supplies, a navigator, and several selected women, and sail to a South Pacific island, hoping thus to escape from all work and responsibilities. To advance their undertaking, they composed a written charter defining the duties of each conspirator and Popov was designated leader, with the title of cornet. Fortunately, one of them, fearing that the plot might fail, disclosed it to Baranov, who unexpectedly appeared in a meeting of the plotters and seized them all. Five of the leaders were sent in shackles to Kamchatka for trial.

Baranov is replaced. The directors were constantly concerned about selecting a man capable of fulfilling the post of colonial governor in case Baranov retired or died. In 1808, with this aim in mind, the board sent Collegiate Assessor Koch to New Archangel, but he died on the way in Kamchatka. Then Collegiate Counsellor Bornovolokov was sent to the colonies, but he died on the *Neva.* In the meantime Baranov, depressed by illness and advancing age, had lost the firmness and unusual strength of character which had distinguished him during his early years in the colonies. To some extent his weakness encouraged many malpractices by his subordinates, who had previously feared to incur his displeasure by the slightest deviation from his wishes.

Moreover, Baranov's constant delays in providing the directors with exact accounting—many items had not been explained since 1808—and the complaints of certain persons concerning him forced the directors to speed his successor's selection. Under these circumstances and anticipating the appointment of a new colonial governor, the directors decided to permit Hagemeister, after his arrival at New Archangel on the *Kutuzov,* to make a preliminary examination of both the administrative and commercial aspects of the company's management. If, upon acquainting himself with local affairs, he should find that the replacement of Baranov would be beneficial to the colonies, he was to present to Baranov the company council's authorization to assume the governorship of that country, approaching the matter with all the care and delicacy that Baranov's long and exceptional service deserved.

In the meantime, on the occasion of the approaching termination of the company's charter, the emperor ordered that Captain of Second Rank Golovnin, commander of the naval sloop *Kamchatka*, who had set out in 1817 for Petropavlovsk to deliver various government cargo, visit all sections of the Russian colonies and make a careful examination of their condition and of the relations existing between the Russian-American Company's employees and the natives. This ship also carried to the colonies Lieutenant Delivron and the civilian navigators Etholen and Schmidt, who were entering company service.

Having familiarized himself with the conditions of the colonial administration so far as time and circumstances permitted, Hagemeister decided to inform Baranov on 11 January 1818 that he was assuming the position of chief manager. This unexpected change must have offended Baranov deeply, especially since he was informed of it almost two months after Hagemeister's arrival in the colonies. Nevertheless, he began with all possible composure to hand over the records and the goods in colonial storehouses to K. T. Khlebnikov, commissioner of the *Kutuzov*, who had been appointed director of the New Archangel office.

The illness from which Baranov long had been suffering, was aggravated by the vexations which he had recently experienced, and prevented him from carrying out the transfer of the goods personally, so Hagemeister had to delegate the accounting to Khlebnikov. Nevertheless, the transfer of the stores was carried out with complete accuracy and all the company property, counted on the spot, proved to be fully in order. Although the bookkeeping methods were not sufficiently accurate, the differences were in an excess of goods rather than in a deficiency.

To put all the accounts in order Baranov planned to stay in the colonies until 1819 and a home was built for him at Ozerskoi redoubt, thirty versts from New Archangel. But Hagemeister, for reasons of health, found it necessary to leave the colonies in the autumn of 1818 and to hand over the governorship of the colonies to Lieutenant Ianovskii. Hagemeister and Golovnin decided to ask Baranov secretly to request permission to sail with them to Russia on the *Kutuzov*. Baranov complied, asking permission only to take with him his nephew and two servants who had served him well during severe attacks of illness. This request was readily granted.

Baranov's condition worsened while he was in Batavia, where he had immediately gone ashore when the ship reached port. Several times the doctor urged him to return to the ship, arguing that the sea air would reduce the high fever which had complicated his original illness during his stay ashore. Baranov, although unconvinced, attempted to return to the ship before its departure from the port, and died on 16 April 1819.[4]

The governorships of Hagemeister and Ianovskii. After assuming the colonial governorship, Hagemeister ordered Khlebnikov, in addition to putting the colonial bookeeping in order, to make a careful list of the colonial employees by occupation, with particular attention to the abilities of each. Then he informed the directors that he had increased the salary of the hunters and completely eliminated the half-share method of allowance, replacing it with a payment of 350 paper rubles per year and, in case of a flour shortage in the colonies, a subsistence allowance of 55 rubles per year. Hagemeister also asked that the salaries of the work dispatchers [*nariadchik po rabotam*] and baidarshchiks be fixed at 600 rubles and the salary of the craftsmen at 400 rubles; and that the payment of male and female servants in kind, which had prevailed up to then, be replaced with a company salary of 120 to 150 rubles for a man and 82 to 100 paper rubles for a woman.

The directors approved the proposed salary payments and ordered that all hunters be paid from 1815, the time of the last share splitting.

Moreover, Hagemeister composed a personnel roster of the colonial offices in Kad'iak, New Archangel, Unalashka, and Ross settlement, which was confirmed by the board of directors, and then proposed rules which should govern the visits of foreign ships to New Archangel. He settled outside the fortress walls several Kolosh who had accepted company protection, and attempted to turn the most capable of them, as well the creoles, to agriculture.

Hagemeister also found the fort quite run down and ordered that it be repaired and its defenses strengthened.

In view of the many drawbacks to sending hunting parties to Vancouver Straits under the protection of a company ship, Hagemeister contracted with Lieutenant Roquefeuille, commander of the French vessel *Bordelais*, to escort an otter-hunting party of thirty baidarkas for a share in the proceeds. A Kolosh attack on the convoy, in which twenty hunters and three women were killed, forced Roquefeuille to return empty-handed. When the board of directors heard of this disaster, they ordered that 350 paper rubles be given to the family of each man killed and a similar sum to each man wounded, depending on the seriousness of his wounds.

In the autumn of 1819 Ianovskii inspected the various colonial districts, visiting Kad'iak, Unalashka, and the Pribylov Islands. He looked into all aspects of the commercial administration and attempted to improve the position of the Aleuts. On Hagemeister's orders he set out the conditions on which Aleuts who were not company employees could be used for various kinds of company work. For example, he ordered that Aleuts sent to hunt birds be given several necessary items on setting out, such as kamleias,[5] shoe material, tobacco, and in addition be given three to five kopeks for each bird they brought back. The kamleias were to be sewn by native women employed by the company, and if there were insufficient women to prepare the necesary number of garments, then Aleuts should be hired and paid fifty kopeks for the sewing of each kamleia or parka.[6] Whale hunters were to be paid ten to twenty rubles for each whale, depending on the size. Aleuts employed in the Pribylov Islands for killing and preparing fur-seal pelts were to be paid twenty kopeks per pelt. In addition, Ianovskii fixed the number of male and female native employees in each section and prohibited the increase of this number without the authorization of the colonial governor.

Beginning in 1819, it was proposed to provide the commanders of company ships plying Northwestern American coastal waters with sea provisions worth 37 paper rubles 50 kopeks per month at colonial prices. Lower ranks assigned to ships were to be given, in addition to their salary, a monthly allowance of 30 pounds of sugar or 1 pud of flour, 15 pounds of meat or 30 pounds of seal meat, 6 pounds 34 zolotniks of groats, 8 pounds of peas, and 7 pounds of butter or fat.

An overland expedition explores the northern part of the American mainland and founds a fort on the Nushagak River. Authorized by the directors; an overland expedition set out from the colonies in 1818 to explore the northern part of the American mainland. It was headed by Korsakovskii, a company employee with some experience in writing descriptions and familiar with the trade relations of the mainland natives. One of this expedition's chief tasks was to found a fort on the Nushagak River and to investigate the rumors concerning Europeans believed to be descendents of Russians who lived somewhere to the north on a river Khiuveren. Many offered as evidence of the possible existence of these men the argument that they might have been descended from the cossacks who had set sail from the mouth of the Kolyma River before 1648 in vessels called *kochi* that were known to have been dispersed by a storm. The fate of several of the *kochi* was described in Müller's account of Siberia, but it was postulated that the other vessels were carried to the shores of America, where they were wrecked. According to this view, the survivors settled in the interior of the continent, in places offering easier living conditions than their previous residence in the far north of Siberia.[7]

When the expedition reached Kenai Bay, it crossed to Lake Iliamna and then followed the Kviichak River to Bristol Bay. Thence it proceeded along the coast to the Nushagak River, where Korsakovskii left part of his men to build a fort and took the rest to the mouth of the Tugiak River and Hagemeister Bay. There they met the cutter *Konstantin* with supplies needed by the expedition. Rounding Cape Newenham they arrived at the Kuskokvim River, where the natives convinced Korsakovskii that the late season would greatly hinder their northward progress because there would be nowhere to get provisions, since the natives had left to winter in distant places. So the expedition turned around. The post on the Nushagak River, which was called Aleksandrovskii redoubt, was completed and successful trading was conducted with the surrounding natives. Ianovskii, however, informed the board of directors of the unsuitability of maintaining a fort on the Nushagak, suggesting that it be transferred instead to the Kuskokvim River. Taking advantage of the presence in those waters of the brig *Golovnin*, Ianovskii ordered the exploration of the Kuskokvim River. The data concerning white men which Korsakovskii obtained from the natives was so contradictory that it could not be relied upon. Therefore it was decided to repeat the investigations, and in subsequent years it was confirmed that the rumors about the presence of cossack descendents in America were completely unfounded.[8]

Captain Golovnin inspects the Russian colonies in America. The sloop *Kamchatka* returned from its voyage somewhat earlier than the *Kutuzov.* Captain of Second Rank Golovnin had visited the company installations on Kad'iak Island, Sitkha Island, and on the shores of New Albion. After his return he gave the government information on the colonies and the native inhabitants under the company's control, including it in his account of the voyage of the *Kamchatka.*

In his remarks on Kad'iak, Golovnin says

In Lisianskii's *Voyage* (on the *Neva*) the condition of the inhabitants in relation to the company is explained in detail and almost everything that they suffer from the company administrators is noted. Here I will merely add that the company's affairs had not gone well under the previous governor. The present governor of the company's colonies (Hagemeister) has taken the most active and stern measures to eradicate the wrongdoing which exists in various areas of the company's activities, despite the best of intentions, and has striven particularly to halt the persecutions and offenses which the inhabitants have suffered from the hunters and to improve their condition. He has already had a great deal of success and for thus the reader should take Lisianskii's remarks as pertaining to the previous state of affairs in that country, not to the present.[9]

In his observations on New Archangel Golovnin speaks particularly

of the harm done to the company's trade by foreign contraband runners, adding:

> Could it be that the directors are not fully aware of the extent of the losses the
> company suffers from the smugglers and the harm they do the colonies and the
> company employees? It would appear almost certain that, if the board of direc-
> tors made the proper representations concerning this wrong and asked for the
> protection of their imperially granted privileges and assistance in protecting their
> property, the sagacious and solicitous government would not deny their re-
> quest.[10]

Moreover, Golovnin notes:

> Three things are lacking in the administration of the company colonies: specific
> duties, distinct ranks, and uniformity of dress or uniform. Foreigners visiting
> the colonies and finding nothing resembling provinces or fortified places be-
> longing to the Russian crown, that is, nothing like a regular garrison, may
> quickly conclude that these places are nothing more than temporary defensive
> fortifications built by hunters to protect themselves against the natives, and con-
> sequently may have no respect for them. In this connection, the good of the
> company demands that men employed in various positions in its service should
> have not only various salaries, but also differing privileges, commensurate with
> their duties, and in addition the road should be open to them to receive rewards
> from the government according to the services which they have performed for
> the nation through the company.[11]

The new charter of September 1821 and other rules for the company's administration, confirmed by the emperor and which exist to
the present day with some changes,[12] awarding considerable privileges
for persons entering its service, eliminated all of the above mentioned
defects.

The company's donation to the hospital for the poor in Okhotsk.
Among other donations which the company made to various government institutions at the time its charter was granted in 1799, the directors with the agreement of the stockholders and on the suggestion of
the commander of the port of Okhotsk, Captain Bukharin, ordered the
Okhotsk office to donate each year goods worth 1,000 paper rubles
for the establishment in Okhotsk of a hospital for the poor. Since it
was difficult to deliver these goods at the designated time, in 1819
the board of directors ordered that the annual 1,000 ruble donation
to the Okhotsk hospital for the poor be made in cash.

The colonial population. As of 1 January 1819 colonial accounts
showed the following numbers of Russians, creoles, and natives under
the control of the company:

Locality	Russians		Creoles	
	Male	Female	Male	Female
New Archangel	198	11	93	111
Kad'iak and neighboring islands	73	—	39	—
Ukamok [Chirikov]	2	—	—	—
Katmai artel' [post]	4	—	—	—
Sutkhom artel'	3	—	1	—
Voskresenskii fort	2	—	—	—
Konstantinovskii fort	17	—	—	—
Nikolaevskii fort	11	—	—	—
Aleksandrovskii fort	11	—	—	—
Ross settlement	27	—	—	—
Pribylov Islands	27	—	—	—
Nushagak	3	2	—	—
Total	378	13	133	111

The number of native adults and children were as follows:

Group	Male	Female	Total
Kad'iak Islanders	1,483	1,769	3,252
Aleuts at New Archangel	285	61	346
Natives of the Aliaska Peninsula	402	467	869
Chugach	172	188	360
Kenais	723	748	1,471
Ugalentsy	51	66	117
Copper River Indians	294	273	567
Fox Islands Aleuts	464	559	1,023
Pribylov Islands Aleuts	188	191	379
Total	4,062	4,322	8,384

Illnesses and their treatment. The only frequent illnesses during the company's first period were scurvy, in some of the newly settled places, and an epidemic which broke out among certain natives at the end of 1819 and which affected all of them more or less severely, killing forty-two in Kad'iak, twenty-five in New Archangel, and six in other places. Despite the efforts of the directors, no physician was stationed in the colonies before 1821 and the sick were forced to use common treatments learned from medical handbooks. During the visits of the ships on round-the-world expeditions it was possible to seek advice from the ships' doctors. The board of directors took care to see that every shipment of goods to the colonies included all necessary medicines and in 1808 sent smallpox vaccine and instructions on its use, ordering the colonial government to make every effort to vaccinate the Russians and as many natives as possible. Doctor Mard-gorst, who was sent to the colonies on the *Neva*, was ordered to demon-strate smallpox vaccination and to teach several capable company employees to administer it.[13]

The Kiakhta trade. In concluding our remarks on the company's activities during its first period, it is appropriate to say a few words on the Kiakhta trade up to 1821. The usual medium of payment for Chinese goods in the Kiakhta market was furs, although coarse (sold-ier's) cloth was also traded. The Chinese goods included black and aromatic tea, nankeen, a small quantity of silk, and sugar candy. Sea otters traded for tea brought 110 to 124 rubles and traded for nankeen brought 55 to 60 paper rubles; beaver tails and young otters brought 3 to 5 rubles; fur seals for tea from 5 rubles 13 kopeks to 7 rubles 20 kopeks, for nankeen from 2 rubles 40 kopeks to 2 rubles 65 kopeks; red foxes for tea 7 rubles 50 kopeks, for nankeen 4 rubles 75 kopeks; cross foxes brought 13 rubles; white polar foxes for tea brought 2 rubles 20 kopeks to 2 rubles 50 kopeks, for nankeen 1 ruble 10 ko-peks; and otters fetched 8 rubles.

Usually the company received two chests of tea for one sea otter and one chest for ten fur seals; four bolts of nankeen were received for one sea otter and one bolt for six fur seals. When these goods were sold, after allowance for all expenses, transportation, and taxes, they gave the following profits: 1 chest of tea from 150 to 180 rubles and 1 bolt of nankeen from 32 rubles 50 kopeks to 57 paper rubles. The average annual trade varied from 100,000 to 150,000 rubles. It reached as high as 270,000 rubles in 1815, when 2,515 chests of tea and 5,011 bolts of nankeen were traded.

The company's capital position and the profits realized from trade. Having set out all the facts relating to the company's administration of its colonies from the time of its founding to the end of its first char-ter, that is from 1797 to 1821, certain data on the company's capital position and on the trading profits it was able to realize in the first period should now be added:

The act of 1797 by which the Russian-
American Company was formed from several
small companies provided for an original capitalization consisting of 723 shares of 1,000 paper
rubles each ....   723,000 r.
  Paid in by new stockholders ....   515,738 r. 78 k.
                                        1 238,738 r. 78 k.

From 1797 to 1820 the return on this capital,
with allowance for expenditures, ordinary losses,
and capital losses ....   7,685,608 r. 57 k.
  By the stockholders' wish all the original prof-
it was added to surplus and, by the terms of the
company charter, a tenth of all profits available
for distribution, which totaled ....   3,331,510 r. 77 k.
  The following dividends were paid to stock-
holders:

1802-3[14]	....	469,791 r. 50 k.
1804-5	....	3,367 r. 30 k.
1805-12[15]	....	364,050 r.
1812-13	....	359,775 r.
1814-15	....	707,670 r.
1816-17	....	1,156,950 r.
1818-19	....	1,195,495 r.

On 1 January 1820 the company's surplus
and capital consisted of ....   4,570,249 r. 55 k.
divided into 7,713 shares, making the book
value of each share 592 rubles and 53 kopeks.
In 1820 the stockholders consisted of 630 individuals from various localities.
  The sale of furs in various places and the barter of furs for tea at Kiakhta brought in a total
of ....   16,376,695 r. 95 k.
  Foreign skippers bartered furs in Canton for
goods and supplies worth ....   3,648,002 r.
  Duty payments totaled approximately .....   2,000,000 r.
  Expenditure for building, purchase, repair,
and equipping of ships for provisions and for
salaries totaled ....   3,841,000 r.
Other articles of expenditure have not been set forth in detail due to
the unsatisfactory methods of bookkeeping in the colonies during this
period.

8. The Settlement of Colonial Borders and Expeditions Sent Out by the Company, 1821–41

The boundaries of the Russian possessions on the northwest coast of America are determined by conventions with the United States and England. The boundaries of Russian possessions on the northwest coast of America, as defined in the company's imperial charter of 1821, had to be slightly amended because of disputes which arose with the United States and England. The conventions which Russia concluded with the American government on 5/17 April 1824 and with the English government on 16/28 February 1825[1] provided that the boundary of Russian possessions in the south should extend from the south end of Prince of Wales Island, 54° 40' north latitude and between longitude 131° and 133° west, north along the Portland Channel to the point where it crosses 56° north latitude. In addition, the first of these conventions provided that United States citizens would have the right to fish in colonial waters and trade with the coastal natives for a period of ten years.

This condition evoked a complaint from the company that its imperial privileges had been violated and that not only the well-being of the colonies, but the very existence of the company was threatened.

In a memorandum to the Ministry of Foreign Affairs Admiral Mordvinov, a stockholder of the company, firmly defended the inviolability of the company's rights, referring to the vagueness of certain points in the convention that could lead to many misunderstandings. The ministry replied that the Russian government had found it necessary to agree to the ten-year concession to United States citizens to trade and fish in colonial waters for two compelling reasons: (1) the government of the United States had reasonably demanded recompense for the considerable advantages permitted Russia in the other points of the convention, particularly in Article 5; and (2) since up to this

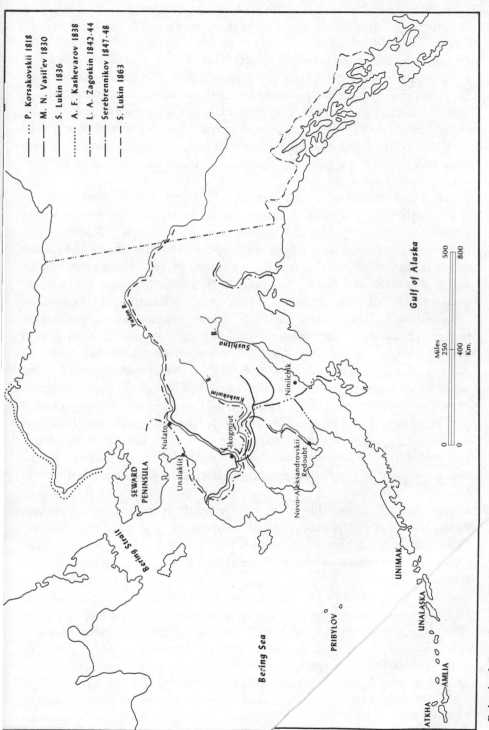

.....	P. Korsakovskii 1818
———	M. N. Vasil'ev 1830
———	S. Lukin 1836
....	A. F. Kashevarov 1838
—·—·	L. A. Zagoskin 1842-44
—·—·	Serebrennikov 1847-48
— — —	S. Lukin 1863

Principal Russian explorations of Alaska, from 1818

Bering Strait

SEWARD PENINSULA

Bering Sea

Nulato

Unalaklit

Yukon R.

Ikogmiut

Kuskokwim R.

Novo-Aleksandrovskii Redoubt

Sushitna R.

Ninilchik

PRIBYLOV

ATKHA
AMLIA

UNALASKA

UNIMAK

Gulf of Alaska

Miles
0   250   500

Km.
0   400   800

time the company had not been able to prevent the long-standing American practice of fishing and trading in colonial waters, it would be incomparably more advantageous to the company to agree formally to this practice than to see its prohibition broken at will and trade and fishing follow their course, as if by some natural and inalienable right. In particular, the granting of this exemption in a formal manner for a definite period of years was significant because in exchange for it the government of the United States was prepared to acknowledge formally that the company, after the period had run, had the full right to prevent and prosecute legally the conduct of trade and fishing in colonial waters by Americans.

Since the convention had not been ratified, the emperor ordered the creation of a special commission to consider the disadvantages which the company claimed would arise from the arrangement. The report of the committee, which was approved by the emperor, explained that the condition permitting United States citizens to fish in colonial waters and trade with coastal natives should not be taken as implying the right to approach the shores of Eastern Siberia and the Aleutian and Kurile Islands, which other powers had long acknowledged as an exclusive Russian possession, and that this condition should pertain only to the disputed lands on the northwest coast of America lying between 54° 40' and 57° north latitude. As a result the minister of foreign affairs and the committee decided that in order to protect the company's rights and to avoid any incorrect interpretation of the convention, the Russian envoy to the United States should be instructed to make a formal explanatory declaration when the ratifications of the convention were exchanged. The envoy replied that he had not found it possible to carry out his instructions, and that he had been able to inform the American cabinet only verbally of the sense of the provision, adding that a formal declaration might cause a serious clash, hinder the ratification of the convention, and produce an effect quite opposite to that intended by rousing conjectures which would otherwise not appear. Thus the convention was ratified by both governments.

Admiral Mordvinov also informed the ministry of the drawbacks which might result from the convention with the English, observing that as early as the 1740s Russia had considered her possessions in northwestern America to extend as far as 55° north latitude, and since then had added to them tribes inhabiting the entire continent as far as the Rocky Mountains, the natural boundary, whereas England had only recently discovered the Mackenzie River, which flowed on the eastern side of the boundaries. He also pointed out that the Committee of Ministers convened in 1822 had acknowledged Russian dominion as far as the fifty-first parallel of latitude, on which basis an imperial manifesto had been issued defining the boundaries of Russian possession in America. The ministry replied that in its opinion the extension of Russian claims toward the interior of the continent to the Rocky Mountains was neither right nor possible, and that such a claim might cause disputes, as well as other more unpleasant occurences, and that, finally, because of the infertility of the soil in this region, there was no foreseeable advantage to such an extension of the boundaries, particularly since contact with a civilized nation was not only harmless, but even profitable for the colonies, offering a new means of emergency food supply.

At the end of the ten-year period of the convention the Washington cabinet petitioned for renewal of the right of American ships to visit colonial waters for fishing and trade. In answer to this petition the vice chancellor informed Dallas, the American ambassador in St. Petersburg, that the Russian government could not agree, since a further extension of the privileges which American citizens had enjoyed in respect to free navigation in colonial waters would not be in keeping with the privileges granted to the Russian-American Company and with the protection which the company had a right to expect from its government.

Dallas then asked the Ministry of Internal Affairs what measures Russia would take at the conclusion of the period permitted by the convention, so that the Washington cabinet might make corresponding arrangements. The emperor instructed the vice chancellor to reply in a note to the ambassador that the government of the Russian colonies on the northwest coast of America had been ordered to insure that no more American ships visited the interior seas, bays, harbors, and inlets lying north of 54° 40′ north latitude, and that Russian vessels had been forbidden to enter corresponding waters south of that parallel. In upholding its rights, however, the colonial government was ordered not to lose sight of the ties uniting both governments and to use measures fully in keeping with the preservation of harmony between the two nations.

Relations with the Hudson's Bay Company. Meanwhile, the misgivings concerning the difficulties which might arise from the close proximity of the English boundaries recognized by the convention of 1825 were partially justified in practice. In this regard certain details concerning the activities of the English Hudson's Bay and Northwest companies up to that time need to be explained.[2]

Despite the destruction of Astor's company and all the advantages obtained since 1812 by the tireless activity of the English against the

Americans, the enmity between the Hudson's Bay Company and the Northwest Company not only decreased the profits which they had previously obtained from the fur trade, but threatened to lead to their complete ruin. For more than fifteen years the companies' realms had been subjected to a shocking spectacle of assorted ravages, thievery, murders, and native rebellions inspired by one side against the other. Finally in 1821, when the mutual enmity had exhausted the means of the two companies, they decided to come to an agreement, and their interests were united under the exclusive direction of the Hudson's Bay Company on the basis of a charter given to it in that year. The rights granted under this charter to exclusive trapping and trade in America included Rupert's Land (granted perpetually and irrevocably to Hudson's Bay Company by the charter of 1617) and the lands lying to the west of the Rocky Mountains, known as the Indian Lands, a considerable portion of which consisted of the northwest coast of America on the Pacific Ocean.[3]

For several years prior to this new charter, the coastal trade, as mentioned above, had been largely in the hands of the United States and Russia and, despite the gradual decline in American activities in those regions, it had brought the English almost no returns. The Treaty of 1818 between England and the United States had provided that the portion of the American continent extending west from the Rocky Mountains, over which both sides had claims, be considered common territory for a period of ten years. The treaty provided equal navigation rights on all rivers, and at the end of that period the treaty was extended for another ten years.

By 1830 the Hudson's Bay Company already had six permanent settlements between the Rocky Mountains and the Pacific Ocean, and in the interior of the continent sixteen, excluding temporary way stations and hunting parties. The fur trade was carried on predominantly in the region between the Rocky Mountains and the Pacific Ocean. The main settlement and trading depot of the company was located ninety miles from the ocean on the northern arm of the Columbia River at Vancouver. The former American post of Astoria had been refounded in 1831 under the name of Fort George. All supplies brought by sea from Europe were introduced through these ports into the interior of the country and all furs and other colonial products were exported to England and other places. Agriculture was carried on along the Columbia River. Generally speaking, the entire American continent south of the Russian possessions to the borders of California had been brought under the exclusive control of the Hudson's Bay Company within ten years of the merging of the companies, so that the Americans were forced to acknowledge that Astor's dream had been realized in a brilliant manner by his enterprising and far-sighted competitors.

The beneficial influence of the unification of the two companies was best reflected in the Hudson's Bay Company's agricultural settlement on the Red River. In 1811, with the aim of establishing an agricultural settlement in the company's own territory, it ceded to the Earl of Selkirk a tract of land at the junction of the Red and Assiniboine Rivers at 57° north latitude and longitude 97° west, where the climate and the soil were suited to wheat cultivation. Settlement of this place with immigrants from England and natives from all regions for the purpose of educating them in the ways of civilization and religion was proposed. On this basis Lord Selkirk went to considerable expense to settle several hundred families on the land that had been ceded to him, but the rivalry which then existed between the two English companies forced the abandonment of the settlement on two occasions. In 1816 twenty-two men were killed and several others wounded there. The dead included Semple, the governor of the company's possessions. In order to rectify the wrong in the best possible manner, the Hudson's Bay Company concluded an agreement with Lord Selkirk's heir by which the settlement was returned to the company in 1821. When the horrors arising from the rivalry ceased, the settlement on the Red River grew rapidly, so that by 1836 the population included 2,000 white men and 3,000 creoles and natives who devoted their efforts to raising grain.

In 1833 the governor of the Hudson's Bay Company in America proposed to Baron F. P. Wrangell, the chief manager of the Russian colonies (1831-1836), that they engage in joint fur trading in order to forestall any interference by the United States. Without flatly refusing the offer of the Hudson's Bay Company, Baron Wrangell ordered Captain-Lieutenant Etholen, whom he had sent to the Kolosh Straits [Alexander Archipelago] on the brig *Chichagov*, to coordinate his activities with the English in trading with the natives, but at the same time in other cases to act completely independently and to make it clear to the English that the Russian-American Company would strongly uphold the strict sense of its rights under the convention to exclusive trade in waters lying within the boundaries of Russian sovereignty. Etholen surveyed the region from Kaigany Strait to the Stakhina [Stikine] River, investigating in great detail the benefits his company might draw from this area and making acquaintances and establishing trade relations with the natives. Shortly after Etholen's visit Baron Wrangell heard rumors that the English had navigated the straits [Inside

Passage] in rowboats as far as the mouth of the Stakhina River, made a detailed inspection and survey, and explored the river for some distance above its mouth. Moreover, they had informed the natives of their intentions to establish a settlement in the upper reaches of the river, which would trade with them at prices considerably more favorable than Russian prices. These rumors were all the more probable since an English settlement in the upper reaches of the river would preclude the transport of beavers from the English territory down the Stakhina to the sea coast, that is into the Russian lands. Consequently, it would increase the profits from the fur trade in the lands under English control. Foreseeing the harm which would inevitably follow if the English established a settlement on the Stakhina River and employed the right of free entry and egress of the river and navigation of the straits under Russian control (Article 6, Convention of 1825), and in reliance on the article of the convention which gave English shipping the right of refuge and berthing in places where Russian settlements were located only with the permission of the head of the settlements (Article 2, Convention of 1825), the governor of the colonies decided to establish immediately a fortification at the very mouth of the Stakhina River. In 1834 with this aim in mind he dispatched two ships, the brig *Chichagov* and the schooner *Chil'kat*, and ordered the commander of the *Chichagov*, Lieutenant Dionisii Zarembo, to prohibit the English from stopping or landing within Russian boundaries, taking care not to viollate anything in the aforementioned points of the convention.

On this basis a redoubt was founded at 56° 40′ north latitude and longitude 132° 10′ west, to be called Redoubt St. Dionysius. In order to carry on unimpeded trade in those regions, it was necessary to build, besides this fort on the Stakhina River, several other fortifications northward of Chil'kat Strait, or, as Vancouver called it, the Lynn Canal. Only then, through the presence of these forts, would the benefits of this trade be assured. The English, fearing Russian trade supremacy in the regions adjacent to their borders, employed all means to hamper our trade and to arm the natives against us. They sent agents who knew the native language to persuade the Kolosh to arm themselves against the Russians, bestowed gifts on the chiefs, and used all available means to achieve their ends. The efforts of the English were not completely fruitless. The hostile intentions of the Kolosh were soon revealed and their plot to destroy the fort almost succeeded. Baron Wrangell had ordered Lieutenant Zarembo to remain there with his brig until another ship came to relieve him, and by Zarembo's efforts the Kolosh designs were averted.

Shortly afterward the English ship *Dryad*, under the command of

Ogden, an agent of Hudson's Bay Company, arrived at the mouth of the Stakhina River with men, cattle, goods, and supplies, and orders to found the proposed settlement. The Russian redoubt obstructed, as it were, the entrance to the river. Odgen could not avoid anchoring in front of the fortification and then, with the help of his rowboats, towing the ship and supplies up the river. He demanded Zarembo's permission to do this, and he, of course, refused. It should be observed that this refusal was limited to a written reply, in which it was pointed out that Article 11 of the Convention would be precisely observed: that is, in case Ogden should resist, no force would be used by the Russians.. Ogden, however, decided not to enter the river, although he had a perfect right to do so under the terms of the convention. He set out for New Archangel for conversations with Baron Wrangell, and unsuccessful in his solicitations there, he informed the Hudson's Bay Company of an alleged violation of the convention by the Russians. Then the directors of the Hudson's Bay Company demanded reparations for the losses, which they claimed to have suffered from this occurrence, in the amount of £21,500 (around 135,000 silver rubles).[4]

Literally interpreting the convention, the Russian Ministry of Foreign Affairs was compelled to acknowledge that the colonial administration was guilty, if not of a positive violation of the essence of the treaty with the English, then at least of a certain vagueness on the part of the commander of the company ship and the commandant of the fort and saw no other way out than to satisfy the English claim.

This was the state of affairs when Baron Wrangell returned to St. Petersburg from the colonies and volunteered to settle the matter if Mr. Simpson, one of the directors of the Hudson's Bay Company, should be appointed plenipotentiary negotiator by the English. The negotiations were approved by the emperor and were held in Hamburg in 1837. The results justified Baron Wrangell's expectations, which were based on the idea that in many cases Simpson would be prepared to agree to any conditions merely to avoid harming the friendly relations between the companies. Simpson had personally directed the possessions of the Hudson's Bay Company for many years and was intimately acquainted with the superiority of the Russian-American Company over the English in the disputed areas and therefore feared giving the Russians a cause to act in their turn to the detriment of his countrymen.

A strip of land in the colonies is leased to the Hudson's Bay Company. The agreement that was concluded provided that the Russian-American Company should lease to the Hudson's Bay Company for a period of ten years a strip of land ten miles in width, to the north and south of the Stakhina River, that is, the portion of the seacoast from

54° 40′ latitude northwestward to a line drawn between Cape Spencer on Cross Sound and Mt. Fairweather. Aside from the fact that English possession of this strip eliminated the cause of clashes and competition with the Russians, it was also particularly important because it made possible for the Hudson's Bay Company the maintenance of a uniform price schedule for furs bartered from the natives, and thus considerably facilitated the control of the English colonial administration over the numerous posts within its jurisdiction.

Generally speaking, this agreement provided that:

1.   The claim of the Hudson's Bay Company to £21,500 in damages for the losses which it suffered because the English vessel had not been permitted to enter the Stakhina River was waived.[5]

2.   The above-mentioned strip of land on the northwestern shore of America, along with Redoubt St. Dionysius located at the mouth of the Stakhina River, would be leased to the Hudson's Bay Company for a period of ten years beginning 1 June 1840. The Hudson's Bay Company would have full and exclusive right to trade in the leased lands and would be obliged to turn over to the Russians at the end of the term all structures and fortifications constructed on the leased strip.

3.   The Hudson's Bay Company would be obliged not to trade or hunt in the islands and other parts of the Russian territory except the leased strip.[6]

4.   The Hudson's Bay Company would pay for the lease with two thousand otter furs (worth around 118,000 rubles at then current prices).

5.   Moreover, the Hudson's Bay Company was obliged to sell to the Russian-American Company each year additional Columbia otter pelts, not to exceed two thousand, for 23 shillings each, and three thousand Hudson Bay pelts for 32 shillings each.[7]

6.   The Hudson's Bay Company would furnish the Russian colonies in America with a certain quantity of food supplies and transport goods on their ships for a predetermined price (see below, section on supplying colonies).

7. In case of a violation, all obligations between the companies would be liquidated without hindrance and the Hudson's Bay Company would be permitted three months to quit the places it occupied.

The agreement was approved by the emperor, and at the designated time Redoubt St. Dionysius and the leased strip were turned over to the English.

Several factors indicate that the leasing of the strip to the Hudson's Bay Company on the above-mentioned terms was quite advantageous to the Russian-American Company. In the first place, it eliminated the expense to the company of maintaining Redoubt St. Dionysius and its garrison, which amounted to 12,000 silver rubles per year; in the second place, it eliminated any cause for hostile clashes, for conflicting claims, and for mutual opposition between the agents of the English and Russian companies, so perilous in those remote regions; and finally it obviated the renewal of the undesirable requests by the United States government to continue the privileges by which American ships were granted the right of free navigation in Russian waters and straits (Article 4, Convention of 1824).[8]

The Kurile Islands are added to the regions under company jurisdiction. On 9 November 1830, a decree of the Siberian Committee, approved by the emperor, provided that the Kurile Islands be placed under the jurisdiction of the Russian-American Company, that a census be made of their inhabitants, that an office be established on Shimushiru Island, and that the imperial rules be applied to the administration of the islands and the conduct of the fur trade.

A detachment was sent from New Archangel in the same year with all necessary materials and supplies to found a settlement at Broughton Harbor on Shimushiru Island. The settlement on Urup, the southernmost of the Kurile Islands, which was abandoned in 1805, was reestablished with permission of the government in 1828. In that year the sighting of sea otters in the Kurile Islands prompted P. E. Chistiakov, governor of the colonies (1826-1831), to send a hunting party of fifty men to Urup with the materials necessary to build various structures. The responsibility for this mission was given to Midshipman Etholen, who succeeded in finishing the necessary buildings before the beginning of autumn.

Hunting on Urup Island brought the company more than 800,000 paper rubles worth of furs during 1828 and 1829.

At that time there were very few native inhabitants in the Kurile Islands: the first island [Shimushu] had two families, the second [Paramushiru] had around thirty families, and the fourteenth [Shimushiru] had ten. The last of these were known as "descenders [*soshlykh*]," since they had resettled there in 1817 from Paramushiru. The census of 1812 showed sixty-seven inhabitants on all the Kurile Islands. Up to the time that the company took over the islands, they had paid an annual iasak of forty-one sea otters, twenty-three foxes, and seventy-four kopeks per capita.

The Atkha District is added to the colonies. Until 1823 the Atkha District was under the control of the Okhotsk office. This had caused many difficulties in providing the section with necessary supplies and in exporting furs. With this in mind the board of directors in 1823 informed Murav'ev, chief manager of the colonies (1821-26), that the Atkha District was being added to the general body of the colonies. Murav'ev was ordered to make necessary arrangements to bring this section under the same administration as existed elsewhere, to provide it with supplies, and to export its fur catch to Russia.

Murav'ev's successor, Chistiakov, visited Atkha Island in 1826 during an inspection of the colonies. He had previously sent a considerable quantity of wood there for new building and for repairing the dilapidated dwellings. Chistiakov found the Atkha settlement in very poor condition and noted many other disorders resulting from the poor administration and carelessness of the Okhotsk office. He ordered the settlement moved to another place, since its location at the foot of a mountain was insecure. Since Atkha offered an easier food supply and day labor with the camp, Chistiakov, agreeing to the wishes of the Aleuts, ordered their settlement on Amlia Island moved to Atkha Island.

In 1827 Khlebnikov, manager of the New Archangel office, visited the islands of the Atkha District on the orders of the chief manager and inspected them. He introduced special rules both for bookkeeping and for the conduct of the fur trade. He also set out the conditions on which the natives might be employed in the company's service and defined their general relationship to the managers of the trading posts. The Aleut settlement on Amlia Island was renewed in 1838 to enable the propagation of the foxes, which had been imported there, to continue.

A proposal to move the colonial capital from New Archangel. Lieutenant Ianovskii, who governed the colonies until the end of 1820, had informed the board of directors that in his opinion it was necessary to move the colonial capital from New Archangel to Kad'iak for several reasons. In the first place, since the time when Sitkha Island was occupied, the fur catch in that region had barely covered a fourth of the expenses which the company bore there. In the second place, maintaining Aleuts there was very expensive, since it was necessary to have at least two hundred at the settlement, each separated from his family. In the third place, the proximity of the Kolosh presented great dangers for the settlement since they were better armed than the Russians, and the fort which they had erected was protected with ten cannon. Finally, there were more furs and more abundant means of obtaining them on Kad'iak. In case the board of directors should accept his proposal, Ianovskii considered it necessary to leave fifty men on Sitkha Island under the command of a trustworthy leader.

Murav'ev also wrote of all the inadequacies of Sitkha and of the excess of expenditures which could be avoided if the settlement were abandoned. He proposed moving the colonial capital to Chatham Harbor on Kenai Bay not far from the site of the former fort Aleksandr, which supposedly presented a great number of advantages, although Murav'ev had not confirmed this through personal observation.

The selection of this location was also advantageous in that it was close to the Aleutian Islands, the chief center of the colonial fur trade.

After discussing this proposal, the board of directors with the confirmation of the council agreed to decrease the number of men in New Archangel and to transfer the main factory from there. They considered it most suitable to move to Kad'iak Island, the homeland of the Aleuts, but left the choice of the future capital to the discretion of Murav'ev, instructing him to begin the resettlement without awaiting further orders, and afterward to inform them of the reasons which prompted him to select one place over another.

Murav'ev, however, did not succeed in beginning the move before the end of his governorship. In 1825 the board of directors opened the question to consideration by a general meeting of stockholders. The meeting unanimously decided to transfer the factory to Paul's Harbor, [the present site of the town of Kodiak] on Kad'iak Island. The new governor of the colonies, Chistiakov, was ordered to make all necessary preparations for this move and, in accordance with the aims of the government, to occupy Ozerskoi redoubt with fifty hunters, renaming it Port New Archangel.

Chistiakov informed the board of directors that in his opinion it would be quite unsuitable to have a hunter's settlement on Ozerskoi Bay because there was not a good anchorage there and it was impossible to enter it with a sailing ship. Furthermore there would be needless expense in sending a ship from Kad'iak every year to provision and to obtain news from the inhabitants of the redoubt, and finally, it would be difficult to transfer cargo from the Sitkha roadstead to the redoubt in rowboats. In 1828 Chistiakov reported that, because of the administrative merger of the Atkha section and the proposed occupation of the Kurile Islands, he would not be able to detach more than twenty-five men for the building operations on Kad'iak until the next shipment of men arrived in the colonies. The work at Kad'iak, however, was going successfully, and he would visit there himself during that year.

Difficulties later encountered in the construction of the factory at Kad'iak and a proposal by the Hudson's Bay Company to establish a settlement near Sitkha caused the board of directors to suspend work at Paul's Harbor until Baron Wrangell could visit the colonies, inspect conditions, and decide whether or not to abandon the main factory on Sitkha Island and transfer it to Kad'iak Island. In 1832 the transfer of the colonial capital from New Archangel was finally cancelled.

Captain Lütke, who sailed around the world from 1826 to 1829 on the sloop *Seniavin*, had the opportunity to familiarize himself with the colonies. His description of the voyage sets out in detail the disadvantages of both Kad'iak and New Archangel, and indicates sufficiently the relative advantages of the latter as a site for the colonial capital.[9]

The company equips a northern expedition of two ships under the command of Khromchenko and Etholen. In order to investigate in greater detail the northernmost regions of the colonies, the company in 1821 mounted an expedition consisting of two ships, the brig *Golovnin* and the cutter *Baranov* under the command of Khromchenko and Etholen, respectively. They were both instructed to survey Hagemeister Island and Hagemeister Strait. Etholen was also ordered to describe Goodnews Bay. After completing these tasks [12 July], the ships followed separate courses. Khromchenko sailed to the north and, although he saw the mainland coast, he was prevented by bad weather from carrying out a survey. Guided by the data which he had obtained from the company's overland expedition to the north [of Korsakovskii, 1819], he discovered Nunivok Island[16-17 July], but various circumstances kept him from describing it fully. Captain Vasil'ev also claimed the discovery of this island, but he did not report his data until Khromchenko had already described several of its shores, and decided that this was the same island first reported by the overland expedition. From Nunivok, Khromchenko proceeded to Norton Sound, where on the west side of Cape Derby he discovered Tachik Bay, surveyed it in detail, and noted what he thought to be an internal water route from there to Shishmarev Bay. He named Tachik Bay after Murav'ev, by whose wishes however it was renamed Golovnin Bay. Because of the lateness of the season Khromchenko decided against making a detailed examination of his discoveries. On the return route he defined several points on Nunivok Island.

Before joining Khromchenko at Hagemeister Strait, Etholen had entered the Nushagak River and described its mouth. After parting from the brig, he entered the Kuskokvim River with great difficulty, explored it for a considerable distance from its mouth, and made many contacts with the natives, including some fur trading. Cautiously leaving the treacherous mouth of the river Etholen set out for Nunivok Island. He had data on it from the overland expedition and from the natives of the Kuskokvim River, although he had not yet heard anything of Vasil'ev and Khromchenko. While tacking off Nunivok he observed the coast of mainland America in clear weather, and, although he wished to cross the strait which separated it from the island, a contrary wind prevented him from doing so. A high cape on the American shore he named Cape Vancouver. He set out around the island, intending to approach the cape from the other side, but bad weather impeded his observations and prevented him from entering Norton Sound. On the return voyage he named another cape on the American shore Cape Rumiantsov [now corrupted to Cape Romanzof]. Continuing the voyage along the shore he reached Cape Vancouver from the northern side and circled the northern shore of the island, making contact with the inhabitants, who had much in common with the Aleuts. On one of the most respected elders, Etholen bestowed a silver medal with the inscription "Allies of Russia," and gave him several gifts, with which he was very satisfied. A shortage of water and firewood forced Etholen to put aside his plan to revisit Cape Vancouver for a more detailed survey, and he returned instead to New Archangel [13 October 1821], where Khromchenko had arrived not long before him [7 September].

This expedition was a complete success. Hydrography was enriched with much information on almost unknown places, while the foundations were laid for trade relations with many native tribes which subsequently were to bring the company significant profits.[10]

The proposals of Lieutenant Romanov and Count Rumiantsov for northern exploration. In 1823 Lieutenant Romanov first proposed to the chief of naval staff an expedition from the Copper River to the Arctic Ocean and Hudson Bay. Upon reviewing this plan, the board of directors informed the admiralty that, although a company expedition had already explored the northern part of America in 1818, if the government wished to mount the expedition, the company would aid this undertaking with all means at its disposal. The plan, however, was not carried out.[11]

In 1824 State Chancellor Count Rumiantsov, with the prior approval of the board of directors, presented the governor of the colonies, Murav'ev, with a request to equip in the colonies, on his account and that of the company, an expedition to explore the northern part of America. Here we present the text of his letter to Governor Murav'ev as an interesting document showing the burning interest with which Count Rumiantsov viewed everything which pertained to the good of the country and also providing certain data on the previous efforts of Russian navigators in this region.

When the *Rurik* was dispatched in 1815 to seek the Northwest Passage, Kotzebue was ordered to proceed overland from Bering Strait to Icy Cape and then along the shore to the east, in order to discover the physical characteristics and direction of the coast, which beginning from Icy Cape is completely unknown to us, and also the direction and strength of the currents: in short, to make preliminary estimates of the possibility or impossibility of undertaking a search for a water connection between the two oceans. The unfortunate circumstance which befell Kotzebue [his illness] prevented him from carrying out this order. Captain Vasil'ev's undertaking was also unsuccessful, and for this reason our geographical knowledge of the northern countries lying to the east of Bering Strait was not increased in the least.

Not seeing at this time any new undertakings on the part of the government to solve this interesting problem, I wish to review the efforts begun on the *Rurik*. It is known from Vasil'ev's report that it is quite possible to circumnavigate Icy Cape. But since this demands a strongly built and abundantly supplied ship, in order that it be in a condition to pass two or three winters on the voyage, and since this kind of outfitting is almost impossible in the settlements of the Russian-American Company, I prefer the mounting of an overland expedition similar to that which I entrusted to Kotzebue in 1815, that is, setting out first for Icy Cape and then eastward along the coast. I consider it superfluous to continue this expedition farther than the mouth of the Mackenzie River, particularly since the noted Captain Franklin will set out on a similar expedition, but from the opposite side. Captain Franklin is ordered to descend the Mackenzie River and then to proceed west toward Bering Strait. He cannot reach the mouth of the Mackenzie earlier than 1826 or 1827 and for that reason it is desirable that our expedition should begin its journey by that time. If it should happen that both expeditions meet, then the glory of a successful undertaking will belong to Russia and to England. Otherwise, if Russia should undertake nothing and the English should succeed in reaching Bering Strait, then the short distance of these regions from our Asiatic and American possessions will give Europe the right to reproach us for leaving such pursuits, in our own waters and around our own shores, to other nations.

Knowing how you love the glory and advantage of our fatherland and having experienced several times the exceptional favor with which you have always been ready to oblige me, I turn to you with full confidence and ask you to take upon yourself the fulfillment of this task and, having considered all the relevant circumstances, to write the instructions to the commander of the expedition. It is my wish to entrust the command to Khromchenko with Etholen as his assistant, but if the demands of the company service prevent Khromchenko from taking the command, then to Etholen. It seems to me that he has all the qualities which might crown the expedition with success. Baron Wrangell's explorations on the ice attest to the possibility of a similar coastal expedition. Last year he trekked around 1,200 miles in only 70 days.

Count Rumiantsov donated 20,000 paper rubles of his own money to the expedition, and the board of directors allocated Murav'ev another 10,000 rubles in case of need.

The death of Count Rumiantsov put an end to this undertaking, since his heir, Count Sergei Petrovich Rumiantsov, would not confirm the expenditure for the expedition, and because the expedition could no longer fulfill the original plan because of the impossibility of meeting Captain Franklin.

Lieutenant Kashevarov's expedition. Immediately after Franklin's overland expedition [1825-26], the English equipped a sea expedition under the command of Captain Beechey to discover a passage eastward through the Arctic Ocean. Franklin's first expedition had got as far as Beechey Point, located at 70° 30′ north latitude and longitude 149° 45′ west. The last point defined by the Beechey's expedition was Point Barrow, at 73° 23′ 30″ north latitude and longitude 156° 21′ 30″ west, that is 170 miles farther than Captain Vasil'ev had gone.[12] Thus, the unexplored portion of the American coast amounted to 6½°, or around 146 Italian miles.

After Baron Wrangell's return from the colonies in 1836, the board of directors proposed an expedition to explore this portion of the coast under the command of Lieutenant Kashevarov, a member of the Corps of Naval Navigators in the service of the company.

According to a plan drawn up by Baron Wrangell the expedition should consist of one twelve-oar baidara and five three-man baidarkas. The crew should, in addition to the leader, consist of an assistant head of the expedition, a medical student, thirteen Russians and creoles one of which might serve as interpreter, and ten Aleuts.

The expedition was to proceed in a company ship to Cape Lisburne, or as far as the ice permitted, and from there to continue in smaller boats or in whatever manner best suited exploring and surveying the region.

Before it left the colonies, the expedition was provided with all necessities, such as warm clothing, leather and wooden supply containers of small dimensions that would be suitable for storing in the baidarkas should it become necessary to leave the large baidara, and finally, surveying instruments.

In the meantime, while preparations were being made for the expedition, the Hudson's Bay Company, under the influence of Simpson, a company director and the governor of its possessions, equipped its own expedition for this same purpose. Two rowboats set out from the mouth of the Mackenzie River westward along Franklin's tracks and in five weeks successfully completed the navigation and survey as far as Point Barrow and back. In this way, England, through the Hudson's Bay Company, obtained the honor of the final exploration of the north coast of America, although the renowned English navigators Beechey and Franklin had been unable to carry this out earlier.

Nevertheless, Captain of First Rank I. A. Kuprianov, chief manager of the colonies (1836-41), wished to provide Russia also with the honor of such an exploration and decided to dispatch an expedition.

On 5 July 1838 the expedition parted from the brig *Polifem* which had accompanied it as far as Cape Lisburne. Beyond Icy Cape,

Kashevrov was compelled to leave the large baidara and proceed in the baidarkas. He succeeded in describing the coast in some detail for thirty-five miles beyond Point Barrow. The first bay found by the expedition, at 71° 13' north latitude and longitude 155° 40' west, was called Prokof'ev Bay [Elson Lagoon]. The cape located at 71° 9' north latitude and longitude 155° 15' west, where the coast turned to the south, was called Cape Stepovyi [Christie Point], and the cape marking the eastern boundary of an enormous bay was called Cape Wrangell [Tangent Point]. The bay itself lying between these two capes was called Kuprianov Bay [Dease Inlet].

The growing boldness of the natives and a planned rendezvous of twenty baidaras at Point Barrow for a probable attack placed the expedition in a very difficult position. Finally, obvious pursuit by the natives and their threats, which by virtue of their large numbers could easily have been carried out and the expedition brought to inevitable destruction, compelled Kashevarov to turn back. On 6 September the expedition joined the brig at Chamisso Island in Kotzebue Sound and returned successfully to New Archangel.[13]

The company sends expeditions northward into the interior and establishes relations with the natives of these regions. Since the founding of Aleksandrovskii redoubt on the Nushagak River in 1820, the manager, the promyshlennik Kolmakov, had established trade relations with the neighboring tribes, converted several of the natives to Christianity, and generally helped to spread the company's influence in that region. But since the activities of the redoubt were confined predominantly to trade, and even then through intermediaries, information on even the nearest places in the interior of the continent and on the peoples that inhabited them were superficial and often contradictory. In view of the necessity of acquiring exact information on this part of the colonial possessions, in 1829 Chistiakov sent a coastal expedition under the command of Ensign [I. Ia.] Vasil'ev of the Corps of Naval Navigators to survey the region between the redoubt and Norton Sound, to collect topographical and ethnographical data on this country, and to extend relations with the natives.

Vasil'ev first went to Kad'iak; proceeding from there across the Aliaska Peninsula to the redoubt [arriving on 1 May]. From the redoubt he ascended the Nushagak River, successfully traversing the rapids to the rivers headwaters, describing the river as accurately as possible. After exploring Lake Nushagak and several other lakes he returned to the redoubt [on 11 July]. His intention to penetrate the mountain range to the Kuskokvim River proved impracticable because of the unfriendliness of the natives and the shortage of willing native

guides. In August of the same year Vasil'ev undertook a more successful exploration of the region west and northwest of the redoubt. With
the beginning of winter, by order of the colonial governor, he returned
to Kad'iak, [arriving 15 January 1830], to increase his complement of
men and take on the supplies and goods necessary for trade with the
natives.

In the spring of 1830 Vasil'ev again set out. Kolmakov had succeeded in engaging as guides to the expedition eleven Kuskokvim natives,
several relatives of whom were left in the redoubt as hostages. The
number of guides, however, quickly diminished to four. The rest refused under various pretexts to accompany the expedition, and even
the remaining four attempted several times to run away. In July,
Vasil'ev reached the Kuskokvim River and visited almost all of the
native settlements along its banks, but the firm refusal of the natives
to accompany him prevented him from reaching the river's source, and
toward the end of the month he turned back. During the journey, he
frequently had had to bear derision, insults, and even threats from the
natives. Facing all their hostile intentions with desperate bravery and
clear contempt of death, qualities highly valued in their eyes, he succeeded in winning the favor of several of their most respected leaders,
and under their protection successfully returned to the redoubt. It
should be noted that during their journey along the Kuskokvim River,
the expedition was constantly on the alert; the men never laid their
rifles down. Some of Vasil'ev's ethnographic observations on the tribes
with which he came in contact—the Aglegmiuts, Kiatentsy, Kuskokvimtsy, and others—supplemented by data obtained later, will appear
in the general survey of natives inhabiting the Russian colonies in
America [see Chapter 20].

As a consequence of Vasil'ev's expedition Baron Wrangell in 1832
ordered a creole named Lukin to found a one-man post on the Kuskokvim River at the influx of the Khulitnak River. Later it was moved
somewhat closer, near the mouth of the river Kvygym and in 1841 it
became the Kolmakov redoubt. From the very beginning, this settlement carried on a very successful fur trade with the natives. Conducting trade along the river, Kolmakov explored it for a distance of around
one hundred miles, designating toens in several places and christening
several natives. Later investigations of various tributaries of the Kuskokvim, carried out by Lukin and Kolmakov's son, permitted the extension of the fort's trade relations to the very source of the river.

In order to obtain more detailed data on the natives inhabiting the
neighborhood of Golovnin Bay and to survey St. Lawrence Island,
Chistiakov in 1830 ordered that Midshipman Etholen, in command of

the brig *Chichagov*, circumnavigate all of Norton Sound from Stuart Island and then proceed to Bering Strait, approaching Aiak, or Aziak [Sledge] Island and Ukivok [King] Island. Etholen was then to visit the settlements of the Chukchi on the Asiatic coast, attempting everywhere to expand the company's trade relations and to gather data on the most suitable means for bartering furs.

Leaving New Archangel on 21 June, Etholen set a course for St. Lawrence Island, but fog and strong winds forced him to put in first at Golovnin Bay. From there he proceeded to Aiak (or Aziak) Island and then to Ukivok Island.

According to Etholen's description Aiak Island is a completely barren rock. "At the first sight of this wild and menacing island," he wrote, "one is amazed that men might settle on it, but the enormous number of walruses around the shores easily explains the riddle. By hunting these animals the natives obtain in exchange all their necessities from the inhabitants of the continent and in this way quite easily secure their livelihood."

The brig arrived at St. Lawrence Bay [Siberia] and anchored there. The next morning large numbers of ice floes were observed in the sea. Astonishingly, these began to drift rapidly into the bay although there was a strong contrary wind. Around noon the entire bay was covered and by evening the ice had reached the brig, so that it was in imminent danger of being broken up by the ice pack or being cast ashore. Some of the ice floes were a mile in circumference. To save the ship from destruction, Etholen was obliged to weigh anchor repeatedly. In this way the crew of the vessel passed fifteen quite exhausting days. Meanwhile, the Chukchi came to the brig from all around, even from as far as Mechigmen Bay, to barter furs and walrus tusks.

Afterwards Etholen set out for St. Lawrence Island, where he traded with the natives of the local settlement, Kukuliak.

There were five settlements in all on the island, two of which, Kukuliak and Kealegak, were somewhat more important than the others. The latter was located at the east end of the island [Southeast Cape]. The inhabitants of both settlements were in constant conflict with each other. Generally speaking the islanders did not have fixed residences. In the summer they wandered here and there in search of food, and only in the winter did they return to their settlements. Their main industry was walrus hunting, which they carried on when the entire island was icebound. Walrus tusks were particularly important in their trade with the Chukchi. They traded them chiefly for essential buckskin clothing. There were no fur-bearing animals except foxes, but their fur was so coarse that the pelts were no better than those of dogs.

According to Etholen, the inhabitants of St. Lawrence Island were identical in physiognomy, language, and culture with the tribes dwelling on the American mainland.

From St. Lawrence Island, Etholen went to St. Matthew Island, but a strong wind permitted him to approach only a tiny island located off the northwest tip where there was a walrus rookery. From there he set sail for St. Paul Island, Unalashka and finally New Archangel.

In his general review of trade relations with the places he had visited on this voyage, Etholen informed the chief manager, Baron Wrangell, that the expansion of trade with the inhabitants of Golovnin Bay, the Kvikhpak River and other neighboring localities would be best served by establishing a redoubt near Stuart Island.

The establishment of such a redoubt followed in 1833. Baron Wrangell sent the sloop *Urup* to the island, under the command of Lieutenant Teben'kov, with materials and prefabricated structures to be used for building the settlement. Sailing around Stuart Island, the sloop put into a bay which Teben'kov had discovered the year before and called Teben'kov Bay. Choosing a site on an island lying on the west side of the bay and next to a native settlement, Teben'kov broke ground for the redoubt, which he named Mikhailovskii [St. Michael], also from his own name. With the help of the natives the redoubt neared completion within ten days. The island on which the fort was built was named St. Michael Island. Having made all necessary arrangements for the construction of dwellings for company personnel and for the performance of essential duties at the redoubt, Teben'kov went to Golovnin Bay. From there he proceeded to Aiak Island, but finding that all of the inhabitants of the settlement had gone hunting, he sailed to Ukivok Island. Here he carried on a small barter with the natives, and then in Mechigmen Gulf he traded for around 435 puds of walrus ivory and 1,012 polar-fox pelts. On St. Lawrence Island the trade was unimportant. Returning to the fort, Teben'kov found many of the buildings already completed, and a short time later he set out for the return voyage to New Archangel.

After the redoubt was established, the colonial government devoted particular attention to scientific and trading explorations of adjacent interior regions of the continent, including the course of the Kvikhpak River and other communication routes which might facilitate trade with the various neighboring tribes. In that year Lieutenant Rosenberg was assigned to explore all the mouths of the Kvikhpak River, but was unable to fulfill this task. He sent the creole Glazunov with baidarkas to explore the lower reaches of the river. Although Glazunov succeeded in entering the river from Pastol' Bay by its northern affluent, the

Apkhun, and went some thirty miles down another arm, he did not succeed in reaching the sea. However, his voyage benefitted the company since many of the native settlements which he visited entered into trade relations, which were subsequently strengthened by the regular visits which the inhabitants made to the fort.

In 1835 and 1836, Glazunov was again sent out to explore the Kvikhpak River and discover its course to the sea. He went down the Kvikhpak where it joined the Yukon River a certain distance and then crossed the tundra to the Kuskokvim River, following it to its junction with the Tkal'khuk [Stony] River. In accordance with his instructions he attempted to make his way down the Tkhal'khuk to Kenai Bay, but nearly perished on the way because of a shortage of provisions.[14]

In 1838 Malakhov, a creole, was sent to explore the upper reaches of the Kvikhpak basin. He reached the junction of the Yukon and Nulato rivers, where the company later founded an odinochka called Nulato. He navigated the entire length of the Kvikhpak to the Apkhun and reached Mikhailovskii redoubt by way of Pastol' Bay. The fruits of this expedition were the considerable number of furs of various kinds acquired in a short time from the natives living on the shores of the Nulato and the strengthening of trade relations.

In 1836 Mikhailovskii redoubt almost fell victim to an attack by the Aiakmiuts, the inhabitants of Aiak Island, but the courageous determination of one of the company's employees, Kurepanov, saved it. The Aiakmiuts had customarily bartered for furs with the natives on the American shore, passing them on to the Chukchi and ultimately to Siberian traders. The establishment of the Russians on Norton Sound led to a considerable diminution in this trade. Ascribing the gradual decrease of their trade solely to the existence of the Russian fort the Aiakmiuts decided to destroy it. Several hundred of them landed on the shore and, not daring to attack the full garrison of the redoubt, awaited some occasion when the Russian forces were divided. Observing that nine men had set out for the forest, they decided to kill them first and then to the redoubt itself. They hid behind the hills, surrounded the party and attacked it. As usual the Russian party carried guns for hunting wild game and several axes. They defended themselves with desperate courage, but in the end the preponderance of strength, being on the side of the natives, would certainly have decided the issue. Seven of the Russian party were already severely wounded and one had been killed when Kurepanov decided to break through to a native baidara which had been beached nearby. He inspired his comrades with the hope of rescue, and they suddenly turned toward the shore. They cleared a way through the crowd of natives with their gun butts and all succeeded in reaching the baidara safely. They dragged it into the water and quickly shoved off. The few arrows which the natives shot after the retreating baidara did not cause much damage, but if the attack had lasted several minutes more, all would have been lost. Most of the wounded soon lost consciousness and Kurepanov almost single-handedly brought the baidara to safety. Under cover of night they reached the redoubt. The natives were amazed by the extraordinary bravery of the Russians. They did not dare follow them, and also feared a counterattack by the Russians and loyal natives in the redoubt, so they quickly set out for their homes. From that time on the Aiakmiuts appeared no more on those shores.

Brave and determined defense always impressed the natives more than the mere size and armament of a garrison. The attack that several Kuskokvimtsy made against Lukin's outpost in 1839 provides a further example of this fact. They intended to destroy it just as they had recently destroyed a similar outpost located near the settlement of Ikogmiut on the Kuskokvim. Forewarned of the natives' intentions, Lukin permitted them to advance almost to his cabin. Observing the instigator of the raid giving his companions the signal to attack, Lukin seized him and threw him back, not touching the others, who silently departed. From that day the natives never again attacked, and even performed frequent valuable services for Lukin.

Surveys of the coasts of Aliaska Peninsula. The company ordered baidara expeditions to survey the shores of Aliaska Peninsula in 1831 and 1837. The leader of the first expedition was Second Lieutenant [I. Ia.] Vasil'ev, who had returned from the Kuskokvim River. He surveyed the coast from Cape Douglas for a distance of eighty miles in as much detail as possible. The second expedition was under the command of Lieutenant Voronkovskii, who was assigned to the service of the company from the Corps of Naval Navigators. He set out from Kad'iak, crossed Shelikhov Strait to the Katmai outpost, and from there followed the shore to Sutkhum outpost and Cape Kumliuk, where Vasil'ev's survey had stopped. From there Voronkovskii surveyed the coast to Cape Khitkuk, a distance of three hundred Italian miles, where he connected with the survey made by Captain Staniukovich on the naval sloop *Moller.* On the way he also surveyed Unga Island and the Shumagin Group. From Unga Voronkovskii proceeded along the southern coast of Unimak Island to Cape Khitkuk and then on to Unalashka Island, and from there back to New Archangel.

The fur trade on the Shantar Islands and surveys of the coasts and islands of the Okhotsk Sea. In 1829 the company decided to hunt furs on the Shantar Islands. For this purpose a detachment of twenty-two men under the command of commoner Serebrenikov was sent from Iakutsk to Udsk ostrog. In the spring of 1830 this detachment successfully crossed to Great Shantar Island, where a settlement was founded on Iakshina Creek, which falls into the bay of the same name. In the course of the year they built essential dwellings and laid in food supplies for the autumn. However, investigation proved that the number of furs which would be obtained in an average year in the Shantar Islands did not exceed three hundred sables and twenty foxes. Therefore, in 1833 the company decided to discontinue the operation.

In 1828 the company planned to survey the shores and islands of the Sea of Okhotsk and to make every effort to find a more satisfactory harbor than Okhotsk. The route then in use for transporting goods for the colonies from Iakutsk to the Sea of Okhotsk involved traveling 1,200 versts overland through Siberia. In his memoranda to Governor-General Iakobii, G. I. Shelikhov had asked permission many times to move the Okhotsk port to another location. Probably the insufficiency of the company's resources and perhaps other circumstances prevented the realization of this goal. The company factory, transferred to a new site in 1820, was very vulnerable. It was situated between the seacoast, only two sazhens above sea level and the mouth of the river. During high tides with winds, the water covered the shore and reached the settlement. Moreover, the shores of this small peninsula were being washed away year by year. Observations conducted over a period of six years showed that the coast had eroded 22 sazhen on the sea side and 5 sazhen on the river side, leaving a space between the buildings and the water of 8 and 105 sazhen, respectively. Under these circumstances the board of directors wished to relocate the factory immediately. Previous observations had shown that there were on the coast of the Sea of Okhotsk three points particularly suitable for the establishment of a port: Uda Bay and the mouths of the Ul'ia and Aldoma Rivers (35 and 140 versts, respectively, from Okhotsk). The board of directors devoted particular attention to these sites.

The expedition equipped for this purpose was sent to the field in two sections. Its leader, Staff Captain Koz'min of the Corps of Naval Navigators, and a detachment of men set out overland for Udsk port in 1829. He was to make a detailed investigation of the route. The second section was sent from Okhotsk to Feklistov Island on the schooner *Aktsiia*, under the command of Klimovskii, a creole navigator. Here he was to await the arrival of Koz'min, who was to cross over to this island from the mouth of the Uda in baidaras. The difficulties which Koz'min encountered in the crossing forced him to winter in Uda Bay. Klimovskii found an anchorage in a small inlet off uninhabited

Feklistov Island and successfully passed the winter there. In the spring of 1830 the schooner arrived at Uda Bay and Koz'min took command of the expedition. During the summer they explored the right bank of Uda Bay, all of Great Shantar Island and a part of Feklistov Island, and wintered at the mouth of Ala River without returning to Uda Bay.

In the spring of 1831 three detachments were sent out to investigate possible routes from the interior of Siberia to the Sea of Okhotsk. One of them explored the overland route from Iakutsk to the mouth of the Aldoma River. The second group inspected a water connection along the Maia River. The third was sent from Okhotsk to survey the Ul'ia River. These explorations showed that the harbor surveyed by Koz'min in Uda Bay was not suitable for ships, which could enter it only with difficulty. For various reasons the mouths of the Ul'ia and Aldoma could not be studied at that time. In the meantime, the detachments sent overland carried out their tasks very successfully. The Maia River and the routes from Iakutsk to Uda and Aldoma bays and to the Ul'ia River were explored and described in detail. These expeditions showed that the routes from Iakutsk to Uda Bay and to the Ul'ia River, from the point where the Aldoma route turned off, were unsuitable and would be difficult to develop. The overland road from Iakutsk to the Aldoma, in its natural condition, presented the same drawbacks, and although it demanded many improvements before heavy loads could be transported during the winter and summer, its location was suitable and it had no points impassable for heavy loads, such as those encountered on the Okhotsk Road. The portion of the Maia River parallel with the Aldoma Road, that is from its junction with the Aldan River to the village of Nel'kan, a distance of 600 versts, was navigable to small vessels and in the winter offered a satisfactory road over the ice, thus eliminating all the difficulties associated with traveling such a great distance over a mountain road. With this in mind, the company had only to construct a 380-verst road from Iakutsk to the junction of the Aldan and Maia Rivers and a 220-verst road from Nel'kan to Aldoma Bay. Construction would be easy on the first segment, but the difficulties on the route from Nel'kan to Aldoma were numerous and could only be overcome in time.

On the basis of these investigations, the Aldoma route was acknowledged the most suitable by the board of directors, and preparations for construction were begun. In 1832 and 1833 Ensign Shilov of the Corps of Naval Navigators, and Uglichaninov, assistant director of the Okhotsk Office, made a detailed survey of Aldoma Bay and the surrounding territory. This survey and other factors led to the selection of another location for the company's factory, on the southwest shore of the Sea of Okhotsk at Aian Bay, located between Okhotsk and Udsk Bay. With the exception of a few changes in the segment from Nel'kan to the Sea of Okhotsk, the road from Iakutsk remained the same. Uglichaninov reported that, although the Aldoma River was suitable for floatage of various kinds and the neighborhood abounded in forests and fish, its drawbacks included wet and swampy soil, few meadow lands, and difficult navigation in summer because of low water. Although the Aian Bay region was surrounded on all sides by mountains and lacked trees, it had advantages. The valleys had good meadow lands, and the soil, mostly chernozem, was suitable for orchards. The Ui River, which could provide enough fish to feed the employees, was also flanked by meadow lands.

There was a fir forest about five versts from the bay and deciduous trees in the river valleys.

Aldoma Bay itself, according to Shilov's description, was not a suitable anchorage, both because of the severe choppiness of the water when the wind was up, and because of the treacherous bottom. Ships that entered this harbor were required to stand at anchor in a place where it was possible to make sail when the wind freshened in order to escape a large number of underwater rocks. Aian Bay, on the other hand, was surrounded on three sides by mountains and on the south was protected by a sandbar and a cape. In addition, the bottom was secure and the chop was mild even under strong winds.

The plan to transfer the factory from Okhotsk to Aian Bay was not realized until the beginning of the 1840s, and for this reason the details of establishing a port in this bay will be covered in the review of the company's activities from 1840 to 1860.

9. *The Dissemination of Religion among the Natives and Improvements in Their Way of Life, and the State of Fur Trading and Shipbuilding in the Colonies*

The Orthodox Church in the colonies. When Archpriest Veniaminov returned to St. Petersburg from the colonies in 1839, he presented to the Holy Synod a survey which he had composed concerning the condition of the Orthodox Church in the Aleutian and Kurile Islands and northwest America[1] along with his views on possible improvements that could be made there. In this chapter, we will present extracts from this survey. In the work of spreading Christianity in this region, Archpriest Veniaminov took a most zealous and beneficial part during his service in the colonies of almost twenty years. Later, his efforts as bishop fully earned him his reputation as the most worthy of the leaders of the Orthodox missionaries.

After the company's imperial charter was renewed in 1821, the board of directors petitioned for the dispatch of several priests from Irkutsk to the colonies. In 1823 Frumentii Mordovskii was sent to Kad'iak to replace Hieromonk Afanasii a member of the first religious mission, in 1824 Ioann Veniaminov was sent to Unalashka, and in 1825 Iakov Netsvetov went to Atkha. Father Aleksei Sokolov had been in New Archangel since 1815.

Thus the religious activity in the colonies was divided among four men. The priest at the Church of St. Michael at New Archangel was in charge of the colonial capital on Sitkha Island and the neighboring redoubts of Ozerskoi and Stakhina. The parish of Kad'iak and the Church of the Resurrection was comprised of the settlements located on Kad'iak and the neighboring islands, on Aliaska Peninsula, and in Kenai Bay and Chugach Bay. The priest at Unalashka had charge of Fox and Pribylov islands and redoubts Aleksandrovskii and Mikhailovskii. The Church of the Ascension on Unalashka was built in 1825. The parishioners of the Church of St. Nicholas on Atkha Island, built in 1827, included the inhabitants of the Andreanov, Rat, Near, Komandorskie, and Kurile islands. The board of directors had proposed that a church be built in the Kurile Islands, but the small population there, ninety-nine natives and a little over one hundred Aleuts and Russians, was insufficient to warrant their separation from Atkha parish. A priest went to the Kurile Islands from Atkha every two years in order to carry out the necessary duties. By 1839 the total number of Christians in the colonies had reached 10,561, including 734 Russians, 1,295 creoles, and 8,532 natives.

In addition to the above-mentioned priests, Friar German of the first religious mission remained on Spruce [Elovoi] Island until his death in 1837, devoting his labors to educating a few Aleut children and to the Christian edification of those natives who came to him.

Besides the four churches in the colonies, there were also several chapels located in remote places, particularly in the Unalashka parish. Here the inhabitants gathered on holy days for prayer, and the liturgy and sacraments were performed when priests visited these places.

The churches and chapels were built and remodeled at company expense. "Each church," writes Veniaminov,[2]

is built with fitting splendor, despite the difficulty of obtaining materials, and provided quite adequately with church plate and a sacristy.

The churches and chapels are maintained from church revenues, which are provided from the sale of candles and from voluntary offerings. These revenues are quite substantial in some churches.

The housing and salary of the priests and sacristans is provided by the Russian-American Company. The sacristans, chosen from the local natives, receive the same salary as other company employees.

The company also pays for the passage of the priests to and from the colonies.

Since each priest, particularly those of Kadiak, Unalashka and Atkha, is obliged to make a circuit of his parish each year in order to visit the inhabitants of the remoter places, the means necessary to make these trips, such as baidarkas with paddles, tents, etc., are also obtained from the Russian-American Company.

Until 1840 the colonial churches were under the control of the Irkutsk diocese. The bishop of Irkutsk gave the first colonial priests special missionary instructions for their guidance. Each priest reported directly to him.

In his survey of religious work among the natives, Veniaminov found the best qualities and most outstanding characteristics and greatest receptiveness to Christian teaching among the baptized Kolosh in the

Sitkha Parish.[3] They were then quite few,[4] twenty souls in all, but the exemplary life of each of them could serve as a guaranty of the future success of the spread of God's word among his people. "Although now [in 1839] there are still only twenty baptized Kolosh," wrote Veniaminov,[5]

> in general they fulfill their obligations to the church quite well. They always attend church when they can, fast and willingly listen to instruction. Except for toion Ionki, who was baptized in former times and does not count here and of whom there is hope that he will yet return, none has reverted to the rites of his former faith. On the contrary, the activity and industry character-istic of all the Kolosh may serve as an example to the Aleuts and creoles, who are not overly active, and their orderly lives may inspire conviction in their Kolosh brethren. I have always been cheered and gladdened by their intelli-gent conversations at confession (the Kolosh, particularly the women, learn Russian very rapidly).

In Veniaminov's opinion, some of the main obstacles to the conver-sion of the Kolosh were the unenviable mode of life of the Christian Aleuts in New Archangel and the firm opinion of the Kolosh that the Aleuts were previously as independent as themselves, but with Chris-tianity had become the slaves of the Russians, "even though the Ale-uts," added Veniaminov,

> live in their own territory, it must be admitted, more independently and more freely than the Kamchadals and even the converted natives of Siberia.[6] Here there is no fur tribute, consequently no tribute collectors, no coercers. The Aleuts are a patient and a mild people: as a result, they have neither courts of law nor criminal investigations, neither judges nor investigative magistrates, whose wages and traveling expenses often have to be paid at the expense of the innocent.[7]

Moreover, Veniaminov attributed the slow increase in the baptism of Koloshes so far to the fact that, until the smallpox epidemic in the colonies, no one had attempted to convert them, let alone the fact that persuading them was very difficult. Veniaminov, battling their prejudices by preaching God's word, always waited for their own free acceptance of Holy Baptism and also asked the permission of the con-vert's chiefs and relatives.[8] In any case, despite the very few converts, Veniaminov found a vast difference in the characteristics and ways of the Kolosh living on Sitkha Island in 1804 when New Archangel was founded and those living there in 1836 and 1837,[9] and firmly hoped that the spread of God's word among these people would bring about a new and beneficial change in their nature.

Of the 6,338 Christians belonging to the Kad'iak Parish, Veniaminov computed from of the reports of the Kad'iak office that there were 514 Russians and creoles, 1,719 Kad'iak islanders proper living in thirty-six settlements, 1,628 Kenais living in twenty-nine settlements, 2,006 inhabitants of Aliaksa Peninsula living in fifteen settlements, and 471 Chugaches living in six settlements.

Everyone has agreed that of all these natives the Kad'iak islanders were the most lax in fulfillment of their Christian duties. Veniaminov attributed this not to their obstinacy or cruelty, but solely to the fact that they had less opportunity than others to apply their Christian teaching. Their attitude toward Christianity was certainly affected most unfavorably by the brevity of Archimandrite Ioasaf's stay among them, the disagreement between the members of the first mission and the colonial government (which has been mentioned above), and the hardly irreproachable life of Hieromonk Afanasii, who remained among them after the other missionaries had left Kad'iak. These effects could only be counteracted by replacing Afanasii with another teacher and consequently presenting the natives with better examples than they had previously had the opportunity to see. This view was fully justified in a short time.

The Unalashka Parish consisted of 254 Russians and creoles, and 1,497 Aleuts, known as Fox islanders.

Veniaminov fully credited Hieromonk Makarii, a member of the first religious mission, with the final conversion of these Fox islanders, which had begun with the first visits of Russian hunters to Unalashka and the neighboring islands around 1760. On the other hand, he stated that these Aleuts "believed in and prayed to an unknown God until a priest lived constantly among them,"[10] because of the brevity of Father Makarii's visit and the absence of good translators who could explain the most elementary ideas of the faith to the new converts. Of course, if the baptism of the Unalashka islanders and their Aleut neighbors without any explanation of its significance could be called conversion to Christianity, this would certainly have to be attributed to Father Makarii. But, be that as it may, their true conversion to the Orthodox faith, particularly to the degree it was afterwards realized, belongs fully to their teacher, Father Veniaminov. His excellent knowledge of the native language, in which he sharply differed from the other priests who preached in that country; his translation of the catechism, sacred history, the Gospel of St. Matthew, a portion of Luke, and the Acts of the Apostles; and his compilation in the same language of all teachings concerning Christian duties significantly advanced the religious education and moral perfection of the inhabitants of

Unalashka and the neighboring islands in comparison with other natives. "When they (the Aleuts) saw books in their own language, the
catechism which I had translated and printed in its first edition," writes
Veniaminov, "even the old men began to learn the alphabet in order to
read in their own language (therefore more than one-sixth of them
know how to read now."[11] We must assume that their characteristic
receptivity also facilitated this, or as Veniaminov puts it, "the cause of
the rapid and true conversion of the Aleuts to Christianity must be
sought in their character and disposition."[12] Without an experienced
and zealous leader the teaching of the Christian faith would surely not
have enjoyed such success among them. "Of all the good qualities of
the Aleuts, none so pleased and delighted my heart," wrote Veniaminov, "as their enthusiasm or, more properly speaking, their thirst
for hearing the word of God, so that the most tireless preacher would
become weary long before their interest and enthusiasm for hearing
the word would weaken."[13] Veniaminov continued,

> The Aleuts perform their church obligations in an exemplary fashion.[14] In
> church and in prayer they stand with astonishing steadfastness. During the
> course of the service, even if it be four hours long, as for example in the first
> days of Holy Week, all of them, even the children, stand without shifting from
> one leg to the other, so that when they leave the church, it is possible to count
> the attendance by looking at the places where they had been standing. I will
> not say many, but some of the Aleuts pray and know how to pray. I do not
> mean to imply merely that they know how to make the sign of the cross and
> kneel and speak certain words of prayer. No! Some of them know how to pray
> from their hearts and do not show off in front of other men or in the church,
> but frequently enter *their storeroom and close the door.*[15]

That the Aleuts improved morally from the time a priest remained
continually among them, that is from 1824, is also clear from the fact
that through 1827 there were at least seven children born out of
wedlock of the thirty-four Aleuts born; but from 1827 through 1839
the number of births was around forty, and none of these was out of
wedlock.[16]

Netsvetov, the priest of the Atkha church, added explanations in
his parishioners' dialect to Veniaminov's translations of the scriptures
into the Unalashka language, since there was some dialectal difference
between the two tongues. Moreover, he translated into the Atkha
dialect the first chapter of the Gospel according to St. Luke and the
first two chapters of the Acts of the Apostles, with an explanation for
the Unalashka islanders.

Of the 782 Christians belonging to the Atkha Parish in 1840, there were 195 Russians and creoles, and 378 Aleuts. As mentioned above, this parish also included 99 Kurile islanders and 104 Kad'iak islanders, and 9 Russians living in the Kurile Islands.

Until the arrival of a real priest, Veniaminov observed, the Atkha islanders were not outstanding for their zeal toward the faith, although they were identical to the Unalashka islanders in character and disposition. "In recent times," he wrote, "all the reliable eyewitnesses unanimously agree that the Atkha islanders are exemplary Christians."[17]

Christian natives living in Aleksandrovskii and Mikhailovskii redoubts and neighboring places did not have their own parish nor belong to any of the American churches, since the Kad'iak priest, whose parishioners spoke the same language as these natives, could not possibly visit them because of the vastness of his parish, spreading over 1,500 versts, whereas the Unalashka priest could visit them only rarely.

With the founding of Aleksandrovskii redoubt on the Nushagak River Christianity was established there, although, because there was no priest, to a very limited extent. The redoubt commander Kalmykov, only baptized eight natives in almost ten years. Father Veniaminov further distinguished himself by spreading the word of God in those regions, having asked permission of the Bishop of Irkutsk to preach the Christian faith in the nothern part of the colonies.

Veniaminov made his first trip to the Nushagak River in 1829 and baptized thirteen of the fourteen natives who were then in the settlement. It is remarkable that, by Veniminov's order, the new converts received no gifts except small copper crosses, not even the white shirts which were customarily given at the font. His aim, of course, was to avoid prompting the natives to be christened from motives of gain, since a shirt was a valuable object for them. The frauds perpetrated in the past by the Chukchi trying in similar circumstances to obtain a few gifts forced Veniaminov to take extraordinary precautions in converting the natives. To avert any impure motive in carrying out such an important matter as Holy Baptism, he abolished this custom, which was so widespread, particularly among the Russians. He also imposed this condition on everyone who baptized natives by their request before a priest had taught them.

On his second visit to the Nushagak in 1832 Veniaminov anointed and gave communion to seventy more men whom Kolmakov had baptized in his absence. Baron Wrangell, the governor of the colonies, who was also present, immediately ordered the completion there of a chapel for common worship.

Those who had joined in 1829, learning of Veniaminov's arrival at the fort, soon came to him, some bringing their families, requesting that he baptize them too, which of course he did not refuse.

Subsequently, Kolmakov, his son, and Father Golovnin, who visited Nushagak in 1838, baptized another 105 converts there. Finally, Father Veniaminov baptized four toions who had voluntarily come to Sitkha from the area lying north of Aleksandrovskii redoubt to be baptized. Thus, by 1840 the number of Christians in the northern part of the colonies, not counting forty Russians and creoles, had grown to 220 according to official records, and reached 320 including those not recorded. In character and other qualities Veniaminov found them very similar to the Aleuts, valuing in particular their desire, not shared by other natives, to accept Holy Baptism without any mercenary motives.

The number of schools in the colonies for native children had grown to eight by 1840, namely four schools for one hundred boys and the same number of schools for girls.

During Murav'ev's governorship of the colonies, the directors instructed him to reopen the Kad'iak girl's school. He ordered a building set aside for this purpose for girls from five to ten years of age, principally the daughters of Russians who had left the children behind in the colonies without means of support. As the head of this school, Murav'ev appointed one of the promyshlenniks' wives, who was a good housekeeper well versed in needlework. Murav'ev also ordered the reopening of the widows' shelter for homeless, elderly widows, particularly those whose husbands had died in the company's service. The colonial reports show that in 1827 there were three boys' schools in the colonies: in New Archangel, in Kad'iak, and in Unalashka. In 1839 the girls' school was moved to New Archangel. All of these schools and homes were maintained at the company's expense.

In his report to the Holy Synod[18] Father Veniaminov attributed the successful spread of Christianity in the colonies "to the blessed cooperation of the Russian-American Company, which has spared neither effort nor expense in this matter." He further reported that the four priests then residing in the colonies were too few to teach the natives and to guide and sustain the many new converts. Also insufficient, because of the remoteness of the country and the wide dispersal of the company and native settlements, were the means to maintain and provide for the priests and other clergy serving in the colonies. In his opinion the following measures were necessary to attain success in this task, which had been so well begun: increase the number of churches in the colonies, form a permanent mission in North America, assign clergy and missionaries, and form an archdeaconate responsible to the dioceasan bishop.

The Holy Synod, finding Archpriest Veniaminov's opinion well founded and consistent with the actual and special needs of the colonial church, above all thought it necessary to give full credit to the Russian-American Company for its good works in contributing to the growth of the Orthodox faith in a land darkened by paganism. Hoping that the company would continue to support the spread of Christian enlightenment in America, it proposed:

1. To establish a cathedral of St. Michael the Archangel in New Archangel with the necessary clergy and a religious school, leaving the other colonial churches with their former staff. Moreover, to organize two traveling churches, assigning to each one missionary priest and the appropriate clerical staff to each of them.

2. The senior priest of the New Archangel cathedral was to be the provost over all the churches and clergy in America and, in general, to supervise all church matters. Since the colonial church was remote from the seat of the diocesan bishop and could not be subject to his immediate control, the provost was to be provided with special instructions precisely defining the rights, obligations, and all relations of the clergy.

Since this reorganization of the colonial church would require an increase in expenditures, the Holy Synod asked the directors to state precisely what the company could contribute for the maintenance of the churches and clergy in America, so that the Holy Synod could further consider this matter.

The directors replied that the company would be willing to assume at its own expense (1) the board of the priests at the Cathedral and the three churches, in the amount of 4,648 silver rubles 85 kopeks; (2) the payment of the school teachers, to the amount of 800 silver rubles; (3) traveling expenses for church work and missions, in the amount of 1,042 silver rubles; (4) the salary of priests and clergy after five years, in the amount of 650 silver rubles yearly; (5) the passages of church members and missions to the colonies and return; (6) the heating of the clergy's quarters; and (7) the construction and repair of the churches. In the opinion of the directors the church's own revenues would cover the maintenance and decoration of the churches and expenditures for the tents and other needs of the traveling churches. This obligated the government to provide the following sums: (1) 2,406 silver rubles for the salary of the clergy, (2) 2,040 rubles for the board of the two missions, and (3) maintenance of the church school.

In addition to the sum of 7,142 silver rubles 85 kopeks provided under the first five points undertakings, the directors gave the colonial church for the expenses of the local churches 6,300 silver rubles accumulated from offerings to the church in the colonies.

Before deciding on this matter, the Holy Synod thought it necessary to ask the directors whether the company would agree "to place at the synod's disposal part of the sums it had pledged for application to other more necessary purposes that might arise in connection with the construction of new churches in the colonies."

When the directors agreed, the Holy Synod informed the company that, besides the matter of building churches in the colonies, it had decided to establish a special diocese consisting of the American churches and those of the Kamchatka and Okhotsk districts, the head to be called the Bishop of Kamchatka, the Kurile Islands, and the Aleutians. The synod also wrote that the establishment of this diocese had been confirmed by the emperor, and that Archpriest Ioann Veniaminov, who had been designated provost of the colonial churches, was to be consecrated as its first bishop, with the consent of the emperor and the blessing of the Holy Synod.

Later, the emperor also approved the Holy Synod's proposals on establishing and building the new cathedral and the diocesan bishop's duties and sphere of activity. In conformity with the needs of the country and the means at hand, the sums pledged by the company were augmented with 1,000 silver rubles per year from the funds of the Office of Religion and Education to maintain schools in the colonies. During his journey through other dioceses His Eminence was permitted to choose suitable men who wished to enter the service of his diocese to serve as priests in the new cathedral and in the churches and missions of the colonies.

Since it was inconvenient to establish a consistory immediately, the three local priests at New Archangel became the church administration for conducting the formal affairs of the eparchy and carrying out, as far as possible, the duties of a consistory. According to the circumstances and needs of the country, the religious school which was to be established in New Archangel was to accept both the children of priests and sacristans and those of laymen, particularly newly baptized natives. One of this school's aims was to improve the religious education of the native parochial clergy. Where there was no school the parish priests were to instill the beginnings of religious education and the elementary domestic instruction of the children. The Holy Synod also provided that legal judgments against the natives should be very simple and very mild, circumspect, and convincingly fair. The bishop was given permission to accept into the parochial clergy capable and reliable baptized natives and creoles who were under the company's jurisdiction on proper terms with the colonial administration, and with the permission of the administration.

At the end of 1840 Father Veniaminov, renamed Innokentii when he assumed the monastic life, was consecrated bishop, and in January 1841, set out for his post. In the same year a seminary was founded in New Archangel in place of the religious school.

The further labors of Bishop Innokentii in spreading the word of God in the colonies, and also the works of other Russian missionaries in that country, will be covered in the survey of the last period of the company's charter.

The smallpox epidemic in the colonies. One of the outstanding oc-curences in the second period of the company's charter was the small-pox epidemic that produced dreadful devastation in the native popula-tion for almost three years, from 1837 to 1839. Despite the vigorous efforts of the colonial administration to prevent smallpox, it spread with terrible rapidity from the borders of California, along the north-west coast of America as far as the Arctic Ocean, and was transmitted from the Indian tribes living in the interior of the American continent to the natives of Kad'iak and Unalashka. In November 1836 smallpox appeared in New Archangel and, despite the best efforts of Doctor Bliashke, the company physician, it gradually spread without regard to sex or age or race. It affected elderly people in particular, and they generally became victims of the disease if they were in the least careless. It was less serious for children. The Kolosh, who had stubbornly re-sisted vaccination, died in whole families at the first appearance of the epidemic, and after three months, four hundred or about half of an en-tire village near New Archangel had perished. Only one Russian, how-ever, took ill, and then only for a short time. In March the disease began slowly to abate, and by April it had completely disappeared. It is interesting to note that the epidemic did not act everywhere with the same intensity. For example, in the neighborhood of the Stakhina River it was quite harmless, and none of the inhabitants of Fort Diony-sius, nor the crew of the company schooner *Chil'kat*, which was sta-tioned there at that time, were affected. In Khutsnov and other Kolosh settlements along Vancouver Straits smallpox devastated some bara-boras [native dwellings] to the last man.

To prevent the disease by vaccination and to give aid to those who had fallen ill in the Kad'iak district, the colonial governor sent to Kad'-iak one of the physicians of the New Archangel hospital, Staff Doctor Volynskii, and three experienced assistants, whom the doctor sent to various parts of the island. The number of victims taken daily by the epidemic increased because the Kad'iak islanders stubbornly refused to take any advice or be vaccinated. They used every possible trick and ruse to avoid it. Some of the natives—736 on Kad'iak alone—died without accepting any medical help. On Aliaska Peninsula, before one of Volynskii's assistants could arrive, the baidarshchik [foreman] Kostylev succeeded in vaccinating 243 natives with smallpox vaccine which he had obtained from the localities where this operation had first been carried out. Thanks to his intelligent foresight, the disease took only twenty-seven natives, who would not be convinced of the necessity of vaccination and had taken no precautions to avoid the disease. As the epidemic approached the Unalashka district, Doctor Bliashke was sent there. His smallpox vaccinations were a remarkable success: 1,086 natives were vaccinated in the various settlements of this section.[19] Of the natives who fell ill only 130 died. Vaccinations were also given to the natives of Kenai Bay and Chugach Bay and Aleksandrovskii and Mikhailovskii redoubts.[20] Throughout the colonies more than four thousand persons were vaccinated. The epidemic finally died out in the colonies in 1840.

Although the majority of natives refused to take the sensible precautionary measures proposed by the colonial medical staff, the chief cause of the rapid spread of the epidemic was no doubt due to the style of life and habits of the Aleuts and Kolosh, which greatly aided the transmission of this disease from one victim to another. Stuffy and often remarkably untidy dwellings, filthy clothing, and intemperance in diet persisted despite the colonial administration's admonitions and efforts, and paralyzed all the endeavors of the most energetic philanthropy. However difficult it was for the colonial administration to see all its persuasion and pains so stubbornly resisted by the Kad'iak islanders and Kolosh, especially at the beginning of the epidemic, it was subsequently rewarded by the fact that its solicitude finally struck a response in many of the natives, including those who had previously opposed it most strongly. Convinced of the necessity of vaccination by the fact that smallpox had not touched the Russians and Aleuts who had been vaccinated, many of the Kolosh and Kad'iak islanders began to approach the company medical staff with requests for aid, and from this time a significant change appeared in their relations with the Russians. The very beginning of the spread of Christianity among the Kolosh, according to Veniaminov, was a necessary result of the awareness, gained by bitter experience, of the superiority of Russian ideas. Until the beginning of the epidemic the shamans had enjoyed unquestionable authority in all spheres of Kolosh life, but doubt concerning the usefulness of incantations and other means which they used to try to avert the epidemic was the first step in the gradual assimilation of truths which the natives had previously rejected with such stubbornness. The contacts between some of the Kolosh and Russians that naturally followed consummated the matter and led to voluntary acceptance of Christian teaching. Some of them even became zealous disciples.[21]

Improvements in the living conditions of the Kad'iak Aleuts. The results of the smallpox epidemic were felt most acutely on Kad'iak Island. Most of the native families lost their chief providers. The company found itself responsible for many widows and elderly, who could not earn their own bread. In general, the Kad'iak district was in a terrible condition after the epidemic, and the board of directors considered it obligatory to take immediate measures to improve the living conditions of the natives of this section in accordance with their needs and ways of life and in agreement with the recommendations of the colonial medical staff and other reliable company employees who had had the opportunity to visit the remotest settlements during the epidemic.

Captain of Second Rank Etholen, who became colonial governor in 1840, energetically undertook this task, and by the middle of 1844 the Kad'iak islanders were unified into common settlements, on the example of the Atkha and Unalashka islanders.[22] The sixty-five places in which the Aleuts had been living or, rather, from which they had been leading a nomadic life over all of Kad'iak and the surrounding islands, were consolidated into seven settlements located at Three Saints Bay, Orlov, Karluk, and Afognak odinochkas, and on Woody Island. The total population of the settlements was 1,375 Aleuts. In addition, one hundred Aleuts lived at the permanent artel' [trading post] on Ukamok [Chirikov] Island. In place of the former low, stuffy, and dirty *zhupan*, large, spacious, and well-lighted *kazhims*[23] were built at company expense. High and dry sites were chosen for these dwellings, and all measures were taken to maintain constant cleanliness in and around the settlements. In addition to the kazhims, various other buildings were erected in these settlements: storehouses for keeping food stuffs; and sheds for baidaras, baidarkas, and all of the Aleuts' hunting supplies, and for livestock. One or two large baidaras, depending on the population were assigned to each settlement. Company cattle were distributed among the settlements and the seeds of various garden vegetables were sent from New Archangel in order to introduce the Aleuts to the benefits of cattle breeding and gardening, which offered a reliable food supply when fish could not be caught, and also brought the natives to a sedentary life. Moreover, measures were taken to care for aged natives and the orphans of Aleuts who had died from smallpox. The company provided them with clothing and many other goods. For the other natives buckskin parkas and *kuklianki* (a kind of *kamleika*, usually sewn from deerskins) were ordered from Okhotsk and Kamchatka and were distributed among the Aleuts at their cost to the company, without any additional charge for freight.

The gathering of the Kad'iak Aleuts into larger settlements was particularly important because it was easier for the local administration to ascertain at all times whether the natives had received from the baidarshchiks and toions full payment for the furs they sold to the company. In the past, because of the wide dispersal of the settlements, it had not always been possible to check this. Moreover, the consolidation of the Aleuts made possible more frequent visits to the settlements by priests, both to administer sacraments and to teach the law of God, which was particularly necessary for the Kad'iak Section because of the character of its inhabitants.

An increase in prices paid to the natives for furs. Even before the smallpox epidemic, one of the company's measures undertaken to improve the natives' living standard was an increase in the prices paid for furs obtained either by using company equipment or independently. The latter rate was one-third higher for the various types of furs taken.

Here we present a comparative table of the rates paid from the early period to the present day.

	Prices According to the Rates Established in the Indicated Year, in Paper Rubles							
FURS	*1804*		*1827*		*1836*		*1850*	
Sea animals	*r.*	*k.*	*r.*	*k.*	*r.*	*k.*	*r.*	*k.*
Adult sea otters, male and female, per pelt . . .	10	—	20	—	30	—	50	—
Young sea otters.	4	—	10	—	15	—	25	—
Prime sea otter pups . .	—	60	2	—	3	—	3	—
Ordinary sea otter pups	—	60	1	—	1	—	1	—
Fur seals, adult bulls and young bulls	—	20	—	50	—	75	—	75
Grey fur seals in general	—	20	—	40	—	50	—	50
Amphibious animals								
River beavers								
1st grade and larger. . . .	1	20	2	50	4	—	4	—
2nd grade, medium								

Prices According to the Rates
Established in The Indicated Year, in Paper Rubles

FURS	1804		1827		1836		1850	
Sea animals	r.	k.	r.	k.	r.	k.	r.	k.
prime and large summer	1	20	2	—	3	—	3	—
3rd grade, small prime and medium	1	20	1	50	2	—	2	—
4th grade, prime pups and small	1	20	1	—	1	--	1	—
Otters								
1st grade or large prime	1	60	3	20	4	60	6	—
2nd grade, medium prime and large summer	1	60	2	40	3	20	5	—
3rd grade, small prime and medium summer..	1	60	1	—	2	—	3	—
4th grade, prime pups and small summer.....	1	60	—	50	1	—	1	—
Products of Sea and Amphibious Animals								
Whale bone, per pud ..	—	75	1	—				
Walrus ivory								
1st grade, per pud.....	—	75	4	—				
2nd grade, per pud	—	75	3	—				
Perineal glands [castors] of beaver								
1st grade, per 10 pairs .	3	—	4	—				
2nd grade, per 10 pairs...............	3	—	3	—				
Island animals								
Silver foxes								
1st grade prime	2	—	6	—	6	—	9	—
2nd grade large, not fully furred	2	—	3	—	3	—	3	—
3rd grade medium summer pups	1	—	1	50	1	—	1	—

*Prices According to the Rates
Established in The Indicated Year, in Paper Rubles*

FURS	1804		1827		1836		1850	
Sea animals	r.	k.	r.	k.	r.	k.	r.	k.
Cross foxes								
1st grade prime	—	80	3	—	4	—	6	—
2nd grade not fully furred large summer . . .	—	80	1	50	2	—	2	—
3rd grade medium summer pups	—	80	—	75	—	75	—	75
Red foxes								
1st grade prime	—	40	2	—	2	—	3	—
2nd grade not fully furred, large, summer . .	—	40	1	—	1	—	1	—
3rd grade pups	—	40	—	50	—	50	—	50
Arctic foxes								
Blue	—	20	1	—	1	—		
Young blue	—	20	—	50	—	50		
White	—	8	—	20	—	20		
Young white	—	8	—	10	—	10		
Muskrats								
Whole prime					—	20	—	50
Mainland animals								
Silver foxes								
High grade					9	—	12	—
1st grade prime	3	—	4	—	6	—	9	—
2nd grade not fully furred large summer . . .	3	—	2	—	3	—	3	—
3rd grade medium summer pups	3	—	1	—	1	—	1	—
Cross foxes								
1st grade prime	1	—	3	—	4	—	6	—
2nd grade not fully furred large summer . . .	1	—	1	50	2	—	2	—
3rd grade pups	1	—	—	75	—	75	—	75

Prices According to the Rates
Established in The Indicated Year, in Paper Rubles

FURS	1804		1827		1836		1850	
Sea animals	r.	k.	r.	k.	r.	k.	r.	k.
Red foxes								
1st grade prime	—	75	1	50	2	—	3	—
2nd grade not fully furred large summer ...	—	75	—	75	1	—	1	—
3rd grade pups	—	75	—	40	—	50	—	50
Sables								
Whole prime	—	20	—	50	—	50	1	—
Torn and in clothing ..	—	20	—	50	—	50	—	50
Summer	—	20	—	40	—	40	—	40
Wolves								
Prime	1	—	1	—	2	—	4	—
Summer	1	—	1	—	1	—	3	—
Bears								
Large black	2	—	4	—	*		5	—
Medium prime and large summer........	2	—	3	—	*		4	—
Small prime and summer medium	2	—	2	—	*		2	—
Cubs prime and small summer	2	—	1	—	*		2	—
Lynx								
Large prime........	—	80	3	—	3	—	5	—
Medium prime	—	80	2	—	2	—	3	—
Small prime........	—	80	1	—	1	—	2	—
Wolverines								
Large prime........	—	80	2	—	2	—	4	—
Medium	—	80	1	—	1	—	3	—
Minks								
Prime	—	20	—	30	—	25	—	50
Summer	—	20	—	15	not accepted			

*In 1836 the schedule of tariffs provided for payment according to quality
rather than according to size.

It should be observed that the prices which the Russian-American Company paid to the Kolosh for furs were almost double those set out in the tariff schedules. The proximity of the boundaries between the domains of the Russian-American Company and the Hudson's Bay Company produced a price competition for furs obtained from the natives, causing the Russian-American Company to pay the Kolosh prices which would make the English trade unprofitable. Of course, in establishing the prices, the fact that a sea otter cost much less in England than it did in Russia was taken into consideration. On this basis the Kolosh were paid 140 to 154 silver rubles in goods or money for a sea otter; 2 to 18 rubles for a beaver; 2 to 18 for an otter; 2 to 36 for a mainland silver fox; 3 to 18 for a mainland cross fox; 2 rubles 50 kopeks to 6 rubles for a mainland red fox; 50 kopeks to 3 rubles for a sable; 2 rubles 50 kopeks to 5 rubles for a wolf; 3 rubles 60 kopeks to 9 rubles for a lynx; 2 rubles 50 kopeks to 5 rubles for a wolverine; 1 ruble 50 kopeks to 18 rubles for a bear; and 45 kopeks for a mink or a muskrat.

The state of the fur trade in the colonies and the export of furs during the second period of the company's charter. A significant decrease in the fur catch occurred during the second period of the company's charter. It is obvious that the continual hunting to which all kinds of fur-bearing animals had been long subjected would have inevitably led to extinction for some species if strict protective measures had not been taken in time, even though these measures were, of necessity, detrimental to the chief source of the company's annual revenue. Prudence could be justified most easily in the case of fur seals. By the beginning of the 1830s their numbers had decreased sharply, compared not only with earlier times, but with even a few years before.

Under these circumstances, the board of directors ordered Baron Wrangell to enforce certain rules in the colonial fur trade. The catch of fur seals, in the strictest sense, was not to affect their present numbers and, insofar as possible, was to be limited to permit their future increase, despite any other requirements, including the profit from their sale. On this basis general hunting on St. Paul Island, one of the main fur seal rookeries, was stopped. In order to improve breeding conditions some of the oldest males, the bulls, which usually control herds of females and prevent the younger males, the bachelors, from approaching, were killed. It should be noted that this plan to some degree, coincided with the opinion of the old hunters, who thought that neglect of the fur seal herds for long periods was ineffective, a view which seems to be confirmed by recent local observations to the effect that too many old males harmed breeding conditions. The decision was to kill only a limited number of two- and three-year old bachelors each year. This experiment was very successful. In 1841 about eight thousand fur seals were taken from St. Paul Island without any risk to the herd, since all observations showed that the number of fur seals hunted in any one year was compensated for by a slight increase in population in the same period. When fur seal hunting was reopened on St. Paul Island, hunting was stopped on Bering and Copper islands, where the fur seals had begun to disappear with alarming rapidity. On St. George Island only the bachelors could be killed, the cows being protected. In this way the subsequent annual export of fur seals would be brought gradually into balance with the rate of their population increase.

The decreased export of fur seals from the colonies in the 1830s was offset by an increase in the availability of river beavers caused by expanded relations between the company and the natives inhabiting the region of the Kuskokvim and Kvikhpak rivers and the lands to the east bordering on Hudson's Bay Company territory. Although the coastal strip that had been leased to the Hudson's Bay Company deprived the Russian-American Company of some river beavers that the natives brought down from the English possessions, this loss was made up by the lease payments: two thousand sea-otter pelts and the right to purchase an additional five thousand. This facilitated the company's barter for tea at Kiakhta, since these pelts commanded a very good price on the Chinese market.

Although there had been no appreciable decline in the export of sea otters from the colonies, because the hunters had moved successively from place to place over a line of outposts along the entire Pacific Coast of the Russian possessions, it could be assumed that the otters would shortly become extinct or at least considerably diminished. The measures of the colonial administration to prevent the natives from destroying these animals indiscriminately, such as refusing to barter for pelts taken too young, and strict sorting of the furs, did not always solve the problems. The obvious decrease in the otter catch of the Kurile Islands forced the company to seek new sources of supply.

In 1832 an effort was made to send hunting parties to places where otters had been plentiful in former times, that is, to L'tua and Yakutat bays, but this attempt proved completely unsuccessful. Failures followed in Trinidad Bay and finally off the shores of Kamchatka, where sea otters were rumored to abound. The chief source of the company's revenue was threatened with almost inevitable extinction. The directors were puzzled as to where to turn next. Fortunately, an increase in the number of sea otters in the Kurile Islands, after their acquisition had virtually ceased for several years, renewed the company's hopes.

Moreover, the introduction of steamboats into the colonies made it possible to conduct a more active barter for all furs, particularly sea otters obtained from the Kolosh living on the Russian borders. This trade was particularly important then because of the need to maintain the Russian trading monopoly among those natives with whom the Hudson's Bay Company had no right to trade, according to the terms of the recently concluded treaty. The steamship *Nikolai I* therefore visited all the main native settlements in the neighborhood of New Archangel in 1840 and 1841 and obtained a good profit for the company. The numerous furs obtained during the ship's voyage through the Kolosh Straits was encouraging, but even more important was the close contact with the Kolosh that resulted in greater influence over them.

Local observations on Kad'iak Island showed a decrease in all kinds of land and amphibious animals, particularly sea otters, seals, and foxes, but also birds, probably caused by the use of firearms in hunting. This prompted the colonial government to prohibit this practice and to discontinue all kinds of hunting for several years.

In order to increase the supply of silver foxes and blue polar foxes, which were so profitable to the company, the directors instructed the colonial governor to transplant breeding stocks of these animals to uninhabited islands where they might find food.[24]

The total number of furs and other products exported from the colonies from 1821 through 1842 was as follows:

Sea otters	25,416	White arctic foxes	13,638
Otter tails	23,506	Blue arctic foxes	55,714
Fur seals	458,502	Bears	5,355
Whalebone	3,455 puds 10 lbs.	Lynx	4,253
Otter	29,442	Wolverine	1,564
Silver foxes	17,913	Mink	15,481
Cross foxes	26,462	Sable	15,666
Red foxes	45,947	Muskrats	4,491
Walrus tusks	6,501 puds 6 lbs.	Wolves	201
Beavers	162,034	Castoreum	124 puds 16 lbs.

Whaling in the colonies. The minister of finance ordered the directors to initiate whaling and fishing around the shores of Kamchatka in order to secure a food supply for the local inhabitants and to prevent foreigners from fishing and bartering with the natives. In 1821 the board of directors asked the Russian consuls in England and Holland to ascertain the cost of fully equipping a whaling ship. However, the company never completed its intention of fitting out its own whaling vessels, probably because of a shortage of funds. In 1826 Chistiakov, the chief manager, informed the directors that it would be useful to send to the colonies a man familiar with whaling, since whale meat constituted one of the chief items of the Aleuts' diet and the colonies frequently suffered from a shortage of fat, which was used to grease baidaras, and to provide fuel for lamps. This proposal was carried out by Chistiakov's successor, Baron Wrangell, who ordered Captain-Lieutenant Etholen to engage an experienced harpooner on one of his visits to California. The American Barton came to New Archangel for that purpose on a company ship in 1833. He was engaged not only to catch whales himself, but to instruct designated personnel in steering whale boats and melting down blubber. All of Barton's activities, in Sitkha Bay, on Kad'iak and Unalashka, and in Nuchek [Boswell] Bay, were unsuccessful. Much more fruitful were the age-old methods of the Aleuts, who shot whales with darts and then waited for them to be washed ashore. Furthermore, the strange belief among the hunters that harpoons only frightened the whales, and the hunters' consequent indifference to whaling expeditions forced the colonial administration to suspend whaling, particularly since Barton's contract with the company was almost completed. In order to encourage the natives in their own whaling, chief manager Etholen doubled the price which the company paid for a whale and appropriately awarded the teacher of each new whale hunter who proved his worth in the chase by obtaining at least three whales. Occasional sperm whales were also taken in the colonies; in 1843 a sperm whale yielding around 90 vedros of excellent spermaceti was washed ashore near a spring not far from New Archangel.

Colonial shipbuilding, the purchase of ships from foreigners, and the loss of several ships of the company fleet. Murav'ev, while chief manager, obtained two American ships for the company, called the *Okhotsk* (174 tons) [former *Lapwing*], and *Baikal* (215 tons) [former *Arab*]. In addition, two ships of around 180 tons each, the *Kiakhta* and the *Volga*, were built at Ross settlement. Murav'ev's successor, Chistiakov, also obtained from the Americans the 150-ton [*Tally-Ho*, renamed the] *Chichagov*.

To help eliminate the difficulties and dangers of carrying supplies by rowboat from the section centers to the various settlements, often remote from each other, Chistiakov proposed to construct several single-decker sailing vessels in New Archangel. These vessels were particularly useful for the colonies since they could carry Aleut hunting parties at sea and through narrow passages without subjecting them to the dangers of long voyages in baidarkas. The first of these craft, called the *Unalashka* after the area where it was built to serve, was launched in 1827. The *Bobr* [beaver], *Sivuch* [sea lion], *Karluk*, and *Aleut* were built on the same plan for service in other sections of the colonies. In

1829 the *Urup*, a 300-ton three-master, was begun in New Archangel, and by the end of that year was ready for sea. Then the directors, knowing the superior structural durability of the timber found near Okhotsk compared with the trees felled at New Archangel and Ross, ordered the Okhotsk office to reinitiate the construction of company ships. Thus the schooner *Aktsiia* (50 tons), the brig *Polifem* (180 tons), and the sloop *Sitkha* (230 tons) were built and outfitted at Okhotsk from 1829 through 1832. To take the place of the *Unalashka*, which had been detached to the Kurile district, Baron Wrangell built a 60-foot, 58-ton schooner in New Archangel. Two other schooners, the *Kvikhpak* and *Chil'kat* were built on the same plan.[25] From the year 1839 through 1841 three other vessels were also built in New Archangel: the brig *Promysel* (75 tons), and the steamship *Nikolai I* (60-horsepower) and *Mur* [Moore] (8 horsepower). The engine for the *Nikolai I* was obtained from the United States. All the engine parts, down to the last screw, for the other steamship were made in the workshops of New Archangel under the direction of the machinist Moore, after whom the ship was named. In addition, the company ordered two ships built in Abo in 1837 for round-the-world expeditions, the 400-ton *Nikolai I* and the 300-ton *Naslednik Aleksandr* (Crown Prince Alexander). A brig of 190 tons was obtained overseas and called the *Velikii Kniaz'* [grand duke] *Konstantin*.

The *Karluk* was wrecked in 1830 in Uganak Bay on the northwest side of Kad'iak Island while on a voyage from Kad'iak to Katmai odinochka. The cargo and crew were saved. Although the cause of the wreck was alleged to be a violent wind, a navigational error by the skipper [*morekhod*] in command may have been partly responsible.[26] The latter supposition is quite probable, since the shortage of real captains in the colonies at that time sometimes made it necessary to entrust smaller ships on short voyages to junior officers or even the more experienced seamen.

In 1831 the *Sivuch* under the command of skipper Ingstrem was wrecked on Atkha Island. The crew was saved and all of the cargo was transported from the wreck in perfect condition in baidaras. This fortunate salvage the company owed to Ingstrem's presence of mind and excellent local knowledge. Therefore it is fitting to present a few details of the incident. As the *Sivuch* left Korovin Bay, she was struck by a strong wind, which forced Ingstrem to remain under storm sail and lie to in darkness. Dawn revealed the vessel almost in the surf of Kan iuga Island. Although the vessel escaped under forced sail, the waves breaking across the deck shattered the washboards.[27] In this condition and with the ever increasing wind, the craft had no possibility of rounding the capes and returning to the inlet, since it might have broken up on either of them with no hope of saving the crew. Then Ingstrem decided to enter one of the coves on the east side of the nearer cape. Fortunately the boat escaped the labyrinth of rocks and held safely on one anchor and a warp [or kedge] [28] at a depth of 5 sazhens, a half cable's length [50 sazhens] from the shore. The other anchor had previously been lost at Amchitka Island, where they had been forced to cut the anchor rope in order to make sail and escape to sea in a freshening wind. Meanwhile, the storm had grown more violent, the sea was running athwart the boat and, finally, the constant jerking broke the anchor rope. The kedge was unable to hold back the ship and it was borne rapidly toward the rocks. The captain was barely able to steer to the sandy shore and when the vessel had run aground, he immediately lowered the launch and carried the crew ashore. Then he saved the cargo of furs and some of the other items aboard. Although the vessel itself could have been repaired, Baron Wrangell ordered that it be broken up and the wood and iron used for other local needs, in view of the impossibility of assigning enough men, who were at that time gathering in supplies for winter, the shortage of structural timber near the wreck, and, finally, the considerable cost of repairs.

In 1837 the company schooner *Chil'kat* under the command of Staff Captain Voronkovskii of the Corps of Naval Navigators was lost near Sitkha with its entire crew and cargo. Fragments of the schooner which washed ashore in the neighborhood of Cape Edgecumbe spoke of the terrible disaster which had overtaken her. The colonial governor sent Lieutenant Zarembo, Navigator Lindenberg, and Navigator Netsvetov to search for any survivors of the lost ship. Despite their careful inquiries of the natives and their detailed search over a wide area, during which they were exposed to many dangers, they returned empty-handed. The schooner's cargo had consisted of furs obtained from the Kurile district and various provisions sent to the colonies by the Okhotsk office. In 1839 the *Aleut* under the command of Kashevarov was driven ashore by a gale in one of the coves of Chiniat Bay. It was not badly damaged, however, and was put back into service after being repaired.

Thus, in 1842 the company fleet consisted of fifteen vessels on active sea duty and five others (*Urup, Sitkha, Kiakhta, Rurik,* and *Aktsiia*) used only for port duty because of their age, as cargo transports in the neighborhood of New Archangel, as tugs for the steamships, and on various occasions as storeships. In 1841 the *Nikolai I* was sold because ships were not needed for round-the-world-expeditions. The other ships which had been part of the company fleet according to the list of 1820 had been turned into blockships or broken up because of their complete unreliability.

10. Supplying the Colonies during the Company's Second Period and More about the Ross Settlement

The seventh round-the-world expedition under the command of Navigators Klochkov and Kislakovskii. The seventh round-the-world expedition, implemented in 1821 at the request of the Kamchatka and Okhotsk administration (see Chapter 5), in order to supply food stuffs to the colonies, was completely unsuccessful and resulted in considerable loss to the company. Two ships were assigned to this expedition: the brig *Rurik*, which had belonged to Count Rumiantsov and which he had placed at the company's disposal after its return from the voyage of exploration in the far north, and the ship *Elisaveta*, built in Hamburg. The directors entrusted the brig *Rurik* and the command of the expedition to Navigator Klochkov; Assistant Navigator Kislakovskii was placed in command of the ship *Elisaveta*. The crew of the brig *Rurik* consisted of three assistant navigators, twenty-four seamen and other lower ranks, and six hunters; the crew of the ship *Elisaveta* consisted of three assistant navigators, eighteen seamen and other lower ranks, and fourteen hunters. In addition to goods being sent to the colonies, the two ships carried 11,000 puds of rye flour, intended primarily to go to Okhotsk.

On the way to the Cape of Good Hope the expedition encountered extremely violent winds, so that for six days the ships could hardly carry even a few of their storm sails. Soon a leak appeared in the *Elisaveta* and throughout several days of stormy weather it became worse. Kislakovskii signaled that he could no longer remain at sea and asked permission of the expedition commander to put into the nearest port. However, the wind abated, permitting him to reach Simon's Bay at the Cape of Good Hope.

In order to begin repairs part of the cargo had to be removed. A shortage of funds forced Klochkov to auction off part of the cargo through an agent chosen by local custom to carry out the sale. Thus the goods had to be sold cheaply and the ship repairs had to be done in an expensive, yet ill-equipped commercial dockyard. As soon as the most essential repairs were finished, the ships put to sea. However, on the very first day the rate of leakage in the *Elisaveta* reached fifteen inches per hour, forcing the ships to return to port. An inspection showed that the *Elisaveta* was completely unsafe to sail farther, forcing its sale. The crew, except for several foreign sailors who were released, was transferred to the brig *Rurik*. The brig left the Cape of Good Hope at the end of May 1822, and on 7 November of the same year it reached New Archangel.

Because of this expedition's difficulties, the colonies obtained very few supplies. Governor Murav'ev had to keep the *Rurik* in New Archangel, rather than sending it to Kronshtadt with a cargo of furs, because it was impossible to provision the ship in the colonies for the return voyage.

Under these circumstances the directors sent additional supplies to the colonies in 1823 on the four hundred-ton ship *Elena*, purchased by Lieutenant Chistiakov for the company in New Bedford. Chistiakov had participated in the fifth expedition to the colonies and the company invited him to take command of the *Elena* for the voyage to New Archangel.

However, this voyage never took place because of a protest by Prokof'ev, manager of the company's Moscow office, who had been made a director in 1823. Prokof'ev found that the abundance of various supplies brought to New Archangel on the *Borodino, Kutuzov*, and *Rurik* made it unnecessary to send more than five hundred additional puds of goods, and it would be quite useless to outfit a special ship for such a negligible cargo. This opinion was confirmed by a general meeting of stockholders, which decided to defer outfitting a ship until a more suitable time and to send a few of the most necessary items through Okhotsk.

When news reached New Archangel that there would be no ship from Russia either in 1823 or 1824, the inhabitants of the colonies were thrown into despair, according to Murav'ev's report. Moreover, the information sent by the company commissioner in California that crop failure and other circumstances would make it impossible to obtain enough provisions there placed the colonies in an almost desperate position. Murav'ev decided to turn for help to the Sandwich Islands and placed Etholen, captain of the brig *Golovnin*, "in charge of seeking the best means of provisioning the colonies."

Despite many difficulties in obtaining food supplies in California at that time, Etholen managed to obtain there and with no custom duties involved in the exchange, for fur seals, at a price quite favorable to the company 1,900 *fanegas* of wheat and 5,000 piasters in cash. He then set out for the Sandwich Islands. Knowing that he would have to pay high prices if he bought from merchants the goods on the list given him in the colonies, Etholen decided to accept the proposal of an American, whereby he obtained the sound and well-armed 220-ton brig *Arab*, renamed the *Baikal*, which the chief manager had ordered him to purchase to augment the colonial fleet, along with its entire cargo, despite the fact that it included some items which the colonies might have done without. The American agreed to sail the ship to the colonies under the company flag and obtain there the rest of his payment in fur seals. Although Etholen had already accepted the cargo, it was secured against loss during the voyage by deducting 1½ percent from the total bill for the vessel and cargo. The company gained 243,000 rubles profit, including 44,000 paper rubles from the cargo itself, for the 36,000 fur seals which constituted the purchase price, a 25 percent profit at current prices. "It is impossible to describe the joy of the inhabitants of Sitkha Island," reported Murav'ev, "at the arrival of the vessels with their rich cargo. Now it will also be possible to barter frieze and blankets with the Kolosh for otters and other furs. Despite all of the unfavorable conditions, Etholen's commercial knowledge, zeal, and ingenuity have exceeded my expectations."

This shortage of necessities in the colonies finally persuaded the directors to dispatch a ship there hurriedly, particularly since the refusal of foreign ships to carry cargoes to the colonies prevented the colonial administration from obtaining necessary supplies, not only for their employees, but also for barter in California for provisions.

The eighth round-the-world expedition to the colonies sails under the command of Lieutenant Chistiakov and returns under the command of Murav'ev, former chief manager. The ship *Elena* was quickly prepared for a round-the-world voyage in the spring of 1824 and by July she was ready to sail. Under Chistiakov's command were lieutenants Balk, Shishmarev, and Stadol'skii; navigators Rodionov and Kristierkin, Assistant Navigator Iakovlev, Surgeon Sakharov, Commissioner Severin, and forty men of lower ranks.

Chistiakov's instructions included several points from a memorandum from the minister of finance to the directors, in which the emperor ordered certain measures to avoid misunderstanding between Russian and American ships in case the frigate *Kreiser* and the sloop *Ladoga* were dispatched to North America:

1. The aforementioned ships which are being equipped here shall be provided

with orders for themselves and for other ships already cruising off said shore to conduct their observations as close to dry land as possible and not to extend them farther than the latitude within which the Russian-American Company has actually enjoyed its hunting and fishing privileges both from the time of its establishment and since the renewal of the charter in 1799.

2. These observations shall have the object of preventing any prohibited trade and any attempt to infringe on the rights of the company by disturbing the peace in places visited by its hunters, and also any other activity aimed at providing the natives, without the permission of their legal government, with firearms, ammunition, or military equipment.

The *Elena* left Kronshtadt on 31 July 1824 and reached New Archangel on 29 July 1825. Having accepted the position of chief manager, Chistiakov surrendered command of the ship to Murav'ev, who left the colonies on 4 November and reached Kronshtadt on 1 September 1826. The return cargo of the *Elena* included 150,000 paper rubles worth of furs and around ten thousand puds of granulated sugar bought in Brazil.

Trade with foreigners is resumed at New Archangel. The sale of these goods and the successful export of 600,000 paper rubles worth of furs to Okhotsk on two company ships were not sufficient to restore the company's profitability, which had been declining seriously for some time. In a memorandum presented to the company council at the end of 1823, Director Prokof'ev ascribed the company's disordered affairs to the rash petition of directors Kramer and Severin to prohibit trade with foreigners in the colonies. He pointed out that Baranov had almost supported the colonies through foreign trade during his governorship, and that goods obtained from the Americans were considerably cheaper to the company than those forwarded by round-the-world expeditions. To support his arguments Prokof'ev presented Murav'ev's report on the shortages in the colonies caused by this prohibition and the impossibility of satisfying the needs not only of the company employees but of the Kolosh, who had formerly obtained their necessities from the Americans. These conditions, in Murav'ev's opinion, could again lead to enmity between the Russians and Americans, since the trading prohibition against foreigners could hardly serve its purpose—the elimination of contraband trade with the natives—since they themselves would go and get firearms if firearms were not brought to them.

The company council asked the minister of finance to petition the emperor for permission to trade with foreign ships only in New Archangel, as a measure necesssary to sustain the company's position under existing circumstances. The emperor, taking into consideration the reason for the board of directors' wish to renew this trade, granted the company's request on the conditions set forth. At the same time the company was relieved of the responsibility of using its ships to supply provisions to Okhotsk and Kamchatka.

Murav'ev reported that "trade with foreigners in New Archangel has been renewed to the obvious advantage of the company and to the satisfaction of the entire population." Late in November 1824 an American brig [*Tamaahamaah*] under the command of Captain Meek arrived, and in the middle of February [1825] another brig [*Lapwing*] from Boston under the command of Captain Blanchard arrived. Essential goods were obtained from both ships. Trading was quite profitable, such that old fur seal pelts of low quality were sold for twelve paper rubles each.

Similar exchanges were carried out from time to time in subsequent years. Until 1829 goods obtained from the Americans were paid for principally in fur seals, but the gradual decrease in these animals in their major habitats forced the colonial government to find more economical means of payment and to purchase goods from foreigners solely with bills of exchange drawn on the directors.

Supplies for the colonies are obtained in California and Chile. The goods obtained from foreigners in New Archangel fell far short of satisfying the colonies' needs. The main articles of supply, consisting of various foodstuffs, could not be obtained from Russia because of the inconvenience and expense of transportation, and California, although undependable, remained the chief source of provisions because of its proximity to the colonies.

After Mexico declared its independence from Spain, a constitution was proclaimed in California and a junta was placed at the head of the government. It consisted of seven deputies chosen from each of the provinces and was under the chairmanship of the governor of Monterey. The former Spanish governor of this province, Pablo de Sola, had been compelled by other important persons in California to take the side of the insurgents. The Mexican viceroy, Marquis Apodaca, left for Europe, and one of the insurgent representatives, General Iturbide, was proclaimed emperor under the name Augustine I and crowned in August 1822.

The change of government in Mexico opened the ports of California to trade with all nations. The duties were raised on imports to 25 percent and on exports to 6 percent, with the exception of wheat, which was taxed at three piasters per fanega, twice the previous rate. Moreover, anchorage duties of two and one-half piasters per ton for each merchant ship, taken along with the other taxes, burdened trade, particularly since many foreign ships were engaged in smuggling, which had a bad effect on the price of goods brought to California on company ships.

Aside from these difficulties, the acquisition of food supplies in San Francisco and other neighboring ports had become even more burdensome because of the newly arisen competition. In 1823 the English company of Beck contracted with many missions to buy locally produced products, primarily hides, tallow, and fat, payment for which was to be made in various goods necessary to the Californians. This arrangement lowered the prices for all objects brought to California from the Russian colonies. The opening of free trade aroused the interest of Californians, who previously had been completely disinterested. Missionaries, officials, and others turned more eagerly toward agriculture, cattle raising, and gardening, since food supplies could be sold very profitably to arriving ships, particularly to those, mainly American and some English ships, along the California coast engaged in hunting fur seals.

However, the constant change of affairs and ruling figures in California at that time brought frequent changes in the laws governing taxes on trade. When Etholen bought grain in Monterey in 1824, he paid no taxes. When Augustine I abdicated from the throne in 1823 and a republic was proclaimed, with a congress modeled on that of the United States, under the presidency of General Santa Anna, a new order in the conduct of trade relations was instituted. When Lieutenant Colonel Don Jose Maria Echeandia was named governor of Monterey with the title and prerogatives of commandant general of both Californias, he promulgated the decrees of the Mexican government forbidding foreigners to trade at remote missions, leaving open only the ports of Monterey, San Francisco, San Diego, and Santa Barbara. When Commissioner Khlebnikov came from the colonies for grain on the brig *Kiakhta* in 1825 he received permission from the governor's assistant, Commissar for Foreign Affairs Guerrero, to sell his goods with no supervision by the Mexican government. No export duties were imposed and food stuffs were purchased by the company quite reasonably—wheat for three piasters per fanega and tallow for two piasters per arroba. Chistiakov's reports of 1826 and 1827 revealed that colonial trade with California was being hampered more and more by frequent visits from foreign vessels able to sell their goods more cheaply than the company could, due to the Mexican government's imposition of large ad valorem import duties, and by other port expenses. As a result, grain could be purchased only for cash. The directors permitted the colonial administration to purchase grain with fur seal pelts, but this measure did not prove completely effective. The number of vessels arriving in California ports greatly increased the demand for local supplies, making it impossible for the colonies to obtain enough provisions in California. In 1828, despite all of the colonial governments, it was impossible to gather a yearly supply of grain in California, although company ships visited all ports. Fortunately, a large quantity of provisions were sent through Okhotsk that year. Although six thousand puds of rye flour were sent from California to the colonies in 1829, new difficulties in obtaining supplies from that source compelled the chief manager to send Etholen to purchase grain in Chile, despite its remoteness from New Archangel.

Before the company brig *Baikal* arrived in Chile, Russian goods were quite unknown there. They occasionally came on foreign ships, but even then they were sold as the products of other countries. On this occasion, however, Russian goods were sold under their own name for the first time and this sale proved quite profitable. Wide linen, various kinds of ticking, and so-called "manorial" sack cloth [*gospodskie kholsty*] sold particularly well. Etholen obtained for the colonies 9,340 puds of wheat and other foodstuffs at lower prices than those in Okhotsk or even in California.

Chistiakov's successor as colonial governor, Baron Wrangell, ordered Khlebnikov, who was sent to California in 1831 on the sloop *Urup*, to inform the missions that Russian ships would proceed to Chile for food supplies if the prices were excessive in California. He wrote the same thing to the governor, hoping thus to hold prices down. His statement achieved its purpose. The *Urup* returned with 2,300 fanegas of wheat purchased for cash at two piasters per fanega. A part of the wheat, however, was exchanged for goods, which cost the company three piasters per fanega.

From then on foodstuffs were obtained from California more regularly. The quantities were sufficient, along with imports from other sources, to satisfy the colonies' needs. The prices for wheat also were encouraging. In 1831 wheat cost the colonies 4 paper rubles 25 kopeks per pud; in 1832, 3 rubles 30 kopeks and 2 rubles 95 kopeks; and in 1833, 2 rubles 87½ kopeks.

For greater convenience in obtaining the supplies from various places along the California coast, the chief manager established an agency in San Francisco under the direction of Hartnell, a local merchant. His commission was 10 percent. However, Hartnell was soon relieved of his duties as agent and was replaced by Kostromitinov, manager of Ross settlement.

In 1835 crop failures in California reduced the food supplies obtained from there to only one-third of the colonies' needs. The next year, 1836, that amount was again halved because of the previous crop failure, and also the death of General Figueroa, governor of California, and the resulting establishment of a ruling triumvirate, which greatly slowed business.

When Baron Wrangell was replaced as colonial governor by Captain of First Rank Kuprianov, he decided to go to Russia via Mexico. The sloop *Sitkha*, under Captain-Lieutenant Mit'kov's command, carried Wrangell to San Blas and then, in June 1836, proceeded to Guaymas. Letters of introduction from Baron Wrangell to several of the most important merchants and his own energetic efforts permitted Mit'kov to carry back to the colonies 1,650 puds of flour and 10,000 puds of salt. The cargo of wood which the sloop had brought from New Archangel was sold in Guaymas at very good prices.

Shortages in California again compelled the colonies to turn to Chile for grain purchases. For this purpose Captain-Lieutenant Etholen, then assistant chief manager, went there in November 1836 on the ship *Elena* with a cargo of timber. The difficulties of trading were so great that Etholen despaired of carrying out his task, but he finally succeeded in obtaining a full cargo for the ship, consisting of 18,000 puds of flour and wheat, and several other smaller items purchased in order to compare their price and quality with similar articles obtained from other sources.

In the following years, the amount of supplies obtained from California greatly exceeded that of former times. In 1839 and 1840, in particular, wheat was imported to the colonies from California in great quantities. On every return voyage each ship carried back 6,300 fanegas. Moreover, Rotchev, then manager of Ross settlement, purchased 1,700 fanegas in various missions in 1840. The contract which the directors concluded at that time with the Hudson's Bay Company, providing that the latter should furnish the colonies with grain in their own ships, terminated purchases in California. By 1841, after 2,000 puds of provisions had been sent to various sections of the colonies and to Okhotsk, a total of over 30,000 puds of wheat remained in New Archangel and Ross. This ensured the colonies a reserve food supply for over one year.

At the same time the directors took all measures at its disposal to provide the colonies with goods necessary for trading, as well as supplies and materials for shipbuilding and other maritime needs. When possible, these items were sent on the government sloops *Krotkii*, *Seniavin*, and *Moller*, with the permission of the admiralty. The freight charge for this service was 10 paper rubles per pud.

The ninth round-the-world expedition to the colonies under the command of Lieutenant Khromchenko. In 1828 the directors again prepared the ship *Elena* for a voyage to the colonies under the command of Lieutenant Khromchenko. The crew consisted of Lieutenants Levendal and Dmitriev; Senior Navigator [Aleksandr] Kashevarov, a creole who had been educated by the company; Assistant Navigator Grey; the company commissioner Arakelov, and his assistant [Vasilii] Kashevarov; Doctor Vebel; and thirty-seven men of lower ranks. The cargo cost almost 500,000 paper rubles. On 3 August 1828, the *Elena* left Kronshtadt, successfully rounded the Cape of Good Hope and arrived at New Archangel on 3 July. The ship left Sitkha on 15 October for the return voyage and arrived in Kronshtadt on 10 July 1830, carrying 1,200,000 paper rubles worth of furs.

In 1831 the board of directors sent to the colonies on the military transport *Amerika*, under the command of Captain-Lieutenant Khromchenko, a large quantity of general cargo worth 467,505 paper rubles 29 kopeks. The freight charges determined by the government were 5 rubles per pud for lower cargo, 7 rubles per pud for middle cargo, and 15 rubles per pud for upper cargo. The transport carried 8,852 puds 16 pounds of lower cargo, 7,014 puds 27 pounds of middle cargo, and 1,582 puds 37 pounds of upper cargo. Ensign [Aleksandr] Kashevarov of the Corps of Naval Navigators, who was being sent to the colonies on duty, was placed in charge of the cargo. In 1834 a company cargo valued at 435,000 paper rubles was sent to New Archangel on the *Amerika* under the same terms, this time under the command of Captain-Lieutenant Shants. On this same voyage the transport took aboard in Portsmouth a load of English woolens which the company had ordered there. On both voyages the *Amerika* brought back cargos of furs from the colonies. The first time they were worth more than 1,000,000 paper rubles, and the second time 340,000 rubles. In 1831, the board of directors chartered the English ship *Caernarvon* to carry a large cargo to the colonies from England and Brazil. In 1835 the company concluded a supply contract with the Boston merchant house of Boardman. The items covered in this contract included tobacco, rum, sugar, treacle, hardtack, calico, etc., as well as a steam engine for a ship to be built in New Archangel for use around Kolosh Straits and the port. The goods and the engine were brought to New Archangel in 1837 in good order, and a similar contract to supply goods and another steam engine was negotiated by the board of directors with the same firm in 1838.

The tenth round-the-world expedition under the command of

Lieutenant Teben'kov. Since it was necessary to send to the colonies many heavy metal objects, such as guns, engines, assorted iron, copper, etc., worth more than 350,000 paper rubles, the directors decided to equip for the voyage the company ship *Elena*, placing Lieutenant Teben'kov in command. The *Elena* left Kronshtadt on 5 August 1835 with a crew consisting of Lieutenant Mashin, who was being sent to serve in the colonies; Ensign Khalizov and Warrant Officer Murashev of the Corps of Naval Navigators; navigators Lindenberg and Netsvetov, who were students of the Merchant Marine Academy; Doctor Volynskii, Cadet Timkovskii; Company Commissioner Rotchev; his assistant Kostromitinov; twenty-three lower naval ranks; and fifteen merchant seamen. The *Elena* stopped in Portsmouth to take aboard forty bales of blankets which had been ordered there, and then proceeded around Cape Horn. After its arrival on 16 April 1836, the ship remained in New Archangel to reinforce the colonial fleet.

The eleventh round-the-world expedition under the command of Captain-Lieutenant Berens. For the eleventh round-the-world expedition, the company acquired a 450-ton ship in Finland and renamed it the *Nicholas I*. The cargo consisted of almost 400,000 paper rubles worth of various Russian goods, supplies, and materials, and also some English woolens, intended partly for trade with California. Captain-Lieutenant Berens was named captain of the ship, and his crew consisted of Lieutenants Zavoiko and Diugamel; Cadet Timkovskii, Warrant Officer Gavrilov, Doctor Fisher; Baron Geiking as supercargo, Merchant Navigator Garder and his assistants Klinkovstrem and Krimmert, the creole Arkhimandritov whom the company had educated, fifteen lower naval ranks, and fourteen Finnish and two Russian seamen. The ship began its voyage on 8 August 1837, sailed by way of Cape Horn and arrived in New Archangel on 14 April. On 9 June 1839 it returned to Kronshtadt with a cargo of furs valued at 300,000 paper rubles.

The twelfth round-the-world expedition under the command of Lieutenant Kadnikov and Captain-Lieutenant Voevodskii. On 20 August 1839 the ship *Nikolai I* under Lieutenant Kadnikov's command was sent to the colonies with a general cargo worth around 500,000 paper rubles. The vessel also carried to New Archangel Captain of Second Rank Etholen, who had been named chief manager. The crew consisted of Lieutenant Bartram; Staff Captain Sergeev of the Corps of Naval Navigators; Doctor Romanovskii; unassigned navigators Krasil'nikov, Kuznetsov, and Stepanov—graduates of the Merchant Marine Academy—and thirty-four lower naval ranks. While in Rio de Janeiro, Etholen purchased a 190-ton brig for the colonial fleet, which he named the

Velikii Kniaz' Konstantin [Grand Duke Konstantin], and arrived in New Archangel on 1 May 1840 with both ships. The brig carried a large cargo of Brazilian foodstuffs for colonial use.

On 14 July 1841 the ship returned from the colonies with a cargo of furs valued at 130,000 paper rubles. On this occasion the *Nikolai I* was under the command of Captain-Lieutenant Voevodskii, whose crew consisted of Lieutenant Mashin, Staff Captain Sergeev, and Ensign Khalizov of the Corps of Naval Navigators, Staff Doctor Bliashke, and thirty-eight naval ranks. Captain of First Rank Kuprianov, who had completed his term of service as colonial governor, and nineteen other passengers also arrived on the ship.

The thirteenth round-the-world expedition under the command of Lieutenant Zarembo. Hoping to strengthen the colonial fleet as much as possible, the directors ordered a 300-ton ship in Abo, the *Naslednik Aleksandr* [Crown Prince Aleksandr]. This vessel set forth for the colonies on 14 August 1840 under Captain-Lieutenant Zarembo's command, carrying a cargo of Russian goods valued at 122,580 silver rubles. The crew consisted of lieutenants Voevodskii and Ogil'vi, Ensign Gavrilov of the Corps of Naval Navigators, unassigned navigators Goman [Öhman?] and Ivanov of the Merchant Marine Academy, Doctor Frankenhaeuser, who had been employed by the company for service in the colonies, twenty-three lower naval ranks, and four Finnish nationals. The ship reached New Archangel on 4 April 1841.

The provisioning of the colonies by ships of the Hudson's Bay Company. The lease agreement of 1839 concluded with the Hudson's Bay Company provided that that company was to deliver to New Archangel the following quantity of goods each year at predetermined prices (in paper rubles):

Wheat	14,000 puds @	3 r. 25 k. per pud
Wheat flour	498 puds @	6 r. 32 k. per pud
Peas	404 puds @	4 r. 90 k. per pud
Groats	404 puds @	4 r. 90 k. per pud
Corned beef	922 puds @	3 r. 78 k. per pud
Butter	498 puds @	20 r. 20 k. per pud
Ham	92 puds @	59 k. per pound

The agreement further provided that:

1. If the Hudson's Bay Company should, for any reason, be unable to provide the designated quantity of supplies, the Russian-American Company would then have the right to obtain them in California or in Chile with its own ship at the Hudson's Bay Company's expense.

2. When the Russian-American Company could not send its own

ships to the colony, they would have the right to send goods and materials there on Hudson's Bay Company ships at a freight rate of £13 per ton.[1]

Salt was sent to Kamchatka on company ships. An order of the Siberian Committee, which was approved by the emperor on 24 January 1828, obliged the company to deliver to the government in Kamchatka from 3,000 to 5,000 puds of salt, depending on the need. For this purpose the brig *Baikal* was sent from the colonies in May of the same year, under Midshipmen Etholen's command. It arrived in Petropavlovsk with 8,000 puds of salt, which was handed over to the government office. Etholen had obtained this salt in the winter of 1827 directly from the salt lakes at San Quentin Bay in Lower California. The purchase of salt in the Sandwich Islands and in California, the main source of its supply, was always very difficult. In the islands a ship sent for salt could never obtain more than 2,000 puds sometimes considerably less, and then with much trouble and for a high price. It was never possible to buy even 1,000 puds at one time in California. Although the seaside lakes abounded in salt, it was never a popular article of trade there and no industry had grown up around it.

While the brig *Baikal* was in Monterey, Etholen persuaded the governor to permit him to obtain salt from the lakes with his own men. He was charged a customs duty of 4 reals per quintal and anchor money of 17 reals per ton. In this way the company obtained fair amounts of salt at one time, although loading entailed special problems and was exhausting work for the crew. The salt had to be carried more than three miles from the lakes to the landing place over a rough, sandy road. Here it was loaded onto rowboats and taken another five miles to the ship, which could not come inshore because of shallow water. In addition, the region of San Quentin Bay was completely uninhabited. Therefore, the mules and drivers that carried the salt from the lakes to the shore had to be hired at San Tomas Mission, 120 miles distant. Fresh water could be obtained only on the opposite side of the bay, from which the ship towed it to the landing in barrels. This complicated operation not only took much time, but also diverted men from their regular work. Fortunately, dry weather helped the mission and the salt was loaded on the ship in perfect condition.

The obligation to provide salt for Kamchatka was also duly performed by the company in subsequent years. Large loads of salt were obtained in Guaymas in 1836 by Lieutenant-Captain Mit'kov on the sloop *Sitkha* and in 1839 by Lieutenant-Captain Voevodskii on the brig *Baikal*, which carried more than 9,500 puds of salt from Del Carmel Island. On these two occasions more than 8,000 puds of salt were brought to Kamchatka, bringing the total amount which the company obtained for the government to more than 16,000 puds.

The administration of the Ross settlement and the export of food from there to the colonies, until its abandonment in 1841. During Kuskov's term at Ross settlement only a few men were engaged in farming, but when the merchant seaman Schmidt took over the administration of Ross settlement in 1820, he devoted special attention to expanding and improving the settlement's agriculture. Schmidt attempted to attract not only all of the Russians and creoles to agriculture, but also the Aleuts, providing them with a large quantity of seed grain for their own use. This arrangement made it unnecessary to supply the settlement with food obtained from California. In those days food shortages frequently occurred in the other company settlements where it was impossible to grow food. Beginning in 1822, constantly increased sowings gave larger yields of grain. In 1825, the average yield was ten times the sowing, and in 1826 the crop of wheat and other grains appeared to be so good that it was proposed to export at least 2,500 puds of grain to New Archangel, after satisfying the needs of the settlement. But rust afflicted the wheat because of the humidity and destroyed these hopes when the grain harvest was reduced to less than half.

The wheat exported from the settlement from 1826 through 1833 totalled around 6 thousand puds, or a little more than 800 puds per year, a quantity far short of satisfying the purpose for which the settlement had been founded. When cultivation was moved from the seacoast to the mountains in 1821, the farming undoubtedly improved. But few places were completely free from the destructive influence of the fog, mainly small plots on the slopes of high and steep hills, accessible only by foot or on horseback. The hard labor of working these hilly fields was increased further by the difficult and slow task of dragging the sheaves to the threshing floors after the harvest, or to places where they could be loaded on horses. Every possible site had to be sown each year, and this so exhausted the soil of many fields that the yield did not even return the seed grain. In these cases the fields had to be abandoned, even though it was impossible to replace them. By 1833 wild oats had grown up in many fields so thick that it choked the wheat, and the only way to destroy it was to pasture cattle there for two or three years, which meant that the settlement lost this arable land for a long period. To make matters worse, attacks by vermin [*myshei i khar'kov*] on the growing wheat caused a considerable decrease in the already sparse crop.

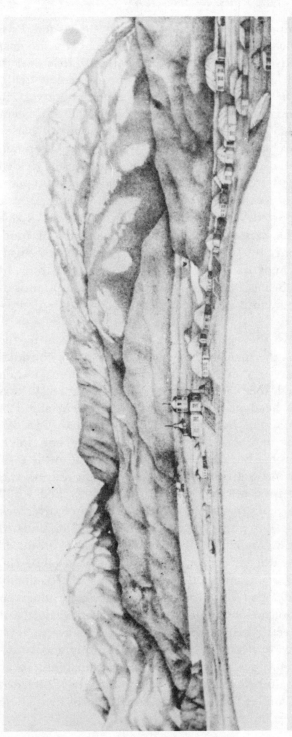

Top, Captain's Harbor, Unalaska, about 1840; bottom, Ross settlement (Fort Ross), California, about 1841

These problems prompted Baron Wrangell when he visited Ross settlement in 1833, to locate the fields elsewhere. He chose a site near the mouth of Slavianka River between the settlement and Little Bodega Bay. In 1833 around 400 puds of wheat were sown on the new fields, and the work of tilling them was rewarded by an abundant harvest. In 1834, after a necessary quantity had been set aside for the settlement and for future sowing, 4,500 puds of wheat and 457 puds of barley were exported to New Archangel. In 1835 there was a general crop failure both at Ross and in California, and 700 puds of seed grain yielded only 3,500 puds for the settlement, instead of the expected 8,000 puds. In 1836, an extremely poor year for crops at Ross settlement, not one grain of wheat was exported. During the last four years of Ross's existence, New Archangel obtained the following quantities of food-stuffs from the settlement: 9,918 puds of wheat, 100 puds of sugar, 939 puds of barley, 20 puds of rye, 243 puds of peas, 246 puds of buckwheat, 109 puds of beans, 38 puds of corn, 4 puds 25 pounds of tobacco, and negligible quantities of flax, linseed, hempseed, mustard, and poppy seed.

Animal husbandry was the second most important item in the settlement's economy. All the species of livestock found there considerably increased from year to year, although the mountainous terrain and the forests prevented the keeping of large herds. In 1821 Ross settlement had only 187 head of horned cattle, 736 sheep, and 124 swine. By 1826 the number of horned cattle had grown to 315. An epidemic had reduced the number of sheep to some 200. The unpleasant smell of the pork, probably caused by the sealion meat in the pigs' diet, made it unsuitable for salting. For this reason pig raising was abandoned. In 1833 the total number of livestock had reached 1,830 head. In the last fifteen years of the settlement's existence, livestock rearing yielded around 6,000 puds of corned beef and 496 puds of butter for export to New Archangel. The settlement also produced much tallow, wool, and leather in its own factory. From a total of 750 bulls and cows, including oxen, and 630 ewes and rams, the company could realize around 8,000 paper rubles worth of various products in a good year, including foodstuffs to be used at the settlement. Without impairing the herd the settlement would have had to have at least 2,000 head of livestock to provide for its own food supply and to export even one-half, i.e. 400 puds, of the colonies' annual supply of corned beef. However, 2,000 head was the maximum total of horned cattle, sheep, horses, and mules that could be conveniently kept there in view of the confining terrain.

One of the main reasons for the insignificance of animal husbandry was the impossibility of carefully tending the herds. From July through November and December the animals wandered for some twenty versts in all directions, seeking new pasturage, since that in the neighborhood of the settlement had already been eaten or burned up by the sun. When the cattle were then rounded up and driven the long distances back to the cattle sheds, they were fatigued and gave very little milk. In 1832, for example, despite all the efforts to improve milk production, 147 milk cows gave only 116 puds of butter. After local needs were satisfied, only 85 puds could be sent to New Archangel.[2]

In addition to agriculture and animal husbandry the other industries of the settlement included:

1. Hunting of fur-bearing animals, such as sea otters, fur seals, and sea lions. When the settlement was founded, these were numerous, but they decreased each year until finally they disappeared. Sea otters could be hunted off the shores of California only with the permission of the Mexican government. On the rare occasions when this permission could be extracted, half of the catch had to be given to the local government. Around the end of the 1830s the sea otter trade became quite insignificant. The fur seals on the Farallon Islands also became completely extinct. After 1833, when only fifty-four were taken, they were no longer hunted. The total numbers of fur-bearing animals taken for the company between 1824 and 1834 by the Aleuts living in the settlement were:

	1824	1825	1826	1827	1828
Sea otters	475	500	287	9	1
Sea otter pups	—	—	13	3	—
Fur seals	unknown	1050	455	290	—

	1829	1830	1831	1832	1833	1834
Sea otters	18	12	112	1	187	220
Sea otter pups	5	4	—	—	34	35
Fur seals	210	287	205	118	54	—

2. Various manufactures, such as rowboats, wheels, cooking dishes, etc., ordered by the Californians. Before California was opened to free trade, such objects were manufactured very profitably at Ross settlement and also New Archangel. In some years the settlement's trading post made up to 6,000 paper rubles profit. Subsequently, these orders decreased in number and became less profitable, because the foreigners

who took over the trade with California imported quantities of all kinds of goods and sold them so cheaply that the colonies could not compete.

3. Shipbuilding. The first two ships built for the company at the settlement in 1817 and 1818, the *Buldakov* and the *Rumiantsov*, proved that the local oak used in their construction lacked durability. Both vessels had to undergo extensive repairs in 1821, and Murav'ev decided in the future to employ pine for ship frames [*shpangouty*] and laurel as sheathing. These experiments, however, were unsuccessful, as shown by the brigs *Kiakhta* and *Volga*. Generally speaking, the ships built at the settlement could only be used five years without complete retimbering. The wetness of the wood caused it to rot early. Finally, ships built at the settlement were more expensive than those purchased from the Americans or built in New Archangel, because of the large number of men that had to be employed to transport the timber from the remote forests to the shipyard. For this reason the company abandoned shipbuilding at Ross.

4. Various articles exported to New Archangel, such as laurel—which was used in shipbuilding—pitch, high-quality brick, made at the settlement factory, and tiles, etc.

From 1825 through 1830 the total outlay for the maintenance of the settlement averaged around 45,000 rubles per year. On the other hand, the average annual export from this settlement totaled 12,883 rubles, 4,138 rubles of which constituted furs, and 8,745 rubles other articles. Therefore, although the export of other goods considerably increased, particularly in the settlement's last year, the complete cessation of fur hunting from 1835 and the increase of expenditures in 1837 to 72,000 paper rubles resulted in an annual loss from Ross settlement to the company of about 44,000 rubles. In 1837 the total value of exports from the settlement was 11,890 rubles 20 kopeks; in 1838, 26,486 rubles 19 kopeks; in 1839, 16,000 rubles 44 kopeks; in 1840, 50,073 rubles 95 kopeks; and in 1841, 12,605 rubles 10 kopeks. (The last two figures represent the proceeds of final liquidation.)

Needless to say, if farming had been successful on the new sites and if livestock rearing had increased in scope, the settlement would have partially fulfilled its function as granary to the colonies, at least in good years. Generally speaking, however, all the other difficulties associated with the settlement's position could have been overcome only if circumstances had favored Baron Wrangell's proposal to annex to the settlement new territory lying beyond the mountain range. This territory consisted of a valley about twenty versts long. Here the soil and other conditions made it entirely possible to expand agriculture enough to satisfy the needs of all the other Russian colonies on the shores of the

Pacific Ocean. But since the very possession of the settlement, even with its present boundaries, was subject to formal confirmation by the Mexican government, and was far from settled, the possibility of annexing new territory was quite doubtful.

As an indication of the new failures experience by the directors in obtaining confirmation of the lands belonging to Ross settlement, we will present its replies to memoranda by the chief manager on the impossibility of improving agriculture at the settlement. In 1827 the directors wrote to Chistiakov:

> Our efforts to gain formal recognition of the territory settled by Russians are still unsuccessful, and, as it appears now, there is no hope that this question will be resolved satisfactorily. As to expanding agriculture, even if the Mexicans are perfectly reasonable, not much good can be expected from it. As Murav'ev states, all the lands suitable for cultivation have already been put under the plow and there are no other fields suitable for sowing near the settlement. It is extraordinarily inconvenient to carry on agriculture at a distance from the settlement. Therefore, the only solution remaining is to maintain the agriculture now being carried on at Ross settlement without expanding it and to improve farming methods through all available means. It is obvious that agriculture at Ross settlement will not be able to meet the food needs of the colonies, and it will still be necessary to obtain grain from California.

In 1829 the directors again wrote to the colonial governor that "all hope for agriculture at the settlement must be abandoned, and therefore any thought of expanding it would be quite futile."

In the meantime, the Mexican government, during the reign of Iturbide, had received no satisfactory reply to their urgent demand, made in 1822 by their emissary Augustin de Vincente, that the Ross settlement be destroyed within a period of six months.[3] The Mexicans were apparently convinced that it was impossible to force the Russians to abandon these lands by using threats. They nevertheless had not abandoned hope that their desire [for the Russians to leave] would somehow be realized. Unable to back up their demands for the settlement's destruction with armed force and perhaps even doubting to some extent their right to the exclusive possession of the shores of New Albion, they turned to a more diplomatic method—the more readily since the influence of Russian power was particularly great in these regions. The arrival in Monterey of the naval sloop *Apollon* was enough to force the deputies who made up the government of California to ask Khlebnikov, the company commissioner, whether it was true that the envoy had demanded the settlement's destruction in six months and had threatened to use force should his demand not be carried out within that time. When Khlebnikov confirmed that this was true, the deputies quickly replied that they were retracting the demand, and would bring the matter to the notice of the highest Mexican authorities.

The Mexican authorities, fearing the southward extension of Russian occupation, then decided to block the Russians' way to San Francisco Bay. Following the example of the Spaniards, who had founded San Rafael Mission on the northern shore of the bay in 1816 for this very purpose, the Mexican government attempted to expand the lands under the control of the San Francisco-Solano and Sonoma Missions, which were founded in 1822. These missions cut off Ross settlement completely from California and so limited its boundaries that it was in no position to inspire either envy or fear.

The colonial government meanwhile pursued its plan to obtain a new strip of land which would make the settlement economically self-sufficient and would strengthen its general territorial position. In 1834 General Figueroa, governor of Upper California, asked Baron Wrangell to accept diplomatic mediation between the Mexican and Russian governments. This gave high hopes that the question of Mexican cession of these lands would be favorably decided, but, as we shall see below, circumstances again led to a different outcome.

General Figueroa wished the Russian government to be informed "that the Mexican nation, having thrown off the dominion of Spain and desiring to maintain friendly ties with all nations, has concluded treaties with many powers. But since diplomatic relations with Russia have not yet been established, they would like to know whether the Russian government recognizes the independence of the Mexican Republic."[4]

When this message had been received, the board of directors and the council decided to bring General Figueroa's proposal to the emperor's attention and to petition for permission to establish relations with Mexico on the same basis as the Berlin government had done; that is, to recognize the independence of the Mexican Republic and to send an envoy there. If permission for negotiation were given, they proposed that this task be entrusted to Baron Wrangell on his return trip from the colonies.

The minister of finance replied that His Majesty had considered the question of recognizing the new order of things in the former Spanish possessions in connection with existing political circumstances, but did not think it proper at that time to grant recognition to the new regime. However, His Majesty hoped that this circumstance would not hinder trade relations between the Russian colonies and Mexico, which were necessary for the colonies' food supply. For this reason he permitted the colonial government to establish such relations with the Mexican government and to attempt to turn to the advantage of our colonies the friendly disposition which General Figueroa had shown to Baron Wrangell. For the same reason he permitted Baron Wrangell to visit Mexico on his return trip to Europe, charging him with determining at first hand to what extent Russian recognition of the Mexican Republic might incline the Mexican government formally to cede the Russian occupied land in California.

Baron Wrangell first set out for Monterey to visit General Figueroa, from whom he hoped to obtain a passport for passage through Mexico and letters of introduction to the President of the Republic, General Santa Anna and to other leading figures in the Mexican government. But when he reached Monterey, Baron Wrangell received the unhappy news of Figueroa's death and immediately set out for San Blas, intending to continue his voyage from there. Baron Wrangell obtained permission to proceed to the mountains where the president lived only through the influence of Barron, the English consul in Tepic, since the passport which he had obtained from the Russian foreign ministry had not been countersigned by a Mexican agent and was not considered valid under Mexican law. After his arrival in Mexico, Baron Wrangell, through the good offices of the Prussian Consul General Gerard, had a private meeting with General Barogan, who was acting as president in the absence of General Santa Anna. His authority to enter into negotiations with the Mexican government on behalf of the directors as private individuals proved insufficient to settle matters officially, and he was obliged to confine himself to verbal understandings. In subsequent meetings with Minister Carro, Barogan's successor, and Foreign Minister Monasterio, Baron Wrangell succeeded in convincing them to cede to the Russian colonies the land which had originally belonged to Ross settlement and the valley which was essential to its economy. This concession was accompanied by the demand that negotiations be conducted in London between the official representatives of Russia and Mexico. To affirm the sincerity of the promises made by the ministers of the republic, Baron Wrangell obtained from them a note to the effect that "the Mexican Government, viewing with satisfaction the wish of the Russian colonies to expand trade relations with California, is fully disposed to confirm these things through a formal treaty with His Majesty the Russian Emperor, for which reason it has instructed its Minister in London to conclude said treaty, should the Russian government be inspired with the same desire."

Upon his return to St. Petersburg, Baron Wrangell presented this note to the minister of foreign affairs and informed him of the results of his verbal negotiations with the representatives of the Mexican government. When the conclusion of Baron Wrangell's mission was reported to the emperor, His Majesty did not consider it opportune to pursue the matter further.[5]

In 1836 Chief Manager Kuprianov informed the directors that several American immigrants had built ranches 30 versts from Ross settlement and at Drake's Cape [Point Reyes] and intended to found other settlements even closer, depriving the settlement of essential territory and erecting insuperable obstacles to our plans for improving agriculture. The directors answered that the vice chancellor had been apprised of this circumstance and had replied "that the colonial government should weigh its actions in the light of local conditions, employing, however, all means it could bring to bear in the area to retain those places we have already occupied and the improvements we have made thereon."

Thus, any hope the company might have had to extract profit from the produce and trade of the settlement disappeared. Moreover, the settlement's distance from the colonies vitiated any strategic significance which it might have, particularly since Bodega Bay did not lend itself to use as a harbor. In this state of affairs the settlement was only a heavy burden for the colonies to bear. It required dilution of the colonial forces, resettlement of large parties of Aleuts, and increased expenditures that promised no satisfactory return in the future. Under these circumstances the directors saw no solution but to abolish the settlement and, with the council's approval, decided to propose this to the minister of finance.[6]

The minister replied that the emperor, on 15 April 1839 had ordered Ross settlement abandoned in accordance with the proposal of the company council, to vacate its trading post, to reassign its employees to other sections, to remove its guns and supplies, and to sell or barter everything else to the inhabitants of San Francisco.

In 1841 all the land, cattle, and buildings at the settlement were sold to Sutter, a Swiss land owner on the Sacramento River, for 30,000 piasters, with the guarantee of the Mexican government that prompt payment should be made in accordance with the terms of the contract with Sutter over the course of the next four years.[7]

In conclusion it should be observed that without the help of the natives living around Ross settlement it would have been impossible to harvest the crops because of the shortage of labor. After the Americans began to settle in California it was quite difficult to count on this assistance. Finally, if the settlement had not been abandoned before the discovery of gold in the area,[8] in all probability the most industrious workers at Ross settlement, drawn by the wish to get rich easily, would have rushed en masse to work the gold deposits, and the settlement, left without workers, could not have been maintained. No worker would have continued to till the soil or herd cattle when he might find his fortune beyond the nearest mountain ridge. Nothing could have bound him to a place where his work was rewarded only with the essentials of life, while he could hope to enjoy comfort from the wealth brought by the discovery of gold.

11. The State of the Company's Trade and Certain Government Actions near the End of the Second Charter Period

The company's finances under the second charter. The company's duty to provide Kamchatka and Okhotsk with grain and, particularly, the directors' untimely desire to prohibit foreign ships from trading in the colonies at the time the second charter was granted caused an acute shortage of supplies in the colonies but also damaged the company's fiscal position. The financial statement of 1820-21 showed a profit of less than 8 percent on the capital investment, and in the next two years (1822-23) the company lost over 82,000 silver rubles.

When foreign trade was again permitted, although it was confined to the chief colonial port, New Archangel, and when the company was no longer obliged to carry grain to the Pacific ports, the expected results followed: not only did the material welfare of the colonies noticeably improve but there was also an improvement in the company's financial position. In 1824, in accordance with proposals made to the company council by the directors Prokof'ev and Severin the company offices and the commissariat in Siberia were reorganized to control expenses; this too must have contributed to the increase in the company's profit. Beliaev, a bookkeeper, was appointed by the board of directors to discuss the needs of these offices with their managers. He found that they could be effectively managed with a total expenditure of 54,000 silver rubles per year. The elimination of the Kamchatka commissariat in 1827 also saved the company 6,000 silver rubles per year.

Such improvements made it seem that the company's affairs might again reach the favorable level that they had formerly enjoyed. But in fact, it developed that such hopes were still far from realistic. A shortage of working capital not only hampered the company in carrying on trade, but sometimes placed it in real difficulties. Although dividends were paid without interruption and at rates of at least 9 percent, and

as high as 11 percent, on the capital, the original budgets always required borrowing from the trading profits of the subsequent period. Thus,
for the period 1824-25 a dividend was paid from the profits for goods
sold in 1826, and so forth until 1842. These untimely payments were a
major reason for the company's increasing difficulties.

A main cause for the lack of working capital was the practice of
sending supplies to the colonies on round-the-world voyages in vessels
obtained for this purpose, despite the quantity of supplies still sent
through Siberia. Thus, although the company purchased large quantities
of goods at very high prices in Russia, the supplies purchased were still
inadequate for the colonies. The markup of 50 percent applied to goods
shipped round the world hardly covered the costs, and the ships used
were always subject to annual depreciation and repairs. Each round-the-
world expedition incurred a loss and also consumed a large amount of
working capital for its equipping and for the initial purchase of a large
cargo.

Additional causes of the shortage of working capital included the unprofitability of paying foreign skippers in furs, the inevitable consequence of the great decrease in the number of fur-bearing animals in
the colonies (as mentioned above in the review of the condition of the
fur trade in this period); the change in the payment scales for furs; and
finally the gradual increase in the cost of maintaining the colonies. Each
of these circumstances deserves further consideration.

Paying foreigners in furs, chiefly in fur seals, was insignificant to the
company when the colonies had abundant supplies, as in the first years
of the company's existence and almost the entire period of the first
charter. But the subsequent decrease in the numbers of these animals
compelled the company to take measures to control hunting. Finally,
the obvious depletion of fur-bearing animals and the threat of their
complete extinction, which would deprive the company of one-fourth
of its revenues, forced the directors in 1834 to confirm a proposal by
the colonial administration to suspend hunting in the major areas for
at least twelve years in order to let the sea otter herds increase, and to
restrict to the utmost the number of these furs sent to Russia. Moreover, the unprofitability of the barter form of payment that the colonies had to use in dealing with foreign ships was now emphasized by
the incomparably lower prices which were obtained in comparison with
sales in Russia. Furs released to foreign merchantmen brought only 2
silver rubles 30 kopeks per pelt, whereas the same pelts would bring
from 4 rubles 30 kopeks to 7 rubles 15 kopeks in Russia. This compelled the colonial administration in 1831 to replace payment for
foreign goods in furs with drafts issued on the directors. This measure

also had its limitations: it did not make it any easier for the company to obtain supplies for the colonies from foreign ships visiting New Archangel. The presentation of the drafts for payment coincided with the arrival of foreign ships in the colonies, for the most part at irregular and often inopportune times. Payment was frequently demanded when the directors had no cash at their disposal or when the cash had been committed to other pressing needs.

In the last ten years of the second period maintaining the colonies cost the company an average over 100,000 silver rubles more than when the second charter was granted. The reasons for this increased cost included more company redoubts; the intensification of hunting inside the country, occasioned by the decrease in the number of fur-bearing animals near the settlements established in the first period; the increase in the salaries of all employees; the enlarged church staff; and finally the increase in schools, hospitals, and other charitable institutions.

Measures were taken to correct this trend in the new contract concluded in 1838 by Baron Wrangell with the Hudson's Bay Company. This contract obliged the Hudson's Bay Company to carry cargoes of goods from England to New Archangel at prices reasonable compared with the previous freightage. The superiority of manufactured goods obtained from English factories over similar goods previously obtained from American ships were also significant. The freight on the Hudson's Bay Company ships from England to the colonies cost the Russian-American Company from 50 to 78 silver rubles 74½ kopeks per long ton, which with the addition of the freight from Kronshtadt to one of the English ports at a price of 15 rubles 15 kopeks per ton (63 puds), totaled only 65 rubles 15 kopeks to 94 rubles per ton, whereas transporting goods through Siberia to Okhotsk cost the company from 540 to 630 silver rubles per ton. Carrying the goods from Kronshtadt to the colonies by the round-the-world route cost from 194 rubles 28 kopeks to 253 rubles 87 kopeks on company ships, and around 180 silver rubles per ton on government ships. Furthermore, forwarding goods on the Hudson's Bay Company ships also assisted the Russian-American Company in that small cargoes of around fifty tons could be sent to New Archangel for the same price and with the same safety as a full cargo taking up one entire ship.

Reorganization of company offices and commissariats in Siberia and abolition of the Kamchatka commissariat. The above-mentioned control of the expenses of maintaining the company offices and commissariats in Siberia was accompanied by certain changes in the duties of these offices:

1. The transfer of funds to the colonies through the Irkutsk office

was abolished and the Irkutsk office was left to control only the funds in its own section. In case of need the offices and commissariats might correspond with each other. The Irkutsk office was not permitted to extend credit to company employees on the way to America, but only to provide them with money according to the written orders of the directors.

2. The transport of goods from Moscow to Kiakhta and return was to be carried out via the Irkutsk office, which had, in case of need, to support transportation only with money and the hire of horses. The Irkutsk office was to sort fur goods brought from the colonies through Okhotsk once a year and send some of them to Kiakhta for barter to the Chinese for tea, and the rest to Moscow. It was also responsible for sending convoys of goods and men to the colonies or to Okhotsk once each year.

3. The Kiakhta office was changed to a commissariat, its duties limited to bartering furs to the Chinese for tea and forwarding the latter on the orders of the directors.

4. The duties of the Okhotsk office included (a) unloading cargoes from ships arriving from the colonies and sending them to Iakutsk, and reloading the ships for the colonies with goods obtained from this purpose from Russia or from Siberia; and (b) keeping accounts of the goods sent from the colonies to Russia and from Russia to the colonies, and supplying reports to the New Archangel and Irkutsk offices and to the Iakutsk commissariat concerning the quantity, nature and destination of the goods. The Okhotsk office was to keep accounts with men proceeding to and from the colonies solely in money received personally by them from the office.

5. The Iakutsk commissariat was responsible for assisting shipments of goods between Irkutsk and Okhotsk and forwarding certain supplies from Iakutsk to Okhotsk.

The establishment of the Kamchatka commissariat in 1803 and the associated supply depot to provide for company ships and their crews was considered necessary to the company then for two main reasons. In the first place the poor condition of the entire colonial fleet meant that ships sailing from Okhotsk to the colonies had to put in at Kamchatka either to supply themselves for the remainder of the voyage or to winter there. Also, the company conducted much trade in Kamchatka essential for the welfare of its inhabitants and obtained numerous furs there.

During the twenty-four-year existence of this commissariat, circumstances changed greatly. Company ships visited Kamchatka only until 1817. In the ten years following only two ships of the colonial fleet visited Petropavlovsk, since the improved condition of the ships permitted the company to instruct vessels plying between the colonies and Okhotsk not to stop in Kamchatka but to proceed directly to their destination, unless unusual circumstances forced them to do so. Although the company continued to conduct business on the peninsula until 1818, for ten years this trade was of no importance, and all its profits were swallowed up by the large debts owed by many of the residents of Kamchatka. The export of furs from there was also insignificant. From 1803 through 1812 furs worth 21,428 silver rubles 75½ kopeks were obtained; but from then until 1827 the value was only 7,000 rubles.

After allowance for all profits from trade in Petropavlovsk and the surrounding area and from the sale in Russia of furs, the company spent more than 135,000 silver rubles to maintain the Kamchatka commissariat. As mentioned above, only two ships visited there after 1818 and the fur catch was insignificant, so that the commissariat office was sometimes left almost idle.

In view of all this and of the possibility of obtaining all necessary help from the Kamchatka naval station in case a company ship should have to put into Petropavlovsk for something, the directors recognized that the company commissariat in Kamchatka was unnecessary and recommended that it be abolished. This was carried into effect in a resolution of the general stockholders meeting of 28 February 1827.

More on company finances. Part of the furs obtained in the colonies was bartered in Kiakhta for tea and nankeen[1] which was sold wholesale in Moscow and on the Nizhnii-Novgorod market. The rest of the furs, along with walrus tusks, whalebone, and castoreum were also sold wholesale in Moscow and St. Petersburg. In the twenty years from 1821 through 1841 the company sold 72,814 chests of tea for 9,316,342 rubles 61 kopeks; 17,319 bales of nankeen for 261,543 rubles 46 kopeks; furs valued at 3,268,648 rubles 37 kopeks; whalebone valued at 111,870 rubles 40-3/7 kopeks; walrus tusks valued at 18,440 rubles 82-4/7 kopeks; and castoreum valued at 23,282 rubles 92 kopeks.

In the period 1821-41 the company revenues from the sale of goods and from other trading activities was . . . .   15,349,905 r. 98—1/7 k.

In this period expenditures were [all values in silver rubles] :

For maintaining the colonies . . . .   4,472,073 r. 92—2/7 k.

For maintaining the colonial churches .   64,780 r. 96—1/7 k.

For maintaining charitable institutions. . . . .   166,301 r. 17—3/7 k.

For maintaining the main office and the company offices and commissions; payments and bonuses to employees and retiring employees; interest payments on bills of exchange and on loans advanced to the company; selling expenses and miscellaneous expenses and losses. . . . . . .   4,341,534 r. 36 k.

Customs duties on tea imported at Kiakhta. . . . .   2,365,340 r. 52 k.

Freight charges for colonial goods from Okhotsk to Moscow, St. Petersburg and Kiakhta; for tea sent from Kiakhta to Moscow and the Nizhnii-Novgorod fair; and for goods sent from St. Petersburg, Moscow, and other places in Russia through Siberia for the Siberian offices and for the colonies . . . .   1,513,491 r. 7–3/7 k.

Donations to the city of Irkutsk for the construction of barracks. . . . .   16,285 r. 7–3/7 k.

For the relief of Iakuts employed in transporting company goods. . . . .   13,714 r. 28–4/7 k.

To the city of Okhotsk for the construction and maintenance of a hospital[2] . . . .   25,714 r. 28–4/7 k.

Dividends paid to stockholders. . . . . . .   2,126,257 r. 85–5/7 k.

Capitalization as of 1 January 1822 . . .   1,323,569 r. 85–5/7 k.

Retained earnings through 1841. . . . . .   235,016 r. 80–4/7 k.

Total assets as of 1 January 1841. . . . .   1,558,586 r. 66–2/7 k.

These assets consisted of goods, supplies, materials, ships, real and personal property, cash, and accounts receivable.

All the buildings in the colonies, the sawmill, the flour mill, etc., charitable and commercial establishments, property for cattle raising and gardening, and doubtful debts owed by Aleuts and others totaled 374,256 silver rubles 97–5/7 kopeks.

Dividends were paid every two years, according to the company's directive, in the following amounts (in silver rubles):

1820-21	– –	22 r. per share
1822-23	– –	None
1824-25	– –	42 r.
1826-27	– –	34 r. 57 k.
1828-29	– –	33 r. 14–1/2 k.
1830-31	– –	34 r. 28–1/2 k.

1832-33	— —	28 r. 57—1/2 k.
1834-35	— —	40 r.
1836-37	— —	34 r. 28—1/2 k.
1838-39	— —	26 r.

There was no dividend paid out in 1840, but the book profit of 7,065 silver rubles 71½ kopeks was added to capital reserves.

The annual maintenance of the colonies cost the company the following amounts:

1821	— —	169,013 r. 53—5/7 k.
1822	— —	150,785 r. 77—1/7 k.
1823	— —	163,444 r. 5—1/7 k.
1824	— —	172,884 r. 43—5/7 k.
1825	— —	164,179 r. 24 k.
1826	— —	224,545 r. 51—3/7 k.
1827	— —	207,791 r. 82—6/7 ,.
1828	— —	194,259 r. 31—3/7 k.
1829	— —	195,218 r. 58—4/7 k.
1830	— —	202,771 r. 1—5/7 k.
1831	— —	200,093 r. 62—4/7 k.
1832	— —	286,980 r. 52—6/7 k.
1833	— —	230,353 r. 57—5/7 k.
1834	— —	256,929 r. 16 k.
1835	— —	229,084 r. 18 k.
1836	— —	289,885 r. 92—1/7 k.
1837	— —	269,476 r. 34—6/7 k.
1838	— —	289,972 r. 18—4/7 k.
1839	— —	267,868 r. 37 k.
1840	— —	304,950 r. 77—5/7 k.

Government decrees relating to the company. The following government decrees arising from proposals of the directors may be added to those already mentioned in this survey of the company's second charter period:

1. *On the method and occasions of use of stamped paper by the board of directors and the company offices.* This question was raised in 1824 by the commandant of the Okhotsk Naval Command, who demanded that the company's Okhotsk office communicate with him and with other government offices on stamped paper and only in the form of reports, not messages, as had previously been the practice.

When the directors learned of this from the Okhotsk office, they communicated with the minister of finance, and after deliberation there, the question was presented to the Committee of Ministers with the following recommendations:

a.   The company's Okhotsk office, in its various dealings with government offices, should be released from the use of stamped paper, except in matters of a legal nature.

b.   The Okhotsk office, since it was not a private person, but an important company office not under the jurisdiction of the Okhotsk Naval Command, should communicate with the latter on an equal basis, in accordance with the company's imperial charter.

c.   Requests by company employees in the colonies to remain for additional terms and their applications for passport renewal should be accepted on plain paper, in order not to overburden these people and to make company service more attractive to them.

d.   In accordance with the imperial decree of 24 November 1821 the Russian-American Company should be obliged to accept requests from individuals to the board of directors and to the company's chief offices in Moscow and Irkutsk only on 50-kopek stamped paper, and the replies to these requests should also be made on this paper.

In its journal of 9 February 1825 the committee approved these recommendations, and on 29 March they received imperial confirmation.

2.   *On the establishment of the post of assistant chief manager of the colonies.* The expanding sphere of activity and the complex duties associated with the post of chief manager convinced the board of directors that these duties could not be successfully performed by one man. In the first place, the chief manager, not having a deputy, found it difficult to leave New Archangel to inspect the various colonial sections, as was necessary to govern this vast country effectively. In his absence, it was difficult to maintain the constant supervision that was nexessary in New Archangel. In addition, the administration of the colonies might be subject to extreme disorganization in case of his death or severe illness. On these grounds the directors recommended to the minister of finance the necessity of establishing a post of assistant chief manager.

On 6 February 1831, in accordance with the recommendation of the council of ministers, the emperor ordered the post of assistant chief manager of the Russian-American colonies to be established on the following conditions:

a.   The assistant chief manager should be chosen by the board of directors from the navy or from some other military or civil service and be confirmed by the high command on the same basis as the chief manager.

b. The assistant chief manager, on the basis of the company's imperial charter, should be considered on active service and upon his appointment should enjoy the privileges permitted to the chief manager by point 9 of the Company Charter of 1821;[3] for greater incentive he should also enjoy these privileges in cases where he is chosen from officials already serving in the colonies.

c. The assistant's salary and period of service in the colonies should be determined upon each appointment by mutual agreement between him and the board of directors.

d. The assistant chief manager, being absolutely subordinate to the chief manager, should fulfill all his orders, and in the case of the chief manager's absence or severe illness should assume his post; the detailed definition of his duties should be left to the directors.

On the recommendation of the chief manager, Lieutenant Etholen, who had been serving in the colonies since 1818, was named to the post of assistant chief manager. His appointment was confirmed with promotion to the rank of captain-lieutenant by the imperial decree of 16 March 1832. After Etholen had served a five-year term as assistant chief manager of the colonies, Captain-Lieutenant Mit'kov was named to that post.

3. *On settlers in the colonies.* Since its formation the Russian-American Company had accepted for colonial service on certain conditions townspeople [*meshchanin*] and peasants [*krest'ianin*]. Some of them, after completing their term of service, returned to Russia. Others, however, burdened by large families, ill health, or advancing years, remained in the colonial service. As a result, by the middle of the second period of the company's charter a large number of old, infirm, and disabled people, many of whom were also burdened by large families, had accumulated in the colonies.

Obviously such people were completely useless to the company and only burdened it. To relieve this obvious problem, the directors ordered Baron Wrangell, the colonial governor, to find means to care for these people in the colonies. His recommendations were carefully considered in joint sessions of the board of directors and the company council and were presented to the minister of finance with a request that the emperor be petitioned for permission to resettle these people in more suitable places in the colonies.

On the basis of a proposal of the Council of Ministers, the emperor decreed on 2 April 1835 that:

a. Freely hired Russian townsmen and peasants serving in the Russian-American colonies who have married creoles or natives, who wish to settle in the colonies for reasons of ill health, advancing age, long residence, familiarity with the climate and way of life, or because they have been left without relatives in Russia, and who make a written request, shall be settled along the Kenai coast of America or in some other place within the Russian possessions designated by the chief manager. The company shall be obliged to build for them suitable dwellings, provide them with necessary domestic and agricultural implements, cattle, fowl, and grain, secure their food supply for one year, and ensure that they shall not suffer from shortages after that time.

b. The company shall inform the appropriate offices to remove these people from the rolls of the former social classes to which they belonged in Russia.

c. Taxes shall be collected from the board of directors for them according to their former status without any further payment by them according to lists obtained from the chief manager.

d. The board of directors of the company shall present these lists of the re-settled migrant townsmen and peasants to the ministry of finance with its annual accountings.

e. The children of these settlers may be accepted into the company service at current wages upon their application.

f. Excess supplies shall be purchased from the settlers at free prices and furs and animals at scheduled prices.

g. Creoles who are leaving the company service and wish to settle and farm the land shall be settled with the Russians on the same basis.

The last such imperial decree appeared in 1844 and will be discussed in detail in the review of the last period of the company's charter.

Changes in composition of the board of directors and the company council. During the second period several changes took place in the makeup of the board of directors.

In the general meeting of stockholders in 1822 the Moscow merchant Ivan Vasil'evich Prokof'ev, who had hitherto managed the Moscow office, was elected to the board of directors effective 1 January 1823. In 1823 Director Kramer retired. Buldakov, chairman of the board, died in 1827. The general meeting of stockholders of 24 June 1824 elected Nikolai Ivanovich Kusov, a merchant of St. Petersburg and member of the first guild, to the board of directors. Rear Admiral Baron Ferdinand Petrovich Wrangell was elected a director by the general meeting of stockholders on 20 January 1842. Since 24 September 1838 he had served as advisor to the directors on matters relating to the colonies. The following stockholders in the company were elected to the company council at various annual meetings: in 1820, to replace the deceased member Vedemeier, Privy Councilor and Senator Gavrilo Gerasimovich Politkovskii; in 1823, on the occasion of the retirement of Vice-Admiral Sarychev, Actual State Councilor German

Ivanovich Rading; in 1825, upon the death of Politkovskii, Commissar-General Captain-Commander Vasilii Mikhailovich Golovnin; and in 1832, after the death of Golovnin and Rading, Admiral Nikolai Seme-novich Mordvinov and Major-General Matvei Ivanovich Murav'ev, former chief manager.

The charter is renewed. In 1841 the company petitioned for a continuation of its privileges for twenty more years. The State Council carefully considered this petition and reviewed the company's activities for the period ending (1819-1841) and, according to the minutes, proposed the following, confirmed by His Majesty on 7 March 1841: "To continue the existence of the Russian-American Company for twenty more years, and, until its new regulations may be reviewed and promulgated, to permit it to conduct itself by the same rules and to enjoy the same rights and privileges as were granted to this company in 1821."

The state council had based its opinion on this subject on the following considerations, communicated by the minister of finance to the board of directors in an extract from the minutes of that council. We present that extract in full.

In respect to continuing the period of privileges of the Russian-American Company the State Council must respect the reasons presented in favor of the company's petition by the Commerce Council and the Ministry of Finance. The breadth and variety of the Russian-American Company's sphere of activity places it in a position that cannot be compared with that of other companies. Aside from a trading and hunting monopoly, the government has granted to the company a portion of its power to govern a distant and extensive country, where it now has the full responsibility for all local administration. In this respect the company is not only a commercial society, but, to a certain extent, a governmental power, and its privileges include not only rights, but also duties. To change this order could hardly be advantageous, and in any case it is questionable whether it would even be successful. If everyone were given free access to the fur trade in our American dominions, this would produce a decrease in revenues, either from the rapid and widespread destruction of fur-bearing animals in conditions of open competition or, on the other hand, from the inadequate application of effort to this trade, if the number of entrepreneurs wishing to risk their capital in this relatively unknown area should be small. On the other hand, if the government should take the responsibility of the local administration of the colonies from the company and assume it itself, it would be burdened with new and large worries and with the necessity of finding additional finances. It is obvious, therefore, that if the privileges are absolutely necessary for the private benefit of the company, they are equally necessary to the nation as a whole, and for this reason it must be admitted that, until the economy of our American dominions is completely reconstructed, these privileges must be continued.

PART TWO

12. *Company Operations in Eastern Siberia*

The port of Okhotsk and the transfer of the company's trading post to Aian. The efforts of the Russian-American Company to find a harbor in southeastern Siberia more suitable than Okhotsk have already been mentioned. The company's exploration of the mouths of the rivers Ulia and Aldoma and of Aian Bay to assess the possibilities they might offer for the berthing of ships and for founding settlements were also noted.[1] Meanwhile, the disadvantages of the company's trading post of Okhotsk became progressively greater year by year and the necessity for removal so imperative that a project for locating another site, regardless of difficulties, was finally confirmed and orders issued.

However, before we touch on the carrying out of these orders it is appropriate to outline briefly the historical background of Okhotsk, to explain fully the reasons which prompted the company to change the site of its trading post.

According to Sokolov[2] the first cossack settlement on the Okhota River was founded three versts upstream from the river's mouth in 1647 under the leadership of the cossack Shelkovnikov, two years after a visit to the region by the cossack Poiarkov, who was the first Siberian to sail down the Amur River into Okhotsk Sea as far as the Ulia River. However, in an article on Okhotsk, based on data taken from local archives, Mr. Polonskii[3] places the foundation of an ostrog [fort] on the Okhota River at a slightly earlier date. Though the abundance of fish and timber in the locality certainly made life easier for the new settlers, the construction of an ostrog was necessary to protect the zimov'ias [winter quarters] of the cossacks from attacks by coastal natives—the Tungus. Subsequently, if bold enough to attack the hated newcomers, the Tungus only fell upon isolated convoys on the trail, never engaging in open warfare, but rather profiting by the carelessness of the travelers or ambushing them.

The ostrog was placed under the jurisdiction of the government office at Iakutsk, while the cossack's duties were limited to collecting iasak for the treasury from the natives. Because the journeys for this, both nearby and in Kamchatka, were all made overland, the construction of a port was never considered. It was only after the cossack Sokolov discovered a sea route to Kamchatka that Okhotsk gained in importance and local ship building commenced to provide for sea crossings. Some of the ships for Bering's first expedition were built in Okhotsk, but, according to Sokolov and Polonskii, the final decision to establish a port on the Okhota River was only taken after the arrival of a crew accompanying Captain Shpanberg, a member of the second naval expedition under Bering's command. To facilitate the outfitting of these ships, Bering put a project before the government, which was subsequently accepted, aimed at reorganizing the region on a new basis and constructing a permanent harbor.

The first port commandant, Skorniakov-Pisarev, an exile in Siberia, former director of the Naval Academy, and ex-attorney general of the senate, arrived in Okhotsk in 1735 accompanied by eighty cossacks and their families. The site he chose for the port was a low-lying strip of land about eighty sazhens wide, at the junction of the Kukhtui and Okhota rivers and slightly above the buildings owned by the second naval expedition. The unsuitability of this location soon became apparent. The construction was not even completed when, in 1736, a strong wind and high water caused the Okhota to overflow, flooding the low-lying ground, boring out a new bed and mouth sixty sazhens wide, and carrying out to sea several buildings and people. Similar inundations had occurred in previous years; in 1731 the old fort and adjoining buildings had barely been saved. Though Bering did in fact issue instructions for relocating the port, the plans put forward either by Shpanberg or the commandant of Okhotsk, Devier, were never implemented, because of their impracticability. Devier suggested moving Okhotsk thirty versts upstream from the mouth of the Okhota to its junction with the river Mal'chikan, while Shpanberg wanted to move it to the Luktur River, which flows with the Urak into the sea twenty-three versts south of Okhotsk. Despite repeated floods, Okhotsk remained where it stood and in 1742, according to Devier's statistical description, it contained over a hundred houses with eight vessels moored in the harbor. In 1772 Okhotsk and Kamchatka were divided into two separate administrative units, while in 1783, at the division of

Irkutsk Gubernia into four oblasts, Okhotsk was made the administrative center of an oblast bearing the same name.

Until 1770 the ships assigned to the fur trade in the Aleutian Islands were built in Kamchatka, but a serious decrease in the population there and consequent labor shortage forced the traders to transfer their wharves to the Urak and Khaibas rivers. The difficulties of shipbuilding there brought them in turn to the Kukhtui River, thirty-five versts above Okhotsk.

In 1799 Captain Fomin's project for moving the port of Okhotsk to Aldoma Bay was officially approved. One of the first tasks undertaken was to lay a wagon road from Iakutsk to the Maia River and from Nel'kan to the mouth of the Aldoma. During Fomin's administration this road was almost completed, but little or no headway was made in building a port at the new location. In the meantime, the danger to Okhotsk steadily increased year after year. Under the direction of Foman's successor, Captain Bukharin, a start was made in moving some of the buildings to the Bulgin, a tributary of the Okhota, but this transfer, too, was soon arrested, while the necessity of taking decisive measures became imperative. The new mouth of the Okhota choked up with sand over this period but cleared once again in 1810, leaving the port of Okhotsk on an island. High tides flowing deep into the harbor greatly hindered obtaining fresh water, requiring the use of boats during the summer months and minimum journeys of eight versts by dog teams in winter. The new mouth of the Okhota was shallow, and the Okhota and Kukhtui poured their waters into the new channel, causing the old mouth to shoal to the extent that ships drawing ten feet could enter the harbor only at high tide and then with great difficulty. Ships sailing into a headwind at high tide were sometimes forced to wait as long as a month before getting another chance to enter the river, while those outward bound could sail only at the beginning of an ebb tide, though even this operation was dangerous because of the narrowness and shallowness of the channel, and the constant shifting of its fairway. Mr. Savin's notes[4] show that there was hardly a ship in the Okhotsk flotilla which had not been damaged one way or another and that some of them had been completely wrecked. The berthing accomodation on the river was inadequate; during the winter the ships had to be dragged on shore.

In 1809 Minitskii, then chief port commandant, unsuccessfully made his own attempt to find a better location for the port. Seeing that it was absolutely impossible to leave the settlement where it was, he obtained permission to move it to Tungus Flat, on the opposite bank, adjacent to the common mouth of the Kukhtui and the Okhota. The transfer was completed by 1815. However, this in no way removed the difficulties facing ships entering or leaving the river. Nor did it improve the living conditions of the inhabitants, whose task of fetching fresh water was made even harder, especially in the summer when the boats they used for this were often swept out to sea by the strong river currents. In addition, the climate on the new site was so bad that many of the settlers fell victim to prevalent local diseases, especially scurvy. Finally, the lack of any kind of vegetation—a few vegetables grown on soil that had to be carried in— never-ending fogs, and harmful effluvia from tidelands contributed little to the attraction of Okhotsk and worsened the general state of the inhabitants.

The offices of the company's trading post, moved in 1820 to the same flat but lower than the harbor installations,[5] were in equal danger. The director of the trading post, Gribanov, informed the board of directors that the rough seawaters had already eroded the enclosure surrounding the buildings, and that there was a grave probability that the river Kukhtui would soon alter its course and find another outlet to the sea, thereby endangering the lives of the company's employees. To remedy this, he suggested moving the company's installations to the Bulgin River, eight versts from the present mouth of the river.

The actual transfer of the company's installations at Okhotsk and the option of choosing a better site anywhere along the southeastern shores of Siberia were left to Lieutenant Zavoiko, who was appointed commandant of the trading post in 1840. On arrival he decided that the transfer to the Bulgin proposed by his predecessor could entail nothing but losses; the remoteness of the location from the unloading point would require an increased labor force, and further, all the navigational difficulties would remain. After studying the previous surveys of the neighborhood he informed the directors that in his opinion moving to Aian Bay, rather than to any other point on the Okhotsk Sea, held many advantages. Chief among these were the shelter offered by the bay during summer to ships of all sizes and the possibility of reducing the number of transports coming yearly from the colonies to Okhotsk with company cargoes. He recognized the difficulties of establishing an overland link between Iakutsk and Aian, but these were not insurmountable, and the resultant route would be easier than the present one to Okhotsk. The road to the mouth of the Maia River built by Fomin was in poor condition but it would nevertheless ease the hardships of the work involved. It would thus remain only to build a road through 250 versts of unexplored territory from Nel'kan to Aian Bay.

Navigation down the Maia River, as previously mentioned,[6] presented no difficulty.

The survey of Aian. Zavoiko, told by the company to act at his own discretion, set out, accompanied by Orlov, an exiled settler and former lieutenant of the Corps of Naval Navigators, for Aian in a whaleboat in May 1842, towing another boat with supplies. About 120 versts out of Okhotsk the expedition was all but crushed by ice floes swept in by a sudden change in the wind and current. Somehow the boats were beached, but Zavoiko and Orlov were forced to wait nine days for a change in the weather. Meanwhile, the time was rapidly approaching when ships would start arriving at Okhotsk from the colonies with company cargoes. It was the commandant's duty to pilot them into the river and personally supervise the dispatch of furs to Iakutsk. Consequently, Zavoiko decided to return on skis along the coast, and he finally reached Okhotsk after crossing flooded rivers on floating ice and enduring many hardships. Left in command, Orlov pushed on to Aian, and after surveying all the bays on the way, mapped out Aian Bay. This survey was completed by Ensign Gavrilov of the Corps of Naval Navigators, commander of the company brig [*Promysel*] sent out to bring back Orlov.

The following year, Orlov was again sent to Aian to make a more thorough survey of the surrounding country. As the trading post had no small rowboats suitable for inshore navigation, he set out in an ordinary fishing boat. By the time he reached the Ul'ia River in May 1843, Orlov knew from experience that his boat was quite unsuited for crossings of this length and in addition was too small to hold the necessary supplies. Consequently, there seemed to be no other choice than to rebuild it. This he did with the help of a Tungus hired for the journey, and by 10 May he was ready to resume his travels. Ten days later, and with no further mishap of note, except, perhaps, the presence of bears, which worried them at night when camping on shore, he and his companion safely reached the Aldoma. On the way they stood alternate watch and thus one at a time at least gained a few hours rest after a day of hard work.

On the Aldoma, Orlov came across a few settled, so-called "sedentary" Tungus and hired two of them as guides. On 25 May they saw Aian. Ice covering the bay forced Orlov to beach his boat in the shelter of a cliff, while he and his companions camped at a nearby lake, better protected from the weather. As a site for the settlement Orlov proposed to adopt one of two main valleys, running north and east, respectively, in the high mountains which surrounded Aian Bay on all sides. A creek

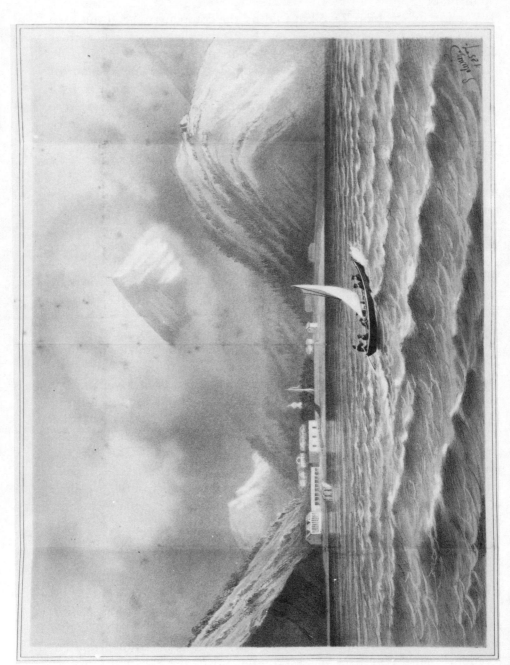

Port Aian, Siberia

ran out of the first of these valleys and was fairly rich in fish, mainly *mal'ma* and humpbacked salmon. In addition a small house and a yurt still stood, the remnants of earlier explorations by the company. The yurt was of course quite derelict but the house was sound and would serve as good shelter in the beginning.

Not wanting to decide on a building site before the arrival of his chief, Zavoiko, Orlov explored the bay and its vicinity. Information supplied by the local sedentary Tungus fully confirmed the fact that the bay, especially during the summer, offered excellent anchorage, that there were normally no breakers until October, and that even in the autumn, with a strong east wind, they were infrequent. The bay froze solidly around Christmas, and by June the sea was clear of ice.

By the time the brig sent out for his use had reached him, Orlov had covered the whole bay area on foot, finished his survey, and prepared his maps. There was nothing left for the brig's commander, Ensign Gavrilov, to do but check on a few details.

Because of the accuracy of the data, Gavrilov left Orlov's findings unamended, only filling in a few soundings here and there, and took the brig back to Okhotsk. Information on Aian Bay based on the reports of Orlov and Gavrilov is given below, as it contributed materially to the survey made by Shilov and Uglichaninov in 1832-33.

Aian Bay lies at latitude 56° 27½′ north and longitude 221° 33′ west, facing northwest and southeast. It is about 2 miles long and 440 sazhens wide between the reef of Larga-Angri, a seal rookery, and Chaiach Rock [*Kekur*]. It is open to the sea between the compass bearings of S by E and SSW, or almost due south. The depth varies, gradually decreasing from a maximum of eighteen sazhens to a minimum of seven and nine sazhens between the cape at the entrance and the center of the bay. The entire bed is either sand or silt. The tide rises thirteen feet, and high tide occurs slightly before the moon reaches the meridian. Incoming tides flow southwest; ebbing tides, northeast. The compass deviation over the whole reach between Iona Island and Aian Bay alternates between 3° and 5° west.

The approaches to the bay are perfectly safe even in fog. In clear weather the shores can be observed from fifty miles away. Entrance to and exit from the bay present no difficulties. The main advantage, however, of Aian over Okhotsk lies in the fact that entry is possible under any wind conditions. The current is negligible after rounding the cape and, thus, towing ships into the harbor in calm weather is comparatively easy. There is good anchorage everywhere below a line stretching from Chaiach Rock to Larga-Angri Reef, despite a heavy swell with an east wind.

Good building timber was sparse around the bay, but up the Ui River, which flowed into Aian Bay, there were many fine trees which could readily be hauled in across the ice in winter. There were lush meadows along the banks, and an abundance of fish in the river promised good fishing. Two and a half versts distant from the northern valley Orlov found a stratum of clay that preliminary tests indicated was suitable for both brickmaking and household pottery.

There is no further need to stress the advantages of the Aian site over Okhotsk or the other locations previously considered as replacements for the Okhotsk trading post. The one point still in doubt was the feasibility of making a road capable of supporting heavy loads from Nel'kan to Aian. To this end, Zavoiko engaged in Iakutsk the services of a townsman named Berezin, and entrusted him with the preliminary survey of the projected work.

Construction of the trading post of Aian. For the intended work at Aian, Zavoiko commissioned an agent in Iakutsk to hire twenty-five Iakuts skilled mainly in carpentry and stovesetting. The agency was to supply them with horses, tools, and other articles required for roughly furnishing the first buildings to go up.

On 11 August 1843 Zavoiko arrived at Aian on the brig *Promysel*, accompanied by the archpriest of Okhotsk cathedral, who was to bless the site in the northern valley chosen for the settlement. Several workmen from Okhotsk were aboard the brig. The timber for erecting the first buildings had already been assembled by Orlov, who from early morning until late at night unremittingly supervised the task of hauling and logging. With this limited labor force and often wielding an ax himself, he accomplished a great deal. Zavoiko writes:

> Even omitting the hazards and difficulties of a sea voyage of 250 miles to Aian in a simple rowboat, no praise is high enough for the selflessness and singleness of purpose with which Orlov tackled every one of his many duties. Having myself made the journey [from Okhotsk] to Aian on foot, and, knowing the surrounding country as I now do, I fully realize all the tremendous difficulties he had to overcome.

Though all the dogs brought by the brig *Promysel* for haulage had died, Orlov never lost heart and carried on with the work at hand. By 1 December 1843, with his crew of eleven, he had both living quarters and facilities ready. The following had been completed at Aian: the manager's and visitors' quarters, 3 sazhens long and 2½ sazhens wide with four windows, three rooms, an anteroom, kitchen, a storeroom, and attendant facilities (the floors were planed planks and the house had an iron stove); a barracks for thirty men with a Russian stove, a

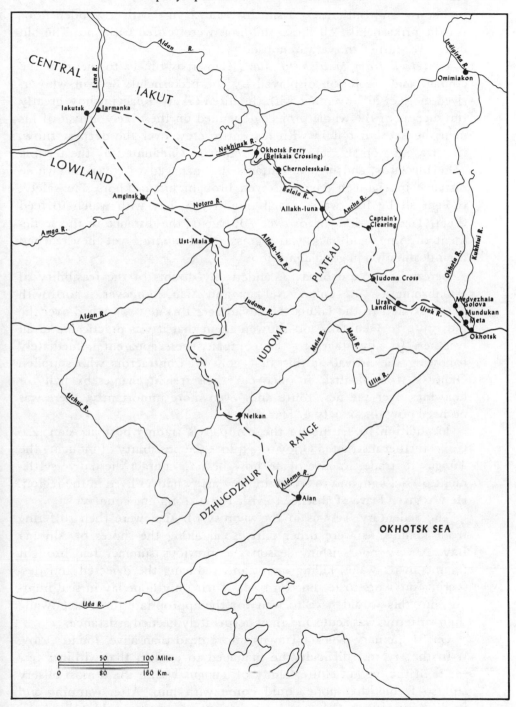

Routes to the Pacific from Iakutsk

bathhouse and outhouses; a smithy; and a yurt with a wooden floor for the prikashchik. All these buildings were roofed with sod. The old house was turned into a warehouse.

First trek from Iakutsk to Aian. Here it is timely to mention the courage and resolution displayed by the prikashchik Berezin who arrived in Aian in November with the hired Iakuts. Realizing how greatly the success of the whole project depended on the timely arrival of his men, he set out boldly with his entire crew over the deepest snow, first traveling on skis and later by reindeer. Undaunted by the terrible cold, blizzards, and high mountains, he managed to cover the whole distance in eighteen days. He even brought his packhorses in safely, though all he had was a small quantity of hay with which to feed them. The only fodder for over 700 versts, the distance to the settlement of Amga and back, was a grass called *sibikta*,[7] yet they reached their destination in good condition.[8]

Berezin's resolute behavior ended any doubts of the feasibility of establishing a route linking Nel'kan and Aian. Moreover, it forthwith demonstrated to the Iakuts the advantages this new route had over the old route to Okhotsk, and showed them that it was practicable in all weather. Its advantages to the company were apparent immediately following the arrival of this first convoy. Contractors who supplied Okhotsk from Iakutsk at once cut their freight charges by half for deliveries over the new route and, even more importantly, there was no need now for anxiety or fear.

In addition to setting up the company's trading post at Aian, Zavoiko further instructed Orlov to explore the possibility of inducing the Tungus to trade, to investigate how best to contact the native settlement of Nel'kan, and to ascertain how many natives lived in the region. He was given leave of absence to visit the surrounding country.

The sedentary Tungus in the vicinity of Aian were then suffering from famine, as were other natives all along the shores of Aldoma Bay. A very poor fishing season the previous summer had brought famine in its wake, killing many and reducing the dejected and despairing survivors to feeding on bark. Their only hope lay in seal hunting, but this would have to wait for the appropriate time. Meanwhile their suffering was acute and they desperately needed assistance.

On 31 January 1844 a Tungus, more dead than alive, found Orlov. With the greatest difficulty he managed to explain that within a few versts of the bay an entire family of Tungus was in the utmost misery and so feeble that none could come with him. After warming and feeding his visitor, Orlov at once set out in search of the others. All the dogs being smitten by distempter, he had to travel over the deep snow on skis and only succeeded in reaching the family's abode by 14 February. One of the Tungus had in the meantime died, and Orlov took the remaining four with him. By now the hungry natives kept coming into the settlement and Orlov's limited supplies forced him to ration to every Tungus only one pound of meat, some bread, and tea. In his report to the commandant of the Okhotsk trading post on the famine around Aian, Orlov stated that though he would issue company supplies to all natives who came to the settlement, he could not bring them in himself over the deep snow without dogteams. The absence of suitable transport also prevented him from providing the natives with powder and lead, though he had ample supplies of both and he knew that the seals had returned to their rookeries.

Foreseeing that the plight of the Tungus might at some future time be ascribed to the fact that a few of the company's employees were lodged in their settlements, Zavoiko sent in a detailed report on the famine to the Okhotsk maritime administration. In doing so, he hoped that his report might ultimately lead to the adoption of measures aimed at helping the natives. For these unsophisticated children of nature, who lived by their hunting, powder and lead were the two prime necessities which ensured success or failure. But these vital commodities were only issued to them through the local police inspector in places convenient for him and often remote from their camps. Long absence from home was always onerous and sometimes impossible for the Tungus. To help them, Zavoiko volunteered on behalf of the company to suppy them with powder and lead.

Although the Okhotsk port commandant, Captain-Lieutenant Trankovskii, knew all about the famine raging among the Tungus from other official sources, he had no means of assistance at his disposal. He was, perforce, limited to sending a report to the governor-general of Eastern Siberia on the desperate plight of the natives entrusted to his care, and of the help rendered them in the company's settlement.[9]

In his report, Trankovskii included information given him by Kapiton Gromov, a Tungus, concerning a caravan of thirty pack-reindeer with goods belonging to a Iakutsk merchant, Struchkov, which he met among the encampments of the nomad Tungus along the Aldoma. To allay starvation Gromov bought some hardtack off him and, according to his statement, was charged plenty for it. When asked by the commandant of Okhotsk to describe what other goods he saw and whether he thought the traders could dispose of all of them to the Tungus, Gromov replied that he had noted daba [Chinese cotton cloth], tea, sugar, tobacco, hardtack, powder, lead, spirits, and other sundries. As regards the conditions of sale, he had no doubts. If the traders could not obtain the desired number of pelts in exchange for their goods, they simply forced the natives to take their remaining goods on credit at unbelievably high prices. By this method the natives were forced into heavy debt. When the creditors returned to collect, the Tungus fled into the forests but seldom evaded capture. The traders used great cunning, and either ambushed the fugitives with the help of hired trackers or just simply rounded them up. Usually the unfortunate victim, weakened by hunger, ended by docilely surrendering to his creditor, praying for mercy, and paying the arrears plus compensation for any losses incurred.

Trankovskii added a few of his own suggestions on the best way to free the Tungus from the clutches of these rapacious traveling traders. On the strength of standing government regulations strictly forbidding the sale of spirits and powder to the natives, he suggested placing the Tungus' settlements out of bounds to the traders, especially those situated at remote places, as at Gizhiga and Aian bays. "This is the only way," he wrote,

of delivering the Tungus tribe, so meek and submissive, not only to higher authorities but, in fact, to every Russian, from oppression by the petty traders. My two trips to Gizhiga convinced me of all the harm wrought among the natives by these traders, particularly to the Tungus, so infinitely loyal to Russia. Knowing the facts, I have no reason to doubt the simple-hearted sincerity of the Tungus Gromov. To put an end to this evil I consider it absolutely essential to restrict trading with the natives solely to places where there is a resident government official, while distant localities should be open to them during the Chukotsk fair and then only if accompanied by a police inspector. Traders on the way to Aian should be permitted to sell their wares only in the native settlement of Nel'kan, where there is a government food store and where the natives coming in to pay their iasak can buy bread, flour, and other commodities at reasonable prices. Quite apart from the advantages to be gained from these suggestions, the natives would be spared a recurrence of misfortunes like the present ones. Their frequency alone leads one to ponder over the fate of the wretched Tungus. A striking example of the full horror of these calamities was given me during my stay in Gizhiga in the winter of 1842-43, when some of the Tungus living near the bay were only saved from death by starvation thanks to the charity of the town's inhabitants.

On my return to Okhotsk, I reported the circumstances to Captain of First Rank Golovnin, former chief of the maritime administration, and later to the Irkutsk civil governor.

Meanwhile, the Iakutsk merchants who traded with the Tungus, sensing that the company might become a dangerous competitor, strove to maintain their influence over the natives and safeguard their revenues. Enticing offers were made and exceptional favors promised to any who would refrain from dealing with the company. Particularly they urged them to move away from the new road, suggesting that no good would come from living near the company's settlement. Some of these allurements had the desired effect. Mistrust of the company's servants was evident even when they went to the rescue of starving natives in a spirit of complete selflessness. Much of this attitude was certainly due to the lack of direct contact, since in so short a period the company had not yet established trade relations over the entire area.

Communications between Aian and Iakutsk. In the spring of 1844 Orlov set forth to establish what was the best route between Aian and Iakutsk. He reported on three possibilities:

1. from Aian along the coast to Nel'kan, a distance of about 300 versts, approximately five days travel; from Nel'kan down the Maia River to its mouth, about 640 versts, around three days; from the mouth of the Maia to the mouth of the Aldan, 900 versts, seven days; and from the mouth of the Aldan up the Lena, about 190 versts, six days. Under favorable circumstances the total time might be cut by two days.

2. from Aian to Nel'kan by light pack transport, about five days; from Nel'kan down the Maia River to the Aldan, three days; and from the Aldan overland to Iakutsk, six days.

3. from Aian to Nel'kan, by light pack transport, five days; from Nel'kan to the Khandikan or Khandyk (a tributary of the Maia), likewise five days; from Khandikan to the Aldan with light loads, three days; and from the Aldan to Iakutsk, six days.

The state of the various routes from Iakutsk to Aian and the distribution of the population along their lengths need to be examined. A wagon road 203 versts in length ran from Iakutsk to the Amga settlement (on the Amga River). It had a number of stations along its length and the inhabitants kept post horses. Then there was also the wagon road built by Captain Fomin in 1806 from the Amga River to the Aldan (180 versts), usable but requiring extensive repairs. There were only a few native habitations along this road. However, on the Aldan River was a large Tungus village where the natives raised cattle. Here a ferry service was planned across the Aldan to the mouth of the Maia. From there to the Khandikan River the country was uninhabited save for a solitary Tungus who lived on the bank and a few who came in summer to fish. Another ferry was planned here. Farther along the route and as far as Nel'kan, where a third ferry was to be installed, there were no habitations.

Supplies could be carried overland by either of two methods: pack-horse, thus saving the expenses of road building except for the initial cost of installing the ferries, or cart, to the Aldan River and then once again by packhorse to Aian.

If the first method were adopted, the labor would be as hard on both men and beasts as over the old Okhotsk route and costs would be about equal; however, the total of 383 versts on this route were easier to negotiate than the Okhotsk route. The cost of hire amounted to about twelve silver rubles per horse, estimating a load at five puds per animal.[10]

If the alternative route were used, the road from Amga to Aldan would have to be repaired at an estimated cost of 3,000 silver rubles. Farther along the stretch, however, the cost was not to exceed one paper ruble per pud. Transportation from the Aldan to Aian would be limited to pack horses, and a road would have to be made along the whole route, as well as a few bridges, costing over 6,000 silver rubles.

Utilizing this route, the cost of hire per horse would be reduced to a maximum of six silver rubles, as against nine paid for transportation to Okhotsk and back.

Water transportation was to be confined to the stretch between Aldan and Nel'kan. The construction, according to preliminary calculations, would necessitate an initial outlay of 10,000 silver rubles, estimating the annual freight at 3,000 puds. A further 15,000 silver rubles per year would be required over the next five years, thus bringing the cost to 6 silver rubles per pud. Later it was hoped to reduce this amount to 5 silver rubles.

After consideration the directors decided, until further research had been completed, to adopt the second route by Orlov as the shortest and most convenient to carry the company's freight. An additional advantage was the possibility of deferring the purchase of a river steamer for the projected river routes. Later surveys, however, showed that because of shallows along certain stretches, carriage in small covered boats (*pávozki*) would be best.

Further organization of the new settlement. On 27 July 1845 the company transferred its establishments to Aian Bay and turned the buildings it formerly occupied at Okhotsk over to the government to be used as a naval hospital.

In any new undertaking even the slightest help is important. A wounded whale, 31½ feet long, stranded on the beach close to Aian Bay at the end of October 1844 proved a veritable boon. Yielding 287 puds of blubber and 125 puds of meat, it provided food for the dogteams over the winter, and thus helped to accelerate the haulage of timber for the post. Otherwise, Second Lieutenant of the Corps of Naval Navigators Savin, acting chief of the settlement in Orlov's absence, would indeed have had a serious problem; supplies for the dogs brought from Okhotsk were inadequate, and the Aleuts in the settlement had killed very few seals.

In June 1845 upon orders from the commandant of the Okhotsk trading post, a company agent was sent from Iakutsk to Nel'kan with instructions to look for land suitable for pasture and tillage. On the way he selected several points, particularly at river crossings and a few other places, and set up posting stations to forward the company's mail from Iakutsk to Aian and back. To run the stations, he settled eighteen hired Iakuts and their families, whom he had brought with him from Iakutsk, and eleven Russian men and eleven women, assigned by the Siberian authorities at Zavoiko's request. All of the Russians belonged to the Skoptsy sect.[11]

By the summer of 1845 the whole system of the company's transport was completed; the ferries were in place at the appointed crossings and the craft designed to carry heavy freight along the rivers were ready. Orlov had made a survey of the Lena River up to its juncture with the Aldan and returned to Aian from the large settlement of Amga utilizing the stations set up by the company along the way.

To insure efficient delivery of overland freight between Aldan and Nel'kan in the future, Zavoiko proposed to build the roads over marshy ground and to cut a clearing through the forest along the whole way. The cost of upkeep was estimated at 2,000 silver rubles annually until such time as the whole road was made serviceable.

In instructing Zavoiko to proceed with the work of establishing a final link between Iakutsk and Aian as he thought best, the company informed him he would be given twenty-five laborers during the course of 1845 and that an additional ten would be sent him annually to replace those who might leave.

The effect that the transfer of the company's trading post to Aian[12] would have on life throughout southeastern Siberia became increasingly evident. Russian and foreign shipping alike could safely shelter in Aian Bay which offered a first-class harbor. As a transit point it held out excellent prospects both for the company and government which could now more readily provision other Russian ports on the shores of the Eastern Ocean. The establishment of settlers along the route from Aian to Iakutsk was bound to bring life to a region so far almost uninhabited. In fact, the region was being given the opportunity to develop its trade and commerce and even its own natural resources. To place the new trading post under the jurisdiction of the general colonial administration seemed undesirable in view of its particular status and distance from other Russian colonies. So, by the very nature of things, it was obvious that the head of the post, a man who was resolute in carrying out his decisions, should have been allowed unfettered freedom of action. This was essential because familiarity with local conditions was necessary to guarantee the welfare of the entire region and the success of the numerous undertakings. In view of the importance of the post, then, and its intended role in the development of the surrounding country, Aian would have to be removed from the overall administration of the company's other installations and enabled to function as a separate and independent unit.

After reviewing the situation, the directors decided to approach the minister of finance and ask for approval of the following changes in the status of Aian:

1. that the trading post being founded at Aian be designated a port.

2. that the commandant of the post, appointed from among officers of the Imperial Navy, be given the title of port commander [*komandir*] with all the rights attached to this position under existing regulations.

3. that in order to render the post of port commander attractive to deserving and gifted officers, they should, on appointment for a term of five years, be promoted to the next superior grade in rank, similar to officers entering the Crown Naval Services at Okhotsk and in Kamchatka.

These proposals received imperial assent on 6 September 1846.[13]

Settlers for the Aian route. Now that the overall system of transport was in operation, the company's next task was to settle a few Iakuts around Nel'kan to convey the company's cargoes to Aian. This was no easy task considering the desolation of the area. Contractors previously engaged had either been forced to default on their agreements or else had demanded exorbitant payment for their services. To eliminate this severe handicap to the functioning of the newly founded post, the board of directors obtained permission from the government to settle forty Iakuts at Nel'kan to transport freight from there to Aian.[14] This plan, however, met with unexpected difficulties unrelated in any way to the company and led to an exchange of correspondence which lasted up to 1848 between the commandant of Aian and the oblast administration of Iakutsk. The innate laziness of the Iakuts was reflected in the small number who volunteered to settle at Nel'kan, while those who did volunteer usually held no property and consequently would not make good settlers. Nevertheless, the company's agency in Iakutsk chanced taking on about ten men and dispatched them to their appointed sectors. Finally, the Iakutsk administration advised the commandant at Aian to select in the native villages a few Iakuts who were in some way a burden to their respective communities.[15] Zavoiko, however, with plenty of experience behind him as to settlers, refused to comply.

The directors, aware of the importance of developing the trade and commerce of the vast region over which it operated, endeavored to impress upon the government the advantages of settling the Iakutsk-Nel'kan route on a larger scale.[16] It pointed out that if Iakuts owning up to a thousand head of cattle and an equal number of horses were placed along the sector, the gain to the government would be considerable. Not only would it lead to a sensible and natural use of the waterways, but would also tend to alter radically the whole manner of life and habits of the native population. It would, on the one hand, facilitate the disposal of grain and other products of the Lena and thereby assist in provisioning the whole Kamchatka region, while, on the other, it would introduce the Iakuts to a more settled way of life. If there were no need for them to leave their homesteads for the whole summer, as at present, they might develop a greater interest in the increase and improvement of their stock. It would, moreover, rid them of the perennial scourge of loss through overwork their one source of wealth—their horses. Finally, agriculture and vegetable growing on the banks of the Maia if introduced would promote the welfare of the region in many other respects.[17]

The government asked for the regional administration's views on the subject. The governor-general of Eastern Siberia, in his reply approving the proposals, indicated that, if desired, he could move to the vicinity of Aian the Nemiugin *nasleg* (the local term for a Iakut village) of the Kangal *ulus* [kinship group], a native settlement comprising 844 men and an equal number of women together with their 1,200 horses and 1,500 head of cattle. The minister for internal affairs, while concurring with the governor-general's views, considered that the cost of compensating the Iakuts for their abandoned yurts and other household goods as well as any cash advances toward new installation should be borne by the company and not the government, because, in his opinion, the entire project was being sanctioned for the sole benefit of the company. The board of directors held a different view. They maintained that the whole southeastern region of Siberia would benefit more from the proposed scheme of settlement than the company. Besides, the needs of the company and of the recently founded harbor were being adequately met by the previously authorized settling of forty Iakuts. The considerable cost of the transfer operation and resettlement, the equipping of the port, and organizing overland and water transport was being defrayed by the company. The board therefore refused to shoulder an additional financial burden, which it felt was not justified in the present circumstances.

The whole matter thus remained in abeyance until General Murav'ev became governor-general of Siberia at the end of 1847. Soon after his appointment the use of Okhotsk as an official port was discontinued.[18] The decision followed to settle the Aian route in adequate numbers and to entrust the execution of government orders in Aian to the resident head officer of the company. An assistant was to be sent to his aid and the company staff reinforced by several employees appointed by the Crown. The majority of the settlers selected for transplanting were Raskol'niki [Old Believers, dissident sectarians] from various parts of Siberia, who were granted special privileges by the government.

Unfortunately, the process of settling the newcomers encountered a number of setbacks, especially during the initial period. Their arrival was delayed until the autumn of 1852, when it was too late to build. Their winter quarters were not provided for and no fodder laid in for their livestock. The families transported to Nel'kan and the surrounding country fared worse than any of the others. Wishing to help the government meet the situation, the commandant of Aian, Captain-Lieutenant Kashevarov, allowed the settlers to use his buildings at Nel'kan and provided them with all the hay they required free of charge. He also gave them all the company grain grown that year and permitted them to buy flour, tea, and other commodities in the company's stores at rates charged to its employees. At the request of the Nel'kan superintendent, he dispatched an assortment of copper, iron, and pig iron articles for housekeeping to the settlement, which were at once bought up. It need hardly be stressed what this relief meant to the settlers.

A personal tour of inspection around Aian convinced Captain-Lieutenant Kashevarov that the settlers would also have to be given cash if they were to obtain the household goods they required. To this end he allowed the settlers at Nel'kan and Khandikan to retain for their own use the ferrying charges levied. He gave to those at Chelazinsk the company's four horses, while those at Aimsk received a large boat on the Nel'kan River. The needs of the settlers on the Maia were to be ascertained. All of them were instructed not to charge the company for ferrying its goods across the rivers, as it was estimated that earnings from private and government freight traffic along the route to Kamchatka and harbors on the Eastern Ocean might be quite substantial.

But despite the company's financial help in providing accommodation and in other ways, the state of the native settlers was pitiable. Their late arrival, exhaustion from the trek, which had often involved towing their belongings against the current of the Maia, the lack of fresh supplies, the inadequacy of the grain ration issued by the government, and, finally, the harshness of the climate combined to increase their misery. Scurvy rapidly developed among them and during the winter claimed many victims. Kashevarov came to their aid with the necessary medicines he had at hand, as well as sauerkraut and other remedies to counteract the onslaught of the disease. A male nurse on the way to Kamchatka interrupted his journey at Nel'kan and did what he could to help the sufferers. The medicines sent by Kashevarov arrived in time to help a great deal. The governor of Iakutsk, probably because of his inability to send aid to the Nel'kan and Kamchatka settlers, who were living together, because of the distance or for other reasons, limited himself to asking Kashevarov to do all that was possible.[19]

Issues of flour, powder, and lead to the Tungus. The proposals put forward several years earlier to supply the Tungus with flour, powder, and lead were at last approved by the government in 1848. The depot at Nel'kan, formerly owned by the company and then handed over to the government for storing stocks of grain, was placed at the disposal of the Aian port authorities for warehousing company supplies. The price charged the Tungus for rye flour by Zavoiko varied between 1 ruble 60 kopeks to 2 silver rubles per pud, whereas the government sold it at between 3 rubles and 3 rubles 48 kopeks.[20] The striking difference in price caused the governor-general of Siberia to ask for an explanation. The reason, as it turned out, was not hard to find. It appeared that the company's supplies were now normally forwarded over the new route from Iakutsk to Aldan at the rate of 43 kopeks silver per pud, from Aldan to Nel'kan by water along the Maia and from Nel'kan to Aian on company packhorses. The government on the other hand still used a routine established in 1818 that followed the setting up of imperial storage depots. The whole area, including the regions of Okhotsk and Kamchatka, was supplied with grain transported by packhorses according to a contract with the Iakuts. Payment was made at the rate of 11 silver rubles 42¾ kopeks per load, that is, per 5½ puds. This basic rate was further increased by the cost of the grain itself, warehouse maintenance, and administrative and other charges. It followed that even given the most favorable conditions of stocking, the cost to the government could not possibly have been lower than 2 silver rubles 61 kopeks or 2 rubles 87 kopeks per pud.[21]

After examining the whole supply situation, the company suggested the following arrangement to the government:[22]

1. The price of grain sold to the Tungus was to be reduced to the lowest minimum possible.

2. Existing stocks of grain in the government warehouse in Nel'kan were to be handed over to the company, and in the future, the amount of grain laid down by regulations, irrespective of stocks was to be delivered to the company warehouse; grain and flour were to be sold at current prices, powder and lead at a rate fixed by the government; credit for these commodities was to be allowed the Tungus only in cases of genuine hardship.

3. The port commandant of Aian was to submit a report three times a year to an appropriate official on grain sold and on hand.

Following the usual procedure, the proposals were submitted to the governor-general of Eastern Siberia. He approved,[23] with qualifications on two items: company credit to the Tungus, and the right of the company to refuse supplies in excess of a quota it had itself fixed. On the first point the governor-general held that credit should be made available to all destitute Tungus alike and should not depend on a means assessment by the company's storekeepers. Moreover, pressure for payment was not to be pushed to a point crippling the native's ability to pay iasak. Regarding the second point, the governor-general agreed to let the clause stand as drafted on condition that early notification be given the Iakutsk regional administration of the company's inability to supply the Tungus so as to allow government stocks to be dispatched in time. An addendum by the governor-general laid down that "in all fairness to the company it should not be saddled with responsibilities greater than those it had undertaken to assume, i.e., to be expected to hold stocks of grain in excess of quantities hitherto considered by the government as adequate."

The proposals, as amended by the governor-general, were accepted by the Council of Ministers and received Imperial assent on 15 February 1849. Meantime, the company had made the necessary preparations well in advance. Trading parties were sent out in 1847 to the ostrog of Udsk and the Tungus encampments lying between Aian, Nel'kan and the Chinese border. The presence of company agents in these areas caused the private traders to scale down their prices in order to meet the competition of the company, thereby making it easier for the natives to purchase necessities.

The net result of three years trading with the Tungus was disappointingly poor, however. No representations by the commandant of Aian to the Siberian authorities could put an end to the peddling of alcohol in the settlements by Iakutsk traders or, for that matter, its open sale in Nel'kan. Everything remained unchanged and the hold of these parasites on the Tungus was as tight as ever. The enticement of alcohol was too strong, and it stripped them of all they had possessed.

Under the circumstances, it was virtually impossible to press charges of coercion or, in particular, of illicit sales of vodka against the rapacious traders, who even when caught red-handed got away free. Proof of their impunity lay in the fact that around Aian alone the sale of spirits rose steeply during the winter of 1849-50. The company had to admit that it was powerless in dealing with the traders, because the Tungus was ready to give up everything for a supply of vodka. Later, of course, the Tungus would turn up in rags at the company's stores demanding food, not as a customer, but as a pauper needing rescue from starvation.[24] The company, therefore, realizing that trying to push trade with the natives any further could not in any way benefit the region as a whole or serve its own interests, sought permission via usual channels to be released from the obligation to supply the Tungus with grain and other commodities and to return the warehouse at Nel'kan to government ownership.

Another reason for this step was the fact that since the abandonment of Okhotsk as a part and the administrative detachment of Kamchatka, the route from Iakutsk to Aian came under government control and the governor-general of Eastern Siberia thought it best to see the natives once again provisioned by the Russian government.[25] Since the route would be used by the company only for transport purposes, there would no longer be any need to stock supplies along it, if the obligations connected with providing for the Tungus were removed.

The Council of Ministers' agreement to the changeover was sanctioned by the emperor on 28 August 1851.

Meanwhile, the governor-general who, in person, was afforded the opportunity "to observe the pernicious effects of dishonest trading by peddler merchants on the life and general status of the Tungus,"[26] was searching for a means to stamp out the evil. A plan put forward by a group of Iakutsk merchants met with his approval. It consisted of holding regular fairs in certain designated localities, and using Aian and the area around it as a distributing center for their wares. The port commandant was approached and the following three places were selected: a site on the river Aldan, seven miles distant from the wharf at Ust'-Maisk; another on the Aian River; and the third at the ostrog of Udsk. For various reasons nothing came of this plan. In 1852 several merchants again informed the governor-general that they needed Aian as a clearing and account-settling center for their dealings in Kamchatka. Further correspondence with the port commandant of Aian was followed by an approach to the directors. They replied that there was no objection to holding an annual fair at Aian, provided proper measures were taken to prevent the importation of liquor by nonresident merchants. But even after this, the fair at Aian was never held, the probable reason being the growing importance of the Amur region as a center of commerce.

Suggestions for transferring the administration of Aian to the government. The increase of the company's staff at Aian, further augmented by the inclusion of a number of state employees, did not, in the views of the East Siberian authorities, measure up to the importance the port was to enjoy as a center of private and state enterprise in the south-eastern parts of Siberia. In October 1853 the governor-general inquired if the company's board saw any objection to handing over to the government the entire responsibility, i.e., the appointment and maintenance of the port administration, for the port of Aian. The company gave its assent, deeming that, as previously in Okhotsk, an office and a few warehouses were all that it really required.

The matter, however, went no further. When, in 1855, the Kamchatka Maritime Board, as well as the government's main trading center on the Eastern Ocean, was transferred to the Amur, the whole project was dropped and Aian continued under company management as it does to this day [1863].

The present situation of Aian port. In these circumstances Aian today is of significance solely to the company, or rather to the colonies under its jurisdiction. Pending the development of trade and commerce in the Amur region, the smooth functioning of the Iakutsk-Aian route and, consequently, of Aian as a transit point, are major concerns of the company. Between 1845 and 1862,[27] the estimated value of goods exported through Aian to the colonies amounted to 450,000 silver rubles, while that of imported furs at colonial prices amounted to 5 million silver rubles. A transit turnover of this magnitude was met by sixty to seventy storekeepers and other workers in addition to the normal administrative port and office establishment, i.e., the port commandant, chief clerk, bookkeeper-treasurer, and correspondent.

The enemy squadron in Aian waters during the late war with England and France. To conclude, we should recall that Aian as a point isolated from other Russian colonies did not come within the terms of the convention signed by the belligerent powers regarding the neutrality and nonviolation of their respective colonial possessions during the late war and, as such, was open in time of war to many hazards. However, landing parties from enemy ships sent ashore in 1855 to inspect the port installations in detail caused no appreciable damage or loss to the company. Two component parts of a prefabricated iron steamboat intended by the company for use on the Amur were all that was destroyed. A schooner on the slips was left untouched after Mr. Freiberg, a bookkeeper accompanying one of the parties, had given an understanding that work on the ship would not proceed until the end of hostilities. In accordance with a proclamation issued upon the squadron's arrival and observed to the letter during the entire stay of the enemy's vessels in port, the inhabitants of Aian and their property were left completely unmolested.

13. *The Exploration of the Amur River, the Building of Settlements, and the Company's Trade in the Amur Region*

The views of Krusenstern and other contemporary navigators on the navigability of the mouth of the Amur River, and projects for exploration of the river and the coast of the Okhotsk Sea. Following the unsuccessful ambassadorial mission to China under Count Golovkin, whose instructions, as previously stated[1] included negotiations for the return of the Amur River to Russia, nothing was undertaken for many years to achieve this end or even to explore the river or its mouth. This indifference was due mainly to the importance attached to navigator Krusenstern's opinion that Sakhalin Island was connected to the coast of Tartary. His assertion that a sandy strip of land connected both shores, confirmed by the English Captain Broughton, as well as the doubts expressed by La-Pérouse,[2] for a long time delayed any attempt to investigate the region. A project for exploring the mouth of the Amur in a small decked vessel was submitted in 1806 by Colonel d'Auvrey, a member of Count Golovkin's embassy who was commissioned by him to collect information on the Amur. The project was never executed, however, probably because of Krusenstern's opinion.[3]

Circumstances eventually proved that Krusenstern's view was false. Krusenstern cited a warning given him in Kamchatka, on his second voyage there, about the difficulties of approaching the shores of Tartary, "for fear," as he said, "of arousing Chinese suspicions and of disrupting the profitable Kiakhta trade." He gave this as his reason for not thoroughly exploring the region, but the excuse is unconvincing. His conviction that the mouth of the Amur was zealously guarded by armed Chinese vessels[4] was flatly contradicted by d'Auvrey, who said, furthermore, that the kind of craft he proposed to build could repel any Chinese attack[5] and make navigation on the river perfectly safe. Finally, the pertinent remarks of Mr. Shemelin, a commissioner of the

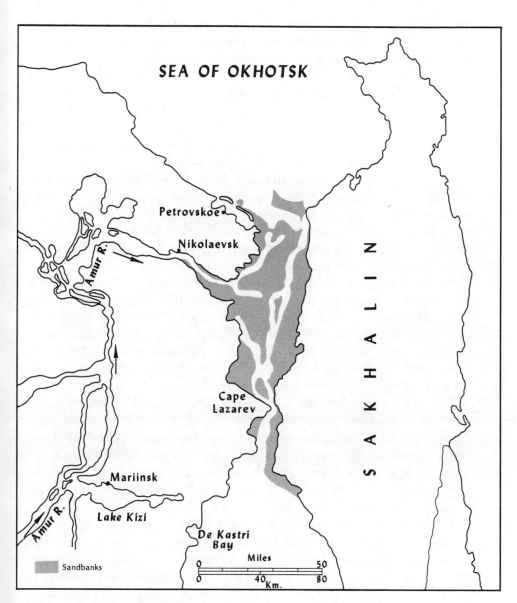

SEA OF OKHOTSK

Petrovskoe
Nikolaevsk

Amur R.

SAKHALIN

Cape
Lazarev

Mariinsk

Lake Kizi

Amur R.

De Kastri
Bay

Sandbanks

Miles
0 ——————————— 50
0 ——————————— 80
40 Km.

The mouth of the Amur River

Russian-American Company who traveled with Krusenstern, definitely confirm the absence of any armed Chinese ships in the region.[6]

Whatever the pros and cons, none of the suggestions proposed either for navigating the Amur or for thoroughly exploring the country round the river's mouth were acted on for over twenty years. Only in 1826 did our government half-heartedly take up the matter, but even then, for various reasons, any concrete decisions were deferred.

In 1826, for example, the State Department of the Admiralty instructed Captain Lütke of the sloop *Seniavin*, which was fitting out for a voyage around the world, to survey the coastline between Sakhalin Island and Udsk ostrog. However, the scope of the plans drawn up for the expedition and the time spent exploring other localities prevented Lütke from ever reaching the Okhotsk Sea.

Then in 1828, the authorities in Eastern Siberia were requested by the Ministry of Foreign Affairs[7] to assemble all possible statistical and ethnographical data about the Amur River. Somewhat later the ministry instructed our mission in Peking to do the same and to make every effort to convince the Chinese government how much both Russia and China could gain from Russian navigation on the Amur.

Privy Councilor Lavinskii, then the administrator of Eastern Siberia, in addition to furnishing the information required, suggested organizing a special exploratory expedition. Of the mass of information supplied by Lavinskii, one item merits special attention: the deposition made by Guri Vasil'ev, a fugitive deportee who voluntarily returned from Chinese territory to Siberia by way of the Udsk region, after living for over six years in various places along the Amur.[8]

The most informative data, however, on the Amur region had been supplied to Lavinskii by Captain Koz'min of the Corps of Naval Navigators. Koz'min, acting on orders from the Russian-American Company,[9] spent almost two years examining the possibilities of a route from Iakutsk to the port of Udsk, and recording a description of the west coast of the Okhotsk Sea and several of its islands. During his work he came into close contact with the natives of the Udsk region and with those living near the Russian border, from whom he learned much about navigational conditions on the river. In his notes, Koz'min particularly mentions the Giliaks, Neidal'tsi (or, as he calls them, "Negidal'tsi") Samagrtsi, or Samagrakh, and the occasional visitors to the Burda River, the Dogurtsi, or to be correct, the Dourtsi [Daurians]. A proposal for exploring the Amur, drawn up by Koz'min in collaboration with Lavinskii[10] provided for building two flat-bottomed boats of the Ostashkov type,[11] twenty to twenty-five feet long, a 200 pud loading capacity.

The crew would consist of a chief, his mate, and twelve other members, two of whom were to be acquainted with the language spoken by the riverside natives, and another two who were to be native Tungus. Referring to the possibility of sailing out of the mouth of the river the draft states:

> If the mouth of the Amur is reached safely the voyage might be prolonged in tow boats by following the coast either to the mouth of the Uda River, Great Shantar Island, or to wherever else directed. In any event the local authorities should be instructed in advance to offer every facility to the new arrivals and to supply them, if in Udsk, with rations drawn from Iakutsk or, if on Great Shantar, from Okhotsk. (The island possesses a settlement of traders and a vessel of the Russian-American Company calls once a year.) To avoid the possible dangers of rowing from the mouth of the Amur to the bay at Udsk, a light sailing vessel might meet the river craft at a date fixed beforehand and help to complete the journey to the point directed.

The main importance of the information gained from Koz'min and Guri Vasil'ev lies in the fact that it proved the accessibility of the river mouth from the sea and ended the theory of an isthmus existing between Sakhalin and the Amur. Henceforth, further research would only have to be directed to a more detailed definition of the coastline, establishing the depth of the fairway and the feasibility of access to the Sea of Okhotsk for ships of a certain class.

Supplied with all this accumulated information, Lavinskii suggested placing Koz'min at the head of an expedition which, in his opinion, would call for a maximum outlay of 20,000 rubles. However, despite the great probability of success, the government decided temporarily to cancel the proposed expedition and to break off negotiations with the Chinese on the subject of the Amur.[12]

The company expedition under command of Lieutenant Gavrilov. In 1843 a special committee, appointed by imperial decree in the Ministry of Finance to discuss measures for maintaining and safeguarding the Kiakhta trade, presented for the emperor's approval a proposal to organize a special expedition from the Black Sea to China and Japan under Rear-Admiral Putiatin's command. The expedition was intended also to survey the southeast coast of the Okhotsk Sea, and the north tip of Sakhalin, and explore the mouth of the Amur. But this scheme, like the others, was deferred by command of the emperor.

This plan was, however, again put forward in 1844. The chairman of the board of directors of the Russian-American Company[13] was informed by the Ministry of Foreign Affairs that "in reply to a report to the emperor on means to implement the existing proposals for exploring the mouth of the Amur, the emperor now desired to see the company approached in order to ascertain whether it would consent to undertake the project by dispatching one of its vessels to Sakhalin and there conducting the necessary explorations, while taking the requisite measures not to alarm the Chinese." Baron Wrangell, the chairman of the board, was further requested to give his personal opinion on the subject and estimate the approximate cost of the expedition.

Baron Wrangell replied that the company would consider it a sacred duty to comply with the emperor's august wish and that it would forthwith dispatch a vessel from the colony with enough rowboats and baidarkas, fully provisioned for a summer cruise and supplied with all the seafaring and astronomical instruments required for the work.

The mission's success, in Baron Wrangell's opinion, would be greatly enhanced if the following methods of procedure were adopted:

1. The rowboats and baidarkas exploring the mouth of the Amur and sounding the fairways should keep closely in touch and not scatter, thus ensuring a safe method of reading signals and of quick assembly for mutual assistance.

2. They should guard against sudden attack.

3. They should show friendliness to the natives when dealing with them, though concealing the real purpose of the work in hand.

4. The mission should terminate exploration and sail back to Aian to report only after the fairway had been definitely charted or its unsuitability for seagoing vessels because of shallowness established.

Baron Wrangell estimated that the expedition would not cost over 5,000 silver rubles.

After further deliberation the board instructed the chief manager of the colony to prepare a sailing vessel by the spring of 1846. The ship was to sail from New Archangel and make the port of Aian immediately upon the breaking up of the ice; operational orders would be sent to Aian.

The company's brig *Konstantin*, manned by a crew of twenty-two and commanded by Ensign Gavrilov of the Corps of Naval Navigators was selected for the expedition by Captain of Second Rank Teben'kov, the chief manager of the colony at the time. The brig was fitted out with the requisite equipment and was provided with rations for five months.[14]

In addition to the orders awaited from Petersburg, Teben'kov found it necessary to furnish Gavrilov with a set drawn up by himself.[15] As stated in the preamble,[16] the primary objective was to mask the real purpose of the expedition and it was considered that the possession of a document of the kind provided might prove useful in subsequent dealings with the natives or Chinese authorities in case of a chance mishap to the ship. However, Teben'kov was at pains to add that "these instructions are binding only insofar as they comply with those sent from St. Petersburg."[17]

The following statement was included in the government instructions on the subject:

> The main task of the expedition for which a sailing ship has been especially fitted out by the chief manager of the colony consists of exploring the mouth of the Amur. As far as is known the river along its entire length is free from any obstacles to navigation. There is, however, a body of opinion which holds that its mouth is silted up by alluvial sands and is, therefore, dangerous for the passage of even relatively small vessels (a fact unsubstantiated by concrete data, as the mouth of the Amur has so far never been properly surveyed). The essence of the task set the head of this expedition and his primary concern consist, therefore, in ascertaining the *navigability of the mouth of the Amur.*

The ways and means for carrying out the work allotted to the expedition have already been described. To avoid repetition, only a few more details contained in the instructions follow.

In addition to exploring the mouth of the Amur it was considered useful to survey (1) the eastern Okhotsk coastline and from the Uda River and the Shantar Islands eastward to Sakhalin, and (2) the northern tip of Sakhalin and the bay embraced by the tip and mainland as well as the narrows separating Sakhalin from the mainland. The government qualified this survey by pointing out that, first, it should be executed with the greatest caution (in particular, at Sakhalin) and, second, if time and conditions made it practicable, *but in no circumstances prior to the completion of the main task of the expedition*, i.e., the meticulous study of the *navigability* of the mouth of the Amur.

To facilitate the work of the expedition a small map made by Middendorf, as well as a description of his voyage to Eastern Siberia, was attached to the instructions.

After completing all the necessary preparations for the forthcoming voyage, on 21 April 1846,[18] the brig *Konstantin* set sail from New Archangel for the Bay of Aian.

On 11 July, having taken on board sundry articles intended as presents for the Giliaks,[19] the *Konstantin* sailed out of Aian and, following the north coast of Sakhalin, anchored on 18 July at the entrance to one of the islands bays, i.e. between Capes Golovachov and Vitovt,[20] on the assumption that the entrance to the river's estuary had been reached. Gavrilov's navigational error was due to the continuous overcast and rain which hindered proper orientation. The next day he weighed anchor and sailed farther ahead. When he reached a depth of eleven feet he moved out to sea and stopped at a suitable depth. From this point he warped his ship in but halted after failing to locate the fairway. When the horizen finally cleared on 21 July, Gavrilov saw that an unbroken shoreline stretched around the brig, "a fact," as Gavrilov notes in his logbook, "which led me to conclude that I had missed the mouth of the Amur which, as I guessed, lay farther to the west. I realized that I had entered another, though extensive bay, as yet unmapped, and, as I was unable to pinpoint my position because of the weather, I resolved to remain another day and continue my exploration."

The following day Gavrilov took soundings of the bay "and so," he adds in his logbook, "having first confirmed my mistake and, second, established the shallowness of the bay, I decided to sail out at the first possible opportunity and endeavor to make up for the four days lost. Though in the appalling weather conditions prevailing, I do not see what else I could have done."[21] At noon on 23 July the brig sailed out of the bay, but due to head winds, strong currents, and a dense fog which prevented astronomical observation, it did not reach the estuary of the Amur until the 26th. On 29 July, while crossing over to the coast of Sakhalin Island, hugged by a deep water channel, the brig grounded on a shallows. In the morning she was pulled clear, and on the 31st sailed up a deep channel which she followed until 3 August at latitude 52° 49 1/5′ and longitude 142° East of Greenwich. Here she halted to explore the Amur and the entrance to the river. Work was held up until 6 August by a strong southerly wind accompanied by fierce gusts. From 6 to 9 August Gavrilov explored the mouth of the Amur and a stretch of the river. On 10 August, in very heavy weather, one of the two anchor-chains parted, though fortunately the second chain held and the brig was able to ride out the storm unharmed. Between 11 and 14 August the approaches to the river were thoroughly sounded, the shoreline surveyed and the data recorded, the channel in the river to the north of the sandbank examined, and sundry distance verified between the ship's position and the coastline of Sakhalin. After returning on board on 14 August, Gavrilov weighed anchor and toward evening halted at the bay's exit. The following day he sailed along the shore and surveyed the coast. In his report, dated 22 August, Gavrilov states:

> The results of the explorations made of the mouth of the Amur and its estuary show that for sailing ships the entrance into the river is definitely impassable. As far as steamers drawing no more than five or six feet are concerned, it is possible to find a suitable passage leading from the bay into the river, but only after thorough investigation, such as is adopted in sounding the skerries of the Gulf of Finland—a task for which I lacked both the time and the means. In the river proper the depth varies between eighteen and twenty sazhens, and the

bottom is hard and the current swift. There are, however, good anchorages with sandy bottom for smaller ships on both sides of the river at a depth of nine or ten feet. The Amur estuary is only navigable by sailing ships drawing no more than sixteen feet. There are no convenient harbors for anchoring anywhere, but the bottom is good everywhere, providing sufficient hold for weathering the fiercest winds on one anchor alone. The surface is never very rough because of the shallowness of the bay. There are settlements of four to ten huts on both sides of the river and on every one of the low-lying promontories of the bay.

After leaving the bay Gavrilov started his survey of the coast but gave up the attempt because of strong winds and fog. On 20 August he returned safely to Aian. From Aian he dispatched a report to Baron Wrangell on what he had accomplished.

Gavrilov's dealings with the Giliaks and some details of his investigation of the mouth of the Amur. From Gavrilov's log of the voyage it would appear that several boats manned by Giliaks visited him on two occasions during his stay in the bay. He made them welcome and gave each member of the crews a little tobacco. The natives asked him to come ashore, pointing to their settlement and women. Lest he should give away the position of the ship to this crew Gavrilov obeyed his instructions on security measures and refrained from asking the natives the course taken by the fairway to the Amur. In conversation, however, he managed to obtain the names of some of the settlements on Sakhalin. "Starting from where I lay," writes Gavrilov, "they were as follows: Chkhuno, Kebo, Muchzhenuo, Puski, Lgzino, and others with names I could not make out. When naming the settlements, the location of Machu and Puir[22] were incidentally mentioned—and that was all I really required."

In the course of his explorations of the river's mouth in a rowboat and two baidarkas, Gavrilov sometimes went ashore for brief spells of rest.[23] "On low-lying ground on the first promontory (Pronge) there is a settlement of six huts." Gavrilov landed some distance away from these. Several natives in baidarkas hastened to the spot where the Russian crews were resting as soon as the approach of their boats was noticed from the settlement. After an endless series of bows the Giliaks stepped out of their canoes and eyed the strangers with great astonishment. They then proceeded to examine the Russians' clothing and proferred tobacco, "the kind," Gavrilov remarks, "which is sold in the colonies and is known as English tobacco." A small mirror given them by Gavrilov evoked a reaction akin to terror and was hastily returned. However, when Gavrilov looked at himself in the mirror and stroked his hair into place, they screwed up their courage and taking it from him, still obviously afraid, started examining themselves. The whole lot were then overcome by a paroxism of a strange, infectious laughter and all Gavrilov's efforts to distract their attention from the mirror by the offer of other trinkets failed, as did his attempt to find out the name of the settlement. Apparently the effect produced by the mirror was too disturbing and he left with his questions still unanswered.

He then proceeded farther along the river. Beyond the promontory at the entrance of the bay, but parallel to it, another one came into view, which Gavrilov calls Tonkii [thin] in his logbook.[24] The boat moored to the west of this promontory. Soon some natives appeared marching toward the boat behind a screen of little boys, none of which was older than five. "One supposes," says Gavrilov, "that this was their way of showing their peaceful intentions and, indeed, none of them carried any weapons." Among this group Gavrilov noticed one man whose features markedly differed from the Mongol type common to all the local inhabitants, and who in all probability was of Slavic origin. Gavrilov also noticed that when he exhibited his mirror the surprise shown by this man lacked sincerity, whereas the natives evinced as much genuine astonishment as had the first group farther up the coast. On the other hand, as Gavrilov himself remarks, his impression may have been quite erroneous. One of the natives took a fancy to the buttons (English, with anchors) on Gavrilov's waistcoat, but he put him off by giving the whole group some trinkets which delighted them. Pretending to be hungry and thus to justify his presence, Gavrilov asked for some fish. A few of them ran off to fetch it and soon returned not only with the requested fish but some women as well. Gavrilov paid for the fish by giving all of them the articles they most fancied.

Gavrilov's journey took him some seventy versts upstream from where his ship was anchored. He turned back from a westerly bend of the river and coasted downstream. Very rough water that threatened to swamp his boat prevented him from following the fairway and forced him to follow the left bank at a distance of one or two sazhens where the water was calm. Toward nine o'clock in the evening he reached a low-lying promontory. Here he halted for the night after taking the necessary steps to ensure his safety, not so much against humans as against wild animals, "probably bears," whose tracks were plainly visible in the sand. With no tents for shelter, Gavrilov and his companions spent a restless night. The next day, heavy rains and a strong wind kept them ashore much longer than he had intended.

Toward evening he again pulled into the bank, never suspecting that he was close to a settlement. After nightfall some natives arrived, as friendly and as affable as usual; they left at once after receiving a few baubles from Gavrilov, and an indication by sign that he wanted to sleep. That night it rained heavily again. By dawn the weather had brightened and the wind moderated; Gavrilov nevertheless decided not to spend another day exploring—"primarily," he says, "because of my anxiety for the safety of my ship and, secondly, because by now the crews were exhausted by continuous rowing and the sealskin of the baidarkas was so sodden that I feared I should never be able to bring them back."

In his notes on some of the places he visited and descriptions of his rest camp, Gavrilov remarks that on the left bank of the river—mostly pine, birch, and aspen—the forest starts at the very edge of the water and climbs up the hills practically to the summits. By the water's edge the timber is thin, but suitable for building small houses. The soil is pure sand—yellow in some places, quite black in others, and small-grained. "Though we dug deep into the ground," adds Gavrilov, "we found no other layer."

After Gavrilov's report to His Majesty on the conclusion of the mission entrusted to him, the following rewards were allotted by imperial command: 2,000 silver rubles to the chief manager of the colonies, 1,500 to Gavrilov, and 1,000 to the crew. The cost of equipping the expedition—5,110 silver rubles 12 kopeks—was refunded by the government.

Results of Gavrilov's explorations. Only a few words need be added on the results of Gavrilov's exploration of the estuary and mouth of the Amur. It is obvious that too great an accuracy cannot be expected of his findings considering the short time employed (three weeks, including the delay in Deception Bay [Bukhta Obmana]), the constant foul weather, and generally unfavorable conditions. Nevertheless, after comparing Gavrilov's chart with those of later surveys,[25] we conclude as follows:

1. The run of the narrow fairway in the direction of the coast of Sakhalin southward from Cape Golovachov as shown by Gavrilov is similar to that of more recent tracings.

2. The existence of a sandbank at the entrance to the mouth of the Amur (drying up in places as shown in the same map) and of channels between the bank and both shores of the river were confirmed by later research based on Gavrilov's findings.[26]

3. The soundings of these channels were carried out in a most efficient manner, especially considering the short time devoted to the work.[27] It follows therefore that the aim of the expedition was, on the whole, achieved, and that Gavrilov's merits were indubitable. A point which needs no stressing is mentioned by Gavrilov in his report

to Baron Wrangell: "I had neither the time nor the means to carry out further or more detailed investigations."

Further proposals for exploring the mouth of the Amur and adjacent areas. The main impetus to further exploration of the Amur was probably a remark made by Emperor Nicholas in the course of a conversation with Major General N. N. Murav'ev, newly appointed governor-general of Eastern Siberia in 1847. During this conversation, His Majesty said that the Amur should unquestionably belong to Russia and that the kind of research carried out so far would probably have to be repeated many times in the future.[28] These words prompted General Murav'ev to consider the best means of turning hopes for the exclusive ownership of the Amur into an accomplished fact, further reinforced by the longstanding universal recognition of the river's importance to the Siberian region. In 1848, after studying in detail the results obtained by previous expeditions to the mouth of the Amur and other available data, the general obtained permission for Captain-Lieutenant Nevel'skoi of the naval transport *Baikal*, to survey the shores of the Okhotsk Sea in the vicinity of the Amur and Sakhalin. The survey was to be undertaken after the delivery of a cargo to Kamchatka and was to be carried out at the captain's own request.

Orlov leads a company trading expedition (1849). At the same time wishing to establish trade relations with the Giliaks, the government requested that the Russian-American Company send a small trading expedition overland from Aian to the mouth of the Amur during the following year.[29]

The company was given a free hand in settling the details of the mission. However, the Ministry of Foreign Affairs particularly requested that special attention be paid to the choice of personnel and pointed out that much, if not all, would depend on the tact of those selected.[30] The ministry also informed the company that in notifying the governor-general of Eastern Siberia of the proposed expedition he had been asked to lend every possible assistance "to an undertaking designed to establish trading relations with the Giliaks through the offices of the Russian-American Company."

Accordingly, on 12 July 1849 the government employee Orlov, appointed by the commandant of Aian to lead the expedition, set out for the mouth of the Amur, accompanied by four assistants in two canoes. Orlov's knowledge of the Tungus language, spoken by the majority of the Giliaks, would be of great assistance to the expedition. The group was supplied with rations for three months and goods intended to be given to and traded with the Giliaks. Following the coast, Orlov first met the Giliaks at the mouth of the Tugur River, which he reached on 1 August.[31] Here the canoes were transported over the isthmus into Konstantin Bay. Orlov then proceeded to the east and to the river Kol' where he found a settlement of forty-six houses inhabited by one hundred men. With the consent of the Giliaks, Orlov's group settled in tents on the banks of the river and within a half an hour was visited by some fifty people. Every native was anxious to examine the Russians' belongings and, aside from extreme curiosity, their behavior was irreproachable. In gratitude for a repast of tea and gruel provided by Orlov, and for his present to each of two leaves of tobacco, the natives returned with berries and fish, for which they were separately paid. Soon the natives got to know the Russians well and sought to please them in every way. Two Giliaks, Pozvein[32] and Dombrano, distinguished themselves by their attention and civility. They also offered their services for either the beginning of winter or in spring as guides to the mouth of the Amur and up the river. By common consent the natives agreed to allow the construction of buildings on their territory and, in his report to the commandant of Aian Port, Orlov stated that "as far as I can gather they are prepared to recognize the suzerainty of our emperor." The Giliaks and their neighbors, the Neidal'tsi, recognized no authority; an insult was washed out by blood or terminated by ransom. "Everything that you were pleased to impart," he wrote, "I personally transmitted to them orally in Tungus without the help of an interpreter and those who were present were apparently well pleased, admitting that the ownership of land and power over it are indivisible."

In fact, during his entire stay with the Giliaks, Orlov met with no animosity whatsoever and he mentions their industry with particular pleasure. Judging by first appearances, he says they show no trace of the laziness and unconcern so typical of the Tungus as to laying in supplies and are forever busy collecting all kinds of herbs and roots for nourishment. Noticing this trait Orlov told them of the nutritive value of our vegetables, and emphasized the value of the potato. They at once asked him to bring some on his next visit and to teach them how to grow them; they also promised to start growing other vegetables. "Judging by the quality of the soil and vegetation," adds Orlov, "their labors should succeed."

Orlov was repeatedly asked to return the following summer and to bring the Giliaks guns, axes, cooking pots, etc. They often deplored the fact that they had been unaware of Orlov's coming and he was assured that "all we trap in the winter we shall keep for you. Had we but known you were coming we would not have traded a single sable to the Chinese." It was apparent from their stories that the Giliaks traded regularly with the Chinese, sailing the Amur by boats in spring, but they were positive that all their neighbors would heartily welcome any Russian traders. They told Orlov that May to September are the best months to trade with the Giliaks; the Neidal'tsi can be reached at any time of the year, but winter is of course best for ease and communications. Basing his information on what he gathered from the Giliaks, Orlov mentions the ugly rumors spread in self-interest by the Iakutsk merchants who habitually traded with the Neidal'tsi. The one most frequently repeated to Orlov by the Giliaks told the danger of dealing with the Russians who allegedly would either kill the natives or deport them upon arrival. Obviously Orlov did his best to refute these stories and largely succeeded. The permanent nature of the dealings between the Neidal'tsi and Iakutsk merchants was patently demonstrated during Orlov's stay with the Giliaks. One of the merchant Novogorodov's clerks arrived in Kol' to graze his master's reindeer, while another took up his summer residence with the Neidal'tsi. At any rate, by the time Orlov left, the Giliaks had a different opinion than they had had formerly about the Russians, "provided it is not ruined by the intrigues of the merchants," says Orlov. His fears were partly confirmed the following year, but, as we shall see, for different reasons.

Orlov's topographic and hydrographic data attached to the same report show that the area between the south of the Kol' River and Lake Chlia, thirty versts distant, offers every facility for making a road for wheeled transport. The passage by boat from Kol' settlement to the river and up to Iskai settlement along the coast takes half a day. The Iskai River flows into the lake[33] in the three branches, the western one being from two to three sazhens deep at low tide, while the river proper is up to four sazhens deep. "At present I should like to examine the passage from the sea into the lake," says Orlov "to see if it might conveniently be used as a harbor." The Giliaks did not try to deter Orlov from going to the Iskai for that purpose, but, being then busy fishing, declined to act as his guides. On these grounds, Orlov decided to postpone his journey to the mouth of the Amur. In addition, the late season rendered hazardous the return journey to Aian by baidarka and he had no reason to expect the arrival of a ship of the Okhotsk flotilla.

Orlov describes the whole stretch of country between Kol' settlement, down the coast to the mouth of the Amur and up both sides of the river as having settlements lying less than thirty versts apart, the entire left bank of the river being populated by Giliak and Neidal'tsi tribes.

The native settlements along the coast from Kol' to the mouth of the river bore the following names: Kol', Iskai, Langr, Machu, Puir, Petikh, Charbakh, and Chnyrakh; along the left bank the names were: Kuegda, Sabakh, Vait, Mago, and others.

In the meantime Captain-Lieutenant Nevel'skoi of the transport *Baikal*, after unloading his cargo at Petropavlovsk, sailed on 31 May 1849 for the east coast of Sakhalin and then went on to the northern and western coasts of the island after verifying some measurements made by Krusenstern. On his way to the Amur estuary, he, like Gavrilov in 1846, sailed into Deception Bay, which he renamed Baikal Bay after his transport. On proceeding he encountered a row of shoals by Cape Golovachov. When all his attempts to find a passage through them into the bay had failed, he altered his course for the northwest, and after circumventing a large sandbank reached the true estuary of the Amur. Accompanied by a few of his officers, Captain Nevel'skoi explored the mouth of the Amur and the river itself, going upstream as far as a low promontory on the left bank, which he named Konstantin Peninsula. On leaving the river he examined and sounded the channel leading south. Back on his transport, Nevel'skoi considered the possibility of taking his ship into the river but after several vain attempts he abandoned the idea and sailed north into the Okhotsk Sea.

On 28 August, on his way back to Aian, Orlov caught sight of the *Baikal*, becalmed off Cape Mukhtel' at the mouth of Usal'ginskaia Bay,[34] and was taken on this vessel to Aian.

When informing the Ministry of Foreign Affairs of the results of Orlov's expedition, the Russian-American Company stated that it intended once again to send Orlov in February 1850 with certain goods for the Giliaks, but this time overland, so as to develop the ties established by his first expedition and to impress the Giliaks with the advantages of dealing with the Russians. It was planned that Orlov should reach Kol' settlement by May, where, as soon as the sea was free of ice, he would be met by a ship of the Okhotsk flotilla conveying rowboats and other goods he might require.[35]

In his reply, Count Nesselrode informed the company that the emperor approved of its actions in every respect, as fully conforming to the policy of the government, and that His Majesty sanctioned the proposals for another expedition to the land of the Giliaks.[36]

Simultaneously, the company was informed that, as regarded further developments in the Amur region, the commandant of Aian would be fully instructed by the governer-general of Eastern Siberia, who would in future coordinate the activities of the company's servants with the government's policies.

In order to develop relations with the natives of the Amur region,

Orlov, on orders from the governor-general, was instructed to build a zimov'ia [winter post] on a suitable site in Giliak territory and to act as company agent.[37] However, it was decided to exclude the banks of the Amur for this purpose and to leave the final decision of its location to Captain-Lieutenant Nevel'skoi, due in Aian on the transport *Baikal* at the opening of navigation in 1850.

For building the zimov'ia ten skilled workmen were chosen from among the Okhotsk crews and ten cossacks were appointed to act as guards. All of them, by order of the governor-general, were placed under the direct command of the company's agent.

On the strength of these developments, Orlov set out on his appointed journey on 23 February 1850 with forty reindeer, three guides, and a six-month supply of goods intended as presents for the natives and for barter with them. Because of early flooding, exhaustion of the reindeer, and unfamiliarity with the route, the detachment did not reach the first Giliak settlement on the Kol' River until 31 May. Again, Orlov was greeted in a friendly manner, although this time with some mistrust. Upset by the appearance of a foreign ship[38] in the Tatar Straits, sounding and surveying the Manchurian and Sakhalin coasts, the Giliaks sought assurance from Orlov as to their safety from the foreigners. When Orlov had set them at rest, by promising that a Russian vessel not only capable of defending them but also laden with goods for barter would soon arrive, the Giliaks were at pains to show their gratitude to Orlov and express their joy at his arrival. Orlov then recruited the services of his former friend Pozvein to act as companion on his journeys in the region and left for the Schast'e [Happiness] Bay, which he reached on 5 June.

Orlov found the bay free of ice, though all the sandbanks round the spit were covered by broken floes brought in by the wind and tides. Lacking the proper equipment for thoroughly studying the mouth of the bay, he could only sound its depth. Hiring three Giliaks and their boats, he and Pozvein rowed up the Amur as far as Alom settlement, from where he started on his return journey. Orlov studied and explored the whole area from Schast'e Bay to the Amur estuary and farther upstream as fully as he could. "Starting from Schast'e Bay and the estuary and all along the left bank of the river right up to the island facing Alom settlement" writes Orlov, "the only suitable place for founding a post is at Cape Kuegda; all other locations which might be considered lie too far inland from the banks of the river and have no coastal connection with Schast'e Bay."

In addition to this hydrographic work, Orlov used every opportunity to foster friendship with the natives and to collect from them information concerning the coasts and shores he surveyed, means of communication, depth of the fairways, etc. In most cases this information has proved correct.[39]

On Orlov's return to Schast'e Bay on 21 June, the transport *Baikal* sailed in and anchored. "The first five days after the arrival of Captain Nevel'skoi" reports Orlov, "were spent in jointly studying the shores of the bay and in trying to find a suitable site for the new settlement. The best location appeared to be an elevated spit of land by the native settlement of Giml'-Rvo.[40]

The founding of Petrovskoe and Nikolaevskii. A settlement, named Petrovskoe, was founded at this point on 29 June. When work on the buildings that were required to house the men, supplies, and goods had been properly started, Orlov and Nevel'skoi left on the brig *Okhotsk*, which had just arrived, for the mouth of the bay where they explored in great detail the channel leading from the Okhotsk Sea to the mouth of the Amur, originally examined by Orlov as mentioned before.[41] Then they went up river as far as the settlement of Tyr, facing the mouth of the Amgun' River (approximately one hundred versts), and studied some of the Amur's secondary channels. On the return journey Captain Nevel'skoi founded the first Russian settlement on the Amur. He chose the site at Cape Kuegda previously recommended by Orlov, and on 6 August 1850 the Russian flag went up for the first time on the lower reaches of the Amur. The newly founded post was named Nikolaevskii. It was temporarily abandoned in the autumn and its inhabitants returned to Petrovskoe settlement to await more favorable circumstances.[42]

In the meantime, work at Petrovskoe settlement was advancing rapidly and by the middle of August most of the essential buildings were ready. Shortly afterward, Captain Nevel'skoi left for Aian on the brig *Okhotsk*, which he at once sent back to winter at Petrovskoe while he himself went on to St. Petersburg. The original garrison of twenty was increased by ten, so that including the brig's two officers and twenty-one ratings, Orlov now had over fifty men under his command.

During the winter the bartering of furs with the natives proceeded fairly satisfactorily, and by the spring all the company goods in the post had either been expended or exchanged. The Giliaks were unfailingly friendly and eager to visit the settlement and trade with the Russians.

In St. Petersburg, Captain Nevel'skoi reported on his actions on the Amur to the governor-general of Eastern Siberia, who had preceded him there, and after explaining why he considered it necessary to found a settlement on the Amur, requested a final decision.

In spite of the governor-general's insistence and the emperor's full approval of Nevel'skoi's behavior,[43] a specially appointed committee on Amur affairs[44] resolved that it was inexpedient to occupy the mouth of the Amur and maintain a settlement there. However, at a subsequent meeting convened by the emperor, the committee, with the heir apparent present, reversed its original decision and passed the following resolution, confirmed by the emperor: "The post on the Amur will be maintained as a Russian-American Company store, until further notice." The broadening of the company's activities in Giliak territory was then also approved. Furthermore, Russian cruisers in those waters were told emphatically to inform any foreign ship attempting to occupy any point in the region that no arbitrary action would be tolerated without the consent of the Russian and Chinese governments and that any such action would entail the gravest consequences.

In order to proceed with its activities on the Amur and to meet all practical requirements, the company decided[45] to increase its personnel, and to build a steamer and enough rowboats for navigation on the rivers in order to broaden and strengthen the existing ties of friendship with the natives. The rate of building in the Amur region was steadily mounting; to meet the demand, the company resolved to keep the region supplied with the materials required which might be difficult to procure locally. Finally, it drew up a special scale of wages for government working crews appointed to guard its trade warehouses, for building and for other needs.[46]

Subject to approval by the governor-general, it was proposed to appoint Captain Nevel'skoi as a liaison officer to coordinate the policies of the local authorities with those of the company—"his relation with the company, as stated in the board's proceedings, to be mutually agreed upon." The work crew and all the company's installations were placed under the command of Orlov.

As soon as Nevel'skoi's appointment had been confirmed by the governor-general, the company gave him full instructions on his duties in the Amur region as its agent.[47] He was also informed of the value to be placed on the company's goods in the event of trade with the Manchurians and the exchange rate for their teas as compared to the prices in Kiakhta.

There remained the settling of the total sum to which the company would be committed over the Amur undertaking. Upon receipt of the first directives issued by the committee on Amur affairs, the company informed the committee that "fully appreciating the great national importance of the undertaking and in the expectation of deriving a measure of profit from trade in the region, the company was prepared to shoulder all the expenditure mentioned above."

However, the company felt bound to qualify the offer by the provision that should trade on the Amur, contrary to expectation, prove unprofitable within the course of the next three years, starting from 1852, or should the company feel it could no longer pursue the undertaking any further, it would submit to the government a detailed statement on the sums disbursed with a view to their recovery.[48]

Accordingly, on orders from the sovereign, the maximum sum the company would be allowed to claim was to be precisely defined. After consultation with the naval and Siberian authorities, the government agreed that, "should the company decide to cease operations, it would pay for any losses the company had incurred to a limit of 50,000 silver rubles—the sum so paid to cover the whole period up to January 1855." In this connection the governor-general of Eastern Siberia stated that in his opinion a special fund, constituted from economies in his department, should be set aside to pay for any losses sustained by the company in excess of the stipulated amount.[49]

Further company activities on the Amur. When sending the brig *Okhotsk* from Aian to Petrovskoe in the fall of 1850, Captain Nevel'-skoi ordered her commander to return to Aian the following spring to load goods and supplies required by the settlement. However, after receding waters in the bay had left the brig high and dry, and the efforts of the few settlers had failed to refloat her.

The vessel's nonreturn at the appointed time lent some substance to rumors that the settlers at Petrovskoe were in grave danger or even, possibly, had all been slaughtered. As soon as Nevel'skoi reached Aian in the beginning of July 1851 (on his return from St. Petersburg) he therefore decided to sail immediately for Petrovskoe in the transport *Baikal*, taking with him as additional support the company's ship *Shelekhov*, just back from the colonies. On board was a group of fifty-seven men appointed to the Amur settlements, several passengers, among them Nevel'skoi's wife, a topographer, an assistant head miner, goods and supplies belonging to the company, and cattle, horses, etc.

The disquieting rumors of Orlov's fate and of those under his command proved false. Relations with the natives all through the winter and spring of 1850 and 1851 were of the friendliest nature. But now a different kind of disaster intervened. Weighing anchor in Schast'e Bay on 19 July, the *Shelekhov*, with Nevel'skoi on board, struck a submerged rock and sank immediately.[50] Thanks to the energy and extreme presence of mind of her commander, the entire crew and all the passengers were saved, and the cattle sent from Aian were brought safely ashore. However, only the waterproof items of the cargo could be saved; the rest, together with the ship, were irretrievably lost in spite of the efforts of her commander, her crew, and the crew of the naval corvette *Olivutsa*, which had arrived on the scene.[51]

Soon after his arrival in Petrovskoe, Captain Nevel'skoi sent one of the company's clerks, Berezin, to Cape Kuegda with instructions to find out if the site where he founded Nikolaevskii post was still unoccupied or if it had been seized either by the Manchurians or by foreigners, now often venturing into the Okhotsk Sea and Tatar Straits. Accompanied by two Tungus, Berezin was instructed to travel through the mountains up the Iskai River and then to cross over to the Lich River, a tributary of the Amur close to the cape. He was told to do his scouting under cover and at a distance during daylight and to approach the place only at night. In case of accident he was to make every effort to avoid capture and was at once to inform Petrovskoe of the fact. After thoroughly inspecting the vicinity and seeing no one except occasionally some natives engaged in fishing, Berezin returned to the settlement.

Captain Nevel'skoi then left for Cape Kuegda with an escort of fifty men, among them Lieutenant Boshniak, Midshipman Chikhachov, Ensign Voronin of the Corps of Naval Navigators, Berezin, a headminer, and topographer.[52] Upon reaching Lich Bay on 8 August, Nevel'skoi brought ashore a Holy Icon and recited a few prayers. He then placed Lieutenant Boshniak in command of the post and put the construction gang under the command of Berezin. About the inaugural ceremony, Berezin says, "A long clap of thunder resounded immediately after our cheers; large drops of rain in bright sunshine sprinkled the ground under our feet and we involuntarily cried out: "God is with us and no one will prevail against us!" Nevel'skoi left for Petrovskoe the same day with twenty men in two whale boats and a large baidara.

Boshniak and Berezin at once set their thirty men to cutting a clearing in the willow undergrowth forty sazhens long on either side, leading from the river to the summit of the hill and down the reverse slope. Every effort was made to clear the center as quickly as possible as a safeguard against the natives. A concealed picket was placed on the hill and by morning a considerable area was free from obstruction. The bewilderment of the natives, who by then had started arriving, was great, so stupefied were they at the thick piles of undergrowth heaped up on four sides blocking passage. However, by cautiously following the water's edge, they approached an opening in the rampart provided for them. Altogether there were about twenty; three of them ventured into the stockade, dropping their bows and spears. They were, of course, made welcome and treated to tea and gruel. There was much animated talk when these three rejoined their comrades. An ejection of heavy stones from inside their clothing followed and then all came up to a designated spot in the center of the clearing. Berezin then gave each a leaf of tobacco, treated them to more tea and gruel, and finally, ripping off a few arshins of pink and blue calico print, tied bits of it to their hair. They thus remained until nightfall when they docilely withdrew when told that their presence here at night would constitute a sin in Russian eyes. On parting, each of them made an offering of sterlet [small sturgeon]. Every day thereafter their numbers kept increasing. Pistols and guns greatly excited their curiosity and they wished to see how they worked; the reports terrified them at first; some of them squatted while others trembled all over and begged for the firing to stop.

Meanwhile work at Cape Kuegda was proceeding apace and by the fifth day after arrival a row of posts three deep surrounded the occupied area. A few days later the area was roofed, walled in with logs, and covered on the outside with sod, like the Iakut yurts. A stove and two open fireplaces were then laid and by 1 September all the working groups and garrison were quartered inside. A three-windowed annex was then added for the officer-in-command and for the stores. The whole structure was, in addition, surrounded by a stockade with loopholes for firing and on the roof of the main building were placed a cannon and a swivel gun. In case of necessity the fortification, such as it was, could offer a stout defense.

Within a month, the Russians learned all about the natives and their ways. Quarrels were studiously avoided; in case of need, persuasion was used, was generally accepted, and was not in the least resented by the Giliaks.

At this point I must mention an event which occurred soon after the coming of the Russians and which did much toward bringing them and the natives closer together.

In November, the Giliak Pozvein arrived at Post Nikolaevskii from Vait settlement with a request for assistance for a severely wounded inhabitant. On the one hand there was the risk of failing to cure the wounded man, and on the other, the obvious advantages to be gained in terms of friendship. After discussing the pros and cons of the matter, Midshipman Chikhachov, then in charge, dispatched Berezin and a medical orderly to the settlement and told them to help the wounded man the best they could. News of the Russians' arrival brought crowds of Giliaks to the yurt where the injured man lay, but excessive curiosity and the terrific din hampered all efforts to help.

The medical orderly did, however, manage to make a brief examination and diagnosed a wound about two inches deep in the left side probably caused by a spear. If treated at once he thought there might be a chance of survival. Berezin, who wanted to get the man to Nikolaevskii post, finally managed to persuade either the patient or the other Giliaks that this was the only course to adopt. On the following day, escorted by a crowd of armed Giliaks, the convoy set out for the post, and twelve days later the patient was able to return home.

This particularly fortunate incident and similar cases, along with the continued help given the Giliaks by the resident doctor at Nikolaevskii post all helped to make a favorable impression on the natives.

By November, two women, the wives of privates in the detachment, arrived at Nikolaevskii; a few head of cattle and two horses were sent from Petrovskoe; and, as Boshniak says in his description of the expedition, "our tiny settlement was just one ten-thousandth of an inch closer to European civilization."[53]

During 1852 several new buildings went up at Nikolaevskii; and the number of its inhabitants gradually increased and spread over a larger area, foretelling what the previously desolate banks of the Amur were destined to become.

Further explorations of the Amur region and company trade with the natives and Manchurians. After Captain Nevel'skoi's arrival other exploratory expeditions to the region followed in rapid succession.[54] The names of his worthy companions—Chikhachov, Boshniak, Orlov, Berezin, and others—will always be remembered in the history of the region. The tireless way in which they withstood hardships and privations, the boundless energy they applied to all they undertook, the legendary distances they covered over wild and desolate country, often with no means of subsistence, all show the self-sacrifice a Russian is prepared to endure in executing his duty, overcoming all difficulties however unconquerable they may appear at first.

Thus, for example, in September 1851 Orlov was sent with a trading party along the Amur and journeyed upstream as far as the Amgun' River and the settlement of a native tribe, called the Samagertsi or Samagrtsi.[55] Apart from gaining factual topographical information, the expedition obtained an agreement with the natives to lead Orlov's trading party over winter trails to the nearest Manchurian settlement for the purpose of entering into trade relations with them.[56]

Some time previously, Chikhachov had left the *Olivutsa* and had gone in small boats to sound the southern channel, i.e., the fairway from the Tatar Straits to the mouth of the Amur and its course southwards.[57] Chikhachov and Voronin surveyed the Tatar coast to Cape

Sushchov, while topographer Popov was engaged in similar work on the mainland. In November, Chikhachov and Berezin, accompanied by a cossack and a Tungus were sent to explore the right bank of the Amur and to find a connection with De-Kastri Bay. Chikhachov was responsible for discovering a route to the bay over Lake Kizi and for a detailed description of the country through which he had traveled.[58] Berezin and Chikhachov, on their return journey, explored the country as far as the mouth of the Amgun' River and farther upstream to its tributaries, the Imelen and Somnen.

On his return to Petrovskoe in January 1852, Berezin was sent off with a posse of five armed soldiers to Vait settlement to investigate the robbery of a Tungus by the Giliaks and to arrest the culprits. On his arrival, he gathered seventy prominent natives into a iurt, under the pretext of a feast, and explained to them the reason of his visit. At this point some of the younger Giliaks adopted a threatening attitude. Never losing his nerve Berezin ordered the elders to take the trouble-makers out of the iurt, and bolstered his demand by drawing his pistols and telling the soldiers to take aim. The results of this resolute behavior were immediate. The thieves, two Giliaks, were at once handed over and he brought them back to Petrovskoe.[59]

A little earlier, acting on Nevel'skoi's orders, Orlov, with a Tungus interpreter and a Giliak, left on two sledges for Chal'm settlement on the Amur via the settlement of Kol' and Lake Chlia. From there he was to proceed farther up the river. In the settlements of Kal'm and Pul' he met seventeen Manchurian traders and agreed that one should deliver tea. In exchange the Manchurians asked for fine black cloth, walrus tusks, little bells, samovars, brass buttons, harmonicas, looking-glasses, and assorted furs. According to Orlov, they were cordial and helpful beyond measure, and he entertained great hopes of establishing trade with them on a friendly basis. Farther than the settlement of Pul' he did not venture; he had run out of food for his dogs and so returned to Petrovskoe.

During this journey, Orlov, in the time he could spare, investigated the Akhchu River and the lake out of which it flows: the Ui River, entering the Amur by the settlement of Ukhte; and the Ugdyl' River. He also investigated means of communication. "The Ui River," says Orlov,

Is one of the best places I have seen not only as to the position of its banks in relation to the Amur of of its depth, which makes it suitable for wintering ships, but also for the facilities it affords for building a wharf. However, the ice pressure both from the Amur and from Lake Ugdyl' would first need careful and detailed investigation. The Bidzha River, which connects with the Amgun',

flows into the northern end of the lake, while the Pil'du river flows into the
southern end and connects with the Amur. There is also a connection between
the Amur and the lake from the settlement of Tus along the left bank of the
river. Up to Ukhte settlement (on the left bank of the Amur 180 versts from
Nikolaevskii) the inhabitants call themselves Guls, but between Ukhte and Pul'
they call themselves Nikhtu.

In the meantime Chikhachov had once again left Petrovskoe on
12 February, taking one sledge and a Tungus to continue his explorations. Berezin and the topographer Popov, followed him for a more
detailed survey of the territory lying between De-Kastri Bay and the
shores of the Amur. Berezin was to inspect particularly localities rich
in building timber, to take every opportunity to trade with the natives
and Manchurians, and lastly to establish what kind of road could be
made between the Amur and Kizi.[60] In a settlement along the
route Berezin met some Manchurians and bartered a few of his supplies,
mainly for sables. Later, as we shall see, such encounters became more
frequent and were invariably friendly. At the same time Chikhachov
was busy surveying the Amgun' River over a length of five hundred
miles upstream,[61] as well as the pass between this river and the Garin
River, and the stretch of the Amur from the mouth of the Garin to
Kizi settlement. In Oda settlement close to Kizi on 29 March, Chikhachov heard from topographer Popov about some sort of vessel which
had been in De-Kastri Bay. He immediately went there and did, in fact,
see a schooner-brig, naval in appearance, lying off the bay waiting for
the ice to clear. He at once sent Berezin to Nevel'skoi for orders concerning this vessel and himself kept a close watch on the ship's movements. The ship did not succeed in making the bay and turned south,
tacking along the coast, apparently surveying the shoreline. According
to the natives at Due settlement (on Sakhalin), which is as far as Chikhachov went following the ship through the straits, and the Giliaks
hunting seals along the passage between the sea and the Amur, this
surmise was correct. Boats from the ship had landed on the Tatar coast
several times and the natives had been closely questioned concerning
the Russians and their settlements about which the strangers knew a
great deal.[62] Here, on his return journey from Petrovskoe with Nevel'-
skoi's instructions, Berezin met Chikhachov on 3 May returning on
foot from De-Kastri Bay with a forty-pound load on his shoulders.
Berezin gave him a lift in his sledge as far as Kizi and stayed there to
watch the breaking up of the ice in the lake and later sounded it,
while Chikhachov returned on the sledge to De-Kastri Bay for closer
exploration and survey. There the natives told him of the existence,
five days' journey south of De-Kastri, of a big bay, or salt lake, as

they described it, called Khodzhi. Circumstances then prevented him from reaching the bay itself, but he did manage to gather some useful information about it from the natives including the best way of reaching it and even arranged with some of them to take him there at the first opportunity.[63]

On his return journey to Petrovskoe, Chikhachov inspected the trail leading from the sea to the Taba River, which flows into Lake Kizi, and which the topographer immediately charted. The trail was barely four versts long over a gentle slope. A clearing, one and a half sazhens wide, very well cut by the natives, offered excellent facilities for hauling boats from the seashore into the river. During his progress farther in the direction of the Tatar coast, Chikhachov's boat was hemmed in by ice in a small bay, close to Cape Sushchov. For five days he and his companions had to wait and suffered greatly after their meager supply of ship's biscuits, divided equally among them, had been exhausted. However, as he felt compelled to push along the coast to the southern channel of the river to inspect the only remaining stretch hitherto unexplored, Chikhachov abandoned the boat and set off on foot with his companions to complete his geological survey. Supplied with maps from the boat and loaded with all they could possibly carry, they set out along the coast over mountains and through forests. After crossing two very large ranges they reached the bay and to their delight saw that a recent gale had broken up the ice, which meant that they could now fight through to their abandoned boat. The topographer and two of their companions cheerfully set about the business and quickly did their job in spite of the heavy swell and surf. Ice and foul weather plagued him as they approached the Amur estuary. In fact, it was only due to the friendly natives who supplied them with food that the survey was brought to a successful conclusion at all. For ten days they subsisted on nothing but seal meat and iukola and finally reached Petrovskoe on 13 June.

During this expedition Chikhachov several times met Manchurians, from whom he obtained much useful information on various localities of the Amur basin and on their trading methods in the region. His first, and by far the most interesting meeting, took place in the settlement of Kondon, on the channel joining the lake of the Samogerts to the Garin River. This group of Manchurians consisted of eight men from the upper Amur who had come there to trade with the natives and to collect outstanding debts. Using the fatigue of his dogteam as a pretext, Chikhachov decided to stay in the settlement for three days, so that he might get to know the traders. This he found quite easy, as apparently they wished for nothing better, judging by their affability, talkativeness, and friendliness at every meeting. By making use of an excellent Amgun interpreter who translated what the Manchurians were saying to a Tungus attached to the Russian expedition, Chikhachov was able to maintain an easy flow of conversation. When he learnt that one of the traders was a merchant, while the rest were clerks, he pretended to be a clerk traveling on business for a Russian merchant of Iskai Bay. At first, trade was the main subject of conversation. The Manchurian was most keen to start business but refused to go farther down the river than Kizi, where he wanted goods to be delivered—mainly gold, silver, clothes, walrus tusks, and mammoth-bone. As regards the likelihood of obtaining tea from the Manchurians, the man said that this time the most he could guarantee was two cases of black Chinese tea—all, according to him, that one could then obtain in the town of Sen-Sin,[64] since the Manchurians use their own tea and not the Chinese variety. In addition to tea he promised to bring woven silk tissues, groats, and peas, and samples of goods obtainable in Sen-Sin, and promised in the future to fill all Russian demands. The Manchurians in general appeared to be well acquainted with the surrounding territory, and readily answered though their knowledge of the upper Amur was more limited. According to them both banks of the river were very sparsely inhabited from the Sungari farther upstream. On the Sungari they were annually visited by the Daurians,[65] who came in fourteen boats to Sen-Sin to buy flour. When Chikhachov expressed surprise at the primitive state and backwardness of the local inhabitants, they retorted by saying that nothing else could be expected of a people ungoverned, unorganized, and with no religion. Anyone, they said, traveling up the Amur to the Sungari River along the whole length of the Ussuri and along the Tatar coast would see exactly the same sort of thing, i.e., savages, who recognized no authority and for whose daily needs the dog and fish sufficed. The Manchurians repeatedly regretted that their own authorities and the Russian government had so neglected this region, thus excluding it from any form of organized trade, while their fear that it might be occupied by some foreign power (not Russian) beggared description. They mentioned with horror and agitation the squadrons of ships and individual vessels cruising along the Chinese coast, which now often entered the Tatar Straits, even De-Kastri Bay, and insistently demanded Chikhachov's views on this subject. Their professed apprehension should of course, be treated with reserve. Many of them acted as willing guides and informants to the missionaries all over the country, while it is obvious that without some form of native aid the latter could never have stayed in the region.

In general Chikhachov met with nothing but good will whenever he dealt with the Manchurians. They wanted the Russians to settle as near them as possible, mainly for trading reasons, but also because of the difficulty of navigating their flat-bottomed boats into the outlets of the Amur and hauling them back against the current.

Berezin's reports of his own dealings with the Manchurians are equally revealing. In his journeys up and down the Amur region he met the same remarkably kind and friendly attitude toward the Russians of the population as a whole: the universal willingness to help, the desire to assist in time of sickness, open hospitality, and demands for trade. The goods offered in exchange were identical with those mentioned to Chikhachov, while a few of the Mancurian traders expressed their intention to visit at all costs Petrovskoe and Nikolaevskii.

In February 1852 Boshniak was dispatched to explore Sakhalin Island. He was instructed to go across the island to investigate localities said by the natives to be rich in coal,[66] and to end his journey on the coast of the Okhotsk Sea, reported to possess an excellent harbor. With a month's supply of biscuits, and some tea and sugar, he set out cheerfully on a dogsled accompanied by the Giliak Pozvein. He traveled from Schast'e Bay to Cape Lazarev, crossing the straits there at the narrowest point, and landing on the island by the settlement of Pogobi. At Tyk, the next settlement to the south, Boshniak found many scattered pieces of coal, while between the mouth of the Viakhtu River and Uandy Bay it was visible in open casts on the surface. The main source of supply, however, was reported by Boshniak as lying in the mountains between the settlements of Mgach' and Niomai. The natives also said the vicinity of their settlement of Duc was particularly rich in coal. Owing to the exhaustion of his dogteam, Boshniak was forced to leave part of his meager supplies at Mgach' and with a lightened sled to follow the Tymi River to the Sea of Okhotsk. He explored the river down to its mouth, a distance of some eighty-five miles. There he sent off Pozvein with his sled and started on the return journey on foot with a hired guide. At the beginning of April, exhausted and footsore from trekking over almost impassible roads Boshniak reached Nikolaevskii.[67]

As soon as he had recovered somewhat from this ordeal, Boshniak was ordered off on another expedition in July 1852. This time he was to find a place on the banks of the Amur suitable for shipbuilding so as to overcome the inconvenience caused by the shallowness of the bay at Nikolaevskii post. Accompanied by a cossack, he was to investigate the Ui River, and Lake Ugdyl', out of which the river flows, for possible sites. He met a few Manchurians and was soon given information on local trade. At Ukhte settlement he found Berezin, sent there to trade with the natives and to study the previously unexplored left channel of the Amur. "I found Berezin" says Boshniak[68] "in a most pitiable condition, alone, in a small boat, with dreadful erysipelas on his foot. Seeing his circumstances and quite sure that he was in no position to carry out his task, I hired a boat and oarsmen and sent him back to Nikolaevskii post. Together with the cossack Parfent'ev, I completed my own work and then went farther up the Amur to complete Berezin's mission." Boshniak returned by way of Ukhte to Nikolaevskii and in 1852, as soon as winter traveling was possible, he was sent to the Amgun' River.

At the close of 1852 and 1853, Berezin, Orlov, and Midshipman Razgradskii were sent out several times along the right bank of the Amur to the Amgun' River, its tributaries, and Lake Ugdyl' to trade with the natives and Manchurians and to study the surrounding country. At the beginning of 1853 Boshniak surveyed Khodzhi Bay, which he called Imperatorskaia Gavan' [Imperial Harbor]. It was visited in August by Captain Nevel'skoi, while Boshniak was given orders to establish a post there [Konstantinovskii] and stay for the winter.[69] Of further explorations the most notable was the establishment in 1853 of a definite navigable course from the Tatar Straits to the mouth of the Amur made by the naval schooner *Vostok* under the command of Rimskii-Korsakov.

The cost of Nevel'skoi's proposals for the immediate expansion of the company's activities in the Amur region far surpassed the amounts stipulated for the undertaking. By the end of February 1852, the company's outlay on the Amur project, inclusive of the value of the wrecked *Shelekhov*, exceeded the 50,000 silver rubles allocated by the government up to 1 January 1855. Consequently Nevel'skoi's request for an increase of personnel in Giliak territory[70] was deferred until further profits had accrued from trade in the region. The company, however, hastened to forward Nevel'skoi's submission to the governor-general of Eastern Siberia.

For some time the company went on with its activities as planned. In April 1853 two imperial decrees followed: one for the company to occupy Sakhalin, and the other transferring the Amur project to the government. The company was asked to submit its final account to the government by 1 January 1854.

The company's outlay on the Amur expedition, from its inception on 12 July 1849 up to 1 January 1854, amounted to 157,926 silver rubles 13 kopeks and another 36,994 rubles 15 kopeks, the value of the brig *Okhotsk* and its cargo, lost to the enemy. The refund paid by the government consisted of 49,767 rubles 65 kopeks silver and a further 36,121 rubles 20 kopeks for the brig *Shelekhov*, which sank in Schast'e Bay with a partial loss of cargo, a total of 85,888 rubles 85 kopeks silver. The value of furs and other items exchanged amounted to 8,077 rubles 24 kopeks (in cash and in kind), disposed of for 17,647 silver rubles 32 kopeks.

During 1854 the company set up its stores in Petrovskoe settlement, Post Nikolaevskii, and by Lake Kizi. Retail trade was very brisk during the year but the exchange trade in furs was negligible. In May the frigate *Pallada* arrived from Japan and up to six hundred members of the crew were sent to winter at Nikolaevskii; they were cared for by the local authorities with goods and supplies furnished by the company on one of its own ships sent from Aian. In 1855 the company's trading operations were equally prosperous, with articles of food, especially, commanding a ready market. Small trading parties dispatched from Aian to various regions of the Amur for bartering furs by the reappointed port commandant, Captain of First Rank Furuhjelm, operated most successfully and supplied the company with 1,200 sables.

Loss of the company brig "Okhotsk" during the war with England and France in 1855. During the war with England and France, the company lost another of its ships near the Amur. The brig *Okhotsk*, dispatched from Aian with a cargo of goods worth 17,800 silver rubles for the Amur settlements[71] was overtaken by the enemy and after removal of the crew was blown up by skipper Iuzelius in sight of the enemy.

The brig left Aian on 22 June and on 1 July was approaching Petrovskoe settlement. Finding the settlement abandoned, the skipper following his orders to go to the Amur, set his course for the north entrance to the estuary. Head winds and fog prevented him from finding the entrance until 11 July, when Lieutenant Voronin reached him from Nikolaevskii and piloted him in. After three days the brig had advanced six miles into the bay, sounding from boats, whenever the weather permitted. That day toward evening, three large enemy ships were sighted. The following morning a screw-propelled, three-masted steamer left the squadron and, preceded by boats, made for the brig. Realizing that defense was useless, Skipper Iuzelius ordered his crew to abandon ship and made ready to blow her up. However, the steamer turned back, and the decision to destroy the brig was abandoned for the meantime.

Next day at dawn the steamer again approached and dispatched

five boatloads of men to attack. Iuzelius then holed his ship underwater, lit a fire by the powder kegs, and fled with the whole of his
crew.

The brig's boats followed the fairway along all of its bends and
twists, while the enemy's boats took a direct line and therefore grounded frequently on the shallows. Nevertheless, the brig's heavy, six-
oared, longboat was soon overtaken and captured. The remaining
enemy boats continued the chase but were halted by a sandbank,
upon which the crews jumped out and started firing at the Russians.
Iuzelius and his crew in a four-oared yawl were no more than seventy-
five sazhens distant from the enemy but escaped uninjured, though
bullets were whistling all round and above them. With two baidaras
he eventually reached Nikolaevskii safely. The second four-oared
boat, under navigator Mansfel'd was, however, closer to the enemy,
and was soon captured. Altogether one navigator, one clerk, two
passengers, and ten seamen were made prisoners-of-war.

Cessation of company operations on the Amur. After the end of
the war with England and France, the company brought most of its
activities on the Amur to a close. Due to an influx of foreign goods,
trade at Nikolaevskii was very slack, though the company remained
convinced that the goods it could offer would be better suited to meet
local demands than those imported from America by private merchants.
Moreover, its business was made awkward by the activities of another
Russian company (the Amur Company) recently founded, with rights
to carry its goods up the Amur and into central Siberia.

It was therefore decided temporarily to halt trading on the Amur
and to limit the activities of the Russian-American Company to the
barter of furs on a restricted scale.

The emperor, upon representations submitted by the governor-
general of Eastern Siberia, ordered his gratitude conveyed to the
company for the zeal it had displayed in implementing the government's policy of bringing the Amur region under Russian control.[72]

14. The Company's Role in the Occupation of Sakhalin Island

The government authorizes the company to take possession of Sakhalin Island and build fortifications there. The dispatch of an American expedition to Japan in 1852 prompted the Russian government to build posts on Sakhalin Island in order to protect our establishments at the mouth of the Amur. It commissioned the Russian-American Company to manage this undertaking.

All of the latest information on this island was studied to determine the best way of carrying out the government's wishes.

The directors first proposed the occupation of two places on this island—one on the west side of the island, and the other on the south side—and the building of a redoubt at each of them like those in the colonies.[1] The choice of sites was to be left to the manager of this undertaking. Occupation of the eastern part of the island was left until later.

Foreseeing that two redoubts might not suffice to prevent foreigners from occupying convenient places on the shores of the island near the Amur estuary, the company offered to build several smaller forts between the two main forts. For this it proposed to use up to two hundred persons from the Amur expedition, sending in addition a crew of skilled workmen, mainly carpenters, from Iakutsk to Aian and from there to Sakhalin. The workmen and construction materials would be transported in company ships. All other supplies and trading goods were to be sent around the world on company ships.

The board of directors proposed that the man chosen to head this undertaking, independent from the Amur expedition, could arrive there in 1854 with employees and one or two company ships for the use of the new establishments.

In conclusion, the directors stated that "even though it still has no

reason to expect profits from this undertaking, the company, in fulfilling the government's wish is ready to bear the expense, being certain
that if after the expiration of three years, the company should be
unable to cover these expenses by profits from local trade, the government will agree to compensate the company for its losses."

At the same time, realizing that this undertaking would involve far
greater expense than the Amur expedition, and not having sufficient
money on hand because of its other duties and undertakings, the
company requested 50,000 silver rubles in advance.

Upon submission of the company's views to the emperor, the sovereign ordained that the company be permitted to occupy Sakhalin and
to administer it on the same basis as the other territories mentioned
in its charter.[2]

Until the arrival from the colonies of the newly appointed manager,
Lieutenant Furuhjelm, the board of directors commissioned Mr. Nevel'-
skoi to supervise the men and construction of the new buildings.
Nevel'skoi received strict instructions that in the occupation of the
south coast he should not disturb the Japanese traders and fishermen
but should take every opportunity to be friendly. He was to explain
to them that the Russians would protect the inhabitants from attacks
and that they could continue their fishing and trade unmolested.

In addition to its orders about hiring clerks and skilled workers
for Sakhalin and purchasing horses and cattle and of seeds for vegetable
gardens, the company gave Furuhjelm the right to choose for the
Sakhalin settlements all the men that he needed from among the
employees in the colonies, preferably volunteers.[3] A mining engineer
and several head miners were hired to explore the mineral deposits
on the island and to mine coal and other minerals.[4] A doctor and a
male nurse were to be sent to Sakhalin on a round-the-world ship.
On receipt of the necessary items from the colonies the doctor was to
prepare a dispensary and a fifteen-bed hospital.

At the same time the chief manager of the colonies was ordered to
send to Sakhalin a well-armed ship with spare sails and rigging, guns
and ammunition for the proposed forts, and implements for trapping
and hunting. A shipbuilder was sent to Aian to build a small sailing
vessel for the Sakhalin expedition.

The company intended to build a main trading post on Sakhalin—
in a place to be determined after studying the local conditions—and
not more than two redoubts, built after the pattern of redoubt Stakhina, besides the one proposed by the Finnish Whaling Company.
Odinochkas [one-man posts] under the company's flag were to be
built in other places on the island if needed, to function only during

the navigation season. During the winter, employees from these out-posts were to return to the main settlement.

The company occupies Sakhalin Island. As outlined in the instruc-tions, the commandant of the port of Aian sent the Company's ship *Imperator Nikolai* commanded by the skipper Klinkovstrem to Petro-pavlovsk in July 1853 to take the detachment to Sakhalin. After taking on board seventy soldiers and one officer, Klinkovstrem sailed with them to Petrovskoe, arriving on 25 August. From there he sailed to Aian with Mr. Nevel'skoi to take on supplies and materials for Sakhalin.

In three days time, after loading supplies worth 21,000 rubles, two dismantled log houses, and tools, Klinkovstrem sailed on 3 September. He bore instructions from the port commandant of Aian to unload the supplies on Sakhalin and winter there with the ship under Mr. Nevel'skoi's orders. If, because of lack of good harbors or sickness on board, it should be found impossible to remain there for the winter, he was, after asking for permission, to sail to the Sandwich Islands and thence in early spring to New Archangel.

Nevel'skoi chose one of the harbors in Aniva Bay for building the first fort on Sakhalin.[5] Anchoring the ship near the main Japanese settlement on 20 September, he went ashore with the two armed boats, taking all precautions against a sudden attack. After exchanging some presents with the Japanese head men, he began negotiations with them about ceding a place for a Russian post. At Nevel'skoi's insistence the head men consented to cede such a place on a hill overlooking some Japanese buildings. Taking the ship nearer the shore, the Russians be-gan to land the men and supplies.

The post was named Murav'evskii. Its garrison comprised the com-pany commander, Lieutenant of the Forty-Sixth Naval Depot Ruda-novskii, and fifty-eight soldiers commanded by the adjutant of the governor-general of Eastern Siberia, Major Busse. On 25 September, the battery of eight cannons (carronades of twelve-pound caliber) was already in place and all the supplies put in a shed purchased from the Japanese. Another shed, acquired in the same manner, was used as living quarters. Six hundred logs were purchased from the Japanese for other construction work.

In spite of friendship expressed by the Japanese, they all disappeared on the following day. Probably they were afraid of being punished by their government for dealing with the Russians. The property which they left behind consisted mostly of provisions, and was saved by Nevel'skoi from the Ainu, (natives of southern Sakhalin) who started to plunder it the moment the Japanese left. Thereafter the distribution of these provisions to the natives took place only by order of the post

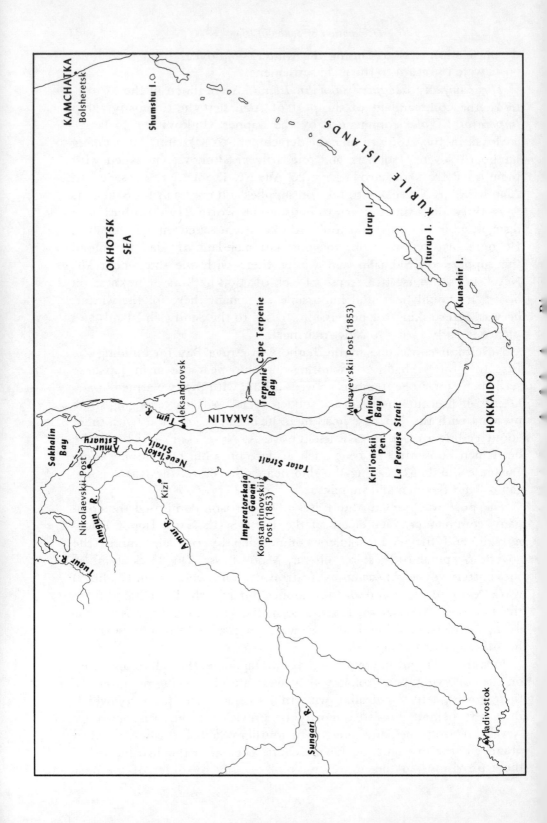

management. Later, some of the Japanese returned and lived quietly in their settlement.

On 26 September, the ship *Nikolai* sailed from Aniva Bay to De-Kastri Bay, arriving there on 2 October. On the way Nevel'skoi stopped at Imperatorskaia Gavan' for several hours to inspect Konstantinovskii post, which was manned by one officer and ten cossacks.

The ship "Nikolai" winters at Imperatorskaia Gavan'. From De-Kastri Bay the ship returned to Imperatorskaia Gavan' with Mr. Boshniak, who was to take charge of the post there, and ɩ company clerk and twelve soldiers who were to occupy the second post.[6] Nevel'skoi instructed Klinkovstrem that if he found the transport *Irtysh* from Kamchatka in the harbor he should sail where the commandant of the port of Aian ordered him; otherwise he should await the arrival of this ship.[7]

The late arrival of the *Irtysh* 11 October, stormy weather, and frost in the following days forced Klinkovstrem to spend the winter at Imperatorskaia Gavan'. On 15 October, the temperature reached 10° below freezing and the harbor became covered with ice, making departure inadvisable. This may have saved the men from an even higher death rate as compared to the calamity that befell them during the first months of 1854. The *Nikolai* had abundant provisions, and, most important, a large stock of wine on board. The transport *Irtysh* arrived at the harbor with a very limited amount of wine and provisions, having unloaded most of them at Aniva at the request of the chief of Murav'-evskii post.[8] However, there were about ninety men in both crews. Due to the shortage of fresh food, a number of men were affected by scurvy beginning early in November. In his report to the company of 27 November 1853[9] Klinkovstrem wrote: "Although they say there are moose, ptarmigans, and heath-cocks, we cannot get them because the woods are impassable and the snow very deep. There are very few natives in the vicinity, so we are unable to procure anything from them and have to live on salted foodstuffs. Crows were the only fresh item of food in our diet, but even they soon left, to avoid extermination."

The situation was getting worse each day. The temperatures reached −20° and −25°. The chief of the establishment managed to construct living quarters for his men, and the remainder lived on board the ships. The company vessel was the better of the two for this purpose. "The strongly built new ship with its double deck above the cabins resisted the cold and −30° was felt less by its inhabitants than by those on the *Irtysh*," writes Boshniak.[10] In spite of all efforts to combat scurvy and the accidental discovery by Petrashkevich, mate on the *Nikolai*, of wild garlic roots (*cheremsha*) under the snow at Cape Putiatin, death cut down the sick. Twelve men, half of the detachment, died ashore. From the crew of thirty-six on the *Irtysh*, one officer and thirteen men also died. Three men died on the *Nikolai*. "Almost everyone else," writes Klinkovstrem, "suffers from some form of scurvy. As of 24 April, five remain in a dangerous condition and eight are convalescent, while the remainder are still weak. How this sad drama will end, we do not know. We hope that after the break-up, God will help us and our health will improve. Most of the men are very thin. Some move and walk like shadows or skeletons. Their faces are as yellow as wax. They need only to close their eyes and they look as if ready for death."[11]

The arrival at Imperatorskaia Gavan' soon afterward of the ships belonging to Vice-Admiral Putiatin's squadron and especially good weather in May completely revived the sick. Their health improved rapidly. Only a small hill not far from Konstantinovskii post testified to the misfortune that had befallen the men who wintered there.

The news of war with England and France, which reached even this region, changed all the plans for occupying Sakhalin Island. By orders of Mr. Putiatin, Murav'evskii post was abandoned, since it could not be defended from enemy cruisers. Part of the squadron which had come from Japan was ordered to sail to the mouth of the Amur to reinforce the establishments there. The frigate *Diana*, which had arrived previously from Kronshtadt, sailed to Japan to negotiate a treaty, and the remainder of the ships, including the company ship *Nikolai*, joined their respective fleets.

After the armistice, the governor-general of Eastern Siberia requested that Sakhalin be transferred to the government. The emperor ordered this transfer effected at once, granting the company the right to have land for its establishments on the island and on the mainland at the mouth of Amur, the land to be alloted by agreement with the local administration. The government retained the exclusive right to mine coal on the island.[12]

The reason prompting the governor-general to request that no exclusive rights be granted on Sakhalin Island and in the Amur region "to any company or individuals, permanently or temporarily,"[13] was his opinion that otherwise the trade and development of this region would be strangled. "The government itself," he wrote, "must not, by premature taxation or by granting privileges, create obstacles to the great future which Russia has a right to expect from her new acquisitions on the Eastern Ocean, and from navigation on the Amur, which connects them with the interior of Siberia. Sakhalin Island, being closely connected with our possessions on Amur, must be under the same administration and have the same defense as the rest of this region.[14]

The governor-general wrote that after receiving 50,000 rubles gratis, the company could not request compensation for the cession of its imaginary possession of this island.[15] "But," added the governor-general, "taking into consideration the assistance the company gave to the government projects on the Amur, and the losses which it suffered during the war, I, as an eyewitness of its activity, can only give it its due for its readiness to be useful to the government and must state that the loss of the ships *Sitkha* and *Okhotsk* and of an iron steamer destroyed by the enemy at Petropavlovsk brought losses to the company which the government should in all fairness share."[16]

As to giving to the company some privileges on Sakhalin and Amur, the governor-general thought that it would be just to give it permission to take timber and coal for its own use, obtaining them by its own means. Such a permission he thought would promote the construction of various establishments and particularly the use of steamers.

Besides this, the governor-general believed that it would be useful to permit to the company free trade and relations with natives under the supervision of local authorities.[17]

However, the company, due to various circumstances and because it did not need Sakhalin coal for its steamers, has so far not used its right to mine coal and has not engaged in trade with the natives. In cases when this coal was needed, the company purchased it locally for between 10 and 16 kopeks silver per pud.

Some statistical and ethnographical data on Sakhalin. It will be useful to give some statistics and ethnographical information taken from reports and notes of persons employed on Sakhalin by the company or who visited the island in 1852-54. Information submitted to the board of directors by Lieutenant Rudanovskii, commander of Murav'evskii post, gathered during his stay at Aniva Bay and during several expeditions in the interior, contains a detailed description of the southern part of Sakhalin Island and of its inhabitants, until now very little known.

The geographical position of Sakhalin is between latitudes 54° 24' 5" and 45° 56' 26" north. A high mountain range extends the whole length of the island, becoming a chain of high hills with deep valleys between as it nears the sea shore. Brush and forests cover the interior of the island. The coastal areas consist mainly of bare and frequently steep cliffs, clearly showing, as some have noted, geological composition and strata. North from Cape Due, from 51° north latitude, the range becomes gradually lower and ends in a low shore sparsely covered with brush. There are scattered mountain ridges on both eastern and western shores of the southern part of the island. Between them lie some slopes which could make good pasture for cattle. The Susue, one of the rivers in southern Sakhalin, flows through lands where grass grows higher than a man's head. The south end of Sakhalin ends in two capes, Kril'ion and Aniva, separated by Aniva Bay. These peninsulas and the hills on them are covered with fir and larch trees. Their geological formations consist of quartz, granite, and clay. To all appearances, the mountains are of volcanic origin. The names given by the natives to some of the shores and capes corroborate this. For instance, the northeastern shore of Aniva Bay is named *Khokui kotan*. The first word means "to burn;" the second, "side" or "earth." However, the natives could tell nothing about earthquakes or the formation of volcanoes. Two rivers of considerable size, the Susuia and Liutoga, not less than 100 versts long, flow into Aniva Bay. There is a portage from one to the other at their source. The Sika, also a river of considerable size, flows into Terpenie Bay. There are many fair-sized rivers in the interior, such as the Tymi, Due, Traisko, and several others, as well as a great many smaller rivers, creeks, and streams. There are several large lakes in the eastern part of the island. The trees on the shores of the rivers are larger than on the mountain peaks. Fir, larch, cedar, some elm, aspen, and birch are the most common. In some places alder, ash, poplar, silver-fir, wild cherry, apple trees, and rowan are found, as well as guelder-rose, raspberries, and other shrubs. Cranberries are particularly abundant. Several kinds of sarana root are found also. There is not much timber for shipbuilding, but according to Samarin, a former company clerk, there are trees along the shores of the Siki River large enough for masts. Mr. Rudanovskii also saw ship timber on the shores of the Susuia River. The soil in southern Sakhalin is chernozem intermixed with layers of clay. According to Rudanovskii, the climate is moderate. During the winter of 1853-54 it was not colder than 14 3/4° below freezing. The snowfall began on 3 November, and the grass and trees started getting green by 9 May.

There are bears, foxes, squirrels, sables, otters, musk-deer, and deer. The bears on Sakhalin are famous for their enormous size and fine fur. There are many foxes, mostly red. The sables are of poor quality in comparison with those in Amur region. The otters are of very good quality and in southern Sakhalin are in great demand and are profitably sold by the natives to the Japanese, Manchus, and Giliaks. The caribou come in big herds to the mouths of the rivers in the winter and are hunted by the natives. Seals, sea-lions, and whales are found along the coasts. Mr. Rudanovskii writes that while traveling along the shore, he saw enormous herds of sea-lions. Sometimes about a hundred of them would lift their heads out of the water not more than five sazhens from the boat and then dive again, all at the same time. According to the natives, there are no sea otters on the shores of Sakhalin, a fact confirmed by the absence of sea-cabbage, which is their food.[18]

There are very many eagles, gray with white wings. Some of them have a wing spread of over a sazhen. In the autumn, flocks of swans cover the shores of the Susui River. There are plenty of grouse, heath cocks, snipe, etc.

Fish abound in almost all the lakes and rivers. Out of many kinds, herring, flounder, nelma, and salmon predominate. Mr. Rudanovskii writes that in the spring of 1845, during the herring run some of the bays were completely blocked by fish. The fish ashore formed a barricade in some places about two versts long, three sazhen wide, and at least one sazhen high. Flounders usually weigh between five and ten pounds.

Most of the fishing on Sakhalin is done by the Japanese. They have stations for this purpose on both sides of Aniva Bay and on the west shore up to the Kusunai River, where they salt and dry fish.

There are at least forty-four establishments of this sort, mainly on the eastern shore. Most of the Japanese fisherman come in the summer but there are winter quarters for them in several places too. The government controls the fishing and a government official supervises fishing establishments. The majority spend the winter on Matsmai Island. While the Russians wintered at Aniva, not more than twenty-five Japanese remained there. It should be mentioned that they and the Russians were on very friendly terms. The natives say that the Japanese take out of Sakhalin at least fifteen boats (about ten tons each) loaded with herring, and five boats with salmon. However, Mr. Furuhjelm believes that because of the number of Japanese establishments on the island, the quantity of salmon taken must be considerably greater.

Besides the information furnished in 1852 by Mr. Boshniak about places on Sakhalin Island where coal is found,[19] additional information was supplied during the cruise in 1853 of the naval schooner *Vostok*, (Captain-Lieutenant V. A. Rimskii-Korsakov, commander). Lieutenant Chikhachov, one of the officers on this ship, the same who had earlier helped to explore the Amur region, was sent to find a convenient place for mining and four miles from Cape Due (Zhonk'er Bay) discovered over twenty layers of coal, each two to three feet in thickness. Near the settlement of Due, Veirikh, the doctor from the schooner, found two layers of coal separated by a thin layer of slate, both layers together measuring about six feet.[20] Lieutenant Orlov found an abundance of loose coal on the left shore of the Noidu River. This coal was probably brought down by the current after being broken from the above-mentioned formations. The natives showed Orlov coal on the Ai River and the company clerk Samarin found on the left bank of the Siki River, at latitude 50°, layers of coal of a considerable thickness which he could not prospect because of deep snow.

The coal at Cape Due proved to be of very good quality. Rimskii-Korsakov found that it burned about 25 percent faster than Welsh coal: that is to say thirty puds of welsh coal equaled forty puds of Sakhalin coal. Rimskii-Korsakov considered Cape Due or Zhonk'er Bay to be the best place on all the west coast for mining coal, because of the proximity of deposits and convenience of floating it down one of the largest rivers on the west coast of Sakhalin.

According to Rimskii-Korsakov and others who have visited the island, the lack of safe, sheltered bays and harbors on the western shore would make coal mining there for commercial purposes difficult. The western shore stretches almost in a straight line, forming rocky inlets only in a few places which, as Mr. Furuhjelm says, should be called anchorages rather than bays. Rimskii-Korsakov believes that because of lack of good harbors, coal mines should be located on the largest rivers, the Due, Tymi, and Neva, the last of which flows from the parts of the island richest in coal.[21]

Besides coal, Samarin found traces of copper ore at the village of Sirooroko, not far from Cape Aniva.

Sakhalin Island is inhabited by three different peoples. The Giliaks live in the northern part: the Orokaty or Orngory, also called the Tazon by the natives, live a nomadic life in the mountains in the middle of the island; and the Ainu or Ainy inhabit the island south of latitude 49° 58″.

The Giliaks on Sakhalin live in the same way and have the same customs as their countrymen in the Amur region. The only difference between them is that the Giliaks on the Amur are more enterprising in trade and do most of the trading on the island. The Giliaks who live on Sakhalin do not like to leave their homes and often sell their furs for a fraction of their cost to the Giliaks from the Amur, who in turn sell them at a considerable profit to the Manchus or Japanese.

The Orngori or Orokati are a branch of the Tungus and resemble their kinsmen in their habits and customs. Their main occupation is hunting fur-bearing animals and reindeer. Keeping reindeer herds and hunting wild deer gives them their main income and food. They fish only when hunting is bad. When they need fish, they barter it mostly from the Giliaks.

The Ainu[22] resemble the Kurile natives and many believe that they are of the same race. These people still live in very primitive conditions and the farther south they are, the poorer they are. They subsist mainly on paltry wages they receive for working in Japanese fisheries. Their belief in the superiority of the Japanese over them is so deep that they consider the Japanese traders their absolute masters. An absolute, and for the most part, humiliating subordination on one side, and a haughty disdain on the other, characterize the relations between the Ainu and the Japanese.

This disdain probably explains the lack of Japanese measures to propagate their religion, mode of life, etc. among the natives. The Ainu receive from their masters the bare necessities, often on credit. In exchange, the Japanese force the Ainu to work for them, collecting even for aid given in time of need.

The Ainu are peaceful and good natured, but they have learned from the Japanese to be hypocritical and treacherous. Although they bitterly hate the Japanese, the Ainu obey them to all appearances without complaint, but are watchful for an opportunity to avenge their insults. Not daring to rebel openly when a Japanese took his wife, an Ainu will still try to avenge himself even if only in an underhanded way. It is notable that this dissatisfaction with the Japanese is widespread. Many of the old men expressed to Mr. Rudanovskii their astonishment at seeing that the Russians could live with the Japanese peacefully. Confidentially, the Ainu offered their help against the Japanese if necessary.

The great leniency and fairness of the Russians in dealing with the Ainu surprised them a great deal and seems to have restored some of their self-respect. Notwithstanding this, however, the Ainu could not avoid being sly even toward their good neighbors, as they considered the inhabitants of Murav'evskii post to be. As proof of this, they seldom told their real names and would not even mention that they had goods for barter until they saw something that they needed. This may have come in part from their fear of the Japanese, but it is most likely a trait of character acquired from the latter. When the Russians first moved to Sakhalin, the Japanese threatened to punish the Ainu for every attempt to trade with the Russians, but at the order of the post officers, the Japanese stopped making these threats and their influence weakened. Because the Russians were fair to them, the natives did not have to use various dodges or cheat them.

The Ainu are of medium and often of small stature. Faces of Mongolian type are seldom found among them. Swarthy complexions and large black beards give a manly appearance to their faces. They shave the tops of their heads and on the sides at the lower tips of their ears. Their hair falls in long strands from the nape of their necks to the shoulders. The women do not shave their heads. Loose, long hair helps their appearance, but their thick lips painted blue, as is done by the married women, and high cheekbones are not attractive. The old women are especially ugly, often with disheveled hair, wrinkled faces, and lips made ugly by paint and black tattoo marks resembling a moustache. The Ainu go about with their heads uncovered, even in the winter. The hands and feet of Ainu women—as one traveler, a good judge of the fair sex, remarks—are outstanding in their small size and beauty. The most obvious characteristic of these natives is their sloven- liness. Their clothes have a smell especially disagreeable to a person not used to it. Clothes of well-to-do Ainu usually consist of several Manchu or Japanese robes. In cold weather the poor dress in a shirt made of elm or aspen bark with a dog skin over it. The women dress in a shirt made of rough blue cloth or a sea-lion hide with the hair outside. The dwellings of the Ainu also have a disagreeable smell. The stench, smoke, and soot in them probably affect the health of the inhabitants. Toward the middle of the island, one finds slightly better dwellings like big sheds or barns. The roof is usually twice as high as the walls, which are faced with birch bark. The well-to-do have mats on the floor. There is usually one or two hearths in such a dwelling, and plank beds and shelves along the walls. Poles under the roof from one end to the other are used to hang clothes and other things. Their household utensils are cast-iron kettles, wooden Japanese cups, and seashells. The Ainu always settle on the coast and leave the interior of the island uninha- bited. The thirty-two villages in southern Sakhalin from latitude 48° 2′ have over 2,400 inhabitants. This figure includes several Giliak families. Men are more numerous than women, probably because of the life of the Sakhalin natives, which being devoid of any comfort is conse- quently hard on women, the weaker sex. The Ainu told Rudanovskii that about twenty years previous an epidemic had killed about half of the population and that women and children had suffered most.

Polygamy is very common among the Ainu. Even a close blood relationship is not an obstacle to marriage. It is only important to be able to give the parents of the bride several presents, such as sable pelts, dogs, etc. Marriage is celebrated by rites of no particular signifi- cance.

The most common disease among the Ainu are eye diseases, scabies, and scrofula. Probably these diseases and the high mortality rate among the children can be explained by the dirt in their dwellings, and by the lack of light and fresh air, which they deprive themselves of in order to keep warm during most of the year. Many of them are blind. Most of the old men are blind or have poor sight. The women have red and purulent eyes, with swollen eyelids. Syphilis also has found its way to the island, but fortunately has not yet spread very far.

The main food of the Ainu is fish, fresh from April until November and dried during the rest of the year. They also eat seal, sea-lion, whale, bear and dog meat, mussels, and some roots, especially sarana, which sometimes surpasses a large onion in size. They freeze it and consider it a delicacy when frozen. Their favorite berries, usually eaten with blubber, are cranberries. Seals are undoubtedly the most useful animals for these natives, because they can be caught year round. Their hides are used for footwear and their meat for food. Leather straps made from sea lion hides take the place of ropes. The Ainu barter rice from the Japanese and enjoy it very much. They sometimes make an alcoholic beverage out of it called *ioski* which some believe is a good antiscorbutic.

The sea provides both the Ainu and the Aleuts with everything they need. But while the Aleuts are famous for being bold, experienced seamen, the Ainu are not. They seldom venture out in their canoes beyond a depth of about three feet, and at the first sign of a storm, paddle ashore as fast as they can.

Every Ainu owns several dogs. They are the only means of communication with other places during the six long winter months. The Ainu seem deeply attached to these animals. A good master will never enter a dwelling before feeding and making his dogs comfortable for the night. Rudanovskii writes that he never saw an Ainu beat a dog mercilessly as do almost all the natives of Kamchatka. If an Ainu has to strike a dog he does it almost with tears in his eyes, because he believes that this dog will die soon.

The Ainu travel very fast. Rudanovskii sometimes traveled with them at a speed of eighteen versts per hour. Even when not in a hurry and over difficult roads, they make eight versts per hour. Between villages which are but a short distance apart, the dogs run at full speed, and great dexterity is required to handle the sled. The sleds of the Ainu are much lighter than those of the Kamchadals and differ from them in having whalebone under the runners, over which wood is fastened when travel on snow is required. In Kamchatka, runners made of whalebone are carried along to be used on ice and in case of a thaw. In southern Sakhalin the dogs are hitched to the sled in single file; this simplifies the harness and prevents them from getting tangled up. In Kamchatka, the dogs are hitched in pairs and often tangle the harness.

The Ainu worship fire, the moon, and the bear. They have no idols but they put up an *inau* as a sign of worship. An *inau* is a green twig of alder, with the bark on the upper part cut in thin strips and curled so that it resembles a curly birch. The *inau* is a requisite of every dwelling and feast and is put at the entrance to a village and in other important places. In a dwelling it is placed by the hearth. When meeting and saying goodby to a guest, the host offers an *inau*. Legends, superstitions, and ritualism seem to play an important part in the life of the Ainu. Every action to be undertaken requires certain rites. Even the most common happenings of everyday life, such as drinking wine, call for ceremony. The oldest and most venerable man among those about to drink from a loving cup takes it in his hand, dips the stem of his pipe or finger into it and, after shaking a few drops from it to the right and left and sometimes before him, says an incantation to the *Kanuiu* (divinity), saying that a sacrifice is made, that they will drink to the health of a certain person, and that he asks God not to get angry at those present and to send them good hunting.

The arrival of a guest is an important event. All the visitor's belongings including his sled are carried into the yurt and the master of the house permits the guest to take his place. Greetings begin only after the guest has rested awhile from his travel. They first touch the hands of one another and then the chest and the beards to show that they feel a mutual liking. After this, the host begins to pray in a low voice to the *Kanuiu*, whom he thanks for enabling him to see his guest. After the last words are spoken, all present stroke their beards and bow to the host. After that comes silence which is interrupted by the guest who begins evenly and in a low voice to tell about the part of the country from which he comes, about his journey, how in a certain place one of his dogs broke loose, how he fell in the snow, and whom he met on the way. This speech is addressed also to the deity and all present listen attentively to it. After the guest finishes his tale, everybody bows to him, and then the usual conversation and eating takes place. The conversation is always conducted quietly in an even voice, without excitement and arguments, and one cannot help but admire the decorum of the Ainu gatherings. The Ainu like to talk sitting by the fire. Sometimes they spend all night like that talking on various subjects. They have a saying: "*undzhi kara, tambaku iku, pirika*" which means "to tend to the fire and to smoke is a pleasant occupation."

A ritualistic killing of a bear is very remarkable. According to Rudanovskii, who saw this ceremony, almost every well-to-do Ainu has a bear cub which he raises for some special occasion and keeps in his hut in a cage. These cubs are usually taken when a female bear is killed and the den is found. An account of a ceremonial killing of a bear follows. About three days before the killing takes place all the neighboring natives of both sexes came to the village. The men engaged in conversation in the yurts, drinking Japanese *saki*. The women sang songs and danced before the bear's cage. On the day of the celebration the village and its inhabitants looked very festive, especially the children. They had put on all the finery they possessed. The place where the bear was to be killed was marked by a hedge of *inau* on which pieces of cloth were tied. Several sazhens within the enclosure a post was placed in the ground to which the bear was to be tied. The bear was led to it in a special manner. Before the cage was opened, a noose of sealion skin strips, the ends of which were held by several men on each side, was put over the bear's neck, and then the top of the cage was opened. When the bear jumped out of it, the ends of the loop did not permit him to run right or left. At the same time one of the Ainu teased him thereby making him move toward the post, to which he was securely tied. The ceremony began when an old man, holding a long *inau* over the bear's head said an incantation to the deity. The bear growled, tried to break loose and to climb the pole, which of course he could not do. The spectators were staring at him all the time and when the animal became tired, three Ainu took aim with their bows and arrows. The first arrow was aimed at the bear's side. With a terrible snarl the bear gathered its remaining strength and broke the arrow with its teeth, the point remaining in the wound. The second arrow followed the first. The bear was still alive but could not move. Finally the third arrow, aimed at bear's mouth, ended his suffering. The moment the bear died, several Ainu ran to him crying and embracing him. After that the bear was laid on his belly and various foods: rice, fish, roots with seal blubber, etc. were placed before him. In making these offerings the Ainu also did not forget to partake. Several days later, they brought to Murav'evskii post the bear's hide and its hind leg, asking Mr. Busse to accept the hind leg as a present from them. The natives usually dry the bear's gall and use it as a medicine.

The main trading place on Sakhalin is Sirakusi, a village on the western coast, latitude 46° 50′. In June and July, Giliaks from the Amur and Manchus and Japanese gather here. The Japanese bring otters, which they obtain by barter or sometimes simply take by force from the Ainu for old debts. They also obtain otters on Matsmai Island. The Japanese also bring cast iron kettles, hardware, rice, sake, wooden and china bowls, pipes, tobacco, and cheap cotton cloth. The Manchus barter silk cloth and robes for otter pelts. Later on they barter furs to other Manchus for vodka, for which there is always a market among the

Amur and Sakhalin natives. The Amur Giliaks sell similar goods which they have procured from the Manchus, as well as blue cotton cloth of Russian manufacture, *boi*, flannel, and eagle tails. They barter these items for Japanese rice, kettles, files, and other hardware. This fair has a peculiar aspect of its own. All native traders arriving at Sirakusi receive from the Japanese official two or three strokes with a cane as a sign that they are Japanese subjects. After that they are allowed to proceed with the trading. The Japanese take all the goods from the Giliaks to a building of their own to look them over. The natives cannot enter this house under any circumstances. All the trading is done under Japanese control and even the prices are arbitrarily fixed by them. The Giliak Pozvein told Mr. Furuhjelm that for one and a half dozen needles, one and a half dozen brass buttons, nine sazhen of blue silk cloth, seven sazhen of red cloth, ten eagle tails of inferior quality,[23] three flannel jackets, two Manchu fur coats, ten pieces of blue cotton cloth, ten strands of large beads, and three pounds of common beads, he received from the Japanese one large cast-iron kettle, one and a half bags of rice, forty otters, twenty-five foxes, and thirty-seven sables. The Japanese were giving five otters, five foxes, and five sables for a piece of silk cloth seven sazhens long and one arshin wide. For an eagle's tail of best quality they gave twelve otters, and for a tail of low grade, an undetermined quantity of rice. Furuhjelm estimates that 2,400 otters, about 1,300 sables, and 640 foxes are bartered at the Sirakusi fair. It must be mentioned here that the Ainu traded more willingly with the Japanese than with the Russians in spite of the fact that goods brought by the company to Sakhalin were better and cheaper. The reason for this is difficult to determine, but it might have been due to force of habit or the fear of being persecuted by the Japanese.

15. *Whaling by Foreigners and Russians in the Eastern Ocean*

Whaling by foreigners, especially Americans, within the Russian colonies, and company measures to prevent this. At the beginning of the nineteenth century, Count Pahlen, Russian minister to the United States, pointed out the inability of the American government to make its citizens obey existing rules and regulations.[1] His words were proven by subsequent actions of the Americans in whaling and probably also in contraband trade in the Russian part of the Eastern Ocean. In this instance the government of the United States at least did all it could to avoid accusations of not keeping its obligations. After the expiry of the ten-year term of the convention negotiated in 1824, the United States not only informed its citizens that free trade in colonial waters had been discontinued, but made it known that Article 2 of the convention strictly prohibited American ships from stopping at places where there were Russian settlements, without permission of the managers of those settlements. As was predictable, however, neither the announcement nor the prohibition brought any results, and the American whalers continued, as before, to do as they pleased in Russian possessions. That the convention had not been kept may be seen from the following facts.

Etholen, who was then the chief manager of the colonies, reported to the company in 1842 that he had met several American ships while on his tour of inspection. The circumstances did not permit him to ascertain what these ships were doing, but by all appearances they were whaling vessels. In corroboration he quoted reports from various districts about frequent appearances of American whalers near colonial harbors and shores.

Among these reports, that of Captain-Lieutenant Kadnikov, commander of the company ship *Naslednik Aleksandr*, is particularly interesting. An interrogation by him of the skipper of an American whaler,

Kodiak islanders whaling

while Kadnikov was on his way from Sitkha to Okhotsk, revealed that the whaler had just arrived from the Sandwich Islands, together with thirty other ships, for whaling along both sides of the western part of the Aliaska Peninsula and adjacent eastern islands of the Aleutian Chain. According to this skipper, up to two hundred whalers were to arrive from the United States during that season. He stated that in 1841 he and fifty other ships had hunted in these waters and that his ship had killed thirteen whales, which yielded about 1,600 barrels of oil.[2]

To an energetic request by the company to prohibit Americans from whaling in colonial waters because it violated the convention, the Ministry of Foreign Affairs replied:[3]

The right to have a "closed sea" (*mare clausum*) in the northern part of the Pacific Ocean, should we wish to apply it, cannot be proven, and according to Article 1 of the Convention of 1824, which is still in force, American citizens have the right to fish everywhere in the Pacific Ocean. According to Article 4 of the same convention, after ten years we can prohibit American ships from entering our territorial waters, harbors, and bays for the purpose of fishing or trading with the natives. This limits our rights and we cannot prohibit American vessels from whaling on the high seas.

Obviously, after such an answer, the company could not put a stop to the high-handedness of the whalers, and therefore they could do as they wished in our colonies. Continuous complaints from the year 1843 up to 1850 prove that the temerity of the whalers became extreme. Landing on the islands of the Aleutian and Kurile groups, they cut wood where they pleased and rendered oil on the beach, thus harming our fur trade since a whiff of smoke is sufficient to frighten away the sea otters. Moreover, in their rowdiness they have often demolished native huts and small company posts, answering with threats or derision when reminded of the existing regulations and of the prohibition against whaling near the shore. According to the whalers, the sea, no matter where, belongs to all, and their flag gives them the right to engage in trade. The American skippers traded with the Kolosh openly, and when the colonial management accordingly expelled some of them from New Archangel, they continued their trading in Sitkha Bay, in spite of all protests. In 1847, when one of the whalers was forbidden to kill sea lions on a small island near Bering Island, the skipper ordered the Russian manager of the island off his vessel and went ashore with his men at once intending to disobey the orders. Only resolute preparations to defend the island forced the whalers to leave, but not before they cut down the shrubbery which had been planted with great difficulty on the treeless island.[4] Not many colonial districts were spared such visits, always accompanied by some sort of violence.

Receiving complaints, the company tried its best to protect the country under its management, but to no avail. In 1843, soon after his first protest, an unusually large gathering of whalers off the shores of Kad'iak caused Mr. Etholen to request that the company give him more definite instructions about the whaling vessels, which threatened to ruin the fur trade, and to define the rights of the chief manager of the colonies relative to the skippers. While waiting for orders, he armed one of the ships of the colonial fleet and sent her to cruise in areas where the foreigners were especially annoying. The commander of this cruiser was instructed to avoid trouble and to confine himself to the supervision of whaling. Only under threat of attack could he take decisive action. Besides taking these steps, Etholen asked the colonial administration for permission to use the navy flag on colonial cruisers, since it commanded more respect than the company flag. Finally, according to him, the foreigners' claims to the right of whaling in Russian waters should be limited by a boundary of three leagues, or nine Italian miles offshore. He pointed to New Holland and other English possessions as an example, where foreign whalers dared not hunt nearer than this distance.

Unfortunately these efforts to defend our rights brought no positive results. At the company's request our Ministry of Foreign Affairs informed the United States government that cruisers in the Russian colonies would patrol the waters to see that foreign ships did not violate the articles of the Convention of 1824, but the company did not receive permission to define the boundaries or to use the naval flag. The government informed the company that all matters regarding foreign ships must be handled very carefully.[5]

The correspondence on this subject was renewed in 1847, following a report by Chief Manager Teben'kov on new transgressions by the whalers. Some time before that, in June 1846, the governor-general of Eastern Siberia asserted that in order to limit whaling by foreign ships it would have been just to forbid the foreign vessels to come nearer than forty Italian miles to our shores, except for Petropavlovsk and Okhotsk, where they should be made to pay one hundred rubles per ship for permission to hunt whales. A naval brig should patrol our waters and see that these regulations were obeyed. The ministry, on the other hand, insisted that "according to both conventions (1824 and 1825), we have no right to prohibit foreign navigation in the part of the Pacific Ocean that separates the east coast of Siberia from the northwest coast of America, or to impose any taxes for the right of whaling." To set up such boundaries, limiting navigation, would mean, according to the ministry, renewing all the former discussions with England and

France on the subject. Only territorial waters within the limits of a cannon shot, that is, about three miles, could not be disputed. In conclusion, the ministry remarked that no power had as yet limited the right to fish on the high seas and that claims of this nature were never recognized by other powers. It hoped that colonial cruisers would help to avoid misunderstandings, and asserted that because these had been in use only a short time, their efficacy could not yet be judged.[6]

The reports of Gavrilov, commander of the company brig *Konstantin*, which cruised in the vicinity of the Kurile Islands, finally prompted the company to request that the government send a navy cruiser to patrol the coast. Gavrilov wrote: "The many whalers hunting in the vicinity of the islands covered the sea with blubber and the shores with carcasses and whales that had died of wounds. Their whale boats approached the shore, especially at night time, and they built fires, the smoke from which frightens away not only the sea otters but the sealions and seals as well."[7]

His Majesty the Emperor ordered all the details on this matter forwarded to the naval chief-of-staff, instructing him to submit his opinion as to how to prevent violation of our rights by the whalers.

The naval chief-of-staff replied that "there would be no difficulty in assigning a navy vessel for cruising in waters of our American possessions in order to prevent foreign ships from engaging in trade prohibited by conventions, provided that all expenses for this would be paid by the Russian-American Company."[8] The Ministry of the Navy estimated the sum needed for fitting out a cruiser at 270,159 silver rubles, 41 kopeks, and annual upkeep at 85,310 rubles, 44 kopeks.[9] This estimate exceeds the company's means for the upkeep of its colonial establishments.

In any case, assignment of a naval vessel became less important for the colonies in American at this time because the whalers transferred most of their activity to the Okhotsk Sea. Later on, some of them visited our colonial waters once again, and in 1849 and 1850 were even caught whaling off St. Paul and St. George islands, but because there were not as many as before, we could defend our possessions locally. Because the names of the vessels and skippers usually remained unknown, our embassy in the United States could not request that individual cases be prosecuted, or ask for damages. As may be seen from embassy dispatches, to which our Ministry of Foreign Affairs forwarded the company's complaints, the American government was powerless, as we had the occasion to state above, to restrict its citizens from arbitrary actions.

In 1850, the navy corvette *Olivutsa* was sent by order of the emperor to cruise in the Eastern Ocean. This circumstance, as well as proposed sailings of other ships for the same purpose, made it imperative to work out definite instructions for their commanders regarding foreign whaling. The company, being the most interested party, was invited to submit its opinion on this subject.

The company believed in the need, if not for complete prohibition of whaling in the Okhotsk Sea, at least for efficient protection by naval cruisers of some of the places where whales abound. The company proposed that the patrol vessels be based near the Shantar Islands and that foreigners be prohibited from hunting in the bays and near the shore.[10]

The company's suggestion to make the Shantar Islands a base for cruisers was not included in the instruction approved by the emperor on 9 December 1853. Instead, it was probably considered sufficient for the cruisers to follow the whalers from place to place during the navigation season. The cruisers had to see that the whalers did not enter bays and sounds nor approach our coasts nearer than three Italian miles.[11] The Okhotsk Sea was declared open for the foreign whalers. In general, the main aim of stationing patrol vessels was to see that whaling was conducted in a manner unharmful to the native tribes subject to Russia, and to see that law and order was observed in waters adjacent to Russian possessions.

To what extent rules for foreign whaling, especially in the Okhotsk Sea, were necessary, can be seen from a general account of the whaling industry in these waters.

Whaling by foreigners in the Okhotsk Sea. As is known from the information furnished by foreign whalers, and from some publications on this subject, the Okhotsk Sea first became important in the whaling industry in the early 1850s. Even before then, as may be seen from reports of Orlov and other company employees, whaling vessels, frequently carrying rich cargoes, were seen in the bays and sounds along the coast of southeastern Siberia adjacent to the mouth of the Amur River. Subsequently, these vessels increased in number each year until finally not a single spot in the Okhotsk Sea was left unexplored.

Until then the foreign whalers and especially the greater part of the New Bedford[12] whaling fleet—the North Pacific Whaling Fleet—had usually sailed north through the Bering Straits. They moved to the Okhotsk Sea because of the discovery of a special kind of whale, the so-called bowhead, in the northern part of this sea, mostly in Tugursk, Ul'bansk, and Usal'ginski bays.[13] Penzhinsk, Gizhiginsk, Tauisk, and Konstantinovsk bays, and others around the Shantar Islands, offered considerable advantages at first to the foreign ships, but Tugursk Bay was considered the best for whaling. A fairly large river flows into this bay and therefore the ice breaks up earlier there than in other places. The whales gather there in large numbers for breeding and are a sure catch, according to all the foreigners engaged in this industry.[14] It is very important, they say, to be in the bay early before too many other ships arrive. The ice does not permit the whalers to enter the bay until the middle of June; and frost and storms force them to leave about the middle of September. Consequently, the whalers are in a hurry to get to the bay. According to the Americans, some of the smaller vessels have even wintered in small bays nearby,[15] but sickness and death and privations of all kinds awaited those who decided on a long stay in that desolate place, forcing them to discontinue such undertakings.

The whalers who managed to enter Tugursk Bay early returned from there with a rich cargo of whalebone and oil. It should be noted that small vessels able to navigate in shallow waters were the most profitable. Recently, some of the whalers have brought small schooners that transferred their cargoes to a large vessel and returned to hunting again.

An average of at least one hundred foreign whaling vessels yearly has visited the Okhotsk Sea during the last ten years. The average quantity of whale oil has been one thousand barrels per ship, but lately with the increased number of whalers this quantity has declined. At first, when the waters were not hunted much, some of the whalers were able to get up to two thousand barrels of oil. As whaling in the Okhotsk Sea has become less profitable, many ships have gone elsewhere. Experienced whalers say that it is not that the number of whales has diminished, but that too many ships have made the whales wary and hunting has become more difficult.

Establishment of Russian whaling in the Eastern Ocean. Attempting to find ways of curbing the abuses of the foreign whalers, the company planned several times to establish its own whaling industry in the Eastern Ocean. Even if such an undertaking could not put a stop to the high-handedness of the whalers, the substantial profits, so far enjoyed exclusively by the foreigners, would compensate the company for some of the losses suffered in its possissions.[16] On the other hand, the failure of the company's petitions to restrict foreign navigation, the large expenditures needed to establish its own whaling industry, and finally the opportunities of putting its capital into safer undertakings, such as trade with California and the Sandwich Islands, made the company extremely cautious.

For instance, a suggestion of General-Lieutenant Rupert, chief of eastern Siberia, was forwarded to the company by the Ministry of

Finance, in which Rupert recommended that the Russian-American or some other company should organize Russian whaling in the Eastern Ocean.[17] The company replied:

> The Company cannot help that it, or some other corporation, will be unable, without government assistance, to take the whaling industry out of foreign hands, when according to the latest information about 200 ships yearly are hunting whales in the Eastern Ocean north of the tropics. If the government will take effective measures to safeguard from foreign ships such parts of the Eastern Ocean that are encircled by Russians possessions,[18] then the company, with some temporary financial privileges, is ready to begin establishing Russian whaling in the Eastern Ocean at its own cost.[19]

The company noted that it had already entered into relations with Bremen whalers about a joint enterprise, but without success.

Meanwhile, several shipowners in Finland proposed to form a whaling company, if the Russian-American Company would take part in it and if the government would grant some privileges necessary for the undertaking's success. A general meeting of the company's shareholders voted[20] to take part in the proposed Finnish company to the amount of 100,000 silver rubles.[21]

The organization of the whaling company was delayed, however, because of obstacles involved in granting the Finns the privileges they hoped to receive. In 1849 they renewed their petition, asking for subsidies. General Murav'ev, chief of East Siberia, who had just returned from a trip to Kamchatka, supported the project.[22]

Thanks to this intervention the Finnish participants received the following subsidies from money authorized for Finland: (1) 20,000 rubles for organization; (2) 10,000 rubles per ship as a premium for outfitting the first four ships; (3) the right to import materials and implements for the first twelve ships from abroad free of duty; (4) the right to import into Finland and to export the products of the whaling industry for a twelve-year term.[23] The code of regulations of this company, to be called the Russian-Finnish Whaling Company, was approved by the sovereign on 13 December 1850,[24] and in August 1851 this company equipped its first ship.

In spite of all these subsidies and privileges, the hopes for a successful undertaking did not materialize. The war with England and France paralyzed the company during its first years. The numerous foreign ships, active, as stated above, even in sheltered bays in the Okhotsk Sea, reduced the number of whales and destroyed all hopes of future profits. Whaling yields did not pay expenses and the company's affairs steadily worsened.

A description of the activities of the whaling company from the time it was founded up to the present follows.[25]

The company's first vessel, the *Suomi*, 500 tons, was built at Åbo but outfitted at Bremen because Åbo lacked the proper facilities. Some of the implements were ordered for America. Its commander was Hagshagen, a citizen of Hanover, and a skillful and experienced whaler. The crew consisted of thirty-six men. Three foreigners were hired to take charge of whaleboats during hunting; three harpooners and two coopers were also hired. This vessel could put down four whaleboats at the same time.

A New Bedford whaleboat, fully outfitted for hunting, served as a pattern for construction of the new whaleboats, which up until then were very unfamiliar to Finnish shipbuilders. There were not enough barrels at Åbo nor could the company find an experienced cooper there to look after them during the expedition. Thus, outfitting the *Suomi* for whaling cost the company the considerable sum of 74,700 rubles.

In order to train men in the whaling business and to make experienced skippers out of them, the whaling company also sent several educated young men on the *Suomi* under Hagshagen's guidance. The Finnish sailors in the ship's crew were to learn from the foreigners how to manage the whaleboats and how to handle the harpoons efficiently. No positive results were attained in this respect because of the short duration of the company's activitites.

During the *Suomi*'s two-year (1852-53) cruise in the Okhotsk Sea, the hunting was good. In the first year, 1,500 barrels of oil and 21,400 pounds of whalebone were acquired and were sold for 88,001 silver rubles. This not only paid for the ship but left 13,601 rubles clear profit.

But the war with England and France, which began shortly before the *Suomi* returned to Europe, had unfortunate consequences for this venture. The vessel barely escaped capture, because skipper Hagshagen, not knowing what had occurred, steered for the English port of Cowes. The pilot coming on board to take the ship into the harbor told of the break between England and Russia, and Hagshagen, helped by a favorable wind, sailed at once for Bremen and luckily reached that port safely.

Fearing for the ship's safety during a prolonged conflict, the company decided to sell it. The allies declared all Russian ships subject to capture, even when sailing under the flag of a neutral nation. This prevented the company from sending the ship on another expedition, and had it not been sold, it would probably have gone to ruin anyhow. The sum of 21,000 silver rubles, obtained with great difficulties, did not correspond to its real value.

The *Turku* (the local name of Åbo), the company's second ship, a little over 500 tons, was sent to the Okhotsk Sea in the fall of 1852. It was outfitted almost entirely at Åbo, except for a few oil barrels purchased in Copenhagen, and two whaleboats in America. Four other whaleboats for the vessel were also built at Åbo. Skipper Scheel of Lübeck was given command of this ship. Its crew consisted of twenty-five Finns. Only the cooper was hired at Denmark. To save expenses, the whaling company took Russian-American Company freight for transportation to the colonies. A collision with another vessel at Falmouth so delayed this ship's sailing that after delivering the supplies at New Archangel it reached the Okhotsk Sea only late in the fall. The crew killed only one whale, which yielded 80 barrels of oil and 650 pounds of whalebone.

Early in 1845 the *Turku*, commanded by Sederblom—a Finn who was the first mate and had taken over the ship because of Scheel's illness—hunted whales in the China Sea off the coast of Japan and later in the Okhotsk Sea after it had cleared of ice. Under the supervision of an American hired in the Sandwich Islands, the hunting was successful and resulted in 1,670 barrels of oil and 23,441 pounds of whalebone. In the fall, after the enemy squadron had left the Kamchatka coast, the *Turku* managed to enter Petropavlovsk Harbor; but expecting another visit from the Anglo-French squadron to avenge the defeat, the skipper sailed to the colonies in early spring 1855. Leaving its cargo at Kad'iak, the ship sailed to New Archangel, a safe refuge under the neutrality convention negotiated by the Russian-American Company with the hostile powers. There the *Turku* remained until the end of the war.

The *Aian*, 540 tons, a third ship of the whaling company, wintered at Petropavlovsk at the same time as the *Turku*. Outfitted in Åbo, it arrived in the Okhotsk Sea in July 1854, commanded by Enberg, a Finn who had been a mate on the *Suomi*.

This ship was not very successful in hunting; several whales were carried away by the current. It acquired only 417 barrels of oil and about 5,000 pounds of whalebone. In the spring of 1855, the chief of Kamchatka's naval administration ordered the *Aian* to transfer its cargo to the *Turku* and to take on board families of employees in Petropavlovsk for their removal to the Amur region. The ship was overtaken and set afire by the enemy before it even left the port.

The *Turku* arrived at Bremen after the armistice, in 1857, with its own and the *Aian's* cargoes. These were sold for 76,618 silver rubles, 50 kopeks. After deducting all expenses, this expedition yielded only 3,075 rubles clear profit.

As may be seen from this short account of the whaling company's activities, the war caused it many losses. Out of its three ships only one remained. The *Suomi*, as stated above, was sold for a song. The supplies, whaleboats, and implements that were made ready for a second expedition had to be sold in Bremen at a big loss. The vessel *Turku* having hunted whales only one navigation season, meanwhile required major repairs and new supplies.

The whaling company's affairs were in such a bad state that it could not have resumed whaling had not the government compensated it for the *Aian's* loss. This gave the company an opportunity to outfit its remaining ship, the *Turku*, and to buy two new vessels. The company management estimated its loss for the *Aian*, implements, and supplies at 97,032 rubles, which the government paid. It seemed that the company had lost nothing, but in fact, several years of inactivity and other circumstances had had such a bad influence that the company fell into complete decay.

In the fall of 1857, the company sent out the ships *Turku* and the newly purchased *Graf Berg*, 600 tons, but the results for both ships were unsatisfactory.

From then on the company's resources declined steadily. The purchase in 1858 of the small ship *Amur,* 276 tons, did not improve matters. Up to the beginning of 1861, whaling had yielded about 2,200 barrels of oil and about 9,000 pounds of whalebone. The ships *Turku* and *Graf Berg* were sent to Europe and sold. The *Amur*, upon advice of Hakfeld & Company, agents for the whaling company in the Sandwich Islands, was left to hunt in 1861 and returned to Europe in May of 1862 with a cargo of 500 barrels of oil and 4,500 pounds of whalebone. This ship has now been sold and the shareholders have started the liquidation of the Finnish Whaling Company.[26]

Thus the first attempt to establish Russian whaling on the Eastern Ocean has failed. However, in studying disinterestedly the operations of the whaling company, it must be admitted that at least part of the misfortunes which it met were not its fault.

Of course, the replacement of experienced whalers by the Finns— even though they had been trained by such experienced men as the skipper of the *Suomi* and the American from the Sandwich Islands who was employed on the *Turku* in 1854—was premature, as it requires long practice to become an expert whaler. On the other hand, it is hard to decide to what extent, considering the state of the company's finances, it could have engaged the services of foreigners—services which required high wages—and whether the foreigners would have paid their way. In the summer of 1854, during the most favorable time for hunting, all the foreign whalers left the vessel *Turku*, out of fear of capture by the enemy, without any consideration of their obligation, or the impossibility for the ship to continue hunting after they quit. The diligence and reliability of the Finns who remained on board resulted in profits from whaling, and was one of the main reasons for entrusting them with perhaps more responsibility than they could handle.

Foreign whaling in the Russian possessions continues without interference just as before, but on a smaller scale. Official notices of sailings of these foreign whaling ships from the Sandwich Islands and sometimes from San Francisco speak for themselves. The whalers themselves probably do not even stop to think if their actions are in accord with the treaties negotiated with Russia. As for the question "Can the Russian-American Company stem the influx of whalers by its own means?"—the answer seems clear!

In concluding this chapter it should be remarked that the company is currently organizing whaling in Tugursk Bay, as an experiment, leaving an expedition there all year round. This undertaking is still in its infancy, however.

16. Supplying the Colonies and Kamchatka with Provisions and Goods, and the Company's Foreign Trade

Supplying the colonies. As specified by contract,[1] food supplies and trade goods of Russian and foreign manufacture were shipped to the colonies on Hudson's Bay Company vessels. However, this arrangement could not fully satisfy the company's expanding requirements during the term of the present charter. The considerable quantity of goods shipped each year to New Archangel on English vessels made it possible to lower the cost of transportation from £13 to £10 per ton.[2] Nevertheless, the company had to find other means to ship its supplies. Formerly, if the colonies experienced a shortage of provisions, they could be brought from San Francisco or from other places on the Eastern Ocean. After the discovery of gold in California, however, the great increase in food prices made the importation of supplies from there difficult and impractical.

On the other hand, the system of chartering ships for the transport of food supplies and trade goods to the colonies, begun by the company experimentally in 1846, proved to be profitable and advantageous as well. It cost considerably less to charter a ship of not less than 500 tons' capacity for 20,000 rubles silver per year than for the transport of goods on Hudson's Bay Company ships. Goods could be carried on a chartered vessel for not more than £5 or £6 per ton. In addition, a ship chartered for a two-year term could be used for four or five months for navigation in colonial waters. Chartering merchant ships also demonstrated the possibility of outfitting company ships for round-the-world voyages economically, giving command to private skippers instead of to navy officers and having much smaller crews.

Changing conditions soon forced the company to find new ways of shipping supplies to the colonies. After ceding its possessions south of latitude 49°—the Oregon territory—to the United States, the Hudson's

Bay Company, in renewing the contract by which it leased the strip of coast belonging to the Russian colonies, was forced to give up transporting food supplies to the colonies.[3] California, as already mentioned, ceased to be a source of grain when everyone there joined the Gold Rush and discontinued farming.

Under such conditions the company had to acquire its own ships for round-the-world voyages. In the course of four years it acquired four ships: in 1850, the *Imperator Nikolai I*, 596 tons; in 1851, the *Tsesarevich*, 650 tons; in 1852, the *Sitkha*, 1,200 tons; and in 1853, the *Kamchatka*, 900 tons. These were sent to the colonies with passengers and cargoes. In addition, the company purchased three vessels (the *Prince Menshikov*, 275 tons; the *Shelekhov*, 270 tons; and the *Kad'iak*, 500 tons) in order to reinforce the fleet in the colonies. Provisions and other goods were also transported on these ships.

Transport of supplies for Kamchatka on company vessels, as suggested by the Ministry of the Navy. Besides supplying the colonies entrusted to its administration, the company undertook, at the request of the Ministry of the Navy, to transport provisions for Kamchatka. During three years (1851-53), about 130,000 puds of rye flour and about 10,000 puds of groats was shipped from the Baltic ports on company ships.

Purchasing manufactured goods and supplies in Hamburg instead of England. In 1850, the company began to obtain manufactured goods and certain supplies for the colonies in Hamburg, where they could be purchased direct from the factories, instead of in London. In 1848, when some goods were purchased experimentally by an agent, the company decided to give Hamburg the preference. This reduced the cost of loading and hauling by almost half compared to London.

Supplying the colonies during the war with England and France. The recent war with England and France created new problems in supplying all parts of the colonies with provisions and protecting company ships. Although sufficient food supplies for 1854 were shipped before the war started, the company had to find means of procuring them in the years that followed, when ships could not be sent around the world because of the war. California, after the gold fever had abated, became a market again and supplies were purchased through the company's agent at San Francisco. A considerable quantity of grain was ordered also in Valparaiso, and shipped from there to California.

The so-called American-Russian Trading Company, formed [in 1852] in San Francisco for the export of ice from Alaska to California, was of great aid to the Russian colonial administration in transporting various cargoes to the colonies. Most of the supplies for the colonies were shipped on vessels of this company.

The vessels of the colonial fleet could not leave the ports, or, actually, the neutral boundary line, without danger of meeting the enemy. Under such circumstances the ship *Siana* [*Cyane*] (now the *Nakhimov*), under the American flag, made voyages safely where formerly company ships had been used. The *Imperator Aleksandr II*, a new screw steamer of 500 tons, built in New York, arrived in San Francisco in 1854, also under the American flag, and sailed from there to the colonies where it was used in the same manner as the *Siana*.

Thus, the colonies were supplied with provisions throughout the war, and all loss to the colonial fleet was prevented. Even though some company ships, such as the *Okhotsk* and *Sitkha*,[4] were lost in the war, the company deemed it a service to the government. These ships and parts of an iron steamer destroyed by the enemy at Aian were not sacrificed on company business in its own territory but in the interests of the eastern part of the Russian Empire.

Before the war the ships of the colonial fleet were busy as usual in sailing to various districts in the colonies and to the Russian ports in the Eastern Ocean. The *Prince Menshikov*, of this fleet, was sent to Japan with Count Putiatin's squadron. The round-the-world ship *Tsesarevich* was sent from New Archangel to Kronshtadt with a cargo of furs. Enroute it stopped at Shanghai to take on a cargo of tea ordered by the company. The ships *Sitkha* and *Kamchatka* were sent from Hamburg to New Archangel and Petropavlovsk with sundry merchandise and with a considerable quantity of provisions ordered by the Ministry of the Navy for the Kamchatka region. In spite of all efforts by the company to have these ships sail under Hamburg flags, they had to sail under Russian colors. They arrived safely, but [on 7 September 1854] the *Sitkha* was captured by the enemy after it left New Archangel to deliver its remaining cargo to Aian and Petropavlovsk.

The skipper of the ship *Tsesarevich* managed to evade very cleverly the enemy cruisers which were waiting for him in the English channel, knowing that the company ship was returning with a rich cargo. After rounding the coast of Scotland, the ship headed for the mouth of the Elbe, and in view of the English ships got through to Hamburg flying the Russian-American Company's flag. The government rewarded Skipper Ior'ian for his exploit with an order of St. Anna third class.

After the armistice the company's fleet was increased with the 300-ton screw steamer *Velikii Kniaz Konstantin*, and the 900-ton clipper ship *Tsaritsa*. After purchase, this vessel was placed at the disposal of the Ministry of the Navy to transport artillery and supplies to the Amur region. After a six-month stopover at Portsmouth for repair of storm damages suffered in the North Sea, followed by a six-month voyage, the cargo was delivered safely to the authorities at De-Kastri Bay.

The ship *Imperator Nikolai I* was also used by the Naval Ministry in 1857 and 1858, as a transport vessel in the squadron which sailed to the mouth of the Amur under Rear-Admiral Kuznetsov.

In 1854, when navigation on the Amur was opened, the Company sent several cargoes, mostly food supplies, to Nikolaevskii post. Thence these cargoes were transported to De-Kastri Bay, where they were loaded on company vessels. Because of the shallowness of the Amur estuary, these vessels had difficulty entering the mouth of the river.

The system of transporting goods overland across Siberia remained in effect as before, except that starting in 1848 the company's freight was taken to Aian instead of to Okhotsk.

Besides the review of the duties of the company's offices and agencies above,[5] it must be noted that goods and supplies purchased for the colonies in Russia were shipped first to Iakutsk and from there under the supervision of company agents to Aian.

Cattle were usually driven to Aian with a caravan of supplies, were butchered there, and the meat salted. Additional meat was brought sometimes to New Archangel from the nearest ports on the Eastern Ocean or shipped by the Amur Company and the Farmers' Society [*Obshchestvo sel'skii khoziain*]. Recently the company has been shipping considerable quantities of preserved meat and vegetables to the colonies. Purchases of rye flour are made mostly in Finland. At present, California again supplies most of the provisions needed for the colonies.

During the last twenty years, including 1862, supplies and trading goods were shipped to the colonies in the following amounts:

> Goods of Russian manufacture . . . 1,975,039 rubles
> Goods of foreign manufacture . . . 2,509,804 rubles 21 kopeks
> Total   4,484,843 rubles 21 kopeks

Supplying of the districts will be reviewed in the chapter dealing with the conditions and the administration during the time of the present charter.

Renewal of the Kamchatka trade. After renewal of the charter in 1842, the company also renewed its trade in Kamchatka. In 1843, goods were sent there as an experiment, and this proved very satisfactory. Even though limited by foreign competition and the poverty of the region, this trade greatly helped the poorer inhabitants, since the company's goods cost less than foreign goods. Because of this the company decided to expand its trade and within five years became the most important source of supplies for the whole region. In 1847, no foreign ships came to Kamchatka, and the inhabitants were dependent on the company's trade. At first all company goods were sold by one of the local merchants on a commission basis. They were to be sold at fixed prices and the merchant had no right to increase prices. Later, the company sent one of its agents to Kamchatka to see that the goods were available for the population even if the foreign competition was unfavorable. This often was the case, but the company did not discontinue its trading operations until 1855, when the naval administration and all the employees were transferred to Nikolaevsk on the Amur.

Beginning in 1851, after acquiring ships for round-the-world voyages, the company shipped goods and provisions to Kamchatka directly from Russia and Hamburg, independently of cargoes shipped to the colonies. This method of purveyance made it possible to ship not only more goods but a greater variety of them, so that when in 1854, no goods could be shipped to the Russian ports because of the war, the warehouses contained an abundance of goods shipped earlier.

During all the time that the company's agency operated in Petropavlovsk, from 1 January 1850, the annual turnover amounted to over 125,000 silver rubles. During this time goods worth 786,92 [*sic*, final digit missing] rubles 97 kopeks were imported, and goods were sold for 824,295 rubles 91 kopeks for prices which included cost of transportation, packing, etc. When the agency was discontinued, goods worth 39,669 rubles 31 kopeks remained on hand.

Export trade. Until the new charter of 1842 was issued, the company's export trade was confined to bartering furs for tea in Kiakhta, trade with California for foodstuffs, and purchasing various goods in foreign ports during the voyages of company ships from Kronshtadt to New Archangel. This also included the sale, mostly in London, of goods exported from the colonies.

Barter of furs for tea in Kiakhta. During the first seven years of the current charter, bartering furs for tea was very profitable, but has since declined. The volume of fur trade with the Chinese has decreased considerably during the last twenty years. The main cause of this decrease is the significant increase in the importation of Russian manufactured goods by China. This caused lower prices on Russian goods, and this combined with the tendency of Russian merchants to acquire as much tea of the various sorts as they could regardless of the prices they received on their goods, making tea consumers pay for their own losses, has made, as might have been expected, a considerable difference in the trading conditions with the Chinese, to their advantage.

From 1842 to 1849, the company bartered 6,700 cases of tea yearly in Kiakhta. From 1849 to 1853, the average was only 3,653. In 1853, because of the political disturbances in China, there was no barter trade at Kiakhta at all and the company had to use what remained of its tea supply acquired in 1852. Because some privileges were granted in 1854,[6] the trade at Kiakhta improved, but even there the quantity of tea bartered by the company during the years following (1855 to 1857) did not exceed an average of 1,300 cases per year. During the last few years (1858 to 1860), trade has increased: 2,335 cases were imported from Kiakhta in 1858; 2,902 cases in 1859; and 2,425 in 1860.

The negotiation of a treaty between England and China in 1861, and, beginning 1 April, 1862, the free importation of tea into Russia by land and sea, has changed trading conditions in Kiakhta considerably and affected all business between the Chinese and the Russians. Plentiful English manufactured goods on northern Chinese markets has affected the sale of Russian goods. Therefore the Russian merchants residing in Kiakhta have decided to send their goods to the fairs near Peking. Persons chosen by the merchants were to transport the goods in caravans and supervise trading. Some company furs from the colonies were sent on a caravan which started from Kiakhta in 1861, but the results of this experiment are still unknown.[7]

An experiment in bartering furs for tea on the western border of China. Difficulties in Kiakhta in 1855 forced the company to experiment with bartering furs on the western border of China, in the towns of Kul'dzha and Chuguchak, which were opened for trade by the special treaty of 1851. In 1853, a caravan with furs was sent to Chuguchak. The Chinese brought much tea there, but the company's furs found no market, because this type of merchandise was new to the Chinese and they did not realize its value. Consequently, when trade in Kiakhta was reopened in 1855, the experiments with trading on the western Chinese frontier were discontinued.

Shipping tea from Shanghai. The increasing cost of maintaining the colonies, without a corresponding increase in income affected the company's finances almost from the time of the charter's renewal in 1842. Obstacles met in Kiakhta, where fur seals could not be sold, and where only part of the other furs could be bartered, as well as the rising price on tea all undermined the company's affairs.

In this plight, the company repeatedly requested the government to grant it certain exemptions from custom duties. For a long time no action was taken. Finally the minister of finance, after studying all the circumstances and consulting with other ministers, found that the company's request merited serious consideration; but he believed that instead of granting duty exemptions, which were nothing more than new trading privileges, it would be better to grant the company a loan to be returned during the term of the current charter.[8]

Even before this was decided, the company had to find some means of improving its state of affairs. For this purpose an experiment in the exchange of colonial furs for tea was carried out in Shanghai. This proved so profitable that the company was convinced that this new market, which made it independent of Kiakhta, was ideal for disposing of furs; and the tea obtained there could be shipped by sea instead of overland. This would not only improve its finances but would even allow it to discharge without any government subsidy its obligations in relation to the colonies. Submitting these considerations to the government, the company asked for permission to ship a cargo of tea from Shanghai to Petersburg, under the same duty as that on tea from Kiakhta.

During the debate, the state chancellor declared "that the company's petition should be granted, because the company has important duties in managing the colonies on the northwest coast of America and has a right to special consideration and help from the government. The merchants of Kiakhta would not suffer any losses because it would not be in company interest to lower the price of tea, and anyway special conditions in this respect could be made in granting the company's request."[9] On the basis, the sovereign authorized the Russian-American Company to import up to 2,000 cases of tea per year from Shanghai for two years. Later on, in consideration of the increased cost of upkeep of the colonies during the war and the company's services to the government, the amount was increased to 4,000 cases per year.[10]

Sale of furs in England and America. Some fur-seal skins were shipped to London in 1843, for such a good profit that in the following year the chief manager of the colonies ordered shipment not only of fur-seal skins but also accumulated stocks of walrus ivory. The high cost of transporting the latter overland across Siberia and the low price received for it in Russia had made disposal of it there unprofitable.

In the same year an opportunity arose to sell fur seals profitably in the United States, where this item came into use for a time and brought a good price. However, the main market for furs of this sort has remained in Russia and Kiakhta.

At the beginning of the war, in 1854, furs could still be shipped to Russia, but in 1855, their export to Russia became impossible. The company shipped the lower grades to Shanghai to barter them for tea, but, because of the disturbances in China, these furs could not be disposed of there. They were then shipped from Shanghai to San Francisco, but could not be sold at a profit. Finally, they were shipped to New York where they brought good prices. Since then part of the furs, mainly fur-seals, have been shipped there every year.

Permission to import beaver and fur seals to Russia. Recently river beaver pelts have begun to be smuggled into Russia from abroad. The Hudson's Bay Company sells many of them in Leipzig, and from there they find their way to other foreign markets and to Russia. Their fur is not as beautiful as that of the sea otter, but is more durable, and since they are sold cheaply, are in demand and interfere with the sale of sea otters. The company could not combat this competition, and even the government was unable to stop the contraband trade. The best solution was to allow the importation of river beavers and fur seals, provided the duty on them would be paid. In 1857, the company petitioned the government to that effect. The proposal was approved, with a new tariff providing for a duty of one ruble twenty kopeks per pound for beavers, and sixty kopeks per pound for fur seals, with 25 percent of the money collected to be given to the company. This arrangement was to be valid until the expiration of the current charter.

Trade with the Sandwich Islands. Seeking to supply the colonies with foodstuffs at low prices and to increase trading operations, the company attempted to establish trade with the Sandwich Islands. From a shipment of goods sent there on a company vessel in 1846, logs, planks, and salted fish brought a good profit. Some of the trading firms in Honolulu ordered more of these goods. In exchange, salt, sugar, molasses, and coffee were brought to New Archangel from the islands. A second shipment brought still more profit. Salt purchased in Honolulu on this occasion cost considerably less than California salt. Taking advantage of the low price, the company bought enough to supply Kamchatka and Okhotsk with salt in 1848. Some Americans who had agreed to ship it to these ports had not done so for some unknown reason, so the Russian government requested that the company do it. In 1848, the company purchased the vessel which was subsequently named the *Kniaz' Menshikov,* and sent it to New Archangel with a cargo of supplies purchased in Honolulu. Three years of experience in trading with the Sandwich Islands convinced the company that this trade was profitable. They agreed with one of the trading firms there to purvey supplies for the colonies at very reasonable prices in exchange for a considerable quantity of lumber and salt fish to be shipped from the colonies. In 1849, among other merchandise, some goods of Russian manufacture were also shipped. When the company resumed its trade with California, however, its relations with the Sandwich Islands began to decrease and finally the war with England and France forced the company to discontinue them altogether. Moreover, the continued migration of inhabitants of the islands to California for work in the gold fields and a decline in the population following an epidemic there changed the conditions on the islands as far as trade was concerned.

Trade with California and the export of ice from the colonies. Even if the company lost the opportunity to buy its food supplies in California following the discovery of gold, the new order of things still made some profit possible especially at first. A cargo of company goods shipped in 1848 brought a considerable profit. In 1850 and 1851, business declined because the stores in San Francisco were full of manufactured goods and other merchandise from almost all the countries in the world, but the colonial products were nevertheless in demand, thus giving hope for the future.

The expansion of the company's affairs in California required the appointment of a special agent to watch and report business conditions and to take care of the company's interests. Companies began to be organized in San Francisco to import ice from the north. The first experiment of this new trade in the colonies took place in the beginning of 1852. The *Bachues*, a vessel belonging to the so-called Ice Company, exported 250 tons of ice from New Archangel, paying the Russian-American Company seventy-five dollars per ton. After this, the company made an agreement with a representative of another San Francisco firm, the American-Russian Trading Company. This agreement provided for the export from the colonies of at least 1,200 tons of ice per year for three years, at from twenty to twenty-five dollars per ton. The American-Russian Trading Company agreed to build at its own expense a place in New Archangel for storing ice and machinery, and to arrange for its loading on board ships.

In order to expand this new trade the company ordered ice to be made on Kad'iak as well. It was easy to obtain a large supply of it in the lakes in the vicinity of Paul's Harbor. Because of frequent temperature changes in New Archangel, it could be procured there only with difficulty, and in limited quantities.

Even before the agreement with the American-Russian Trading Company expired, another was substituted. After personal negotiations in St. Petersburg with Mr. Sanders, president of the American-Russian Trading Company, the Russian-American Company entered into partnership for a term of twenty years for the supply of ice, lumber, coal, and fish from the Russian possessions on the northwest coast of America for sale in the ports of the western United States and Australia. The period for which this agreement was negotiated exceeded the term of the present charter, but the emperor gave the company special permission to make this agreement with the Americans, and an exclusive right to export ice from all of the Russian possessions on the northeast coast of Asia.

From 1 June 1854, when the agreement became valid, the company did everything in its power to supply the required quantity of ice. After installing the necessary machinery in New Archangel and Kad'iak, it could procure 5,000 to 6,000 tons of ice per year. At the same time, coal mining began in English Bay on Kenai Bay under the supervision of an experienced mining engineer. For this purpose a crew of workers was imported from Russia and tools and machinery from abroad. The salting of fish for the California trade was also improved, and a supply of lumber was readied.

In spite of all this, three years of partnership with the American-Russian Trading Company and the export of ice did not measure up to expectations. Lacking sufficient capital to survive competition, this company had to evade the contract terms of allowing payments to the Russian-American Company to become overdue, and sometimes acting arbitrarily and without explanation.

Despite the fact that the company always had a surplus of ice in San Francisco and could supply all that was required, this trade gradually diminished. A business depression in California at this time contributed to the condition, but with better management of the American-Russian Trading Company's finances, the difficulties in the ice trade might have been prevented.

A partnership agreement under such conditions not only restricted the activities of the Russian-American Company, but the long term of the agreement deprived it of all hope of compensation in the future for its expenses in promoting this trade.

With affairs in such a state, the company ordered Captain of First Rank Furuhjelm, the new chief manager of the colonies, to stop over in San Francisco on his way to New Archangel to take up this matter personally with the directors of the American-Russian Trading Company. Furuhjelm had instructions to insist decisively that the Americans fulfill all the conditions of the agreement, and in case they said that they were unable to do so because of the depression, to renegotiate the agreement.

Negotiations were soon concluded to the satisfaction of both sides.

The first agreement was annulled and replaced by another on 9 January 1860. The Russian-American Company agreed to sell to the American Company 3,000 tons of ice per year up to 1 January 1863 at seven dollars per ton at the loading point in New Archangel or Kad'iak. Except for such stipulated places as California, Oregon, and Mexican coasts, where the ice could not be sold for less than twenty-five dollars per ton, the Russian-American Company retained the right of free trade.

This time the Americans were more scrupulous in fulfilling their obligations. They have kept to the letter all the conditions of the new agreement. Sometimes by mutual agreement the vessels of the Russian-American Company have been used to transport ice from the colonies to California, the freight being eight dollars per ton for the ice loaded on board the ship. From the beginning of this trade in 1852 up until 1 July 1862, 27,500 tons of ice have been exported from the Russian colonies. Company income from this item, counting the freight charges, so far has amounted to 250,000 dollars.[11]

Relations between the company and Japan. In conclusion to this review of the company's export trade an account must be given of its repeated attempts to establish relations with its neighbor, Japan.[12] The complete isolation of this country, except for its minor trade with Holland, cannot and must not continue. The generally accepted ideas of international relations are bound to penetrate into Japan in spite of its isolation from the rest of the world and its immersion in traditional customs and superstitions. Even in Rezanov's time some Japanese statesmen advised establishing friendly relations with other countries, and now after several decades the number of such advocates is certain to have increased. The favorable opportunities that presented themselves remained to be used to establish good relations between the two countries. This problem was taken care of by the company as far as circumstances permitted.

The best pretext was the return of shipwrecked Japanese to their country. Their boats, not very seaworthy, were often wrecked and the crews were sometimes rescued in the colonies. The company's first attempts at this were failures, but the gratitude of the shipwrecked Japanese for kindness and return to their fatherland, and the friendliness of many Japanese toward their neighbors played a definite part in the final accord between the two nations.

But before we speak of the expeditions sent by the company in these cases, we must first follow the history of the relations between Russia and Japan following the imprisonment of Captain Golovnin.[13]

After Golovnin was freed, the Japanese government prohibited

Russian ships from approaching the coasts of Japan. At the same time, however, there was a hope that relations would improve. This hope was founded on the following circumstances. After the governor of Matsmai Island had freed the Russian prisoners, the governor of Irkutsk sent him a letter of thanks and made a new proposal for negotiations to define the boundary line and establish relations between the two empires. The governor of Matsmai replied that he had no right to answer such an important question himself, but that he would forward this proposal to the government. At the same time he gave instructions as to where and when an answer could be received.

Captains Golovnin and Rikord wrote letters to two of the governor's aides to the effect that, upon receipt of permission of the Japanese government, our ship would arrive at Iturup Island. In 1813, a ship was sent there, but as the Japanese did not appear, the ship sailed back after waiting for several days. In order to settle this matter somehow, the governor-general of Siberia ordered another ship to be sent from Petropavlovsk, but this expedition had no luck either. After that all relations with Japan ceased for over thirty years. Our government strictly prohibited the company from sending "ships or baidaras under any pretext farther than Urup Island."[14]

This prohibition was based on the opinion of Captain Golovnin, who believed any further attempts on the part of Russia to establish relations with Japan would be untimely.

As proof that he was right, Golovnin pointed to an unauthorized attempt by a Russian priest in 1808 to propagate Christianity among the Kurile and Japanese inhabitants of Iturup Island. This priest, according to the Kurile natives, distributed crosses and icons to the natives of Iturup Island, and at the same time collected from them fox and other furs. This attempt made the Japanese government conclude that besides Khovostov and Davydov's expedition the Russian government was sending such missions to do still more harm to Japan. "If, while Golovnin and others were prisoners in Japan," wrote the governor-general of Siberia, "a priest had arrived at the Kurile Islands to propagate the Faith in a similar manner and had been seized by the Japanese, or if the ikons had fallen into their hands, this priest would have been most severely punished because of their hatred of the Christian religion, and the fate of Golovnin and his assistants would have been most difficult because it would have been impossible to convince the Japanese that such missionaries travel about on their own volition."[15] To prevent even more unfortunate happenings, the governor requested that until more reliable priests would be found, attempts to propagate Christianity among these people should be discontinued.

In spite of all this, the company decided to try again at the next opportunity. The return to their native country of four Japanese who were shipwrecked in 1835 and who had been brought from Okhotsk to New-Archangel[16] at least gave hope that Japan would be convinced of Russia's readiness to help. The company tender *Unalashka* was outfitted with government permission and sailed under command of Second Lieutenant of the Corps of Naval Navigators Orlov, to take the Japanese to Atkiz Bay on Matsmai Island. In case it should be found impossible to land the Japanese there, the vessel was to sail to some other place on the Japanese coast. Unfortunately, no amount of argument could persuade the Japanese authorities to accept the shipwrecked men. The Japanese batteries opened fire and forced Orlov to leave the bay. As for the poor Japanese passengers, he managed to land them at the village of Urbych at Samo Bay on Iturup Island.

This first failure did not diminish the company's determination to establish relations with Japan. Eight Japanese brought to the Sandwich Islands in 1842 by an English whaler after they were shipwrecked were cared for by the company, and taken to New Archangel.

The emperor granted the colonial management permission to return the men to their country, and they were shipped on the company brig *Promysel*, commanded by Ensign of the Corps of Naval Navigators Gavrilov.[17]

The Japanese were outfitted with all the necessities for the voyage and two boats of Kolosh manufacture covered with seal skins were shipped with them. In case, as had happened previously, the Japanese would not permit them to land in some port, these boats could carry the Japanese themselves and all their baggage. Gavrilov had instructions to land them either on Matsmai or Iturup Islands. He was to keep out of reach of a cannon shot, to avoid the same trouble the *Unalashka* had had.

This expedition had much better luck, even though the inhabitants of the settlement in Atkiz Bay on Matsmai Island fled, and the Japanese who were landed returned to the ship. The pursuit of a Japanese vessel, to which the Japanese begged to be transferred, took much time and took Gavrilov to Iturup Island.

The first assistant of the governor of the island met the ship and was very pleased when he saw his countrymen on board. Learning that bringing the shipwrecked Japanese was the sole reason for the Russian ship's arrival he offered at once to help obtain supplies for the further voyage. Gavrilov explained that returning the Japanese to their country now, as before, was done to prove the sincere wish of the Russians to be on friendly terms with the Japanese.

"If some of the Japanese would visit the colonies," Gavrilov told the Japanese official, "they could be sure of being received there as good neighbors and citizens of a friendly power."

In reply, without any requests by Gavrilov, the Japanese official promised that in case Russian vessels had to stop at Kunashir, Iturup or the Nippon Islands, they would meet a friendly reception and the Japanese would provide everything they needed. After exchanging some presents, the official gave Gavrilov a paper which stated that "the first assistant of the chief of the settlement on Iturup, Kvaitomai, in the name of Kuvaise-Asangori, received eight Japanese returned by the Russians to their country 8 June 1843 on the brig *Promysel*, belonging to the Russian-American Company, as proof of the friendly intentions of Russia toward Japan." After leaving the ship, the official stopped at some distance from the ship to wait for the Japanese brought by the Russians, "who then were saying farewell to us with tears of unfeigned gratitude," writes Gavrilov. "The attention and good care given them during their stay in the colonies and finally their return to their own country, affected them strongly."

Such a satisfactory ending of this expedition and the assurances of the Japanese official led the Russians to believe that Japan intended to forego its complete isolation, if not at once, at least gradually. The company therefore felt itself obliged to pursue its aim and requested the government to repeal the prohibition on visiting the Japanese coasts and to authorize the dispatch of a new expedition to Iturup Island under command of Gavrilov.[18] The company proposed that he be furnished with a paper, signed by the manager of the Okhotsk office, to the chief of the settlement on Iturup Island expressing gratitude for the permission given by him to stop at Nippon, Kunashir, and Iturup islands and asking that he designate places there where the ships could stop. In case the Japanese official could not give a definite answer, Gavrilov was instructed to inquire where he could come for an answer the following navigation season.

This expedition sailed in 1845, carrying presents consisting of Russian manufactured goods for the Japanese officials and a letter from Admiral Rikord, with portraits of him, addressed to a prominent Japanese of his acquaintance. Arriving at Kvaitomai village, Gavrilov learned that the official who was in charge of Iturup Island in 1843 had died and that all the officials there were new. Negotiations with them lagged. The Japanese brought by Gavrilov in 1843 had learned some Russian during their stay in the colonies and had helped a great deal in negotiations, but now lack of interpreters forced them sometimes to revert to sign language. Two Kurile natives who could understand the dialect of the so-called "hairy Kuriles" acted as interpreters for the expedition. The "hairy Kuriles," the natives of Iturup and several adjoining islands, differ from other Kurile natives in having especially long hair and beards. They have regular relations with the Japanese but as was proven during negotiations, the Japanese know very little of their language. As far as could be understood, the Japanese did not refuse to supply the company's ship with water and provisions, but they definitely refused pay and presents.[19]

A new occasion for visiting Japan arose only five years later, in 1850, when seven shipwrecked Japanese were brought to Kamchatka. The emperor ordered the Russian-American Company to take them to Japan, and ordered the treasury to pay the expenses.[20]

In order to avoid the difficulties experienced by Gavrilov's second expedition because of lack of interpreters, the company requested that the shipwrecked Japanese be brought from Petropavlovsk to New Archangel and that the departure for Japan be postponed until the navigation season of 1852. During this time they were to study Russian, and an employee of the company was to learn Japanese from them. The chief manager of the colonies, Captain of Second Rank Rosenberg, ordered living quarters assigned to the Japanese together with a navigation apprentice. The results of mutual studying of languages exceeded all expectations.

The Japanese could have acquired an even better knowledge of Russian if only they could have been persuaded to learn to write it, but this they always refused to do, saying that the shapes of the letters were too difficult, that they were not used to a pen, etc.[21]

The company decided to send the Japanese to the port of Simodo on Nippon Island and outfitted the ship *Kniaz' Menshikov*, commanded by Skipper Lindenberg. A letter signed by the chief manager of the colonies was sent with him addressed to the governor of Simodo. In this letter, after pointing out the existence of trade relations between Japan and Holland, it was suggested that Japan enter into similar relations with Russia since the two countries were close neighbors. Various presents for the Japanese, and some samples of goods of Russian manufacture, in case the Japanese would allow trade relations, were part of the ship's cargo.

The ship reached Nippon Island 22 July 1852. As it neared Simodo, several boats went to meet it. The men in them, by shouting and gesticulating tried to tell the Russians not to sail any farther. Paying no heed, Lindenberg entered the harbor in order to forestall the Japanese from more formally prohibiting entry. As soon as the ship stopped, visitors came from all sides, several hundred in number, and filled the deck and cabins. To preserve some order, Lindenberg was forced to request his guests to take turns and not to come all at once, but they replied that as soon as the governor arrived, they would have no further chance to examine the ship. Soon the governor appeared, with many officers and officials. He interrogated the Japanese who were brought by the Russians and looked over the ship. His assistants made minute notes of everything. Lindenberg invited the governor into the cabin, explained to him the purpose of his visit, and handed him the letter from the chief manager of the colonies. The governor replied that although he appreciated all that the Russians had done for his countrymen, he could accept neither the letter nor the shipwrecked Japanese until he had received an order from Edo. However, he asked for permission to make a copy of the letter. Lindenberg decided to comply, believing that otherwise the governor might perhaps not mention the letter when writing to Edo. Before leaving the ship the governor told Lindenberg that according to their laws he would have to place boats around the ship to keep watch and requested that none of the crew members go ashore. "However," he added, "if the commander himself would like to visit Simodo, I beg that you let me know and I myself will accompany you." Unfortunately, the approach of darkness prevented Lindenberg from accepting the governor's offer. The next day the governor came aboard again, and re-examined everything, expressing particular interest in the rigging.

In the meantime, artists were making sketches of the ship from the boats. Others were making descriptions and sketches of what impressed them on board. The governor was as polite as before, but when Lindenberg expressed a wish to go ashore, he replied that it could not be arranged.

With each passing day the Japanese tightened their watch. The number of boats surrounding the ship increased. Nobody was permitted inside their circle. Even the visits by the officials stopped. Soldiers began to arrive at Simodo and several batteries of artillery were placed behind the trees.

Several days later the governor of the town, Odovari, visited the ship. Gathering around him the Japanese who had been brought on board he made a long speech. The substance of his address was that the shipwrecked Japanese could not be accepted. It is easy to imagine how astounded by this news the poor wanderers were. No amount of persuasion by Lindenberg could change the governor's decision and his only concession was a suggestion to try Nagasaki. When Lindenberg told him that having come with the sole purpose of bringing the shipwrecked men back, he must land them on the Japanese coast, the governor thought that he intended to do that in the harbor, and wanted to run ashore. After quieting the governor, Lindenberg told him that he had no intention of breaking the Japanese rules, but that he would have to do what he was sent to do and that he would be forced to land the Japanese after leaving the harbor.

To this, the governor answered that he was not responsible for what happened after the ship left the harbor and asked them to do so as quickly as possible. Here the negotiations ended. Lindenberg, afraid to injure future relations between Russia and Japan by persistence, decided to obey the governor's request. After the ship left the bay the Japanese asked to be landed near the port and Lindenberg, choosing a small bay about five miles from the harbor of Simodo, landed them in the two Kolosh boats. Before their departure the Japanese knelt and with tears in their eyes thanked the Russians for the good care that they had received on board the ship and in New Archangel. "The memory of the Russians' care and solicitude toward us," they said, "will always be with us and will be remembered in our families from generation to generation. Our neighbors not only took care of us but gave us a chance to see our country once more."

Finally, exactly fifty years after Rezanov's ambassadorial mission, Russia and Japan were brought together and accord between them was established. An expedition of three navy ships commanded by Admiral Putiatin, sent by order of the emperor, negotiated a trade treaty. The company took part in this expedition by lending, free of charge, the *Kniaz' Menshikov*, belonging to the colonial fleet. Among other matters, this treaty defined the boundary between the two countries. The line was set between the islands of Urup, belonging to Russia, and Iturup, belonging to Japan.

17. *The Colonies under the Current Charter*

The charter of 1844. Before we review present conditions in the colonies, some information must be given about the charter approved by the emperor on 11 October 1844.[1]

This charter supplements many of the old rules and regulations concerning company management, both in Russia and in the colonies. Without abolishing former procedures, the new rules define more precisely the policy to be followed by company representatives. The company management itself was reorganized to conform more closely to modern conditions.

Thus, to the four directors of the company was added a fifth. One of the members elected by the shareholders to the post of chairman of the administration [*predsedatel' pravleniia*], was to preside during all shareholders' meetings. Apart from management, his duties included supervision of accounting and correspondence, selection of persons for company offices, and execution of measures for improvements in the colonies.

Another member of the board became an executive in matters of trade and supplies. His duties took him everywhere that the company conducted trading. Having more authority than other company agents, he could independently, by quick decisions, benefit the company more than if the usual, often slower, courses were taken.

One of the most important supplements to the charter required the directors to have a uniform accounting system. It also made rules regulating bookkeeping and audits, and made the administration itself accountable to the shareholders.

With regard to the colonial administration, the administrative, judicial, and economic duties of the chief manager of the colonies were expanded and defined more precisely. For extremely important affairs a council was created, composed of the chief manager, his nearest assistants, and several navy officers or government employees in company service. Besides this, the duties of various offices in the colonies were defined and the rules on native self-government, the company's relations with independent natives, and the rules about the creoles were supplemented.

The colonial staff. During the last ten years of the term of the second charter, the cost of maintaining the colonies increased considerably, as has been explained above.[2] The company was depending on future expected profits from the expansion of trade and trapping in the interior to compensate for these expenses.

The largest item in these expenses, the increased number of employees in the colonies due to expansion, did not always bring desired results. Although the number of persons employed in managing the colonies exceeded local needs, the number of persons needed on the staff had not been defined, and there were persons in it no longer useful in active service. In the interests of the region the company had to balance the number of employees against actual needs, and had to choose according to ability. Yet the company was also responsible for security and welfare of employees when they lost their strength and health.

To remedy these conditions the directors instructed the chief manager of the colonies to estimate the number of staff actually needed. No salary cuts were proposed and economy was to be attained by employing only persons who were actually needed. Since projects for expanding the fur trade were left in force, this measure was not a curtailment of the company's activities.

The estimate called for 949 employees in all parts of the colonies, including 613 Russians and creoles, 237 Aleuts, and 99 native women workers.

The Unalashka and Atkha offices were liquidated. Instead, managers of Unalashka, Unga, and Atkha islands were to be under the supervision of the New Archangel office.

Because of improved communication with the interior, the Aleksandrovskii redoubt on Nuchagak River was replaced by an odinochka. This change made it unnecessary to send supplies by ship.

The staff of the New Archangel office was increased by several accountants in order to audit more frequently the books of managers of the islands, forts, and trading posts. After collecting data on the Kuskokvim and Kvikhpak rivers it was decided to supplement the new trading posts in these localities with experienced men. The number of skilled workers and laborers in the port was increased.

The upkeep of the colonies was estimated at 236,000 rubles per year, not counting what was paid to the Aleuts for furs. It must be remarked that with the expansion of colonial industry in the last ten years, the cost of upkeep has increased considerably.

Welfare measures for ill or aged company employees. It has been stated above how important the right kind of personnel was for the success of colonization. Limiting the number of persons employed left others without work. The following measures were taken in order to make the future of these persons secure: (1) settlement in convenient places in the colonies after houses were built for them at company expense and after everything necessary for housekeeping was provided in order to give them a start;[3] (2) annual pensions for life; and (3) subsidies.

Pensions and subsidies for colonial citizens and colonial settlers. Only persons who had served at least fifteen years after arriving at the colonies were given the right to settle there. Creoles born in the colonies had to serve the company for twenty years, beginning at the age of sixteen, to acquire these rights. The former were called "colonial citizens"; the latter, "colonial settlers." The first settlements of this kind were established on Spruce Island and Afognak Island. Later, other places were chosen for the same purpose.

Persons entitled to receive a pension for life included the following: (a) persons who had been in the company's employ at least twenty years, and who because of illness, old age, or other reason could not support themselves and had no families to take care of them, or, in other words, all who could not qualify as "colonial citizens" or "settlers,"[4] but who would like to remain in the colonies; (b) those entitled by poor health or accident to receive pensions before having served twenty years, (c) widows of the above-mentioned persons and of all who died while employed by the company, who were given pensions in proportion to their needs and to the positions occupied by their husbands while in company service.

Retired employees entitled to pensions but who did not want to settle in the colonies were given subsidies not exceeding twice the amount of their salaries. These subsidies were paid by the company office nearest the desired place of settlement. Transportation expenses were also paid by the company.

This disposed of about one-fifth of the unserviceable persons in the region. Out of eighty persons forced to retire because of old age or sickness, twenty-three and their families became settlers, thirty remained in the colonies and received pensions, and twenty-three, at their own request, were sent back home. Besides giving them subsidies, the company annulled their debts.

As proposed by Etholen, chief manager of the colonies at the time of this reform, funds for these purposes were acquired by slightly increasing the prices of some of the company's goods.

Aleut communes on Kadiak Island and other native villages and regulations for the administration of the natives. Hopes that improvement would follow the consolidation of the Kad'iak Aleuts in large villages[5] were soon realized. No doubt the changes in their mode of life contributed to the spread of Christianity among them and even stimulated closer ties between them and the Russians. From this time on they began to change in every way, and thus the Kad'iak natives of today differ greatly from those of twenty-five years ago.

In case population increases and shortages of local food supplies in winter force some of the Kad'iak villages to be split in two, as now seems necessary, it is to be hoped that they will not forget their new way of living. Here is what Doctor Govorlivyi, who served in the colonies, says about their mode of life in his review of health conditions.[6] "The Aleuts on Kad'iak live with their families. Each family has its own barabara. In my visit to Kad'iak in 1852, I noted that these barabaras have been improved, since besides the room (*zhupan*) where the whole family sleeps in the winter, special rooms have been built of thick slabs of wood and with wooden floors. They are clean and tidy. Most of the sleeping rooms also have wooden floors."

The same applies to other native dwellings on the Aleutian Islands, even in places where there are no trees. We will quote another passage from Doctor Govorlivyi's account describing living conditions on the Fox Islands:

Here is my impression of Unalashka: Construction of iurts [dwellings], at least in places which I visited in Iliuliuk and Imagnia, is suitable as far as hygiene is concerned, being adapted to climatic conditions. A dwelling must give protection from the weather and the air in it must be pure. Both conditions are met in the construction of the local iurts, and as far as hygiene is concerned, they are satisfactory and are well suited to the Aleut way of living. They are much better than the barabaras of the Kolosh, where even with abundance of wood for fuel, people perish from the cold. The cleanliness I found in all the Unalashka iurts contrasted sharply with the general impression I had acquired from hearing stories of the "dirty, slovenly Aleuts."

To protect the Kad'iak natives from oppressive treatment by officials, Mr. Etholen gave a written instruction to the manager of the Kad'iak office and rules for the toions chosen to govern the natives.[7] These rules were also adopted by other colonial offices. Besides instructions on how to guarantee a supply of food, they explained the hunting and trapping of fur-bearing animals with their conservation in view.

Lieutenant Zagoskin's expedition establishes relations with the natives of the interior. In spite of all the exploration and survey work carried on by the company in various parts on the mainland of North America prior to the term of the last charter, much remained to be done.

The vicinities of the Kuskokvim and Kvikhpak rivers remained either unexplored or completed exploration had failed to furnish the precise data required for expanding the company's activities. For this reason chief manager Etholen commissioned Lieutenant Zagoskin, who was in company service, to explore the region in the vicinity of both rivers, from Mikhailovskii redoubt to their sources, the Chageliuk River, a tributary of the Kvikpakh, said to abound in beavers, the Buckland River, which flows into Kotzebue Sound, and other waterways which could be used for trapping purposes. The expedition was also to choose places for company trading posts and become acquainted with the natives.

This expedition accomplished a great deal. During two years of his travels (1842-44), Mr. Zagoskin made statistical, ethnographical, geological, and botanical observations; surveyed the Kvikhpak River for a distance of 600 miles, and the Kuskokvim River for a distance of 250 miles; and explored the most important tributaries of the Kvikhpak for a distance of 100 miles.[8] Zagoskin also defined the position of more than forty outstanding landmarks by means of astronomical observations, and explored the areas between the rivers with all possible accuracy.

In this manner the company learned of the natural resources of the region, the extent of the population became known, and prospects for future trade relations were studied.

In order to better understand Mr. Zagoskin's expedition we will include here some information drawn from his account of this expedition and its results.

On 4 May 1842, the company brig *Okhotsk* sailed from New Archangel to Mikhailovskii redoubt with Mr. Zagoskin and five company employees on board. Upon arrival Mr. Zagoskin made ready for a journey to the Kvikhpak River to make a survey of the river and of the native villages on the coast. The mouth of the Unigaklit [Unalakleet] River, which flows into Norton Sound a little above Mikhailovskii redoubt was the first place to be explored. Because of the importance of this river in relations between the natives of the northern part of Norton Sound and the natives along the Kvikhpak, Zagoskin decided to establish a small trading post there. He also moved the dogs there that had been used for hauling goods to the company establishment on the Kvikhpak River. He sent part of the supplies and trading goods for the expedition from the redoubt to the Nulato River with men assigned to the trading post.

Trading in Mikhailovskii redoubt was not of great volume. The demand was limited to tobacco, hardware, copper utensils, and a small quantity of dry goods, which were bartered for furs. The subsequent establishment of other trading posts in the interior diminished further the amount of furs and goods bartered there.

Trade among the natives consisted mainly of the barter of sea animal blubber, deer skins, baidaras, and baidarkas by the coast natives for furs and wooden utensils of the Kvikhpak River natives. Trade between the natives of Norton Sound and of the islands in the Bering Sea, by which a certain amount of furs found their way to the Chukchi and from them into the hands of the Siberian merchants, fell off considerably after the company built its trading posts in this region.

The expedition started in December with five sleds and twenty-seven dogs. On 10 January, after many stopovers because of soft snow and bad weather, the expedition arrived at the village of Khogoltlinde on the left bank of the Kvikhpak River. The natives were very friendly. After staying for a while to become better acquainted with this part of the country and for trading, the Russians arrived on the fifteenth of the same month at the Nulato River, where a company establishment had been built in 1839, destroyed by the natives, and rebuilt in 1841. Zagoskin stayed there until the winter cold was broken, and then started for Kotzebue Sound via the Kuiuk or Kuiak [Koyukuk] River, which flows into the Kvikhpak above Nulato, but after following one of its northern tributaries he had to turn back, because he had no guides to lead him through the pass to the native village on the Buckland River. It was caribou hunting time then and the natives could not go as guides, but otherwise communication between these two places offers no difficulties. After obtaining a supply of food and building a baidara for six men, the expedition started at the beginning of June 1843 up the Kvikhpak River which [above Nulato], had the name Iun'a. After going over one hundred miles by boat the expedition had to turn back because even the natives had never gone as far as this river's source and their knowledge of it was very confused. Some of them who had traveled sixty miles farther up from the place where the expedition finally turned back assured them that there were rapids. They thought that the source was at least three hundred miles farther.

After preparing for the journey at the Nulato establishment for about a month, Zagoskin and his men floated down the river as far as Ikogmiut village [Russian Mission], from where the portage to the

Kuskokvim River is the shortest. There he remained until winter travel was feasible.

Zagoskin chose for his travel to Kolmakov's redoubt the portage at Paimiut, a short distance up the river. He used Ikogmiut only for his headquarters. He did this because the manager of the fort informed him that the natives living along the former portage were hostile and Zagoskin did not want to endanger his expedition. He planned in the first part of February to explore the Innoko River, at least as far as the place Kolmakov reached in 1839. After the breakup on the Kuskokvim River, he wanted to travel to its source and from there float down to Ikogmiut and then return to Mikhailovskii redoubt.

Thus, the results of the second part of this expedition consisted in the exploration of summer and winter communications between the Kvikhpak and Kuskokvim rivers, the survey of the vicinity of Kolmakov's redoubt, the making of topographical and ethnographical observations, the study of trading conditions, and the survey of many places on the Innoko River.

During his survey of the Kuskokvim, Zagoskin corrected mistakes made in Vasil'ev's survey of this river[9] as far as the place where the Khulitnak River flows into it. Zagoskin did not reach the source of the Kuskokvim because more men than he had with him were necessary for such a long voyage, and it was inconvenient to take men from the redoubt. He simply gathered all the information he could from the natives about this region. According to this information, the upper reaches of the Kuskokvim are formed by many small tributaries, the largest being the Togtychagno River, which takes its course in the direction of Kenai Bay.

Because transporting goods to Kolmakov redoubt is difficult, little is shipped there. Half of what is received has to be used to purchase provisions for the redoubt's employees and to pay the natives for transporting the company's furs to Nushagak. The remaining half of the trade goods is bartered for beavers, caribou skins, seals, etc. Mr. Zagoskin says that trade between the Kenai natives and the tribes inhabiting the upper reaches of the Kuskokvim deprive the redoubt of almost half the furs, of which the company gets sometimes only a few, because during difficult travel over the mountains in bad weather, the natives are compelled after exhausting their food supplies to eat the beaver skins.

At present most of the natives living along the Kvikhpak and Kuskokvim are partly dependent on the company. They remain free but frequently have recourse to its protection and help.

Attempts on the Russians have sometimes been made here as well, but they were rare and were made by the more remote tribes. For example, in 1851, the natives from the Kuiuk River attacked the trading post at Nulato,[10] killing Deriabin, the company's manager, mortally wounding Bernard,[11] an English lieutenant who happened to be there at the time, and one Aleut, and burned and plundered the native village of Nulato.

It was found later on that the attack occurred because of the protection which the Russians were giving to the Nulato natives, with whom the Kuiuk natives had a feud.

A similar incident took place in 1855. Savages from the so-called robbers' village plundered Andreevskii odinochka, located south of Mikhailovskii redoubt and three versts from the mouth of Nychyglik River,[12] and killed two company employees who were in the bathhouse at the time of the attack. The third employee, who was in the trading post, fled, but upon becoming exhausted from hunger and cold would undoubtedly have become a victim of the robbers had not one of the natives sheltered him and later brought him to the redoubt. The redoubt's manager, Andreianov, immediately took measures to find the murderers. Finding their hiding place, he surrounded it, and forced them to surrender and return their booty.

Relations with the independent Kolchani and Copper River natives. Besides Zagoskin's expedition, two detachments were sent in 1843 to explore the route to Lake Plavezhnoe northeast of Kenai Bay and to extend influence over the tribes inhabiting the southeastern part adjoining the English possessions.[13] Establishment of trade with the Copper River natives and with the Kolchani or Gol'chani, also called tundra Kolosh (the name originated from the word "kkhyltshan," which means "far away, on the tundra"), would be important since it would give the company many beavers and other furs which were sold to the English.

One of the two detachments had instructions to follow the Sushitna River and the other, the Tishlina (or Tlishitna), because these rivers, the former flowing into Kenai Bay and the latter into the Copper River, were apparently the waterways used for trading in this region.

It was found that many rapids and the swift current of the Sushitna made navigation on it very difficult, especially for baidaras carrying goods. The going was easier on the Tishlina, although it is very swift and there are rapids in some places. In all, 1,250 versts were covered before reaching the lake. The second detachment met no serious obstacles.

The results of this expedition were disappointing. Very few furs were bartered, and the survey of trapping and hunting in this region promised little in the future. The expedition did not reach the Kolchani territory as it found that they lived much farther in the interior than was at first expected. Trading with them is done even now through the natives of Kenai and Chugach Bays, or when they visit company establishments in these places themselves.

In 1848, the Kolchani killed the creole Serebrennikov and three employees sent by the colonial administration to make a detailed survey of Lake Plavezhnoe and the Copper River region.[14] Serebrennikov probably rashly went too far into the interior without finding out first if the natives there were friendly; or perhaps, as rumors said, the natives had turned against him because he showed disrespect for their customs.

According to the Copper River natives who were accompanying Serebrennikov, the tragedy occurred 200 versts north of the small company post in the first village of the Kolchani. They had attacked while the Russians slept. Serebrennikov and two of his men were killed on the spot. One shot his way out and escaped in the forest where he disappeared without leaving a trace. Serebrennikov's journal indicates that the last place where he made observations was at 62° 48' 43" north latitude. On his way back to the Copper River he had explored Lake Plavezhnoe and the Tlishitna River. According to his information the fur trade in this region is very limited because the natives are poor and most of their furs find their way to Nikolaevskii redoubt and to the trading post on Copper River, brought by Kenai and Copper River natives.

In the future, the Knyk River [flowing into the head of Kenai Bay] should become the center of the company's fur trade in this region. An experienced manager will be sent there for the winter each year.

Trade with the Copper River natives is conducted generally from Konstantinovskii redoubt in Chugach Bay. Goods are sometimes given to the Copper River natives on credit, and the accounts are settled the following trapping season. The toion from Copper River arrived at the redoubt in 1858 and said his people and the Kolchani wanted to trade with the company at a post on the Copper River. A clerk, escorted by the natives themselves, was sent there with supplies, and after the trading was done returned safely to the redoubt.

The Kolosh. From all that has been written on the relations between the Kolosh and the Russians, it seems almost certain that friendly relations between the two will not soon be achieved. The characteristics of this warlike and completely savage people have blocked all the efforts of the colonial administration to change and to develop their moral qualities. The occupations, mode of life, and social order of the Russians remain just as alien to the Kolosh as they did sixty years ago. Plundering and thievery at every opportunity, treachery, and revenge are considered to be superior qualities among them even now. To protect its establishments from such restless neighbors, the company must pursue one of two courses; it must either begin a long and bloody war, of doubtful outcome, or, trying at all costs to live in peace with them, be condescending, and to compromise in some matters when their childlike vanity is affected. The example of the late Baranov, who with forces insignificant compared to those now available, could always keep them at least in order, if not in terror, and later experiments favor that course. Relations with the Kolosh have always depended on the influence which the chief managers of the colonies had on them, and on their ability, when necessary, to insist sternly on their demands and rights but with due discretion.

Even if this policy did not always bring the expected results, it at least helped to avoid major encounters with the Kolosh for many years. In studying the management of the colonies during the term of the present charter, very few hostilities by the Kolosh can be noted. It should be remarked in all fairness that these cases resulted either from too much complacency by the colonial management or from not acting in time to prevent native conspiracies. For instance, the treacherous murder in 1852 by the Sitkha Kolosh of forty of their countrymen from Stakhina when the latter arrived at their village to end a long-standing feud could have been prevented by sternness on the part of the chief manager of the colonies. Plundering by the Stakhina Kolosh of a company establishment at the sulphur springs, where they were seeking their enemies, also could have been averted.[15]

The armed outbreak by the Sitkha Kolosh in 1855 also could have been prevented. This outbreak ended in a complete defeat of the natives but also cost the lives of several Russians.[16] The Kolosh attacked without provocation a Russian sentry who would not let them steal the company's firewood and wounded him with a spear. Chief Manager Voevodskii demanded the guilty parties give themselves up but the Kolosh answered with threats. Two cannon shots aimed along the shore did not frighten them. An armed mob of savages attacked the fort and began to cut down the palisade. One of them shot at a company employee who was on the battery and wounded him fatally.

Gun and artillery fire were opened, but failed to halt the Kolosh. Some of them tried to reach the port but luckily were stopped. Others occupied the wooden church which had been built for services in the native language and began to shoot from the windows. After two hours of firing, which depleted their ranks, they gave hostages and the firing was discontinued.[17] Two Russians were killed and nineteen wounded in this action; about sixty Kolosh were killed or wounded. This ending had its good side, however. For some time, because of extreme leniency of the colonial management, they had thought that our forces were weak but now they learned that every hostile action on their part would be severely punished.

The Kolosh show no hostility toward the Russians at present, but their nature and qualities remain unchanged. If only Christianity, as well as a gradual understanding of the civilized world, would ever take root among these people, their customs would become more humanitarian. Such changes would be more effective than force.

Some progress can be noticed even now. The Kolosh do not refuse medical help anymore and often come for it voluntarily. They consent to be vaccinated. They apply for work in the port. They do not kill their slaves during celebrations or wakes, as they used to, but permit the company to ransom them, etc. The Kolosh tribes in the straits have helped the company on many occasions. Assistance given by them in helping to salvage the company's goods from the steamer *Nikolai*, which was wrecked in 1861, and their hospitality in taking care of the crew until help was sent from New Archangel are proof of their friendliness. Some of the Kolosh, following the Russians' example, have vegetable gardens and sell their surplus to the company.

It is interesting to compare the Kolosh attitude toward the Russian-American and Hudson's Bay Companies.[18] The stronger Russian influence on the Stakhina natives can be seen from the fact that when in 1846 the Dionis'evskii redoubt was turned over to the English under the agreement leasing a strip of Russian possessions on the sea coast, the natives besieged it and cut all communication. Only appearance of a steamer at the fort manager's request and the arrival of messengers from our company persuaded the Kolosh to stop the quarrel which, as the English themselves admitted, probably would have ended in complete destruction of the fort.[19]

In 1862, one of the navy officers in the company's service sent by the chief manager of the colonies to the mouth of the Stakhina River had to suppress the disorders which took place, in spite of the presence of an English steamer, between the natives and the English who were on their way to gold fields discovered in Hudson's Bay Company territory. The toion of Stakhina and other chiefs promised this officer that order would be restored at once.[20]

An order given by both companies at the beginning of the term of the present charter, prohibiting the sale of alcoholic beverages in their possessions should be mentioned. This measure is still in force and the managements of both companies believe that it prevents drunkenness among the natives, to which they have a particular inclination, to the impoverishment of the country. The Kolosh still obtain rum and whisky from foreigners who visit these coasts, but because liquor is now considered contraband, both sides have to be careful in these transactions. This prevents at least some of the harm which the colonies would suffer if the import of liquors were free.

To promote more order among the independent natives living near the Russian colonies and to acquire all possible influence, the company created the title of "chief Kolosh toion" [*glavnyi koloshenskii toion*], confirmed by the Sovereign on 6 December 1842. Upon the representation of the directors this position was given to Mikhail Kukkhan, a baptized Kolosh who by descent was one of the most prominent of this tribe. A similar election of a chief toion took place at Stikine in 1862, with the approval of the colonial management.

Some changes in the contract with the Hudson's Bay Company regarding the lease of a strip of the coast and renewal of this contract. The contract between the Russian-American and the Hudson's Bay companies for lease of a strip of land belonging to the former for a term of ten years starting 1 June 1840, was renewed by mutual consent, to be effective until 1 June 1859. Some of the conditions in the agreement were changed even during the first term. The English—being short of employees and workers, most of whom had joined the gold rush in California or gone to the Oregon territory which had been ceded to the Americans—had to liquidate the Dionys'ius redoubt in 1847, and refused to continue supplying the Russian colonies with provisions. The Russian-American Company, because the quantity of goods it imported on Hudson's Bay Company ships had increased, managed to persuade them to lower the freight rate from £13 to £10 sterling per ton. Later on, when our company began to charter ships for navigation in the colonies, it was decided to send provisions on these ships at a lower rate.[21]

When the term of the first contract ended, the Hudson's Bay Company wanted to lower the amount it paid for the lease, pointing out that it was suffering losses because of the fewer furs it acquired in the leased territory,[22] but the Russian-American Company refused to consent to that. Since temporary use by the English of this part of the Russian possessions had been granted in compensation of a claim for damages, the Russian-American Company proposed to take the region back upon expiration of the contract term. Only the arguments of Baronet Pelly, representing the Hudson's Bay Company, and the soundness of his idea that "the renewal of the lease is the only effective way to preserve friendly relations between both sides" persuaded the company to yield to the wishes of the English.[23]

In 1856 both companies agreed to replace payments for the lease in otter pelts for payments in money, to the amount of £1,500 per year.

The contract with the Hudson's Bay Company was extended first until 1 June 1863, and then for two years more until 1 June 1865.

Conditions were the same except that the new agreement did not allow the Hudson's Bay Company to export from the leased territory ice and other items which were included in the Russian Company's agreement with the company of American merchants in San Francisco.

The convention of colonial neutrality. During the war with England and France, the friendly relations between the Russian-American Company and its neighbors had an important influence on the negotiations that led to guarantee by the convention of the neutrality of the colonies of both sides.[24]

During the time of the rupture with England in 1807, and the wars with France, no hostilities occurred in our colonies, but this was because the colonies themselves were then of no great value. Subsequently the expansion of the company's establishments, the development of many branches of the local trade, and the increasing number of ships in the colonial fleet, which visited not only the Eastern Ocean ports, but all the seas were sure to attract the attention of the hostile powers. During the war with England and France these powers would have used circumstances favorable to them to destroy everything the company had created in this remote country. The means of defense in the colonies were inadequate for the repulsion of enemy forces of any size. Adequate defense measures would have required great sacrifices and expenditures on the company's part with little hope of success.

To prevent such a disaster, the company had only one recourse, and that was negotiation of a convention. This convention was signed due to efforts of the Hudson's Bay Company directors who saw the desirability of such a measure for their own possessions. By this convention, confirmed by the governments of England and Russia, possessions of both companies were declared neutral, but Article 2 of the petition—safety of ships and cargoes on the open seas being subject to international law and requiring an approval by the English parliament—could not be included in the convention. The French government was not notified officially of this agreement in the hope that as an ally of England it would comply with the obligations to which England agreed. This expectation was fully justified.

Neutrality of the colonies was observed throughout the war. An attack in 1855 by two enemy ships, one English and one French, on Urup, the last of our islands of the Kurile chain, should not be interpreted as a violation of the convention. As became clear later on, this attack arose from a misunderstanding, a belief that this island was out of the neutral zone. The losses suffered by the company were small and the services rendered by the English made it impossible to ask for compensation.

In 1855 the English squadron cruised for some time in view of Sitkha Island, probably to blockade the coast. The admiral in charge went by steamer to New Archangel itself, and upon receipt of information from an envoy of the chief manager that no naval ships were in port was quite satisfied and returned immediately to the squadron.

The fur trade and the export of furs from the colonies during the term of the current charter. In order to conserve fur-bearing animals in the colonies, orders were given at the beginning of the current term to trap and hunt in alternating localities and to have closed seasons. Results from this measure have justified expectations.

Sea otters. The number of sea otter pelts taken in the Kad'iak, Unalashka, and especially in the Atkha districts has increased during recent years, due to the organization of hunting parties in such a manner so as not to interfere with the breeding of these animals in certain places for a period of several years. It must be remarked that this order was in effect only temporarily during the closed season. At present in the Kad'iak district, the hunting is conducted alternately in three places: at Tugidak Island, in Kenai Bay, and along the coast of Aliaska. The crews of the Unalashka and Unga districts hunt in the same places every year. Unalashka hunters go to Umnak and Sannakh islands. From Unga Island one crew sails to Semenovskii and Chernoburyi [black-brown] islands and Cape Kuprianov, and the other goes also to Sannakh Island but only after the Aleuts from Unalashka have quit hunting. The Four Mountains Islands belong to Unalashka district, but hunting there is done by the Aleuts from Atkha.

The number of sea otters has not diminished from this continual hunting and has even increased at Umnak Island. The only difference has been in their moving farther offshore and because of that the hunting crews cannot make more than two trips.

A long closed season in the Urup Island area, where in the early 1840s the sea otters disappeared completely, also remedied the situation and the hunting at this island is now quite good. A volcanic eruption on Simushir Island (Prevo Peak) frightened the sea animals away but at least this misfortune was compensated for by an increase in the number of sea otters at other islands of the Kurile chain. Some say the sea otters never became extinct in the Kurile Islands, but disappearing in one place they appeared in some other. For instance, the unsuccessful hunting at Urup was compensated for by good hunting at Shumshu or at Thirteenth or Fourteenth Islands, etc., although of course, not always in the same degree. Lately, frequent earthquakes and volcanic ash have caused the sea otters to move from one place to another.

Repeated experiments at sea otter hunting on the Kamachatka

coasts, even during winter, in spite of predictions by old timers of good results, failed, and the hunting crews were sent elsewhere.

Fur seals. Company orders to hunt fur-bearing animals with a view to their conservation brought very good results on the Pribylov Islands. Fur seals on St. Paul Island increased very rapidly. Ten years after killing was discontinued it became possible, without decrease in their number, to kill up to 30,000 of these animals per year. Their number has now risen to 70,000. While Etholen was manager of the colonies an experienced hunter was sent to St. Paul to teach the method of closed seasons employed on the Commander Islands, where this method had shown good results.

Dried and salted fur seal skins. The skins of fur seals are prepared for export by drying and by salting. At first, they are scraped of grease, stretched, and dried at a certain temperature. For salting they are not scraped, but two skins are folded together after being salted, fur inside, and are rolled tight to keep the salt from spilling. A bundle is made of several such rolls.

Fur seal oil. During Mr. Voevodskii's management, the virtual end of whale hunting, which had formerly furnished most of the oil used in the colonies, caused an increase in the production of oil from fur seal carcasses. Whale blubber is not only the favorite food of the Aleuts but is widely used for greasing baidarkas, machinery ashore, and engines on the steamers. The preparation in 1858 of about 1,000 gallons of fur seal oil on both the Pribylov Islands saved the company about 3,000 rubles which it would have had to pay in buying this oil. The skins of the small (gray) fur seals, from which most of the oil is obtained, have no good market as yet, but they can be used for making light warm clothes, very durable and of good appearance, which could be very useful in damp and cold climates.

Sea lions. The sea lions have increased considerably on St. Paul Island but it is becoming harder to hunt them on St. George Island. At present their breeding places are at the foot of steep capes and approach to them is very difficult.

Walrus ivory. Walrus tusks come at the present time mostly from Moller Bay on the northwest side of the Aliaska Peninsula, where the largest breeding places are. Some tusks are bartered from the natives of Bristol Bay. The amount paid to the natives for ivory has now almost doubled over what it was in former years.

Foxes. Extensive hunting and trapping of foxes has caused them to become smaller in size and their fur to become coarser. This deterioration was especially noticeable in the Unalashka district. Mr. Etholen found it advisable to prohibit shooting these animals and allowed only the use of traps. Besides this, the directors ordered black-brown and other high-grade foxes introduced on the principal islands of Unalashka and Atkha districts. Later, alternating closed seasons were established to conserve these animals. The quantity of foxes acquired in the colonies varies each year, depending upon the climate. For instance, it is difficult to find fox trails in winters without snowfall. On the other hand, too much snow covers the traps completely and renders then harmless. Severe cold following rain makes them freeze, etc.

The same is true of trapping blue and white foxes. During the past ten years the color of the fur of the so-called blue foxes has changed slightly for the worse, becoming paler or more gray, and their value has decreased. A higher price paid by the company to the natives for blue foxes made them spare the white foxes, the number of the latter increased and in mixing with the blue foxes brought about this change in color. In order to exterminate the white foxes, their trapping and hunting was allowed all year round, beginning in 1858, and the purchase price was made equal to that of blue fox pelts.

Ground squirrels, beavers, mountain sheep, otters, and other animals. During Mr. Teben'kov's management ground squirrels were brought to Attu Island for breeding purposes and beavers and mountain sheep were introduced on Kad'iak Island, but the experiments failed.

The export of land otters during the time of the current charter exceeded two and a half times the quantity exported during the twenty years. Most of these were furnished by the Hudson's Bay Company as payment for the land they leased. Lately, as was stated above, payments in otter pelts were discontinued and the purchase of otters and beavers has been considerably decreased because of lower sale prices.

Other furs, such as muskrat, mink, lynx, wolverine, wolf, etc., are purchased by the company in small quantities and, like ground squirrels, are used mostly for local consumption with the exception of bearskins, which are exported to Russia.

Although the quantity of furs of all kinds, except sea otters, has decreased, there is hope that this quantity will remain the same for a long time to come and will not be subject to various unfavorable changes as happened in the past. On the other hand it is easy to see that continued trapping and hunting in the colonies over so many years was bound to decrease the number of fur-bearing animals by a certain extent. It may be seen   clearly   that had it not been for strict and necessary conservation measures taken by the company, many kinds of fur-bearing animals which are now found in the colonies would be only a memory.

From 1842 to 1862 the following furs were exported from the colonies and from the Amur:

Sea otters	25,899	Bears	1,893
Foxes	77,847	Wolves	24
Blue and white foxes	54,134	Muskrats	6,570
Fur seals	372,894	Wolverines	10
Beavers	157,484	Mink or skunk	872
Otters	70,473	Beaver castors	103 puds, 21 lbs.
Lynx	6,927	Walrus ivory	765 puds, 34 lbs.
Sables (from the colonies)	12,782	Sea otter tails	25,797
(from the Amur)	7,185	Legs of various animals	40,588

Shipbuilding in the colonies and the present state of the company's fleet. During this period the following vessels were built in New Archangel: the 58-ton boat *Kamchadal* ordered by the port of Petropavlovsk, the 35-ton schooner the *Klinkit*, for a private party, and two steamers for use in New Archangel. Their hulls after a while were replaced by others also built in New Archangel. The other vessels for the company's fleet, as previously stated, were purchased abroad. Caulking and repairs of sailing vessels and steamers are done in New Archangel workshops.

At present the company's fleet consists of the following vessels, all of which are sheathed in copper:

Screw Steamers:

1. *Imperator Aleksandr II*, 70 hp, 500 tons, built for the company in New York in 1855. Armed with 6 guns.

2. *Velikii Kniaz Konstantin*, 75 hp, 300 tons, built for the company in Newcastle in 1856. Armed with 6 guns.

Paddle-Wheel Steamers:

3. *Imperator Nikolai I*, 60 hp, built in New Archangel in 1833 of local cypress, engine imported from the United States.

4. *Baranov*, 30 hp, built in 1860 of local cypress, engine imported from the United States.

Sailing Vessels:

5. Ship *Imperator Nikolai I*, 595 7/8 tons, built for the company in

New York in 1850 of white oak and yellow pine. Armed with 8 guns.

6. Ship *Kamchatka*, 900 tons, built in Hamburg in 1852. Armed with 8 guns.

7. Ship *Tsesarevich*, 529 tons, built for the company in Lübeck in 1852. Armed with 8 guns.

8. Ship *Tsaritsa*, 946 tons, built in Portsmouth in 1854, of oak and pine and purchased by the company in 1858. Armed with 8 guns.

9. The *Kniaz' Menshikov*, 273 tons, built in Massachusetts, in 1845, of oak and purchased by the company in 1848. Armed with 8 guns.

10. The *Nakhimov*, 287 tons, built in Maryland, United States, in 1848, of oak and pine, purchased by the company in 1856. Armed with 5 guns.

11. Brig *Shelekhov*, 270 tons, built for the company in 1848 in Hamburg, in Ofel'genn at Altona. Armed with 2 guns.

12. Brig *Velikii Kniaz' Konstantin*, 170 tons, built in Boston in 1850 and purchased by the company the same year. Armed with 6 guns.

13. Schooner *Aian*, 60 tons, built in Aian in 1861 of pine.

14. A schooner of 60 tons for whaling in Tugur Bay, built in Åbo.

Loss of the company brig "Chichagov," the ship "Kadiak" and the steamer "Nikolai I." During the last twenty years the Russian-American Company has lost, as a result of various misfortunes, two brigs, a ship, and a paddle-wheel steamer.

On 15 May 1845 the brig *Chichagov*, 200 tons, which had been assigned by the colonial administration for navigation in the Atkha district and Kamchatka, was wrecked during a severe storm at Mednyi Island. Two days before the disaster, the furs from the island had been taken on board, provisions and supplies unloaded, and the brig was ready to put to sea. At midnight of 14 May the north wind became stronger and squalls followed one after another, accompanied by snow and poor visibility. To secure the ship, skipper Klinkovstrem dropped anchor at a depth of 3½ sazhen, and had a chain 60 sazhen long and two hawsers which held the ship from the shore, ordered two more ropes to be taken ashore and two more anchors to be used, one on a chain 40 sazhen long and the other a cable length. After taking these measures, Klinkovstrem was sure that the anchors would hold under any circumstances, but this did not prove to be true.

The next morning the waves became bigger and the wind blew with extraordinary force. For greater resistance the ropes which had been holding the ship's stern were fastened to the bow. They soon broke and the ship began to drift. There was at least 2½ sazhen of water under the keel, and the ship was drawing no more than 8 feet of water, but due to waves it hit the bottom and lost the rudder. After that one of the anchor cables broke. The other anchor began to drag more and more, and the fury of the storm simultaneously reached its peak. The harbor was covered with foam and the waves were so large that a rock nearby, about fourteen feet above the water in good weather, could not be seen at all.

Seeing that the anchors would not hold and that delay would bring about the wreck of the ship without hope of saving the crew, because the place toward where the ship was drifting was full of submerged rocks, Klinkovstrem decided to release the anchors and hawsers, and run toward a sandy beach. The stay-sail and mizzen sails which were put up for this purpose were torn away by the wind and the ship heeled to her port side after reaching the shore. To keep it in this position, all the ballast, consisting of rocks, was transferred from the starboard side, and ropes were tied to the mast tops and taken ashore.

In this position the brig was hammered by the waves and began to leak. The waves sometimes lifted her up or rolled over her. The storm continued so fiercely that even the birds could not find shelter, dropping from exhaustion and not even trying to fly away if approached on shore.

Under such circumstances the crew was taken ashore. Many were carried by waves into deep water but with help from the shore all were rescued, together with the furs and most of the provisions.

At the first opportunity the ship was examined, and it was found that besides the damage suffered during the storm its condition after being in long service was such that without a complete overhauling she would be unsafe. Having no facilities for repairs on the spot and believing that shipping of materials and men for this purpose from New Archangel would be too costly, Klinkovstrem decided to break up the ship without waiting for an order from the colonial administration. Sending a report of what had happened on a whaling vessel which was on its way to Kamchatka, Klinkovstrem got busy building living quarters for his crew and laying in enough food that could be obtained locally to last him all winter in case they had to winter there. His idea was sound because only in the following spring did the company brig *Konstantin* arrive to take him and his crew to New Archangel.

The wreck of the brig *Shelekhov* in Schast'e Bay in 1851, has been described in the chapter dealing with the exploration of the Amur.

Another ship the *Kad'iak* (500 tons) was transporting ice to the American-Russian Company in San Francisco in 1860. After taking on a cargo of ice at Woody Island this ship struck a rock when leaving the island on 30 March and suffered a hole in its bow. The hold of the ship began at once to fill with water and skipper Arkhimandritov ordered the crew ashore in rowboats. He himself remained until the last, and even when the vessel was filled with water he stayed nearby in a rowboat trying to find a means of salvaging it. In spite of all efforts of the captain and of men sent by the Kad'iak office to tow the ship into the harbor, using all available launches and baidaras, the fresh wind and waves prevented this. On the third day the ship sank about 100 sazhen from Spruce Island in water over 10 sazhen deep.[25]

On 1 November 1861 the steamer *Imperator Nikolai I*, commanded by skipper Kadin, was sent from New Archangel to the Vancouver or Kolosh Straits for trading purposes. Leaving Asanka Harbor [in the Kolosh Straits], where a large supply of wood and vegetables for the needs of the port had been gathered and crossing to Keku Straits on 8 November the steamer struck rocks 2½ miles from Nal'tushkan village. The weather was stormy and murky.[26]

The smoke stack fell when the steamer struck the rocks. Pipes leading to the condenser broke and water filled the vessel, stopping the engine. After several hours the skipper and the crew were forced to abandon ship taking with them provisions, arms, powder, and all they could load on boats. They went ashore and the next day, with the help of the Kolosh inhabitants of Nal'tushkan village, the steamer was towed close to shore and more of its cargo salvaged.

Upon arrival of another steamer, a schooner, and more boats in tow for the salvage of the engine of the wrecked steamer, it was found lying on its side in shallow water. Its hull was badly damaged but the engine parts were found undamaged and were loaded on the rescue vessels.

The company ship "Naslednik Aleksandr" in distress. Besides the wrecks described above there is left to mention the misfortune which befell the company ship *Naslednik Aleksandr* in 1842 on its return voyage from California to New Archangel. Navigator Arkhimandritov, who took command of the ship after the death of Captain Kadnikov, and crew members described this accident during the investigation that followed.[27]

On 27 September the wind was blowing from the southeast. The ship was making eleven knots, sailing nicely before the wind. The waves were large but regular. Toward evening the barometer began to fall. Giving orders to mate Krasil'nikov as to how to handle the ship in case the wind became stronger, the commander went into the cabin to change his clothes, which had become soaked from the continuous rain. Soon after that an enormous wave rolled over the ship from the starboard side and made the ship turn, exposing it to the full fury of the storm. From pressure on the sails and from waves, the ship was almost lying on its port side. Krasil'nikov, two helmsmen, and an apprentice were washed overboard and a Kolosh crewman was killed. The main boom, gaff, wheel, binnacle, all lifeboats, and skylights were broken or washed away, and the ship was half filled with water.

In this critical moment the commander was in his cabin, with Chernykh, a company employee. The ship was rolling so much that they were thrown from one side to the other and could not reach the upper deck. Kadnikov kept presence of mind and encouraging his companion he managed to give orders through the hatch. Then from water pressure, partitions of the cabin broke. In water and among broken lumber and pieces of furniture, Kadnikov was carried from side to side. The other navigator, Arkhimandritov, was in another cabin in no less a desperate situation. Knowing the ship's great danger and hearing the commander's voice and the sailors shouting that Krasil'nikov and several more had been washed overboard, he tried desperately to swim to the upper deck. Wreckage barred his way everywhere, but finally he managed to reach the deck, and running to the steering gear ordered the ship close hauled and sent men to rescue the commander. The mass of wreckage, constantly moving with the pitching of the ship, endangered the lives of the rescuers who could not get hold of the two unfortunates. Only pieces of Kadnikov's and Chernykh's clothing remained in their hands. Kadnikov's voice was becoming weaker and weaker and his last words were: "Chernykh, hold the head higher. . . . Is the ship on its course? Keep her on course!" After that he was heard no more. Chernykh was luckier. Water threw him toward the hatch, and he managed to get hold of a piece of canvas and was pulled out.

After the water had been pumped out, Kadnikov's body, all bruised, with clots of blood on his head and face, was found in a corner of the cabin under the wreckage. Beside him lay the dead Kolosh. Arkhimandritov ordered immediate burial. The storm continued for two days more but grew weaker and the ship could be put more or less in order. Most of the cargo and provisions had to be thrown overboard because of saltwater damage. On 5 October the ship arrived safely at New Archangel.[28]

Supplies for the colonial districts and their sale. Supplies and trade goods for local consumption and barter are brought on ships of the colonial fleet, which are sent from New Archangel to all the colonial districts at least once a year. At the same time furs accumulated during the year are brought to New Archangel. Some trading posts also ship items necessary for use of the hunters, such as sealskins and whalebone for baidarkas, and intestines of sea lions and the parts of their hides covering their throats, which are used for hunters' clothes and footwear. Requisitions for future needs are then sent to the New Archangel office. This office prepares all needed items for shipment in advance, sending its requisitions to the directors. This mostly applies to trading goods, as the approximate quantity of provisions needed for the population is usually known, and is mainly purchased by the board of directors in California and in other ports of the Eastern Ocean.

The population buys its supplies from the managers of the trading posts for the tokens which are used in the colonies instead of money,[29] or takes them on credit or barters furs for them. Some items are sold at fixed prices and below cost. Other prices are increased, as will be explained later, by adding to the cost of freight, such things as insurance, commission, packing, and a certain percentage for profit.

The first includes rye and wheat flour, salt meat, and some other important food supplies. For example, a pud of flour is sold in the colonies for the fixed price of 1 silver ruble 42½ kopeks while during the last four years the same quantity has cost the company at least two silver rubles per pud and formerly more. Buying food supplies in California has lowered their cost considerably but the constant changes in economic conditions there make this unreliable. Corned beef is sold at 25 kopeks and 50 kopeks per pound, depending on where it was shipped from. The lower grades are shipped from Aian by the Amur company. The average cost of the first grade is 3 silver rubles 57 kopeks per pud and the other is 3 silver rubles and 1¾ kopeks. The best corned beef is imported from California. It cost the company 7 rubles 40 kopeks per pud in 1860 and 4 rubles 43 kopeks in 1861. As the sale of alcoholic beverages to the natives is prohibited, they are sold at higher prices and for a higher profit than other goods.

The following figures represent the principal supplies for the colonies used yearly, and the prices at which they are sold (in silver rubles):

25,000 puds of rye flour at 1 r. 43 k. per pud . . . . 35,750 r.

2,500 puds of wheat flour at 2 r. 86 k. per pud . . . . 7,150 r.

750 puds of buckwheat and barley at 2 r. 86 k. per pud . . . . 5,720 r.

500 puds of peas at 1 r. 37 k. per pud . . . . 685 r.

75 puds of beans at 1 r. 37 k. . . . . 102 r. 75 k.

1,500 puds of corned beef at 5 r. 71½ k. . . . . 8,565 r. 75 k.
(This is the price of corned beef imported from California. Corned beef from Aian is sold at 2 r. 86 k. per pud.)

700 puds of rice at 4 r. 58 k. . . . . 3,206 r.

1,500 puds of butter at 11 r. 43 k. . . . . 8,001 r.
(This is also the California price. Butter from Iakutsk costs 8 r. per pud.)

10,000 puds of salt at 1 r. 15 k. per pud . . . . 11,500 r.
(Part of this salt is used for salting fish.)

365 puds of black tea at 1 r. 43 k. per pound . . . . 20,878 r.

    2,500 puds of sugar from 27-30 k. . . . . 27,000 r.
                    (Crushed and refined sugar 8 r. 57½ k. per pud.)
    500 puds of molasses at 3 r. 43 k. per pud . . . . 1,715 r.

The above-stated quantity of flour, however, is insufficient to supply the demands of the native population. Even now bread is only a supplement to their native food. On the other hand, if the natives had to depend entirely on flour for their diet, the company would have to import at least four times more than it does now, which would require a larger colonial fleet and would make expenses higher than the company could afford. Besides this, shipping, mostly under sail, loading and unloading, and the need in such a case to build large and weatherproof warehouses in all the districts, often in places where no wood is available, would require heavy expenditures.

The company also limits the sale of sugar and tea to the Aleuts. This measure has nothing to do with profits and losses, as far as the company is concerned, for more could in fact be imported without loss. This limitation is imposed in the interests of the natives since they like tea so well and use so much that the moment they earn a little money they spend it on tea; the measure helps some of them to use their money to better purpose. Without this measure the natives would often return home empty handed, even after good hunting or after completing a profitable job, without any savings. The limitation does not affect those Aleuts, who in receiving their pay from the company,[30] as we will see below, think first of their families' needs.

Generally speaking, the sale price of all goods is 77 percent higher than their original purchase price. Of this, 35 percent is profit, but this increase above cost is not uniform for all goods. Manufactured and luxury goods are priced higher. Necessities such as clothes and footwear for workers are sold at cost plus freight, and sometimes for even less. Such a mark up is necessary to pay for the loss due to the slow turnover of capital in trading operations. From the time goods are purchased by the company until they are sold, the capital spent does not bring any returns. It takes three years to sell some goods, and four years to dispose of provisions, independent of the loss which results from the usual below cost selling price. Money for purchasing supplies is discounted, and the discount rate is especially high now. Finally, the cost of shipping and storage of the goods and supplies is an important item in determining the prices at which they are sold in the colonies.

*Price list of the New Archangel office for goods shipped around the world
and delivered to the colonies in the spring of 1860 (in silver rubles)*

Dradadem [cloth] , all colors, best quality 1 arshin . . . . 2 r. 57 k.
Thick woolen cloth, gray and black . . . . 5 r. 71½ k.
Wool cloth, light gray and black . . . . 3 r. 43 to
                                                            5 r. 71½ k.
Wool cloth, heavy gray and black . . . . 1 r. 68½ k. —
                                                            2 r. 28½ k.
Velvet [dradeveliur] , light grey and striped . . . . 5 r. 71½ k.
Shirts, wool 1 doz. . . . . 30 r. 85 k.
Shirts, flannel (cotton) . . . . 28 r. 85 k.
Calico grey, 1 arshin, from . . . . 11½ k. to 25 3/4 k.
Calico, blue . . . . 34½ k.
Cambric, various colors . . . . 34½ k.
Prints . . . . 28½ k.
Shirting [cotton cloth] . . . . 28½ k. to 34½ k.
Handkerchiefs, 1 doz. . . . . 5 r. 14½ k. to
                                                            6 r. 86 k.
Overcoats, wool, each . . . . 16 r. to 35 r.
Suits . . . . 12 r. 85 k. to
                                                            14 r.
Jackets . . . . 5 r. 71½ k. to
                                                            8 r. 57½ k.
Trousers . . . . 2 r. 85½ k. to
                                                            5 r.
Baize and flannel, double width, 1 arshin . . . . 1 r. 14½ k.
Blankets, wool, one . . . . 5 r. 14½ k.
Leather soles, 1 pound . . . . 74½ k.
Leather, iufta, 1 pud . . . . 27 r. 43 k.
Boots, calf-leather [opoikovyi], pair . . . . 4 r. 28½ k.
Boots, calf-leather [vyrostkovyi] , pair . . . . 3 r. 57 k.
Boots, iufta, pair . . . . 2 r. 85 k.
Candles (tallow), 1 pud . . . . 8 r.
Candles (stearin) . . . . 22 r. 85 k.
Soap, grey . . . . 6 r. 85½ k.
Tobacco, Circassian . . . . 17 r. 14½ k.
Tobacco, Virginian . . . . 17 r. 14½ k.
Powder for rifles . . . . 11 r. 43 k. to
                                                            17 r. 14½ k.
Lead and shot . . . . 5 r. 71½ k.
Flints, per thousand . . . . 55 r. 71½ k.
Kettles, iron various sizes per pud . . . . 11 r. 42½ k.
Kettles, cast-iron . . . . 6 r. 85 k.
Axes (Kolosh pattern), each . . . . 1 r. 42½ k.
Axes (Aleut pattern), each . . . . 85½ k.

All provisions and goods shipped to New Archangel as well as
shipped from various districts are stored in one large warehouse known

as the colonial stock warehouse. Supervision and distribution of this warehouse is entrusted to the New Archangel office manager and to a commission composed of the assistant-manager and several clerks, in whose presence the good are checked. These rules were made by Mr. Etholen when the warehouse was built. A complete inventory is taken at least twice every five years. There are four distributing departments in connection with the warehouse: the trading [torgovoe], public [obshchestvennoe], stock [material'noe], and the spirit or rum departments. Goods are requisitioned for these departments in small quantities, approximately a one month's supply at a time. The same system is used for the mercantile store where goods and supplies are sold to the workers.

Local foodstuffs. Fish is the main item in local diet. They are caught everywhere in the colonies during most of the year and generally in quantities sufficient for the entire population. Besides fish, the natives eat, in summer and fall, the meat of fur seals, sea lions, and various birds, as well as bird eggs, berries, roots, clams, sea cabbage,[31] etc. Some of these are preserved for winter. Dried fish (iukola) is a main item. The natives use whale oil with all of their food, or, if there is not enough of it, fur seal oil.

The colonial administration has to see that the natives stock enough food for the winter. The Aleuts seldom think ahead and when there is plenty they eat with no thought for the future. A native family sometimes runs out of food at the beginning of winter when no amount of effort can provide even the bare necessities.

In order to prevent starvation, all company establishments keep a reserve of food out of which they give the Aleuts fish and oil until they can procure food for themselves.

Fishing for salmon and herring at New Archangel is very good, especially recently. In 1861, for instance, 106,000 salmon were caught. Out of this number 90,000 were salted for local consumption and for sale in California.

There have been years when there was hardly enough fish for the port's inhabitants. During the last ten years, however, the average catch in New Archangel and Ozerskoi redoubt has been over 70,000 fish per year.

The Aleuts raise only a few vegetables because they spend most of their time at the more profitable occupations of hunting and trapping and the rest of the time they are busy getting food for themselves and their families.

Only colonial citizens and settlers have vegetable gardens and engage in other branches of farming. The vegetable supply raised in the settlements on the right shore of Kenai Bay sometimes exceeds even local needs, and then the vegetable growers sell their produce to the nearest company stores. Potatoes and other vegetables are raised in New Archangel, but not enough for all of the inhabitants of the port.

Because of this shortage, vegetables are shipped from Kad'iak and the colonial administration buys potatoes from the Kolosh as well.

The Kolosh of Sitkha bring wild goats [*iaman'*] and halibut to New Archangel to sell—almost the only fresh food there in the wintertime. There was a shortage of goat meat during the first ten years of the present period, but there has been plenty in recent years. During the winter of 1861, deep snow in the mountains forced the goats down to low ground, where the Kolosh had no trouble getting them. They brought 2,774 into port, an unbelievable quantity compared to that of the past.

The Kolosh bring all these foodstuffs to the so-called marketplace in New Archangel where a company agent buys them at a fixed rate. They are then sold at the same rate to the inhabitants of the port, who to avoid trouble are not allowed to trade or bargain with the Kolosh.

Besides these fresh foods, cattle, fruits, and other food are shipped from San Francisco and sold by the company at cost.

Food supplies for the employees, workers, and ships' crews. All company employees receiving salaries of less than 1,000 paper rubles are entitled to a bread allowance and meals. Instead of bread they can have two rubles fifteen kopeks allowance and buy baked bread at two kopeks per pound. Married crown seamen receive six puds of flour per year for each child below six years of age and twelve puds for each child from seven to fourteen. Liquor is distributed during big holidays, and during bad weather. The average is fifty cups of rum per person per year.

The crews on board ships of the colonial flotilla receive the following provisions per maritime month (twenty-eight days) per person: hardtack, thirty-five pounds; corned beef, fourteen; butter, five; peas, eight; groats, eight; sugar, three; tea, thirty-five zolotniks; and rum, nineteen cups. Potatoes and dried vegetables are given as required. Besides this, salted fish is cooked sometimes, or fresh fish upon arrival in colonial harbors. During stays in Aian or California, fresh meat is given instead of corned beef. The ship commander and mates receive seven rubles fifteen kopeks per month food allowance while the ship is at sea.

The crews of ships on round-the-world voyages receive slightly more food: thirty-six pounds of hardtack per month or seventy-two pounds of bread; twelve pounds of corned beef and twelve pounds of pork (if there is no pork, sixteen pounds of corned beef are substituted); three pounds of sugar; and three-fourths pound each of tea and coffee. The crews have salted fish, potatoes, and dried vegetables when needed, as well as kvass or small beer in ports where it is available. At sea, instead of kvass, vinegar or cheap claret and a little mustard are given. Every day a large glass of rum is issued, and in bad weather two. On holidays the commander has the crew issued puddings, coffee, pies, and punch and may increase the meat allowance[32] if he desires.

During round-the-world voyages the ship commander receives, besides his salary, a double allowance of food. Mates and passengers get the usual amount.

An allowance for rain clothes are given the ship crews on each voyage to the colonies, calculated at seven months duration, at a rate of two silver rubles per man per month or a total of fourteen silver rubles.

Salaries, wages, and contracts with employees. Every person entering the company service in the colonies (except the chief manager) must sign a written contract with the general administration. The usual term of service is five years from the date of arrival. The salaries are paid according to the position or by previous agreement. Salary increase in case of promotion depends upon the chief manager of the colonies. Rewards after termination of service are decided by the directors. Rewards of more than one thousand rubles to persons who were especially useful to the company are decided upon at shareholders' meetings.

Workers are accepted for colonial service on contract terms with wages of one hundred rubles per year, transportation, board, and living quarters. During the voyage to the colonies and return, they receive four silver rubles per month and the same food allowance as the sailors. Persons hired in Irkutsk or other Siberian towns are given transportation back home after they leave the colonies. Aleuts in company employ receive eighty-six silver rubles per year and food.

The natives and settlers who are assigned at Paul's Harbor on Kad'iak Island to go on company business in baidarkas are paid according to distance from two paper rubles fifty kopeks to fifteen paper rubles. For the use of baidarkas for sea otter hunting, the company pays the Aleuts fifteen paper rubles for a three-hatch baidarka and ten paper rubles for one with two hatches. Aleuts hired to get ice on Woody Island are paid one paper ruble per day and their food, and get vodka in cold and bad weather. When preparing food supplies for local consumption, the men are paid twelve paper rubles and women ten paper rubles per month. Aleuts hired for work at Unalashka, Atkha, and Unga districts receive fifty kopeks paper per day.

Navy sailors entering company service in the colonies receive 100 silver rubles per year; sergeants receive 143 rubles, plus 25 rubles 71½ kopeks for rations, and 5 rubles 84 kopeks (lately 6 rubles 34½ kopeks) for clothes. They all receive meals in the mess room.

Soldiers of the Siberian line battalions, constituting the New Archangel garrison since 1855, receive from the company double the wages paid them by the government as well as food money: sergeants receive fifty silver rubles; soldiers receive twenty-five silver rubles per year. While working, they are paid on a contract basis. They receive a uniform and ammunition allowance to the sum of seven rubles eighty-four kopeks. The officers receive double the government wages and 250 rubles for board per year in addition to transportation costs both ways.

The company provides all employees with quarters, fuel, and light.

Medical help and epidemics during the current period. There are two hospitals in the colonies: one with forty beds in New Archangel and one with ten beds at Paul's Harbor on Kad'iak Island. In other districts the sick get medical treatment at home. Medical help in the colonies is supervised by two doctors, with their headquarters in New Archangel, who visit all the districts when there is an opportunity or need. One of them supervises the hospital and pharmacy in New Archangel while the other visits the sick in their homes. A surgeon's assistant [*lekarskii pomoshchnik*] is in charge of the hospital on Kad'iak. Because of his long experience and knowledge of local diseases he is able to treat the natives very successfully. There are surgeon's assistants [*fel'dsher*] in other districts, supplied with instruments and medicines.[33] The medicines are shipped to New Archangel from St. Petersburg at the request of the doctor in the colonial hospital.

Smallpox did not again occur in epidemic scale among the native tribes subordinate to the company. In 1862 this disease appeared only among the Kolosh, spreading from south to north. As most of the Sitkha natives did not object to vaccination, the epidemic was not severe around New Archangel. The natives were vaccinated in all the districts especially during the first and last five years of the current charter. While Mr. Etholen was chief manager, 1,200 adults and children were vaccinated. Recently, Mr. Furuhjelm has ordered fresh vaccine from California to be shipped to all the districts. The doctor accompanying Furuhjelm during his inspection tour supervised the smallpox vaccination and the natives were provided with vaccination facilities in all parts of the colonies.

Among other epidemics in the colonies during the last twenty years the most serious has been measles, from which about three hundred persons died in 1848 on Unalashka, Unga, and Sitkha islands and on the Aliaska Peninsula, mainly because the majority of the natives refused medical help. An epidemic of scurvy in 1853 and typhus in 1855, which resembled yellow fever, was brought to New Archangel on a round-the-world ship, but halted without doing much harm. In the scurvy epidemic 9 out of 64 who were ill died, and in the typhus 13 out of 341 died. Out of 398 persons who suffered in 1855 from grippe (influenza) only one old man, aged sixty, died and of 81 persons who had scarlet fever none died.[34] Energetic measures are taken to prevent syphilis, which makes its appearance among the Kolosh women and crews of the ships arriving at New Archangel.

The colonial population. The population of the colonies includes Russians, Finlanders, some of the foreigners in the company's employ, creoles, and subordinate native tribes.

As of 1 January 1863, the population figures were as follows:

Nationality	In New Archangel and Ozerskoi redoubt		Kad'iak district		Unalashka district	
	male	female	male	female	male	female
Russsians, Finlanders, and foreigners	480	50	129	1	4	—
Creoles	210	300	480	489	131	125
Aleuts and Kuriles	36	31	1010	983	749	835
Dependent tribes on the American mainland	—	—	1520	1245	—	—

Atkha district		Kurile Islands		Northern district	
male	*female*	*male*	*female*	*male*	*female*
2	–	1	–	32	–
94	106	4	5	25	21
367	342	126	108	14	11
–	–	–	–	9	12

Founding a social club in New Archangel. In 1840, A. K. Etholen, then chief manager of the colonies, founded a social club in New Archangel. All company employees in this port are grateful to him for this. First, it was the best if not the only measure by which to develop social life. Second, getting persons who in Russia were in different social strata together in a club was morally useful. Finally it helped single men arriving to work in the colonies in starting housekeeping if they could live in pleasant rooms attached to the club and have their meals in the mess room.

The New Archangel club still retains the same rules laid down when it was founded. It is managed by a special board elected each year on 5 November, the day when the club was founded.

Construction work in New Archangel and in the districts. Most of the buildings and establishments now existing in the colony were built during this period [from 1844]. The following were built during the five years while Mr. Etholen was managing the colonies [1840-1845]: a new pier at New Archangel, on a stone foundation, and armed with twelve cannons, constituting the lower battery of the port; a stock warehouse; a building for the library; a depot for charts and astronomical instruments and for magnetic observations; living quarters for the observatory personnel; a Lutheran church; a social club; barracks for married soldiers; a powder magazine; a laundry; a new church on Kad'iak Island; and a sawmill and flour and water mill, for which water had to be raised laboriously in the lake by means of sluices and a dam on the opposite shore. During Mr. Voevodskii's management, the sawmill was enlarged and converted to steam operation. Now either water or steam can be used for power. The sawmill includes a planer, and machines for making blocks, cornices, window frames, and shingles. Patterns for the foundry are also made here and machines for the foundry, sheet metal shop, and blacksmith shop. A new flour mill was built in New Archangel because the mill in Ozerskoi redoubt could not be depended upon since the dam was often damaged and communication with New Archangel was difficult in the fall.

During Mr. Etholen's management a tannery was also built for wild goat skins [*iaman'ikh shkur*]. It was intended to use these and sealskins instead of leather imported from Russia. The brickyard at Kenai Bay was enlarged.

During Mr. Teben'kov's management [1845-1850], a sawmill run by water power was built in Serebrennikov Bay on the Kirenga River, about an hour's travel from New Archangel, to replace the sawmill in Ozerskoi redoubt that had been built by Baron Wrangell. The battery of eight cannons aimed at the Kolosh village was renewed. A market for trading with the Kolosh, and some other port establishments were built. A good road was built from the pier to the creek, and several wells were dug. On Kad'iak Island a road five versts long was built from the settlement to the mill, and on Unalashka a house was built of unbaked bricks as an experiment.

During Mr. Voevodskii's management [1854-1859], several workshops were built in the port. New barracks were built for the workers and construction of a house for the port office, which had been started during Rosenberg's and Rudakov's time, was finished. A scow with a thirty hp steam engine was built for sawing lumber in places far from the port. On Woody Island and in New Archangel three icehouses for six thousand tons of ice, a road for hauling ice from the lake, a pier, and a sawmill for preparing the sawdust used in packing ice on the ships were built. At Kenai Bay everything necessary for coal mining was provided; machinery was installed and barracks for seventy men, a chapel, various workshops, and fifteen houses for employees and workers were built.

Recently, during Mr. Furuhjelm's management [1859-1863] another icehouse, a two-story barracks for workers, and a large store have been built on Woody Island, and in New Archangel houses belonging to the company and private individuals have been rebuilt and repaired.

The principal hydrographic surveys. During Mr. Etholen's management, Kashevarov, first mate of the brig *Okhotsk*, surveyed the mouth of the Anadyr River, and Orlov and Second Lieutenant of the Corps of Naval Navigators Gavrilov surveyed Aian Bay.

During Mr. Teben'kov's management, skipper Arkhimandritov surveyed the coast between Anchor Cape in Kenai Bay and Suklia Island in Chugach Bay; all of Kad'iak Island; and of Sitkhinak, Tugidak, and other islands south of it. Skipper Kashevarov surveyed Resurrection [Voskresenskii] Bay. Ensign of the Corps of Naval Navigators Benzeman surveyed Afognak, Marmot, and other islands; Chichagov Bay on Attu Island and the east part of this island; Semichi and Agatu Islands; and the western coast of Sitkha Island between Omuni [Ommaney] and Edgecumbe capes. In this last survey, special attention was paid to all the bays, especially Whale (Banks) Bay. Navigator Kuritsyn surveyed Umnak Island, Unalashka, Akutan, Akun, Unimak, and other islands. Salamatov, an apprentice seaman, surveyed all the Andreanov Islands east of Gorelyi Island to Siguam Island. Captain Zarembo, assistant chief manager, surveyed the mouth of the Anadyr River. Skippers Pavlov, Garder, and Klinkovstrem defined by astronomical observations various places in colonial waters. Pavlov worked mostly in Norton Sound and in Bering Strait; Garder, in the Shumagin Islands and in some of the places on the Aliaka Peninsula and Unimak Island; and Klinkovstrem, up to the western islands of the Aleutian chain and on the Komandorskie Islands. Lieutenants Rudakov and Skipper Lindenberg surveyed the southeast entrance to the second Kurile strait and defined the most important places on Urup Island relative to the islands north of it.

All these surveys and astronomical observations together with the former surveys were compiled by Mr. Teben'kov in his *Atlas of the Northwest Coast of America from Bering Strait to Cape Corrientes and of the Aleutian Islands, With the Addition of Certain Places of the Northeast Coast of Asia*. The charts, thirty-nine in number, were engraved in New Archangel by the creole Terent'ev. Notes written by Mr. Teben'kov describing the colonies from hydrographic, statistical, and historical viewpoints formed a supplement to this atlas. All the surveys and observations have since been corrected on every occasion by company skippers.

Geological surveys. Doroshin, a mining engineer who entered the company's employ in 1848, made a geological survey of Sitkha Island up to Icy Strait, Kad'iak Island, and the eastern part of Kenai Bay. He found limestone on Sitkha Island and coal and formations in which he believed diamonds could be found on Khutsnov Island.

On Kad'iak, coal and graphite were found in many places. Coal found along the shore of Kenai Bay proved to be of much higher grade than the coal on Kad'iak. Traces of gold were found in the Kaknu River.[35]

Coal mining at English Bay on Kenai Bay. Because the company's steam vessels had to be supplied with coal and because a high price for it could be gotten in California and in other ports of the Eastern Ocean the company started mining coal in Kenai Bay. The report of mining engineer Furuhjelm, who supervised this work, shows that the largest coal deposits are in Kachetmak Bay, also called Chuchachik Bay. Coal can be traced for fifty to sixty miles north and judging from its surface formation it extends very deep. Farther north the quality of the coal deteriorates and it disappears before Nikolaevskii redoubt (latitude 60°32') is reached. It was decided after further surveys to start coal mining on English Bay, a short distance south from Kachetmak, because Kachetmak Bay freezes sometimes, while English Bay is free even from floating ice. The shore there rises steeply to a height of fifty to sixty feet. The coal formation on English Bay is in the bed of the old straits and barely touches the foot of adjacent mountain ridges. The layers of coal can be seen at the entrance to the bay at low tide and mining can be done only by means of a shaft.

Coal mine and settlement, English Bay, Kenai Peninsula

A small indentation in the north shore of the bay, called Coal Bay, was chosen for operations. In 1857, almost in the middle of the coal deposit, shafts for lifting coal and for pumping water were started. On the edge of the coal deposit a gallery 1,687 feet long from the seashore was dug for temporary coal mining for local needs. Of the total length of the gallery, 1,589 feet were built in coal.

At present a considerable quantity of coal is ready, but it cannot be shipped to California since coal deposits have been discovered not far from San Francisco.[36]

Magnetic observations at New Archangel and other scientific research suggested by the Russian Academy of Science. At the request of the Academy of Sciences the company took part in magnetic observations which were conducted by the Russian and English governments. For this purpose an observatory was built on Japonskii Island, not far from New Archangel, according to plans furnished by the academy. The academy also furnished the instruments. The observations are conducted by a director and his aide, both chosen by the academy, and paid by the company.

At the academy's request, a search was made in the colonies for the bones of a very remarkable animal, the northern sea cow (*Rhitina borealis stelleri*), which had inhabited the waters adjacent to Kamchatka and had become extinct in the middle of the last century. In 1847, bones of this animal were found on Bering Island, and in 1857 a complete skeleton was found. The company recently has donated similar skeletons to the universities in Moscow and Helsingfors. In 1858, also at the academy's request, a skull of a sperm whale [*plavun*] and a complete skeleton of a grampus [*morskaia kasatka*] were shipped from Bering Island, and a skull of a sperm whale was shipped from Copper Island.

The company gave extensive aid to Mr. Voznesenskii, who was assistant at the Zoological Museum (and now in charge of it), commissioned by the academy in 1839. During ten years of work in this region, Voznesenskii made many valuable finds for natural history and ethnography.[37]

18. *Further Propagation of Faith among the Natives, and Schools for the Children of Company Employees*

Arrival of the Most Reverend Innokentii in the colonies and some of his measures. After the Most Reverend Innokentii arrived in the colonies on 26 September 1841, and assumed the administration of the bishopric, he introduced many useful measures. One of the most important of these was the transfer of the seminary from Kamchatka to New Archangel. Until then there had been no native clergymen in the colonies. After this transfer, the son of a creole or an Aleut could study, become a priest and then propagate the faith among his countrymen. Their knowledge of the language, customs, and the country in general helped them to become successful missionaries. By 1 April 1842, twenty-three creoles and natives were studying in the seminary.

The Most Reverend Innokentii also ordered the propagation of the faith in remote places not yet visited by the missionaries. However, before a discussion of the increase in the number of Christians in the colonies, we must give briefly some information about the natives who were not Christians at the beginning of the present charter term.[1]

The Kolosh, affected less by Christianity than other natives of the region, required special attention by the missionaries. Their mode of living, customs, mistrust of the Russians, and finally their treachery, apparent in many instances, required taking many precautions before baptizing them. The Most Reverend instructed that in case a Kolosh asked to be baptized, the missionary must first be certain that the truths of Christianity had left a deep impression in his soul. "About eighty of them want to be baptized now," wrote the Most Reverend to Metropolitan Filaret on 30 April 1842, but I will not hurry. The more they know about religion, the safer it will be. An archpriest is diligently discussing religious matters with them."[2]

In their degree of religious enlightenment, the Kad'iak natives were nearly the same as the Kolosh. One of the reasons for this was lack of good missionaries among them until 1840. The Kad'iak islanders adhered to the customs and beliefs of their forefathers, and in this respect were among the last of the tribes under company influence. After they were organized into communes, the priest Peter Litvinov was sent among them. His influence and the help of the colonial management in the person of Innokentii Kostromitinov, manager of the Kad'iak office, brought about a quick change in their moral development. The number of people attending church increased rapidly. "Formerly, only about one out of a hundred Kad'iak natives ever went to church" wrote Most Reverend Innokentii.

> They did not even know what the preparation for the sacrament by devotions and fasting meant, but now the church is full of people on holidays, and during Lent 400 prepare for the sacrament. They come for that even from distant places. Concubinage (common law marriages of which there were many) is now rare. The figures show how badly the Kad'iak parish was neglected. Out of 3,700 persons, according to the census of 1861, more than 1,000 were not Christians. Even now there are about 100 children from two to nine years old who are not baptized. Many of them died without being baptized, especially during the epidemic of smallpox, when about 2,000 died in the Kad'iak district.[3]

Natives who inhabited the region from Mikhailovskii redoubt and the trading post on Nushagak River up to the upper reaches of the Kvikhpak and Kuskokvim rivers also required much attention on the part by the missionaries. Until 1841, Christianity penetrated only the places near the above-mentioned forts. Several hundred baptized Nushagak natives were only a small part of the population of the northern American mainland. The natives living around Nushagak did not belong to a separate parish and thus had no priest.[4] Clergymen from other parts of the country, having large districts to cover, could seldom visit them. Future missions and parishes had to be planned in this region. At present, because of the time required to learn local dialects and cope with other difficulties, the work here requires much labor by even the most zealous and tireless missionary.

The Nushagak mission. One of the first orders of the Most Reverend was to send an ecclesiastical mission to Nushagak under the authority of the priest Ilia Petelin. The Christians at Nushagak, numbering about two hundred in 1842, rose to six hundred during the next three years. As may be seen from the missionary's journal, all whom he visited listened attentively and were baptized. To prove the sincerity of their conversion they threw in the river or burned before the missionary the masks which they often used and the idols to which they had made sacrifices.[5] Some of these new Christians used every opportunity in later years to see the missionary and their answers to him about faith and salvation showed understanding of these concepts. Some of them even surprised the missionary by their piety and diligence. During the next six years, or by 1 May 1851, the number of Christians reached 1,448. Of course, some returned to their old ways. "We decided to be baptized" the Kiatentsy (natives of the village next to Nushagak) told the missionary, "but we live in the same way as before, with a shaman, etc."[6] However, except for these natives, the results of teaching the faith in the Nushagak parish were most gratifying. Many of the natives from distant villages came to listen to the missionary. Among the natives around Nushagak, the Aglemiuts were the best Christians. "Even their dwellings are clean, contrary to the prevailing custom," wrote the missionary, "and the people themselves are friendly in their manner."[7]

The Kvikhpak mission. The Kvikhpak mission, sent in 1845 to teach the faith along the Kvikhpak and Kuskokvim rivers and their tributaries, cooperated with the Nushagak mission in the northern part of the American mainland. To the number of natives who were baptized in 1838,[8] the priest from Unalashka added 163 more in 1843, during his journey to the Mikhailovskii redoubt and neighboring villages. The next year he had an opportunity to see them. "The majority," writes Most Reverend Innokentii,[9] "endeavor to keep the promises they made when they were baptized. None returned to the ways of paganism, and some of the most religious persuaded many of their countrymen to become Christians."

The priest Iakov Netsvetov, a creole, was in charge of the Kvikhpak mission. He chose Ikogmiut [Russian Mission], one of the native villages about two hundred versts up the Kvikhpak River from Mikhailovskii redoubt, as his headquarters. When the mission arrived the natives in this village were not baptized. The missionary and his aide spent the first winter in a small, cold yurt and the next year, with very little help from the natives, built themselves a good sized house. Flour and other supplies were shipped to them from the company's store in Mikhailovskii. They had to prepare fish by themselves, as it was difficult to find help among the natives, who were unaccustomed to steady work. The missionary felt himself lucky when he could find guides for his travels to the native villages.

During two years of travel on the Kvikhpak River and along the seacoast, in baidarkas in summer and on foot in winter, the Kvikhpak missionary added 437 natives to the Orthodox church. A smallpox epidemic, which killed many of the population in 1836 and 1837, was one of the biggest obstacles to propagation of the faith in this region. The epidemic spread at a time when the colonial management had been making efforts to have the natives vaccinated. Many natives thought that the missionaries wanted to vaccinate them and were afraid of this. This prejudice gradually weakened, however.

It must be noted that the example and conviction of newly baptized natives concerning the need to teach the faith and the thought that salvation cannot be attained by those who do not believe in Christ greatly influenced the natives along the Kuskokvim and Kvikhpak rivers. In a letter of 1 July 1849,[10] the Most Reverend relates how one of the chiefs of the Anulakhtakhpagmiut settlement, on the Kvikhpak River, who was baptized in 1847, so influenced his country-men by his example that as soon as the missionary arrived, all ninety-three of the natives, young and old, asked to be baptized. His example affected the chief of the Ingeliks, the tribe inhabiting the shores of the Kvikhpak and the Chageliuk rivers, who happened to be in the village when the missionary arrived. He asked to be baptized and persuaded forty-six of his people to become Christians. "This occurrence on the Kvikhpak River is unprecedented," writes the Right Reverend.[11]

In the village where the missionary lived and in places where he could visit often, the natives began to live more and more as Christians should. Many of their pagan customs, shamanism, and superstitions diminished, and they performed willingly all rites of the Orthodox Church. Of course, not all of them were eager to become Christians. On the other hand, there were some people living on the shores of the Pastol' who, after being baptized in 1843 and 1844, refused soon after-ward to listen to sermons or to obey the rules of the Church. Natives of another village in the same locality first agreed to be baptized, but then refused. One of the old men told the missionary, "We did not know God before and we don't want to know him now."

As the missionary states, the circumstances were unfavorable to teaching the faith. During his visits the natives were busy in the day-time trading with travelers and at night they were hunting belugas. However, in 1851 they sent for the missionary, met him in a very friendly fashion, and from that time on have adhered to both the Christian religion and way of living.

Many Ingelik and Ingalit, at least 137 of both sexes, joined the Orthodox Church in 1851. During the missionary's journey to the Kuskokvim River, many natives living along the river were converted. As of July 1852, 203 were baptized. As Netsvetov reported, the Church influence was stronger in places that were near his residence. In places the priest visited seldom or never, Christianity made little progress.[12]

In contrast to other places, of the natives belonging to the Kvikhpak mission, none of the newly baptized became recreant.

In 1853, there were 1,720 converted natives in the Kvikhpak mission, and a church was built there in 1851.

The Kenai mission. The Kenai mission was formed in 1845, headed by a monk, Nikolai. In two years, this missionary visited all the villages of the Kenai natives and of the Chugach, baptizing four hundred people, not counting children. He actually baptized these natives a second time because most of them had already been baptized by laymen before his arrival. In spite of his eagerness to propagate Christianity, the missionary was careful not to increase the number of the baptized natives without sufficient reason. The Kenai natives, according to the missionary, willingly became Christians and obeyed the teachings of the Bible. They listened attentively, and obeying the missionary's wish they abandoned their old dances and songs, substituting religious songs that had been translated into their language. All of their shamans became baptized and most of these became the best Christians. The Most Reverend writes: "Their abandonment of some of their superstitions, beliefs and habits upon the advice of the missionary astonishes everybody who formerly knew them and who sees them now."[13]

The missionary writes of the character of the Kenai natives: "[They] are stubborn, and if they do not want to do something, nobody can force them to do it. But they are true to a given promise and, it must be added, lazy like all the Aleuts."[14]

In general, teaching the faith among the Kenai natives is remarkable because of the many cases of great devotion.

Many of the Kolchani people asked to join the church.[15] In 1846 and 1847, about sixty families came to the fort and to one of the villages on Kenai, but unfortunately the missionary was away then and they had to be baptized by laymen. .

New Archangel parish. As of Easter of 1843, 102 Kolosh natives, among them 2 shamans, had become Christians. This last circumstance seemed to be an important step toward Kolosh enlightenment because nowhere were shamans more fanatical than among these people. Many Kolosh women asked the priests to baptize them and it seems that their husbands, fathers, and brothers had no objections to this. Many of the baptized Kolosh voluntarily prepared their families to become Christians. Their kinsmen from Vancouver Straits willingly listened to the sermons of the missionaries and were impressed by the conversion of the Sitkha natives and by the baptismal rite.[16] It was hard to suspect that the Kolosh in asking to be baptized had mercenary aims in their minds because they received nothing except crosses and icons.[17] Even if we admit that some of them expected presents, still it is hard to believe that for a small profit they would abandon their boundless freedom to be limited by the rules of the Church. On the other hand, considering their nature and inclinations it is hard to believe that they were converted due to a firm conviction regarding religious truths. Probably their conversion was a temporary fascination, because their subsequent actions, during their fight with the Russians in 1855, made their faith appear rather suspect. When the Kolosh, many of them Christians, occupied the Orthodox Church they showed no reverence for holy things and demonstrated how little they could be relied upon.

This church was built in 1849 for services in the Kolosh language. The main prayers, the Gospel and sermons before every mass were accurately transmitted to the natives. The priest Litvintsov, who had transferred from Kad'iak to New Archangel, was active in missionary work among them. During five years (1847-52) he baptized about 150 persons of both sexes, not counting children. At this time the baptized Kolosh numbered over 350. The Right Reverend stated in a letter, dated September 1853,[18] that an upperclassman of the seminary was studying their language and could converse freely with them even on abstract matters.

By 1860, according to Kostlivtsov's report,[19] there were 12,028 Christians in the colonies (6,314 males and 5,714 females):

Nationality	Males	Females	Total
Russians	576	208	784
Creoles	853	823	1,676
Aleuts (Unalashka, Atkha, and Kadiak)	2,206	2,185	4,392
Kenai	430	507	937
Chugach	226	230	456
Ugalentsy or Ugalakhmiuts	73	75	148
Copper River	17	1	18
Magmiuts)	18	1	29
Aglemiuts)	19	20	39
Aziagmiuts)	105	101	206
Kuskokvimtsy) Northern peoples	755	640	1,395
Kvikhpaktsy)	226	153	379
Agul'miuts)	19	20	39
Ingelik and Ingalit)	263	213	476
Kol'chani	97	93	190
Kolosh	221	226	447
Kuriles	63	48	111
Tungus	1	1	2
Total	6,314	5,714	12,028

In spite of their obvious successes, however, the missionaries could not succeed everywhere. The country is too large and there are too few missionaries. Most of their journeys are undertaken in summertime because in winter, stormy weather prevents travel in baidarkas, the principal means of transportation. For long voyages, company ships are of course used, but the missionary must wait for an opportunity, which does not come very often. A priest can visit places such as the Commander and Near Islands only once every two or three years.

Mr. Kostlivtsov, who was sent in 1860-61 by the emperor to survey conditions in the colonies, reported that

> the missionaries are forced to travel in baidarkas and walk long distances over mountains, tundra, and forests. While making these portages their guides carry baidarkas, provisions, and camping equipment on their shoulders. Often they have to endure cold and hunger and live in tents for long stretches in rainy weather. Because of the sparse population and the severe climate these inconveniences cannot be avoided. The company helps the priests and missionaries by providing them with baidarkas and guides.

Backwardness and superstitions among some of the natives are another obstacle to conversion, according to Mr. Kostlivtsov. According to the local clergy the following obstacles delayed the spread of Christianity:

1. Polygamy, which they do not want to give up.
2. Shamanism, sustained by charlatans who persist in it among the pagans for mercenary reasons, enjoying such confidence among the artless savages that often the baptized natives resort to them.
3. Difficulty of travel in the interior in the wintertime when quantities of provisions, without which one might perish from starvation, must be carried.
4. The nomadic life of many of the tribes, which makes missionary contact with them difficult.
5. The savagery of the interior tribes, where some practice cannibalism, according to rumors. Missionaries can find neither guides nor interpreters to accompany them to these places.

Besides the above-mentioned causes, Kostlivtsov attributed the slow progress in conversion of the Kolosh and some of the other independent natives to a lack of knowledge of native dialects by the missionaries, their lack of training for missionary work, and finally a lack of Kolosh clergymen (the children of the Aleuts and creoles are prepared for ecclesiastical vocations). But here the following questions arise: considering these people's characteristics and their indifference to Christianity, would a few clergymen of Kolosh origin have enough influence on their people? Would a priest not belonging to a toion's family have any influence among them? Would the aristocracy consent to send their children to the seminary to be prepared as priests, when Christianity does not suit their war-like inclinations? Only time and experience will answer these questions.

"However," concludes Mr. Kostlivtsov, "it must be stated that everything done in the colonies for teaching Christianity since the founding of the Russian-American Company, unquestionably deserves praise." The Right Reverend Innokentii, in a memorandum written to the Holy Synod in 1859, expresses his gratitude to the company for its assistance and donations, and requests that the Synod report this to the emperor. In this memorandum he mentions the following company contributions during the nineteen years that he supervised the missions and churches in the colonies.

1. For maintaining the clergy in America 7,902 silver rubles have been paid yearly out of company funds over a nineteen-year period, a total of 150,138 silver rubles.

2. Living quarters have been provided, including fuel and light amounting to at least 10,500, or a total of at least 15,500 silver rubles.

3. A servant is assigned to the Most Reverend and each of the seven priests. These servants have received a total of 13,000 rubles in wages from the company during the nineteen-year period.

4. The company erected the following buildings during this time: (a) the bishop's house in New Archangel at a cost of about 6,000 rubles; (b) the cathedral, with an iron roof and a belltower, at a cost of about 8,500 silver rubles; and (c) four churches, at Aian, Kad'iak, on Unalashka Island, and on the Nushagak River, respectively. These churches cost about 12,000 silver rubles.

5. Thirty chapels were built in the colonies during this period, at least twelve by the company. The rest had been built by the parishes with company help, at a cost of about 2,000 silver rubles.

6. Until the treasury began to assist priests going to America or returning from there, the company had been giving them this assistance, the total for nineteen years amounting to 5,000 silver rubles.

7. The company has donated 100 rubles per year for destitute clergymen for nineteen years.

8. Everything needed for the churches—books, candles, vestments, etc.—is shipped by the company around the world free of charge. This has cost 1,000 silver rubles.

9. The directors have accepted and paid interest on ecclesiastical funds, not for the company's profit, but for the benefit of the missions. Because of this aid the seminary now has capital of over 20,000 silver

rubles. The funds for destitute ecclesiastics, which in 1859 were 19,150 silver rubles, have accumulated at least 7,500 silver rubles interest. The general capital of the American Churches, which at present amounts to 36,000 rubles, received at least 12,500 rubles in interest. The total interest on all ecclesiastical funds is over 40,000 silver rubles.

Of course this capital would receive interest if it had been left in government institutions, but it would have brought one-fifth less income if it had been left there, and besides considerable money would be spent for transfers of money and correspondence so that this capital would bring less than 10,000 rubles income. The remaining accumulation should be considered a donation by the company.

The full amount contributed by the company for the missions during nineteen years, not counting 30,000 rubles interest amounts to at least 230,000 silver rubles, or 12,000 rubles per year. The company also gives much aid that cannot be appraised in monetary terms, such as helping the priests and missionaries in their travels and housekeeping each year. For voyages of the archbishop and his retinue, the best ships and the best quarters have always been assigned, without cost. This has saved the treasury at least 15,000 silver rubles.

Equally it would have been hard to build a house for the seminary in Sitkha without the company's help, at least it would have cost the Ecclesiastical Department much more.

All the provisions for the seminary students were sold at the same prices as company employees are charged, sometimes below cost.

In order to clearly show the magnitude of these contributions it can be said that since 1841, our Russian America has been provided with a well-furnished bishop's office, an ecclesiastical administration, nine churches (not counting the one in Aian), and thirty-five chapels, several of them very well decorated. There are nine priests (not counting one at Aian), two deacons, and a number of church attendants. They are all well paid and cost the treasury only 881 silver rubles 43 kopeks per year, while their salaries alone amount to from 8,500 to 9,500 silver rubles (not counting the church at Aian).

Education of Aleuts and other natives. It may be seen from the brief report of the most Reverend Innokentii on the state of the Orthodox Church in America[20] that literacy is so widespread among the Aleuts, especially on the Fox and Pribylov Islands, that in some places everyone except small children can read books in the Aleut language. In 1848, books were printed in the Kad'iak language. At present the Kolosh also have many prayers, the mass, the gospels of St. Matthew and St. John, and the ten commandments translated in their language. Besides this many words and sentences used in conversation have been printed in alphabetical order. Considering this success, it can be predicted confidently that prayers and articles on religious subjects will soon appear in the dialects of the natives living on the shores of Bering Sea and along the Kvikhpak and Kuskokvim rivers. At least, as the Most Reverend wrote in his report, "a start has been made."[21] It would not be surprising if literacy spread there as quickly as it did among the Aleuts. As far back as 1848, the missionary at Nushagak wrote that many married men and women natives in his district wanted to learn to read.[22]

It is needless to explain how much literacy aids the spread of Christianity among the natives. The Aleuts are the best example. As Mr. Kostlivtsov writes (his report, page 72): "Translation of books on religion in the Aleut language and the study of this language by the clergy has contributed greatly to the success attained in the spread of Christianity."

Colonial schools for children of both sexes. The translation of books into the Aleut language also contributed to the successful education of the native children. In January 1844, The Most Reverend himself began gathering boys and girls at his home to teach them religion. This example was followed by other clergymen in the colonies and in this manner over four hundred children were educated in 1844. Later on, schools were organized in connection with all churches and many chapels, in which writing, religion, and reading were taught.

Independent of these were the schools founded before 1844—two schools for forty boys and twenty-five girls in New Archangel; two schools for twenty boys and ten girls on Kad'iak Island; and two schools in Unalashka for five boys and five girls.

In the boys' schools, reading, writing, religion, grammar, and arithmetic were taught. In the girls' schools the studies were limited mostly to needlecraft and housekeeping.

The best pupils from the boys' schools were sent after graduation to St. Petersburg to complete their education in the merchant marine school,[23] or were trained in various trades.[24] Some of them were given jobs as pilots and apprentices on vessels of the colonial fleet, while boys of more average ability were given jobs as sailors and cabin boys.

During the reorganization in 1844, all the schools, with the exception of the parish schools, were merged into one school for boys and one for girls in New Archangel. It was decided to have fifty pupils and ten cabin boys, but the average did not exceed forty. The same subjects were taught as before. On coming of age at seventeen, the pupils enter company service as clerks or skilled workers. The most capable and gifted get skippers' jobs on company ships and attend the general colonial school for this purpose. The annual upkeep of the school for boys, exclusive of quarters, fuel, light, books, and paper, comes to 1,850 rubles.

In 1842, before the reorganization, it was decided to increase the number of pupils in the girls' school to forty. But even here the average enrollment was only two-thirds of the proposed number. Most of the girls live in the school under a matron's supervision. The same subjects are taught as in the school for boys, but needlework and housekeeping are emphasized. There is a sale of the girls' handiwork once a year and money received from these sales forms a capital from which the girls upon marriage or on some other important occasion receive from 150 to 300 paper rubles (43 to 85 silver rubles). Upkeep of the girl's school costs about 1,750 silver rubles per year.

Renewal of the vicarage in the colonies and the founding of the general colonial school. In 1858 the seat of the bishop of Kamchatka was transferred to Iakutsk and from there to Blagoveshchensk on the Amur. The vicarage was reinstated in the colonies and the Archimandrite Peter, superintendent of the seminary in New Archangel, was ordained bishop of New Archangel. With the Most Reverend Innokentii's transfer to Iakutsk, the seminary was also moved to Iakutsk.

At the same time, at the request of the company's board of directors, a school for the children of company employees was founded in New Archangel. This school, called the general school [*obshchoe uchilishche*] of the Russian-American Colonies, is organized on the following lines:

1. It has the status of an uezd school [*uezdnoe uchilishche*]. The chief manager of the colonies provides general supervision. Qualified teachers have civil service status, are considered to be in government service under the Ministry of Education, and have the same rights as the teachers in the uezd schools in Siberia.[25]

2. The term and the subjects taught are the same as in the three-grade uezd schools in Siberia, i.e., religion, church history, Russian language, arithmetic, geometry (as far as stereometry) geography, Russian history, and abridged world history. In addition there will be special subjects for the children of ecclesiastics who intend to complete their education in the seminary, namely, the Slavic language, additional church history, and church singing. Students intending to enter company service in the colonies are also taught bookkeeping, mathematics, navigation, and astronomical observations, German, English, and some of the other sciences necessary for commerce and navigation. [Modern] languages are optional for theology students.

3. Graduates who enter the company's service receive, after six

years, the title of honorary citizen, this being non-hereditary. To pay for their education they must remain in the company's employ for ten years.

4. The company will pay the cost of construction and upkeep of the building, all student expenses, and teachers' salaries. Salaries for teachers of religious subjects to the children of ecclesiastics are paid from sums authorized for missionary work.

The cost of maintaining this school is estimated at 7,000 rubles per year plus 1,000 rubles from the funds of the Holy Synod.

The benefit to the colonies from a school of this type is evident. The opportunity to give their children a good education and resulting rights for employment, will probably persuade many useful employees experienced in colonial management to remain for a longer time. During the brief existence of this school, this expectation has already been justified. Later, after improvements through time and experience, the possibility of acquiring good educations in the colonies will undoubtedly attract even better employees there.

At present there are seventeen employees' children and two ecclesiastics' children attending the college.

The boarding school for daughters of company employees. Good results can be expected from the reopening of a boarding school for girls in New Archangel. This school was founded while I. A. Kuprianov was manager and was considerably improved by A. K. Etholen. The school was closed for some time because of the lack of a qualified teacher, but it has now reopened. According to the last report of the chief manager of the colonies there are fifteen girls studying there. The subjects include religion, Russian language, geography, history, and needlecraft.

19. *The State of the Company's Resources, Internal Trade, and Income, and Changes in the Board of Directors during the Current Charter Period*

The state of the company's financial resources. After renewal of the company's charter, a meeting of shareholders elected a special committee to investigate the state of its finances and to suggest possible improvements. The committee found that the formation of a fund of reserve capital would not only improve the company's credit, but would also insure fixed capital, and would be useful in case of emergency.

It was proposed to set aside 98,000 rubles for this purpose—a sum originally set aside from profits in 1818 to secure the stock from accidental losses. It was decided to put this reserve capital in circulation when necessary, but under condition that starting 1 January 1843, it should be increased by 6 percent each year. It was also decided to increase the reserve capital by adding to it 10 percent of the net income. At the same time the committee suggested payment of dividends to shareholders every year instead of once every two years as before. These proposals were approved by a meeting of shareholders.

In issuing new shares, as per Paragraph 35 of the last charter, and in stating their value in silver money instead of paper money, it was decided to set their value at 150 silver rubles each instead of 500 rubles each in paper money.

In this manner the capital stock was divided into 7,484 shares amounting to 1,122,600 silver rubles. In 1844 the company had reserve capital of 132,511 silver rubles 41 kopeks and floating capital, accumulated over many years, of various company assets worth 451,837 silver rubles 87 kopeks.

Besides this, beginning in 1853, a special insurance capital was formed. Until then company ships and cargoes had been insured abroad and in Russia. In eight years' time 155,038 rubles were spent for this purpose, without loss. In order to save unnecessary expense, the company decided to limit insurance to important items only, such as, furs shipped from the colonies to Aian and tea shipped from Shanghai to Kronshtadt. The amount that would have been spent on insuring cargoes and ships was set aside to form an insurance capital which earned bank interest. Accidental losses were to be reimbursed from this capital and in case the losses exceeded it, the shortage would be paid from the reserve capital. In nine years the insurance capital increased to 144,372 rubles and 96 kopeks. According to the last audit, which took place 1 January 1862, the amounts were:

Reserve capital .... 660,511 r. 58 k.
Floating capital .... 737,745 r. 55 k.
Insurance capital .... 174,372 r. 96 k.

Internal trade. The company's internal trade during the last period has been limited to selling furs imported from the colonies and tea carried on company ships from Shanghai or imported overland from Kiakhta. Tea from Kiakhta has been sold mostly in Moscow or at the fair at Nizhnii-Novgorod and the tea brought by ship has been sold in Petersburg. The furs have been sold wholesale, except for sea otters, which for sometime have been sold retail for making coat collars, and which have been stamped with company's seal in special warehouses in Petersburg and Moscow. During the last two years, the sea otters have been sold by agreement to one of the local merchants who is entitled to use the company's trademark.

Company income and expenditures. From 1841 to 1862, 20,205,681 silver rubles 8 kopeks have been realized from the sale of these goods and from other commercial operations.

During the same time the upkeep of the
colonies has cost the company a total of ....   6,334,747 r. 26 k.
Upkeep of the churches and clergy ....   172,963 r. 92 k.
Upkeep of hospitals and welfare institutions .....   367,240 r. 88 k.
Expenses for: board of directors, offices and
    agencies; awards and relief to employees;
    transport of workers; and employees to
    the colonies, etc. ....   3,030,874 r. 14 k.
Import duty paid to the treasury for tea pur-
    chased in Shanghai and Kiakhta ....   4,406,243 r. 30 k.
Freight and packing of tea ....   1,811,395 r. 71 k.
Freight and packing of furs ....   481,085 r. 61 k.
Insurance for tea and furs ....   211,978 r. 54 k.

Expenses for transporting goods to the ship-
ping points, packing, and other expenses . . . . . .   670,066 r. 44 k.

Losses sustained during the last war . . . .   169,706 r. 20 k.

Dividends paid to shareholders . . . .   2,722,664 r. — k.

Set aside to form the reserve capital . . . .   253,640 r. 62 k.

Set aside to form the reserve insurance capital . . . .   163,455 r. 71 k.

Set aside to form the reserve funds for destitute . .   12,618 r. 75 k.

Goods, chattels, and fixed property. The last audit[1] shows that the company owns property in Russian worth 357,522 silver rubles 78 kopeks; in the colonies, 477,513 rubles 88 kopeks; in seagoing vessels, the sum of 568,664 rubles 63 kopeks; and in trading goods and supplies, 2,223,401 rubles 8 kopeks. Company debts amount to 2,068,703 rubles 52 kopeks.

Annual dividends. Dividends on shares have been paid as follows:

For 1840 and 1841 . . . .   27 r. 50 k. per share

For 1842[2] . . . .   15 r.

For 1843 . . . .   15 r.

For 1844 . . . .   15 r.

For 1845 . . . .   15 r.

For 1846 . . . .   15 r.

For 1847 . . . .   15 r.

For 1848 . . . .   15 r.

For 1849 . . . .   15 r.

For 1850 . . . .   15 r.

For 1851 . . . .   18 r.

For 1852 . . . .   18 r.

For 1853 . . . .   18 r.

For 1854 . . . .   18 r.

For 1855 . . . .   18 r.

For 1856 . . . .   18 r.

For 1857 . . . .   18 r.

For 1858 . . . .   20 r.

For 1859 . . . .   20 r.

For 1860 . . . .   20 r.

For 1861 . . . .   16 r.

The cost of upkeep of the colonies. Upkeep of the colonies has cost the company the following amounts:[3]

Year 1841 . . . .   657,915 r. 75 k.

Year 1842 . . . .   488,122 r. 68 5/7 k.

Year 1843 . . . .   309,204 r. 22 k.

Year 1844	283,704 r. 94 k.
Year 1845	267,934 r. 77 k.
Year 1846	272,391 r. 20 k.
Year 1847	229,581 r. 55 k.
Year 1848	250,612 r. 70 k.
Year 1849	239,035 r. 51 k.
Year 1850	266,767 r. 06 k.
Year 1851	253,140 r. 87 k.
Year 1852	136,313 r. 62 k.
From 1 July 1852 until 1 July 1853	206,972 r. 27 k.
From 1 July 1853 until 1 July 1854	257,263 r. 94 k.
From 1 July 1854 until 1 July 1855	268,059 r. 40 k.
From 1 July 1855 until 1 July 1856	235,922 r. 81 k.
From 1 July 1856 until 1 July 1857	276,965 r. 58 k.
From 1 July 1857 until 1 July 1859	309,775 r. 18 k.
In 1859	292,115 r. 72 k.
In 1860	291,165 r. 97 k.
In 1861	335,127 r. 12 k.

Changes in the staff of the company's board of directors and the committee for government affairs and matters of extreme importance. A shareholders' meeting held on 19 December 1844 elected as members of the board of directors the following: commercial councilors I. V. Prokof'ev and A. I. Severin: Rear-Admiral Baron F. P. Wrangell: Colonel V. G. Politkovskii; and Civil-Councilor N. I. Kusov. The meeting asked Baron Wrangell to preside at the meetings of the board of directors. In 1845, Prokof'ev died and Lieutenant-General V. F. Kliupfel was elected in his place. In 1846, Severin was discharged and Captain A. K. Etholen was elected in his place. In 1848, Baron Wrangell resigned his post as chairman, and in 1850, Major-General Politkovskii, a member of the board of directors, was elected in his stead. Civil-Councilor Baron V. E. Wrangell was elected to take the place of Kusov, deceased. In 1858, Rear-Admiral V. S. Zavoiko replaced Rear-Admiral Etholen, who resigned because of illness.

The following were elected members of the committee for government affairs and matters of extreme importance: privy-councilors Pozen, Borovkov, and Kovalevskii, Adjutant-General Knoring and Adjutant-General Grinval'd; in 1854, Pozen, Borovkov, and Kovalevskii retired and Vice-Admiral Baron F. P. Wrangell, Major-General Prince A. Ia. Lobanov-Rostovskii and Actual State Councilor S. N. Dargomyzhskii were elected members of the committee.

Government order of a survey of conditions in the colonies. In 1860, because the charter term was about to expire, a survey of conditions in the colonies was ordered in the sovereign state. Councilor Kostlivtsov and Captain-Lieutenant Golovin were appointed to make the survey. In 1860 they visited New Archangel, and in 1861, some of the other districts in the colonies. The company's privileges were prolonged until a decision on the question of a new charter could be made.

20. Some Statistical and Ethnographical Data on the Russian Colonies

Boundaries of company holdings.[1] The Russian possessions controlled by the Russian-American Company or, in other words, the Russian colonies on the Kurile and Aleutian islands and on the northwest coast of America, are bounded on the north by the Arctic Ocean; on the west by the southeast coast of Siberia, the Sea of Okhotsk, and the island of Iturup (by the treaty with Japan of 29 January 1855); on the south by the Eastern Ocean; and on the east by the English possessions along the American coast.[2]

The Russian territories include part of the northwest coast of America from 54° 40' north latitude up to the Arctic Ocean; all islands of the Aleutian and Kurile chains up to Iturup Island; and islands north of the Aleutian chain such as Nunivok, Ukivok, Matvei [St. Matthew's], the Pribylovs, the Commanders, and others. These territories lie between longitude 132° 39' and 209° 48' west of Greenwich[3] or, more precisely, 210° 5'.

Districts and administrations. For convenient management, these possessions are divided in two districts [*otdel*] : Sitkha and Kad'iak; and ten administrations [*upravlenie*] subordinate to the Sitkha district. These administrative subdistricts comprise (1) the Northern administration, subdivided into the administrations of the Mikhailovskii and Kolmakovskii redoubts; (2) Unga; (3) Unalashka; (4 and 5) the Pribylov Islands; (6) Atkha; (7) Attu; (8) Bering Island; (9) Copper Island; and (10) the Kurile administration, subdivided into the administrations of Shumshu and Urup islands.

The Sitkha district includes the American mainland from Cape St. Elias south to 54° 40' latitude and the adjoining islands.

The Kad'iak district includes the shores and islands of Kenai and Chugach bays; the northern part of the Aliaska Peninsula up to the meridian of the Shumagin Islands; the islands of the Kad'iak archipelago; Uka-mok (Chirikov) Island and other adjoining islands; and to the north the shores of Bristol Bay, the Nushagak River area, and several places near the Kuskokvim River.

The Northern administration manages the coast of Norton Sound, the basins of the Kuskokvim and Kvikhpak rivers, and adjoining places.

The Unga administration includes the southern part of the Aliaska Peninsula and the Shumagin islands.

The Unalasha administration includes the Fox Islands up to and including Amukhta Island.

The Pribylov Islands administrations, independent of each other, include St. Paul and St. George islands.

The Atkha administration includes the Andreanov and Rat islands.

The Attu administration includes the Near Islands.

The administrations on Bering and Copper islands each manage those islands and the administration on Bering manages the small adjacent islands.

The Kurile administration is sub-divided into separate administrations centered on Shumshu and Urup islands.

A general topographic and climatic description of the Russian posses-sions in America and of the islands in the Eastern Ocean. The main topographical characteristic of the Russian possessions in America and on the islands is their mountainous and volcanic formation. The moun-tains on the Aleutian Islands run west to east, that is, the southwestern and western parts of the islands are lower than the eastern so that, with two exceptions (Amchitka Island, on which the northwestern side is higher than the northeastern, and Unalashka, with Mount Makushin, also in the northwestern part), all the main elevations face northeast. The coastal mountain chain on the American continent consists of high mountains, the largest being Mount St. Elias (17,000 feet). The tops of these mountains are always covered by snow. Some of them emit smoke and at times fire. Volcanic action is especially noticeable on the islands of the Kurile chain, some of which have changed considerably in appearance. In the mountain valleys are many lakes, from which flow rivers, which are sometimes of considerable size and navigable. There are many hot springs. The shores slope steeply toward the sea, ending, in most places, abruptly. The soil is mainly tundra, with some mead-ows. Sand and gravel occur in comparatively few regions.

Thus, various regions of the Russian possessions have much in com-mon, but as should be expected, the country is so large that parts of it differ considerably. For instance, there are dense coniferous forests on the American mainland but the Aleutian Islands and all the islands north of them are devoid of trees. Only dwarfish, stunted willows grow on some of them and larch forests grow in places on the Kurile Islands. There are forests on Kad'iak Island and on the islands north of it, but they are of limited extent. The climate on Sitkha Island is moderate, but damp. Sea winds and the proximity of a great, dense forest cause almost continuous fog, sleet, and rain. On Kad'iak Island, the climate is severe but drier and in the spring the meadows are covered with very fine grass. High winds are frequent in the more elevated portions of the island. The shores and vicinity of Kenai Bay have a good climate, but the shores of Chugach Bay are nearly always damp and shrouded in mist. The Aleutians and especially the Kurile Islands are damp and foggy most of the year and the climate there is colder than on the American mainland. Snow remains on the islands until May, and in the mountain valleys until June and sometimes even July.

Rivers. The largest rivers on the American mainland are the Kvikhpak, Kuskokvim, and Nushagak, flowing into the Bering Sea; the Copper River, flowing into the Eastern Ocean; and the Chil'kat, Taku, and Stakhin rivers, flowing into the Kolosh straits.

Lakes. Iliamna or Shelikhov[4] Lake, in the northern part of the Aliaska Peninsula, is the largest lake in the colonies. There are also many other large lakes on this peninsula and around Kenai Bay. The largest lakes in the interior are Mintokh [Minto], Nushagak [Beverly?], Plavezhnoe [Tazlina], and Mil'tinbota [Klutina?]. The southwestern and eastern parts of the northwestern region of the American continent are covered with lakes. There are several sizable lakes on the islands of the Kad'iak archipelago, namely on Woody Island and on Afognak Island—the most notable being Lake Nerpich'e ["hair seal," probably the present L. Afognak] on Afognak.

Mountains and volcanoes. All the peaks in this country are volcanoes, some of them active. Some become dormant temporarily but after awhile emit fire and smoke again. Mount St. Elias is the highest. The next highest on the American mainland are Dobraia Pogoda [Mt. Fairweather] northeast of L'tua Cape. On the Aliaska Peninsula, the highest are Chigiinagak, at least 10,000 feet; Iliamna, 12,066 feet; Douglas (Chetyrekhogolovaia), a volcano which erupted in 1857; Pavlovskaia Sopka [Pavlof Volcano], about 6,000 feet; and Redutskaia Gora [Redoubt Volcano], 11,270 feet. On Unimak Island, the highest are Shishaldinskaia [Mount Shishaldin], 8,775 feet; Pogromnaia [Pogromni Volcano], 5,522 feet; and Issanakhskaia, over 8,000 feet. On Sitkhin Island, the highest is Snezhnaia Gora [Snow Mountain, now Great Sitkhin Volcano], 5,033 feet. On Akutan Island the highest is called Akutan. On Unalashka Island, the highest is Makushinskaia,

5,474 feet. On Atkha Island there is Korovinskaia [Mount Korovin], 5,000 feet.

An explosion in Shishaldinskaia in 1856 caused a large crack to form at the foot of the mountain on its north side. This crack was about three versts long and emitted fire and ashes for three days. Aleuts on the island at the time told how the creeks were so full of ashes that one could not see the water in them. The subterranean noise and rumbling continued for almost two weeks. The explosion was heard on Unalashka Island, which is at least sixty Italian miles (100 versts) from Unimak Island. It is remarkable that, according to Shaeshnikov, the priest on Unalashka, the explosion was not heard on the north side of the island.

In former years explosions on Shishaldinskaia were frequent. In 1825 and 1826, the mountain was broken in many places by powerful explosions. The ashes in the air were so thick that it was hard to distinguish objects even a short distance away. During the eruption in 1826, the natives of Unimak Island had to remain in their yurts for ten days using artificial light. The ashes were falling so thick outside that they filled eyes and nose and caused severe headaches.

The volcanic island of St. John the Theologian. This island rose from the sea in an eruption west of Unalashka and north of Umnak in 1806. Khlebnikov, quoting Davydov,[5] says that this occurred in 1802. Although many periodicals mentioned this island in the issues of 1818, we will report here what Khlebnikov has written about it:

> On 1 May 1806 a severe storm came from the north and the sky darkened. The storm and darkness continued all day and became worse during the night. During the next two days noise was heard like distant thunder. On the third day the storm diminished and the sky cleared. Then flame, and later on smoke could be seen coming out of the sea between this island and Umnak Island to the north. This phenomenon continued for ten days. On the tenth day a small, round, whitish eminence appeared above the sea level and began to increase in size very rapidly. In a month the flame disappeared but there was even more smoke than before. The smoke carried with it a substance like soot and small burned stones. This island was surveyed by Kriukov, manager at Unalashka, who went in a baidara to look it over. He named the island Sv. Ioann Bogoslov [St. John the Theologian].

Later on a lagoon formed which became a breeding place for sea lions. Natives from Unalashka used to come and hunt them. Hunting was extremely dangerous because of rockfall from the high mountain. After a while the low beach crumbled and the sea lions disappeared.

The Kurile Islands. Nearly all of the Kurile Islands are of volcanic origin, most of them still smoking and erupting flame. Eighteen of these islands belong to Russia. The first island, off the Kamchatka Peninsula, is Shumshu where there is a small company establishment and a native settlement under a company manager. The population numbers about one hundred natives. Alaid Island, from which a volcano rises about 6,000 feet in height, is on the same latitude as Shumshu, but is not included among the islands of the Kurile chain. Paramushir, fifty-six Italian miles long and eight to twelve miles wide, the largest island of this group, is separated from Shumshu Island by a narrow strait. Several natives live in one of the small bays on the island. In September 1859, a thick and suffocating smoke rose from the craters of Paramushir volcanoes, which according to the manager of Shumshu Island dimmed the sun and caused the inhabitants to suffer from headaches and giddiness. This lasted for five days. Further west and to the south lie Shirinki, Makairushi, Onekotan, Kharamukatan, Shiashkotan, Ekarma, Chirinkotan, the Musig islands (or, as Krusenstern called them, the Rocky Traps [Kamennye Lovushki]), Raukoke, Matau, Rashau, two Ushisir islands, Ketoi, Simushir, Chirpoi, and the last and eighteenth island, Urup, nearly the size of Paramushir. Volcanoes are constantly smoking on Shiashkotan, Ekarma, Chirinkotan, Matau, and Chirpoi. Raukoke Island is the remnants of a mountain which exploded in 1777, changing the appearance of the island. There are many hot springs on the Ushisir Islands, from which steam rises like smoke. On Simushir Island two active volcanoes constantly emit smoke and flame. The largest of them is called Prevo Peak. Broughton Harbor, in the northern part of Simushir Island, is convenient for small boats. Kolokol [Bell] Mountain is the highest peak on Urup Island. The shores of this island are steep and rocky. The company's settlement there is on the eastern side of the island in a small bay. The superintendent and about 150 people live there.

Most of the Kurile Islands are devoid of forests. Only in a few low spots do birch, poplars, alders, mountain ash, and cedars grow. Wild cherries grow on Urup Island. There are fish in the lakes on Shumshu and Paramushir islands but not on the other islands. The inhabitants of the islands eat the meat of sea animals, whales and birds, and certain sea plants mixed with the blubber of sea animals. Quantities of sarana [root][6] are gathered on Kharamukatan Island. Many geese, swans, ducks, ptarmigans, and sea birds live on Chirinkotan. Red foxes live on all islands, and black-brown ones are found from Rashau Island south. There are wolves on Paramushir Island. The sea otters, as explained before, move from island to island because of the frequent volcanic eruptions accompanied by smoke and the smell of sulphur, which they cannot endure.

The Komandorskie Islands. The islands in the Eastern Ocean nearest the southeastern coast of the Kamchatka Peninsula are called the Komandorskie [Commander] Islands in honor of Commander Bering, chief of the first maritime expeditions, and who died on one of these islands, which was thereafter called Bering Island.[7] The other is called Mednyi [Copper] Island because pieces of copper were found on it by some navigators who believed they were virgin copper, but which were proven later to have come from Japanese ships wrecked on this island.

Bering Island is about fifty Italian miles long and about twenty-two miles wide at its northern tip. It is lower in the western part and forms a small bay where there is a company settlement. To the east stretch pastures covered with rank grass. The sandy soil is intermixed with sea shells. There is no timber of any kind on this or on Copper Island. Only in the ravines between the mountains and along the creeks are willows and mountain ash to be found. Much driftwood is left on the shores by storms, most of it from Kamchatka. West of Bering Island are two small islands called Toporkovye and Arii Kamen' [Tufted Puffin Rock and Murre Rock], because of the great number of those types of birds which are found there.

Copper Island is separated from Bering Island by a strait about thirty miles wide. It is higher than Bering Island, about thirty miles long and only five miles wide. Ten miles from its northwest tip is a small bay with a company settlement. Above the harbor rises a high, conical mountain covered with everlasting snow but this does not seem very high in comparison with the elevation of the island itself. There are no active volcanoes on either of these islands, but earthquakes are frequent. Recently, in 1859, a slight earthquake occurred on Bering Island, and in 1861 a large rock broke off near the settlement on Copper Island after a severe earthquake. It is never very cold on these islands, but the snow is deep in the wintertime and blizzards are frequent. In January and February the west and northwest winds bring much floating ice. It is clear when the wind is north or northeast, and overcast when the wind is east or southeast. The spring is usually cold and foggy. The snow melts in June or July. The best weather is in August.

For food the natives use sarana, borshch, and several other roots, and the herbs nettle, spinach, and parsley. Cloudberries and crowberries are abundant, and sometimes cranberries and raspberries as well. The principal land animals are foxes, mostly blue. The principal sea animals are fur seals, sea lions, and hair seals. There are a few sea otters on the north side of Copper Island. Ptarmigans live on the islands. Geese do not stop there, but swans do and sometimes remain half of the winter. There are many sea birds such as murre, tufted puffin, cormorant, and others. Many fish, including sea trout, and red and silver salmon enter numerous creeks on Bering Island from the sea. Codfish and small halibut are caught in the sea. The abundance of local foodstuffs make Bering Island the best of the islands in the northern part of the Eastern Ocean.

About three hundred persons live on Bering Island. From 1842 to 1861, 6,496 foxes and 9,526 fur seals were shipped from this island. About ninety people live on Copper Island.

The Aleutian Islands. The Aleutian Islands lie between latitude 55° 5′ and 51° 15′ north, and longitude 127° 34′ and 163° 20′ west of Greenwich. They are divided into groups of islands named either from their location, or their first discoverer, or some local peculiarity. For instance, the islands nearest the coast of Asia, from where the first expeditions sailed, were called the Near Islands. The Andreanov Islands, as mentioned, were named after the merchant Andrean Tolstykh, who explored them.[8] Fox Island was named because of the abundant foxes; the Rat Islands from the numerous rats, believed originally to have come from a Japanese vessel which was shipwrecked there; and the Shumagin Islands, in memory of a sailor of the Bering expedition who was buried there. By tradition the word Aleut or Aleutian is a corruption of Teleuty, the name of a tribe of Mongolian origin inhabiting the gubernia of Tomsk in Siberia. The first navigators found some similarity between them and the inhabitants on the islands.

The Near Islands consist of Attu, Agattu, and Semichi. Attu Island is thirty-two miles long and up to eight miles wide, and mountainous, especially in the north. The shores are rocky and high. There are two harbors for sailing vessels: Ubiennaia [Massacre Bay] and Port Chichagov [Chichagof Harbor], connected by a narrow neck of land. Besides these, there are two bays on the north side: Khaptunov and Gol'tsovyi [Holtz] bays, convenient enough as an anchorage, but open to the north wind. The native village and the company's buildings are within Port Chichagov, encircled on almost all sides by mountains, some of which are volcanoes. The tops of these mountains are bare and enveloped by fog. It rains all of the time. Strong gusts of wind strike frequently from out of the mountains and from the lake behind the settlement.

Agattu is slightly smaller than Attu, about thirty miles long, but wider, mountainous with many small lakes and creeks. Its shores are hardly indented and there is not a single harbor or bay on this island. Probably because of this peculiarity of its shore, it is sometimes called Kruglyi [Round] Island.

The Semichi islands consist of three small islands separated by narrow straits which are dry at low tide.

Vegetation on the Near Islands is very poor. Only in a few places do small willows and mountain ash grow. There is much driftwood as well as edible roots and berries on these islands. Only foxes live on Attu, and on the other islands no land animals of any kind can be found, not even mice. There are sea otters and a few sea lions and hair seals. Dead whales are sometimes cast ashore. Formerly these were mostly sperm whales.[9] There are plenty of fish of various kinds, such as, red salmon, humpback, silver salmon, codfish, halibut, and salmon trout. Sea birds, the murre and tufted puffin in particular, are mostly on Agattu and Semichi islands. There are a few on Attu Island. Geese visit these islands in the spring and fall, and swans arrive in the fall and stay all winter. There are hawks of various kinds, some of them pure white, and ravens. Except for Attu Island, which has 240 inhabitants, the Near Islands are uninhabited. From 1842 to 1861, 2,421 sea otters and 2,503 foxes were exported from the Near Islands.

The Rat Islands include Buldyr, Big Kiska and Little Kiska, Tenadakh, Chugul, Little Sitkhin, Rat, Amchitka, and Semisopochnoi. Amchitka, the largest island in this group, does not have much elevation above sea level, but there are high mountains on its west side. It is forty-one miles long and up to seven miles wide. There is a bay on this island called Konstantin or sometimes Finliandiia [Finland] Bay. Semisopochnoi Island is about thirty miles in circumference, Little Sitkhin, twelve miles, and Rat Island, ten. The rest of the islands are from three to five miles in circumference. All these islands are mountainous with the exception of the southwest side of Big Kiska Island and of the east of Little Kiska Island, which are low and flat. There is a bay on Big Kiska about three versts long.

According to Teben'kov, Amchitka has the best food supply of the Aleutian Islands on it.[10] Salmon also enter four creeks on Big Kiska Island. Halibut and cod are caught year-round. Buldyr Island also can provide some food. Half-rotten driftwood is piled up on the shore of Amchitka Island in some places forty and fifty feet above the high water mark.[11] Except for rats, there are no land animals on these islands, but there are sea animals such as sea otters, sea lions, and hair seals. Sea lions breed on Big Kiska and on the adjoining rocks. There are no permanent inhabitants on these islands.

The Andreanov Islands consist of Gorelyi [now Gareloi], Amatygnak (the southernmost of the Aleutians), Iulakh [Ulak], Kavalga, Unalga, Tanaga, Bobrovyi [Bobrof], Kanaga, Adakh, Kagalaksa [Kagalaska],

Tannakh [Little Tanaga], Chigul [Chugul], Igitkhin, Ulakh, Tagalakh, Sitkhin [Great Sitkin], Atkha, Amlia, Koniuzhii [Koniuji], Kosatochi, Siguam [Seguam], and some smaller islands.

Atkha, the largest in this group, is about fifty-six miles long and comprises several small mountainous islands connected by narrow, low isthmuses. Its north tip is formed by two mountains with a narrow neck of land between. The northern mountain, Korovinskaia, is an active volcano. The summits are covered with snow. There are few level places on the island and no streams of any size, only brooks and small creeks flowing from the mountainsides. There are a number of lakes. Several bays offer more or less convenient anchorage, including Korovin Bay on the west side of the isthmus, and Nazan Bay on the east side. The natives carry their baidarkas from one bay to the other over a portage of four versts. Korovin Bay gives the best shelter for ships. Bichevin, Kaurov, and Banner bays, to the west, are smaller, but are convenient for anchorage. There are layers of coal among the rocks on the east side of Korovin Bay.

The native settlement of Nikol'skoe and the company's establishments at Korovin Bay have been moved recently to Nazan Bay. Only the church and the house for the priest and his attendants have been left in the old village. The natives move back and forth from one village to another. The company manager and about ninety people, apart from ecclesiastics and their families, seven men and eight women in all, live on Atkha Island.

Amlia Island is separated from Atkha by a narrow strait. This island is about thirty-six miles long and three to four miles wide. It is composed of high conical mountains, whose summits are covered with snow and enveloped in fog. These stretch west to east, terminating in a high, almost perpendicular drop. On the south side of the island is Sveshnikov [Sviechnikof] (or Ovechkin) Harbor, protected by a small island. Many lakes and small creeks dot this island. The population numbers about two hundred persons of both sexes.

Siguam Island, which lies northeast of Amlia, is about twelve miles long and not more than six miles wide. It is composed of a chain of mountains, some of them active volcanoes. A considerable quantity of sulphur has been found around one of the extinct volcanoes. The east side of this island is higher and rockier than the west side. The straits between Siguam Island and Amlia Island and between Amlia and Atkha are dangerous for baidarkas because of the strong current.

Adakh is next in size in this island group, followed by Kanaga Island and Tanaga. All the Andreanov Islands are high and rocky, and there are active volcanoes on many of them. One of these is on the small island of Gorelyi, west of Tanaga. Only Adakh and Tanaga islands have good harbors. Sarychev, our noted hydrographer, visited one on Tanaga in the ship *Slava Rossii* and named the harbor in honor of his vessel.

There are no woods on the Andreanov Islands, only brush. There is plenty of grass which is suitable for cattle. Roots used for food included sarana, snakeweed, sweet grass [*borshch*], spinach, and wild parsley. Foxes are found only at Atkha. There are no land animals of any kind on the rest of these islands. The sea animals include sea otters, sea lions, and a few hair seals, and sea birds include the tufted puffin, horned puffin, murre, and cormorant. They are most numerous on Siguam Island; and there are a few on Atkha Island. Fish are abundant on the Andreanov Islands, especially on Atkha Island. Salmon enter the creek flowing into Sarannaia Bay [Sarana Cove] and enough can usually be taken to last all winter. On Amlia Island the salmon run is not dependable. Other fish caught around these islands include cod, halibut, greenling [*terpuga*], perch, and other small fish. Herring caught around Atkha Island are excellent, better than imported herring when properly prepared and salted. The main staple in the diet of the Andreanov islanders is seafood of various kinds, such as sea turnips [*morskie repki*], *mami, baidarki,* and round crabs [*Kruglye raki—* King crabs]. The crabs can weigh as much as twenty pounds. Their legs measure up to one and one-half feet long, and their bodies are eight to ten inches across. These crabs are very tasty but the Aleuts catch them only in May, June, July, and August. During the rest of the year they do not eat them. From 1842 to 1861 the company exported 1,188 sea otters and 1,685 foxes from the Andreanov Islands.

The Fox Islands stretch from Siguam Island to the Aliaska Peninsula. They are Amukhta, Chugul, and Iunaska [Yunaska]; the Chetyrekhsopochnye Islands [Islands of the Four Mountains] (Chugulakh, Ul'mega, Chuginadak, and Kagamil); Umnak and the small island of Samalga; the small islands that make up the Vsevidov group, of which Uegakh is the largest; Unalashka and adjoining small islands; a group of small islands and rocks called the Iaichnymi [Egg] Islands; Unalga; the Krenitsyn group (named after Krenitsyn, who described them), Aektak, Avatanok, Tigalda, Ukamak, the two small rocky islands of Akun, and Akutan; and Unimak Island.

Unalashka is the largest island of this group, measuring about seventy miles long and thirty miles wide in its northeastern part. The volcano Makushinskaia, the highest mountain on this island, lies between Makushin Bay and Kapitanskaia [Unalashka] Bay. The latter provides the best refuge for ships in this part of the country. Other bays on Unalashka are Kolekhta Bay, on the northeast side of the island; Bobrovaia

Bay [Beaver Inlet], on the east side; and Kashigin [Kashega] Bay and Chernov Bay [Chernofski Harbor], on the west side.

A company establishment, Port Illiliuk, is located on a cape in Kapitanskaia Bay. The manager of the island lives there, as well as about 102 natives; Port Illiliuk also has a church, employing seven men and four women. About 368 Aleuts live in a village called Imagnia at the entrance to Kapitanskaia Bay.

On the west shore of Unalashka Island, there are Aleutian villages at Makushin Bay near Cape Kovrizhska and at Kashigin Bay. There are about 60 inhabitants in the first village and about 110 in the second. Unalga and Spirkin Islands lie northeast of Unalashka, and Umnak Island lies to the west of it.

Umnak is about fifty miles long and fourteen miles wide at its north end. The mountains on the island are higher toward the north, the highest being Tulikskaia and Vsevidovskaia. Umnak Island has no harbors except for one small bay, an excellent anchorage for small vessels. About eighty-six natives of both sexes live on Umnak.

Akutan Island, forty miles in circumference, lies east of Unalga. It consists of high mountains, the largest of which is about 3,300 feet high and emits smoke.

Unimak Island, the last of the Fox Islands to the east, is also the last of the Aleutian Islands before the American mainland, separated from the Aliaska Peninsula by Issanakh Strait. Unimak Island is sixty-two miles long and about twenty miles wide, and has several active volcanoes. The highest, Shishaldinskaia, is one of the largest in this region. Unimak has rocky shores and the south shore is higher than the northern. There are two bays, one with two small islands in it, one on the east side and the other on the west side. About sixty natives inhabit the village of Shishaldinskoe, on the north shore.

There are about 165 natives on Akun Island. On some of the other small islands of the Fox Islands, such as Tigalda and Avatanok, the natives stay only temporarily.

The Fox Islands are treeless. Low bush--willow and alder--grows at the foot of the mountains and on the plains. Willow grows in the northeastern part of Unalashka, and alder on islands in the eastern half of the group. The lower slopes of the mountains are covered with scant vegetation; their upper parts are barren except for moss. Of some fir trees brought in 1805 from Sitkha to Unalashka and planted in the vicinity of Illiliuk village, only those planted on Amakhnak Island survive. According to Veniaminov,[12] these trees grew at first more in thickness than in height, but in recent years began to grow noticeably higher.

There is plenty of driftwood on the Fox Islands, used by the inhabitants for firewood or for making charcoal. Brush is also used for fuel. Berries and mushrooms of several kinds are picked for food. The grass on low ground grows high and thick, but, as Veniaminov writes,[13] its nourishing qualities are low, probably from too much humidity and salt from the sea. Almost all known vegetables are grown on these islands. Wheat, peas, and barley (except for one variety which is grown near the sea), do not ripen, however, as experiments have shown.

The climate of the Fox Islands is subject to quick changes depending upon the wind direction; but they are drier than the other Aleutian Islands. Rain and foggy weather are infrequent, but there are few clear days during the year. Freezing begins in October and sometimes in September; the snow begins to fall then and remains sometimes until June and even July. These islands never get very cold, but constant winds lower the temperature considerably. The warm weather in summer also depends upon the wind, which can change suddenly and make even the warmest day very cold. The best weather is in August.

A large supply of various fish is gathered in the company's main establishment on the Fox Islands, but the run starts earlier in the creeks in the vicinity of Makushin village and Cape Veselov [Cape Cheerful] where fishing is also conducted for the Illiliuk settlement. In addition to salmon, codfish is dried on Unalashka Island. When whales appear in the vicinity, the Aleuts living in the harbor kill them with darts. A wounded whale does not remain in the water long and is usually cast ashore. He then becomes the property of the man whose dart killed him. As explained previously, the frequent visits of foreign whalers to these waters have caused a decline in whale hunting, and the natives are sometimes in great need of whale oil, whalebone, and sinews. The colonial management is, therefore, forced to substitute seal oil for whale oil, or to purchase it as well as other items.

Besides a few cattle in the main settlement, the inhabitants raise pigs and poultry, but because both of the latter are fed mainly on fish, the pork, chicken flesh, and eggs all have a repulsive, fishy taste.

Foxes, sea otters, land otters, and sea lions are hunted on the Fox Islands. The best marmots are found on Unimak Island. From 1842 to 1861, 5,686 sea otters, 329 land otters, 19,671 foxes, and 536 puds of walrus ivory were exported from the Fox Islands.

Unga, about twenty-five miles long and about twelve miles wide, is the largest of the Shumagin Islands. Unga is mountainous, like all the islands in this group, though compared to the mountains on the neighboring Aliaska Peninsula, those on the Shumagin Islands seem low.

There are two harbors on Unga Island—Zakhar'ev [Zachary] on the north side, and Unga or Delarov's Harbor on the southeast side where all of the company's establishments are.

This island, all of the Shumagin Islands, and the adjoining region on the Aliaska Peninsula are supervised by a district manager. There is an Aleut village at Delarov Harbor. Four hundred and ninety-five persons of both sexes inhabit this island. The population figures in the colonies include the natives of Unga Island as well as the population of the Unalashka district. None of the other Shumagin Islands is inhabited.

Popov Island, east of Unga Island, is sizable. There are two small islands in the strait between Popov and Unga. Two larger islands Buldyr [Karpa] and Korovin, are in the strait between Popov Island and the Aliaska Peninsula. Southeast of Unga is Nagai, and farther, in the same direction, lie Koniuzhii [Koniuji] Island and many small islands and rocks.

All of the Shumagin Islands are rocky. Between the mountains on Unga and other islands are many low places. There are several lakes and many creeks on these islands, many containing fish. The vegetation on the islands consists of alder, which grows on the northwest side, and willows, on the east side. All of the berries found on other islands grow here, with the exception of cloudberries. Foxes live on Unga Island; ground squirrels, mink, otters, hair seals, and sea otters are found on all of them. Sea birds also nest on these islands. There are deposits of coal and slate on some of the islands, mostly on the northwest shore of Unga. There are also quartz crystals on Unga, and a grotto with stalactites.[14]

From 1842 to 1861, 3,611 sea otters, 979 land otters, and 5,731 foxes were exported from these islands.

East of the Shumagin islands lie the treeless and uninhabited Evdokiev or Semidi Islands.

Near the southeast side of Aliaska lie Sannakh, Ikatok, and other small rocky islands.

The Pribylov Islands. The Pribylov Islands lie north of the Aleutian Islands, opposite the Fox Islands. They are named after skipper Pribylov, who discovered them in 1786.[15] There are two islands in this group: St. Paul and St. George, and near St. Paul a small rocky island called Bobrovyi [Otter] Island and a large, low rock called Morzhovyi [Walrus] Rock. St. Paul Island is the largest, measuring about ninety miles in circumference. Its east and north sides are low and the shores are sandy with a gentle slope, but the west side is high and the shore is rocky. The main elevation is in the middle of the island. The summits of the mountains have crumbled, showing that at some time these islands were subjected to earthquakes. On top of one of these mountains is a lake about 1½ versts in circumference. The soil is sandy in low places, and clayey with iron ochre on higher parts of the island. The rest of the soil is lava of various kinds. There are no large rivers, but small brooks run down the slopes of the mountains and a creek flows from the lake. On a small bay in the southwest part of St. Paul Island the company has established a settlement. Inhabitants of the settlement number 276 of both sexes.

St. George Island lies south of St. Paul Island. It is much smaller in size than St. Paul, about ten miles long and three and one-half miles wide. The shores, except for rare places, are rocky and steep. About 140 people live in the company settlement on the north shore.

The climate on these islands can be severe,[16] depending on the wind direction. North winds bring ice and cold weather to the islands. South and east winds usually bring rain and fog, and cause the ice to drift away from the shore and the weather to become warmer. The first snow falls in October and ice stays from October until as late as June sometimes. The fogs from May until August are so thick that it is often impossible to see objects several feet away. There are few clear days and the sun is rarely seen.

Only small willows grow on these islands, but thick grass occurs in ravines and everywhere on low ground. Plants include *polyn'* [wormwood], *pyrei*, and *tysiachilistvennik* [literally, thousand-leaved plant]. A few crowberries and cloudberries can be found. Many roots are gathered for food and a few vegetables are grown.

The Pribylov Islands are rich in fur seals and sea lions. At present, as stated above,[17] about 70,000 fur seals are killed each year on St. Paul Island without depleting them, and about 6,000 are killed on St. George. Sea lion hunting on St. George is becoming more difficult each year. Foxes are also trapped on these islands. Walruses stay temporarily on Walrus Rock, but strangely, no females are found among them. Presumably the females remain in the places farther north from which the males migrate. A species of mouse on these islands, yellow-brown, small and tailless, feeds on roots.

Whales sometimes come here but are seldom cast ashore. There are many halibut and codfish. The former is caught during the summer months from July until September, and the cod in the springtime. There are no salmon. Aleuts living on the islands use round crabs (the so-called sea spiders and sea-turnips) for food.

Murres and other sea birds abound on these islands. There are many murres on St. George Island, particularly on East Cape. A vessel nearing land in the fog can determine its location by the number of these birds.

The Aleuts use murre meat for food and preserve the eggs in fat for winter. Sea ducks [*glupysh*] remain mostly in swift current, their flocks sometimes covering an area of two square miles. Their eggs are similar to duck eggs. In the fall they get so fat they cannot fly. Large numbers of geese, ducks, and snipe also live on these islands.

From 1842 to 1861, 277,788 fur seals, 10,508 foxes, and 104 puds of walrus ivory were exported from St. Paul and 31,923 fur seals and 24,286 foxes from St. George.

The Kad'iak Archipelago. The Kad'iak archipelago consists of Kad'-iak Island, the adjacent islands of Afognak, Elovyi [Spruce], Lesnoi [Woody], Dolgoi [Long], Sitkhlidak, the Gusinye [Geese] Islands, Malinovyi, Govorushechii or Ketoi [Whale], and nearby to the north, Shuiak and the Bezplodyne (Peregrebnye) [Barren] Islands. To the east lies Marmot [Evrashechii] Island, and, to the south, Sitkhinak, Tugi-dak, and other small islands.

Kad'iak, the largest island of this archipelago, is ninety miles long. It is hilly but has no high mountains. Its shores have many deep indentations, the most remarkable being Marmot Bay, between this island and Afognak Island; and Chiniak, Kiliudin, and Igak bays on the west side. Chiniak is composed of three smaller bays: Kal'sin, Sredniaia [Middle], and Bab'ia [Women's] Bay (sometimes called English Bay). Kad'iak has no large rivers, but the Karluk and Sapozhkova [Buskin] rivers are noted for their abundance of fish.[18] The climate is not very good. Earthquakes occur quite frequently. The earthquake of 1844 was severe and lasted at least two minutes. A rumbling noise underground and the trembling of the earth terrified the natives. Many fled their dwellings believing that the earthquake would destroy them. Even the old men do not remember so strong an earthquake in previous years.

The harbor of St. Paul, on the northeast side of Chiniak Bay, is one of the principal places in the Russian colonies. Most of the local food-stuffs for all the Kad'iak district and for some of the other establishments are procured around the harbor, and, in addition, it also serves as a center of the fur trade, and most of the ice for the California trade is out here. The harbor consists of a narrow strait about 60 to 140 sazhens wide protected from winds by a comparatively high treeless island. This strait narrows from its beginning due to a sandy cape, leaving a passage only forty sazhens wide for ships. A small battery of guns on a rocky cape of Kad'iak Island protect the harbor. The west entrance to the strait is even more inconvenient because of its narrowness and the difficulty of avoiding rocks that are invisible in high water. In the summer months only five vessels can shelter in the harbor but in the fall and winter not even this number can be accommodated. Northeast and northwest winds predominate then. They blow so along the strait sometimes that they break hawsers and anchor chains, smash rowboats left on the shore, and tear off roofs. Two such cases occurred in 1858. On 24 November, both anchor chains of the steamer *Imperator Aleksandr II* were broken and she was barely kept from striking a rock on the opposite shore by means of two hawsers from shore. New roofs on the buildings next to the strait were torn off and even carried by the wind across the strait onto the small island opposite. On 24 December many roofs were also damaged, and the roof and rafters from one house were torn off.

The settlement is built on a high rocky shore. To the north is a mountain, with a lake at its base. There are many other small heights around, treeless but covered with dense grass in summer. There are fir woods in the east part of the settlement. Farther inland the ground becomes marshy. A church surrounded by poplars stands on a hill. Besides the main altar of this church there are two chapels. One of these was built by the Most Reverend Innokentii, and the other was built at the expense of the former manager of the Kad'iak office, F. I. Murgin. The settlement also includes a large warehouse, a hospital with a separate wing for women patients, barracks for the employees, a building which serves as the office and as the manager's residence, an officers' club, workshops, a carpenter shop, a blacksmith shop, and other company buildings. The population includes the office manager and several clerks, the clergy, a medical functionary, and various company employees (mostly creoles and a few Russians). There are about 360 people of both sexes. Company establishments around the harbor include one on a point eight miles from the harbor, on the banks of the Sapozhkova River, where cattle are kept and in summertime fish are dried. At Women's Bay (or English Bay) hay is made for the cattle, which are kept there in the wintertime. Cattle are also kept at Kal'sin Bay. A flour mill operates at Popov Bay, six versts from the harbor. Bricks are made from local clay at a brick factory at Middle Bay. Mr. Teben'kov remarks that "the seawater penetrating the clay probably makes the bricks porous. They crumble easily, and so are used only in extreme need."[19] There is a small tannery on the west shore of Uiak Bay.

Besides its other functions[20] the Kad'iak office organizes hunting crews for this district, provides the hunters with the necessities, and settles accounts. Workers steadily employed by the company are always busy, depending upon the season, in cutting down, hauling, and sawing logs and in construction work. In summer they gather hay for the cattle and store firewood; during the fishing season they catch fish and prepare it for the winter.

When the need arises, Aleuts from neighboring villages are hired on a daily basis after they return from hunting in order to help company workers. The company supplies these Aleuts with food.

Humpback salmon, dog salmon, and silver salmon are caught in Paul's Harbor by purse seine during their annual run. Besides the daily distribution of fresh fish among the inhabitants, a supply of not less than 50,000 fish is salted for the winter. After the salmon run, special native fishermen are hired to fish with hook and line for cod, *kalaga*, and sometimes halibut. They are paid for each fish caught. In a good (not stormy) winter enough of the latter fish is caught for all of the local population and the salted fish is then cooked in the community kettle only when the weather prevents fishing.

Besides this, in the odinochka on Karluk Creek, between 100,000 and 150,000 iukola [dried salmon] are prepared for the Aleuts living in the harbor and in other places under company management and for their families in case of famine. Part of this supply is shipped to New Archangel and to U̇kamok Island. King salmon [*chavycha*], a very tasty fish, enter Karluk Creek from the sea. The bellies of this fish are salted and the backs smoked, but through press of other work, few of these fish are so prepared.

Potatoes, two hundred barrels (a barrel is about four chetveriks) of which were purchased lately from the settlers, are the main item of local diet. Some are set aside to be sent to New Archangel and for consumption by the harbor population; the rest are issued in the spring to the inhabitants for seed. Formerly, potatoes were grown on Kad'iak Island in company vegetable gardens, but since the settlers came, the company's gardens have been discontinued so that the settlers can sell the company vegetables and other products. Sometimes there are mushroom crops on Kad'iak, but not enough for the whole population.

Various berries including crowberries, cloudberries, stone-bramble [*kostianika*], cranberries, and raspberries (the last are very watery and flavorless, grow in ample quantities for the population. The Aleuts and creoles preserve crowberries[21] for the winter, pouring melted fat over them. Saran roots are also gathered.

From spring until fall there are many geese on Kad'iak Island, mostly in its southern part. At first their meat is very tough but later in summer they get fatter. They are salted and in the winter are given away on big holidays. Many kinds of ducks remain until late fall. Ptarmigans are hunted even in the winter.

The Kad'iak office supervises the following settlements and odino-chkas:

1. A village on Chiniak Cape, with a population of about 300 of both sexes;

2. The Orlov odinochka in Igak Bay with a village of about 320;

3. The odinochika of Three Saints in the strait between Kad'iak and Sitkhlidak Island near an Aleut village of 557 inhabitants. Much whale meat and oil is prepared here, though less than in former times; from 40,000 to 50,000 pieces of iukola are dried, and berries—cranberries, cloudberries and crowberries—are picked by Aleut women hired by the company.

4. The Karluk odinochka and a village of about 300;

5. An odinochka and a village of 160 inhabitants on Ukamok (Chiri-kov) Island, a small island south of Kad'iak. Humpback, dog salmon, silver salmon, and red salmon enter the creeks on Ukamok Island.

Woody Island is about one-half mile east of Kad'iak. It is 2¼ miles long and 1¼ miles wide and is covered with dense forest. Mr. Teben'-kov remarks that the island appears attractive, but its soil is unsuitable for cultivation.[22] However, some of the Aleuts living there have vege-table gardens. There are several lakes on this island, from one of which up to 5,000 tons of ice is exported to California,[23] as stated above. According to McPherson, an American engineer who was employed here, this lake can provide up to 30,000 tons of ice. A native settlement inhabited by 190 people lies on the west side of the island. Near the village there are icehouses and a wharf for loading ice.

One-quarter of a mile east of Kad'iak is Spruce Island, the west side is high, and the east side low and covered by forest. There are company settlements, vegetable gardens, and cattle on this island. The Monk Herman, the last member of the first ecclesiastical mission, lived here a long time. He died in 1827 and was buried near Archmonk Ioasaf, who also died here. Father Herman organized a school in his house for native girls and also spent much of his time gardening. According to Khlebnikov, he had between 150 and 180 beds of potatoes. There are about seventy-five natives on Spruce Island, living in two villages.

Northeast of Kad'iak, across a narrow strait, is Afognak Island, thirty-one miles long and twenty-five miles wide in the north. This island is mountainous and abounds with fir, larch, poplar, birch, and mountain ash. Its shores have many bays of different sizes. On the east side are Perenosnaia [Portage] Bay, Nerphich'ia [Seal] Bay, and a bay called "Beyond the Thin Cape" [*za tonkim mysom*, probably referring to modern Tonki Cape Peninsula]. As harbors for sailing ships, how-ever, these bays are inconvenient. Nerpich'e [Seal] Lake and several smaller lakes and the creeks flowing from them abound with fish. The salmon run starts here earlier than at Paul's Harbor and the natives acquire their first fish of the season here, but not much iukola is prepared. There are many foxes, mostly black-brown. There is an odinochka here and three colonial settlements, where vegetables are raised. About 410 persons inhabit this island.

The channel separating Kad'iak from Malinovyi [Raspberry] Island is strewn with small islands and rocks where water fowl live. The natives gather their eggs for winter.

Raspberry Island, sixteen miles long and seven miles wide, abounds with berries, especially raspberries.

Marmot [Evrashechii] Island, east of Afognak, is seven miles long and four miles wide, and treeless. It is so named probably because marmots are hunted there.

Among other islands of the Kad'iak archipelago should be noted Tugidak Island, near which are hunting grounds for sea otters, and Aekhtalik Island, where the company sends special hunters for geese.

Between 1842 and 1861 places supervised by the Kad'iak office yielded 5,809 sea otters; 85,381 river beavers; 14,295 sables [marten]; 14,313 muskrats; 1,175 mink; 1,296 puds 22 lbs. of walrus ivory; 26,095 pairs of beaver castors; 712 parkas made of marmot skins; 1,276 wolverines; and 58 wolves.

The northwest coast of America. By the northwest coast of America, we understand the Aliaska Peninsula, Kenai and Chugach bays and adjacent places, and the coast from Chugach Bay down to the southern boundary of the Russian possessions, including the Vancouver Islands.

The Aliaska Peninsula. The Aliaska Peninsula stretches from Issanakh Strait, separating it from Unimak Island, to the Kviichak River. From Cape Douglas to the mouth of the Kviichak the peninsula is 320 miles long and 115 miles wide. At Issanakh Strait it is only 20 miles wide. A chain of high mountains, many of which are volcanic, nearer to the southeast side and sloping toward the northwest extends the entire length of this peninsula. There are many lakes on the peninsula from which large and small rivers flow. The most noteworthy are Kviichak, Naknek, and Ugazhak. There are eight bays on the southeast side of the peninsula and three on the northwest side. The largest of these, Pavlov Bay, is almost sixty versts long. Pavlov Mountain rises on the peninsula's west side. The end of the bay turns northeast where it is separated from Beaver Bay by a narrow strip of land. There are company odinochkas and native villages at Katmai Bay, with 457 inhabitants, and at Lake Iliamna, on the Iliamna River, with 140 inhabitants.

Starting about midway on Aliaska, forests fill the ravines—birch, alder, and fir in the south, and coniferous trees in the northern part. Most of Aliaska abounds with forests and most of the ground is covered with lush grass. Berries of all varieties grow in abundance. Sarana and many other roots suitable for food are found there. There are many varieties of land animals including red foxes noted for their excellent fur. Earlier there were many caribou [*olen'*] but they have now disappeared completely. Sea lions, walrus, and hair seals are hunted along the coasts. There are many beavers around Katmai. Very infrequently, whales are cast on these shores. Khlebnikov states that graphite, rockcrystal, and lime spar are found on the shores of Aliaska and small pieces of red amber are found in some of the bays. Granite, basalt, and coal are also found.

Kenai Bay. Kenai Bay, called Cook Inlet by the English, and Summachin in the Kenai dialect, is bounded on the west by part of the Aliaska Peninsula, and on the east by part of the mainland that forms the west shore of Chugach Bay. Cape Douglas on the west shore and Cape Elizabeth on the island next to the east shore, forty-six miles apart, form the entrance to this bay. There are many indentations in the shores of this bay, the main ones being Kamyshak Bay on the west shore and Chugachik or Kachetmak Bay on the east shore. A short distance south of the latter is English Bay, in a small cove of which, called Ugol'naia [Coal] Bay, the company mines coal. North of Cape Elizabeth is Port Chatham. The west shore of the bay is made up of the high mountains of the Aliaska Peninsula, the largest being the Iliamna and Redoubt volcanoes. The east shore is much lower, with a gentle slope and low hills. There is fine pasture in level places between the hills. The soil is mostly tundra. Layers of coal, as we have already stated, extend for almost seventy miles along the east shore of the bay, north of English Bay. Traces of gold have been found at the mouth of the Kaknu [Kenai] River, where the redoubt Sv. Nikolai is. Formerly forts Resurrection [Voskresenskii] and George [Georgievskii] were situated between Kenai and Chugach bays, but they have been abandoned.

The climate around Kenai Bay is more temperate and better than in other places in the Russian colonies. It is moderately warm and clear in the summer. In the winter the cold sometimes reaches 40°. Rain and fog seldom occur and for a short time only, and therefore the air is healthy and fresh. North and south winds predominate. East winds are rare but very strong in the fall and the weather then is usually bad. As Mr. Teben'kov remarks,[24] navigation on the bay at this time requires great care.

Fir, pine, larch, alder, poplar, and, in the northern part, birch grow on the shores of Kenai Bay, and many berries—crowberries, raspberries, frostberries, cranberries, and red currants. The settlers raise potatoes, turnips, radishes, beets, lettuce, onions, and garlic. Wheat and barley grow very well in some places but do not ripen. Mr. Murgin wrote the following in his journal after he visited the small bay of Ninil'chik (between redoubt Sv. Nikolai and Kachetmak Bay) in 1855:

> Among other agricultural experiments I saw a patch of oats sowed by the settler Kvasnikov. The young growth looked very good and Kvasnikov told me that oats ripened completely last year, but that wheat and barley did not during all the three years he experimented with them. If the settlers as Ninil'chik had been peasants from our agricultural provinces, the soil would have been better prepared and the experiments could have been more businesslike. The company would have to furnish only the necessary implements and seeds. But what can be accomplished by a former city dweller who left his country thirty years ago and has hardly seen any farming done, or even more so a creole who is unfamiliar with this work or the implements used for it? Still, oats ripened on a spaded plot prove that a good crop of oats could be had in properly cultivated fields around Ninil'chik, farther away from the seashore. Even if only oats would ripen, they could be used for making porridge—an improvement compared to a fish diet.

The many rivers flowing from the mountains abound with king salmon, red salmon, silver salmon, trout, and various small fish.

Trapping beavers is the main occupation of the natives of Kenai Bay. They trap and hunt them in the fall and winter after locating the beaver houses in the summer. They use beaver meat for food, and Mr. Murgin remarks that the meat is so white and tasty that if they would only bring it to the redoubt everybody would want it. Besides beavers, they trap foxes, river otters, and bears.

In a brickyard near the redoubt, about 50,000 bricks of good quality are manufactured with the help of local natives who are hired by the company as part-time workers. Most of these bricks are shipped to New Archangel, except for a small quantity, which is shipped to Kad'iak.

There are 958 natives living on Kenai Bay. About twenty small villages are scattered on both sides of the bay; on the east side from English Bay to the Knyk River, and on the west side from that river to the West Foreland cape. There is a church in the redoubt where the Kenai missionary resides.

The number of furs exported from here was included with the furs from the Kad'iak office, since the redoubt is managed by it.

Chugach Bay. The north and west shores of Chugach Bay are covered by a very high mountain chain that starts from Cape St. Elias. Its east side is low. Near the southeast side of the bay is Khtageliuk

[Hinchinbrook] Island, with an indentation in its shore known as Nuchek [Port Etches] Bay. Beside the smaller Bay of Sts. Constantine and Helen [Constantine Harbor], which forms a part of Nuchek Bay, is the company's redoubt of the same name, with 80 inhabitants in it and 427 in the neighborhood. Another 200 natives live near a small company trading post on the Copper River.

The soil here is mostly wet tundra. The shores of Chugach Bay present a cheerless picture. They and the high snow-capped mountains hovering above the shore are enveloped by eternal fog accompanied by a continuous sleet or drizzling rain. The ice in the ravines and crevices in the mountains never melts. There is bad weather here at least three quarters of the year. The thermometer does not rise above 12°. Part of the mountains and ravines between them are covered with woods, mostly fir, larch, alder, and poplars. Berries here include raspberries, bilberries, cranberries, red currants, and crowberries. Sarana root also grows here. Potatoes will grow in vegetable gardens. Fish, mostly king salmon, enter the many small creeks on Khtageliuk Island from the sea. The constant dampness greatly hinders preparation of iukola for the fort. To overcome this, large covered sheds have been built, where the fish are hung from several rows of poles, placed one above the other. On the ground is kept a smouldering fire of rotten wood. The smoke dries the fish before it has time to spoil and it keeps well.

Land animals found here include various foxes, wolverines, black and brown bears, minks, porcupines, and, farther in the interior, rabbits, deer, squirrels, ermine, and mountain sheep [*gornyi* or *dikii baran*]. The meat of these animals is salted for Kad'iak. The amphibious animals are beavers and river otters. (The quantity of furs exported is shown together with the furs from Kad'iak.) Shore birds in this region include eagles, ravens and magpies; seabirds include murres, cormorants, tufted puffins, and sea ducks; and migratory fowl include geese, ducks, and cranes.

The coast from Chugach Bay to Icy Strait. A very high mountain chain follows the northwest coast of America between Chugach Sound and Icy Strait. Mounts St. Elias and Dobraia Pogoda [Fairweather] are the highest. In many crevices in the mountains the ice never melts. Ice sliding off the mountains floats in L'tua Bay the year round. Low-lying ground at the foot of the mountains is partly covered with coniferous forest and grass. Some of the creeks, for instance Icy Creek at the head of Yakutat Bay—the so-called Bering Bay—between L'tua Bay and Chugach Bay, make their way between heavy ice or have their sources in the glaciers.

Very little is known about the natural history of the region. According to Baranov's notes,[25] and those of his subordinates, silver salmon, halibut, herring, and other small fish were caught year-round on the shores of Yakutat Bay, where up to 1805 a Russian settlement stood. "There are plenty of berries," writes Baranov, "raspberries, blueberries, bilberries, salmon berries, arctic bramble [*kalina*], and perhaps other varieties. There are also many hair seals in the bay and mountain sheep [*baran*] on the ridge. The natives rely on these for fat." According to navigator Shield's report to Baranov in 1796, "except for halibut there are no fish in L'tua Bay. Sea lions live on the rocks in the winter. There are very few hair seals. To the north there is a sizeable run of fish in a small creek which flows from the lake. The berries are the same as at Yakutat but they were not yet ripe in July."

Sea otters are found in L'tua and Yakutat even now, but there are not nearly as many as there used to be. Besides, entrance to these bays is very dangerous so the company no longer sends hunters there.

The coast from Icy Strait to the southern boundary of Russian territory, including the Vancouver Islands. Mr. Teben'kov writes in his notes on hydrography:

> From Icy Strait, so-called because of ice floating there almost year round, as far as the strait of Juan de Fuca, the coast of America breaks up into a multitude of islands, islets, and rocks. Compared to the gigantic size of these islands and the straits which separate them from each other, the rocky island of Finland and the fjords of Norway are mere imitations. Vancouver, the English navigator who explored and put them on the map has an undeniable claim to fame. Timber, coal, fish, and finally, traces of gold on the Queen Charlotte Islands and on the shores of Kaigany Strait are resources which, if worked by the natives, promise considerable profits.[26]

The port of New Archangel. The port of New Archangel on the west shore of one of the largest of the Vancouver Islands is the administrative center for the Russian colonies in America and for the islands in the Eastern Ocean. In addition to what has been stated of the reasons that compelled Baranov to make his headquarters here, and of the history and present state of this port,[27] the following can be added:

New Archangel offers all the conveniences of a harbor for ships and a trading center. It is free of ice year-round, has several entrances which are safe from obstruction, is large enough to accommodate a whole fleet and give protection regardless of the wind direction. The armaments and fortifications at New Archangel, although insufficient for protection from an attack by large vessels, are nevertheless adequate against any hostile attack by the savage native tribes, who ever since

Novo-Arkhangel'sk (Sitka), about 1860

Murav'ev managed the colonies have lived under the very walls of the port. There are about sixty cannon on all the forts and batteries at New Archangel, among them several for shooting explosive bombs. Another eighty-seven are in reserve, ranging from cannon capable of shooting bombs of two puds down to one pound falconets. The main fort built on a high promontory where the chief manager's house is built, is armed with seventeen cannon from twelve to twenty-four pounds caliber. The port is separated from the Kolosh village by a high palisade extending from the seashore to the north of Swan Lake and for about thirty sazhens on its opposite shore. Where the palisade begins on the seashore, the port is protected by a blockship with three guns; and by the so-called Kolosh battery of six guns. There are four towers three stories high at the corners of the palisade; in the second story are placed from three to six cannon depending upon the size of the towers. A battery of twelve cannon from six pounds up to one pud caliber is in the harbor, the cannons directed toward the Kolosh village. The garrison is made up of all the male adults in the settlement, numbering 550. This includes about 180 soldiers from the Siberian infantry regiments and about 90 sailors from the navy and the merchant marine. Every man knows his duties in case of alarm and has firearms.

The constant humidity in New Archangel has already been mentioned. Only during two months in the winter, when the wind blows from the snow-covered mountains to the northeast is there a perceptible dryness in the air, accompanied by cold. Doctor Govorlivyi in his review of health conditions in the colonies writes:[28] "an inhabitant of New Archangel can be compared to an amphibian. His body is submerged not only in a mass of air as are the bodies of other people, but also in a cold steam bath. This condition cannot be beneficial even to a native and is harmful for a European who has not yet become acclimatized." On the other hand, Govorlivyi finds some benefits for the natives, who are inclined to have weak lungs, in this combination of humidity and temperate climate. Southwest winds coming from the sea, he claims, clear the air of germs that breed on the tundra in the surrounding mountains. According to him, winds from the mountains bring inflammatory diseases, particularly of the throat. Meteorological observations set the average temperature in New Archangel at + 6° 5′.

Sitkha Island, of volcanic formation, consists of tundra and rock, covered by a thin layer of black soil. Hot sulphur springs flow in many places, those about twenty-five versts from New Archangel being the best known. The company has built a small sanatorium there for persons suffering from rheumatism, impure blood, and other diseases.

Earthquakes are frequent at New Archangel. Those which occurred in December 1843 and in March 1848 were of considerable magnitude. During the first of these there were two vibrations which lasted about three seconds. The last earthquake continued over twenty-five seconds, was accompanied by loud rumbling underground, and reoccurred several times during the next two weeks but more mildly. This earthquake cracked stoves in many houses and knocked down some chimneys but did little other damage.

The mountains surrounding New Archangel average at least 3,000 feet in height. They are covered almost to their summits with gigantic conifers. (Mr. Teben'kov writes in his notes that some of the logs used for construction of the warehouse in 1826 were up to twenty-two sazhens long, and even more remarkable, were absolutely straight.) The speed and vigor of tree growth in these parts is astonishing. According to Teben'kov, brush or various creepers fill all the space between the trees. Trees grow on Sitkha Island and on other islands of Vancouver Straits on the fallen decayed tree trunks of several preceding generations. They include fir, larch, silver-fir, *dushmianka* (American cypress), and wild apple trees. Nevertheless, the lumber is of low quality, the wood not being just damp but watery, with the exception of the American cypress, which is very dry, even when the tree has just been cut. Besides being watery, the wood at Sitkha is flabby and contains no resin. Because of the difficulty of logging even enough for company settlement, only a little is exported to the nearest foreign ports. The best trees near the port and the seashore have already been cut down and at present the logging is done in places thirty and fifty versts away. During the last ten years, about 9,500 logs were cut down around the port, not counting some of the lumber for shipbuilding.

Almost all known varieties of vegetables are raised at New Archangel. Bread grains, as many experiments conducted around the port prove, do not ripen, probably due to the climate.

Berries here include raspberries—very large but, as everywhere in these parts, watery and tasteless—amberberries, blueberries, bilberries, and sometimes Arctic bramble [*mamura*]. Strawberries grow at the foot of Mount Edgecombe. Notably, berries growing beside the hot springs ripen two weeks earlier than elsewhere, although the vegetation in these spots is poorer than around New Archangel.

All species of sea birds known in the colonies are found in this area. Besides these there are two species of eagles—one with a white head—appearing mainly when the herring come, the blue magpie with a topknot, grey woodpeckers, and small birds like sparrows. Migratory birds include swans, geese, hummingbirds, thrushes, the so-called redbreast [*krasnobriushka*], snipes, and sometimes woodcock [*bekasy*]. Fish caught include red salmon, dog salmon, silver salmon, humpback, and king salmon. Halibut is caught year-round. Herring are caught mainly during February and March, but sometimes appear in the fall. (So numerous are they during their periodic runs that around small islands and in narrow straits the water takes on a milky color. One need only put into the water a pole with nails driven into one end to pull out several fish at once.) Mountain goats [*iaman'*] sometimes in considerable numbers, are found on the heights around Sitkha and on other islands. The only fur-bearing animal on the Vancouver Islands is the brown bear, but on the mainland, especially around the Stakhin, Taku, and especially the Chil'kat rivers there are many beavers, muskrats, sables, foxes, wolves, and porcupines. At times raccoons are also seen. Near the Chil'kat River are found lynx, rabbits, squirrels, and mountain sheep [*dikii baran*], the wool from which the natives use for making mantles. A few sea otters appear at Cape Edgecombe and at the hot springs. Hair seals abound in the straits.

Besides various buildings and living quarters, New Archangel contains three Orthodox churches and one Lutheran church; two hospitals [*lechebnitsa*], one for men and one for women; the main colonial school [*glavnoe kolonial'noe uchilishche*] for boys and a boarding school [*pansion*] for girls; two schools for children of both sexes, including orphans, of the company's employees and workers; and the colonial and ecclesiastical administrative offices. In the port, as was stated above, are concentrated all the facilities for construction and repair of vessels belonging to the colonial fleet.

Ozerskoi redoubt is situated fifteen versts southeast of New Archangel. It was built for protection against attacks by the Kolosh, on a small lake in which fish abound. At present the main purpose of this establishment is to supply New Archangel with fish. About forty persons, counting women and children, live in this fort.

The northern part of the American mainland. This is the region north and northwest of Kenai Bay and the Aliaska Peninsula, bounded on the south and southwest by the Bering Sea. The report of Zagoskin's journey to the Kuskokvim and Kvikhpak rivers has indicated the extent of exploration by the company. We will submit here only some topographical and statistical data on the company's establishments in this region.

The country around Bristol Bay and the Nushagak odinochka. One of the largest bays in the northern part of the American mainland, Bristol Bay, stretches from the west shore of the Aliaska Peninsula to Cape Newenham. Two small shallow bays, Chagvan and Port Dobrykh Vestei [Good News Bay] are to the west, between this cape and the mouth of

Ozerskoi Redoubt

the Kuskokvim River. The shores of Bristol Bay itself contain several smaller indentations of which the most important are formed by the Nushagak and Kviichak rivers. The Nushagak River, originating in a lake of the same name (known to the natives as Naianak), is at least two hundred versts long and in some places is up to two versts wide. This river's current is very swift, especially at the mouth, because of tides. The Nushagak River forms several estuaries at its mouth.

At certain sports on the sandy and partly rocky shore of Bristol Bay grow small poplars, willows, alders, birch, and various shrubs. The soil consists of wet and frozen tundra and gravel. Heights in the interior contain many lakes some of which are considerable in size. The country around the Nushagak River is much better than the other places on the bay. The plains are covered with thick grass and in some places there is black soil or sand well suited for gardening. Khlebnikov writes of the speed with which vegetables grow in many of these places and the fecundity of the soil. He gives as an example a very good potato crop. The woods on the shores of the Nushagak River are like those in other places near the bay, but also include mountain ash. Birch suitable for firewood grows near the mouth of this river. The berries are red bilberries, cloudberries, blueberries, and crowberries. Good brick clay occurs on the river banks. Beyond lowlands and plains extending for a long distance up the Nushagak River, a chain of high mountains begins, many of them bare or covered with snow. The climate sometimes is rather severe. Fall and winter last from September until April. Summer is usually pleasant but fogs and rains also occur. The rains are sometimes accompanied by lightning and thunder. There are no volcanoes in this region and earthquakes never occur.

Walrus, sea lions, and hair seals are found in the vicinity of Bristol Bay, especially at Hagemeister Island. Amphibious animals are beavers, land otters, and muskrats. Land animals are bears, wolves, mink, porcupine, sable, fox, and caribou. The latter appear at certain times of the year in herds and provide good hunting for the natives. Shore and sea birds include eagles; hawks; cranes; ptarmigans; ravens; magpies; swans; white, grey, black, and dove-colored geese (the latter on Hagemeister Island and in Tugiak Bay); snipe of various kinds; ducks; loons; cormorants; and sea gulls. The natives make parkas out of eagle feathers. Fish entering rivers and lakes from the sea include king salmon, silver salmon, dog salmon, humpback, red salmon, and smelts, while particularly in the Nushagak and Alegnak rivers, and in the lakes are also pike, *syrok*, *motuk*, graylings, eelpout [*nalim*], salmon trout [*gol'tsy*], *semga*, and yet another fish, which, according to Khlebnikov, has no name. The fish run continues from May until August. First trout enter the rivers, then smelt, and after that king salmon and others. Belugas are found along the coast.

Khlebnikov states that mammoth ivory is found in this region in the river banks and sometimes in fields, underground. Some tusks brought to New Archangel were two arshins long but the ivory was mostly of poor quality, crumbling. The natives scrape blue paint from these bones. Some of this ivory has become petrified and the blue substance forms layers in the bone itself. Layers of blue clay are found at Ekuk Cape, and white clay at Aleknagak Lake and River. Pieces of amber are found on the shores of Nushagak Bay and in a small bay nearby.

Nushagak odinochka, previously called Aleksandrovskii redoubt, is situated on the east shore of the bay, near a native village. Trading is confined to bartering furs from the neighboring natives, mostly Aglemiuts. A manager is in charge of the post and several employees. The fur trade is conducted on a small scale because of the indifference of the Bristol Bay natives and because more important trading posts exist in Kenai Bay.

The trading goods in greatest demand are tobacco, some dry goods and cast-iron kettles of sizes from ¼ to 1½ vedros. Beads, formerly much used, are bartered now only in small quantities and only red, black, and white ones of large size.

There is a church at the Nushagak odinochka and mission. There are about 20 company employees of both sexes at the post and about 1,260 natives in the neighborhood.

The west coast from the mouth of the Kuskokvim River to the north end of Norton Sound and the region around the Kuskokvim and Kvikhpak rivers. Part of the American mainland between the mouth of the Kuskokvim and the end of the Norton Sound represents a lowland cut by the many mouths of the Kvikhpak River. This river and the Kuskokvim rise far in the interior. The Kvikhpak is deep at its right shore and the whole river is deep between the villages of Ikogmiut and Nulato, dotted in many places with large and small islands, on some of which are lakes with many fish. The left shore of the Kvikhpak is rather low, with meadows and tundra. Along its shores about ten miles inland, and along some of its tributaries, grows a large forest of fir, birch, and poplars, and farther inland tundra and lakes. In some places are small larch trees, willows, and alders. Near the village of Ikogmiut is the jagged Illivit group of mountains and the volcanic cone Mount Chiniklik. The Innoka, one of the tributaries of the Kvikhpak, flows on a large low plain covered by small trees. These places abound in beaver, otter, caribou, moose, foxes, wolverine, rabbits, grouse, and ptarmigan. Groups of mountains of two thousand feet or more are scattered along the upper reaches of the Kvikhpak. On the river itself are many small wooded islands. The trees are of the same species as in other places on the river. Red and black currants, raspberries, sweet briar, and guelder rose grow here. Edible plants include angelica [*lesnoi diagil'nik* or *puchki*].

In places the shores of Norton Sound are lined with rocky hills. About thirty miles from the sea, stretches a chain of sizable mountains. The natives say that in the volcanic cones on some, which are from five hundred to one thousand feet high, are large lakes abounding in fish. This mountain chain separating the Nulato River from Norton Sound consists of large rocks and steep hills covered by fir forests up to their summits. Birch, poplars, and alder grow in ravines. The shores of the Nulato River are low.

By expanding its fur trading activities to this region the company is trying to prevent the furs from being bartered by the natives living there to the natives of the islands in the Bering Sea and by them to the Chukchi. As stated above,[29] in 1833, the company founded Mikhailov-skii [St. Michael] on a small island of the same name in the southern part of Norton Sound. This island is separated from the mainland by a narrow channel with small Teben'kov Bay in its east shore. The soil on the island and on the mainland shore is tundra covered with moss, and in some places small thin birch and willows. As Mr. Zagoskin remarks, the tundra on St. Michael Island thaws not more than three or four inches, but in the village of Unalaklit north of the redoubt on the main-land and at the mouth of the Nulato River it thaws up to two feet in the sun. A twenty-one foot well dug at the fort shows alternating layers of slimy clay and clear ice. Winter begins in these parts in the middle or end of September. The ice goes out in June.

Timber is procured from the interior over twenty miles away. The natives use some roots and herbs for food, including snakeweed [*mak-arsha*] and small black nuts, *kytkhyt*, which grow at the roots of goose grass and are dug by the natives from burrows made by mice. On dry ground and on the slopes grow crowberries, frostberries, blueberries, and red huckleberries. A few amberberries grow on the lake shore.

Fish for the redoubt, mostly humpback salmon and dog salmon, are caught at Unalaklit. A few fish are also caught at the redoubt itself. Whitefish, *nel'ma*, *nerka*, silver salmon, and king salmon enter the mouth of the Kvikhpak River from the sea. Nel'ma here reach an extra-ordinary size of over two puds. Farther north, in the shallows of Pastol' Bay the natives hunt beluga. Hair seals, including a particular variety, *makliaki*, are sometimes seen. Numerous heards of caribou roam the shores of Norton Sound. Red foxes and wolves live on St. Michael

Island. Beavers, otters, and muskrats abound on the shores of the Kvikhpak, Innoko, Nulato, and other rivers, south of the redoubt. Sables, rabbits, etc. are found in the interior. There are black and brown bears and lynx around the Nulato River. Migratory waterfowl include swans, geese, and cranes, on the shores of the Kvikhpak, St. Michael Island, and the Nulato River. Ptarmigans and grouse are live in these places.

At present there are sixty-five persons of both sexes at the redoubt. In addition, natives are hired to get in a winter food supply. From 1842 to 1861, the export of furs to New Archangel amounted to 49,398 beavers, 4,954 otters, 10,216 foxes, 183 bears, 1,007 lynx, 8,853 sables [marten], 4,688 muskrats, 330 minks, 52 wolverines, 2 puds, and 36 lbs. of walrus ivory, and 3,315 pairs of beaver castors.

The following odinochkas are managed from Mikhailovshii redoubt: Andreevskaia [Old Andreafsky] at the mouth of the Nugaklik River in the lower reaches of the Kvikhpak (seven inhabitants), Nulato on the Nulato River in the upper reaches of the Kvikhpak (eight inhabitants), and Unalaklit on the shore of Norton Sound (seven inhabitants).

According to Zagoskin, the shores of the Kuskokvim are much more picturesque than the shores of the Kvikhpak, but the Kuskokvim on the other hand cannot compare with the Kvikhpak in abundance, size, and tastiness of fish. The right shore of the Kuskokvim is rocky; the left is covered with forest, through which flow many mountain streams. A chain of mountains up to two thousand feet high, stretches parallel to the river separating it from Nushagak. The space between the mountains and the river is covered by tundra and partly by woods. There are many lakes, with fish. The shores of the upper reaches of the Kuskokvim are stretches of tundra and low hills with many lakes between them. The shores of Khulitnak River, one of the tributaries of the Kuskokvim, are rocky. A chain of mountains up to one thousand feet high stretches to the southwest of this river. Near Kolmakovskii redoubt, which is situated in the middle reaches of the Kuskokvim, the earth is sand and clay covered by a foot of black soil. Meadows are covered by fine grass. In the wintertime very large burbot [*nalim*], a fish measuring from 1 to 1½ feet in length, are caught from under the ice. This fish is followed by whitefish [*sis*], and in summer by king salmon and silver salmon. The oil from sea animals is brought from the Kvikhpak for use by the natives. Hair seals are found at the river mouth, mostly at Cape Avinov.

Furs bartered in redoubt Kolmakov include mostly beaver and fox. Beaver castors are bartered here in large quantities. From 1842 to 1861, 32,396 beaver pelts, 1,165 otters, 3,590 foxes, 320 white foxes, 93 bears, 327 lynx, 2,098 sables [marten], 26 puds of walrus ivory, and 6,836 pairs of beaver castors were exported from here. There are thirty-six inhabitants of both sexes in this fort.

Natives inhabiting the northwest coast and parts of the American mainland owned by Russia. The Kolosh are the most important of all the native tribes inhabiting the northwest coast of America and parts of the mainland owned by Russia. This tribe occupies the region from Vancouver Straits up to Chugach Bay, but the Kolosh living north of the Vancouver Islands differ from the rest in dialects spoken and in certain customs. These branches of the tribe have different names such as Ugalentsi, Yakutat, Kolchani, tundra Kolosh, etc. The Kolosh belong to Indian tribes entirely different from other savages inhabiting the mainland north of Chugach Bay and the islands in the Eastern Ocean. These tribes are related to the Eskimos of Greenland. The Kolosh themselves claim descent from two ancestors of particular stock: one wolf, and the other crow. Because of this they are divided into two branches: the crow people and the wolf people, each in turn divided into several clans. The wolf people, or the clan of Kukhontan, inhabiting Sitkha and the Chil'kat settlements, are considered the most important, not because they are more warlike specially distinguished but because of their numbers. The total number of the Kolosh is unknown, but some believe that it is around 40,000. Others, including Veniaminov, estimate their numbers at only 25,000. We will give here only the number of Kolosh in the well-known settlements, borrowing this data from Mr. Verman's notes:

		Kolosh		Kalgi (slaves)	
		men	women	men	women
Sitkha settlements (near New Archangel)		715	535	51	43
Khutsnov	)	280	280	20	20
Chil'kat	)	728	728	80	80
Kek	)	210	210	13	12
Taku	) In Vancouver	335	337	20	20
Genu	) Straits	195	197	10	9
Tanga	)	154	154	13	12
Icy Strait	)	154	154	13	10
Asanka Harbor	)	56	56	3	3
Kuiuts	)	126	126	5	5
Stakhin settlements		308	308	41	40
Kaigan settlements (Near Prince of Wales Island)		280	280	99	99
L'tua Bay		265	267	29	29
Yakutat		163	168	25	24
	Total	3,974	3,700	422	406

The number of natives such as the Ugalentsi or Ugalakhmiuts, living on the coast south of the Copper River, the Copper River natives living on the river, the Kolchani and Tundra Kolosh living in the interior, and the Kenai natives from the east shore of Kenai Bay to the upper reaches of the Kvikhpak and Kuskokvim is unknown except for those figures already mentioned. Some of the differences in the various Kolosh tribes will be pointed out. The Kolosh language can be divided into three dialects: Sitkha, Yakutat, and Kaigan. These dialects differ according to the distances separating various tribes. The dialects of the Ugalentsi, the Copper River natives, and the Kolchani are entirely different from the dialect of the Vancouver Islands Kolosh, but the similarity of certain words indicates that they all have a common root.[30]

Most of the Kolosh have regular features; their eyes are black and have an open look. They are of medium height and seldom tall. They look self-confident. Many of the Kolosh women are pretty and were it not for the various ornaments that they insert in their lower lips they would compare favorably in looks with the women of other races. The men almost from birth are trained by their parents to bear all kinds of privations. They become so hardened that when they grow up, they can bathe in icy water and stay outdoors in intense cold without any clothes other than a mantle over their shoulders. Their indifference to pain is quite remarkable. The tortures to which the Kolosh subjected themselves voluntarily in olden times and sometimes even now, to show their bravery before others, proves that when circumstances demand it, a Kolosh is capable of anything. In short, we will only say that with these qualities and skill in using firearms, which are smuggled in freely by foreign ships, hostile Kolosh can be determined and dangerous enemies.

We wrote above in the review of the colonial missionary work about the extent of Christian influence among the converted Kolosh. It remains here to describe the religious beliefs of the non-Christian Kolosh. The most important of these includes a belief that everything on earth has been created by a mythical Elia, or Man-Raven, and a belief in the shamans teachings that good and evil spirits are the intermediaries between the Supreme Being and men. Veniaminov writes in his notes on these natives[31] that the story of Elia, known not only to the Kolosh but to other American tribes as well, repeats biblical events corrupted by fiction. A legend about Kanuk or Man-Wolf, who is older and more powerful than Elia, also plays an important part in Kolosh beliefs and justifies the Wolf tribe's claim of importance.

The shamans greatly influence their countrymen even now. Their importance gradually weakens, however, when our medicines prove superior over the magic and incantations of the shamans in case of sickness. The Kolosh are asking for medical help more often now than formerly. This change in their attitude, replacing their former determination to reject everything offered by Europeans gives hope that shamanism will be weakened gradually even if it does not completely disappear in the near future.

At birth a Kolosh is usually given two names: one chosen from his mother's family and the other from his father's. The name day is always accompanied by a big feast. Some Kolosh, mostly the rich, have several wives, who are always taken from among the women of some other clan. Their marriages are devoid of any ceremony. Russian marriages seem strange and funny to them, remarks Veniaminov.[32] Thus, even the baptized Kolosh seldom worry about church weddings.

Dead Kolosh, if they were prominent in life, are cremated with all possible solemnity, but the bodies of dead slaves are unceremoniously thrown on the beach or in some other place. If the dead tribesman was prominent, the Kolosh would either kill one or two slaves to serve the deceased in the life after death, or would free them. Some of the Kolosh tribes now let the company ransom the slaves thus condemned to death, but the Kolosh themselves free slaves during some other important celebrations. A male slave costs sixty blankets, plus other goods amounting to one hundred paper rubles. A female slave costs only forty blankets plus seventy-five rubles worth of other goods. The Kolosh measure their prosperity by the number of slaves they own, acquiring them from their countrymen in war or by purchase.

Feasts of various kinds are frequent among the Kolosh, particularly among the well-to-do, and are accompanied by singing, dancing, and eating. At dances and when going to war the Kolosh use masks and various ornaments, paint their faces with soot, etc., trying to look particularly frightful. A Kolosh of means wants everybody to know that he is hospitable, sometimes spending most of what he has for entertainment. Due to the rivalry between hostile tribes their feasts sometimes have the most tragic endings. It would be wrong, simply on the basis of the Kolosh passion for feasts, or their ancient custom of treating their countrymen to free food, to judge them as profligate. The opposite would be truer, and the main reason for their wild spending is either vanity or fear of losing their standing among their tribesmen.

Admittedly the mental faculties of the Kolosh and their aptitude for any kind of work far surpasses that of the other tribes living in the Russian possessions in America and on the islands in the Eastern Ocean. Among their handicrafts, their boats hollowed out of a single log, their ornaments and carvings on wood and slate and household utensils, and their other things woven from roots of young fir trees or from cedar bark are remarkable. They are apt traders and in this and at home their women help them greatly, losing no opportunity to profit from the smallest transactions.

The food of the Kolosh consists of dried and fresh fish; the fat and meat of sea and land animals; various birds; clams; sea cabbage; fresh, dried, and leavened berries; potatoes; and roots. They buy bread, molasses, and various cereals eagerly, but only as a delicacy to supplement their usual diet. They like tea and sugar very much but do not buy it, especially the tea. Tobacco, as with all savages, is their first necessity. They are particularly fond of alcohol. For making clothes, they buy from the company cotton prints, woolen blankets of various colors, red woolen cloth, and cotton kerchiefs. They buy ready-made European clothes, hardware, cast-iron kettles, mirrors, vermilion paint, and mother-of-pearl buttons.

Their dwellings [*barabora*] consist of log sheds, partitioned in compartments when housing several families. The fire is usually built in the middle of the floor. No furniture is used in these dwellings except chests owned by the well-to-do.

The Kolosh at Yakutat are identical in every way with the Kolosh living on the islands of Vancouver. The Ugalentsi and Copper River natives, although they belong to the same tribe and are similar in their mode of life, beliefs, and legends, are much more peaceable and not as treacherous as the Yakutat natives. The Ugalentsi and Yakutat natives are related. The Ugalentsi come to Konstantinovskii redoubt to trade with the company. Caribou hunting is the main occupation of the Copper River natives and failure to secure enough caribou meat reduces them to the most pitiful condition—sometimes even to death from starvation, as in 1828 when about one hundred of them died from famine. Some of the Kolchani who live nearby trade with the Copper River and Kenai natives.

The more distant Kolchani and the Tundra Kolosh are known only by rumor. It is said that some of them are very warlike and ferocious and that some even practice cannibalism.

At present only the natives of Yakutat and L'tua Bays hunt sea otters, because there are more otters there than in other places along the northwest coast of America. The early spring before the fishing season begins is the best time for hunting. About then the Kolosh gather from their villages in a certain place and from there hunting parties, sometimes over one hundred boats, start for the hunting grounds. The natives of Yakutat and L'tua Bays allow only their relatives and the most prominent toions from the villages in Vancouver Straits, where there are but few sea otters, to take part in the hunting. Like the Aleuts, the Kolosh make a circle around a herd of sea otters but do not kill them with arrows as the Aleuts do, but by shooting. The Kolosh from Sitkha obtain a few sea otters near the sulphur springs and at Cape Edgecombe.

Before hunting sea otters, the Kolosh, particularly those from Yakutat and L'tua, follow certain customs. They believe that their success in hunting depends upon strict observance of these customs.[33]

Two months before the hunters are to start, while the moon is full, they take up a collection and hire a shaman who forecasts whether the hunting will be good or not and if they will all return home safely. The shaman keeps a strict fast for eight days, eating not more than once a day and drinking quantities of sea water before eating another meal so that the new food will not mix with that eaten before. Fresh fish, sea cabbage, crabs, and other shell fish are prohibited not only for him, but to all other hunters as well, and they believe that failure and even danger to hunters' lives may follow if these rules are not obeyed. During this fast, the shaman and hunters live apart from their wives.

On the eighth day the hunters all gather in one barabora in the middle of the floor where a fire is lighted. The shaman enters and begins to walk slowly around the fire and everyone present must touch him with his hand. After that the shaman starts to perform his rites and prognostications. In order not to lose presents, the shaman usually predicts good luck. Even if his prediction does not come true, he keeps the presents or at least half of them because he attributes bad luck in hunting or misfortunes which befall the hunters to their not keeping strictly the rules of abstinence. In case of an unsuccessful hunt half of what was given to the shaman may be taken back, but only if the hunters return within twenty days. If they remain away longer, the shaman has ownership of everything that was given to him. Sometimes, bad luck is blamed on the hunters' wives for their alleged failure to obey the rule of temperance, etc. In case of accident, as when a hunter is wounded by another, not only the guilty but his wife's relatives are held responsible.

The hunters and their wives dress in clean underclothes, and blankets or mantles made of skins and do not change them until their return. Washing clothes during sea otter hunting is strictly forbidden to men and women and any deviation from this rule can bring very bad luck.

Formerly, the Kolosh traded in two channels: one was trade with the southern Kolosh tribes such as the Kaigantsi, and the other was with the natives of the Queen Charlotte Islands. From them they procured most of their slaves. The slaves were captured by the southern tribes during their raids in Columbia and Oregon. While purchasing slaves, the Kolosh bartered various goods from the English who lived there. They also disposed of their furs by bartering them to the Russian colonial management at New Archangel where the Kolosh from Sitkha were the usual intermediaries. An active competition and sometimes trickery by Hudson's Bay Company employees have been the main reasons why the Kolosh have not sold any sea otters to our company in recent years. In their travels in the straits, the Hudson's Bay Company employees spread rumors that the Russians had authorized them to buy the furs from the Kolosh, or paid them much more than our set price. Sometimes they supplied them with goods prohibited by the agreement between the two companies, such as alcoholic beverages, firearms, lead, powder, and knives of the dagger type. It also happened that the English bartered goods that the Russians did not have available: earthenware, and blankets of the lowest grade and price. They could of course give more of these goods for a sea-otter pelt. As far as the other furs are concerned, the Hudson's Bay Company did not pay higher than the Russians and sometimes they paid less. For instance, one blanket was bartered for two beavers or ten sables [martens], or four cross or red foxes, or one black-brown fox, or five lynx.

The Kenai natives also belong to the Kolosh tribe. The legends of their origin, customs, mode of life, etc., often resemble those of the Kolosh. At the same time they are different in nature and disposition. All Kenai natives around Kenai Bay are Christians and are gradually forgetting their old beliefs, which live on only among a few old men who cannot forget the old delusions. The "Kenai natives live in worse conditions than the Aleuts," writes Golovin in his travel notes,[34] "but have more energy, and move faster. Their dress shows that they are hunters of land animals. They are like one of the American Indians seen in pictures. They wear their hair long, tying it as our women do in a thick bun on the napes of their necks. This hairdress and a skin shirt (parka) makes it difficult to distinguish a young boy from a girl and I was very astonished when a toion in introducing his family to me said that these were his sons, while I thought all the time they were his daughters." The Kenai natives barter with the natives of the interior and receive sables sewn into mantles or parkas. Fairs are held for this purpose in several places on the mainland. Natives gather there from far away places and barter their furs for Russian goods. For this purpose a company employee accompanied by the Kenai natives is sent there from Nikolaevskii redoubt.

The Chugach natives, living around Chugach Bay northeast of Kenai Bay, are of the same origin as the natives of Kad'iak, but, being related by intermarriage to the Kolosh from Yakutat, resemble them in appearance. They believe that they are the descendants of the dog, not of the wolf or raven like the Kolosh, and some believe they migrated from Kad'iak Island during the tribal wars in the middle of the past century. Their legends are very like those of the Kad'iak natives and their language, being of the same origin, seems to confirm this belief. On the other hand there is so much difference between their dialects that they can hardly understand one another. Their clothes differ from clothes worn by the natives on the mainland. Instead of being dressed in deerskins, the Chugach make parkas like those which the Aleuts make of bird skins, and kamleis [rain shirts] made of sea-animal intestines.

They are by nature peaceable, just like the islanders, but probably because of intermarriage with the Kolosh they are more ambitious than the islanders and require careful handling. Their dwellings are not distinguished by cleanliness. As Golovin writes: "Upon entering one of the Chugach huts we had to leave it at once—dizzy from a strong fishy smell pervading everything. One more minute there would have made me sick, but the Chugach seem to be unaffected by this smell—they are all saturated with it."[35]

Part of the American continent to the north and to the west from Kenai Bay is inhabited by peoples also belonging to the Kad'iak stock—meaning that is, to those who came from the north, as the legends of these peoples tell us.[36] It is still uncertain, however, to which of the two main races, Mongoloid or Greenland, they belong. Their language also is similar to that of the people of Kad'iak, which in turn is identical to the language of the sedentary Chukchi living on the Asiatic shore across Bering Strait,[37] and similar to the language of the Eskimos. At the same time, all the dialects of the North American natives differ more or less from the Kad'iak language, which is considered the basic language.

Various tribes, or rather, various branches inhabiting the northern part of the American continent are distributed as follows: Aglemiuts on the shores of Bristol bay; Kuskokvim natives along the Kuskokvim River; Magmiuts between Capes Avinov and Rumiantsov; Agul'miuts from the latter cape up to the central estuaries of the Kvikhpak River; Aziagmiuts from there to the Shakhtolik River and around redoubt Sv. Mikhail; Malemiuts from this river up to Kotzebue Sound and farther; and Ingeliks and Ingalits along the Kvikhpak and Kuiuk rivers.

Vasil'ev and Zagoskin found some similarity in the features of the natives living in the southern part of Norton Sound to the features of the Chukchi and Kamchadals. At the same time, they notice that the latter move and walk quicker than the Aleuts. "But," writes Zagoskin,[38] "like the natives of the interior, these people have straight or aquiline noses, high foreheads, and eyes set only at a slight angle. They are taller and more slender than the Aleuts."

The faces of the Kuskokvim and Kvikhpak men are puffy, but Zagoskin thinks they look better than their women. The latter can boast of white skin which is not unlike the skin on Caucasians, but have prominent cheekbones and flattened noses. Some have blond and even red hair. Some of the men wear beards and mustaches, but either shave their heads or closely crop their hair. Both men and women wear various ornaments in their noses and below their lower lips and have tattoo marks on their chins.

The other tribes resemble in their general characteristics those mentioned above, depending upon the region and distance separating them and differ very little in customs and mode of life. (In the 1780s, says Zagoskin, when the first Russians met them, all the tribes were living in the same places which they now occupy.) Presumably, however, that in olden times many of the now separate tribes in this part of the mainland were one people which became disunited because of various circumstances. They gradually lost their ethnic unity by intermarrying with their new neighbors of a different race, but never absorbed completely all the characteristics of this race. For instance, the Aziagmiuts are probably a mixture of Kalemiuts and Ingcliks or perhaps belong only to the former, who for some reason were forced to leave their birthplace. Zagoskin found no difference between the Agul'miuts and Magmiuts, living on the coast of the Bering Sea from the mouth of Kuskokvim River up to one of the central branches of the Kvikhpak, and the Kvikhpak natives. Their resemblance seemed so great to him that hc named both branches Agul'miuts. The natives on the Kuskokvim and Kvikhpak rivers are also very similar. Because of this similarity, we will speak of all the natives in this region as one unit, pointing out at the same time the differences existing between some branches.

In an economic sense, the natives of the northern mainland have in some respects a considerable advantage over the Aleuts. Zagoskin writes that the Kuskokvim River natives possess a high degree of staunchness and paticnce for work.[39] All these natives are sedentary. Every family has a separate household and both man and wife work for mutual welfare. "But there are black sheep in most of the families," remarks Zagoskin, "the lazy are kept by the industrious but are scorned by them."

Every village has a community building called the kazhim, corresponding in size to the village and sometimes accommodating up to five hundred people. Men hold their councils and sleep there at night. The old men, women, and children remain in their yurts.

The winter dwellings of the Kvikhpak and Kuskokvim river natives are better than those of the coastal natives, probably because of the abundant wood and dry ground. The winter hut differs from the summer hut in being set in a hole in the ground. Posts are then put in, and walls of hewn slabs. The summer hut is built on the surface without excavation. The walls of the winter hut are covered with earth in pyramid shape, with an opening on top which has a small frame with sea animal gut stretched across to give light. In a summer hut, the windows are made in the walls. A narrow underground tunnel closed by a palisade serves as an entrance to the winter dwelling. Benches along the wall take the place of furniture. Provisions are stored about ten feet above ground to protect them from dogs and other animals.

Household implements and untensils of the Kvikhpak natives are nicely finished and clean. The natives of several villages along the Kvikhpak and Kuskokvim are very skillful in carrying and in making various knick-knacks and masks used at dances. The coastal natives do not use such masks and only paint their faces with graphite or charcoal during religious ceremonies.

Most of the natives in this region, as we stated above, have become Chirstians.[40] Among those who have not been converted, the shamans have great influence as intermediaries between men and good and bad spirits. "There are traces of idolatry among the natives on the Kuskokvim and Kvikhpak rivers" remarks Zagoskin. "Evidence can be seen in their dance masks, in the dummies or dolls which they honor in place of people who are absent and which are paid homage, and finally in the special ceremony which the natives celebrate in their own villages without inviting guests from neighboring villages." The essential part of this ceremony or rite is a sacrifice before the idols and a ritual dance. After this ceremony, the natives hide the idols in a sacred place until the ceremony is repeated. The old natives say that even their fathers did not know when these idols were made.

The shamans are so highly esteemed by the Kvikhpak and Kuskokvim natives that they consider it an honor for a girl to belong to a shaman before her marriage. This fact alone gives her a right to attend religious celebrations thereafter.

Non-Christian natives bury their dead, with knees flexed, in four-cornered boxes. These boxes are set on posts about five feet above the ground. The deceased's occupation is depicted on one side of the box. The coastal natives cremate some of their dead or just pile wood over them after they are taken to the burial grounds. There are no special marriage ceremonies, and polygamy is rare. The coastal natives do not practice it. Most of the natives are good family men and divorces are very rare. Parents are very tender with their children, who have absolute freedom but are trained from infancy to follow occupations suitable to their sex. These natives eat the same food as the Kolosh.

Natives living in wooden regions hunt and trap beavers, muskrats, river otters, sables, bears, foxes, mink, and caribou; they also catch fish in the rivers and lakes. Natives living on the barren seashores hunt and trap foxes, mink, caribou, and sea animals, including hair seals and *makliaki*, a large species of hair seal. In addition, they fish in the rivers and sea and hunt beluga. The Aglemiuts also hunt walruses. Many undertake long trading journeys, in summer traveling in baidarkas, and in winter with dog teams. They trade not only with our redoubts and trading posts but with other native tribes as well, even with the Chukchi. The Malemiuts are considered to be the most enterprising. They barter furs from other tribes and sell them to the Chukchi and to foreign ships. All of these natives wear clothes made from the skins of fur-bearing animals or caribou. They make waterproof clothes from the intestines of sea animals and bears. Thus, they buy very few manufactured goods from the company, limiting their purchases to a few prints and kerchiefs; and hardware such as knives, kettles, hatchets, and iron and copper wire for making bracelets, needles, and beads. Russian tobacco is in great demand and is highly valued by the natives. Firearms have appeared lately in great numbers among the Malemiuts, Ingeliks, Aziagmiuts, Kuiukans, and also the Kenai and Copper River natives. They procure these from the English possessions. The Malemiuts provide the main supply to other natives, since they barter powder, lead, rifles, and alcohol from the foreigners engaged in contraband trade.

Natives of Nunivok and Ukivok should be included with the natives of the northern part of the American mainland. Nunivok Island lies northwest of Bristol Sound and is separated from the mainland by Cook's Strait. Ukivok Island is northwest of Norton Sound and south of Cape Spencer. Both of these islands are barren. The shores of Ukivok are steep and rocky, and near the shore the water is deep. On Nunivok live up to four hundred inhabitants of both sexes, in sixteen known villages. On Ukivok there are about two hundred inhabitants. (These natives, being independent of the company, are not entered in the data on colonial population.) The natives on Nunivok Island do not do much hunting and trapping of fur-bearing animals although there are many foxes on this island. Their main occupation is hunting large hair seals, or makhaki, walrus, and caribou, and catching fish offshore. These islanders lead a sedentary life, coming to the mainland in the summer to barter sealskin blubber, and a few foxes for tobacco from the local natives. They know very little about cloth and do not use it for clothing.

The natives of Ukivok Island are just as enterprising in trade as the Malemiuts and make long journeys along the American coast and to Asia. Without this barter it would be difficult for them to survive on a barren island. Only walrus are killed here and a very few other sea animals and fish, so the islanders have to buy dried fish on the mainland. They buy only manufactured goods that are strictly necessary for home use. They also buy beads, but their favorite barter is for firearms and alcohol.

In concluding this information on the natives of the northern part of American, we must mention the natives living north of Kotzebue Sound. This information is taken from the report of an expedition sent out by the company under Lieutenant of the Corps of Naval Navigators Kashevarov.[41]

At latitude 56° 30′ N. there is a native village called Kavaliagmiuts, who were very hostile to the expedition. On the Ukutak River, which flows at latitude 70° N. into a long lake, is the village of Utakagmiut. The language of the inhabitants according to Kashevarov, is similar to that of the Aglemiuts. On the north side of Icy Cape is a village called Kaiakshivigmiut, whose inhabitants were friendly toward the expedition. The natives in the village of Kilamytakagmiut, at latitude 63° 33′, were hostile to the Kakligmiuts who live near the Arctic Ocean and warned the expedition against them. Kashevarov found the inhabitants of a large village in Tutagvak Bay particularly hostile. The first Kakligmiut village is on Cape Belcher. According to one of the toions of this tribe, beyond Point Barrow on the shores of the Arctic Ocean, the natives lived on the coast only during summer and moved onto the tundra in the fall toward their winter quarters. (He said that the farther one went along the coast the wilder they were, and they would attack anybody.) On Cape Smith is a large village of the Utkiagvigmiuts. The hostility of the natives was confirmed during Kashevarov's journey farther east. The inhabitants of the large village of Nugmiut and other places were ready to attack, forcing the expedition to turn back.

The Aleuts and their life today. The natives of the Aleutian Islands differ considerably in appearance from those living on the mainland. Continuous life on the sea, in a narrow baidarka, makes the Aleut clumsy on land. Constant rowing develops the upper part of his body disproportionately to the lower part, which is always immobile in the narrow hatch of a baidarka. All his movements and even his walk are different and seem clumsy to people raised on land. But on the sea, and especially while hunting sea animals, the most experienced hunter and trapper on land cannot compete with the Aleut in dexterity or resourcefulness. Surrounded sometimes by several hundred sea lions or walrus, an Aleut bravely blocks their way to the sea, armed only with a club or a spear, or sometimes single handedly attacks a large whale, while the best American whalers start on such a hunt in a whaleboat in parties of at least five men. If an Aleut could throw a harpoon into a whale and then follow it, as is usually done in this kind of hunting, instead of waiting for the wounded whale to be cast ashore, he could probably hold his own in this kind of hunting too. However, owing to its construction a baidarka, so indispensable to him at sea, is not fitted by its construction for whale hunting, and forces him to follow his old way of whaling.

The faces of the Aleuts are of a definite Mongol type—narrow eyes, low forehead, high cheekbones, and straight stiff black hair— are typical to all these islanders. Some of the women are not bad looking though very few have good figures. They seldom have more than three or four children.

With the spread of Christianity on the Aleutian Islands, the native way of life has changed greatly. Almost all of the old superstitions, beliefs, and legends have lost their importance and meaning, and now all the Aleuts and their families assiduously perform their church duties. As for whether they are real Christians or whether their innate obedience and meekness explains their conversion, it should probably be stated that they show a real and sincere interest in religious matters. The more stubborn and stern natives of the Kad'iak archipelago after long waverings gave up superstitions which at the beginning of the 1840s seemed central to their beliefs, not by compulsion, but by their own conviction. The more susceptible and meeker Aleuts embraced Christianity wholeheartedly and with full understanding.[42]

According to the colonial clergy and many persons who have lived among the Aleuts for a long time, these natives are among the best followers of the Orthodox Church. There is so much in the Aleuts' character and customs that serves as a good foundation in assimilating Christianity that all suspicions of hypocrisy and indifference are groundless. Besides Veniaminov's opinion,[43] our well-known writer on the way of life of the Aleuts, N. V. Alekseev, former manager of the Unalashka office, who served in the colonies about thirty-five years, writes in his notes of the islands he managed:

An Aleut is extremely patient even in the hardest circumstances. They never quarrel or fight between themselves and when there are some differences between one family and another, they last only until a whale is killed; then the former antagonists become friends again. When a catch is divided, shares are alloted to those who could not come and take part in the distribution. Sharing what he has with those who are in need often impoverishes an Aleut. He owns his food only when he is taking it home in his baidarka. The moment his boat is beached, he ceases to own his property, especially fish, sea animal meat, etc. Each of his countrymen takes what he wants, and in case this is not done the Aleut himself takes the food to the various huts. It is impossible to convince an Aleut that he has to save for a rainy day. "Yes," he will answer, "you have your land, but God gave us the sea and the day [i.e., the present in which we live]." Is this carelessness or a deeply rooted feeling of obligation toward their fellow men?

As to the Aleuts' performance of religious duties it is noteworthy that when they receive their pay from the company for hunting or other work, they always contribute within the limits of their resources to the chapels in their villages and to the parish churches. They also buy candles, frankincense, and other items necessary for church service, although they are poor. The Aleuts built almost all of the chapels, and many of the objects in them such as vestments, books, and bells were acquired through their donations and contributions. We have described the self-government by toions chosen by common consent.[44] It remains only to add here that all business matters, differences, and disputes are settled among these natives at communal gatherings.

Crime is usually punished with a verbal reprimand of the offender by the company's local manager either in the presence of a toion or privately. Sometimes he is assigned some extra work. There is no corporal punishment, and in all fairness an Aleut never deserves such punishment and could not bear the ignominy.

Except for the carefree quality mentioned above and laziness about continuous work, and Aleut at home possesses many qualities which make him a good family man. A peaceable disposition is his most outstanding characteristic. Fathers love their sons more than their daughters. Mothers love their daughters most. A son learns to help his father in his occupations long before he is of age. At the same time he studies at school and sometimes at home. Daughters help their mothers with housework beginning at an early age.

Aleut dwellings, because of the limited wood supply, lie partly below ground level, while the baraboras of the Kolosh stand above ground. Most Aleut dugouts are well finished inside.[45] Each has one or two windows. Walls and ceiling are faced with planks and painted with white or yellow clay. Some have stoves. Floors are usually present only in the middle of the huts. Along the walls *uruny* (plank beds) are constructed. Each household has a quantity of cast-iron and copper cooking utensils. They have kettles for cooking, tea kettles, some china, glasses, knives and forks, etc. Guns and clothes hang on the walls. European clothes—overcoats, jackets, women's calico dresses, mantles, etc.—

are found together with the native kamlei, parkas, *torbasa* [boots], wooden hats, etc.

Some huts have shelters with a small fireplace on which are two stones. Water for tea, if the Aleut has it, is almost always boiling. Near the dugout is the *labaza*, in which fish are hung to dry, and in which whale, sea lion, and seal meat is kept, along with bladders of oil, fish eggs, and liver, tubs of berries, hides, and kettles for melting blubber. Baidarkas with one and two hatches, with paddles, are kept there, as well as darts, of which the largest has a *maut*, or cord made of whale sinews or walrus hide, half the size of a finger in diameter. The large dart is thrown with a bladder attached to keep it on the surface. There is also fishing tackle and throwing boards which are used for throwing darts at sea otters, other animals, and birds. Next to the *labaza* are piled *tsireli* (woven hats), dry grass, and firewood. Potatoes, other vegetables, and roots are kept underground.

The only poultry the Aleuts keep are chickens, but because they are fed on fish, due to a lack of other food, they are very tough. The natives keep a few hogs, but the meat has a repulsive fishy taste.

The Aleuts are well known for their hospitality, especially if their supply of food is not exhausted and if they do not have to feed themselves and their families at company expense. When some prominent person visits their dugouts they always offer their favorite food, crowberries mixed with fat. The guest must taste this dish, even if he finds its taste repulsive, so as not to offend his host.

The Aleuts work mainly at hunting and trapping sea and land animals and at providing food for their families. In spring the best hunters go great distances to hunt sea lions and seals. This expedition is usually undertaken before making baidarkas ready for future hunting. At the same time the old and middle-aged together with the youngsters catch fish in the sea,[46] repair baidarkas, and build new ones. The Aleut women sew kamlei, parkas, boots [*torbasa*], coverings for baidarkas, and make lines of whale sinews for darts used in sea otter hunting. The old men make arrowheads out of stone, slate, and bone, paddles, wooden hats, and baidarka frames. Many of these objects and implements are painstakingly carved, painted in various colors with ochre, decorated with sea-lion whiskers, feathers, beads, and painted ornaments. The boys help to make the wooden parts, split whalebone, make paint, grease the seal skins and baidarka frames, etc.

The outfitting and dispatching of Aleut sea otter hunting crews. Arrangements for sending Aleut hunting crews on sea otter hunts are made by the Kad'iak office and other agencies as early as the fall, when they return from the previous hunt. After consulting the toions or elders of all the Aleut villages, the managers set the time, usually about the middle of April, when the Aleut hunters are to gather in a certain place. At the same time they order the *baidarshchiks* [village elders] to submit lists of the Aleuts who will participate in the hunt, with their names and the materials they will be able to furnish for outfitting baidarkas and making kamlei. To those natives who have no sealskins or intestines for kamlei, the management issues what they need from company warehouses and sees that everything is made ready for the hunt.

After the hunters gather, the company gives them provisions, consisting usually of iukola, whale meat, and blubber. Fish hooks and lines are also furnished in proportion to the number of baidarkas and men, and several rifles with ammunition for shooting sea lions and seals for food during the voyage. A *partovshchik* [foreman] is appointed to oversee distribution of provisions, etc., during the hunt. Besides these provisions, the partovshchik also receives 7½ pounds of flour and 1½ pounds of leaf tobacco for each man in the crew and, if the Aleuts prefer it, tea and sugar instead of wine, which is given to them at the start of the hunt.

When the crew is outfitted, the partovshchik gets instructions from the office as to how the crew will hunt at the appointed place, the procedure for issuance of provisions, and the way to keep a journal during the voyage, entering in it daily the party's position, weather conditions, the number of good hunting days, and the number of sea otters killed.[47] After these preliminaries, the crew receives orders to sail on a certain day, depending upon the weather. If, for instance, the gathering place chosen was Paul's Harbor, on the morning of the day set for sailing from 80 to 100 baidarkas[48] are lined in the strait, their bows touching the shore. A priest is invited to pray for the expedition's success and to sanctify the water in the lagoon. After the service, the Aleuts kiss the cross, the priest sprinkles them with holy water, and they man the baidarkas. After that the crew begins to paddle out of the harbor, firing a salute from their guns to the company's flag, to which the fort's cannons answer with three shots.

In addition to what we have already written about sea otter hunting,[49] we should add that the hunters paddle sometimes up to forty versts offshore. The moment one of them sees a sea otter, he quickly paddles to the spot where it dived and lifts his paddle upright. After that he does not move. All the crew, which until then was moving in a line, keeping such a distance between the boats that a sea otter can be seen, form a circle around the baidarka with the hunter who raised his paddle. He moves then to a place where he expects the sea otter to surface.[50] When it appears, the hunter throws darts at it. The first seldom takes effect. The sea otter disappears again and the hunters narrow the circle made by their baidarka. The sea otter dives and comes to the surface more often. Darts fly from all sides and finally the exhausted and wounded animal becomes the prey of the hunter whose dart struck nearest to its head.[51]

About the middle of August, the Kad'iak crew returns to Paul's Harbor. The foreman at once makes a detailed report to the office with a list of acquired pelts, which, if the weather permits, are retained for a day or two by the hunters for drying. After that the pelts are brought to the warehouse to the manager. The latter makes a record of the hunters' names, the number of pelts brought by each one, and their grade. Sea otter skins are dried without being cut open.

After the furs are accepted, the manager pays the Aleuts at set prices[52] and at the same time gives orders to issue the required goods and supplies from the warehouses into the store.

The main purchases of the Aleuts are manufactured goods, such as, prints, grey and blue calico, blue fustian, white flannel blankets, cotton kerchiefs, snuff boxes, cheap earrings, crosses, leaf tobacco, powder, and lead. The Aleuts also buy other trifles which are not really necessary for them. Well-to-do Aleut hunters first of all supply their families, and no matter how little money they receive for furs they buy prints for dresses or kerchiefs for their wives, then something for the children, etc. Finally with what remains of their money, they purchase some tea and sugar, and if even some money is left, they buy other goods, never forgetting to leave something for church services, especially if a christening, marriage, etc., is expected in the family.

Selling to the Aleuts always takes a long time because they hesitate a great deal in choosing what they want. Of course some have to hesitate because of bad luck in hunting. Some unfortunates do not have a single sea otter pelt to their credit. Their entire income consists of pay by the company for the use of their baidarkas while hunting, and this only if they did not have to use seal skins belonging to the company. In such a case the luckier hunters often give the poor man the skin of a small sea otter and sometimes even a large one. Unlucky hunters usually stay voluntarily in the harbor and get work in the fall. The average Aleut's income from sea otter hunting amounts to forty silver rubles for the season.

After all accounts are settled, the toions are treated at company expense, and a council is held concerning sea otter hunting the following year and the dispatching of parties of fox trappers during the coming fall.[53]

Bird hunting. After the crew leaves to hunt sea otter, the Kad'iak office dispatches another crew to hunt sea birds: murres, tufted puffins, cormorants, and horned puffins, whose skins are used for making parkas, in former times worn by all Aleuts.[54] Large crews used to be sent out, but after smallpox reduced the population on Kad'iak Island, and when the Aleuts began to wear European clothes, the demand for parkas declined, and now the crews hunting birds are only half as large as formerly.

At present, only a few men from each village are sent out for this purpose, mostly old men or men unfit for other work, with not over twenty men to a party. A company baidara and two or three baidarkas take them to the hunting grounds. These are chosen either near the the former Sutkhum odinochka, on the Aliaska Peninsula, or on the Peregrebnyi Islands and in Kenai Bay.[55] The management supplies this expedition with provisions for three months according to the number of men taking part, and outfits them on the same line as the sea otter hunting crews.

The birds are caught in snares, made from pieces of whalebone issued to the hunters. When they arrive at the place where they will hunt birds, the Aleuts tear the whalebone in thin strips not heavier than a horse's hair, make snares of these strips, and set them on rocks where the birds are. When they reach for bait—a branch of berries or something else—the birds are caught, and in trying to get away choke to death.

Every Aleut leaving with the bird crew has to furnish the company with enough birds to make from five to ten parkas—each parka requiring forty birds. He is paid six kopeks in paper money per bird and has a right to catch enough birds to make two to three parkas for himself. But because this party is sent under the supervision of a steersman who is also an Aleut, the hunters often bring fewer birds for the company, keeping enough for the parkas to which they have a right.

The company pays seventy-five kopeks silver for tanning and sewing enough skins to make one parka. These are issued to Aleuts who remain temporarily in the harbor for work or in other places in the Kad'iak district. The surplus is given to trappers as part of the outfit furnished to them by the company at a price of six paper rubles apiece.[56]

After the crews sent to catch sea birds return, the Aleuts are paid for birds they have taken and for the use of their baidarkas if some were privately owned. The bird hunting crews trade for goods in the same manner as the sea otter hunting crew.

Trapping foxes and otters. Plans for trapping foxes and otters are made beforehand after consulting the toions. In the fall, after the return of a sea otter hunting crew, the office confirms these plans and outfits the trappers with parts for making traps.[57] It also supplies them with provisions and issues one and a half pounds of tobacco per man, two strips of skins from sea lion throats for making *torbasa* [boots], two pairs of soles, and a glass of vodka after the trapping is over. The men are placed on trapping grounds belonging to various villages and build dugouts for their living quarters. After locating fox and otter trails they set the traps and begin trapping in the middle of October. There are usually two or three men living in every dugout during the trapping season who examine the traps every day. Trapping requires much attention. The traps must be made correctly in every detail and must be in perfect shape, or nothing will be caught. A good trapper has ten to twelve traps and examines them twice each day. Only thus can he hope for success.

The length of the trapping season depends entirely upon the weather. A long and dry fall is the best for trapping foxes and otters. Rainy days followed by frost are harmful because the sinew used as springs in the traps gets wet, freezes, breaks, and must be replaced. An early deep snow and blizzards make trapping impossible. Trapping is continued sometimes until the middle of December. In unfavorable years it lasts only until November.

In former years when there were more men and more fur-bearing animals on Kad'iak Island, a party of hunters was dispatched in January or February, independent of the trappers, to shoot foxes. The company furnished guns and ammunition and the hunters shot foxes on the seashore on moonlight nights. Now with only a few good riflemen left and, still more important, because of the declining qualities of foxes,[58] this hunting has been almost entirely abandoned. It occurs now only in years when early deep snow makes trapping poor.

Aleut trappers do not all arrive at the harbor at the same time after the trapping is finished, due to weather conditions and distances which they have to travel. Paying them off at set prices and settling accounts continues sometimes until spring.

The Kurile natives. The handful of inhabitants of some of the Kurile Islands are only a very small particle among the other tribes in the Russian possessions. The nomadic Kuriles reside mainly on Shioshkotan Island, from which they come to Ekarmu, Chirinkotan, Kharamukotan, Onnekotan, and Musir islands for their food supplies. Only on Shumshu and Paramushir do several families live in sedentary fashion and breed cattle.

The lack of food on the islands often forces these natives to move from one place to another. The Kuriles do not hunt sea otters offshore in baidarkas the way Aleuts do. The company pays one-fifth of the value of these furs to the Kuriles when the Aleuts hunt sea otters at these islands. In summer the nomadic Kuriles shoot sea otters and in winter catch them with nets. They barter furs to foreign skippers, mostly for alcohol. When catching sea otters with nets, they eat a special diet believing that it brings success.

The natives of the Kurile Islands are tall and well built. Their customs and mode of living are identical to those of their countrymen living on Sakhalin Island.[59] They are very meek and ready to please, but timid, lifeless, and inert. In the winter they live in sod huts, and in summer they mostly live under their baidaras. They eat fish, some roots, and meat and fat of sea animals. With few exceptions, they have no cattle and do not engage in agriculture because of the climate and other unfavorable conditions. Well-to-do Kuriles wear European clothes, and the poor wear parkas of bird feathers and animal fur, but, as Teben'kov remarks, nearly all have linen underwear. Their language is different from the languages of the Kamchadals and Aleuts. Many of the Kuriles in frequent contact with company employees have learned to speak Russian and are adopting European customs.

The creoles. The creoles form a separate group in the native population. They are the result of intermarriage between Eurpoeans and Aleuts and other aborigines of this country. Their descendants will probably predominate over the Aleuts proper and perhaps in the future will completely replace them. They form a class of their own having the same rights as the *meshchanstvo* [townsmen, or lower middle class] in Russia, but the additional advantage of exemption from taxes.

The creoles' duties are limited to an obligation that if they have been educated and raised at company expense, they must remain in the company's employ for ten years. With the Aleuts fast diminishing in number, creoles will have to replace them in all their occupations, especially in the occupation on which their very existence depends, namely, the hunting and trapping of fur-bearing animals. It must be remarked that at present most of the creoles are trying to evade this occupation unless they are given authority over other natives. Most of them give the impression that they are ashamed of their descent, and their main characteristics are sensitivity and irritability in certain situations. All of the creoles have good faculties. Many are employed in company colonial offices and some, mostly after serving for a certain time, are settled and given by the company as previously stated, all necessities for their household, etc. They are known as "colonial citizens."[60]

Data on the native population dependent on the company during its last two charter periods. As is known, the first reliable data on the native population in the colonies, including natives more or less dependant on the company, was submitted in 1817 by Captain Golovnin, who was sent by order of the emperor to investigate the conditions there, and in the company's reports of 1 January 1819.[61] This population, including creoles, amounted to 8,629 persons of both sexes. By 1830, a little over ten years, the number of natives had increased to 9,800; and by 1 January 1837, to almost 10,500. An epidemic of smallpox that raged in the colonies about this time so reduced the native population that reports made at the beginning of the current period—1 January 1842—gave their number as only 6,800. From then on, in spite of the measles epidemic in 1848, which killed three hundred persons, the population of the colonies has increased, and by 1 January 1863, not counting the 1,880 Kuskokvim River natives, Aglemiuts, Chugach, Copper River natives, and other mainland tribes, has reached the figure of 8,000 persons of both sexes. The average number of Russians and Finlanders in company employ during the last 20 years has been about 530 men. With them were about sixty women and children.

The following is a list of all the population in the Russian colonies from 1830 to 1863, taken from the company's annual reports:

Date	Persons of both sexes	Date	Persons of both sexes
1 January 1830	10,327	1 January 1847	7,874
1 January 1831	10,453	1 January 1848	8,707
1 January 1832	10,493	1 January 1849	8,892
1 January 1833	10,800	1 January 1850	9,081
1 January 1834	10,670	1 January 1851	9,273
1 January 1835	10,867	1 January 1852	9,452
1 January 1836	10,989	1 January 1853	9,573
1 January 1837	11,022	1 January 1854	9,514
1 January 1838	10,313	1 January 1855	9,660
1 January 1839	8,070	1 January 1856	9,725
1 January 1840	7,574	1 January 1857	9,792
1 January 1841	7,580	1 January 1858	10,075
1 January 1842	7,470	1 January 1859	9,902
1 January 1843	7,581	1 January 1860	10,121
1 January 1844	7,896	1 January 1861	10,136
1 January 1845	7,224	1 January 1862	10,156
1 January 1846	7,783	1 January 1863	10,125

Some additional remarks on fur seals, sea lions, and walrus. A fur seal is similar to a hair seal. It has powerful front flippers. The hind flippers are joined. A *sekach* or old fur seal, male, has dark-brown fur, and is three to four times larger than the females. It is said that a large sekach weighs up to eighty puds. The sekach and *polu*[semi]-*sekach* [a mature but younger male] differs from a *kholostiak* [bachelor, or male with no females] in having shaggy hair on the upper part of the body. In defining the age of sekachi, it should be remembered that some fur seals even when they are twenty years old or older do not become *sekachi*, while some become sekachi before they are five years old.

The hair of the females is almost the same color as that of the sekachi, but with more red in it. The seal rookeries are on rocky sloping places. Kholostiaki are not as strong as the sekachi and are afraid of them. After their arrival at the seal rookeries, the kholostiaki lay down on special places near those chosen by the sekachi. These stay near the water and while waiting for females, occupy an enormous area of ground. After the females arrive in the middle of May, the sekachi begin to call them. The females gather around them on the beach and form separate families. Strong and alert sekachi sometimes have up to one hundred females; old and weak ones, only one or two. Sometimes the females desert and move from one male to another. In such a case, a fight between rivals ensues and often one of them is killed. The sekachi on the beach are always looking around, afraid of losing their females. The females on the beach give birth to one pup, rarely to two, and until then stay on the shore. Only after giving birth does the mother enter the water, probably with permission of the sekach, for the pup is left in his care. The mothers feed their young only on the beach. They must be at least one month old before they have their first swimming lessons. The mother takes her pup in her teeth, takes it a little way from shore, and throws it into the water. The pup, of course, tries to crawl on the beach, but is thrown again in the water.

Fur seals are usually killed early in the morning when it is colder and the grass is covered with dew, otherwise they tire quickly when they are driven away from shore. After the slaughter is finished, the females bellow for several days trying to find their young. Small seals who have managed somehow to save themselves from the hunters remain the longest on the island. The sekachi sometimes remain also until the ice comes.

Fur seals feed on fish and shellfish. It is said that when they come to the islands too late in the season, the pups are born while the females are in the sea and are lost.

Sea lions. A sea lion's body is covered uniformly with short, stiff hair. They do not have a mane or shaggy hair on their necks, but the hair on their chests and shoulders is only slightly longer than the hair on the rest of their bodies. Their hide is very thick. Their mustaches reach two feet in length, and the hairs are as thick as the base strings of a guitar. The females are smaller than the males, and their hair is of even length everywhere. Sea lions feed on fish and shellfish, as do fur seals. While swimming, they lift their heads and chests high. A sea lion is much stronger than a fur seal, and killing them is dangerous for the hunters so that instead of a club or a spear a gun is almost always used while hunting them. The sea lions are not so attached to the same places on shore as fur seals, but scatter more. If a sea lion sees blood on the beach, it will never return to that place. The sea lions are divided into several grades in the same way as fur seals. Males come to the breeding places in the latter part of March, and the females come later, staying all winter with the young males. The previous year's pups go into the sea. Soon the females return and join the sekachi. It is said that a strong sekach will have up to twenty females in his herd. Pups are born near the water, and after their birth the females move farther up the beach. The bachelors who have returned with the females stay higher on the shore to avoid the jealous old sekachi. After staying with his herd until the middle or the end of July, a sekach goes into the sea. The females remain on the same places until the young sea lions learn to swim and then move to other places nearby. The young males (kholostiaki) gather as before around the females and remain there until the lawful lords and masters return again.

Sea lion intestines are used for making kamlei and baidarka coverings. The meat of young sea lions is used for food. A dish prepared from sea lion flippers (something like gelatin) is considered a delicacy.

Walrus. The walrus has small and short flippers and loose skin. This animal is very clumsy and moves place to place with the help of its tusks, which it sticks in the ground. A walrus skull is stronger but smaller than a sea lion's. Khlebnikov and Veniaminov remark that, according to the hunters, walrus blood is so hot that spears' thrust through the heart become so heated after being given several twists in the wound that the iron bends into a ring. Walrus like to lay on the flats near water. Walrus hide is so thick that it requires special tanning.

Notes

Chapter 1

1. Emperor Peter I ordered the first Northern Sea Expedition (1725-30) to survey the adjacent coasts of Asia and America.

2. According to A. P. Sokolov, the author of the account of Bering's voyage "Severnaia ekspeditsiia 1733-43 gg." [The northern expedition of 1733-43] *Zapiski Gidrogragicheskago departamenta* [Notes of the Hydrographic Department] [St. Petersburg, 1851], ch. 9, the honor of discovering the American coast belongs to Second Navigator Fedorov, commander of one of the vessels of Captain Pavlut-skii's expedition of 1732. The Diomede Islands (in Bering Strait) should bear his name.

3. A. P. Sokolov, ibid.

4. Data on the first voyages to the Aleutian Islands has been taken from V. N. Berkh's *Khronologicheskaia istoriia otkrytiia Aleutskikh ostrovov, ili podvigi Rossiiskago kupechestva* [Chronological History of the discovery of the Aleutian Islands, or the exploits of Russian merchants] (St. Petersburg, 1823) [translation, *A Chronological History of the Discovery of the Aleutian Islands, or The Exploits of Russian Merchants* (The Limestone Press, Kingston, Ontario, 1974)], I. E. Veniaminov, *Zapiski ob ostrovakh Unalashkinskogo otdela* (Notes on the islands of the Unalashka district) (St. Petersburg, 1840), and the archives of the Russian-American Company. [See also R. V. Makarova, *Russkie na Tikhom Okeane vo vtoroi polovine XVIII v.* (Moscow, 1968), translation, *Russians on the Pacific, 1743-1799* (The Limestone Press, Kingston, Ontario, 1975), based on extensive archival research, which adds significantly to what is known of this period.]

5. Bering and Chirikov also saw this island, which Chirikov named Saint Feodor's Island.

6. On 2 March 1766, Empress Catherine II sent the following decree to Chicherin, the governor of Siberia:

> Denis Ivanovich! I have been pleased to read your account of the discovery and submission of six Aleutian islands, previously unknown, as well as a copy of the report by the cossack Vasiutinskii. This acquisition pleases me greatly. I am only sorry that the detailed description and the census books have been lost. I approve your decision to return to the merchant Tolstykh one tenth of the iasak collected from those islands, in accordance with the privileges which I have bestowed upon companies completing such voyages, and I order you to fulfill this promise and also to elevate the cossacks Vasiutinskii and Lazarev to the local nobility so that they may be encouraged. God grant that they

complete happily and successfully the voyage which they are undertaking this spring! I would like to know: Have the inhabitants of those islands told them of any Europeans who had been there, and have they seen any wrecked ships there? . . . .

Her Imperial Majesty added the following to the original in her own hand: "Make it clear to the promyshlenniks that they are to treat their new brothers, the inhabitants of these islands, kindly and without the slightest persecution or deceit." [From *Polnoe sobranie zakonov rossiiskoi imperii* [complete collection of laws of the Russian Empire, hereafter PSZ], 17(1765-66), Law #12,589.]

7. [A. P. Sokolov's negative assessment of Krenitsyn and Levashov's expedition in "Ekspeditsiia k Aleutskim ostrovam Kapitanov Krenitsyna i Levashova (1764-69 gg.) [Captains Krenitsyn and Levashovs' expedition to the Aleutian Islands, 1764-69] *Zapiski* (1852), pp. 70-103, has governed views of this venture until recently. However, a reassessment by I. V. Glushankov, in "Aleutskaia ekspeditsiia Krenitsyn i Levashova," *Priroda* 12(1969): 84-92, translated as "Krenitsyn and Levashov's Aleutian expedition," *Alaska Journal* 3, No. 4 (Autumn 1973): 204-11, shows that there is valuable material in the expedition records.]

8. Shares (*pai*) were of two kinds: investment (*valovoi*) and donative (*sukhovoi*). There were three types of investment shares: (1) those belonging to the promyshlennik and half to the owner (for the latter's vessel and his expenses in outfitting it and the promyshlenniks); (2) those belonging entirely to the owner, who was thereupon bound to pay his promyshlenniks an agreed annual wage; and (3) those belonging entirely to the promyshlennik, in which case the share was said to be given "on landing" (*na skhod*). Donative [*sukhovoi* or "dry (land?)"] shares belonged neither to the owner nor to his worker-promyshlenniks, but were given to the Holy Church or to a sea captain or a company director for his services; or, with the general agreement of the company, they were assigned to useful persons, i.e., those able to influence the course of the undertaking.

9. Data on Shelikhov's voyage are taken from the published journal of the voyage or from his reports to Iakobii, governor-general of Irkutsk. [First published as *Rossiiskago kuptsa Grigor'ia Shelekhova stranstvovanie v 1783 godu....* Journey of the Russian merchant Grigorii Shelekhov in 1783] (St. Petersburg, 1791). In 1793 this was combined with an account by Bocharov and Izmailov of their voyage of 1788 and "An historical and geographical description" compiled from various sources, and published as *Rossiiskago kuptsa imenitago ryl'skago grazhdanina Grigor'ia Shelekhova pervoe stranstvovanie s 1783 po 1787 god iz Okhotska po Vostochnomu okeanu k Amerikanskim beregam. . . .*[The first voyage of the eminent citizen of Ryl'sk, Grigorii Shelekhov, a Russian merchant, in the years 1783 to 1787 from Okhotsk over the Eastern Ocean to the American shores. . . .] (St. Petersburg, 1793), and as *Puteshestvie G. Shelekhova s 1783 po 1790 god iz Okhotska po Vostochnomu Okeanu k Amerikanskim beregam, i vozvrashchenie ego v Rossiiu. . . .* [The voyage of Mr. Shelekhov in the years 1783 to 1790 from Okhotsk over the Eastern Ocean to the American shores and his return to Russia . . . .] (St. Petersburg, 1812). See Avrahm Yarmolinsky, "Shelekhov's voyage to Alaska. A bibliographical note," *New York Public Library Bulletin*, 36(1932): 141-48.]

10. Baidarkas are native canoes, made of sealskins sewn together, with one, two, or three round apertures for oarsmen. Accordingly, they are referred to as one-hatched, two-hatched, and three-hatched. Baidaras, similar to launches, are also made of sewn sealskins. They were introduced into the colonies by the Russians and serve for transport of large numbers of people or heavy cargoes.

11. Many think that this number is exaggerated at least ten-fold, but it is unknown by whom, since the number of Koniagas on the islet is not mentioned

in Shelikhov's reports to Iakobii, and the journal of his voyage was published without his knowledge.

12. Instruction of the Admiralty College to Captain Mulovskii, 17 April 1787.

13. Instruction of the Admiralty College to Captain Billings, who in 1785 was named head of a geographical and astronomical expedition to the northeastern parts of Russia. [For text, see G. A. Sarychev, *Puteshestvie po severo-vostochnoi chasti Sibiri, Ledovitomu moriu, i Vostochnomu okeanu* [Voyage to Northeast Siberia, the Arctic Sea and the Eastern Ocean] (Moscow, 1952), pp. 279-94, and Martin Sauer, *An Account of a Geographical and Astronomical Expedition to the Northern Parts of Russia....* (London, 1802), Appendix, pp. 29-49.]

14. An extract from Iakobii's report of 30 November 1787. [A condensation. For the complete text, see A. I. Andreev, ed. *Russkie otkrytiia v Tikhom Okeane i Severnoi Amerike v XVIII veke* [Russian discoveries in the Pacific Ocean and North America in the eighteenth century] 2d ed. (Moscow, 1948), pp. 250-65. In his quotation, Tikhmenev modernizes the original language and changes the order of certain sentences.]

15. Probably the determination of the iasak to be taken from the Aleuts was based on its collection from Siberian tribes under Russian sovereignty, from whom it was taken in amounts varying for different tribes, depending on local conditions. The seventeenth article of the instruction to Captain Billings stated: "In surveying the islands, shores and capes belonging to the Russian Empire, you will in addition to your responsibility for describing them, find out as truly as possible the number of male inhabitants of these places and establish the basis for the future collection of iasak or tribute from them." On this basis a commission of naval officers and officials was appointed during the expedition's sojourn at Unalashka in 1791 and was charged with carrying out the instruction relating to the collection of iasak from the Aleuts. "The Aleuts," wrote Sarychev, "readily agreed to pay iasak and promised, after winter had set in, to bring it both for themselves and for all who were able to trap animals; moreover, they undertook this payment of their own free will. Heretofore the iasak had been imposed on each settlement on two or three men selected by their fellow trappers and called tribute payers [*iasashnymi*]." G. A. Sarychev, *Puteshestvie*, pt. 2, p. 123 [in 1952 edition, p. 195].

16. [Evidently an error by Tikhmenev. Instead of latitude 49-60° and longitude 53-63°, the text given by A. I. Andreev, *Russkie otkrytiia*, p. 259, indicates latitude 15° to 65° and longitude 40° to 73° *reckoned from Okhotsk*. The thirty-three degrees of longitude would encompass the Fox Islands, the Alaska Peninsula, and territory eastward almost to Mt. St. Elias. The 15° latitude may be an error in the original; perhaps 51° was meant.]

17. [Agaekhtalik in Andreev, *Russkie otkrytiia*, p. 260.

18. [Report, governor-general of Irkutsk, Iakobii, to empress, 30 November 1787, in Andreev, *Russkie otkrytiia*, pp. 259-61. Tikhmenev's "extract" has been revised and corrected.]

19. Report of the College of Commerce, March 1788. [Full text in Andreev, *Russkie otkrytiia*, pp. 269-79. Tikhmenev's quotations differ from the document in Andreev.]

20. Veniaminov, in his *Zapiski*, pt. 2, pp. 187-94, describes the excesses of the Russian traders in the Fox Islands:

When Glotov returned from Kad'iak to Umnak Island, instead of the friendship with which he had parted from the Umnak Islanders, he encountered hostility and for this reason he brought them fire and sword, rather than peace and amity. Partly because of their insubordination, he destroyed all of the settlements along the south side of Umnak and on the islands of the Four Mountains and Samalga, leaving hardly a trace. When Solov'ev arrived at Unalashka from Kamchatka and lay at anchor in Koshiga Bay, be behaved with great brutality toward the poor Aleuts, also under the pretext of avenging the death of other Russians. Natrubin, a comrade and worthy disciple of Solov'ev, slaughtered unarmed and often guiltless Aleuts on Avatanak Island. When the Russians returned in the years 1770 to 1790 and saw how their predecessors had treated the islanders, they too sometimes committed extremes of cruelty, especially the parties of Ocheredin and Polutov.

21. [See letter, 4 September 1788, Bezborodko to Viazemskii, in Andreev, *Russkie otkrytiia*, pp. 283-84, regarding the empress' decision to issue the citations, *Senate ukaz*, 28 September 1788, in Andreev, ibid., pp. 284-85, and citation text, 11 October 1788, to be published in P. A. Tikhmenev, *Documents on Russian America*, hereafter referred to as Tikhmenev, *Documents*, no. 4a.]

22. Shelikhov's reports to the acting governor-general of Irkutsk and Kolyvan, Pil, and the latter's reports to the empress. [See Andreev, *Russkie otkrytiia*, p. 289 ff.]

23. [For journal of Izmailov and Bocharov's voyage of 1788, see second part of Shelikhov's *Puteshestvie*.]

24. Here we reproduce a few words from Governor-General Pil's report to the empress concerning the activities of Shelikhov's company, dated 14 February 1790. [For complete text, dated 13 February, see Andreev, *Russkie otkrytiia*, pp. 295-304]:

The two noted merchants Shelikhov and Golikov, who are already known to Your Majesty through their unceasing efforts in behalf of the State, have again shown their zeal on your behalf by pursuing their occupation in North America at their own risk and expense and by successfully navigating those waters in ships they themselves have built. For this reason I am sending Your Imperial Majesty two descriptions of this voyage, a map and four plans. The first is an account of a voyage along the coast of America, and the second is a description of this new part of the world, including the inlets and bays therein and the native tribes. Special plans indicate the places where my predecessor placed emblems of your Empire.

I must also point out to Your Majesty the praiseworthy behavior of the explorers toward the natives, in accord with Shelikhov's wise instructions. Shelikhov's company also conscientiously placed in appropriate places the markers entrusted to them by the government.

This company's devotion to the welfare of the pagan American tribes and its efforts to establish peaceful relations with them oblige me to mention also that these means are now being pursued solely through the zeal of this company, for, thus placing your Majesty's interests higher than their own, they furnish an example to their countrymen in similar pursuits and are obtaining for Russia greater riches than any so far brought from America.

I must conclude that the sums obtained from the imposition of iasak are not as important as the establishment of the rights of Your Majesty's Empire, *for last year, which was the first, your treasury received from this company no more than 3,500 rubles* [stressed phrase omitted by Tikhmenev, included in Andreev, *Russkie otkrytiia*, p. 299]. And since the above-mentioned map actually proves that your subjects have sailed from Kad'iak Island southeast to a latitude between 57 and 59 degrees, I am confident that the many islands which they have discovered off the coast of America and the two harbors which they have found (which rank with those previously known at Kad'iak and Chugach Bay) will justify my hopes.

25. In those times the word "company" was used not only in its modern sense but also to indicate a loose association of traders [*promyshlenye*] who carried on their occupation together.

26. Probably on the shores of Kenai and Chugach Bays. Unfortunately data on Delarov's term as manager of the company settlements does not include exact locations where forts were built, and deals with other matters quite superficially.

27. Their only settlement in Nootka Sound was destroyed according to the terms of the Spanish-English treaty of 1790.

28. Kolosh: the term for the tribe living from Yakutat Bay to latitude 52°. All of the Kolosh have the same customs and ways, but their language, especially those living some distance from one another, are quite different.

29. [See letter, Baranov to Shelikhov and Polevoi, from Pavlovsk Harbor, 20 May 1795, Tikhmenev, *Documents*, no. 18.]

30. [Cf. ibid. The passage in the text does not appear in the reference to Vancouver's ships in this letter; it may be from another document.]

31. [PSZ, vol. 23, #17,171, 21 December 1793.]

32. [First letter, Shelikhov and Polevoi to Baranov, from Okhotsk, 9 August 1794, in Andreev, *Russkie otkrytiia*, p. 337.]

33. [Second letter, Shelikhov and Polevoi to Baranov, from Okhotsk, 9 August 1794, Tikhmenev, *Documents*, no. 17.|

34. [Report, Shelikhov to Governor-General of Irkutsk Pil, 18 November 1794, in Andreev, *Russkie otkrytiia*, p. 362.]

35. [Ibid.]

36. [Ibid., pp. 365-68.]

37. [Report, Governor-General of Irkutsk Pil, to empress, 20 November 1794, in Andreev, *Russkie otkrytiia*, pp. 373-74.]

Chapter 2

1. From letter, Shelikhov to Baranov, 9 August 1794 [given in full in A. I. Andreev, *Russkie otkrytiia v Tikhom Okeane: Severnoi Amerike v XVIII veke* (Russian discoveries in the Pacific Ocean and North America in the eighteenth century) (Moscow, 1948), pp. 336-53.]

2. [Tikhmenev, *Documents*, no. 19, Archimandrite Iosaf to Shelikhov, from Kad'iak Island, 18 May 1795, which states: "Zaikov told me that Baranov incited the Chugach to massacre his party."]

3. This was probably Tlikh [Kruzof] Island, one of the inlets of which was called Krestovskaia [Cross] Bay.

4. "Barabora" is the local term for a hut, usually built without stones, with a large opening in the roof. The front is covered with thin planks. The other sides usually consist of staves bound together with tree bark.

5. [K. T. Khlebnikov, *Zhizneopisanie Aleksandra Andreevicha Baranova, Glavnago pravitelia Rossiiskikh kolonii v Amerike* (Life of Aleksandr Andreevich Baranov, chief manager of the Russian colonies in America) (Moscow, 1835), p. 38.]

6. According to Baranov's reports, Father Juvenal demanded that natives with several wives dispose of all but one. [Father Juvenal's colorful "journal," quoted at length in Hubert Howe Bancroft, *History of Alaska* (San Francisco, 1886), pp. 365-74, may have been fabricated by Bancroft's assistant, Ivan Petroff.]

7. *Polnoe sobranie zkonov rossiiskoi imperii* (Complete collection of laws of the Russian empire) [Hereafter *PSZ*], 1797, #18,076, 5 August; and #18,131, 8 September.

8. [Tikhmenev, *Documents*, no. 49.]

9. Because of good profits, the company's shares had risen to that value.

10. [For earlier versions of the *Sv. Zosima's* epic voyage, see G. I. Davydov, *Dvukratnoe puteshestvie v Ameriku morskikh ofitserov Khvostova i Davydova* (Two voyages to America of the naval officers Khvostov and Davydov) (St. Petersburg, 1810-12, 1:158; and V. N. Berkh, *Khronologicheskaia istoriia otkrytiia Aleutskikh ostrovov* (Chronological history of the discovery of the Aleutian islands) St. Petersburg, 1823), pp. 119-23.]

11. [Tikhmenev, *Documents*, no. 50 and 51.]

12. [Tikhmenev, *Documents*, no. 52.]

13. These "previously prescribed rules" probably refer to articles 15, 16, and 17 of the instructions to Captain Billings, dealing with the extension of Russian sovereignty over newly discovered lands and the rules to be observed in dealing with their inhabitants.

14. *PSZ*, 1800, #19,611, 19 October 1800.

15. *PSZ*, 1801, #19,982, 17 August 1801.

16. The board of directors, however, issued secret orders concerning promyshlenniks who had long and faithful service with the company. They could sell their share of furs [to the company] at a freely negotiated price or dispose of them otherwise as they wished so long as their furs did not fall into the hands of outsiders.

17. Such an increase in the cost of goods for transport is known in the colonies as a *pritsenka*.

Chapter 3

1. The fort was dedicated in the name of the Archangel Miachael.

2. [Tikhmenev, *Documents* no. 34.]

3. [See report, Kuskov to Baranov, from Yakutat, 1 July 1802, in *K istorii Rossiisko-Amerikanskoi Kompanii. Sbornik dokumental'nykh materialov* (For the History of the Russian-American Company. A Collection of Documentary Materials) (Krasnoiarsk, 1957), pp. 106-23.]

4. This vessel was under the command of the Englishman MacMeister, who had commanded merchant vessels in the Pacific Ocean and to Chinese ports, and who had proposed a plan for the Russian colonies to trade by sea with China. The company proposed to retain MacMeister in the colonial service and to buy a ship to strengthen the colonial fleet. However, for some reason MacMeister was never taken into the company's service, apparently on the advice of Count Ruminatsov, who wished to combine the profit of sending a ship around the world to the colonies with the honor of Russian discoveries of new lands.

5. It is probable that this honor, which was bestowed on Baranov over and above the just recompense for his services, was also intended to exalt the chief manager's rank in the eyes of his subordinates. Most of these were the kind of men for whom a leader's lack of rank is an obstacle to carrying out orders, no matter how reasonable those orders might be.

6. These Japanese were saved by Delarov, the former manager of Shelikov's company, who happened to be on the same Aleutian island where the Japanese ship ran aground. Delarov took them to Okhotsk and from there sent them to Irkutsk. Apparently they had little hope of returning to their native land, since some of them, according to accounts of that time, accepted Christianity. Shelikhov persuaded Lieutenant Laksman's father, one of the German scientists who were employed at some factory in Irkutsk, to propose to the Empress a project for returning the Japanese to their homeland, with the aim of entering into relations with Japan. The Empress approved this plan and ordered a ship fitted out and a

mission named and provided with a letter from the governer-general of Siberia and suitable gifts. Laksman's son, Lieutenant of the Guard Adam Laksman, was named envoy and Navigator Lovtsov was placed in command of the ship.

7. Several sources of that time show that Laksman might have obtained much better results in his dealings with Japan. First, he declined, for some unknown reason, an overland trip to Edo, which was proposed to him by Japanese officials who had come from there to his wintering place on Matsmai Island for negotiations with the Russian mission. Instead, he decided to proceed to Hakodate, a harbor nearer the capital, but only on his own ship. Second, he refused to go to Nagasaki to petition the government to permit Russian trade with Japan, since the response which was given him in Hakodate and the general manner in which the mission was received had given him high hopes of success, that is, of the exclusion of Russians from the general law of the Japanese Empire forbidding relations with foreigners. In short, Laksman did not understand in the least his government's purpose in sending him to Japan. The empress ordered that a second expedition be equipped, but, for unknown reasons, this plan was dropped after her death.

Shelikhov appears to have followed the course of the negotiations with Japan with great interest, and provided the first news of the ship sent there.

The heir to the throne, Grand Prince Paul Petrovich, thanked G. I. Shelikhov for information concerning this mission in the following two letters, which are preserved in the company archives. We present them in full:

"Mr. Shelikhov! I have received your letter and read it with pleasure, for which I thank you. I remain yours benevolently. 17 January 1794."

"Mr. Shelikhov! I have received and am most grateful for both the map of the Kurile Islands and that of Lieutenant Laksman's voyage to Japan. Wishing you good success, I remain yours benevolently. 22 May 1794."

8. The original supplement, defines the relations which were supposed to exist between the minister and Krusenstern:

As a supplement to Point XVI of these instructions the board of directors informs you that His Imperial Majesty has consented to entrust to His Excellency Chamberlain N. P. Rezanov the leadership of the proposed mission to the Japanese court, in his capacity of minister extraordinary and plenipotentiary, and all matters concerning trade and the organization of Russian America. For this reason the board of directors, having relied on the chamberlain ever since the company was organized, to intercede for it at the Imperial Court and to guard its interests, is now pleased to confirm its confidence in him, appointing him plenipotentiary, during the voyage and in America. As a result he has been provided with special credentials in the name of the entire company. Thus, the instructions given to you now pertain in several respects to the person of His Excellency, leaving to your full disposition the control of the ships and crew during the voyage and the preservation of His Excellency, as an area relating solely to your art, knowledge and experience. Now we add to this only that, since all trade dealings, the observation of places suitable for profitable trade and all of the company's interests are fully entrusted to him, the board expects from you and from your officers that you, as commander, in your zeal for the good of the Russian-American Company, so closely related to the good of the nation, will be guided by his advice in all those matters which concern company interests and profit. The board of directors has also informed His Imperial Majesty of this matter.

The second point of the instructions to Rezanov, confirmed by the emperor, also states:

Leaving to Captain Lieutenants Krusenstern and Lisianskii, under the leadership of the former, the command of the vessels and crews during your voyage, as an area relating to their particular skills, you for your part have the duty, particularly in reference to Captain Krusenstern, of seeing that entry is made into port only in case of absolute necessity and that all provisions are made for the protection of the crew and for the most rapid attainment of the goals set for you.

9. One of these commissioners, the Moscow merchant F. Shemelin, is well known for his detailed description of this voyage: *Zhurnal pervago puteshestviia rossiian vokrug zemnago shara* [Journal of the First Russian Voyage Around the World] (St. Petersburg, 1816).

10. Due to certain circumstances, the originally planned route of the expedition was changed. Instead of going around the Cape of Good Hope, it was decided to sail by way of Cape Horn.

11. See Shemelin's *Zhurnal*. Without going further into this sad epoch in the history of Russian navigation, we will state that Shemelin's evidence is fully confirmed by all available data on the first Russian round-the-world expedition. Some may wish to attribute the difficulties between the minister and the commander of the ships to the former's insufficient firmness in maintaining the prerogatives of his position, which is so necessary in such cases. Rezanov's assertion that if he had acted otherwise he might have done serious harm to the work to which he had devoted his life, and might even have failed to reach the colonies, would seem sufficient justification for his behavior.

12. [See also Tikhmenev, *Documents* no. 38, letter, Rezanov to Chichagov, from Brazil, 17 May 1804, and no. 39, report, Rezanov to Emperor, from Petropavlovsk, 16 August, 1804.] From the accounts of Japanese officials who were apparently in sympathy with Rezanov's position, it seems that the Russians' wish to establish trade relations with Japan would have succeeded if the mission had arrived right after Laksman's visit. The chief minister of the empire at that time was well disposed toward foreigners, particularly such close neighbors as the Russians, and awaited impatiently a renewal of the Russian proposals for a rapprochement. All Japanese, especially the merchant class, shared the minister's opinion. The secular emperor had expressed his particular sympathy with the conclusion of a trade treaty with Russia. But unfortunately this minister died and Rezanov arrived in Japan under completely different circumstances. His successor held opposite convictions and was particularly opposed to deviation from the rule that Japan should remain apart from the civilized world. The Russian mission, however, found support for its aims in a favorite of the secular emperor who was sincerely devoted to the plans of the previous minister, and over the present minister's opposition, Rezanov's affairs were most satisfactorily concluded in the Japanese state council. Then the new minister, determined to have his own way, tackled the matter from another side. He succeeded in convincing the spiritual emperor that the council's decision was a dangerous threat to the established religion, violated the basic customs of the nation and, consequently he demanded the interference of the head of the faith. The spiritual ruler of Japan, envious of the power of the secular emperor and offended by the fact that the previous government had not consulted him in issuing to Laksman the letter granting the Russians permission to come to Nagasaki for negotiations, announced he could agree in no way to the religiously harmful accord with foreigners and opposed with his full authority the violation of the basic law of the empire. The government had to accept such an order silently and Rezanov, after being assured from all sides of the certain success of his proposals, received a blunt and unexpected refusal.

13. One of this mission's objectives was the indispensable cession to Russia of the Amur River. The thought of the return of this important and natural route between central Siberia and Russia's Far Eastern boundaries is also attributable to Rezanov and thanks to the support of Count Rumiantsov it may have been close

to realization, had not coincidental, and unfortunate circumstances broken off negotiations at the very beginning.

Chapter 4

1. Tribal divisions and native names are taken directly from Baranov's reports without any change.

2. In 1804 the board of directors sent a large supply of medicines to the colonies according to Dr. I. O. Timkovskii's prescriptions along with his instructions for their use and for the treatment of various diseases. But, despite their efforts, the company was unable to find a doctor for the colonies.

3. All later experiments confirmed the impossibility of expanding agriculture in the Russian colonies. This subject was covered by the learned Russian seafarer, V. A. Golovnin, in his notes on Kad'iak Island. Golovnin visited this region in 1808, and in 1818 he inspected, at the order of the emperor, the possessions controlled by the Russian-American Company. His findings are reported in his *Puteshestvie vokrug sveta . . . na voennom shliupe Kamchatke*, (Voyage around the world on the naval sloop Kamachatka) pt. 1, p. 194.

> The quality of the soil is quite suitable for agriculture, but the climate is unfavorable. Agricultural efforts will always be doomed to failure by the almost constant fog and the extremely frequent rains, which occur at least two or three days in a row every week. The head of the local mission, Father German, tried to sow wheat and barley on Elovoi [Spruce] Island. During the year the barley grew fairly well, but the wheat never ripened and was completely unsuitable for seed. Cabbage will leaf out but does not form heads, although potatoes, turnips, radishes and horse-radish grow very abundantly, but the frequent rains impart a watery taste to all the locally grown vegetables.

In his "Notes on New Archangel" *Voyage*, pt. 1, p. 212), Golovnin says, "Despite the mildness of the local climate, there can never be agriculture here because of the frequent, almost ceaseless rains. Grain will not ripen and even ordinary garden vegetables do not attain their full size when grown out of doors."

4. Wild goats [*iaman'*] are found in fair numbers on Sitkha Island and on the mainland, although not in herds, like deer, but in pairs.

5. *"Kleptsy"* were a type of trap [*kapkan*] or snare [*lovushka*] invented by Siberian promyshlenniks.

6. As a supplement to this outline, we present here a list of the major species of fur-bearing animals hunted by the company and a short account of some of the hunting methods and of the habitats of each species.

Fur-bearing amphibious animals include beavers, sea otters, fur seals, sea lions, seals, and walruses. Land animals include deer, bears, wolves, foxes, wolverines, lynxes, minks, polar foxes, and muskrats.

Sea otters are still hunted in almost exactly the same way that Baranov described. To the extract from Baranov's reports we will add only that the best time for sea otter hunting is in the early months of summer, when there is almost no wind. Rarely, nets and rifles are used. The latter method is now forbidden, since rifle fire frightens the otters and makes them abandon the place where it is used. There are three types of otters, by age, the full-grown male or female otter [*bobr samets or bobrovaiamatka*], young otters two to three years old [*koshlok*], and pups [*medvedok or shchenok*]. Sea otters are now hunted chiefly in the Alexander

Archipelago, in the islands of the Kurile and Kad'iak districts and throughout the Aleutian Islands. The toions assign the Aleuts to fur hunting parties, taking into consideration the number of males in the tribe, and depending on a voluntary summons to join the party.

River beavers and otters, except for a few acquired in the Fox Islands, are purchased from the natives living on Kenai and Chugach bays, near Sitkha, and particularly along the Kuskokvim and Kvikhpak rivers. Nulato River (a tributary of the Kvikhpak) and the Pikhtalmik River (near Mikhailovskii redoubt) are considered good beaver rivers. In the days of the private companies and Baranov a very destructive method of acquiring beavers was followed in respect to the conservation and reproduction of the species. This method consisted of destroying the beaver lodge and indiscriminately killing every beaver inside, regardless of age, with a thick metal hook set in a long wooden handle. At present beavers are usually caught with a leather net placed at the mouth of the lodge. This trapping generally takes place in the winter, when the beaver's pelt is especially valuable. In this form of trapping the ice is cut open above and below the lodge. When it swims out into the river, the beaver is ensnared in the net, although it sometimes escapes through ventilation holes in the ground. For this reason, the hunters try to find these air holes and place traps in front of them. However, there are cases of beavers which, when they notice the trap—particularly if they have managed to escape from one before—will stick a piece of wood in it and, when it snaps to, will climb past it to freedom. The remarkable intelligence of the beaver is evidenced in many such ways. The males hunt for food and gather twigs, pieces of wood, etc. for the construction of the lodge. The females gather the earth and build the lodge. Old beavers very rarely leave their lodge, but the young sometimes go out into the river and wander from place to place. Then the natives hunt them with bow and arrow. They also lie in wait for them at the exit of their lair and beat them with sticks.

Beaver castors are also bartered from the above-mentioned natives.

The otter is hunted with nets and with bows and arrows. Sometimes the hunter manages to catch an otter by the hind legs and rips open its belly on the spot. The fur of the otters caught on the east side of the Rocky Mountains, called Columbian otters, is very highly prized. Otters acquired in the vicinity of the company's northern redoubts (Mikhailovskii and Kolmakovskii) are also characterized by more valuable furs than those from other regions.

Fur seals mostly inhabit the Pribylov Islands, with a few found in the Fox and Commander Islands. There are five kinds: bulls [*sekach*]—males at least five years of age, dark gray in color, over twice the size of a pregnant fur-seal cow; half-bulls [*polusekach*]—males from four to five years old without a harem, lighter in color than true bulls; bachelors [*kholostiak*]—young fur seals no more than two or three years old, light gray in color; cows [*matka*]—females at least twice the size of ordinary young fur seals, almost the same color as bulls; and finally, pups [*kotik* or *seryikot*] both male and female, gray, only a few months old. Pups are born black. Fur seal rookeries are located on sloping rockless shores. The seals are hunted in the autumn with clubs. For this purpose the whole herd of fur seals is surrounded and driven away from the shore, then, as far as possible, the cows and bulls are isolated and set free. When they notice the free passage, they return to their former places or settle down a bit closer to the sea. The remaining fur seals are driven farther from the shore and, after being given a slight rest, they are clubbed to death. The pelts are stretched, dried and then tied into bales. Nowaday some pelts are salted, especially for export to America. Fur seals go to sea at the beginning of November and return to their rookeries in the spring. The bulls leave their places last and return first.

Sea lions are especially useful to the natives in many ways. Their hide is used for sheathing baidaras and baidarkas, their meat for food; clothing and waterproof boot tops are made from their throats and their flippers serve as the boot soles. In some areas the sea lion's intestines are also made into clothing. A sea lion is larger than an ox. These animals are found in considerable numbers on one of the Privbylovs, St. George, and are hunted by being driven away from the shore, like fur seals. Then they are clubbed on the snout and stabbed in the heart. Sometimes sea lions are hunted with guns, in which case the hunters try to shoot them either in the mouth or in the head near the ear, since other places on the head are invulnerable to bullets.

Common seals [*nerpa*-hair seal- or *tiulen'*] inhabit many places in the colonies, but not in large numbers. In hunting seals, the hunter attempts to lure the seal toward the shore by placing a dummy seal (the native term is *manshik*) on a rock and imitating its cry. Then he throws a harpoon with a rope attached, drags the seal onto the shore and clubs it to death. Near the company's northern forts *makliaks* (a particular variety of seal), are hunted with bow and arrow and leather nets. Seal hide is well suited to baidarka-making, particularly the skin of the makliat, which is even thicker than that of the sea lion.

Walruses are hunted in the colonies primarily for their tusks. These tusks are more than two feet in length and each weighs fifteen pounds or more. The walrus is almost double the size of the sea lion. The thickness of walrus hide makes it unsuitable for working. This animal lives primarily on Aliaska Peninsula and on some of the islands of the Bering Sea. Walruses are hunted by surrounding the herd and killing those closest to the water with an iron spear.

To Baranov's account of foxes it may be added that dark or black ones are called silver foxes [*chernoburyi*], yellow or reddish ones are called red foxes, and cross foxes [*sivodushka*] are a cross between silver and red. Foxes are also divided into island and mainland types. The island type includes those obtained on Kad'iak Island. Their fur is of a lower quality than that of the mainland type. The best furs are from the mainland type, obtained chiefly by barter from natives living on the American mainland, particularly near Norton Sound and Mikhailovskii redoubt. In some years many red foxes appear near the latter. The foxes caught in the Fox Islands are also of the mainland type. The fox furs taken from the Sannakh and Unga Islands are also almost as valuable as mainland furs. Foxes are hunted with rifles and steel traps. Traps are constructed in those places where the animals usually pass and have sharp iron teeth which drive into the animal's paw with great force. Foxes are hunted primarily before and after the end of winter. At these times the fox is obtaining a new and full coat. Sometimes foxes are taken in the winter, but this is unsatisfactory in a number of respects.

Polar foxes [*pesets*] are found on St. George Island, Atkha, and the Komandorskie Islands and are divided into blue and white varieties according to the color of the fur. A cross between these two varieties completely spoils the color of the animal's fur, so to avoid this, measures have been undertaken to exterminate the white variety. Polar foxes are hunted with firearms, steel traps, and many other types of traps.

Bears inhabit the Aliaska Peninsula and several other places in the colonies. Bear fur, with a few exceptions, is of low quality. Most bear skins, as well as the pelts of wolves, lynxes, wolverines, minks, marmots, and muskrats, are acquired from the natives inhabiting the banks of the Kuskokvim and Kvikhpak rivers and the vicinity of Norton Sound. Bears abound particularly on the lower reaches of the Kvikhpak. Marmots are also found on Marmot Island and Chirikov Island. The furs on the latter are of the highest quality. An experienced hunter can sometimes obtain more than a thousand marmot pelts in one three-month season. There are many wolves on St. Michael Island. Wolverines are found around many lakes of the same island, most frequently in places where there are many beavers. Small numbers of brownish-gray squirrels, ermines and other animals are taken along the Nulato River and in all the above-named places.

Hunting methods vary but consist primarily of the bow and arrow and kinds of traps best adapted by experience and local conditions to the taking of each kind of animal.

7. [Letter, Rezanov to the emperor, 18 July 1805, in Tikhmenev, *Documents*, no. 40.]

8. Ibid.

9. [From letter, Rezanov to board of directors, 6 November 1805. See Tikhmenev, *Documents*, no. 42.]

10. [I. F. Krusenstern, *Puteshestvie vokrug sveta v 1803, 1804, 1805 i 1806 gg.* (Voyage around the world) (St. Petersburg, 1809-13), pt. 2, pp. 120-22.

11. Iu. F. Lisianskii, *Puteshestvie vokrug sveta v 1803, 4, 5 i 1806 godakh na korable "Neva,"* [Voyage around the world in 1803-06 on the ship "Neva"] (St. Petersburg, 1812), 2 vols., vol. 2, p. 209.

12. G. I. Davydov, *Dvukratnoe puteshestvie v Ameriku* [Two voyages to America] (St. Petersburg, 1810-12), 2 vols., vol. 1, p. 192.

13. F. P. Litke [Lutke], *Puteshevstvie vokrug sveta na voennom shliupe "Seniavin" v 1826-1829 gg.* [Voyage around the world on the naval sloop "Seniavin" in 1826-29] 3 vols. (St. Petersburg, 1834-36), pt. 1, p. 130n.

14. From a comparison of these numbers with the Kad'iak population recorded by Baranov in 1796, it appears that in ten years the natives decreased by almost half. According to Veniaminov, the depopulation of the Aleuts in this period was caused by their resettlement to other places and, in particular, by epidemics. In his *Notes on the Unalashka District*, pt. 2, p. 197, he observes: "Although there were epidemics in the Unalashka District, they seem never to have caused as many deaths as on Kad'iak. The date and exact nature of these epidemics are unknown."

15. This includes domestic service and other labor in the settlements, with the exception of those especially assigned to hunting parties. Native men and women employed thus were known respectively by the local name of *kaiur* and *kaiurka*.

16. Rezanov also compiled a dictionary of the Japanese language, which he forwarded to Petersburg from Kamchatka with the note that although it was incomplete, he felt that it might help students of the Japanese language in the Irkutsk school, and that he would try to gather more data for it in Japan. [See Ol'ga Petrovna Petrova, "Slovar' iapanskogo iazyka Nikolaia Rezanova, neuchtennyi rezul'tat ekspeditsii v Iaponii v 1803-1805 gg." (Nikolai Rezanov's Japanese dictionary, a little known result of the expedition to Japan in 1803-05), *26-i Mezhdunarodnyi Kongress Vostokovedov. Doklady delegatsii SSSR*, 14-ii doklad (26th International Congress of Orientalists. Reports of the USSR delegation, 14th report [Moscow, 1963], 15 pp.)]

17. [See also letter, Rezanov to Minister of Commerce, from New Archangel, 17 June 1806, in Tikhmenev, *Documents*, no. 46; G. H. Von Langsdorff, *Voyages and Travels in Various Parts of the World, During the Years 1803, 1804, 1805, 1806, and 1807*, (2 Vols., London, 1814), Vol. 2, pp. 136-220; and R. A. Pierce, editor, *Rezanov Reconnoiters California, 1806, A new translation of Rezanov's letter, parts of Lieutenant Khvostov's log of the ship Juno, and Dr. Georg von Langsdorff's Observations* (San Francisco, 1972).]

18. [See also William S. Hanable, "New Russia," *Alaska Journal*, Spring, 1973, Vol. 3:2, 77-80.]

19. [See also Letter, Midshipman Davydov to Baranov, 7 August 1807, "written while under house arrest," Tikhmenev, *Documents*, no. 47.]

20. [See also Report, Midshipman Davydov to the Board of Directors, 18 October 1807 (extract), in Tikhmenev, *Documents*, no. 48.]

Chapter 5

1. [See Instruction, Baranov to Hagemeister, November 1808, in *K istorii Rossiisko-Amerikanskoi Kompanii. Sbornik dokumental'nykh materialov* [materials for the history of the Russian-American Company. Collection of documentary materials] (Krasnoiarsk, 1957), pp. 160-66.]

2. [See letters, Hagemeister to the directors of the Russian-American Company, 1 May 1809 and 20 June 1809, in R. A. Pierce, *Russia's Hawaiian Adventure, 1815-1817* (Berkeley, 1965), pp. 37-40.]

3. [The *H. M. S. Cornwallis* called at the Sandwich Islands in December 1807, *before* Hagemeister's visit, en route from the west coast of South America to the East Indies. The purpose of the visit is not clear.]

4. [Regarding the tribulations of Captain Pigot, see Kenneth W. Porter, "The cruise of the *Forester*: Some new sidelights on the Astoria enterprise," *Washington Historical Quarterly* 23 (October 1932): 261-85.]

5. [See correspondence in *American State Papers: Foreign Affairs*, 1:5, pp. 438-43; and documents in *Vneshniaia politika Rossii XIX i nachala XX veka. Dokumenty Rossiiskogo Ministerstva Inostrannykh Del* (Foreign policy of Russia in the nineteenth and early twentieth centuries. Documents of the Ministry of Foreign Affairs.) seriia pervaia, 1801-1815 gg., 4 (July 1807-March 1809): 241-43, 246-47, 267, 323-26. See also S. B. Okun, *The Russian-American Company*, trans. Carl Ginsburg (Cambridge, Mass., 1951, pp. 75-77.]

6. [See text of Astor proposal, *Vneshniaia politika Rossii*, 6:711-14.]

7. Information on the English fur-trading companies and the activities of the Americans have been taken from *Copies or Extracts of Correspondence Relating to the Charter of the Hudson's Bay Company* and the *North American Review*.

8. [Kenneth W. Porter, *John Jacob Astor, Business Man*, 2 vols. (Cambridge, Mass., 1931), pp. 252-53.]

9. [Text of Astor proposal, *Vneshniaia politika Rossii*, 6:711-14; letter, board of directors of Russian-American Company to Minister of Foreign Affairs N. P. Rumiantsev, 26 September (8 October, O.S.) 1811; *ibid.*, 6:180-81; letter, Astor to A. B. Bentzon, 21 January 1811, Porter, *John Jacob Astor*, pp. 454-59.]

10. [Letter, minister of foreign affairs to board of directors of Russian-American Company, 4 (16 October O.S.) 1811, *Vneshniaia politika Rossii*, 6:191.]

11. [Convention, American Fur Company and Russian-American Company, St. Petersburg, 20 April (2 May O.S.) 1812; ibid., 6:385-88.]

12. [Porter, *John Jacob Astor*, pp. 175-78; letter, Ebbets to John Jacob Astor, 11 January 1811, from Macao, ibid., pp. 448-53.]

13. [Letter, Baranov to John Jacob Astor, 13(25 August O.S.) 1811, from New Archangel, ibid., pp. 469-74.]

14. [V. M. Golovnin, *Puteshestvie na shliupe Diana iz Kronshtadta v Kamchatku v 1807-1811 gg.* (Voyage on the sloop "Diana" from Kronshtadt to Kamchatka . . . in 1807-1811) (Moscow, 1961); from editions of 1819 and 1861, pp. 324-26. Porter, *John Jacob Astor*, p. 176.]

15. Unfortunately, the company archives contain neither Baranov's report on the assignment of the *Suvorov* nor Lazarev's letters to the directors from San Francisco explaining his departure from New Archangel, letters to which he refers in his subsequent reports. Data on the proposed voyage of the *Suvorov* were borrowed from letters of Doctor Schäffer and supercargo Molvo, written prior to Lazarev's departure from New Archangel and from other private sources.

16. After the *Suvorov* returned to Kronshtadt, the admiralty appointed a commission to investigate the factors which prompted Lazarev to leave New Archangel without the permission of the governor of the colonies. There are reasons to suppose that as a result of these investigations the board of directors authorized

Hagemeister, commander of the next round-the-world expedition, to relieve Baranov as manager of the colonies *if he should find this desirable.* [*M. P. Lazarev. Dokumenty* (M. P. Lazarev. Documents), (Moscow, 1952), vol. 1, contains "Iz 'istinnykh zapisok moei zhizni' Leitenanta S. Ia. Unkovskogo," (From Lieutenant S. Ia. Unkovskii's 'A true account of my life'), pp. 11-60. This contains some interesting remarks on Russian-America, but all of the portions concerning Baranov and Lazarev's quarrel have been excised. The original manuscript is in the Central State Archive of the Navy (TsGAVMF), f. 1152, d. 2, folios 3-69. The same volume, *M. P. Lazarev. Dokumenty*, contains (p. 70) "Iz sledstvennogo dela po obvineniiu M. P. Lazareva v zloupotrebleniiakh vo vremia krugosvetnogo plavaniia na korable 'Suvorov' " (From the investigation of accusations against M. P. Lazarev of offenses during the round-the-world voyage of the ship *Suvorov*), from a manuscript in TsGAVMF, f. 166, d. 4767, folios 29-30, exonerating Lazarev of Baranov's charges; and "Iz ob'iasnitel'noi zapiski M. P. Lazareva po povodu pred'iavlennykh emu pravleniem Rossiisko-Amerikanskoi Kompanii obvienii v zloupotrebleniiakh po sluzhbe vo vremia krugosvetnogo plavaniia na korable 'Suvorov' " (From M. P. Lazarev's explanatory memorandum regarding the accusations presented to him by the main office of the Russian-American Company concerning accusations of offenses in its service while on the round-the-world voyage of the ship *Suvorov*) (pp. 70-76). This is from a copy in TsGAVMF, f. 212, d. 3735, folios 133-158. Again references to the quarrel have been excised, however the complete text may be seen in TsGAVMF, f. 212, d. 3735, folios 133-158, and in the Russian-American Company *Correspondence*, 1817, no. 182, 22 March 1817, Main Office to Baranov, enclosure, folios 17-40, in the U. S. National Archives.]

17. [See F. W. Howay, "The Last Days of the *Atahualpa*, alias *Behring*," Hawaiian Historical Society, *Forty-First Annual Report* (1933), pp. 70-80.]

18. Previously King Kamehameha had been a minor chief in the northern part of Oahu Island. With the assistance of fugitive foreigners he killed other chiefs, including Kaumualii's father, who had ruled five islands. Kaumualii fled to Kauai Island, retaining only the two islands that lie north of Oahu. All of his policies, particularly in respect to foreigners, were governed by his constant enmity to his father's murderer, his wish to avenge him at the first suitable opportunity, and his desire to regain his father's dominions. [For documents regarding Schäffer's mission and his activities in the islands, see Pierce, *Russia's Hawaiian Adventure*, and S. B. Okun, "Tsarskaia Rossii i Gavaiskie ostrova" (Tsarist Russia and the Hawaiian Islands), *Krasnyi arkhiv*, no. 5 (no. 78) 1936), pp. 161-68. See also N. N. Bolkhovitinov, "Avantiur Doktora Sheffera na Gavaiiakh v 1815-1819 godakh" (Doctor Sheffer's adventure in the Hawaiian Islands in 1815-1819 godakh), *Novaia i noveishaia istoriia* (Moscow), 1972:1, 121-36.]

19. On 1 February 1820 Count Speranskii reported on this subject to Count Nesselrode:

On 12 November 1819, I had the honor of informing Your Excellency that in my predecessor's records I found no evidence of Dobello's proposals or the answers given him. From the contract and the letter which I have now obtained, I must conclude that he was either instructed or permitted to attempt to establish whale fishing on the shores of Kamchatka, and consequently this matter has already been considered and settled by the government. For this reason it is now necessary only to review the conditions of this contract. But if for some reason this matter has not already been settled both in detail and in essence, the following observations could be made: The undertaking could have two advantages, the more immediate being the improved food supply of the natives of Kamchatka. This advantage could be quite important in times when they catch few fish, almost their sole item of diet. From the attached excerpt of the report of the Okhotsk manager, Your Excellency may see with what pleasure the Tungus occupying the Okhotsk coast came upon the carcasses of whales which had been washed ashore last autumn. The second advantage is the eventual building of our own whaling ships. This benefit is far in the future, and if the government proposes to undertake this enterprise, then it is not likely to have any success, since only ten sailors or workers are going to be trained in whaling. We are still a long way from the establishment of such an industry; we will need vessels, equipment, money and most of all expert supervision. But even if we suppose that this last benefit is possible and even probable, permitting this industry to fall into foreign hands still presents the following disadvantages:

1. Everyone knows of the Russian-American Company's complaints about the efforts of American citizens to trap and trade on their own account, and even to provide the natives with fire arms; these complaints are justified, but the matter cannot be helped. To try to get the American government to prohibit this would be in vain and against the spirit of that nation's trading rules. The company has only one recourse: to attempt to place its own establishments at key points. At the least, the government should not favor this foreign-owned trade. But it undoubtedly will be favored by the establishment of whaling on the eastern shores of Siberia. This would both foster and support it.

2. Although for various reasons animal trapping in Kamchatka and Okhotsk has diminished in significance, present and future hopes of the trade still depend on Russian hunters. But if foreign establishments are set up on the shores, it will undoubtedly pass into foreign hands. In these sparsely populated regions it would be impossible to maintain close surveillance or to prohibit the importation of alcoholic beverages, if this trade were permitted.

3. For the unity and completeness of its enterprise, the Russian-American Company should attempt to establish whale fishing, if not with its own employees, then at least with its own capital. At present its capital position is not only strong, but even excessive, and for this reason its enterprises require expansion. But a contract with foreigners would impose an insurmountable obstacle to this expansion.

4. Rikord asserts in his letter that if the foreigners wished to carry on whaling in those regions we would lack the forces to prevent them. First, the disproportionate weakness of our forces is questionable. The timely appearance of one well-armed ship would subdue and scatter all of these whalers. Second, if they are able to appropriate this industry by force, why should we support their force with contractual rights?

After these remarks on the essence of the proposal, one may ask the following questions concerning the details of the contract:

1. If Pigot is asking for no more than local and temporary permission to carry on whaling off the coast of Kamchatka, then why not confine this to simple permission, which could be summarily and arbitrarily withdrawn? Why is a ten-year contract necessary? Certainly a contract could not and should not compel him to carry on whaling if he should find it unprofitable. How many pretexts could he find to violate or nullify a contract which was to our sole advantage, in that it served to teach our own people whaling?

2. Why was it necessary, instead of "Kamchatka," to use in the contract the indefinite phrase "Eastern Siberia," a phrase which extends these whaling rights not only to the Sea of Okhotsk, but also to the Kurile Islands, which our Russian-American Company would then certainly be compelled to disclaim?

3. Why must we give these whalers the Russian flag? The audacity and violence of these Americans has been displayed on almost every one of their voyages. Why should they be able to hide behind our flag among the Chukchi, in Japan

and everywhere else? In place of strength, which Rikord is seeking, here we find only responsibility for the actions of others, the more dangerous because the governor of Kamchatka will have no means to limit it. If the thoughtlessness of one Russian officer (Khvostov) could rouse the Japanese to ideas of war when we were seeking peaceful relations, how can we put our flag into the hands of men accustomed to dare everything for profit?

[For more on the Dobello proposal see V. I. Vagin, *Istoricheskie svedeniia o deiatel'nosti grafa M. M. Speranskogo v Sibiri s 1819 po 1822 g.* (Historial data on the activities of Count M. M. Speranskii in Siberia from 1819 to 1822), 2 vols. (St. Petersburg, 1872).]

Chapter 6

1. [See also Hubert Howe Bancroft, *History of Alaska, 1730-1885* (San Francisco, 1886), reprinted, New York, 1960; *History of California*, 7 vols. (San Francisco, 1886), vol. 2; and *Quarterly of the California Historical Society*, vol. 12, no. 3 (September 1933), a special issue devoted to the Russians in California.]

2. [Letter, Director of Russian-American Company M. M. Buldakov to Emperor Alexander I, 28 January 1808 *Vneshniaia politika Rossii*, [Russian foreign policy] 4:163-64 (and extract in V. A. Potekhin, *Selenie Ross* [the Ross settlement] (St. Petersburg, 1859), pp. 3-5); letter, Minister of Foreign Affairs N. P. Rumiantsev to Minister Plenipotentiary in Madrid G. A. Stroganov, 20 April 1808, *Vneshniaia politika Rossii*, 4:235-36.]

3. [Bancroft, *History of California*, 2:295, gives the text of the message to the Spanish authorities, written at St. Petersburg by Mikhail Buldakov and Benedict Kramer on 15 March 1810 from Spanish and Latin versions in Spanish California state papers. An extract of most of the Russian text is given in Potekhin, *Selenie Ross*, p. 8. Whether Ayres himself acted as an emissary of Baranov in 1812, or merely transported an emissary, name unknown, is unclear.]

4. [For an extract from Kuskov's report of the future site of Ross, see Potekhin, *Selenie Ross*, pp. 8-9.]

5. [Ibid., p. 21.]

6. [Ibid., p. 22.]

7. [Extract, letter of Hagemeister to governor of California, ibid., pp. 23-24.]

8. [Extract, board of directors to Minister of Foreign Affairs Count Nesselrode, January 1820, ibid., pp. 25-26.]

Chapter 7

1. [See Sobstvennoi Ego Imperatorskago Velichestva Kantseliarii. *Sbornik istoricheskikh materialov izvlechennykh iz arkhiva Pervago otdeleniia.* (His Imperial Majesty's Office. Collection of historical materials from the archive of the First Section), Vyp. 1, "Vsepoddaneishee donesenie glavnago pravleniia Rossiisko-Amerikanskoi kompanii s predstavleniem vypisok iz protokolov po raznym predmetam" (Report of the Main Office of the Russian-American Company to His Imperial Majesty with extracts from memoranda on various subjects), pp. 137-48.

This states that in response to a proposal by Baranov, the Main Office authorized such tokens on 20 June 1803, more than a decade earlier than indicated by Tikhmenev. The first issue was to comprise 10,000 rubles each in denominations of 1, 2, 5, 10, and 20 rubles, printed on parchment. It was felt that if coins were used, the natives would use the metal for other purposes. See also A. Doll and R. A. Pierce, "Alaskan treasure—the Russian skin money," *Alaska*, November, 1969.]

    2. Confirmed by the emperor for company ships on 6 September 1806.

    3. I. Veniaminov, *Zapiski ob ostrovakh Unalashkinskago otdela* (Notes on the islands of the Unalashka district) (St. Petersburg, 1840, 2 vols.), vol. 2, p. 371.

    4. Here are a few more words on Baranov, taken from the notebook of one of the officers of the sloop *Kamchatka*, during that ship's voyage.

As soon as we dropped anchor in the roadstead of New Archangel [19 August 1818], Lieutenants Ianovskii and Podushkin and Commissioner Khlebnikov came out to us. When we sat down to dinner, they announced the arrival of Baranov. The extraordinary life and deeds of this extraordinary man had aroused my curiosity and I had a great desire to see him. Baranov was of slightly less than average height. His age and his labors had left few traces of that fire which had inspired him in former times. His face was covered with wrinkles, he was hairless, his gait was hesitating, but with all this it was impossible to think he was eighty years old, particularly if one knew of his laborious and unsettled life. On the next day he invited us to dine. When the meal was completed, a chorus of singers appeared on the scene, who spared neither their own throats nor our ears to entertain their foremost chief. When they began singing a song of his own composition, *The Russian Mind Has Gone to Work*, the eighty-year-old Baranov [sic. He was then 72] could not help following a custom which he had had for twenty years. He stood in a circle of his comrades and joined them in proclaiming their common exploits in the new world. It would be appropriate here to say a few words on this old man's way of life. He arose early and ate one meal a day, but at no fixed time. Some might say that he was imitating Suvorov in this, but I am sure that Baranov has never imitated anyone, with the possible exception of Pizarro or Cortez. During his entire administration he behaved with unprecedented disinterestedness. He never gave general accounts to the board of directors, and therefore had a real opportunity to line his own pockets. But he never did so. When Hagemeister took over from Baranov, he compared the information which Baranov gave him on the transactions with foreign ships with the invoices which the captain usually gave, and found no discrepancies except in the case of rum, where there was a small quantity missing, but even this Baranov had not used for his own benefit. Baranov's unique position compelled him to start a custom which later he could not break. Namely, he surrounded himself with a band of loyal ruffians, ready to go through fire and water for him. The only way he could hold these men was to give them frequent feasts at which they could drink all they wished. They consumed large quantities of rum, which Baranov was in no position to buy and consequently had to take on the company's account, not indicating that in his reports. He has been reproached for his strictness and even for his former cruelty; but God knows that he could not have gotten by otherwise in those days. Before the company that we know today had come into existence, Baranov was not the leader of any well-organized society, but of a band of cutthroats, each of whom considered himself Baranov's equal. Most of them were either exiles or profligates, ruined men who could not find a place for themselves in Russia. Such men could not live in peace. They plotted unceasingly against Baranov, his life was in constant danger and the only way he could keep these hoodlums in order was always to behave decisively, strictly, and sometimes perhaps even cruelly. The hunters of that time could not love him—it was necessary that they fear him. When the Russian- American Company was formed and regular communication was established between Russia and the colonies, circumstances changed and Baranov became another man. . . .

[Baranov's song, mentioned here, was published by L. A. Zagoskin in the journal *Moskvitianin* (1849) no. 5, book 1, section 6, pp. 1-4, and has been reprinted in the modern edition of Zagoskin's principal work, *Puteshestviia i issledovaniia leitenanta Lavrentiia Zagoskina v Russkoi Amerike v 1842-1844 gg.* (The travels and explorations of Lt. Lavrentii Zagoskin in Russian-America in 1842-44) (Moscow, 1956), pp. 379-81. See also Alexander Doll and R. A. Pierce, "Songs of Russian America," *Alaska Review* (Anchorage), Spring and Summer 1970, Vol. 4:1, pp. 24-32.]

5. A "kamleia" is a kind of hooded shirt, usually made from the intestines of sea lions, or sometimes bears, walruses, or whales.

6. A "parka" is also a type of shirt, but with a standing collar, usually sewn from bird skins or seal skins.

7. [The Khiuveren or Kheveren River first appears on a map prepared by Nikolai Daurkin, a cossack of Chukchi origin, sent to the Diomede Islands in 1763. His map shows the river south of Cape Prince of Wales, with a fort and an inscription stating that it was inhabited by bearded men, dressed in furs, speaking a language unlike Chukchi. See A. V. Efimov, *Iz istorii russkikh ekspeditsii na Tikhom Okeane. Pervaia polovina XVIII veka* (On the History of the Russian Expeditions in the Pacific Ocean. First Half of the Eighteenth Century) (Moscow, 1948), pp. 138, 147. Efimov believed the Khiuveren to be the Yukon, but from its position on several other eighteenth century Russian maps, it could as easily have been—if it existed at all—the Kuzitrin or Koyuk on the Seward Peninsula. See Svetlana G. Fedorova, *The Russian Population in Alaska and California, Late 18th Century–1867* (Kingston, Ontario, 1973) for an extensive analysis of this question, and Dorothy Jean Ray, "Kauwerak, lost village of Alaska," *The Beaver* (Winnipeg), Autumn, 1964, pp. 4-13.

8. Korsakovskii's diary of the expedition of 1818 (27 April-4 October) is in the Manuscript Division of the Lenin Library, Moscow, f. 256 (N. P. Rumiantsev), R. 487, folios 1-50. It has never been published, but is described by Fedorova, op. cit., pp. 66-68, 308-10. The journal indicates that the 1818 expedition left on 27 April by baidara from Kad'iak for Katmai artel on the south shore of the Alaska Peninsula, and from there went to Bristol Bay. From there Kolmakov led a detachment by way of Kvichak and Nushagak bays to Cape Newenham, and back to the Eskimo village of Ekuk at the mouth of the Nushagak River. On 21 July, Korsakovskii, leaving Kolmakov and a few others at the mouth of the Nushagak, led a detachment up the Kvichak River to Lake Iliamna, Lake Clark and the upper reaches of the Mulchatna River, a tributary of the Nushagak. On Lake Iliamna Korsakovskii met Eremei Rodionov, a local trader, who offered to lead a group north to find the "Kheuveren" River. This party apparently reached the Kuskokvim River near the mouth of the Khulitna and proceeded downstream to the Mulchatna, then ascended that river and returned to Kad'iak Island on 4 October by way of Lake Iliamna and the Kenai Peninsula.

As Fedorova states, what Tikhmenev describes as Korsakovskii's expedition of 1818 actually took place in the following year, 1819.]

9. V. M. Golovnin, *Puteshestvie vokrug sveta na shliupe "Kamchatka" v 1817, 1818 i 1819 godakh flota kapitana Golovina* (A voyage around the world on the sloop "Kamchatka" in 1817, 1818 and 1819) (St. Petersburg, 1822), pt. 1, p. 200.

10. Ibid., pt. 1, p. 220.

11. Ibid., pt. 1, p. 222-24. [See also V. M. Golovnin, "Zapiska Kapitana 2 ranga Golovnina o sostoianii Rossiisko-Amerikanskoi kompanii v 1818 godu" (Notes by Captain of Second Rank Golovnin on the condition of the Russian-American Company in 1818), *Materialy dlia istorii russkikh zaselenii po beregam Vostochnago okeana* (Materials on the history of the Russian settlements on the Eastern Ocean) (St. Petersburg, 1861), pp. 48-126. L. A. Shur, *K beregam Novogo Sveta. Iz*

neopublikovannykh zapisok russkikh puteshestvennikov nachala XIX veka (To the shores of the New World. From unpublished writings of Russian travellers at the beginning of the 19th century) (Moscow, 1971) includes the journals of two other officers on the *Kamchatka* during its voyage of 1817-1819—F. F. Matiushkin and F. P. Litke (Luetke)—with valuable editorial notes.]

12. [See P. A. Tikhmenev, *Documents*, 1977, no. 55 and 56.]

13. During his stay in the colonies, Doctor Schäffer discovered sulfur springs a verst from New Archangel. He considered the waters better than those of Teplice.

14. The profits for the years 1797 through 1802 and most of the profits for 1802 and 1803 were added to the capital surplus.

15. The small profits for the years 1804-12 were caused by (1) the loss of the *Phoenix* with a valuable cargo, which halted hunting and other company activities, and (2) the loss of more than a million fur seal pelts through the ignorance of the hunters, who dried them in bath houses.

Chapter 8

1. See Tikhmenev, *Documents*, 1977, no. 57 and 58.

2. [See *Arkhiv grafov Mordvinovykh* (Archives of the Counts Mordvinov) (St. Petersburg, 1902), vol. 6, for correspondence between Mordinov and Nesselrode regarding the conventions. See also English translation, letter, Nesselrode to N. S. Mordvinov, from St. Petersburg, 11 April 1824, in *Fur Seal Arbitration* 8:334-40 (corrected version).]

3. [*Copies or Extracts of Correspondence Relating to the Charter of the Hudson's Bay Company.*]

4. [See the official, though unfortunately undocumented, *History of the Hudson's Bay Company, 1670-1870*, 2 vols. (London, 1958, 1959); and John S. Galbraith, *The Hudson's Bay Company as an Imperial Factor, 1821-69* (Toronto, 1957). See also "McLoughlin's Statement of the Expenses Incurred in the 'Dryad' Incident of 1834," with an introduction by W. Kaye Lamb, *British Columbia Historical Quarterly* 10(1946):291-97.]

5. So that the substance of the charges against the company may be clearly defined, we will present the words of the contract on the indemnification of this claim, concluded between the two companies:

> The Hudson's Bay Company shall relinquish their claim now pending on the Russian Government, the Russian-American Company, or whomever else it may concern, for injury and damages said to be sustained by the Hudson's Bay Company arising from the obstruction presented by the Russian Authorities on the northwest coast of America to an expedition belonging to the Hudson's Bay Company at the entrance of the river Stakine on the northwest coast of America in the year 1834, outfitted and equipped by the said Hudson's Bay Company for the purpose of forming a commercial station in the interior British territory on the banks of the said Stakine River.

6. Sea otters found in waters adjacent to the leased strip of land were reserved for the benefit of the Russian colonies, since they were not a resource of the mainland.

7. A profit margin of about 100 percent could be realized on otters purchased by the company under these terms and resold in Russia.

8. [See Donald C. Davidson, "Relations of the Hudson's Bay Company with

the Russian-American Company on the Northwest Coast, 1829-67," *British Columbia Historical Quarterly* 5(1941):33-51; and Willard E. Ireland, "James Douglas and the Russian-American Company, 1840," ibid., 5:53-66, the latter including Hudson's Bay Company documents concerning execution of the agreement.]

9. [See Frederic Lütke, *Voyage autour du monde . . . dans les annees 1826, 1827, 1828 et 1829* (3 vols., Paris, 1835), vol. 1.]

10. [In the following year, 1822, the Russian-American Company sent out a second expedition under Khromchenko. Etholen, who the year before had commanded the cutter *Baranov*, went along to survey coastal areas with baidarkas. On 22 April 1822 the Golovnin left New Archangel. After looking around the Pribylov Islands to see if there was another island nearby, Khromchenko went to Hagemeister Island and surveyed it, then went to the Nushagak River, then on 9 June again sought the non-existent island near the Pribylovs. Then back to Nunivak Island, through Etholen Strait to Stuart Island. On the voyage back the Golovnin stopped at the Pribylovs and Unalashka to pick up furs and returned to New Archangel on 29 August. See "V. S. Khromchenko's coastal explorations in Southwestern Alaska, 1822," edited with an introduction by James W. VanStone, translated by David H. Kraus, *Fieldiana Anthropology*, vol. 64, 1973. The original journal is in the Perm oblast archive, U.S.S.R. This is a translation of the only portion of the journal ever published, in *Severnyi Arkhiv* (St. Petersburg), in seven installments, in 1823.

Chief Manager Murav'ev was dissatisfied with the results of the 1822 expedition, particularly the limited use made of the baidarkas, but recommended that Khromchenko be granted a medal and Etholen a promotion. See Russian American Company, *Journals of Correspondence*, 1823, no. 45 (11 February) and no. 106 (2 April).]

11. [See V. P. Romanov, "Mysli o puteshestvii kotoroe mozhno predpriniat' ot reka Mednoi po sukhomu puti do Ledovitogo moria i do Gudzonova zaliva" (Thoughts on a journey which might be taken from the Copper River overland to the Arctic Sea and Hudson Bay), *Severnyi Arkhiv*, 1825, part 17, section 3; and Glynn R. Barratt, "The Russian interest in Arctic North America: The Kruzenshtern-Romanov Projects, 1819-23," *Slavonic and East European Review*, Vol. 53, no. 130, January 1975, pp. 27-43.]

12. [See F. W. Beechey, *Narrative of a voyage to the Pacific and Beering's Strait . . . in the years 1825, 1826, 1827 and 1828* (London, 1831).]

13. A detailed report by Kashevarov on the expedition was printed in *Syn otechestva* (1840), and excerpts from the diary which he kept during the expedition appeared in *Sankt Peterburgskie vedomosti* (1845), nos. 190-93.

14. [See J. W. VanStone, "Russian exploration in interior Alaska. An extract from the journal of Andrei Glazunov," *Pacific Northwest Quarterly* 50, no. 2 (1959):37-47.]

Chapter 9

1. [Veniaminov, later known by his monastic name of Innokentii, first published his survey under the title "Sostoianie pravoslavnoi tserkvi v Rossiiskoi Amerike" (Condition of the Orthodox Church in Russian America), in *Zhurnal ministerstava narodnago prosveshcheniia* (Journal of the Ministry of Education), Vol. 26, No. 6 (1840), pp. 16-48, and it was reissued later that same year as an offprint by the Printing Office of the Imperial Academy of Sciences. A. S. Sturdza

included it in his *Pamiatnik trudov pravoslavnykh blagovestnikov russkikh s 1783 do 1853 goda* (Monument to the Labors of the Russian Orthodox Missionaries from 1783 to 1853) (Moscow, 1857); and Ivan Barsukov, Innokentii's biographer, included it in his three-volume collection of Innokentii's works: *Tvoreniia Innokentiia, Mitropolita Moskovskago i Kolomenskago* (Works of Innokentii, Metropolitan of Moscow and Kolomna) (Moscow, 1886), II, pp. 1-42. This survey has been translated by Robert Nichols and Robert Croskey, "The Condition of the Orthodox Church in Russian America," *Pacific Northwest Quarterly*, 63, no. 2, (April 1972): 41-54.]

2. *PTPBR*, pp. 210-11.

3. In 1834, at Baron Wrangell's order, Father Veniaminov was transferred from Unalashka to Sitkha, where his Christian zeal was offered a broader field of action.

4. The parishioners of the Sitkha church consisted of Russians, creoles, seventy-eight Aleuts, and twenty Kolosh.

5. *PTPBR*, p. 213.

6. Ibid., p. 214.

7. Ibid., p. 214n.

8. Ibid., p. 220.

9. In 1837, on the advice of the Russians, Kuatkhe, one of the Kolosh chiefs on the Stakhina, gave his people the first example of freeing a slave (*kelgi*) condemned to death by Kolosh custom to honor the souls of the dead. By request of the board of directors the emperor bestowed on him a brocade caftan and a cap.

10. *PTPBR*, p. 226.

11. Ibid., pp. 228.

12. Ibid., p. 226.

13. Ibid., p. 227.

14. Ibid., p. 228.

15. Ibid., p. 229.

16. Ibid., p. 232.

17. Ibid., p. 234.

18. Report of the High Procurator of the Holy Synod to the board of directors, 28 May 1840, no. 3018.

19. According to Veniaminov (*Zapiski*, 2:322), the Unalashka Aleuts accepted smallpox vaccination willingly, and cooperated as far as possible.

20. In the neighborhood of the Aleksandrovskii and Mikhailovskii redoubts, and on the Kuskokvim River, 200 of the 550 afflicted died.

21. Here it would be appropriate to recall certain measures taken by Etholen as chief manager (1840-45) to bring about closer relations with the Kolosh. In 1841 he arranged at New Archangel a kind of fair with entertainment, the so-called "games" [*igrushki*]. When the news reached the surrounding Kolosh settlements that an entertainment had been planned for them, where they could also barter necessary supplies, about five hundred of the most important Kolosh gathered in a specially constructed barabora next to the fort. This entertainment, which satisfied the vanity so characteristic of these natives, apparently made a very favorable impression on them and had quite good results on subsequent relations. When the board of directors received word of Etholen's undertaking, they wholly approved of it and proposed that these games be occasionally repeated or even turned into a yearly fair, if that should be possible.

22. By the early 1830's the Unalashka and Atkha Aleuts were finally united in common settlements with chiefs appointed over them. When Captain of First Rank Kuprianov, the chief manager, visited Atkha and Amlia in 1838, he spoke very highly of the way of life of the Atkha Aleuts, especially those living on Amlia Island. After carefully examining the local living quarters and outbuildings, as well as the chapels which the Amlia Islanders had built, Kuprianov wrote:

I will not trouble to express in full my extreme satisfaction with the condition of the local Aleuts, which I have found praiseworthy in all respects. Here I was simply a disinterested visitor like any other, since I regret to say that I am not able to attribute to myself or to my assistants any of the things which I saw. The basis for all this had already been laid by my predecessors and by the local supervisors. Recalling very well the *kazhims* (houses) of the Aleuts at New Archangel, which I had inspected in 1823, I must confess that here also I expected to encounter the same thing, perhaps with minor improvements. When I entered them, I was first struck by the unexpectedly clean air inside, and in the second place by the unusual orderliness, which apparently had long been the rule. Of course, all of this must be attributed to the efforts of the wise Atkha toion, Dediukhin, and the good advice of the spiritual leader of the local Aleuts, Iakov Netsvetov, who has won universal respect by his exemplary life and his concern for the natives. The storage barabora was full of supplies and prosperity was obvious everywhere. Supplies are laid up jointly under the supervision of the chief. In this way the food supply is not subject to chance nor dependent on the arbitrary actions of idlers. Although there are few cattle, they are kept in good condition. Most of the cattle are obtained from the offspring of those sent by the company when the local natives were gathered into common settlements. The toion has left some of the cows in the possession of those Aleuts who have shown themselves the most knowledgeable and most industrious cattle raisers. . . .

To this report Kuprianov added a sketch on the Unalashka Aleuts made by Doctor Bliashke [Blashke], who had the opportunity to become intimately acquainted with their way of life when he visited the settlements of this district during the smallpox epidemic. We reproduce several lines of his notes:

All of the Unalashka Aleuts build their baraboras almost identically. They are of timber or plank construction, rarely more than twenty-one feet in length or fourteen feet in width. Their height rarely exceeds that of a man. They are covered on the outside with sod and divided into two sections, one in the nature of an entrance hall, where the cooking fire is kept and supplies of dried fish, fat, etc. are stored, and the other the living quarters with plank beds along the walls. Although the first room is not always clean, the living room is always kept neat, the floor is strewn with straw and covered with straw mats, as are sometimes the plank beds and the walls. One never enters the living room in wet clothing, but leaves it in the entry, in order not to increase the humidity which inevitably evaporates from the ground after the frequent rains. Light is usually admitted from above through a frame that is covered with an animal membrane in bad weather. One or two families live in each barbora, depending on the number and ages of their members. The toions and well-to-do Aleuts have well-built baraboras, sometimes divided into two or three rooms, but very few have glass windows, aside from those of the baidarshchiks. In the village of Nikolaev on Umnak Island the natives have built a beautiful chapel, resembling more a church.

The usual Aleut dress is a birdskin parka, which the poor wear over their bare body. Most Aleuts, however, wear a canvas shirt underneath. The parkas are washed quite frequently and in general the Aleuts keep themselves clean. Baths, of which some are quite comfortable, are located at every house. The Aleuts are great lovers of bathing and have become accustomed to frequent hot steam baths.

Food supplies are found in abundance in the Unalashka section. Special so-called "company" baraboras have been built in every village in order to avoid a shortage of winter supplies of dried fish and fat, the chief and essential objects of the Aleut diet. This potential shortage is a result of over-consumption, particularly at their games. Half of the entire supply of iukola is placed in the barabora under the control of the baidarshchik, and when the shortages begin, he gives it out to the needy, as well as sharing it with other villages where the provisioning was inadequate. In this way the almost annual spring famine of previous years is averted.

Needless to say, the tidiness in home life and dress, as well as the methods of food provisioning, the number of skilled hunters, and the resulting prosperity are not the same everywhere. Nevertheless, the number of well-run villages considerably exceeds the number of poorly run ones, of which there are only two.

[From Eduard Blashke, "Neskol'ko zamechanii o plavanii v baidarkakh i o Lis'-evskikh Aleutakh" (Some notes on a baidarka voyage and about the Fox Island Aleuts), *Morskoi sbornik*, 1848, no. 3 & 4, pp. 115-124, no. 5, pp. 160-65. [See also Blashke's *Topographia medica portus Novi-Archangelscensis, sedis principals rossicarum in Septentrionali America* (*Medical topography of the port of New Archangel, the Russian capital in North America*) (St. Petersburg, 1842).]

23. A *kazhim* is a wooden hut, built as far as possible according to the customs and preferences of the natives. Properly speaking, the Aleut *kazhim* is an earth hut in which there is usually a section set aside for sleeping, called a *zhupan*.

24. The colonial administration at various times had pairs of foxes transported to many of the Aleutian and Kurile Islands, and it was to their offspring that hunting in those places owed its beginning.

25. Among the other shipbuilding projects carried out in New Archangel during Baron Wrangell's administration an American ship renamed the *Lady Wrangell* was retimbered in the dockyard there. It is remarkable that until the construction of a navy yard in San Francisco recently New Archangel had the only shipyard on the entire northwest coast of America where United States citizens could have the needs of their ships looked after. The fine workshops and other shipbuilding facilities in this port enabled foreign vessels to repair damage and to obtain all necessary supplies.

26. *Morekhod* was the name applied to experienced sailors who had obtained satisfactory practical knowledge of navigating during long voyages.

27. *Fal'sh-borty*, or washboards, are the side of the ship raised above the upper deck.

28. A *verp* (warp, or kedge) is a small anchor used mainly for warping, that is, hauling the vessel from one place to another, when it is impossible to make such a move under sail. For this purpose the warp is usually placed on the assigned point with a rope attached, by means of which the vessel is hauled to the new place.

Chapter 10

1. In Russian money this price totals 78 silver rubles 74½ kopeks per ton, or using the accepted rules of conversion for each class of goods, 3½ kopeks silver per pound of sugar or tea, 31 kopeks per gallon of liquid, and 98¼ kopeks per cubic foot of dry goods.

2. [See reports on agriculture in California by E. L. Chernykh in *Zhurnal sel'skago khoziaistva i ovtsevodstva* (Journal of agriculture and sheep raising) (Moscow, 1841), one of which has been translated as "Agriculture of Upper California: A Long Lost Account of Farming in California as Recorded by a Russian Observer at Fort Ross in 1841," *The Pacific Historian* 11, no. 1 (Winter, 1967):10-28.]

3. [See V. Potekhin, *Selenie Ross* (Ross Settlement) (St. Petersburg, 1859), p. 32.]

4. [Condensed version of message given in more complete form in ibid., pp. 33-34.]

5. [For Wrangell's own account of the journey from Sitkha by way of Mexico, see L. A. Shur, *K beregam Novogo Sveta. Iz neopublikovannykh zapisok russkikh puteshestvennikov nachala XIX veka* (To the shores of the New World. From unpublished writings of Russian travellers at the beginning of the 19th century) (Moscow, 1971), pp. 169-277 (diary text, pp. 190-259) with appendices and editorial notes. A popularized version was published as F. P. Vrangel', "Puteshestvie iz Sitkhi v Sankt-Peterburg," (Journey from Sitkha to St. Petersburg), *Severnaia Pchela*, 1836, No. 240-46, 259-64, and as F. P. Vrangel', *Ocherk puti iz Sitkhi v S. Peterburg* (Sketch of a journey from Sitkha to St. Petersburg) (St. Petersburg, 1836).]

6. [See document, board of directors to minister of finance (extract), Potekhin, pp. 38-41.]

7. [For documents of local Mexican and Russian authorities concerning the sale and relinquishment of Ross, see Clarence J. DuFour, "The Russian Withdrawal from California," *California Historical Society Quarterly*, 12, no. 3 (September, 1933): 240-76.]

8. Auriferous gravels were discovered in the regions lying beyond the mountain range separating the inhabited coastal strip from the interior plains.

Chapter 11

1. The company stopped selling nankeen in 1826.

2. The general meeting of stockholders of 2 October 1821, decided to make these contributions as a token of the company's loyal recognition for the imperial favor which had been shown it during the period of its charter. According to the imperial decree of the minister of finance concerning these contributions, the emperor was graciously pleased to accept them, a fact which was also communicated to the board of directors at the same time. Moreover, in view of the poverty of the citizens of Okhotsk, the board of directors granted their request in 1828 to make an annual distribution from the Okhotsk office of goods worth 85 silver rubles, 57½ kopeks per person. In 1840 they granted the request of the Okhotsk town governor's request to pay the city 1 3/7 silver kopeks (5 kopeks in bank notes) for each pud of company goods which proceeded through Okhotsk, on the grounds that this amount had been realized from the merchants trading in the port.

3. "If the chief manager is an official serving in a military or civil capacity at the time of his appointment to this post, he shall enjoy the privileges stated in the ukaz of March 21, 1810, for officials appointed to positions in the Siberian gubernias." (Paragraph 9 of the Imperial charter of September 13, 1821).

Chapter 12

1. See Chapter 8.

2. A. P. Sokolov, *Zapiski gidrograficheskago departamenta* [Journal of the Hydrographic Department], no. 9 (1851).

3. *Otechestvennyia zapiski* [Fatherland Notes], no. 6 (1860).

4. Sokolov, *Zapiski,* no. 9 (1851).

5. See Chapter 8.

6. Ibid., p. 292.

7. *Sibikta* is a green grass with black joints, about six inches high. In this region it grows all the year round, mostly on mountain ridges in damp spots produced by the seepage of mountain streams. According to the natives it is very nourishing, but there is a particular knack in caring for horses whose diet consists of this grass. In winter horses get at it through the snow.

8. Iakut horses are noted for their ability to carry heavy loads over seemingly impassible terrain. Climbing up the sides of high mountains or along steep descents they often fall head over heels, yet at the end somehow manage to stand up. They can be seen bogged down in marshes fighting to reach firm ground, or yet again, they can be found with hooves bleeding and unshod plodding along a stony shore straining at the end of a towline. Altogether, one is forced to admit that they serve their masters better than any other breed of horses in Russia.

9. Report dated 4 June 1844, No. 1273, Russian-American Company Archives, File of 1843, no. 6, pp. 85-91.

10. In 1844 the cost per horse had increased by ten paper rubles.

11. The settlers were given three cows per homestead and furnished with what necessities they required. The conditions of service laid down by Zavoiko also provided for the grant of a raft and two boats per river station and permission to levy and retain the following ferrying charges per single trip: six kopeks per passenger, twenty-four kopeks per ox, and thirty kopeks per horse. They were supplied with sundry tools, an annual issue of garden seeds, an initial grant of four puds of flour per household and half the yearly estimated ferrying income, calculated from the date of their arrival at the Aldan river. Their duties consisted of building a log house, the proper maintenance of the rafts and boats given them, and the obligation to have them serviceable at the end of winter. Later, they were required to furnish new craft to replace those past repair. Trading-post personnel were to be conveyed unimpeded from station to station on payment of 5 kopeks per verst per horse. In addition they were given the option of carrying the company's mail in winter at the same rate and a provision of three horses per station. The cattle they received from the company were not to be slaughtered until they had increased twofold.

12. A church was built at the trading post after its removal to Aian. All the natives in the surrounding country were included in the parish and could now attend services without trekking for miles as before, often at great inconvenience.

13. The imperial ordinance subsequently issued directed that (1) the trading post transferred from Okhotsk to Aian be known henceforth as "The Russian-American Company Port of Aian," similar to the altered designation of the Port of New Archangel; and (2) the post of Commandant of Aian Port be open exclusively to officers of field rank in the Imperial Navy and that, subject to the maintenance of existing relations between the company and the department of marine, they should retain all the rights, duties and responsibilities provided for in paragraphs 142, 143, 144, 145, 148, 156, and 158 of the Russian-American Company's charter relating to its chief manager.

The promotion of naval officers holding the posts of chief manager of the colony, his deputy, and the commandant of Aian port to higher rank was discontinued after 1859 by imperial ordinance following the general cancellation of such promotion for all naval officers taking service in Siberia.

14. The cost of settling areas was to be assumed by the company up to a limit of 3,000 silver rubles, payable immediately. The duties of the settlers were to consist of caring for three hundred horses and the necessary number of cattle, and the conveyance of the company's cargoes over a distance of 250 versts by pack

animals in summer at the rate of 3 silver rubles per horse and by sleigh in winter at 40 kopeks per pud. Passengers and mail were to be carried between stages at the established rates.

15. Iakutsk oblast administration to company commissioner in Iakutsk, 18 March 1846, no. 1902, Company Archives, File of 1843, no. 1, pp. 131-25.

16. In his frequent reports, Zavoiko had in fact requested the board to direct the attention of the government to the need of settling Iakuts along the route, a policy he believed would have a most beneficial effect on that part of Siberia.

17. In 1844 experimental sowings of winter and spring grain and of many varieties of wheat had amply proved the suitability of the region to agriculture. Vegetables of all kinds, and cabbage in particular, were grown with great success.

18. The Imperial Ordinance of 2 December 1849 abrogated the use of Okhotsk as an official port, terminated the functions of the local maritime board, incorporated the area into the oblast of Iakutsk, and established an entirely new oblast, that of Kamchatka. The former Okhotsk Maritime Board was transferred to Petropavlovsk, on Kamchatka. Below we given an extract from General Murav'ev's report on the pressing need of transferring the installations at Okhotsk to some other locality:

I feel it my duty to inform you that should the reasons advanced thus far for the immediate transfer of Okhotsk be found insufficient, extensive repairs [of the port installations] will have to be undertaken forthwith. Practically every single building of the naval and other departments owned by the crown is literally in ruins. To restore them to a state of worthiness will cost far more than the figures submitted in the estimates, whereas the temporary accomodation at Petropavlovsk is perfectly adequate to store government supplies, as I have personally verified. Moreover, it is extensive enough to quarter our troops in no worse conditions than in Okhotsk. The expenditure on future construction work in Petropavlovsk would be no greater than in Okhotsk, in spite of the distance over which building timber would have to be hauled, provided the work is done under the supervision of a single, competent, and independent overseer.

In hastening to report to Your Serene Highness immediately upon my return from the shores of the Sea of Okhotsk I have perhaps failed to comply with the accepted procedure of appending sundry estimates and detailed data to my report. Should I have done so, much valuable time might have been lost in endless queries and correspondence on a matter which has been hanging fire for over a century, while the high mortality rate among the garrison of Okhotsk and the unprotected position of Kamchatka demand speedy and less involved measures.

In Aian I had occasion to observe the speed and efficiency with which matters of this kind can be tackled provided they are untrammelled by the tiresome formality of accounts, estimates, and certificates.

In the annual report of the Russian-American Company you may have seen a reproduction of the buildings erected. I have examined these buildings on site and have as well inspected the road between Aian and Nel'kan now being built, with over 250 versts laid down by Mr. Zavoiko. I saw nothing of the kind on my way to Okhotsk, although the above mentioned report will have shown you the meager means needed to obtain such results.

19. Company Archives, File of 1853, no. 5, pp. 4-8.

20. Governor-general of Eastern Siberia to minister of interior, 7 June 1847, no. 881. Company Archives, File of 1845, no. 5, p. 63.

21. Journal, Council of Main Administration of Eastern Siberia, 5 December 1846, no. 148. Company Archives, File of 1845, no. 5, pp. 17-25.

22. Ibid., pp. 32-60.

23. Ibid., pp. 67-71; acting governor of Eastern Siberia to minister of interior, July 1848, no. 1192.

24. Report, commandant of Aian Port to board of directors, 31 December 1849, no. 321, Company Archives, File of 1845, no. 5, pp. 110-2.

25. Minister of interior to minister of finance, 23 February 1851, no. 269, Company Archives, File of 1845, no. 5, p. 110.

26. Governor-general to commandant of Aian Port, 7 October 1849, no. 199, Company Archives, File of 1852, no. 11, p. 6.

27. In 1855 and 1856 the bulk of food supplies for the colonies was shipped down the Amur.

Chapter 13

1. See Chapter 3.

2. I. F. Krusenstern, *Puteshestvie vokrug sveta v 1803, 1804, 1805 i 1806 gg.* [Voyage around the World in 1803, 1804, 1805 and 1806], pt. 2, pp. 200-5.

3. Here are a few words from d'Auvrey's project:

After navigating the channel, this vessel would reach the ostrog of Udsk under canvas and would at the same time explore the coast between the mouth of the Amur and the Uda. At this point the navigators would find a supply of food and possibly a larger ship for the voyage to Okhotsk.

But before undertaking this expedition some very important questions would have to be answered: Is it possible to sail a ship in and out of the mouth of the Amur, or is the entrance blocked? What would be the best type and draft of vessel for such a voyage? Finally, what course should be followed in order to leave the mouth of the river? These questions can be answered only after Krusentern's return.

(Archives of the Department of Asiatic Affairs) (Original in French).

4. Krusenstern, *Voyage*: pt. 2, pp. 196-97.

5. D'Auvrey remarks on the subject as follows:

The Russian fugitives, Dunaev and Rusinov, who made their escape by the river, emphatically deny in their statements having encountered any Chinese vessels powerful enough to face the craft we propose to build locally. It should be noted that Rusinov's route, which took him over seven weeks to cover, led him far beyond any Chinese towns situated on the right bank of the river. The contention that the suggested type of vessel would never be halted by the Chinese is further strengthened by the fact that neither of the escapees was captured by Chinese sentries in spite of the frailness of their respective craft: driven by hunger Rusinov gave himself up to the Chinese five hundred miles upstream from the mouth of the river, while Dunaev was captured by surprise after mooring alongside a Chinese post on the left bank, mistakenly taking it for a Tungus hut.

6. Shemelin refers to the subject in his *Zhurnal pervago puteshestviia rossiian vokrug zemnago shara.* [Journal of the first Russian voyage around the world], (2 parts, St. Petersburg, 1816-1818), pt. 2, pp. 259-60 in these terms:

The Chinese maintain a number of guard posts and mounted patrols on both sides of the river, but only in the vicinity of towns, settlements, trading posts, or administrative, military, or government offices lying close to the border; uninhabited country is left unguarded. The routes followed by Russian and Chinese patrols meet in the Nerchinsk region at the confluence of the Shilka and Argun' rivers, which after joining are called the Amur. As the Chinese frontier here crosses to the left bank of the river, looking downstream, and runs through uninhabited regions up to the Stanovoi range of mountains which extend to the Sea of Okhotsk, it follows that the river over its entire length flows through Chinese territory and, consequently, requires no guarding. Further, the inhabited localities mentioned above all lie deep inland, and the frontier line is purely imaginary, never having been defined by the bordering states, while, probably, the Chinese themselves have no conception of its extent. As the mouth of the river and the neighboring coastline and bays have never been explored by anyone except Mr. Krusenstern, the Chinese government would not have been troubled by reports on the region and would have no reason for maintaining armed ships to protect it. Besides, the existence of such ships has never been reported, and their presence has never been mentioned by any traveler.

A. F. Middendorf, in his *Reise in den aüssersten Norden und Osten Sibiriens während d. j. 1843-44* (St. Petersburg, 1847) [Journey to the north and east of Siberia in 1843-44] (pt. 1, p. 169n), mentions by name those who insisted on the need to navigate the Amur and notes that in 1816, Shemelin, the chief commissioner of the Russian-American Company, went so far as to uphold in print his opinion on the vital necessity for Russia to own navigational rights on the Amur and the river itself. (Shemelin, *Zhurnal*, pt. 1, p. 201) As Middendorf remarks, not until 1830 was a similar suggestion ever again published.

7. Archives of the Asiatic Department.

8. We now borrow a few words from Guri Vasil'ev's statement relating to his sea voyage from the mouth of the Amur while escaping from the Manchurians, as transmitted from Irkutsk to the Directorate of the Asiatic Department by Baron Shilling von Kanshtat on 16 January 1832, no. 1:

Traveling on foot, Vasil'ev succeeded in reaching the mouth of the Amur by the summer of 1826. Turning right he followed the coast for a few days, and then halted for the winter and built himself a small shelter on the land dividing the Giliaks and the Kugs. From the former, who supplied him with dried fish, he often heard of Russians who allegedly lived north of the river, and so in the spring of 1827 he decided to sail back to its mouth. Crossing over to the left bank he sailed farther north, always hugging the coast. Within thirty-five versts of Tugur, he broke his journey to winter with the Giliaks. In 1828, during Lent, he left with the Giliaks by dogteam for Ust'-Tugur, and then in the company of some Russian Tungus traveled on to Udsk ostrog where he reported to Mr. Uvarovskii. Throughout his journey round the bay he could see a large island, about sixty versts offshore to the eastward.

9. See Chapter 8.

10. This project and the information supplied by Koz'min was transmitted by Lavinskii to the Asiatic Department on 26 December 1831, no. 7.

11. Boats of this kind were built in the Ostashkov and Vyshnevolotsk uezds of the gubernia of Tver. The overall length from stem to stern was twelve to sixteen sazhens; the beam was four sazhens. The boats were usually tarred and hence were called "black boats." Their draft, with a full cargo of 7,000 puds, was 12-15 vershoks.

12. Following this the well-known scholar on Japan, Dr. von Siebold, published a map of Sakhalin Island and the opposite coast of Manchuria, copied from an 1808 original by the Japanese astronomer, Mamio Rinzo (See note to map 1). Rinzo, as indicated on the original map and in the description of these places in Siebold's

work (*Nippon*, I, erste Abtheilung, pp. 26, 127, and 139; and *Nippon*, VII, p. 167, Nachrichten über Krafto und das Amurland") named and described the mouth of of the Amur and many places on the island of Sakhalin and the Manchurian coast, including Lake Kizi. Thus, Rinzo named the straits between Sakhalin and the mainland after the Japanese astronomer Mamiano Seto; the capes at the entrance to the river on the right bank he called Wasi and Firoke; the first tributary at the southwest bend of the river, Honko; and so forth. These facts are also mentioned by Middendorf (Ibid., pt. 1, p. 173). He draws attention (note 2, p. 173) to information given him by [Johann Ch.] Stuckenberg (*Hydrographie des Russisches Reiches*, 6 (1849): 177) concerning Admiral Nagaev, who, he states, had mapped the mouth of the Amur, and to Stuckenberg's surmise that the map was shelved in the archives of our Admiralty. He also remarks incidentally that Nagaev was commissioned merely to coordinate the findings of Bering's and Spanberg's earlier surveys.

Here I feel compelled to dwell briefly on Mr. Middendorf's contribution to the exploration of the Amur and the eastern regions of Siberia generally. In 1842, after completing a research mission sponsored by the Academy of Science, he decided on his own responsibility to return from the shores of the Okhotsk Sea by following the banks of the Amur. Though coming close, he never actually reached the mouth of the river because of the lateness of the season. As he remarks in the account of his travels (pt. 1, p. 185): "To my sorrow I dared not entertain the idea of staying any longer and was compelled reluctantly to abandon my impatient desire to reach the mouth of the Amur, only three days distant from the eastern tip of Academy Bay, Umelongte Cape, on Muktel' Peninsula. We had to prepare for our return journey and I hastened back to the mouth of the Tugur. On 22 September 1844, with nothing to keep us back, we set out over the Amur region on our long route home." Had Middendorf's wish been fulfilled, we should long ago have had a perfectly true and accurate description of a region over which so many doubts were expressed and arguments engendered. Middendorf's explorations in various regions of Siberia and the detailed account of his efforts, substantiated by a surprising amount of research into ancient and modern sources of information, speak for themselves. Middendorf evaluates Koz'min's exploratory work around the shores of the Okhotsk Sea on behalf of the company, completed before his own, as follows (Ibid., pt. 1, p. 104):

> The precise knowledge and definitions we now possess of the Shantars are entirely due to Koz'min, this worthy officer of the Corps of Naval Navigators and Wrangell's traveling companion on his journeys from the mouth of the Kolyma River. For over two hundred years Okhotsk, by incurring heavy losses and exacting an excessive toll in human life, had proved to be one of the most worthless harbors in the world. The government either ignored the constant drain on shipping and other resources or tried to provide for the future by searching for a new harbor. However, the quest proved fruitless and Okhotsk remained a port. For obvious reasons the North-American (i.e. the Russian-American) Company, as a business concern, could not put up with this state of affairs and, in 1829, entrusted Koz'min with the task of locating a site for a new harbor between the Uda and Tugur rivers, i.e. on the southern shores of the Okhotsk Sea and possibly, even farther. As Koz'min's diary was published two years after my return, his detailed, thoroughly accurate charts, as well as a brief account of his sailings, description of the coast, mainland and islands are now at everyone's disposal.

13. 12 December, no. 89, Company Archives, File of 1844, no. 1, pp. 1, 2.

14. In a letter to Baron Wrangell, (20 April 1846, no. 331. Company Archives, File of 1844, no. 1, p. 25), reporting in detail on the work of equipping the ship, Teben'kov says: "With God's help, the expedition is so well equipped that were I

to join it myself I doubt if I could find anything lacking. The ship is of the best, her captain an experienced and efficient officer, and his mates and the crew all healthy and experienced men. Instruments, rowboats, canoes, everything in fact, has been seen to. The one thing left us is to hope for the successful outcome of the enterprise."

15. 17 April 1846, no. 121, Company Archives, File of 1844, no. 1, p. 31.

16. Ibid., no. 120, p. 29.

17. Text of Teben'kov's instructions to Gavrilov (Company Archives, File of 1849, no. 1, relating to an expedition for sounding the mouth of the Amur River, dispatched on behalf of the Ministry of Foreign Affairs, p. 31.):

Our government has learned from Tungus wandering on the shores of the Okhotsk Sea that a number of Russian fugitives and vagabond tramps, either fleeing the law or simply tired of wandering, have drifted to the mouth of the Amur and have settled there. You are probably acquainted with happenings of a similar nature at the beginning of the eighteenth century, when a number of people of that ilk, likewise on the Amur, founded the town of Albazin and, having fortified it, proceeded to pester the Chinese. In doing so they greatly inconvenienced our government, which was forced to take the punitive measures of which you are aware, and the Chinese government suspected that the whole thing was a ruse used by us to expand our possessions.

In order to forestall a repetition of such events our government has requested that the board of directors of the Russian-American Company dispatch a ship from the colony on a mission of enquiry. This ship is to enter the mouth of the Amur and ascertain on site whether such Russian settlements do in fact exist and, if so, the extent of the possible annoyance they might cause.

To allay possible Chinese suspicions or prematurely warn the fugitives you must disguise the identity of your ship. Nothing on board should betray her nationality and you will, therefore, take the necessary steps to mask her Russian origin as well as that of you and your crew. I shall furnish you with a flag which you will hoist and fly after leaving Sakhalin. The composition of your crew will not give them away; on assignments try to pick your crews so as to conform to the stated need of concealing their Russian nationality.

When at work, order your boats to keep together and not to scatter over a wide area, so precluding the possibility of a surprise attack by natives. As far as possible avoid contact with the natives either personally or through your crews. If you cannot avoid doing so, adopt a friendly attitude, pretend you are engaged in fishing and looking for a deep-water current. In case of danger, instruct your boats immediately to rejoin their parent vessel. Be particularly careful about allowing anything from your vessel to fall into the hands of the natives. Should circumstances force you to appeal to them for fish, barter with them in goods common to all Europeans and only in your own presence. Their greatest need is tobacco; when handing it out in exchange use the Virginian, not the Circassian, variety.

Having thus formulated the aim of your mission and the security measures you should adopt to preserve overall secrecy or prevent any leakage to the Chinese, I hereby instruct you to enter the bay of the Amur River and to locate its mouth. You will probably find a bar at the entrance, a feature common to most rivers. Cross the bar and proceed upstream to where the river flows over a true bed. At this point you will halt and make as detailed a hyrographic survey of the surroundings as you can. You will make the same kind of survey of the bay along the coast from Sakhalin to the entrance of the bay, supplementing it with your observations relative to the risks involved in entering the river and the accessibility of it, these latter being the main objectives of the mission with which you are entrusted.

When you reach your destination you will first of all ascertain whether there are, in fact, any Russian settlements on the Amur. If there are, assume the role of a foreigner and, I repeat, do not let them suspect you are Russian and, morever, certainly make no demands on them. Try and work out their numbers as best you can. In intercourse with them, strictly prompted by necessity, tell them that you have learnt to speak Russian on the Okhotsk Sea, while engaged in the fishing trade—that, too, being the reason for your venturing into the Amur.

You are instructed to continue your exploratory work until you have located the fairway or definitely established that, because of shallow water, you cannot bring your ship into the river. Only then return and, if time permits, on your way out to the mouth of the bay examine the main features of the mainland or the Sakhalin peninsula within the bay. You will maintain unceasingly the security measures you have followed by avoiding intercourse with the natives or revealing the fact that yours is a Russian ship. After returning to Aian Bay proceed to New Archangel.

[Further] instructions to Gavrilov:

The board of directors of the Russian-American Company, while directing me to dispatch a vessel for hydrographical research, with which I entrust you, inform me that this expedition is being undertaken by imperial command and that the emperor expressly desires that full security be maintained. I bring this point to your attention for consideration on all occasions.

To this end I suggest that you reveal your destination (which will be detailed to you from St. Petersburg and handed to you by the Aian office) to no one, and that having sailed from Aian you continue to withold this information and reserve the knowledge to yourself, thus even keeping your officers in ignorance as to where you intend to sail. It is understood that for doing so you will have to find some suitable pretext.

I have mentioned that in Aian the local office will hand you your orders from St. Petersburg defining the aim of the expedition. In all probability, the various circumstances which may pertain to its achievement will have been foreseen. It only remains for me to advise you to follow meticulously the instructions you receive from St. Petersburg. However, I think it appropriate to remark that I am furnishing you with a set of instructions of my own explaining your presence in foreign waters should you by mischance fall into the hands of the natives (which God forbid). No doubt this fact will be mentioned in the directives you receive. I recommend that you regard my own instructions as a general guide to your activities, and only insofar as they comply with your orders from St. Petersburg. Should, however, the fact be omitted from your official orders, you may use them in the improbable event of the loss of your ship when you will, perforce, fall into the hands of the natives. For the reasons mentioned above I attach a passport for your ship and your crew which you should only use in the event foreseen (which God forbid) or in case you receive no passport from St. Petersburg to meet the occasion.

18. Report to the board of directors of the company by the chief manager of the colonies, 15 May 1846, no. 331: Company Archives, 1844, no. 1, p. 23.

19. Gavrilov's report to the chairman of the board of 21 August 1846 and the brig's logbook. Ibid., p. 96-129.

20. See Gavrilov's chart: Exploration of the bay and mouth of the Amur, included with log book.

21. Some of the details given above, the excerpts from Gavrilov's log, the official orders he received and Teben'kov's directives are here quoted mainly in order to clear Gavrilov's memory of the unjustified assertions by Mr. Romanov. In an

article entitled "The Annexation of the Amur by Russia" published by the journal *Russkoe slovo*, nos. 4, 6, 7, 8 (1859) Romanov tries to prove that Gavrilov's expedition did little to further the work of later explorers of the mouth and bay of the Amur.

22. The names of the settlements are here transcribed literally as they appear in Gavrilov's logbook. The settlements of Puir and Machu are located on the Tartar shore, between the mouth of the Amur and Schast'e Bay.

23. "From my ship," writes Gavrilov, "I steered W by S ½ W., keeping the baidarkas at a distance of a verst to north and south. The first promontory lay N by N; the depth at first shallowed from four to two sazhens, then gradually increased to five sazhens and finally dropped again to one sazhen. The deep water channel, where it is from two to two-and-a-half sazhens wide, is no longer than a mile. Thereafter the depth varied from ½ to one sazhen, but 400 sazhens offshore we struck three sazhens, the first promontory lying N by W. After this and right up to the shore the overall depth is one sazhen."

24. We quote from Gavrilov's logbook on the first soundings of the Amur River: "Immediately after pulling away from the first promontory to ENE an increase in depth was observed and at a distance of half a verst it equalled six sazhen. An effort was made to locate the channel in the bay but with no effect. Shallowing gradually down to three sazhens, the stream is broken by a sand-bank. Altering our course to N (over a depth of 6½ sazhen) we steered for the promontory at the entrance of the bay and about a mile away found a two-foot sand-bank, which stretches across the mouth of the river and terminates within a mile of the entrance promontory. Here the depth increases abruptly: 1, 3, 6, 8, 7, 6, 5 and 4, sazhen at 100 sazhen from the promontory."

25. See Gavrilov's map.

26. "Therefore, the deep channel along which the ship was sailing," says Gavrilov, "is not connected to the river and the northern stream of the river flows along its bank constantly diminishing in depth until it, probably, reaches the three-sazhen depth by the low-lying cape; here it is only broad enough to admit the passage of a boat (Gavrilov's log entry of 14 August).

27. I had intended to investigate the north and south flows, a task I completed before dinner. As the river reaches the bank it divided into two branches, one flowing along the north shore, the other the south, the depth decreasing by a third, though deeper in the north branch, i.e., from seven to eight sazhen. The depth in the south branch is only six sazhen; there are many sandbanks and the bottom is very uneven, thus after six it is suddenly three sazhen, then one, and back again to six. The bottom of the north branch is, however, quite even. Having finished with the south branch I moved over to the north intending to row down it into the estuary and ascertain the point of entry.

(Gavrilov's log entry of 7 August). Gavrilov's map indicates that this north branch peters out at a sand-bank somehwere down the middle of its course, whereas later surveys show that the flow is uninterrupted. The error can be explained, as previously mentioned, by the lack of time for detailed exploration.

28. "The annexation of the Amur by Russia," *Russkoe slovo*: 7(1859): 93.

29. The Ministry of Foreign Affairs defined the aim of the expedition in the following terms (Asiatic Department, 15 February 1849, no. 151, Company Archives, File of 1849, no. 4, p. 7): "We are particularly anxious to establish relations with the Giliaks, living on the left bank of the Amur near its mouth. The Giliaks and their kinsmen apparently do not recognize the sovereignty of China. Encounters with the Chinese should in any case be avoided."

Concerning this independence Middendorf says: (Ibid. pt. 1, p. 167) "Prior to my voyage all of the tribes living along the lower reaches of the Amur were regarded as Chinese subjects, but during my sojourn there I had occasion to note that the Giliaks do not consider themselves subject to China. The fact that the Chinese themselves recognized their independence is proved by 'lettre de'Andre Kimarkim, diacre coreén, datée du 15 decembre, 1844 in *Nouvelles Annales des Voyages* 1(1847): 81. Here I should add that, in my time, this de facto independence also included the Tungus tribes of the Amgun' river basin.'

Another likely reason for the company's dispatch of a trading expedition to the mouth of the Amur was the information supplied by Orlov in 1848 about some of the Amur natives whom he had had occasion to meet during his trading travels. He reported that "in the course of the present winter (1847-48), having left a store-keeper at Udsk ostrog to deal certain goods, I traveled among the settlements as far as what the Tungus call Cape Burukan on the Tugur River about two-hundred versts upstream from its mouth. On Burukan I met a gathering of Tungus and twenty Neidal'tsi of both sexes. The Neidal'tsi are a different people from the Tungus, living on the Amgun' River, one of the left-bank tributaries of the Amur. They are not Russian subjects but they do not recognize the Chinese government. Emissaries of this government are rumored to visit them in winter to collect taxes. However, the first Neidalets [singular form] they meet is generally stripped of what they consider adequate and no individual collection of taxes is ever made. The Neidal'tsi mostly trade furs and moose for manufactured and sundry other goods required by the Asians, they trade either with Russians on Burukan, the neighboring tribes of Samagrtsi and Chukchagiry, or with petty Chinese merchants from the Amur. One of the Samagrtsi on Burukan tried to induce me to go the Amgun'; he advised me on how to trade with the Neidal'tsi, made me familiar with local prices, and even appointed a place where I might meet them for commerce. Though I am aware that our merchants and Russian Tungus trade as far as the Amur, I did not venture that far, partly because I had no positive knowledge of the Chinese frontier, but mainly because of heavy snowfalls. The Neidal'tsi, Samagrtsi, and Chukchagiry are industrious peoples. They not only refrain from hindering the traveling merchants but, by general agreement, invariably make them welcome in their habitations." (Report of the commandant of Aian Port, 17 May 1848, to the Board of Directors).

Besides the above, letters from the Kamchatka Bishop Innokentii to the Metropolitan of Moscow, Filaret (*Pamiatnik trudov pravoslavnykh blagovestnikov russkikh* [Memorial of the Works of Russian Orthodox Evangelists, hereafter *PTPBR*], p. 263.), show that some of the Neidal'tsi and other Amur natives embraced Christianity as far back as 1845. He says, "the light of the Gospel is beginning to penetrate from our side into the confines of China, though in this I had no part. The priest at Udsk reports that in the course of journeys around his parish he meets at Burukan Nigidal'tsi (Neidal'tsi) and other natives who live in China but who come here for trade and commerce. At each meeting his discourses have borne fruit. In 1845, when the church at Udsk was joined to the See of Kamchatsk, nine of these natives were baptized; and later, in 1846, three more. One, in particular, was very insistent in his wish to be baptized.

30. Memorandum, 15 February 1849, no. 151.

31. Orlov's report of 4 September 1849: Company Archives, File of 1849, no. 4, pp. 28, 44.

32. Pozvein subsequently took part in practically every Russian expedition to the Amur region. According to Orlov, Pozvein and the other Giliaks, Gaivrano and Dombrano, were well off and enjoyed the respect of the natives; Middendorf (ibid., p. 161, pt. 1) writing about Pozvein's Tungus origin, calls him "a hybrid of genius."

33. Or, more properly speaking, into Schast'e Bay, first noted from the transport

Baikal on 1 August 1849 and as outlined in the transport's logbook, examined by the ship's captain and two officers on 2 August.

34. Renamed Sv. Nikolai [St. Nicholas] Bay by Nevel'skoi.

35. Board of directors to vice-chancellor, 12 January 1850, no. 26: Company Archives, File of 1849, no. 4, p. 43.

36. 10 February, No. 584, ibid., p. 46.

37. Instruction to Orlov by Aian Port commandant of 16 June 1850: no, 18, ibid., p. 60.

38. Probably one of the whalers who sometimes sailed into the straits from the Okhotsk Sea.

39. "From Cape Tabakh," writes Orlov, "i.e., from the final tip of the left bank of the Amur, I sounded the whole distance to the northern roadstead. Opposite Cape Puir, a rising wind and the stubbornness of my Giliaks forced me to abandon operations and to land. Along the entire length of the channel in the estuary the depth varies from five to eleven sazhens at low tide, except for a side run into which I was brought against my wishes. Judging by the depths encountered and by the assertion of the Giliaks living along the shores of the estuary, the existence of a connection between the river and the Okhotsk Sea is quite obvious, with a minimum depth of four sazhens. The Giliaks' statements may be trusted unreservedly as they have proved correct on repeated occasions." (Orlov's report to Aian Port Commandant, 30 June 1850, no. 2: Company Archives, File of 1849, no. 4, p. 72.)

40. Ibid., p. 73.

41. "On 15 July," writes Orlov in his reports to the Commandant 15 August 1850, nos. 13 and 14 (Orlov's journal), "we went as far as the fishing poles standing north of Cape Puir, waited for the ebb tide and rowed into the Okhotsk Sea at an overall depth of 3½ sazhens. Once out to sea, we halted at a depth of four sazhens. The average depth of the channel joining the Amur River to the Okhotsk Sea is six sazhens, except over the bar, where it does not fall below three."

42. "The Annexation of the Amur by Russia," *Russkoe slovo*, 7(1859): 118, gives a detailed account of the reasons which prompted Nevel'skoi to found a post on the banks of the Amur, thus contravening the expressly stated prohibition in his instructions—namely, "anywhere but on the banks of the Amur." In the absence of documentary evidence we limit ourselves merely to recording the founding of Nikolaevskii post on the strength of the material at our disposal.

43. Romanov, "Annexation of the Amur by Russia," *Russkoe slovo*, 7(1859): 120.

44. This committee was formed by imperial decree, already in 1849.

45. Proceedings of the company's board of directors of 13 February 1851. Company Archives, File of 1851, no. 8, pp. 4-6.

46. It was proposed to keep the complement of this works unit to a minimum of sixty men, composed mainly of tradesmen in addition to crews off ships of the Okhotsk flotilla. These ships, a minimum of two for 1851, were used for cruising in those waters and for maintaining communications. For guarding its trading posts and for convoy duty, the company proposed to recruit the best cossacks of the Iakutsk Regiment and the Okhotsk Company. Over and above government pay, the men were to receive 30-40 silver rubles per year and their officers, employed as works overseers, were to receive a board allowance of 150-200 silver rubles per year. In general, the company proposed in 1852, that it assume the maintenance charges of shore and ships' crews alike against a government refund at the ordinary rates of pay.

47. Company instructions to Nevel'skoi, 16 February 1851, no. 196, and memoradum to governor-general of Eastern Siberia of same date, no. 197: Company Archives, File of 1851, no. 8, pp. 10 and 17.

48. Letter from the chairman of the company's board of directors to the governor-general of Eastern Siberia, February 13, 1851, no. 183: Company Archives, File of 1851, no. 8, p. 8.

49. Copies of correspondence exchanged between the governor-general of Eastern Siberia and the chief of the naval staff, and between the state chancellor and governor-general March 7, no. 768: Company Archives, File of 1851, no. 8, pp. 32, 33.

50. Letters of 24 and 30 July 1851, from Captain Nevel'skoi and the *Baikal's* commander, Captain-Lieutenant Garnovskii, to Commandant of Aian Port Captain-Lieutenant Kashevarov. Also report of 25 July, by the Commander of the *Shelekhov*, Lieutenant Matskevich, on service with the company, (no. 17: Company Archives, File of 1861, no. 9, pp. 1-13.) The *Shelekhov* was an oak-timbered ship of 234 tons, built in Bremen in 1845.

51. The government later paid the company 36,000 silver rubles for the loss of the *Shelekhov*.

52. I have borrowed the details on the inauguration of post Nikolaevskii and of some of the expeditions into the interior of the region from Berezin's diary, kept by him while on the Amur and from instructions given him by Captain Nevel'skoi. We are equally indebted to Berezin for preserving the diaries and sundry other papers of the late Orlov referring to his explorations in the Amur region, excerpts from which have supplied much of the material included herein on the activities of the expedition sent to the region.

53. *Morskoi sbornik* [Naval Journal] 12(1858).

54. The limitations of this treatise and the absence of much documentary data prevent making a detailed account of the exploration in the region of the Amur. We are confined to giving a list of the most important works contributing to a greater acquaintance with the facts on the territory, and to describing certain events relative to this exploration.

55. The settlements of the Samagrtsi extend from the mouth of the Amur to the settlement of Kevrety.

56. "The natives obtain their clothes, khandzha (Manchurian vodka), wooden and earthenware house utensils, tobacco, mats, millet, and lengths of Chinese cloth from the Manchurians. In exchange they are given furs (common fox and sable pelts), dried sturgeon spine, glue, sturgeon and sterlet gristle, jerked fish, small bells, and articles made of copper. The Japanese, via the inhabitants of Sakhalin, supply the natives with iron cooking pots, copperware, and lead. Manchurian tobacco, eagle tail feathers, live eagles, and bearskins are given in exchange." (Letter of Captain Nevel'skoi, 2 November 1851 to the board of directors of the company, no. 150: Company Archives, File of 1851, no. 8, p. 68, note on native trade with the Manchurians and Japanese).

57. The straits up to the cape bearing his name were earlier studied by Nevel'skoi.

58. We give a brief extract from Berezin's diary about his search for De-Kastri Bay: "On April 23, we found in Aur settlement, a Giliak shaman named Saiaga and from his stories about a large bay to the south called Nol'mar, visited long ago by two vessels, concluded that this must be De-Kastri Bay, visited by La Perouse. We made friends with the Giliak, and took him with us; seven days later we were there. We entered at high tide and were nearly wrecked on a cliff. The chart of the bay made by La Perouse was very accurate."

59. The general rule applied to natives convicted of theft, robbery, or similar offenses consisted either of the return of the stolen articles to the owner, payment of their value, or a term of labor in the Russian settlement.

60. Nevel'skoi's instructions of 15 April 1852. No. 44: [Company Archives?]

61. The natives living along the Amgun' are just ordinary settled Tungus. They have the same customs, speak the same language, and wear the same kinds of clothes. Sustained intercourse between Russians and Tungus, to whom they are related, has acquainted them with Russian customs and forms of administration, and Chikhachov often heard them express regret at not being properly administered by anyone and left defenseless against the ferocity of the Giliaks. Some of the Amgun' inhabitants had been converted to Orthodoxy in Burukan; there were also a few Tungus families who had settled on the Amgun' long ago but who, nevertheless, still sent their iasak [tribute] to Udsk ostrog.

62. The fact that the ship used the direct passage from the open sea into the Amur tends to prove close knowledge of the vicinity. Another remarkable fact was the pains the ship's landing parties took to instill fear of the Russians into the natives, the constant refrain being, "when the Russians settle in your midst, they will hang you all." The great number of foreign missionaries scattered over the Amur region served, of course, as an excellent source of information for the ships now frequently sailing along those shores under the guise of whalers. The missionaries in the region were a varied collection—preachers, sorcerers, shamans; sometimes they passed themselves off as Russians, and all wore native clothes. Their constant efforts to breed mistrust of the Russians among the natives and Manchurians were not without effect; when Chikhachov came to the mouth of the Garin River it was rumored that the Russian goods were poisoned and that the first Manchurian to don a jacket made of Russian cloth would wither immediately. Soothsayers predicted the certain death of a native if and when the Russians drove through a village, etc. The Manchurians told Chikhachov about a missionary who had elected to dwell in one of their prayer houses on the Sungari River. When asked who he was and why he was there he replied that he was a higher being, whom everyone must worship and, consequently, he had every right to live in the prayer house. This answer cost him his life. In the account of his expeditions to the Amur region (*Morskoi sbornik* 2[1859]:338), Boshniak also mentions three Catholic missionaries who were killed close to the settlement of Sabakh by the Giliaks out of greed for the silver articles in their possession. At a later date he was told by an abbot of the Catholic mission in Hong Kong that one of the missionaries killed was the well-known Labrumiere, who had gone to the mouth of the Amur to preach the Gospel.

63. When Chikhachov returned to Petrovskoe he was sent by Nevel'skoi to Khodzhi Bay in a locally built boat of 35 tons (later christened *Babushka* [Grandma]). Once again he failed to reach the bay, this time because of the unseaworthiness of his craft.

64. A town on the Sungari River at its confluence with the Khurga River, the starting point of all goods sent into Giliak territory on the Amur.

65. Natives from the vicinity of Lake Kizi.

66. "As early at 1850 (Nevel'skoi to the company's board of directors, 2 November, 1851, no. 150: Company Archives, File of 1851, no. 8, p. 64), Orlov informed the natives that a reward would be given to anyone bringing a sample of coal or describing the locality from which it came. The response was rapid; a few days later a Giliak presented a lump of coal which, on testing, was found to be of excellent quality. The Giliak who brought it said the natives obtained it on Sakhalin Island, to the south of Pogobi settlement, i.e., twenty miles from De-Kastri Bay and that it lay there in great quantities, by the seashore. The Giliaks used it for making a kind of clasp." This information proved entirely correct.

67. See report, Boshniak to Nevel'skoi, 15 April 1852, in A. I. Alekseev, *Amurskaia ekspeditsiia, 1849-1855 gg.* (The Amur expedition, 1849-1855) (Moscow, 1974), pp. 183-88.

68. *Morskoi sbornik* (1859).

69. Further information concerning this post [Imperatorskaia Gavan'] will be given in the next chapter.

70. Nevel'skoi in his submission of 2 January 1851, no. 150, pp. 72-74, petitioned for six assistants: 1 accountant for Orlov, 6 clerks, an expert shipbuilder, 5 fishermen, 6 experts in various trades (these he had already engaged), and 110 laborers.

71. After leaving Petropavlovsk in April, Rear-Admiral Zavoiko's Kamchatka squadron had by this time reached the shores of the Amur.

72. Ukaz, Governing Senate, 14 August 1859, no. 36,769. [For further information on the events covered in this chapter, see G. I. Nevel'skoi, *Podvigi russikh morskikh ofitserov na krainem vostoke Rossii* (Exploits of Russian naval officers in the Russian Far East) (St. Petersburg, 1878); and Alekseev, op. cit.]

Chapter 14

1. A note on the occupation of Sakhalin, 22 March 1852, submitted by the board of directors to the Ministry of Foreign Affairs (Russian American Company Archives, File of 1853, no. 12, pp. 1-6).

2. Memorandum from chief of the naval ministry, 12 April 1853, no. 617: ibid., p. 7. Other principal articles of the imperial order placing Sakhalin under company control were: (1) a promise to assign officers and soldiers to the company for the defense of its establishments on Sakhalin; (2) an agreement that the company would occupy, in 1853, such places as might be found most important (from 1854 it would have a special manager, subordinate in all political questions to the governor-general of Eastern Siberia or other government officials as designated by the emperor); (3) an understanding that the company would not permit any foreign establishments to be built on Sakhalin either by unilateral decision or by mutual consent, and that this island could only be transferred back to the government; (4) an agreement that the government could use coal from Sakhalin free of charge, but would mine it at its own expense; (5) a promise that the company would undertake to maintain a sufficient number of ships for the protection of the coast and harbors, but in case of attack could request armed government forces; (6) an understanding that officers and men assigned for service on Sakhalin would be taken there on company ships and at company expense from the places of their former service; (7) a promise to assign this year not less than one hundred men from Kamchatka, provided the company would arrange their transportation; and (8) a promise to give the company 50,000 silver rubles at once for the expenses of this undertaking from sums assigned to the governor-general of Eastern Siberia for affairs concerning the Giliaks, and that the company would not be required to account for this sum.

3. These employees were to include several persons acquainted with bookkeeping, the fur trade, and general trade and merchandise; two pilots' mates experienced in coastal survey work; several workers, literate if possible, capable of serving as foremen; and a crew of experienced Aleut hunters for the exploration of the coasts with regard to the fur trade. This crew was to have twelve baidarkas, carrying two or three men each. Wives of the Aleuts wishing to accompany their husbands to Sakhalin were to sew [sealskins for] baidarkas and do other work for which they were suited.

4. The mining engineer and the head miners were employed later on for coal mining on Kenai Bay.

5. From the report of the company to the governor-general of Eastern Siberia (Company Archives, File of 1853, no. 486), "to establish the first settlements in one or two places on the western and eastern shores of the island, in its southern part, where ships could arrive safely, but not in the estuary, where navigation is less convenient and where foreigners cannot be expected to appear." Mr. Murav'ev gave corresponding instructions to Nevel'skoi, in which he confirmed that Nevel'-skoi was "not to disturb the Japanese traders and fishermen in the southern part of the island, but to be friendly with them." (Para. 1 and 2 of 15 April 1853 instruction, no. 125). Mr. Boshniak writes (*Morskoi sbornik* [Naval Chronicle] 9[1859]:396) that Nevel'skoi was instructed to occupy a place only on the western or eastern shore of the island, but *not* in Aniva Bay, but there is nothing of this kind in the instruction to Nevel'skoi. As may be seen from his communication to the commandant of the port of Aian (1 September 1853, no. 287: Company Archives, File of 1853, no. 12, p. 67): "the governor-general orders me to occupy two or three places in the southern part of the island at my discretion." Nevel'skoi was fully convinced that his occupation of the shore of Aniva Bay was strictly in compliance with the wish of the governor-general and the company administration.

6. Nevel'skoi reported to the board of directors 15 October 1853, no. 336: Company Archives, File of 1853, no. 12, p. 109) that he founded a second post on Sakhalin named Il'inskii, but as can be seen from other documents, he had no time to do this because it was so late in the season. Orlov, who was sent by him to Sakhalin to find a convenient location, arrived on the transport *Irtysh* and soon went to Petrovskoe. The men wintered in Kostantinovskii post. Orlov's journey in Sakhalin took him from Cape Notoro over the mountain ridge to the eastern shore on the Okhotsk Sea by the Many River, thence following the coast to Mordvi-nov Bay and from there to Murav'evskii post. On 28 November Orlov started by sled from Imperatorskaia Gavan' to Petrovskoe with one guide. Following the coast, he reached the Tumdzhi River. Following this river, he overtook a party of ten Giliak traders, who were walking on skis and dragging five sleds loaded with goods and provisions. Such companions were priceless, since, in spite of all efforts of Mr. Boshniak, the natives had refused to accompany Orlov such a long way as to the shores of the Amur. At first, Orlov and his companions made slow progress, carrying such heavy loads that the Giliaks could not make more than fifteen versts per day. Large unfrozen patches of water warmed by the swift river current in spite of 25° below freezing tempratures, slowed them down at almost every step. When 180 versts from the mouth of the river they began to follow the Sololi River. As they approached the pass in the mountains the snow became deeper and deeper, finally reaching a depth of four feet. The descent into the valley of the Khoial River was an almost vertical 1,500 feet. They followed the Khoial as far as the Iai or Iava River, and on 28 December arrived at Mariinsk post on Lake Kizi. "In view of the formation of the coast," writes Orlov, "and the almost constant obstacles from the many rivers, a trail for saddle horses can hardly be built. In the wintertime, given a sufficient supply of food for the dogs, communication by dogteam would be possible, although the pass over the mountains is very steep. The surface is mostly tundra." (Report of Orlov to Nevel'skoi, 25 January 1854, no. 1).

7. To this order Nevel'skoi added that in case the *Irtysh* should arrive so late that leaving the harbor would be dangerous (assuming that the newness of the place and inaccuracy of the charts would make sailing dangerous after 15 October), the *Nikolai* would have to spend the winter in Imperatorskaia Gavan'. In case the *Irtysh* should not arrive at all, the *Nikolai* was to sail again to Sakhalin Island, and remain under orders of the chief of Murav'evskii post. (Instruction, Nevel'skoi to Klinkovstrem, 30 September 1853, no. 14. Russian-American Company Archives, File of 1853, no. 12, p. 113).

8. *Morskoi sbornik* 10(1859):403.

9. Company Archives, File of 1853, no. 12, p. 166.

10. *Morskoi sbornik* 10(1859):406-7.

11. Report, Klinkovstrem to board of directors, 24 April 1854: Company Archives, File of 1853, no. 12, p. 231.

12. From His Imperial Majesty to the Chief of the Naval Ministry, 9 April 1856, no. 12,500: Company Archives, File of 1853, no. 12, p. 251.

13. From communication, governor-general of Eastern Siberia to chief of the naval ministry, 5 May 1856, no. 323: Company Archives, File of 1853, no. 12, p. 260.

14. Ibid., pp. 251-59.

15. Ibid., p. 363.

16. The vessel *Sitkha* was captured by the enemy squadron in 1854, at the entrance to Avacha Bay, Kamchatka peninsula, with a cargo for Petropavlovsk. The company lost 91,529 rubles 30 kopeks, counting the cost of the ship and the cargo. The company's expenses for the occupation of Sakhalin Island were 29,619 silver rubles 32 kopeks, not counting the 50,000 rubles given by the government.

17. This view of the governor-general was shared by the grand duke, according to Chief of the Naval Ministry Baron Wrangell and reported to the board of directors. 8 May 1856, no. 12,625: Company Archives, File of 1853, no. 12, p. 259.

18. Sea cabbage is a species of seaweed, found on rocky shores or on shoals covered with water at high tide. Sometimes sea cabbage grows very high above the sea bottom. Several kinds are used for food.

19. *Morskoi sbornik* 12(1858):184, 185, 194.

20. Ibid., p. 14.

21. Ibid., p. 45.

22. The word "Ainu" means "man" in their language. More detailed information is given here about the Ainu in comparison to other natives of Sakhalin because the Russians living at Aniva Bay had a better opportunity to study the mode of living, customs, and religion of the natives of southern Sakhalin.

23. The tail of an eagle with a red beak is valued highly by the Japanese. The tail of an eagle with a black beak is considered of inferior quality and brings a low price.

Chapter 15

1. See Chapter 5.

2. A barrel contains 31½ gallons. One gallon equals 32½ Russian charkas, so a barrel is equivalent to 10½ vedros.

3. Department of Manufacturing and Internal Trade, 14 December 1842, no. 5191: Company Archives, File of 1842, no. 14, p. 7.

4. Ibid., pp. 9-11.

5. In the ministry's words: "Setting up a limit within which foreign ships should not approach our shores for whaling would be incompatible with the spirit of the Convention of 1824 and our Convention of 1825 with Great Britain. Taking a measure of such nature without preliminary explanations and negotiations with other powers would cause friction because of the lack until now of a clear and uniform definition of territorial waters among nations. As far as the colonial cruisers are concerned, His Majesty the Emperor did not give his consent to use the naval flag. He also ordered it to be known that the commanders of these cruisers must be very careful in their actions and as far as possible avoid occurrences that can lead to

complaints on the part of the foreigners." Ministry of Finance to board of directors, 26 May 1845, no. 2518: ibid., 37a.

6. Minister of foreign affairs to minister of finance, 4 June 1847, no. 4575: ibid., pp. 62-65.

7. Gavrilov's report to the Board of Directors, 3 July 1847: ibid., pp. 83-84.

8. Department of Manufacturing and Internal Trade to Company, 8 November 1848, no. 5254: ibid., p. 102.

9. That is, as expressed in the letter of the naval chief-of-staff to the minister of finance of 24 February 1849, no. 8244: ibid., p. 108

> that from detailed accounts of the naval commissariat it appears first that complete fitting out of a forty-four-gun frigate for cruising in waters of the Russian possessions in America (including the cost of the frigate's crew, all its armament and annual reserve) amounts to shipbuilding, 182,648 rubles 79 kopeks; commissariat, 56,017 rubles 62 kopeks; and artillery, 31,493 rubles; or a total of 270,159 rubles 41 kopeks. Second, annual upkeep of such a cruiser requires: shipbuilding, 9,886 rubles 6 kopeks; commissariat, 63,318 rubles 38 kopeks; and artillery, 12,106 rubles; or a total of 85,310 silver rubles 44 kopeks.

10. The original communication of the company on this to His Imperial Highness the head of the Naval Ministry (16 November 1853, no. 970: ibid., p. 181) included the following: "For protection of whaling in the Okhotsk Sea from complete ruin, it would be extremely useful, at least until it is possible to forbid foreign whaling in these waters entirely, to base one of the naval cruisers continually in the Shantar Islands to keep foreign whalers away." Shortly before that the company wrote to the Ministry of Foreign Affairs (22 March 1853, no. 368: ibid., p. 163: "if it is inconvenient to cut off foreign whaling in the Okhotsk Sea, would it not be possible at least officially to forbid whalers from putting in to our coasts and hunting in bays and near islands, and to assign one of the cruisers of the Kamchatka flotilla to enforce this?"

11. That is, the coasts of Russian America (north of 54° 41' north latitude) the Kamchatka peninsula, and Siberia, to the islands of the Kad'iak archipelago, the Aleutian chain, the Pribylov, Commander, and other islands in the Bering Sea and the islands of the Kurile chain, Sakhalin, the Shantar Islands, and others in the Okhotsk Sea north of latitude 46° 30' north. The commanders of the cruisers were instructed to bear in mind "that our government not only does not wish to prohibit or restrict whaling in the northern part of the Pacific Ocean, but even allows foreigners to hunt in the Okhotsk Sea, *the geographical position of which*, as noted in the instructions, *makes it an inland Russian sea*."

12. New Bedford is a city in America in the state of Massachusetts. Most of the population, of about 25,000 inhabitants, are engaged in whaling.

13. The whalers have given these bays their own special names. Thus, Ul'bansk Bay became known as Potter's Bay in honor of the American whaler Potter, who had particular success there in 1849; Usal'ginsk Bay became Mercury Bay after an American vessel that operated there; Tugursk Bay became Shantar Bay, etc.

14. Information on whaling in the Okhotsk Sea is furnished by the acting commandant of the port of Aian, Captain-Lieutenant Elfsberg, and Doctor Schneider, the physician there.

15. The *Caroline*, a small schooner owned by the American whaler Long, wintered in 1854 in little Mamga Bay in Tugursk Bay. Four men left with the ship for the winter died from scurvy. The schooner itself suffered no damage and was used for whaling the following year.

16. Teben'kov, chief manager of the colonies, in his correspondence with the board of directors proposed to establish littoral whaling by clippers and schooners

in three places: at Kad'iak Island (near Afognak Island); on Shumagin and Commander islands; or, if more convenient, near Kamchatka. Teben'kov proposed
importation of whalers from the United States and to sell the oil in the Sandwich
Islands. The word *littoral* in this case means that blubber is not melted on board
the ship, but at an establishment ashore where it is put in barrels. The formation
of the Russian-Finnish Whaling Company forced abandonment of this project.

17. This is the copy of a communication from the governor-general of Eastern
Siberia to the minister of finance, 7 March 1846:

> Desiring to improve conditions in the province entrusted to me by the sovereign,
> I suggest the immediate restriction of the freedom of foreign ships to fish and
> hunt whales in Russian waters of the Eastern Ocean, which they do to the
> detriment of the interests of the natives, subjects of Russia. The number of
> foreign whaling ships is increasing each year. They pitilessly destroy whales
> and fish, which are the sole food supply for the Aleuts and Koriaks, almost at
> the Russian shores.

> For this purpose, the Russian-American Company should be requested to
> establish a Russian whaling enterprise either at its own expense or by issuing
> new shares; or, after the expiration of the charter another company should be
> given this opportunity and thus an important industry now completely in the
> hands of foreigners will pass into ours. If prominent Russian merchants join
> such a company, it will bring large profits.

> I humbly request Your Excellency to submit my information to the emperor
> and to inform me of his wish.

18. The Bering Sea north of the Aleutian chain and the Okhotsk Sea west of
the Kurile Islands.

19. Board of Directors to Department of Manufacturing and Internal Trade,
8 May 1846, no. 937: Company Archives, File of 1846, no. 11, p. 3.

20. "Journals of the session of the general meeting of stockholders," 15 March
and 22 April 1847: Company Archives, File of 1847, no. 21, pp. 57, 94.

21. Several stockholders disagreed with the decision of the general meeting,
considering it useful instead to employ the allotted sum to strengthen the coastal
defenses where the whaling took place, to base one or two company cruisers there,
and to increase the salaries of crews assigned to this duty. Finally, they proposed
that contraband be kept out by not admitting any outsiders, such as Finns, to our
harbors, and that instead creoles should be taught to use whale boats, under the
tutelage of experienced Americans. Ibid., pp. 97-177.

22. On 26 September 1849, Murav'ev wrote to the naval chief-of-staff: "this
year there were at least 250 whaling ships in our Sea of Okhotsk alone. They were
all of large tonnage and had large crews. I met them constantly during my voyage;
often there were several ships together. Nevel'skoi and Korsakov met them also.
My own figure of their number is more conservative than any which I heard from
the whalers themselves."

23. Copy, from governor-general of Finland to the chief of the Ministry of
Foreign Affairs, 13;25 July 1850, no. 2966. Company Archives, File of 1847, no.
21, p. 204.

24. See Appendix 1.

25. Company Archives, File of 1851, no. 3.

26. [For more on the Russo-Finnish Whaling Company, see Ernst Lindberg,
Åbosjöfarts Historia (A history of Åbo seafaring) (3 Vols., Åbo, 1928), Vol. 3, pp.
99-139; and Sven Andersson, "Finländsk valfångst på 1850-talet" (Finland whaling
in the 1850's), *Nordenskiold-Samfundets Tidskrift* (Helsingfors), Vol. 14 (1954),
pp. 3-28.]

Chapter 16

1. See Chapter 11.

2. Ibid., p. 352.

3. A letter from Baron Pelly, director of the Hudson's Bay Company, to the board of directors of the Russian-American Company, 22 October 1848. Company Archives, File of 1838, no. 24, p. 81.

4. See Chapter 13.

5. See Chapter 12.

6. By order of the sovereign, 6 August 1854, it was permitted to barter to the Chinese objects made of silver, but only together with other goods, in an amount not to exceed one-third of the value of the manufactured goods bartered at the same time, or not more than half if furs should be the other item.

7. In reviewing the trade in Kiakhta, it should be noted that sea otters of lower grade, some beavers, all land otters, foxes of lower grades, blue foxes, and some fur seals are bartered for tea there.

8. Department of Manufactures and Internal Trade, 4 September 1848, no. 4172. Company Archives, File of 1849, no. 6, p. 4.

9. Ibid., p. 33.

10. Ibid., 20 February 1850, no. 3046.

11. [See E. L. Keithahn, "Alaska Ice, Inc.," *Pacific Northwest Quarterly* 36 (April 1945): 121-31; reprinted in Morgan B. Sherwood, *Alaska and Its History* (Seattle, 1967), pp. 173-86.]

12. Company Archives, File of 1843, no. 24.

13. [See also George A. Lensen, *Report from Hokkaido: The Remains Of Russian Culture in Northern Japan* (Hakodate, Japan, 1954), pp. 23-53.]

14. Decision of the Committee of Ministers, 25 April 1815, in relation to granting the right to display the navy flag on the brig *Rurik*, dispatched by Count Rumiantsov (Company Archives, File of 1843, no. 24, pp. 31-37). According to Golovnin, the Japanese government believed that the natural boundary line between Russia and Japan was between Iturup and Urup islands, the first of which belonged to Japan, and the second to Russia.

15. Company Archives, File of 1843, no. 24, pp. 31-37.

16. Ibid., File of 1835, no. 36.

17. Ibid., File of 1843, no. 24, pp. 1-22.

18. Because of this petition, temporary relations between the company and Japan were allowed by the emperor on 5 February 1844 as an experiment. The prohibition of 1815 against visiting the Japanese coasts remained in force because, in the words of the vice minister of finance: "Only the results of this undertaking will influence our actions toward Japan and will show if the prohibition should be repealed or not." Company Archives, File of 1843, no. 24, pp. 40-41.

19. Ibid., pp. 65-86.

20. Ibid., File of 1850, no. 19, pp. 1-67.

21. While the Japanese were at New Archangel, Rosenberg ordered the compilation of (1) a Russian-Japanese dictionary of 1,650 words. (Each page of this dictionary was divided into five columns in which were placed, respectively, Russian words, Japanese words spelled with letters of the Russian alphabet, the same Japanese words spelled in the Japanese old and new alphabets, and finally the pronunciation of the Japanese words in Russian letters); (2) a simplified Japanese alphabet composed of forty-eight letters, twenty one of which are pronounced differently when dots are added to them, and a Russian pronunciation guide to all sixty-nine letters; (3) Japanese numerals and corresponding arabic numerals, along with a Russian pronunciation guide; (4) the complex old Japanese alphabet and principal words of the Japanese language written in Japanese with the

pronunciation of every character or sign explained in Russian; (5) a description of Japanese coins, with drawings of some of them; and (6) two notebooks with statistics of the Japanese state, the first written in Japanese and the second in Russian, explaining the meaning and pronunciation of all the Japanese words used in the first notebook. The company gave all of these works to the expedition of Admiral Putiatin, who sailed to Japan in 1852.

Chapter 17

1. Tikhmenev, *Documents*, 60.
2. See Chapter 11.
3. Ibid., p. 382; Order of the Sovereign, 2 April 1835.
4. See Chapter 11.
5. Ibid.
6. *Zhurnal ministerstvo vnutrennykh del* (Journal of the Ministry of Internal Affairs), part 48, section 2, 1861:1; and report of the company for 1860.
7. Tikhmenev, *Documents*, 61, 62.
8. L. A. Zagoskin, *Peshekhodnaia opis' chasti russkikh vladenii v severnoi Ameriki* [Exploration on foot of part of the Russian possessions in North America] (St. Petersburg, 1847). [Republished, with additional material, as *Puteshestviia i issledovaniia leitenanta Lavrentiia Zagoskina v russkoi Amerike v 1842-1844 gg.* (Travels and explorations of Lieutenant Lavrentii Zagoskin in Russian America during 1842-44), (Moscow, 1956). The latter edition has been translated as *Lieutenant Zagoskin's Travels in Russian America, 1842-44: The First Ethnographic and Geographic Investigations in the Yukon and Kuskokwin Valleys of Alaska*, Henry N. Michael, ed. (Toronto, 1967).]
9. See Chapter 8.
10. Company Archives, File of 1852, no. 1.
11. Lieutenant Bernard belonged to the crew of the English sloop *Enterprise*, which had been sent to search for Captain Franklin. Captain Collins, the commander, heard rumors in 1850 that savages living beyond Mintokh Lake on the mainland had killed twelve Englishmen who had arrived in a baidara. To investigate this, Captain Collins landed Lieutenant Bernard, Doctor Adams, and a sailor at Mikhailovskii redoubt. The latter two remained at the redoubt, but Bernard went to Nulato trading post with Deriabin, its manager, who was returning there after bringing some furs. Deriabin persuaded the lieutenant to remain in the trading post until a company employee returned with one of the Kuiukan natives who knew of rumors of the massacre. This employee became the first victim. After that the Kuiukan natives approached the trading post stealthily at night, killed Deriabin, and mortally wounded Bernard and the interpreter.
12. Company Archives, File of 1856, no. 32.
13. Ibid., File of 1846, no. 42.
14. Ibid., File of 1845, no. 38.
15. Ibid., File of 1852, no. 15.
16. Ibid., File of 1855, no. 8.
17. After a detailed report had been submitted, the emperor expressed his pleasure at Captain Voevodskii's prompt action in suppressing the outbreak, he granted the order of St. Anna of the fourth degree to Second-Lieutenant Baranov of the Siberian infantry regiment, and ordered one military cross and four medals to be distributed to the most deserving wounded soldiers or company employees.
18. To supplement the information given on the Hudson's Bay Company up to the granting of its second charter (See Chapters 5 and 8), we will state here

briefly the changes which occurred then. The company's rights and trade monoply in the same territory were renewed by the charter granted by Queen Victoria on 30 May 1838, for the term of twenty-one years, the only limitation being that lands suited for settlers could be appropriated if necessary. In 1849, the English government transferred Vancouver Island to this company, together with a right to sell land suitable for settlement at a stipulated price.

Before the expiration of the charter in 1858, the Act of British Columbia administration was inaugurated, that is, the province formed from the lands held before 1821 by the Montreal Company and acquired from the Americans [Indians]. Rupert's land, according to the charter of King Charles II, remains in eternal and hereditary possession of the Hudson's Bay Company, with all the rights then granted. Although this company continues to trade in British Columbia, it does so without special rights, and on an equal basis with other English subjects. The company has in all these lands a total of 136 posts, besides mobile hunting and trading parties. The company administration is centered in the port of Victoria on Vancouver Island. (Details on the composition of the company administration, population, etc. may be found in a brochure, *Svedeniia ob angliiskoi gudsonbaiskoi kompanii* [Facts about the English Hudson's Bay Company] (St. Petersburg, 1861).

19. Company Archives, File of 1841, no. 16, pp. 49-53.

20. Ibid., File of 1862, no. 15, report of chief manager, 15 November, no. 449.

21. See Chapter 16.

22. Here is the account submitted by the Hudson's Bay Company of its income and expenditure for a three-year period in the Stakhina district and Fort Durham:

Stahkina district

Year	Acct. paid £	s.	d.	Employee's Salaries	Totals			Received from sale of furs			Losses			Profits		
1843	961	19	3	561.10	1523	9	3	2071	18	6	—			548	9	3
1844	1443	18	5	526	1969	18	5	1728	12	8	241	5	9	—		
1845	1111	10	2	548	1659	10	2	2086	5		—			426	14	10

Fort Durham

Year	Acct. paid £	s.	d.	Employee's Salaries	Totals			Received from sale of furs			Losses			Profits		
1843	730	11	8	227 1 8	957	13	4	1334	7	9	—			376	14	5
1844	730	11	8	113 10 10	844	2	6	1334	7	9	—			490	5	3
1845	730	11	8	113 10 10	844	2	6	1334	7	9	—			490	5	3

23. Letter of Baronet Pelly to Baron Wrangell, chairman of the board of directors, 3 December 1847. Company Archives, File of 1838, no. 14, pp. 85-89.

24. Ibid., File of 1854, no. 16.

25. Ibid., File of 1860, no. 24.

26. Ibid., File of 1862, no. 6.

27. Ibid., File of 1843, no. 13.

28. Skipper Arkhimandritov, to whom the company was indebted for saving the ship, was rewarded by the emperor, on behalf of the board of directors, with a gold medal to be worn on the ribbon of the order of St. Anna; several crewmen who took part in the rescue were rewarded with silver medals. The mothers of Kadnikov and Krasil'nikov received pensions from company funds.

29. See Chapter 4.

30. See Chapter 20, section on outfitting and pay of hunters.

31. Sea cabbage is seaweed, the leaves of which resemble cabbage. It grows in shallow and rocky places underwater.

32. Instruction to commanders of company ships during round-the-world voyages.

33. As of 1 January 1862, there were three doctors (one in Aian), eleven surgeon's assistants and orderlies, five apprentices, two midwives, and two assistants.

34. Review of health conditions in the colonies by Doctor Govorlivyi, *Zhurnal Ministerstvo vnutrennykh del* (Journal of the Ministry of Internal Affairs), part 47, sec. 2, bk. 1, 1861; company report for 1861.

35. [See also P. P. Doroshin, "Neskol'ko podrobnostei o rasprostranenii zolota v russkikh Severo-Amerikanshikh vladeniiakh" (Some facts about the distribution of gold in the North American possessions) *Gornyi Zhurnal* (pt. 1) (St. Petersburg, 1866), pp. 277-400; and "Kamennyi ugol v byvshikh amerikanskikh vladeniiakh Rossii (Coal in Russia's former American possessions) Ibid., pt. 4 (1868), pp. 45-57. Frank A. Golder, "Mining in Alaska before 1867," *Washington Historical Quarterly* 7(July 1916):233-38, reprinted in Morgan B. Sherwood, *Alaska and its History* (Seattle, 1967), pp. 149-56, is based on Doroshin's second article and on other material.]

36. [See also R. A. Pierce, "The Russian Coal Mine on the Kenai," *Alaska Journal*, Spring, 1975, Vol. 5, No. 2, pp. 104-108, containing a translation of Enoch Hjalmar Furuhjelm's description of several years spent in developing the mine. The enterprise was liquidated in 1865, a major financial loss for the Russian-American Company.]

37. [See also K. K. Gil'zen, "Il'ia Gavrilovich Voznesenskii. K stoletiiu so dnia ego rozhdeniia (1816-1871)," (Il'ia Gavrilovich Voznesenskii. The hundreth anniversary of his birth (1816-1871), *Sbornik Muzeia antropologii i etnografii*, (Collection of the Museum of Anthropology and Ethnography) Vol. 3, 1916, pp. 1-14; E. Blomkvist, "Risunki I. G. Voznesenskogo (Ekspeditsiia 1839-1849 gg.)" (I. G. Voznesenskii's sketches (Expedition of 1839-1849), *Sbornik MAE*, Vol. 13, 1951, pp. 230-303 (translated by Basil Dmytryshyn and E. A. Crownhart-Vaughan, "A Russian scientific expedition to California and Alaska, 1839-1849," *Oregon Historical Society Quarterly*, June 1972, Vol. 73, No. 2, pp. 100-170; B. A. Lipshits, "O kollektsiiakh Museia antropologii i etnografii sobrannykh russkimi puteshestvennikami i issledovateliami na Aliaske i v Kalifornii" (On collections of the Museum of Anthropology and Ethnography collected by Russian travellers and scientists in Alaska and California), *Sbornik MAE*, vol. 16, 1955, pp. 358-369; R. G. Liapunova, "Ekspeditsiial. G. Voznesenskogo i ee znachenie dlia etnografii Russkoi Ameriki" (I. G. Voznesenskii's expedition and its significance for the ethnography of Russian America), *Sbornik MAE*, Vol. 24, 1967, pp. 5-33; Morgan B. Sherwood, "Science in Russian America, 1741 to 1865," *Pacific Northwest*

Quarterly, Vol. 58, No. 1, 1967, pp. 33-39; and R. A. Pierce, "Voznesenskii, Scientist in Alaska," *Alaska Journal*, Winter, 1975, Vol. 5, No. 1, pp. 11-15.]

Chapter 18

1. This information and the account of subsequent propagation of the Faith is taken from Innokentii's letters to Filaret that were published in the *Pamiatnik trudov pravoslavnykh blagovestnikov russkikh* (Memorial of the works of Russian Orthodox evangelists) (Moscow, 1857), [hereafter, PTPBR]; from his report submitted to the company after terminating his service in the colonies [published in the *Otchet Rossiisko-Amerikanskoi Kompanii za 1857 god* (Report of the Russian-American Company for 1857) (St. Petersburg, 1858, pp. 40-52, translated by Robert Croskey as "The Russian Orthodox Church in Alaska. Innokentii Veniaminov's Supplementary Account (1858)," *Pacific Northwest Quarterly*, Vol. 66, no.1, January, 1975, pp. 26-29]; and from the report by Mr. Kostlivtsov, who was sent recently by the government to inspect the colonies. Also some other sources.

2. *PTPBR*, p. 245.

3. Ibid., p. 246. Later records show that soon after this letter was written, chapels were built in all the villages in the Kad'iak district and, as the Most Reverend wrote, were filled with people on holidays.

4. See Chapter 9.

5. *PTPBR*, pp. 256, 258.

6. Ibid., p. 279.

7. Ibid., p. 278.

8. See Chapter 9.

9. *PTPBR*. p. 258.

10. Ibid., p. 274.

11. A miraculous cure of one of the Kvikhpak River natives from fits of madness had, according to the Most Reverend, a strong influence on others: "For instance, in one village where up until then some of the natives would not even listen to the missionary and others refused under various pretexts to be baptized, they now requested to be baptized, and when asked why indicated the man who had recovered."

12. *PTPBR*, p. 285.

13. Ibid., pp. 265-66.

14. Ibid., p. 266.

15. Ibid., pp. 269-70.

16. Ibid., pp. 251, 270.

17. Ibid., pp. 255, 259.

18. Ibid., p. 295.

19. Company Archives, File of 1860, no. 7, pp. 2-7.

20. Ibid., File of 1857, p. 50.

21. Ibid., p. 51.

22. *PTPBR*, p. 278.

23. Later some of the young creoles who were sent from the colonies to merchant marine school were also sent to other schools. During the term of the current charter, four have graduated from pilot's school, four from the school of commerce, two from the technological institute, one from the medical academy, and ten from the merchant marine school. At present nine boys and three girls are studying in various schools at company expense.

24. During the same period, two were trained in watchmaking in St. Petersburg,

one in gunsmithing, one in tailoring, one in fur-dressing, one in the Izhorsk naval factories, one for work on a turning lathe, and two in the foundries.

25. Statute of the Siberian Committee, confirmed 19 March 1859.

Chapter 19

1. *Otchet Rossiisko-Amerikanskoi Kompanii za 1861 god* (Report of the Russian-American Company for 1861) (St. Petersburg, 1862).

2. In determining the amount of a dividend, the company usually holds back a constant approximate figure rather than an exact sum because of the impossibility of basing this sum solely on a year's operations. The complex turnover and calculations to which the company's capital is subject, and the nature of the business compels it to enter in the annual accounts the furs and goods acquired during two or three years, as well as expenditures corresponding to turnover in various periods.

3. This includes expenses for missionary work and for charity institutions.

Chapter 20

1. This chapter is based on K. T. Khlebnikov's *Zapiski o koloniiakh* [Notes on the colonies], written in the 1830's. The statistical and ethnographical information therein has been revised and supplemented by information from F. P. Litke's "Geographical and navigational description of the American coast and the Aleutian Islands," in his *Puteshestvie vokrug sveta na shliupe Seniavin* [Voyage around the world on the sloop *Seniavin*] pt. 2 (St. Petersburg, 1835); Baron F. P. Wrangell's "Zapiski o zhiteliakh Ameriki" [Notes on the inhabitants of America] *Syn Ote-chestva* [Son of the Fatherland] St. Petersburg, 1839, vol. 7; Veniaminov's *Zapiski ob unalashkinskom otdele* [Notes on the Unalashka District] (St. Petersburg, 1840); Zagoskin's *Peshekhodnoi opi si chasti russkikh vladenii v Amerike* [Exploration on foot of part of the Russian possessions in America] (St. Petersburg, 1847), and the reports of his forerunners in this work, navigator Vasil'ev and the company employees Glazunov, Grigor'ev, and others; M. D. Teben'kov's *Gidrograficheskie zamechaniia* (Hydrographic notes) (St. Petersburg, 1852), supplementing his atlas of the northwest coasts of America and the Aleutian Islands; the same author's *Kratkie statisticheskie svedeniia o koloniiakh* [Concise statistical data on the colonies] (St. Petersburg, 1852); S. A. Kostlivtsov's and P. N. Golovin's reports on their recent inspection of the colonies, and the latter's *Putevye pis'ma* [Travel notes] *Morskoi Sbornik* [Naval Journal] (1863), vols. 5 and 6; and the "Zapiski" [Notes] of the company employees F. I. Murgin, acting manager of the Kad'iak office, N. V. Alekseev, manager of the Unalashka office, Captain-Lieutenant F. K. Verman, who commanded several ships of the colonial fleet, and the "Zamechaniia" [Remarks] of A. Ia. Rutkovskii, former secretary of the chief manager of the colonies. I am especially indebted to the last four for information concerning recent changes in the native's mode of life, hunting, etc.

My aim has been to present concisely, and as fully as possible, a picture of the present state of the Russian colonial possessions from statistical and ethnographic viewpoints. How well I have succeeded, I cannot judge, but at least I have presented in condensed form all that I have found in others' descriptions of the colonies. Such information, which was unavailable when I published the first part of this work, is included in the second part.

2. See Chapter 8.

3. The longitude of the company's settlement on Urup Island; its latitude is 45° 56′.

4. [In the first part of his work Tikhmenev] spelled the name of the founder of the colonies "Shelekhov" after certain documents and the signatures of some of his descendants. However, from the colonial archives and some signed papers and letters, it is apparent that it should be spelled "Shelikhov." [This form has been used throughout the present work. However, the other spelling is used for the vessel *Shelekhov*.]

5. *Dvukratnoe puteshestvie Khvostova i Davydova v Ameriku* [Two journeys of Khvostov and Davydov to America] pt. 1, p. 176.

6. Sarana is a small root which looks like an onion covered with small peas. These latter are gathered by the Aleuts, cooked a little, and mixed with whale oil. When boiled, these peas become soft and the taste reminds one of truffles. Above the root, sarana is violet in color.

7. Bering died on this island in 1741 on the way back to Kamchatka after his voyage to the Aleutian Islands. Severe storms, fog, and cold weather with frequent rains reduced his ship, the *Sv. apostol Petr*, and its crew to a pitiful state. The shrouds were breaking continuously, all the rigging was loose, the sails were falling to pieces, the crew was completely exhausted, and scurvy was ravaging the ship. Every day one or two sailors died from it. The supplies of hardtack and wine were exhausted and only fifteen barrels of drinking water remained. Bering was so sick he was unable to leave his cabin. the officers were also ill and relations between them were strained. Because astronomical observations could not be taken due to bad weather, the navigation was left to chance. Finally, on 4 November, they sighted a steep high shore and took it for the shore of Kamchatka. It was decided after a council to sail nearer to shore and anchor the ship in open water strewn with rocks. The rotten ropes could not hold the ship, and it was carried toward the rocks, but luckily it managed somehow to get over them and stopped in smooth water. Unfortunately, the shore proved not to be Kamchatka but uninhabited and inhospitable. The sick men were taken ashore immediately. Many died while being transported. Those who were alive were put in holes dug in the ground and covered with sails. Bering, half buried in the sand, because he felt warmer there, died on 8 December. In addition, the navigator, the mate, the supercargo, and twenty-seven sailors died. (Sokolov, *Zapiski gidrograficheskago departamenta* [Notes of the Department of Hydrography] (St. Petersburg, 1851), vol. 9. Bering's grave is located on the east side of the island, nineteen versts northwest of Cape Khitrovo. (Teben'kov, *Atlas severozapadnykh beregov Ameriki* [Atlas of the northwest coasts of America] (St. Petersburg, 1852).

8. See Chapter 1.

9. The natives have names for different kinds of whales: *plavun, kulema, polosatik, alemak,* and *magnidak*. The kulema is the largest of them, measuring from four to twelve sazhen in length. Sperm oil is procured from the head of the plavun or *cachelot* [sperm whale]. The blubber and meat of the polosatik is used in the colonies for food. The blubber of the kulema and of the plavun is used for lamps. The magnidak and alemak belong to the polosatik species.

10. Teben'kov, *Gidrograficheskie zamechaniia k atlasu* [Hydrographic notes to the atlas], p. 123.

11. "This circumstance and the large quantity of driftwood on the shores of Alaska and Norton Sound," writes Teben'kov (ibid., last page) "is attributed by the natives to the terrific earthquake of 1737, which shook Kamchatka and the Kurile Islands."

12. Veniaminov, *Zapiski*, pt. 1, p. 54.

13. Ibid., pt. 1, p. 55.

14. Ibid., pt. 1, p. 266.

15. See Chapter 1.

16. The west tip of St. Paul Island is 57° 10′ 2″ latitude, longitude 170° 1′ 1″; the west tip of St. George Island is 56° 38′ 3″ latitude, longitude 159° 27′ 5″.

17. See Chapter 17.

18. A description of products and foodstuffs for local consumption by the islanders of the Kad'iak archipelago will be given in the description of the most important establishments, especially of Paul's Harbor on Kad'iak Island, the administrative center of these islands.

19. Teben'kov, *Gidrograficheskie*, p. 78.

20. Tikhmenev, *Documents*, no. 61.

21. It is remarkable that the Aleuts and Creoles call only crowberries [*shiksha*] "berries;" the rest are just called by their own names. In years when there are few crowberries but plenty of other berries in the marshes, the natives say, "this year there are no berries, God did not provide them!" The crowberry grows mostly on the tundra, almost level with the ground. It has soft needles instead of leaves on the branches. The berries are small and black, their juice has an agreeable taste and quenches the thirst.

22. Teben'kov, *Gidrograficheskie*, p. 66.

23. See Chapter 16.

24. Teben'kov, *Gidrograficheskie*, p. 66.

25. Journal of Baranov's voyage in 1795 on the cutter *Ol'ga*. [This journal is probably no longer in existence.]

26. Teben'kov, *Gidrograficheskie*, p. 36-41.

27. See Chapters 3, 7, 8, 17.

28. *Otchet Rossiisko-Amerikanskoi Kompanii za 1860 god* [Report of the Russian-American Company for 1860] (St. Petersburg, 1861), pp. 71-74.

29. See Chapter 8.

30. [These linguistic classifications are of course long outmoded. Eds.]

31. Veniaminov, *Zapiski*, supplement, pt. 3, p. 51.

32. Ibid., p. 94. The Kolosh bride and groom take no part in the feast and keep a strict fast for four days. After this they can stay together but do not consummate the marriage for four weeks.

33. These customs were described by N. M. Koshkin, secretary to the chief manager of the colonies.

34. *Morskoi Sbornik*, 6:316.

35. Ibid., p. 317.

36. Zagoskin, *Peshekhodnoi*, pt. 1, p. 42.

37. The following are theories from the notes of Baron Wrangell regarding the origin of the natives of the northern part of America and nearby islands in the Eastern Ocean and the differences between the dialects. Baron Wrangell has studied these questions thoroughly and is an authority on this subject.

All of these people (the natives of the northern part of America) speak the same language and belong to the same race, which extends northward geographically along the American coast, as Captain Beechey remarks, to latitude 71° 24′. Beechey sets the southern boundary of the race, which he calls Western Eskimos, at latitude 60° 34′, and finds a close connection in language, facial features, and customs with the Eastern Eskimos of Hudson's Bay, Greenland, Igliulik, and the north coast of America in general. He also found a similarity between the Western Eskimos and Chukchi, whose descendants he thinks the Western Eskimos are. Cook saw in the Chugach and the Aleuts of Unalashka Island a branch of the Greenland Eskimos. The natives on Kad'iak Island speak a language almost identical to that of the Chugach. [People who have lived a long time among the Kad'iak natives and the Chugach and have learned their languages say that the difference is, as we stated above, quite considerable—P. T.] and the language of the natives living along the coast between Bristol Bay and Norton Sound. Thus, we find the Eskimo language in Bering Strait and along the American coast south as far as Chugach Sound, east to Greenland, along the whole chain of the Aleutian Islands, and on Kad'iak. But in making a thorough study of the dialects of these people as related to one another, comparing their customs, folklore, and their appearance, we find striking differences. The islanders of the Aleutian chain from Attu Island up to the Aliaska Peninsula differ in many respects from the Kad'iak and Chugach natives. There are only a few similar words in the languages of these natives. A native from Unalashka does not understand a native from Kad'iak. Words typically Eskimo do not coincide in their dialects.

At first glance one sees Asiatic, Mongol, or Manchu aspects in an islander from the Aleutian chain. Japanese who were taken from the ship wrecked at the Sandwich Islands and brought to New Archangel resembled the natives of Unalashka. On the other hand the Kad'iak natives look more like the natives belonging to the American tribes and are entirely different in their appearance from the Eskimos or Asiatics. They probably became intermixed with the American tribes, and though they perserved their language, they lost their Asiatic type. Their legends state that the Kad'iak natives, Chugach, Kuskokvim natives, and other neighboring tribes all came from the north to the places they now occupy; but the natives on Unalashka came from the west. If we consider these tribes as belonging to the Eskimos, we should divide them, considering differences in dialects, appearance, and folklore, into Northern, Southern, and Western Eskimos. The first would be the Eskimos in the Bering Strait and all along the northern coasts of America as far as Greenland. The second would be the Eskimos south of Bering Strait (beginning with Cape Rodney) up to the Aliaska Peninsula including Kad'iak and Chugach Bay. The last would be the islanders of the Aleutian chain. . . ."

Veniaminov writes of the origin of the Aleuts on the Fox Islands (*Zapiski*, pt. 2, p. 3) thus-

Mr. Bliumenbach believes them to belong to the Mongol race together with the Yakuts, Tungus, and other tribes on Kamchatka. Mr. Forster relates them to the Greenland Eskimo and so does Chamisso, who finds great similarities between the Aleut and Eskimo languages. On the other hand, Fater, the famous linguist, is doubtful as to the question of the Aleuts being descendants of the Eskimos. Bory de St. Vincent, using his own definition, numbers them among the "*lejotrichi*" and "hyperborean" race, to which he also adds Yakuts, Chukchi, Koriak, Kamchadals and others.

It seems to me, that scientists who think that the Aleuts are of Mongolian origin are right, because they greatly resemble the Yakuts in appearance. . . . In their language and mode of life, on the contrary, they resemble the Eskimos of Greenland, not that the language is identical, but in comparing the Aleut language with the Kad'iak language, which is entirely different from the Aleutian in appelations and endings even if the general construction is the same.

Veniaminov also writes (ibid., pt. 1, p. 113): The faces of the Aleuts bear close resemblance to the Japanese and this makes one believe that they are of a Mongol race. It is quite probable that they originally lived on the mainland of Asia in the vicinity of Japan, and being hard pressed by other tribes, moved to the northeast along the Kurile chain. Finally, coming into contact with the people of Kad'iak stock or Kad'iak natives themselves in Kamchatka, and seeing that the natural resources farther north were poorer, they moved to the islands which they now occupy.

38. Zagoskin, *Peshekhodnoi*, pt. 1, p. 48.

39. Ibid., pt. 2, p. 20.

40. See Chapter 18.

41. See Chapter 8.

42. There is a considerable difference in the mental and moral characteristics of the Kad'iak natives and the inhabitants of other islands of the Aleutian chain. The last are much kinder and good-hearted. This partly explains why Christianity has spread quicker on the Fox and other western Aleutian Islands than in other places in Russian-America.

43. We have already had occasion to quote Veniaminov (*Zapiski*, p. 299): "The Aleuts are a patient and mild people. As a result, they have neither courts of law nor criminal investigations, neither judges nor detectives, whose wages and traveling expenses often have to be paid at the expense of the innocent."

44. See Chapter 17

45. Golovin writes in letters about his voyage (*Morskoi Sbornik*, 6:315):

During these days we went about in baidarkas visiting the Aleuts, and the Russian and creole settlers on nearby islands (the islands of the Kad'iak archipelago), and I confess that we found all of them, especially the settlers, living quite comfortably. It is true that the Aleut houses are half-underground, but such is their manner of building them and they prefer such huts to large log houses, which they feel are too spacious. The settlers are well off. They have large well-lit houses with closets, sheds, vegetable gardens, etc. Many have the walls finished inside with wallpaper or painted canvas. Their houses are clean inside and comfortable. All settlers formerly employed by the company receive pensions of from 150 to 700 paper rubles.

46. According to some of the company's employees, the Aleuts in the Kad'iak district observe the same prohibitions when fishing as the Kolosh, when the latter are on a sea otter hunt. This custom, mentioned above, includes not washing their clothes, the floors of their yurts, etc.

47. We speak here mainly of the Kad'iak crew, because it has the largest catch, and is dispatched as a whole at the same time. The first crew from Unalashka and Unga sails around 10 April. It returns by 1 July, but other hunters leaving at this time remain until 15 August. The number of baidarkas sailing from neighboring villages varies. The office at Unga sends out about forty-five, the office at Unalashka up to one hundred one- and two-man baidarkas. Usually, the best hunters are assigned to the hunt, excluding a number of men left to obtain food for local consumption and to hunt birds. The Atkha Aleuts, from the islands of Siguam and Four Mountains, sometimes hunt sea otters at Amukhta and Iunaska islands, and at the latter shoot them instead of using arrows, because in this particular spot the sea otters escape among the rocks when wounded by arrows. The hunting crew sails here in the last part of March and returns in August, September, and sometimes even in October, depending upon where the hunting is done. This crew sails in a large baidara belonging to the company that holds from twenty to twenty-five men and four to eight women, and from sixteen to twenty one- and two-man baidarkas. While on the way to the hunting grounds, the baidarkas are loaded into the large baidara. On the return voyage the baidarkas are taken apart, because the large baidara is usually filled with blubber and meat of sea animals. In addition to this crew, five or six one-man and two or three two-man baidarkas are sent to Adakh Island. They return in August. The Aleuts from Attu Island sail to the hunting grounds in two large baidaras having with them about seventy one-man baidarkas corresponding to the number of hunters. They usually sail to Semichi Island.

48. This depends upon whether a party of Chugach from Konstantinovskii redoubt is included. When the Kad'iak crew sails to hunt in the vicinity of the

abandoned trading post [*odinochka*] at Sutkhum village the Chugach hunt in their territory.

49. See Chapter 4. We also include here a description of a sea otter taken from Veniaminov (*Zapiski*, pt. 2, pp. 336-42):

Like other amphibious animals—river otters, beavers, hair seals, fur seals, sea lions, and walruses—the sea otter is a mammal. All these animals have strong teeth, especially the sea lions. Beavers and otters have short legs reminding one of a wolf's legs. Otters have longer legs than the other animals and can move faster on land. The other animals mentioned have flippers instead of forelegs, resembling fish fins or short human arms with five long fingers, but which are more like feet than hands. The skin of all these animals is loose around the body, and sea otters, river otters and fur seals have soft, short, fluffy hair underneath the longer, while the sea lions, walruses, and hair seals have stiff, coarse hair. The sea otter has a round head and flat chest. The forepaws resemble human hands, and the sea otter uses them so dextrously that after retrieving seashells from the sea bottom, it opens them by breaking them with a stone. These animals are very clever. The females love their little ones, have them always nearby, and when necessary fight for them until the very last. All amphibious animals have an acute sense of smell, but their eyesight is weak, especially in clear weather. They are born on land and learn to swim gradually. They feed on fish and seashells. On land they are clumsy.

50. When it dives the first time, a sea otter can stay underwater for twenty minutes. After the first dive, the time it can stay underwater becomes shorter and finally it cannot stay more than a half a minute. A sea otter usually swims on its back.

51. It must be noted that sea otters were sometimes found in the wintertime on the shore, where they came to rest. In this case, the hunter approached the spot cautiously in his baidarka against the wind, and, quickly jumping ashore, killed the animal with a club or shot it. In Atkha District, the sea otters formerly were caught with nets.

52. See Chapter 9. Oppressive treatment by managers of company offices and by foremen was eliminated by Baron Wrangell during his management of the colonies. The natives were also indebted to him for lowering prices on goods sold to them. Until then, company goods were shipped from Russia around the world, and prices were so high that one could buy some of them more cheaply at Okhotsk. Baron Wrangell found means of purchasing many of the goods abroad, and repeatedly pointed out in his reports to the main office the great gap between the high prices and the small compensation received by the natives from the company.

53. In the Unalashka and Unga district offices, the councils planning a sea-otter hunt for the coming year are held during the Christmas holidays, after all hunting and trapping for the current year is finished.

54. The great number of migratory birds in the colonies is witnessed by the fact that, for instance, on St. Paul's Island from April until late in the fall, four hundred birds are used for food per day. Some of the birds most frequently hunted include: (1) the murre [*ara*], which is the size of a hen. It has black wing feathers, a white belly; a pointed beak, like the beak of a magpie, and legs resembling those of a loon. This bird lays two eggs, and if one of them is taken, it lays another. It feeds on fish. Murres arrive in May and remain until fall; (2) the tufted puffin [*toporok*], is about the same size as the murre, with black feathers, a red bill, and a green and yellow flat tip (hence the term *toporok* ["hatchet"]). It is also called a sea parrot. It has on its head two tufts [*kosy*] of small feathers, like hair, coming down to its neck. Its legs are red, and it has webbed feet. This bird is found on rocks and in crevices. It lays the same number of eggs as the murre, and

feeds on fish. When diving, it flaps its wings underwater; (3) the horned puffin [*ipatka*] is slightly smaller than the tufted puffin. Its feathers are black, with white on the belly. Its bill is almost identical to that of the tufted puffin. It feeds on fish, and arrives and leaves almost at the same time as the murres. Among the sea birds hunted in the colonies is the cormorant [*uril*], the size of a small wild goose. It has a long neck, and a long bill, narrow and sharp, slightly bent at the end. Its feathers are black with some green on the neck and back. It lives among the rocks and lays three to four eggs. These eggs do not become hard when boiled. It feeds on fish and shellfish and does not fly a long way from shore. Other birds are the sea duck [*glupysh*] and kittiwake [*govorushka*]. The sea duck is of two kinds, blue and gray; the latter is the more numerous. It is the size of a freshwater duck. It has a bill with a hump and a bend and feeds on whale oil floating on the water. The kittiwake resembles a seagull but is smaller. It flies fast and screams all the time as if trying to tell something. It lives among the rocks and feeds on fish and meat, but never dives underwater. Geese are of two kinds, gray and white. Some of the grays have yellow and some black legs. There are various species of sea ducks and snipe.

55. Aleuts living on the islands managed by the Unalashka and Unga offices hunt birds on Amak and neighboring islands. Some of the sea-otter hunters sail to hunt walruses to the northern part of the Aliaska Peninsula and remain there until 15 August after the return of the sea-otter hunting crew.

56. Aleuts wear these parkas with feathers outside. Such a parka, with a kamleika of sea-lion skin underneath is the best protection obtainable from severe cold and driving rain.

57. Traps [*kliaptsy* or *kleptsy*] as Veniaminov describes them, consist of three main parts: the stock [*kolodka*], the lever [*motyr*], and the ropes [*guzhi*]. The stock is a block of wood (about eight vershoks long), hollowed out, with a slot in the middle. The lever is a hardwood stick about fourteen vershoks long with three iron spikes on one end. These prongs are three vershoks long. The ropes are of twisted whale sinews about two vershoks thick. Placed inside of the hollow block and stretched on both sides with wedges, they have the action of a strong spring. The lever is inserted in the ropes and in the slot of the stock. This trap is set near the fox's trail so that the iron spikes on the lever will lie on the trail. It is lifted and set on the other side, a stick fastened to the end of the stock being used for this purpose. A string is fastened to the trigger stretched across the trail and tied to a peg. The moment the string is touched, the lever strikes the trail with such force that the iron spikes can go right through a man's foot.

58. See Chapter 17.

59. See Chapter 14.

60. See Chapter 17 and Tikhmenev, *Documents*.

61. See *History*, I:252, 253.

Glossary

Artel:	A work crew; in Russian-America a large group of hunters
Baidarshchik:	Head of an artel and of the territory in which it operated
Peredovshchik:	Foreman
Prikashchik (or prikazchik):	In Siberia a local administrator; in Russian-America an agent of the chief manager, or the supercargo on a vessel
Promyshlennik:	A Russian trapper, hunter, or trader
Toion (or toën):	Kamchadal word for chief, carried from Siberia to Russian-America
Amanat:	Hostage
Kaiur:	Kamchadal word meaning post driver or driver of a dog team; in eighteenth-century Russian-America a native worker (female worker: kaiurka)
Iasak:	Tax in furs paid by Siberian tribesmen; applied in Aleutian Islands until abolished by order of Catherine II
Kalga:	A Kolosh (Tlingit) slave
Yurt:	In Siberia a felt or skin tent on a dome-shaped wooden framework; in Russian-America a driftwood hut or an Aleut dugout dwelling
Barabora (or barabara; pl. barabory):	From a Kamchadal word for a hut put up for summer camping; in Russian-America applied to dwellings and other buildings of the natives
Kazhim:	A communal house of Aleuts and Eskimos
Kamlei (also kamleia or kamleika):	Chukchi word for a hooded outer garment worn in bad weather, or when hunting at sea, or worn by itself as a summer garment; originally made of sea mammal intestines or fish skins
Parka:	A type of shirt, similar to kamleika, with a standing collar, usually sewn from birdskins or sealskins

Baidara:	Originally a Russian term for river boat; in Russian-America a skin boat holding 20-25 people
Baidarka:	An Eskimo or Aleut kayak, holding one, two, or three persons
Shitik:	A decked boat with side planking sewn with willow wands instead of nails or pegs, used in the first voyages from Siberia to the Aleutian Islands
Otdel:	A section or district, one of several administrative divisions in Russian-America
Koshlok:	A young sea otter, not yet a year old
Medvedka:	A young sea otter, still without full growth of fur
Laftak:	Dressed hides of sea animals; sometimes used interchangeably with lakhtakh, properly a type of seal, the sea hare
Odinochka:	A one-man post
Zimov'e:	A winter camp
Redoubt:	A small fort
Pud (or pood):	36.11 pounds avoirdupois
Fanega:	A dry measure in Spain (1.58 bu.) and Spanish America (varies); about 135 lbs.
Arroba:	Spanish dry measure; 25.36 lbs.
Verst:	.6629 mile or 1.067 kilometers
Arshin:	28 inches
Sazhen:	7 feet, or 1.16 fathom
Ruble:	If silver, in early nineteenth century, approximately U. S. $0.50; a paper ruble (assignat) was worth 68 kopeks in 1794, 25 kopeks in 1810, and 20 kopeks in 1815
Kopek:	1/100 ruble
Piaster:	A Spanish peso or dollar of the early nineteenth century equivalent to about U. S. $1.00 of the time

Chief Managers of the Russian-American Company Colonies

Alexander Andreevich Baranov	[?] 1790 to 11 January 1818
Leontii Andreanovich Hagemeister	11 January 1818 to 24 October 1818
Semen Ivanovich Ianovskii	24 October 1818 to 15 September 1820
Matvei Ivanovich Murav'ev	15 September 1820 to 14 October 1825
Peter Egorovich Chistiakov	14 October 1825 to 1 June 1830
Baron Ferdinand Wrangel	1 June 1830 to 29 October 1835
Ivan Antonovich Kupreanov	29 October 1835 to 25 May 1840
Adolf Karlovich Etholen	25 May 1840 to 9 July 1845
Mikhail Dmit'rivich Teben'kov	9 July 1845 to 15 October 1850
Nikolai Iakovlevich Rosenberg	15 October 1850 to 31 March 1853
Alexander Il'ich Rudakov	31 March 1853 to 22 April 1854
Stepan Vasil'evich Voevodskii	22 April 1854 to 22 June 1859
Ivan Vasil'evich Furuhjelm	22 June 1859 to 2 December 1863
Prince Dmitrii Petrovich Maksutov	2 December 1863 to 18 October 1867

Index

The following is a list of abbreviations used in the index:

RAK   Russian-American Company (*Rossiisko-Amerikanskaia Kompaniia*)
CNN   Corps of Naval Navigators (*Korpus flotskikh shturmanov*)
HBC   Hudson's Bay Company
Kr.   Kronshtadt
NA   New Archangel (Novo-Arkhangel'sk)
RA   Russian America

Separate listings for the categories "Ships" and "Indigenous Peoples" follow the main index.

Academy of Sciences, 378
Afanasii: hieromonk, 36, 189, 192
Afognak I., 17, 81, 200, 413
Agattu I., 10, 402
Agriculture, 30, 41, 42, 58, 83-84, 157, 368-69, 458n
Aiak I., 182, 183
Aian Bay, 247, 251, 253, 375
Aian port, 187, 251, 253, 254-56, 260-62, 268
Akun I., 406
Akutan I., 11
Alcohol: sale of, prohibited, 354
Aldoma R., Sib., 187-88, 247-49
Aleksandrovsk fort, Kenai Bay, 25, 81, 174
Aleksandrovsk redoubt, Nushagak R., 158, 180, 194, 345

Alekseev, N. V., 439-40
Aleutian Islands, 402-8
Aliaska Peninsula, 10, 81, 185, 414-15
Amakhnak I., 406
Amchitka I., 210, 403
American Fur Co. project, 115-19
American-Russian Trading Co., 328
American trading vessels, 61-62, 151; posts on Columbia R., 132; rights in 1824 convention, 164
Amgun' R.: Amur area, 290, 291-92
Amlia I., 10, 174, 404
Amur Co., 298, 330
Amur R., 270, 273-74, 298
Andreevskii post: attack on in 1855, 351
Andreianov Islands, 10, 403-5
Andreianov, manager Mikhailovskii redoubt, 351
Arakelov: RAK commissioner, *Elena*, 220
Arbuzov, Lt., 74
Arguello: Doña Concepcion de, 97, 98; José de, acting governor, 137; Luis de, 96
Arillaga: governor of California, 97, 98, 137
Arkhimandritov, 221, 375; *Kad'iak* wrecked at Spruce I., 362-63; *Naslednik Aleksandr* mishap, 363-64
Artela, Spanish captain, 26
Astor, John Jacob, 115-18, 167
Astoria: American Fur Co. post, 118, 168
Atkha Co., 51, 57, 404
Atkha I., 10, 89, 173-74, 345, 396, 470n